Written by
Brian Shields & Kevin Sullivan

ENCYCLOPEDIA

THE DEFINITIVE GUIDE TO
WORLD WRESTLING ENTERTAINMENT®

TO THE WWE UNIVERSE

I am proud to share with you our first-ever encyclopedia detailing the complete history of World Wrestling Entertainment. The exciting images and dynamic text that bring these pages to life serve as the first-ever official documented history of the WWE. World Wrestling Entertainment's unique form of entertainment has translated into an international language, uniting people of all ages, genders, races, colors and creeds. In this all-encompassing work, you will read about our groundbreaking 45 years, and those few who have had the privilege to perform before our audiences to deliver unmatched excitement and drama. I hope you enjoy reading about our incredible history as much as we enjoyed being part of it.

CONTENTS

LONDON, NEW YORK,
MELBOURNE, AND DELHI

Senior Development Editor
Ken Schmidt

Lead Designer
Doug Wilkins

Production Designer
Tracy Wehmeyer

Cover Designer
Eli Zigdon

Editor-In-Chief
H. Leigh Davis

Publisher
David Waybright

Licensing Director
Mike Degler

Marketing Director
Debby Neubauer

International Translations
Brian Saliba

**Director of Business Development
and New Markets**
Michael Vaccaro

First UK Edition, 2012
12 13 14 15   9 8 7 6 5 4 3 2 1

Published in the United States by DK/BradyGAMES, a division of Penguin Group (USA) Inc.
800 East 96th Street, 3rd Floor
Indianapolis, Indiana 46240

ISBN 978-1-4093-8238-6
ID: 001-WD178-SEPT/12
Printed and bound by Hung Hing, China

ABOUT THE AUTHORS

Brian Shields is the author of *Main Event: WWE In The Raging 80s*. He began his professional career marketing WWE video games and later collaborated on the launch of the WWE Legends Program. A 1980s Hulkamaniac, Brian most recently worked as Marketing Director for Game On, Inc. developing a line of WWE licensed video game accessories.

Kevin Sullivan is a graduate of Fairfield University in Connecticut, just a few miles north of WWE's Stamford headquarters. During his senior year in college, Sullivan landed an internship with the worldwide leader in sports-entertainment, which ultimately resulted in a full-time position. He spent the next 10 years splitting time between WWE.com and WWE Magazine. His most recent position was Director of Content Development for the company's website.

Sullivan currently lives in Milford, Connecticut, with his wife, Caryn.

In an industry defined by larger-than-life personalities performing acts both heinous and heroic, it is a nigh-impossible task to condense almost 50 years of history into any number of pages. However, what you hold in your hands is an attempt to do just that: take the history of World Wrestling Entertainment, from 1963 through 2008, and catalog the people and events into over 350 pages.

Not every event in each Superstar's career is covered, but what's inside touches on triumphs and tragedies, rivalries and partnerships, and championship reigns. Regardless of whether they were met with cheers or jeers, the men and women on the following pages worked hard to entertain you, the fans, night in and night out, on the road and away from home, hundreds of nights each year.

Superstars are listed by the name for which they are most famous (for example, look in the "R" entries for The Rock instead of Rocky Maivia, and "Hacksaw" Jim Duggan is included with the "H" entries). Those Superstars who are more well-known for tag team accomplishments in WWE than individual accolades appear under the name of their tag team (Arn Anderson and Tully Blanchard are both in the Brain Busters entry, for example). If you're having trouble finding a specific topic, use the index at the end of this book which lists all the Superstars that appear in these pages, alphabetized by last name (or only name in the case of someone like Yokozuna).

For most Superstars, the background color of their entry indicates the decade in which they first appeared (see the following chart). For the Superstars whose careers helped define the eras in which they competed, they have been given colors that allow them to stand out from the crowd. The entries with black backgrounds are most often television shows, types of matches, special events, and title histories.

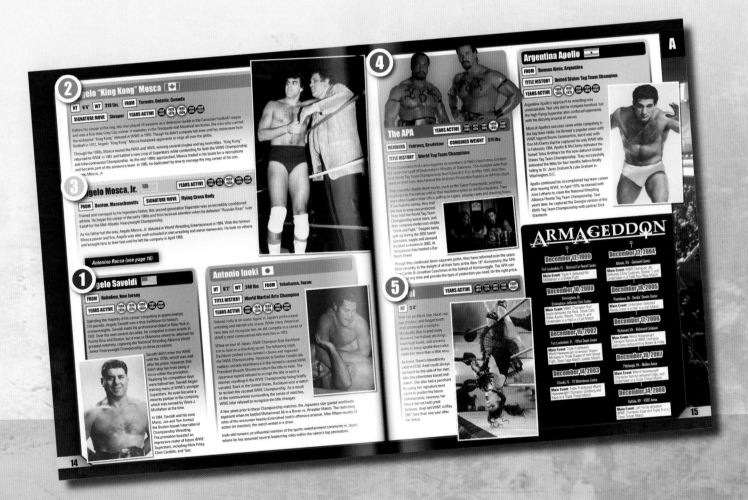

① 1960-1969   ② 1970-1979   ③ 1980-1989   ④ 1990-1999   ⑤ 2000-PRESENT

3-Minute Warning

| MEMBERS | Rosey, Jamal |
| COMBINED WEIGHT | 939 lbs. |

YEARS ACTIVE

1960-1969 · 1970-1979 · 1980-1989 · 1990-1999 · **2000 PRESENT**

Even the most casual WWE fan knows that Eric Bischoff abused his authority while serving as *Raw* general manager. To make matters worse, his decisions were oftentimes made just so he could let out a hearty laugh. One of the best (or worst) examples of this is 3-Minute Warning.

In July 2002, Rosey & Jamal made their debut when they jumped the crowd barrier to decimate D-Lo Brown & Shawn Stasiak. The attack opened many eyes and also cured Bischoff's boredom from watching Brown & Stasiak compete. In the months that followed, Bischoff continued to entertain himself by giving Superstars a warning of three minutes before Rosey & Jamal would put a painful end to segments the GM deemed dull.

The most memorable moment of 3-Minute Warning's brief WWE career saw them invade *SmackDown* to crash Billy & Chuck's highly publicized commitment ceremony. Shortly after the invasion, Rosey & Jamal competed in a high-profile Tables Elimination Match at *Survivor Series*. With Rico as their partner, they fell victim to Jeff Hardy, Bubba Ray & Spike Dudley. The duo never bounced back from the loss, and they went their separate ways shortly after.

Abe "Knuckleball" Schwartz

| HT | 6' | WT | 240 lbs. |
| FROM | Brooklyn, New York |

YEARS ACTIVE

1960-1969 · 1970-1979 · 1980-1989 · **1990-1999** · 2000 PRESENT

During the Major League Baseball strike of 1994, WWE did their part in bringing the national pastime to fans when they introduced Abe "Knuckleball" Schwartz (sometimes referred to as MVP). With a baseball painted on his face and sporting a double-zero numbered uniform, he gave fans a piece of that baseball action they were missing.

Accompanied to the ring by a slightly demonic version of "Take Me Out to the Ballgame," Schwartz had big-league aspirations. Unfortunately, however, he struck out when it came to WWE. The closest he came to any fame was competing in a Battle Royal where the two Superstars left standing would face off for the Intercontinental Championship. Schwartz made it halfway through before being eliminated by Owen Hart.

Adam Bomb

HT	6'6"	WT	290 lbs.
FROM	Three Mile Island
SIGNATURE MOVE	The Meltdown

YEARS ACTIVE

1960-1969 · 1970-1979 · 1980-1989 · **1990-1999** · 2000 PRESENT

In May 1993, World Wrestling Entertainment faced a nuclear threat. Introduced to fans by Johnny Polo, Adam Bomb was a powerhouse whose intent was to win the coveted WWE Championship. Four months into his career, he relieved Johnny Polo of his managerial duties and replaced him with the ever-slippery Harvey Wippleman.

However, his relationship with Wippleman soured, and Adam Bomb began receiving the support of fans. By August 1995, this apocalyptic threat was defused as Adam Bomb left WWE. Though he spent only a few years with the organization, Adam Bomb will always be remembered as an unrelenting force in the ring.

"Adorable" Adrian Adonis

HT	5'11"	WT	298 lbs.
FROM	New York City
SIGNATURE MOVE	Sleeper Hold

TITLE HISTORY

World Tag Team Champion

YEARS ACTIVE

1960-1969 · 1970-1979 · **1980-1989** · 1990-1999 · 2000 PRESENT

With a nickname of "Adorable," some might expect Adrian Adonis to be a bit soft in the ring, but those people would be dead wrong. Despite displaying an overtly feminine persona later in his career, Adonis was one of the toughest men of his time.

Adonis arrived in WWE in the early 1980s, alongside his tag team partner, Jesse Ventura. When injuries prevented Ventura from competing regularly, Adonis joined forces with fellow tough man Dick Murdoch. The duo captured the World Tag Team Championship in April 1984. They held the titles for nine months before losing to the U.S. Express.

Following the loss, Adonis' rugged biker persona gave way to a more flamboyant one. Despite the effeminate makeover, Adonis remained a force in the ring. He proved this right away with a convincing victory over Uncle Elmer at *WrestleMania 2*.

In addition to excelling in the ring, the "Adorable One" also hosted his own interview segment dubbed *The Flower Shop*. Adonis' copycat tactics infuriated Roddy Piper, causing the two Superstars to engage in a memorable rivalry. Their heated rivalry culminated in a Hair vs. Hair Match at *WrestleMania III*, which saw Piper get the win and Adonis get a haircut.

Adrian Adonis & Dick Murdoch

COMBINED WEIGHT 527 lbs. **TITLE HISTORY** World Tag Team Champions

Adrian Adonis & Dick Murdoch couldn't have more different backgrounds. Adonis, a loud-mouthed, leather-wearing biker, grew up on the mean streets of New York City, while Murdoch, a man who let his actions in the ring do his talking, spent his early days on a sprawling 17-acre Texas ranch. In the ring, however, they shared one very similar characteristic: they liked to hurt people.

The wrecking crew of Adonis & Murdoch made their debut as a unit in late 1983 after the New Yorker's original tag team partner, Jesse "The Body" Ventura, was sidelined due to injury. With Murdoch by his side, Adonis captured his only piece of WWE gold when the tandem defeated Rocky Johnson & Tony Atlas for the World Tag Team Championship in April 1984. They held the titles for more than nine months before being derailed by the U.S. Express, Mike Rotundo & Barry Windham.

Shortly after the loss, Adonis & Murdoch went their separate ways. The rough and tumble biker transformed his image into a flamboyant cross-dresser, while the big Texan took his talents to the Mid-South.

Ahmed Johnson

HT 6'2" **WT** 305 lbs. **FROM** Pearl River, Michigan **SIGNATURE MOVE** Pearl River Plunge

TITLE HISTORY Intercontinental Champion

In 1995, World Wrestling Entertainment was greeted by a powerhouse from the streets of Pearl River. Ahmed Johnson was all business in the ring. During his *Monday Night Raw* debut, he showed he was for real when he bodyslammed Yokozuna. Ahmed had one of the most impressive starts in WWE history and continued handing opponents quick lessons, including a win over Buddy Landell at *In Your House: Season's Beatings* in less than 45 seconds!

At the 1996 *King of the Ring*, he made history when he defeated Goldust to become the first African-American Intercontinental Champion. He also formed an alliance with the "Heartbreak Kid" Shawn Michaels and battled Camp Cornette. Unfortunately, a serious kidney injury at the hands of Ron "Faarooq" Simmons forced him to vacate the title. When Ahmed returned to action, he had an on-and-off relationship with the Nation of Domination.

His WWE career ended in 1998 as a brother in arms to the Legion of Doom and Ken Shamrock. This mountainous Superstar went wherever he pleased and refused to be intimidated by anyone. Ahmed Johnson didn't vanish from the spotlight entirely. In 2001, he appeared in the movie *Too Legit: The MC Hammer Story*.

Al Perez

HT 6'1" **WT** 245 lbs. **FROM** Tampa, Florida

SIGNATURE MOVE German Suplex

YEARS ACTIVE 1980-1989 1990-1999 2000-PRESENT

Al Perez began wrestling as an amateur in high school and became one of the top athletes in the state of Florida. Trained by the famous Boris Malenko, he made his pro debut in 1982 and made a name for himself in the mid 1980s as "The Latin Heartthrob" in World Class Championship Wrestling. In 1989, he arrived in WWE. With his amateur background and ring savvy, it looked like Perez would be a major championship contender.

He entered the ring against a variety of competitors, including the Brooklyn Brawler, Koko B. Ware, the Red Rooster, and Bret "Hit Man" Hart. In the beginning of 1990, Al left WWE and appeared in WCW. He spent the rest of the decade competing in independent promotions throughout the United States before retiring in 2002.

Al Snow

HT 6'1" **WT** 235 lbs. **YEARS ACTIVE** 1960-1969 1970-1979 1980-1989 1990-1999 2000-PRESENT

FROM Lima, Ohio **SIGNATURE MOVE** Snowplow

TITLE HISTORY World Tag Team Champion, European Champion, Hardcore Champion

Al Snow's quirky persona made him stand out and brought him success. Despite owning impressive in-ring skills, the delusional Superstar's actions oftentimes made fans scratch their heads, especially when he would talk to his Head (his mannequin head, that is).

While competing in ECW, Snow developed a close relationship with a mannequin head named Head. The popularity of Snow and Head eventually caught the attention of WWE. With Head in tow, Snow moved to WWE in 1998 where he became an immediate fixture in the promotion's budding hardcore division.

Using the experience he gained while competing in ECW, Snow went on to capture WWE's Hardcore Championship six times. In November 1999, Snow teamed with the equally deranged Mankind to capture the World Tag Team Championship. While the reign lasted only four days, it remains one of the brightest moments of Snow's career.

The unpredictable Snow is also known for his time spent on the show *Tough Enough*. Working as one of the show's trainers, Snow was responsible for molding many WWE hopefuls into legitimate Superstars. His impressive list of students includes John Morrison, the Miz and Maven.

Albert

YEARS ACTIVE | 1960–1969 | 1970–1979 | 1980–1989 | **1990–1999** | 2000–PRESENT

HT 6'7" **WT** 331 lbs. **FROM** Boston, Massachusetts **SIGNATURE MOVE** The Baldo Bomb

TITLE HISTORY Intercontinental Champion

This former Superstar and NFL player is perhaps best remembered for his body hair and piercings. Albert debuted in WWE in 1999 as Prince Albert. He joined a short-lived trio that went by the name "the Pierced Pals." After the group disbanded, Albert formed a team with Test. Managed by the seductive Trish Stratus, these two big men were known as T & A.

In 2001, Albert formed an alliance with X-Pac and Justin Credible, known as X-Factor. When the group separated, Albert teamed with Scotty 2 Hotty. Dubbed the "Hip-Hop Hippo," the team lasted until April 2002. In late 2002, Albert formed the most powerful alliance of his career. Now billed as A-Train, he was paired with Big Show and Paul Heyman. In singles competition, A-Train faced Undertaker at *SummerSlam 2003,* and continued to appear on *SmackDown* until he was traded to *Monday Night Raw* during the March 2004 Draft Lottery. That November, this pierced powerhouse parted ways with WWE.

Aldo Montoya

YEARS ACTIVE | 1960–1969 | 1970–1979 | 1980–1989 | **1990–1999** | 2000–PRESENT

HT 6'1" **WT** 225 lbs. **FROM** Portugal

Clad in his country's colors of green, red, and yellow, Aldo Montoya arrived on the WWE scene to much fanfare in late 1994. Dubbed the "Portuguese Man O' War," the proud Superstar from Portugal used his quickness to turn back foes.

A few months after Montoya's debut, Superstars were able to scout his speed and incorporate counters into their game plans. As a result, it wasn't long before he found himself getting tossed around the ring by larger, more skilled opponents like Vader, Goldust, and Hunter Hearst-Helmsley. As the losses began to mount, people began to tease Montoya, claiming the mask he wore over his face resembled an athletic supporter. Montoya was never able to attain the level of success many expected from him upon his WWE arrival. By 1997, Montoya began to compete in fewer matches before disappearing from WWE completely.

Alexis Smirnoff

YEARS ACTIVE | 1960–1969 | 1970–1979 | **1980–1989** | 1990–1999 | 2000–PRESENT

HT 6'3" **WT** 255 lbs. **FROM** Russia **SIGNATURE MOVE** Heart Punch

Entering WWE in the early 1980s, Alexis Smirnoff used his "Mad Russian" persona to strike fear into audiences nationwide, while his paralyzing Heart Punch instilled terror through WWE locker rooms.

Though his WWE legacy will never equal that of fellow Russians Ivan Koloff and Nikolai Volkoff, Smirnoff will be remembered for setting lofty goals for himself. Upon entering the promotion, he immediately sought out the top stars, which resulted in memorable rivalries with Rocky Johnson and former World Tag Team Champion Ivan Putski.

Alicia Fox

YEARS ACTIVE | 1960–1969 | 1970–1979 | 1980–1989 | 1990–1999 | **2000–PRESENT**

HT 5'9" **FROM** Tampa, Florida

A new kind of Diva from the Sunshine State, Alicia Fox debuted in June 2008 on *SmackDown*. As the wedding planner for Edge and Vickie Guerrero, Alicia needed to make sure everything was perfect for their special day. When footage aired of her in a lip-lock with Edge the day before the wedding it created issues between the betrothed.

At *The Great American Bash* Fox attempted to interfere in the Heavyweight Championship match between Champion Triple H and Edge. After she dodged a spear, the Rated-R Superstar leveled Vickie Guerrero.

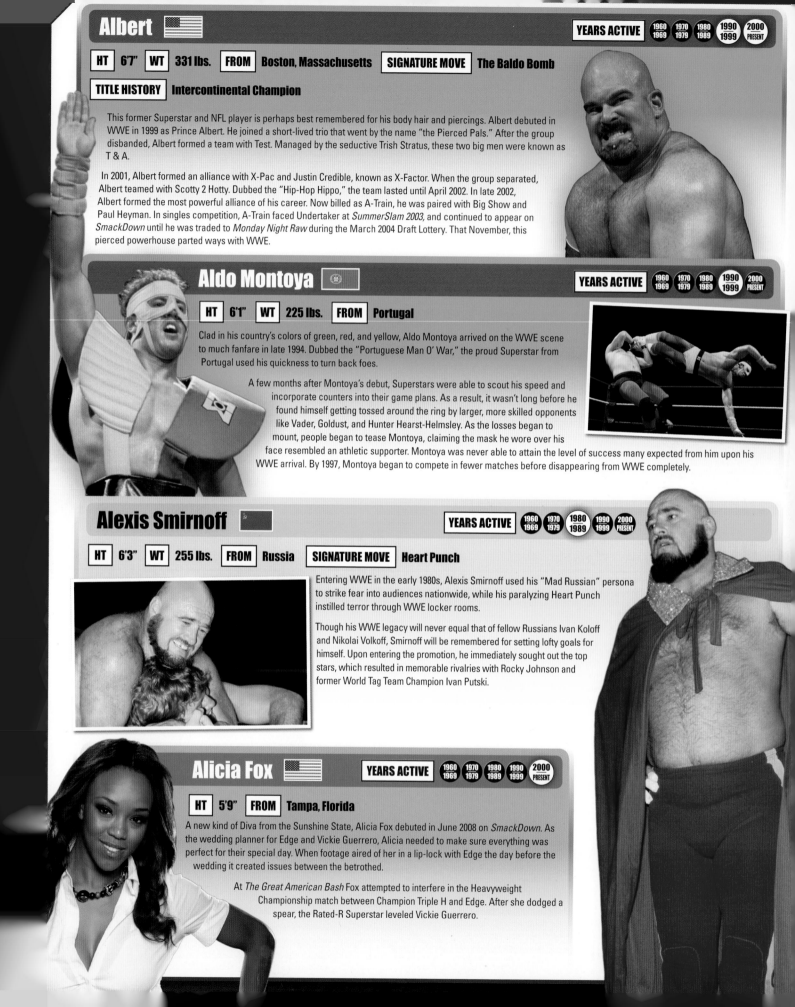

THE ALLIANCE

This menagerie formed in July 2001 as members of Shane McMahon's newly acquired World Championship Wrestling came together with the hope of taking over World Wrestling Entertainment. WCW talent like Lance Storm, Hugh Morrus, and Diamond Dallas Page were led by Shane and interrupted WWE broadcasts and events.

On the July 9, 2001 episode of *Monday Night Raw*, WWE was under another attack. This time WWE's flagship program saw the television return of ECW stars Rob Van Dam and Tommy Dreamer as they jumped the guardrail and attacked Kane and Chris Jericho. During the melee, Lance Storm and Mike Awesome suddenly sided with their former hardcore brethren. WWE Superstars rushed the ring and opposed the quartet of Van Dam, Dreamer, Storm, and Awesome. As the standoff continued, the Superstars suddenly turned around and the odds become 10-on-2. Paul Heyman then left the *Raw* broadcast position and announced to the world that the "Invasion" had just become extreme. After Shane McMahon broke the pact he had with his father to keep ECW out of WWE, the one-time corporate rivals WCW and ECW joined together in violent unison to eliminate WWE. Before *Raw*

went off the air, Shane made one more unbelievable announcement as ECW and WCW stood together in the ring. He introduced the new owner of Extreme Championship Wrestling, Stephanie McMahon-Helmsley.

For the next few months, other individuals made their presence felt for both sides, and some defected from one entity to the other. Superstars also fought for both WWE and WCW championships in numerous battles. Perhaps the most shocking moment in the conflict came at the *Invasion* pay-per-view, when Stone Cold Steve Austin turned his back on WWE and became the Alliance leader. The callous trio of Shane, Stephanie, and Paul Heyman devised plans for Austin and his followers to carry out. In November 2001, this war was finally settled at *Survivor Series* as Team WWE defeated Team Alliance in a winner-take-all 10-man tag team elimination. Though WWE survived this hostile corporate takeover attempt and continued to prosper, some still bear the scars today from the battles of yesterday.

Allied Powers 🇺🇸 🇬🇧

Fate brought these two pillars of strength together during a January 1995 episode of *Monday Night Raw*. History repeated itself as England's British Bulldog and America's Lex Luger combined forces and battled Ted DiBiase's Million Dollar Corporation. The

MEMBERS	British Bulldog, Lex Luger
COMBINED WEIGHT	525 lbs.
YEARS ACTIVE	1960 1969 · 1970 1979 · 1980 1989 · **1990 1999** · 2000 PRESENT

duo became World Tag Team title contenders after an impressive win at *WrestleMania XI* over Jacob & Eli Blu.

Despite heated bouts with then-World Tag Team Champions Owen Hart & Yokozuna, British Bulldog & Lex Luger were unable to win the titles. That August saw a sad turn of events take place during *Monday Night Raw*. When Luger couldn't compete due to a sudden family emergency, Bulldog recruited Diesel to be his partner. After the make-shift duo lost in a valiant effort, British Bulldog turned on Diesel. Unaware of his partner's actions, Luger returned days before *SummerSlam* expecting to reconnect with his partner. To the disappointment of WWE fans all over the world, the Allied Powers were no more. The British Bulldog joined the ranks of Camp Cornette.

Alundra Blayze 🇺🇸

HT	5'10"	FROM	Tampa, Florida

SIGNATURE MOVE	Bridging German Suplex

TITLE HISTORY	Women's Champion

YEARS ACTIVE	1960 1969 · 1970 1979 · 1980 1989 · **1990 1999** · 2000 PRESENT

Alundra Blayze's dangerous combination of athleticism and sex appeal made her the ultimate female force in the ring. When WWE reintroduced its Women's Championship in December 1993, Blayze appeared from out of nowhere to win a tournament to crown the new titleholder. The buxom blonde went on to dominate the division for nearly one year before being toppled by Bull Nakano in November 1994.

Early the next year, Blayze gained her revenge by upending Nakano on *Monday Night Raw* to regain the title. Unfortunately, however, she was derailed by yet another colossal competitor when Bertha Faye defeated her at *SummerSlam 1995*. The loss to Faye proved to be just a blip on the screen, as Blayze quickly recaptured the gold in less than two months.

Blayze held the title until she defected to WCW in December 1995.

ANDRE THE GIANT

HT	7'4"	WT	540 lbs.	FROM	Grenoble, France

SIGNATURE MOVE	Sitdown Splash	YEARS ACTIVE	1960 1969	1970 1979	1980 1989	1990 1999	2000 PRESENT

TITLE HISTORY	WWE Champion, World Tag Team Champion

As Andre Rousimoff played soccer on the streets of Grenoble, France, he never thought one day he'd grow up to be the largest professional athlete in the world. In the mid-1960s, a promoter introduced him to then-wrestler and future WWE commentator Lord Alfred Hayes. Audiences were beside themselves at Andre's amazing size, remarkable agility and immeasurable strength. He could even throw dropkicks and leap from the top rope. Since most of his matches lasted a few minutes, he was often showcased in handicap matches against two, three, or four opponents. Soon his fame reached the lights of Paris and he went by the name "Monster" Eiffel Tower. When Andre met Edouard Carpentier after an event, the French-Canadian mega-star saw Andre's natural skill and agreed to train him. Fresh from Carpentier's teachings Andre traveled to Japan in 1969 and frightened everyone as "Monster" Rousimoff.

While there, doctors diagnosed him with Acromegaly, commonly known as "Giantism," an endocrynological disease that causes one to grow at an accelerated rate beyond the age of physical maturity. Andre never told anyone of the diagnosis and remained the fun-loving figure both in and out of the ring.

WORLDWIDE FAME

After his successful Asian tour, Andre connected with his mentor and appeared in French-speaking areas. Though wrestling was broken down into regional territories at the time, Andre quickly became the world's most popular attraction. Now at 7'4" and more than 500 lbs. of awesome power, Andre was referred to as "The Eighth Wonder of the World," a moniker that stayed with him his entire career.

In 1971, Andre met with Vince McMahon, Sr. and was contracted to work in the then-World Wide Wrestling Federation. On March 26, 1973, he debuted in Madison Square Garden and for the first time was called Andre The Giant. Through the 1970's Andre broke into the mainstream. In 1974, he turned down a lucrative contract offer from the National Football League's Washington Redskins to remain in the squared circle. Soon Hollywood knocked on his door and he appeared on television programs including *The Tonight Show*, *The Merv Griffin Show*, and in 1975 he made his acting debut as Bigfoot on *The Six Million Dollar Man*.

"THE EIGHTH WONDER OF THE WORLD"

BOXER VERSUS WRESTLER

At the 1976 *Showdown At Shea*, he fought the 6'5" "Bayonne Bleeder" Chuck Wepner in a "Boxer vs. Wrestler" contest. Wepner looked like a mere toddler next to Andre and ended up being launched into the third-row seats. In 1980 Andre returned to Shea for another epic showdown against Hulk Hogan, who at the time donned a cape and retained the services of "Classy" Freddie Blassie. In a new decade, Andre continued to sell out arenas and in 1981 was featured in Sports Illustrated. However, Andre became revered for his interests and accomplishments outside the ring as well. He acted on both the small and silver screens, played and performed music, was a masterful cards player, raised horses at his farm in North Carolina, and amassed one of the largest private cellars in the world as a connoisseur of fine wines.

Andre continued to travel and briefly appeared in the territories of the National Wrestling Alliance, where he held several regional tag team championships. When he returned to World Wrestling Entertainment, the feared Killer Kahn was waiting for him. During their match Kahn jumped from the top rope and broke Andre's ankle, putting him out of action. Andre recovered and got retribution when he defeated his attacker in a "Mongolian Stretcher Match."

As The Eighth Wonder of the World headed into the mid-80s, a combination of new and familiar faces stood in his path. Andre's rivalry with the Heenan Family began when Big John Studd, Heenan, and Ken Patera schemed to "rape Andre of his dignity," as commentator Vince McMahon famously referred to it, on national television. During a tag match, Patera threw Andre's partner S.D. Jones out of the ring, crashing into the metal guardrail. The two henchmen then ganged up on Andre and beat him unconscious. In an act of humiliation the Heenan Family cut Andre's hair. Fueled by revenge, Andre first took out The Olympic Strongman during a match at Madison Square Garden. His ongoing battle over who was wrestling's true giant culminated at the first *WrestleMania*. Andre met Big John Studd in a $15,000 Body Slam Challenge. Andre emerged victorious but the victory was somewhat bittersweet when an outraged Bobby "The Brain" Heenan jumped into the ring and took the bag of money from Andre as he threw it to the crowd. Andre's historic undefeated streak continued and he was often referred to as wrestling's "Uncrowned World Champion." At *WrestleMania 2,* he added another victory to his record-setting number of battle royal wins when he eliminated The Hart Foundation in the 20-man WWE/NFL Battle Royal.

In 1986, Andre again was the focus of a Heenan Family plan when then-President Jack Tunney suspended him for not appearing at matches on WWE cards. As a result of the suspension, Andre was banned from WWE television and live events. However, while he served his suspension under strong protest, a three-man team from Sapporo, Japan called The Machines debuted. Their largest member, Giant Machine, became the target of a witch hunt conceived by Bobby "The Brain" Heenan. After battling with the Heenan Family, the Machines left World Wrestling Entertainment and their identities were never discovered.

WINNING A TITLE BY ANY MEANS NECESSARY

In 1987, Andre returned to Hollywood and co-starred in the hit film *The Princess Bride* as the gentle giant Fezzik. When he came back to WWE, Andre's appearance and demeanor had changed. He shocked fans worldwide when he appeared on an episode of *Piper's Pit* with Bobby "The Brain" Heenan at his side. Andre issued a challenge to his longtime friend, Hulk Hogan, to a WWE Championship match at *WrestleMania III*.

In front of a record-breaking 93,173 fans at the Pontiac Silverdome, the irresistible force met the immovable object. The friendly, warm giant that made fans smile for decades now stood in the ring as a towering, stoic figure dressed in black. In the end, the power of Hulkamania bested Andre the Giant and his fifteen-year undefeated streak was broken. That November, their rivalry carried over to team warfare at the inaugural *Survivor Series* where Andre was the sole survivor. The momentum from that dominating showing led to a WWE Championship rematch. It was set for February 5, 1988 and was a primetime national television broadcast of *The Main Event*.

During the bout, Andre suplexed the champion and attempted a pinfall. Referee Dave Hebner made the three-count despite Hulk Hogan raising his left shoulder. As Hogan disputed the outcome, Andre was presented the championship belt with his hand raised. Seconds later, Andre surrendered the title to DiBiase who pronounced himself the new WWE Champion.

THE AFTERMATH

Andre left the ring and taunted a fallen Hulk Hogan when suddenly another referee appeared who looked exactly like Dave Hebner. As the two officials argued, the one who called the match sucker-punched and kicked the man out of the ring who later was identified as the real Dave Hebner. Then-WWE President Jack Tunney ruled that when Andre handed the championship to DiBiase he forfeited the belt. The WWE Championship was considered vacant and a new, undisputed champion would be crowned in a tournament at *WrestleMania IV*. Andre and Hulk Hogan met in the first match of the second round. With no regard for the rules or themselves, the match ended in a double-countout.

That summer the two Superstars met in the main event of *WrestleFest '88* in a Steel Cage match in front of over 25,800 screaming fans. The next major match between them was in the main event of the first-ever *SummerSlam*. Andre had his partner, "Million Dollar Man" Ted DiBiase, and Hogan had his, then-WWE Champion Randy "Macho Man" Savage.

REDEMPTION IN THE END

Andre started to team with fellow Heenan Family member Haku and formed the Colossal Connection. On December 13, 1989, Andre and Haku defeated Demolition to capture the WWE World Tag Team Championship. At *WrestleMania VI*, Ax and Smash regained the titles when a double-team move gone wrong sent Andre into the ropes and Haku was pinned. After the match, a furious Bobby Heenan berated Andre. After venting his frustrations on his now former manager and tag team partner, Andre left the SkyDome to his first *WrestleMania* ovation in four years. Weeks later he appeared in a sold-out Tokyo Dome for *The Wrestling Summit* where he teamed with *purorseu* legend, Giant Baba, against Demolition. Andre continued to appear at WWE events through 1991 as well as in Japan and Mexico. His last in-ring appearance was in 1992 for All-Japan Pro Wrestling. Andre's last television appearance was on Septmeber 2, 1992 at World Championship Wrestling's *Clash of Champions XX* as he, along with Jim Ross and Gordon Solie, celebrated twenty years of professional wrestling broadcasts on WTBS.

Sadly on January 27, 1993, while back in France for his father's funeral, this amazing human being passed away in his sleep, at the age of forty-six. The disease that was responsible for his size proved to be too much for his body to endure. Shortly after his death, Andre was inducted into the WWE Hall of Fame. The privilege of being the first person acknowledged into sports-entertainment's elite group was fitting for the man who was the industry's first and arguably most recognizable global icon.

Angelo "King Kong" Mosca

HT	6'4"	**WT**	319 lbs.	**FROM**	Toronto, Ontario, Canada

SIGNATURE MOVE Sleeper **YEARS ACTIVE** 1960-1969 1970-1979 1980-1989 1990-1999 2000-PRESENT

Before his career in the ring, this man played 14 seasons as a defensive tackle in the Canadian Football League and was a five-time Grey Cup winner. A mainstay in the Stampede and Montreal territories, the man who carried the nickname "King Kong" debuted in WWE in 1970. Though he didn't compete full-time until his retirement from football in 1972, Angelo "King Kong" Mosca brutalized opponents in rings all over the globe.

Through the 1970s, Mosca toured the NWA and AWA, winning several singles and tag team titles. "King Kong" returned to WWE in 1981 and battled a new crop of Superstars while contending for both the WWE Championship and Intercontinental Championship. As the mid-1980s approached, Mosca traded in his boots for a microphone and became part of the announce team. In 1985, he dedicated his time to manage the ring career of his son, Angelo Mosca, Jr.

Angelo Mosca, Jr. YEARS ACTIVE  1960-1969 1970-1979 **1980-1989** 1990-1999 2000-PRESENT

FROM	Boston, Massachusetts	**SIGNATURE MOVE**	Flying Cross Body

Trained and managed by his legendary father, this second generation Superstar was an incredibly conditioned athlete. He began his career in the early 1980s and first received attention when he defeated "Russian Bear" Ivan Koloff for the Mid-Atlantic Heavyweight Championship.

As his father led the way, Angelo Mosca, Jr. debuted in World Wrestling Entertainment in 1984. With the famous Mosca power and fire, Angelo was also well-schooled in mat wrestling and aerial maneuvers. He took on villains and brought fans to their feet until he left the company in April 1985.

Antonino Rocca (see page 16)

Angelo Savoldi

FROM	Hoboken, New Jersey

YEARS ACTIVE 1960-1969 1970-1979 1980-1989 1990-1999 2000-PRESENT

Spending the majority of his career competing at approximately 210 pounds, Angelo Savoldi was a true trailblazer for today's cruiserweights. Savoldi made his professional debut in New York in 1937. Over the next several decades, he competed in main events in Puerto Rico and Boston, but it was in Oklahoma where he attained his greatest notoriety, capturing the National Wrestling Alliance World Junior Heavyweight Championship on three occasions.

Savoldi didn't enter the WWE until the 1970s, which was well after his prime. However, that didn't stop him from being a force within the promotion. Realizing his competitive days were behind him, Savoldi began training many of WWE's younger Superstars. He even became a minority partner in the company, which was owned by Vince J. McMahon at the time.

In 1984, Savoldi and his sons Mario, Joe and Tom formed the Boston-based International Championship Wrestling. The promotion boasted an impressive roster of future WWE Superstars, including Mick Foley, Chris Candido, and Tazz.

Antonio Inoki

HT	6'2"	**WT**	240 lbs	**FROM**	Yokohama, Japan

TITLE HISTORY World Martial Arts Champion

YEARS ACTIVE 1960-1969 1970-1979 1980-1989 1990-1999 2000-PRESENT

Antonio Inoki is an iconic figure in Japan's professional wrestling and martial arts scene. While many American fans may not recognize him, he did compete in a series of WWE's most controversial title matches in 1979.

While on tour of Japan, WWE Champion Bob Backlund lost to Inoki in a shocking upset. The following night, Backlund cashed in his rematch clause and regained the WWE Championship. However, to further complicate matters, outside interference in the rematch caused WWE President Hisashi Shinma to return the title to Inoki. The Japanese legend refused to accept the title in such a manner, resulting in the WWE Championship being briefly vacated. Back in the United States, Backlund won a match to reclaim the vacated WWE Championship. As a result of the controversies surrounding the series of matches, WWE later refused to recognize the title changes.

A few years prior to these Championship matches, the Japanese star gained worldwide exposure when he battled Muhammad Ali in a Boxer vs. Wrestler Match. The restricting rules of the encounter heavily diminished Inoki's offensive arsenal. After fifteen rounds of action (or inaction), the match ended in a draw.

Inoki still remains an influential member of the sports-entertainment community in Japan, where he has assumed several leadership roles within the nation's top promotions.

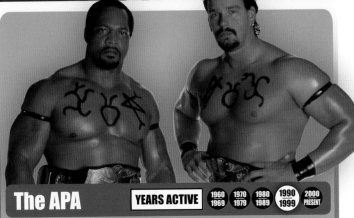

The APA

YEARS ACTIVE 1960-1969 1970-1979 1980-1989 **1990-1999** 2000-PRESENT

MEMBERS Faarooq, Bradshaw · **COMBINED WEIGHT** 574 lbs.

TITLE HISTORY World Tag Team Champions

These Superstars first came together as members of Hell's Henchmen, but then fell under the spell of Undertaker's Ministry of Darkness. The Acolytes won their first World Tag Team Championship from Kane & X-Pac in May 1999. After they went on their own, they formed the Acolytes Protection Agency, or APA for short.

Their powerful double-team moves, such as the Super Powerbomb, sent foes crashing into the canvas and as their reputation grew so did their business. They were often found in their office puffing on cigars, playing cards and downing beers.

If you had the money, they had the time to keep you protected. They held the World Tag Team Championship twice more, and their company motto was simple, "Drink and Fight." Despite being split-up during the 2002 brand extension, supply and demand dictated a reunion in 2003, At *Vengeance,* they hosted a Bar Room Brawl.

Though they continued down separate paths, they have reformed over the years. Most recently, to the delight of all their fans at the *Raw 15th Anniversary,* the APA beat Carlito & Jonathan Coachman at the behest of Hornswoggle. The APA can reform at any time and provide the type of protection you need, for the right price.

Ariel

YEARS ACTIVE 1960-1969 1970-1979 1980-1989 1990-1999 **2000-PRESENT**

HT 5'4"

With her jet-black hair, blood-red eye shadow, and fanged teeth, Ariel possessed a vampire-like quality that scared many. However, her fishnet stockings, knee-high boots, and uncanny ability to hang upside down also made her more than a little sexy.

As Kevin Thorn's bloodthirsty valet in ECW, Ariel could always be found by the side of her man, who she oftentimes kissed mid-match. She also had a penchant for using her signature tarot cards to predict the future. Unfortunately, however, her future did not hold great fortunes. Ariel left WWE in May 2007, less than one year after her debut.

Argentina Apollo

FROM Buenos Aires, Argentina

TITLE HISTORY United States Tag Team Champion

YEARS ACTIVE **1960-1969** **1970-1979** 1980-1989 1990-1999 2000-PRESENT

Argentina Apollo's approach to wrestling was unmistakable. Not only did he compete barefoot, but the high-flying Superstar also confused opponents with his dizzying arsenal of moves.

Most of Apollo's success came while competing in the tag team ranks. He formed a popular union with WWE legend Bruno Sammartino, but it was with Don McClarity that he captured his only WWE title. In February 1964, Apollo & McClarity defeated the famed Tolos Brothers for the now-defunct United States Tag Team Championship. They successfully defended the titles for four months before finally falling to Dr. Jerry Graham & Luke Graham in Washington, D.C.

Apollo continued his accomplished tag team career after leaving WWE. In April 1970, he teamed with Jose Lothario to claim the National Wrestling Alliance Florida Tag Team Championship. Two years later, he captured the Georgia version of the NWA Tag Team Championship with partner Dick Steinborn.

ARMAGEDDON

December 12, 1999
Fort Lauderdale, FL - National Car Rental Center

Main Event: Triple H defeated Mr. McMahon in a Street Fight

December 10, 2000
Birmingham, AL
Birmingham-Jefferson Civic Center

Main Event: WWE Champion Kurt Angle defeated the Rock, Stone Cold Steve Austin, Rikishi, Triple H, and Undertaker in a Hell in a Cell Match

December 15, 2002
Fort Lauderdale, FL - Office Depot Center

Main Event: Triple H defeated World Heavyweight Champion Shawn Michaels in Three Stages of Hell (Street Fight, Steel Cage Match, Ladder Match)

December 14, 2003
Orlando, FL - TD Waterhouse Centre

Main Event: Triple H defeated World Heavyweight Champion Goldberg and Kane in a Triple Threat Match

December 12, 2004
Atlanta, GA - Gwinnett Center

Main Event: WWE Champion JBL defeated Eddie Guerrero, Booker T, and Undertaker in a Fatal Four Way Match

December 18, 2005
Providence, RI - Dunkin' Donuts Center

Main Event: Undertaker defeated Randy Orton in a Hell in a Cell Match

December 17, 2006
Richmond, VA - Richmond Coliseum

Main Event: World Heavyweight Champion Batista & WWE Champion John Cena defeated King Booker & Finlay

December 16, 2007
Pittsburgh, PA - Mellon Arena

Main Event: World Heavyweight Champion Batista defeated Edge, and Undertaker in a Triple Threat Match

December 14, 2008
Buffalo, NY - HSBC Arena

Main Event: Jeff Hardy defeated WWE Champion Edge and Triple H in a Triple Threat Match

ANTONINO ROCCA

| HT | 6' | WT | 224 lbs | FROM | Buenos Aires, Argentina | SIGNATURE MOVE | The Argentine Backbreaker |

| YEARS ACTIVE | 1960 1969 | 1970 1979 | 1980 1989 | 1990 1999 | 2000 PRESENT | TITLE HISTORY | United States Tag Team Champion, International Heavyweight Champion |

Antonino Rocca was one of the most beloved heroes of all-time. His amazing array of maneuvers astounded millions around the world, and his signature repertoire has proven to be timeless. His influence has transcended generations and cultures, which is a testament to the quality of man and the limitless scope of his vision. Rocca is credited with bringing past fans back to professional wrestling and welcoming new ones, as well as being one of the greatest innovators in the history of the art form. He was one of the biggest stars responsible for wrestling's first "Golden Age." His fearless nature in the ring ushered in a new wrestling style that high-flyers of the squared circle will surely study forever.

Born in Trevino, Italy, this trailblazer grew up in Argentina and started his career in professional sports as a soccer player. When a leg injury ended his career, he yearned for another outlet to showcase his charisma, heart, and unparalleled athleticism. Trained by Stanislaus Zbyszko, Rocca received the teachings he needed to succeed in the ultra-competitive world of professional wrestling.

He debuted in South America in 1942 and competed as he felt most comfortable: barefoot. Unlike anything ever seen before in the ring, Antonino was in constant motion and beautifully executed exciting maneuvers both in the air and on the mat.

To frustrate opponents and delight fans, Antonino used to slap his opposition in the face with his feet.

" ARGENTINA "

THE UNITED STATES AND THE NWA

In the late 1940s, Rocca arrived in the United States and started wrestling in Texas, where he was a main event star as the NWA Texas Heavyweight Champion. It was then that promoter Kola Kwariani introduced Antonino to former wrestler and Goldust Trio member Joseph Raymond "Toots" Mondt, the kingpin of wrestling in the Big Apple. Rocca was brought to Manhattan and shared with other promoters in the region, including then-newcomer from Washington, D.C. Vincent J. McMahon. The barefoot boy of Argentina was a breath of fresh air. With his elegant balance, showmanship and energetic poise, he put Madison Square Garden back on the map as the ultimate venue for professional wrestling. Hurricanranas, flying dropkicks from any angle, victory rolls and flying body presses dazzled audiences who were accustomed to athletes who never left their feet. His finishing move, the Argentine Backbreaker, brought crowds to a frenzy and dastardly foes to submission as they yelled in incredible pain. From the Empire State Building in New York City to the Grand Olympic Auditorium in Los Angeles and all places in between, "The Amazing Rocca" was king. He was the most dynamic performer the industry had seen to that point and a legitimate phenomenon.

Shows at Madison Square Garden that hosted the NWA Champion saw the Argentine acrobat in the main event. During this period in wrestling history only Gorgeous George was a bigger star. Rocca's ethnicity played a role in his following as well. He was of Italian heritage and hailed from Latin America, which made him a huge attraction for two of the New York area's largest immigrant populations. His fans were so devoted to him, that when Dick The Bruiser split him open during their match in Madison Square Garden, a violent riot ensued. Soon after, an image from the melee taken by a brave photographer was featured on the cover of *LIFE* Magazine.

GREATER SUCCESS AND FAME

As time went on and Rocca's popularity grew, McMahon convinced him to join his outfit full-time. In 1956 Antonino created a team with Puerto Rican Superstar Miguel Perez, and on March 30, 1957 the duo became the first holders of the United States Tag Team Championship when they defeated Don and Jackie Fargo. During this era, the Argentine Superstar feuded with the likes of Hans Schmidt, The Kangaroos, Eduard Carpentier, Johnny Valentine, Don Leo Jonathan, and Lou Thez. He also took on Gene Kiniski, Skull Murphy, Pampero Firpo, Dr. Jerry Graham, and future WWE Hall of Famers Eddie Graham, Killer Kowalski, Verne Gagne and "Classy" Freddie Blassie. In July 1959, Argentina bested future WWE Hall of Famer "Nature Boy" Buddy Rogers in the tournament finals for the International Heavyweight Championship, which he turned into the longest reign of any International Heavyweight Champion.

Rocca's fame carried him into the early 1960s as his numbers of fans continued to grow. After he graced countless magazine covers, in August 1962, DC Comics featured him on the cover of the Superman #155 comic book throwing The Man of Steel out of the ring. On television, Rocca even grappled with the "King of Late Night" Johnny Carson on *The Tonight Show*. A Latin music LP by famous artist Billy Mure was released on MGM Records titled, *In This Corner, the Musical World of Argentina Rocca* and showed the Superstar performing a dropkick on the album cover.

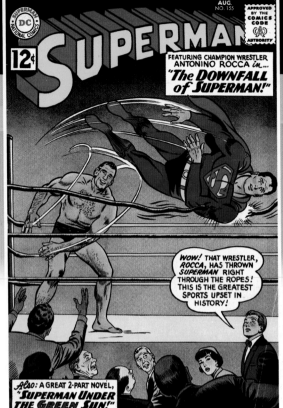

"Superman" # 155 © 1962 DC Comics.

CHANGING OF THE GUARD

By the time the World Wide Wrestling Federation was independent from the National Wrestling Alliance, Rocca relinquished his title as the company's top Superstar to Bruno Sammartino. In one of his last bouts with the company, he once again stood across the ring from "Nature Boy" Buddy Rogers in a tournament finals. This time, it was in Rio de Janeiro, Brazil for the newly created World Wide Wrestling Federation Championship. On that evening it was Rogers' turn to lift a gold belt into the air in victory. For the remainder of the decade Argentina wrestled and officiated for the Japanese Pro Wrestling Association. In the early 1970s, he worked for New Japan Pro Wrestling and officiated the classic bout between Antonio Inoki and Karl Gotch. Rocca returned to North America in 1976, and in November of that year he made his silver screen debut in *Alice, Sweet Alice* starring Brooke Shields.

Over a decade since his last appearance, Antonino Rocca returned to the World Wide Wrestling Federation as an announcer. Each week he called the action with Vince K. McMahon, the legendary promoter's son. On February 25, 1977, he donned the referee's shirt and was the man in the middle of a boxing match that pitted future WWE Hall of Famers Gorilla Monsoon and Andre the Giant at Madison Square Garden. Tragically, on March 15, 1977, this uniquely gifted individual suddenly passed away at Roosevelt Hospital in New York City after complications following an infection.

The greatest honor Antonino Rocca would receive came in 1995, when then-WWE Champion, Diesel posthumously inducted the father of aerial assault into the WWE Hall of Fame, permanently marking his place amongst sports-entertainment's elite figures.

ARNOLD SKAALAND

HT 6'	**WT** 240 lbs.	**FROM** White Plains, New York

TITLE HISTORY United States Tag Team Champion

YEARS ACTIVE   1960 1969 · 1970 1979 · 1980 1989 · 1990 1999 · 2000 PRESENT

There was nothing Arnold Skaaland couldn't do. He was an accomplished wrestler, legendary manager, brilliant promoter, and cherished friend to countless names within the wrestling industry. This rare combination of greatness lead Skaaland to one of the finest careers in sports-entertainment history.

After representing the U.S. Marines in World War II, Skaaland kept in shape by competing as an amateur boxer. He proved to be a force within the ropes, but never believed he could make a living in the sport. Instead, he focused his efforts on wrestling, an up-and-coming profession that was gaining popularity thanks to television.

Skaaland made his professional debut in 1946, competing mainly in the Northeast. His speed, toughness, and overall intelligence quickly earned him the nickname "The Golden Boy." By the early 1960s he earned several opportunities at what was then considered the industry's leading title, the National Wrestling Alliance (NWA) Championship.

In 1963, Skaaland began working for Vincent J. McMahon's newly-created WWE. It was here that he gained his greatest success. Not only did Skaaland enjoy a reign as one-half of the United States Tag Team Champions (with Spiros Arion), but he also became a shareholder in McMahon's company. As part owner, Skaaland was responsible handling a great deal of the company's finances.

During this time, Skaaland also made a successful transition into the managerial ranks. Behind his supreme level of wrestling knowledge, he guided Bruno Sammartino and Bob Backlund to three of the most remarkable WWE Championship reigns in history. In fact, aside from ten months in the late 1970s, Skaaland's men held the WWE Championship uninterrupted from December 1973 to December 1983.

Skaaland's managerial career came to an end shortly after he threw in the towel on Backlund's reign in his loss the Iron Sheik in December 1983. From there, he assumed several backstage responsibilities until his retirement in the early 1990s. In 1994, Skaaland's tireless efforts to the sports-entertainment industry were recognized when he was inducted into the WWE Hall of Fame.

Armando Estrada

HT 6'2"	**WT** 230 lbs.

FROM Havana, Cuba

YEARS ACTIVE 1960 1969 · 1970 1979 · 1980 1989 · 1990 1999 · 2000 PRESENT

Originally a successful Cuban businessman, Armando Estrada came to WWE in April 2006 as the manager of the savage Umaga. Under Estrada's shrewd leadership, the "Samoan Bulldozer" became known as one of the fiercest competitors in all of WWE.

After leading Umaga to the Intercontinental Championship and the famous Battle of the Billionaires Match at *WrestleMania 23*, Estrada left his protégé's side in May 2007. After a brief hiatus, he resurfaced in ECW as the brand's General Manager. As GM, the powerful dictator made life hell for many ECW stars, most notably Colin Delaney.

In June 2008, Estrada was relieved of his GM post by Theodore Long. Unemployed, the Cuban set out to make a living in the ring. Ironically, it took some help from rival Delaney for Estrada to defeat Tommy Dreamer and earn his ECW contract.

Ashley

HT 5'5"

FROM New York, New York

SIGNATURE MOVE Starstruck

YEARS ACTIVE 1960 1969 · 1970 1979 · 1980 1989 · 1990 1999 · 2000 PRESENT

A bad girl from the Big Apple, this punk chick started to get attention when she was crowned Miss Hawaiian Tropic USA in 2002 and Miss Hawaiian Tropic Canada in 2005. She entered WWE that June when she won the Diva Search contest. From there, she became one of the most popular Superstars on *Raw*.

As she fought off Divas Candice, Melina, and Torrie Wilson, she aligned herself with Trish Stratus and became a tough competitor. She ended her first year in WWE gracing the cover of December's *Flex Magazine*. She started 2006 by stopping the hearts of men everywhere when she appeared in *Maxim*.

As she went from *Raw* to *SmackDown*, Ashley showed her verbal skills behind the broadcast booth. In April 2007, she answered the pleas of men everywhere when she appeared in *Playboy*. She also appeared on an episode of *Smallville* and that summer branched out further as a pop-culture personality and was a contestant on *Survivor: China*.

Ashley and World Wrestling Entertainment parted ways in July 2008. Though her time in WWE was brief, the pierced princess made quite an impact as a Diva.

Avatar

HT 6' **WT** 235 lbs. **FROM** Parts Unknown

SIGNATURE MOVE Frog Splash

This enigmatic competitor combined martial arts with high-flying moves, and made his debut on *Monday Night Raw* in October 1995. Unlike most masked Superstars, he didn't put on a mask until he was in the ring, and removed it after a victory. His version of the Frog Splash was a bit different. To begin, he'd stand on the sternum of his fallen opponent, then jump from their body and land on them with a body splash.

Avatar became a fan-favorite as he battled villains like Sycho Sid, Isaac Yankem DDS, Brooklyn Brawler, and Bradshaw. During his stay in WWE, he also formed an exciting tag team with fellow aerialist Aldo Montoya. By March 1997, Avatar vanished from WWE. Even if it was only for a brief period of time, Avatar showcased his talents where only the select few are given the opportunity.

B

BACKLASH

April 25, 1999
Providence, RI - Providence Civic Center

Main Event: WWE Champion Stone Cold Steve Austin vs. The Rock, Shane McMahon as special guest referee

April 30, 2000
Washington, DC - MCI Center

Main Event: WWE Champion Triple H vs. The Rock, Shane McMahon as special guest referee

April 29, 2001
Rosemont, IL - Allstate Arena

Main Event: WWE Champion Stone Cold Steve Austin & Intercontinental Champion Triple H vs. World Tag Team Champions Undertaker & Kane

April 21, 2002
Kansas City, MO - Kemper Arena

Main Event: WWE Champion Triple H vs. Hulk Hogan

April 27, 2003
Worcester, MA - Worcester Centrum

Main Event: Goldberg vs. The Rock

April 18, 2004
Edmonton, Alberta, Canada - Rexall Place

Main Event: World Heavyweight Champion Chris Benoit vs. Shawn Michaels vs. Triple H, Triple Threat Match

May 1, 2005
Manchester, NH - Verizon Wireless Arena

Main Event: World Heavyweight Champion Batista vs. Triple H

April 30, 2006
Lexington, KY - Rupp Arena

Main Event: WWE Champion John Cena vs. Triple H vs. Edge, Triple Threat Match

April 29, 2007
Atlanta, GA - Philips Arena

Main Event: WWE Champion John Cena vs. Randy Orton vs. Edge vs. Shawn Michaels, Fatal Four Way Match

April 27, 2008
Baltimore, Maryland - 1st Mariner Arena

Main Event: WWE Champion Randy Orton vs. Triple H vs. John Cena vs. JBL, Fatal Four Way Match

BAD BLOOD

October 5, 1997
St. Louis, MO - Kiel Center

Main Event: Shawn Michaels defeated Undertaker in a Hell in a Cell Match

June 15, 2003
Houston, TX - Compaq Center

Main Event: World Heavyweight Champion Triple H defeated Kevin Nash in a Hell in a Cell Match with Mick Foley as Special Guest Referee

June 13, 2004
Columbus, OH - Nationwide Arena

Main Event: Triple H defeated Shawn Michaels in a Hell in a Cell Match

The original *Badd Blood* was an *In Your House* event that featured the very first Hell in a Cell Match and the debut of Kane. *Bad Blood* returned in 2003, but was replaced by *One Night Stand* in 2005.

Bad News Brown

HT 6'2" **WT** 271 lbs. **FROM** Harlem, New York **SIGNATURE MOVE** Ghetto Blaster

In 1977, this Olympic Bronze Medalist in Judo entered the ranks of professional wrestling. Trained by Japanese legend Antonio Inoki, Bad News Brown first made waves in WWE in 1988 and showed why he was one of the meanest, nastiest, most violent Superstars in WWE history. Bad News also showed he could be a persuasive swindler when he double-crossed Bret "Hit Man" Hart and eliminated him to win the Battle Royal at *WrestleMania IV*. Bad News also never hesitated to display his inability to coexist with others when he walked out on teams during the first two *Survivor Series* events. Bad News posed a serious threat to the reign of then-champion Randy "Macho Man" Savage.

In 1990, Bad News vanished from World Wrestling Entertainment after he accosted then-WWE President Jack Tunney on *The Brother Love Show*. He spent the rest of the decade primarily competing in Mexico, Japan, and Canada, but when a chronic knee injury intensified, he hung up his boots in 1999. Brown briefly owned and operated his own training facility in his adopted home of Calgary, Alberta in 2005.

Tragically, on March 6, 2007, Bad News Brown passed away. Brown's legacy in amateur athletics and sports-entertainment continues to resonante, as he is widely regarded as one of the toughest men to enter the ring.

Balls Mahoney

HT 6'2" **WT** 305 lbs.

FROM Nutley, New Jersey

SIGNATURE MOVE

Nutcracker Suite

YEARS ACTIVE

1960 1969 | 1970 1979 | 1980 1989 | **1990 1999** | 2000 PRESENT

Mahoney started his career in 1987 and toured the United States, Canada and Puerto Rico. Mahoney won numerous singles and tag team championships on the indepedent circuit, and in 1996, Balls Mahoney arrived in ECW. He was quickly embraced by the promotion's demanding fans. Mahoney formed a tag team with another purveyor of pain, Axl Rotten, collectively known as the Chair Swingin' Freaks. When ECW went out of business in early 2001, Mahoney returned to tours of the United States and Asia.

In 2005, he surprised fans everywhere when he appeared at *ECW's One Night Stand* in a brawl with the Blue World Order. Mahoney was the first Extremist signed for the resurrected ECW. While Balls shared the ring with some familiar faces, he faced new challengers, as well. Balls even caught the eye of Diva Kelly Kelly. In April 2007, he was an advisor on the Sci-Fi Network's reality show, *Who Wants To Be A Superhero?*

BAM BAM BIGELOW

HT 6'4" **WT** 390 lbs. **FROM** Asbury Park, New Jersey

SIGNATURE MOVE Slingshot Splash, Greetings From Asbury Park

YEARS ACTIVE 1960 1969 | 1970 1979 | 1980 1989 | 1990 1999 | 2000 PRESENT

The "Beast From The East" wowed audiences with the agility of a gazelle, forward rolls, cartwheels, and devastating moves off the top rope. His colorful ring attire was topped off with a fireball tattoo that covered his entire skull. In 1987, most WWE managers competed for the employment this powerful newcomer. As the "Battle for Bam Bam" continued, the world stood still when Bam Bam Bigelow selected Sir Oliver Humperdink to guide his career. This fan favorite was tough as nails, and he was selected as a member of Hulk Hogan's team at the first *Survivor Series*. Outnumbered 3-to-1, Bigelow managed to eliminate King Kong Bundy and One Man Gang before finally being eliminated by Andre the Giant. His last appearance of the decade was in the WWE Championship Tournament at *WrestleMania IV*.

Bam Bam returned to WWE in 1992 and later became a member of The Million-Dollar Corporation. In 1995, he made his silver screen debut in *Major Payne*. He then met pro football Hall of Famer Lawrence Taylor in the main event of *WrestleMania XI*. After a stint in Japan, Bam Bam surfaced in Extreme Championship Wrestling and later in WCW. After World Championship Wrestling was purchased by WWE in 2001, Bigelow returned to the independent scene.

On January 19, 2007, Bam Bam Bigelow passed away. Bigelow was considered a physical phenomenon and one of the greatest big men to ever set foot inside the ring. He entertained millions around the world. He commanded an audience, a match, and respect like few others in sports-entertainment.

Bam Neely

HT 6'7" **WT** 275 lbs.

FROM

Robbinsdale, Minnesota

YEARS ACTIVE

1960 1969 | 1970 1979 | 1980 1989 | 1990 1999 | **2000 PRESENT**

Bam Neely comes from a town rich in ring tradition. Hailing from Robbinsdale, Minnesota, the former border patrol agent shares the same zip code as the late, great WWE Legends Rick Rude and Curt Hennig. In the ring, however, Neely shares no likenesses with his renowned predecessors. Instead, he substitutes pure power for their technical ability. His overwhelming strength caught the eye of Chavo Guerrero, who brought Neely in to serve as his bodyguard in April 2008. On occasion, Neely will also team with his boss, combining a lethal amount of speed and power.

Barbara Bush (B.B.)

YEARS ACTIVE 1960-1969 1970-1979 1980-1989 **1990-1999** 2000-PRESENT

This buxom blonde first appeared as an EMT tending to injured Superstars. For weeks, fans in the crowd suddenly claimed they needed medical attention. She appeared again after the first-ever Gravy Bowl Match on *SmackDown* and got into it with Ivory. Her fights with the then-Women's Champion continued and B.B. participated in the Four-Way Evening Gown Match at *Armageddon 1999*. At the Holiday Topless Top-Rope Match against Terri on *Raw*, she was in Val Venis' corner and Terri in Hardcore Holly's. This match stipulated every time one of the Superstars was thrown over the top rope, his female representative must remove an article of clothing. The first woman to be topless lost the match for "her man." Venis was tossed over twice and Triple H was the judge to make sure she peeled it all off.

B.B. continued to captivate WWE audiences until late 2000, when she left the company. Audiences and Superstars will always remember this energetic EMT who was dedicated to making people feel better.

Barbarian

HT 6'2" **WT** 300 lbs. **FROM** The Isle of Tonga

SIGNATURE MOVE Kick of Fear

After years of competing as one-half of the intimidating Powers of Pain tag team, the Barbarian washed the paint from his face and went his own way in search of singles success in 1990.

The Barbarian's quest to make it solo began when his manager, Mr. Fuji, sold the big man's contract to Bobby "the Brain" Heenan. Under Heenan's tutelage, the Barbarian altered his image, trading in his leather and chains for a skull-and-antler headdress and warrior-like fur robes. The makeover paid early dividends, as the new-look Barbarian got off to an impressive start, defeating Tito Santana at *WrestleMania VI*.

Unfortunately for the Barbarian, *WrestleMania VI* is where the winning stopped. He spent most of the following year coming up short against the likes of Big Boss Man and Bret "Hit Man" Hart. Realizing a solo career might not yield big benefits, Heenan paired the Barbarian with Haku in hopes of recreating some of the strong man's earlier tag success. The Barbarian's return to the tag scene proved just as futile as his singles efforts. After his team lost to The Rockers at *WrestleMania VII*, the Barbarian struggled to get back on track. By mid-1992, he left WWE.

THE BARBER SHOP

DEBUT 1991

In 1991, Brutus "The Barber" Beefcake introduced audiences to the place where he would regularly "cut and strut." *The Barber Shop* became one of the most popular talk show segments in WWE, as Superstars were answering questions, and at times being held accountable for their actions by one of their own.

Whether it was a showdown between The Nasty Boys and The Legion of Doom, or Ted DiBiase's Million Dollar Team coming out in full to predict their 1991 *Survivor Series* dominance, fans were guaranteed to see something exciting take place when the Shop opened for business.

Perhaps the most talked-about moment during the show's existence came in January 1992, when Shawn Michaels threw partner Marty Jannetty through the *Shop's* glass window and ended the almost decade-long partnership of the Rockers. Later that year, the show set was destroyed by a crazed Sid Justice after he decided the time for answering questions regarding his deeds toward Hulk Hogan was over.

Baron Mikel Scicluna

HT 6'3" **WT** 256 lbs. **FROM** Isle of Malta

SIGNATURE MOVE Use of foreign objects

TITLE HISTORY World Tag Team Champion, United States Tag Team Champion

YEARS ACTIVE **1960-1969** **1970-1979** **1980-1989** 1990-1999 2000-PRESENT

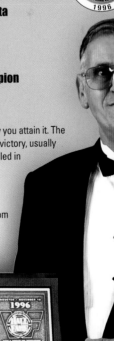

For Baron Mikel Scicluna, a win's a win, regardless of how you attain it. The WWE Hall of Famer made a career out of cheating to gain victory, usually by thumping opponents with a roll of coins he kept concealed in his boots.

Upon entering WWE, Scicluna was thrust into a rivalry with Bruno Sammartino. Scicluna failed to pry the WWE Championship from Sammartino, but that didn't stop him from eyeing other golden opportunities. In late 1966, Scicluna enjoyed a three-month reign as United States Tag Team Champion with partner Smasher Sloan. Six years later, he teamed with King Curtis to claim the most prestigious prize in tag team wrestling: the World Tag Team Championship.

Scicluna continued to wrestle for WWE until his retirement in 1984. Twelve years after hanging up his coin-filled boots, Scicluna was awarded the ultimate honor when he was inducted into the WWE Hall of Fame by longtime nemesis Gorilla Monsoon.

Baron Von Raschke

HT 6'3" **WT** 281 lbs.

FROM The Republic of Germany

SIGNATURE MOVE Iron Claw

YEARS ACTIVE 1960 1969 1970 1979 1980 1989 1990 1999 2000 PRESENT

Most of Baron Von Raschke's career was spent competing in the AWA and NWA. However, news of his devastating Iron Claw made its way to WWE locker rooms, causing many Superstars to fear locking horns with him during one of his rare WWE appearances.

A skilled amateur wrestler, Raschke excelled immediately upon his debut in the mid-1960s. By the mid-1970s, his German goosestep earned him the reputation as one of America's most hated Superstars. Northeast fans feared the worst when Raschke earned an opportunity at Bruno Sammartino's WWE Championship in 1977. Just a few years removed from Ivan Koloff's frightful victory over Sammartino, WWE fans feared another title loss to a hated opponent. Luckily for Sammartino's fans, Raschke's temper got the better of him, as he was disqualified after using a steel chair on the champion.

In 1988, Raschke made a return to WWE as the manager of the Powers of Pain tag team. Known simply as the Baron, he lead Barbarian & Warlord to early success before moving over and letting Mr. Fuji take control of the team. Raschke's career began to wind down following his managerial stint in WWE. Though his WWE efforts were minimal, he will long be remembered as one of sports-entertainment's most fear-provoking Superstars.

Barry Horowitz

YEARS ACTIVE  1960 1969 1970 1979 1980 1989 1990 1999 2000 PRESENT

HT 6' **WT** 221 lbs. **FROM** St. Petersburg, Florida **SIGNATURE MOVE** The Cloverleaf

Barry Horowitz was a touted high school amateur wrestler and later competed collegiately at Florida State. Trained by the legendary Boris Malenko, he made a brief WWE stop in 1983. Barry returned to WWE in 1988, appearing on programs such as *Prime Time Wrestling*, *All-Star Wrestling*, and *Wrestling Challenge*.

After he recovered from a serious neck injury, Barry's shining moment came when he defeated Bodydonna Skip at *SummerSlam 1995*. That year, he also won *Pro Wrestling Illustrated*'s "Most Inspirational Wrestler of The Year" Award. He maintained a place on WWE cards through 1997, when he moved to WCW, where he stayed until 2000.

One of the most well-traveled ring veterans ever, Barry Horowitz has appeared in promotions all over the world, patting himself on the back each step of the way. In a career that spanned 21 years, Barry is considered by ring aficionados as one of the toughest and technically sound competitors to step inside the ring.

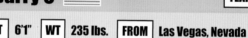

Barry O

YEARS ACTIVE  1960 1969 1970 1979 1980 1989 1990 1999 2000 PRESENT

HT 6'1" **WT** 235 lbs. **FROM** Las Vegas, Nevada

With "The Big O," Bob Orton, Sr. as his father, many sports-entertainment insiders forecasted greatness for Barry O. Unfortunately for the younger Orton, those predictions never turned into reality.

Unlike his brother, "Cowboy" Bob Orton, Barry O had a difficult time getting his WWE career off the ground. While brother Bob was competing with the likes of "Rowdy" Roddy Piper and Hulk Hogan, Barry O struggled against opponents like Outback Jack and Corporal Kirschner.

Despite his WWE troubles, Barry O did manage to gain some success while competing for Stu Hart's Stampede Wrestling in Calgary. Competing under a dark mask, Barry O called himself The Zodiac, which was a tribute to his father, who wrestled under the same name during the 1970s. While today's WWE fans may not recognize the name Barry O, they certainly know his nephew, "The Legend Killer" Randy Orton.

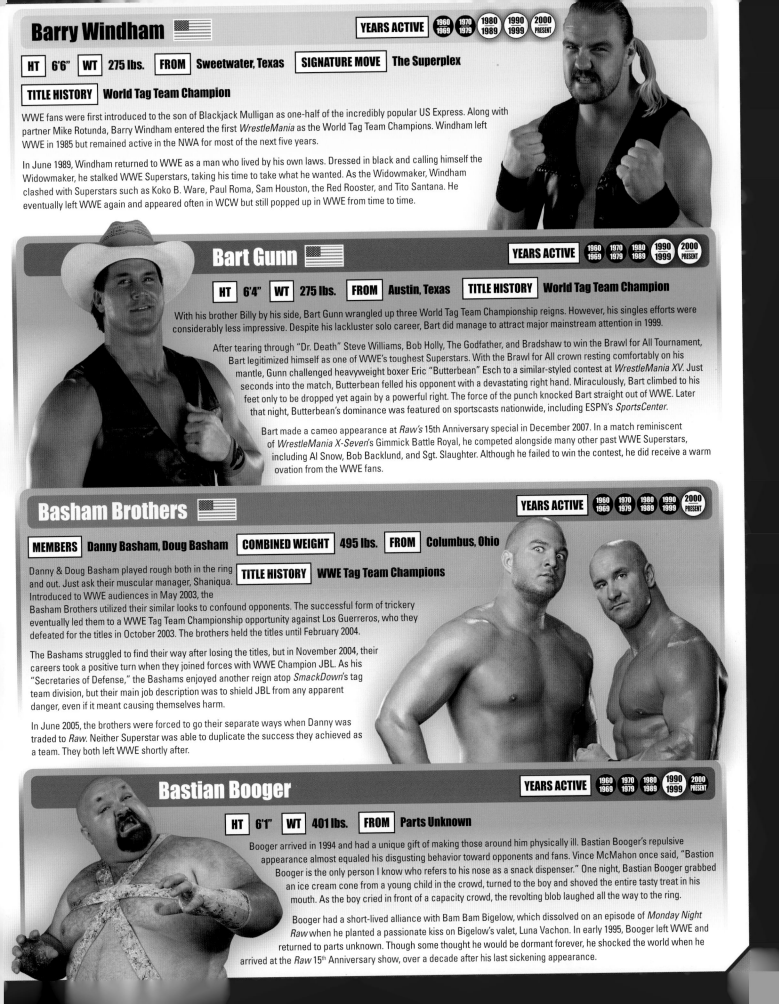

Barry Windham 🇺🇸

YEARS ACTIVE | 1960 1969 | 1970 1979 | 1980 1989 | 1990 1999 | 2000 PRESENT

HT 6'6" **WT** 275 lbs. **FROM** Sweetwater, Texas **SIGNATURE MOVE** The Superplex

TITLE HISTORY World Tag Team Champion

WWE fans were first introduced to the son of Blackjack Mulligan as one-half of the incredibly popular US Express. Along with partner Mike Rotunda, Barry Windham entered the first *WrestleMania* as the World Tag Team Champions. Windham left WWE in 1985 but remained active in the NWA for most of the next five years.

In June 1989, Windham returned to WWE as a man who lived by his own laws. Dressed in black and calling himself the Widowmaker, he stalked WWE Superstars, taking his time to take what he wanted. As the Widowmaker, Windham clashed with Superstars such as Koko B. Ware, Paul Roma, Sam Houston, the Red Rooster, and Tito Santana. He eventually left WWE again and appeared often in WCW but still popped up in WWE from time to time.

Bart Gunn 🇺🇸

YEARS ACTIVE | 1960 1969 | 1970 1979 | 1980 1989 | 1990 1999 | 2000 PRESENT

HT 6'4" **WT** 275 lbs. **FROM** Austin, Texas **TITLE HISTORY** World Tag Team Champion

With his brother Billy by his side, Bart Gunn wrangled up three World Tag Team Championship reigns. However, his singles efforts were considerably less impressive. Despite his lackluster solo career, Bart did manage to attract major mainstream attention in 1999.

After tearing through "Dr. Death" Steve Williams, Bob Holly, The Godfather, and Bradshaw to win the Brawl for All Tournament, Bart legitimized himself as one of WWE's toughest Superstars. With the Brawl for All crown resting comfortably on his mantle, Gunn challenged heavyweight boxer Eric "Butterbean" Esch to a similar-styled contest at *WrestleMania XV*. Just seconds into the match, Butterbean felled his opponent with a devastating right hand. Miraculously, Bart climbed to his feet only to be dropped yet again by a powerful right. The force of the punch knocked Bart straight out of WWE. Later that night, Butterbean's dominance was featured on sportscasts nationwide, including ESPN's *SportsCenter*.

Bart made a cameo appearance at *Raw's* 15th Anniversary special in December 2007. In a match reminiscent of *WrestleMania X-Seven*'s Gimmick Battle Royal, he competed alongside many other past WWE Superstars, including Al Snow, Bob Backlund, and Sgt. Slaughter. Although he failed to win the contest, he did receive a warm ovation from the WWE fans.

Basham Brothers 🇺🇸

YEARS ACTIVE | 1960 1969 | 1970 1979 | 1980 1989 | 1990 1999 | 2000 PRESENT

MEMBERS Danny Basham, Doug Basham **COMBINED WEIGHT** 495 lbs. **FROM** Columbus, Ohio

TITLE HISTORY WWE Tag Team Champions

Danny & Doug Basham played rough both in the ring and out. Just ask their muscular manager, Shaniqua. Introduced to WWE audiences in May 2003, the Basham Brothers utilized their similar looks to confound opponents. The successful form of trickery eventually led them to a WWE Tag Team Championship opportunity against Los Guerreros, who they defeated for the titles in October 2003. The brothers held the titles until February 2004.

The Bashams struggled to find their way after losing the titles, but in November 2004, their careers took a positive turn when they joined forces with WWE Champion JBL. As his "Secretaries of Defense," the Bashams enjoyed another reign atop *SmackDown*'s tag team division, but their main job description was to shield JBL from any apparent danger, even if it meant causing themselves harm.

In June 2005, the brothers were forced to go their separate ways when Danny was traded to *Raw*. Neither Superstar was able to duplicate the success they achieved as a team. They both left WWE shortly after.

Bastian Booger

YEARS ACTIVE | 1960 1969 | 1970 1979 | 1980 1989 | 1990 1999 | 2000 PRESENT

HT 6'1" **WT** 401 lbs. **FROM** Parts Unknown

Booger arrived in 1994 and had a unique gift of making those around him physically ill. Bastian Booger's repulsive appearance almost equaled his disgusting behavior toward opponents and fans. Vince McMahon once said, "Bastion Booger is the only person I know who refers to his nose as a snack dispenser." One night, Bastian Booger grabbed an ice cream cone from a young child in the crowd, turned to the boy and shoved the entire tasty treat in his mouth. As the boy cried in front of a capacity crowd, the revolting blob laughed all the way to the ring.

Booger had a short-lived alliance with Bam Bam Bigelow, which dissolved on an episode of *Monday Night Raw* when he planted a passionate kiss on Bigelow's valet, Luna Vachon. In early 1995, Booger left WWE and returned to parts unknown. Though some thought he would be dormant forever, he shocked the world when he arrived at the *Raw* 15th Anniversary show, over a decade after his last sickening appearance.

BATISTA

"THE ANIMAL"

YEARS ACTIVE 1960-1969 1970-1979 1980-1989 1990-1999 2000-PRESENT

HT 6'6" **WT** 290 lbs. **FROM** Washington, D.C. **SIGNATURE MOVE** Batista Bomb

TITLE HISTORY World Heavyweight Champion, World Tag Team Champion, WWE Tag Team Champion

The mere sight of him instills fear in opponents. His rock-solid physique, uncontrollable rage, and overwhelming power have propelled him to many of sports-entertainment's biggest wins in recent memory. He is Batista.

He spent his formative years finding trouble on the streets of Washington, D.C. and San Francisco, and was living on his own by the age of 17. For the next 10 years, he divided his time between bodybuilding and bouncing at nightclubs. An encounter with two rowdy patrons ignited his volatile temper and resulted in an arrest and a year's probation.

GETTING ON THE RIGHT TRACK

The event prompted Batista to make some serious changes in his life. It was then that he turned to wrestling. After WCW officials told him he didn't have what it took to succeed in sports-entertainment, Batista worked even harder to pursue his newfound dream. Fearing a return to bouncing, he completely redesigned his training and mental outlook. His dedication eventually earned him an opportunity with WWE.

Batista made his WWE debut on *SmackDown* in May 2002, but it wasn't until he moved to *Raw* later in the year that he began to turn heads. Within weeks of changing to Monday nights, he scored two major victories over Kane.

The wins impressed Ric Flair and Triple H, who were looking to align themselves with the industry's brightest new stars. After a lengthy search, they identified Randy Orton and Batista. Collectively, the four Superstars became known as Evolution.

EVOLUTION OF A CHAMPION

With Triple H and Flair leading the way, Batista learned firsthand what it meant to be a champion. In December 2003, he finally earned his first piece of WWE gold when he teamed with Flair to defeat the Dudley Boys for the World Tag Team Championship. For the better part of the next year, Evolution painfully proved its dominance over the rest of the *Raw* roster.

At WrestleMania 21, Batista dethroned Triple H for the World Heavyweight Championship. Proving his victory was no fluke, he went on to defeat "The Game" at the following two pay-per-view events, which included a bloody Hell in a Cell Match at Vengeance 2005.

By 2005, paranoia began to take over Triple H. After Batista last eliminated John Cena to win the *Royal Rumble*, "The Game" began to see his Evolution cohort as a serious risk to his World Heavyweight Championship. In an attempt to protect his prize, Triple H began to devise plans that would derail Batista's success, but there was no stopping the leviathan known as "The Animal."

Batista's reign, which saw him turn back such noted challengers as JBL and Eddie Guerrero, came to an untimely end when a triceps injury forced him to relinquish the title in January 2006. The injury, which occurred at the hands of Mark Henry, kept "The Animal" out of action for more than six months. When he returned, however, he set his sights on regaining what he believed was rightfully his.

After several failed attempts to reclaim the title, Batista finally regained the World Heavyweight Championship when he defeated King Booker at *Survivor Series 2006*. Four months into his second reign, Batista was forced to do the impossible in order to keep the gold around his waist: defeat Undertaker at *WrestleMania 23*. Like Triple H, Ric Flair, and many others before him, Batista came up short that night, losing his World Heavyweight Championship to the "Deadman." He reclaimed the title five months later when he defeated The Great Khali and Rey Mysterio in a Triple Threat Match at *Unforgiven*. In June 2008, Batista was drafted back to *Raw* which ultimately led to a confrontation with John Cena at *SummerSlam*, an encounter won by Batista.

Clearly, Batista's insatiable desire to be the best has propelled him over mountains of adversity. His perseverance and dedication kept him going when other men might have walked away. In the end, his commitment to excellence has resulted in one of the most impressive careers of the new millennium. With years of dominance left ahead of him, there's no telling how large his legacy will grow.

Battle Kat

HT	5'10"	**WT**	225 lbs.

FROM Parts Unknown

SIGNATURE MOVE Moonsault

YEARS ACTIVE

In October 1990, WWE was introduced to a man with the martial-arts skills of a ninja, the high-flying acrobatics of a gymnast and superior technical wrestilng skills. His identity hidden behind a mask, Battle Kat displayed his abilities against the Barbarian, Boris Zhukov, Pez Whatley, and "Playboy" Buddy Rose. Battle Kat disappeared from WWE soon after his debut. Reports at the time speculated that he traveled to Japan to compete there.

Today, the identity of this man remains unknown. Though he was only in WWE for a brief period of time, he will always be remembered as a talented performer.

BATTLE ROYAL

Recent WWE history has seen the advent of such revolutionary matches as the Elimination Chamber, Hell in a Cell, and the Ladder Match. While these new matches have been the source of some of the most exciting in-ring action ever, none have the ability of conjuring up such nostalgia as the classic Battle Royal.

The rules are simple: A pre-determined number of Superstars enter the ring (usually 20). An elimination occurs when a Superstar is thrown over the top rope and his or her feet hit the arena floor. Eliminations continue in this manner until there is only one person left standing. That Superstar is declared the winner of the Battle Royal.

The grand stage of *WrestleMania* has hosted many of WWE's greatest Battle Royals. In 1986, *WrestleMania 2* was the home of the first-ever pay-per-view Battle Royal. Andre the Giant last eliminated Bret "Hit Man" Hart to win the event, which also featured NFL stars, including William "Refrigerator" Perry and Bill Fralic. The match was also Bruno Sammartino's only *WrestleMania* match.

Fifteen years later, *WrestleMania X-Seven* was the site of the Gimmick Battle Royal, which featured many great names from the past. In the end, the Iron Sheik outlasted such memorable personalities as Doink the Clown, Brother Love, and Gobbledy Gooker. Ironically, the Iron Sheik was also a participant in the *WrestleMania 2* Battle Royal.

On rare occasions, a Battle Royal is used to crown a new champion. In January 2006, Kurt Angle last eliminated Mark Henry to claim the World Heavyweight Championship. The same prize crowned a new titleholder in July 2007 when The Great Khali simultaneously tossed out Kane and Batista. Both historic matches took place on *SmackDown*.

While the Battle Royal is a great platform to crown a new champion, it's also equally effective in cramming scores of beautiful women in one ring. The most high-profile Divas Battle Royal saw Beth Phoenix last eliminate Michelle McCool at *SummerSlam 2007*. Beth went on to capture the Women's Championship six weeks later.

Battman

| HT | 5'10" | WT | 240 lbs. |

| FROM | Gotham City |

| SIGNATURE MOVE | Abdominal Stretch |

| TITLE HISTORY | International Tag Team Champion |

| YEARS ACTIVE | 1960-1969 | 1970-1979 | 1980-1989 | 1960-1969 | 2000-PRESENT |

In 1966, the Battman debuted in Buffalo to the joy of fans and dismay of villains everywhere. Opponents were taken aback by his physical conditioning, wrestling skill, intellect, and his acts of escape artistry. He quickly amassed an impressive win-loss record, and would co-hold the International Tag Team Championship with two different partners. The first reign saw him hold the belts with then-WWE Champion, Bruno Sammartino. For the second, he teamed with Latin Superstar Victor Rivera. He maintained order across WWE during the turbulent late 1960s and into the next decade.

The Beast 🇨🇦

| HT | 5'10" | WT | 255 lbs. | FROM | Dorchester, New Brunswick, Canada |

| YEARS ACTIVE | 1960-1969 | 1970-1979 | 1980-1989 | 1960-1969 | 2000-PRESENT |

With a big, bushy beard and wild hair, The Beast certainly appeared to be well named. He even played the role in between the ropes with his savage in-ring approach. However, behind the wild exterior was a man with close familial ties. Believe it or not, the untamed Superstar is the oldest of four wrestling brothers. His younger, more-refined siblings, Rudy Kay, Bobby Kay, and Leo Burke all made a living inside the ring.

The Beast toured the globe seven times during his nearly 40-year career. His undomesticated style attracted huge crowds in Australia, and even landed him in a match against the legendary "Giant" Baba in front of 45,000 rabid fans in Japan. It was in Canada that The Beast gained his greatest notoriety. In 1966, he defeated Dave Ruhl for Calgary's National Wrestling Alliance Canadian Heavyweight Championship. He also held Toronto's version of the NWA United States Heavyweight Championship for five months after defeating Johnny Valentine in October 1963.

Beaver Cleavage

| HT | 6' | WT | 243 lbs. |

| YEARS ACTIVE | 1960-1969 | 1970-1979 | 1980-1989 | 1990-1999 | 2000-PRESENT |

Despite having a shelf life of less than one month, the controversy created by Beaver Cleavage is still being talked about today. In the summer of 1999, Beaver debuted in several black-and-white vignettes filled with double entendres. Fans' jaws hit the floor when the sexy Mrs. Cleavage appeared alongside Beaver. The controversy surrounding Beaver's innuendos failed to prevent him from entering the ring. In June 1999, he defeated Christian in his first in-ring appearance. A few weeks later, he disappeared from WWE television.

Bertha Faye 🇺🇸

| HT | 5'8" | FROM | Walls, Mississippi |

| SIGNATURE MOVE | Sit Out Powerbomb |

| TITLE HISTORY | Women's Champion |

| YEARS ACTIVE | 1960-1969 | 1970-1979 | 1980-1989 | 1990-1999 | 2000-PRESENT |

Bertha Faye may not have been the most attractive woman to set foot in the ring, but she may have been the most loved. Despite the fact that she dwarfed him, Harvey Wippleman adored Bertha Faye with every ounce of his being.

Wippleman first introduced fans to Bertha Faye in April 1995 when she attacked Alundra Blayze on an episode of *Monday Night Raw*. As a result of the assault, Blayze suffered a broken nose, which ultimately ignited an intense rivalry between the two competitors. At *SummerSlam 1995*, Bertha Faye flattened her rival with a sit-out powerbomb, enabling her to capture her first-and-only Women's Championship.

Two months after winning the Women's Championship, Bertha Faye found herself on the losing end of a *Monday Night Raw* rematch with Blayze. After losing the Women's Championship, Bertha Faye was rarely seen in a WWE ring again.

Beth Phoenix

| YEARS ACTIVE | 1960 1969 | 1970 1979 | 1980 1989 | 1990 1999 | **2000 PRESENT** |

HT 5'7" **FROM** Buffalo, New York **SIGNATURE MOVE** Hanging Fishermen's Suplex

TITLE HISTORY Women's Champion

Beth Phoenix grew up with a dream to be a part of sports-entertainment and to be a force in the industry the likes that had never seen before. She became the first female amateur wrestler in her high school's history to compete on its varsity team. Beth traveled the country for training necessary to make the transition from amateur wrestling to sports-entertainment.

In May 2006, Phoenix debuted on *Raw* and assaulted then-Women's Champion Mickie James. As WWE fans searched for more information on her background, Trish Stratus provided some insight on Beth's past with Mickie. Weeks later, Beth was announced as the newest WWE Diva. Unfortunately, she suffered a fractured mandible in a match against Victoria, an injury that sidelined her for over one year.

She returned to *Raw* as a "Glamazon" who was on the hunt for gold. After unsuccessful attempts at winning the Women's Championship from Candice, Phoenix finally picked up the win in October and ruled for five months. She lost the prize to rival Mickie James, but she regained the title in a "Winner Take All Match" at *SummerSlam 2008*.

Time after time, the "Glamazon" has proven that she can overcome any adversity and will take on any challenger. As time goes on she will only become more dangerous.

The Berzerker

HT 6'8" **WT** 323 lbs.

FROM Parts Unknown

SIGNATURE MOVE Big Boot

| YEARS ACTIVE | 1960 1969 | 1970 1979 | 1980 1989 | **1990 1999** | 2000 PRESENT |

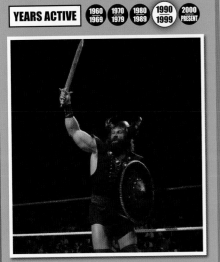

Unleashed on WWE by Mr. Fuji in 1991, this crazed Superstar was first known as the Viking. However, due to his irregular behavior and spontaneous shouting, this Nordic beast changed his name to something more appropriate. He had an unusual means of communicating with his manager that included unidentifiable hand signals and a dialect that remains untranslatable to this day.

Despite his baffling ring presence, this sword-swinger won many matches by throwing opponents over the top rope, leaving them on the arena floor unable to return to the ring before a ten-count. A consistent championship contender, the Berzerker faced off against Tito Santana, Jimmy "Superfly" Snuka, Bret "Hit Man" Hart, and Greg Valentine.

In early 1993, The Berzerker left WWE and has not been seen since. Today, fans' curiosity is still piqued when archived footage is shown of his matches and interviews. He'll always be remembered as one of the most unique and dangerous personas in WWE history.

The Beverly Brothers

MEMBERS Beau, Blake **COMBINED WEIGHT** 514 lbs.

| YEARS ACTIVE | 1960 1969 | 1970 1979 | 1980 1989 | **1990 1999** | 2000 PRESENT |

During interview segments that aired in May 1991, the Beverly Brothers proclaimed to WWE, "The Bevs want it all and we'll get it all." The Beverly Brothers, with their deadly finishing move called Shaker Heights Spike, quickly became contenders for the World Tag Team Championship.

After a series of impressive showings, Beau & Blake fought the Natural Disasters for the World Tag Team Championship, but were ultimately unsuccessful in defeating Typhoon & Earthquake. The team disbanded in early 1993 after Blake left WWE.

The Beverly Brothers were another example that a team can emerge onto the scene and shake up the tag team division in short order. No matter who led them to the ring, or who stood across the ring from them, opponents of the Beverlys were in for a long night.

BIG BOSS MAN

YEARS ACTIVE 1960 1969 | 1970 1979 | 1980 1989 | 1990 1999 | 2000 PRESENT

HT 6'7" **WT** 330 lbs. **FROM** Cobb County, Georgia **SIGNATURE MOVE** Side Slam

TITLE HISTORY Hardcore Champion, World Tag Team Champion

Managed by the "Doctor of Style," Slick, Big Boss Man gave new meaning to the term "Protect and Serve" as he wielded his nightstick and destroyed anyone in his path. After a dominating victory over Koko B. Ware at *SummerSlam 1988*, Boss Man teamed with Akeem to form the Twin Towers, one of the largest teams in WWE history. Big Boss Man became a threat to Hulkamania, and on October 1989, they settled their score in a Steel Cage Match on *Saturday Night's Main Event*. After he showed he couldn't be bought, the former prison guard's rivalry against "Million-Dollar Man" Ted DiBiase made him a fan favorite. Big Boss Man then battled members of the

Heenan Family and taught "The Brain" not to talk bad about people's mothers. Boss Man then entered into an ideological dispute over law and order with The Mountie. After he won their Jailhouse Match at *SummerSlam 1991*, Mountie spent a night in a New York City lockup. Boss Man showed he was the true protector of WWE when he returned to the ring from an attack by one of his former inmates, Nailz, and won a Nightstick Match at *Survivor Series 1992*.

In October 1998, after time overseas and in WCW, Big Boss Man returned to WWE as the head of personal security for Mr. McMahon. Wearing S.W.A.T.-like attire, he happily displayed an updated version of "hard time" suitable for the Attitude Era. After he returned from an injury in 2001, Boss Man formed brief alliances with Bull Buchanan, Booker T, and Mr. Perfect before leaving WWE in 2003.

Sadly, Big Boss Man passed away in September 2004. He is remembered as one of the most agile big men and toughest Superstars to ever enter the ring.

Big Bully Busick

HT 6' **WT** 265 lbs. **FROM** Weirton, West Virginia

YEARS ACTIVE 1960 1969 | 1970 1979 | 1980 1989 | 1990 1999 | 2000 PRESENT

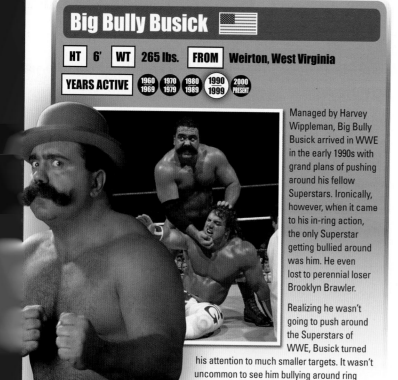

Managed by Harvey Wippleman, Big Bully Busick arrived in WWE in the early 1990s with grand plans of pushing around his fellow Superstars. Ironically, however, when it came to his in-ring action, the only Superstar getting bullied around was him. He even lost to perennial loser Brooklyn Brawler.

Realizing he wasn't going to push around the Superstars of WWE, Busick turned his attention to much smaller targets. It wasn't uncommon to see him bullying around ring announcers and kids in the audience. He once went so far as to steal a youngster's balloon. The mean-spirited act turned heartbreaking when he popped the colorful balloon right in front of the little girl.

Big Daddy V

HT 6'9" **WT** 487 lbs. **FROM** Harlem, New York

TITLE HISTORY World Tag Team Champion, Hardcore Champion

YEARS ACTIVE 1960 1969 | 1970 1979 | 1980 1989 | 1990 1999 | 2000 PRESENT

ECW has a way of bringing the extreme out of its Superstars. Covered in curious tattoos, Big Daddy V was brought into ECW to protect Matt Striker from Boogeyman. After ridding Striker of his worm-eating nemesis, Big Daddy V went inter-promotional, focusing much of his devastation on the bigger Superstars of *SmackDown*, including Undertaker and Kane. Over the next several months, he had a difficult time besting the Brothers of Destruction, but did manage to defeat Kane in an Extreme Rules Match in November 2007.

Big Dick Johnson

YEARS ACTIVE `1960 1969` `1970 1979` `1980 1989` `1990 1999` `2000 PRESENT`

"Lock up your daughters, lock up your wives. Lock up the back door and run for your lives…"

Those words come from the revolting exhibitions brought to WWE courtesy of Big Dick Johnson. Appearing when fans least expect it, Big Dick loves prancing around WWE events showing off his finest features. He has appeared on ECW with the Sandman, wished everyone a Merry Christmas at *Armageddon 2006* and at one point was even considered among the possibilities of being Mr. McMahon's illegitimate son.

No matter where you are in the world, when you hear the beat to his familiar theme music, you know who's coming through to give a little something special to all of you: Big Dick Johnson!

THE BIG EVENT

LOCATION Exhibition Stadium, Toronto, Canada

DATE August 28, 1986

With a record 64,000 in attendance, the Big Event pitted Hulk Hogan against "Mr. Wonderful" Paul Orndorff, who lost the match when Bobby Heenan attacked Hogan with a stool.

With nearly a dozen matches on the day, many legendary names made appearances at the show including Junkyard Dog, the Killer Bees, the Funks, and "King" Harley Race. There were two special matches at the event: a Snake Pit match between Ricky Steamboat and Jake Roberts, and a Six-Man Tag Team Match that had Big John Studd, King Kong Bundy & Bobby Heenan face Giant Machine, Super Machine & Lou Albano.

BIG JOHN STUDD

YEARS ACTIVE `1960 1969` `1970 1979` `1980 1989` `1990 1999` `2000 PRESENT`

HALL OF FAME 2004

HT 6'10" **WT** 365 lbs. **FROM** Los Angeles, California

During WWE's magical mainstream renaissance of the 1980s, Big John Studd proved himself as a larger-than-life villain. With an awe-inspiring frame and standing nearly seven-feet tall, he thwarted countless attempts by the fans' heroes to chop him down to size. With each passing conquest he further cemented his legacy as one of sports-entertainment's greatest giants.

Studd made his professional debut in 1976 after being trained by WWE Hall of Famer Killer Kowalski. In the early 1980s, he started working with WWE. Upon entering the company, he was managed by Freddie Blassie, but quickly switched to Bobby Heenan. By 1983, Studd began promoting himself as WWE's only true giant. The claim obviously didn't sit well with the 7'4" Andre the Giant. Over the course of the next several years, the two Superstars engaged in a bitter battle designed to crown WWE's elite giant.

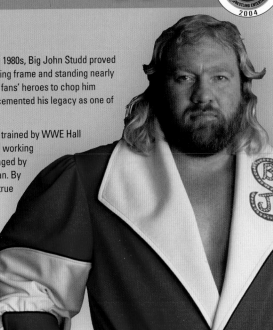

Studd gained a favorable advantage in his rivalry with Andre when he cut his foe's hair in December 1984. The stunt eventually lead to a $15,000 Bodyslam Challenge between the big men at the first-ever *WrestleMania*. In the end, it was Andre lifting Studd over his head and slamming him to the ground for the win. After the match, Andre attempted to share his $15,000 with the capacity crowd, but a lightning-quick Heenan swooped in to steal the giant's winnings.

The following year, Studd walked into the *WrestleMania 2* WWE/NFL Battle Royal as one of the favorites. After eliminating William "Refrigerator" Perry, it appeared as though Studd would coast to the end, but "The Fridge" eventually outsmarted Studd when he pulled him out of the ring under the guise of a handshake. Studd left WWE soon after.

Studd made a brief return in late 1988. This time, however, the fans took a liking to the big man after he turned his back on the devious Heenan. His second WWE stint was highlighted by a victory in the 1989 *Royal Rumble* Match. Big John Studd, one of the greatest giants sports-entertainment has ever seen, was honored with induction into the WWE Hall of Fame in 2004.

Big Man Steel

| HT | 6'3" | WT | 384 lbs. | SIGNATURE MOVE | Bearhug |

| YEARS ACTIVE | 1960-1969 | 1970-1979 | **1980-1989** | 1990-1999 | 2000-PRESENT |

A protégé of the "Doctor of Style" Slick, this monster of a man appeared in WWE in June 1989. A villain of the most brutal kind, Big Man Steel shook the very foundation of the Convention Center in Niagara Falls just by entering it. When he set foot in the ring during the episode of *Wrestling Challenge,* everyone in attendance watched in awe as he manhandled rugged veteran Tom Horner.

Big Man Steel and his manager had a falling out following the match and what was supposed to be the beginning of an era of dominance, turned out to be a one-time experiment.

Big Show & Kane

| COMBINED WEIGHT | 767 lbs. | YEARS ACTIVE | 1960-1969 | 1970-1979 | 1980-1989 | 1990-1999 | **2000-PRESENT** |

| TITLE HISTORY | World Tag Team Champions |

Prior to *Taboo Tuesday 2005*, Big Show & Kane found themselves in opposite corners several times throughout their careers, but at the annual pay-per-view, the fans' voting forced them to compete as a team. The massive duo instantly clicked, using their size advantage to dethrone World Tag Team Champions Lance Cade & Trevor Murdoch. The victory gave Kane his ninth reign as World Tag Team Champion; it was Big Show's third.

Over the next several months, Big Show & Kane breezed past WWE's top teams. They even won a Champions vs. Champions Match at *Armageddon*, defeating *SmackDown*'s WWE Tag Team Champions, Batista & Rey Mysterio.

After turning back Chris Masters & Carlito at *WrestleMania 22*, Big Show & Kane looked as though there was no WWE duo that could stop them until they signed on to defend against Kenny & Mikey of the Spirit Squad. Unfortunately for the champs, Nicky, Johnny, and Mitch also weaseled their way into the match. The five-on-two disadvantage proved to be too much for Big Show & Kane, as Spirit Squad successfully dethroned the mighty duo.

BIG SHOW

| YEARS ACTIVE | 1960-1969 | **1970-1979** | 1980-1989 | 1990-1999 | 2000-PRESENT |

| HT | 7' | WT | 441 lbs. | FROM | Tampa, Florida | SIGNATURE MOVE | Chokeslam |

| TITLE HISTORY | WWE Champion, United States Champion, Hardcore Champion, World Tag Team Champion, ECW Champion |

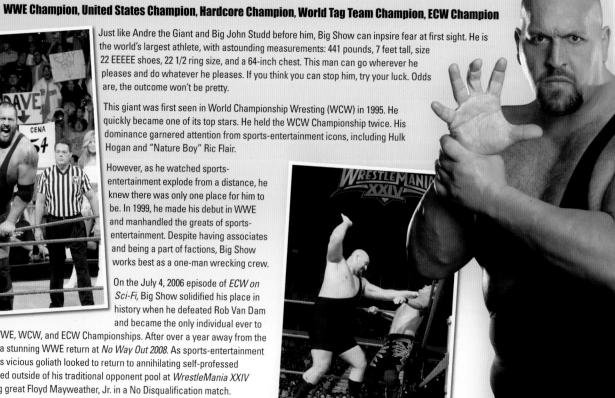

Just like Andre the Giant and Big John Studd before him, Big Show can inspire fear at first sight. He is the world's largest athlete, with astounding measurements: 441 pounds, 7 feet tall, size 22 EEEEE shoes, 22 1/2 ring size, and a 64-inch chest. This man can go wherever he pleases and do whatever he pleases. If you think you can stop him, try your luck. Odds are, the outcome won't be pretty.

This giant was first seen in World Championship Wresting (WCW) in 1995. He quickly became one of its top stars. He held the WCW Championship twice. His dominance garnered attention from sports-entertainment icons, including Hulk Hogan and "Nature Boy" Ric Flair.

However, as he watched sports-entertainment explode from a distance, he knew there was only one place for him to be. In 1999, he made his debut in WWE and manhandled the greats of sports-entertainment. Despite having associates and being a part of factions, Big Show works best as a one-man wrecking crew.

On the July 4, 2006 episode of *ECW on Sci-Fi*, Big Show solidified his place in history when he defeated Rob Van Dam and became the only individual ever to hold the WWE, WCW, and ECW Championships. After over a year away from the ring, Big Show made a stunning WWE return at *No Way Out 2008*. As sports-entertainment was put on notice, this vicious goliath looked to return to annihilating self-professed contenders. He stepped outside of his traditional opponent pool at *WrestleMania XXIV* when he faced boxing great Floyd Mayweather, Jr. in a No Disqualification match.

Bill DeMott

HT 6'2"	**WT** 280 lbs.	**FROM** Trenton, New Jersey			

SIGNATURE MOVE No Laughing Matter

YEARS ACTIVE (1960-1969) (1970-1979) (1980-1989) (1990-1999) (2000-PRESENT)

For years, fans only knew Bill DeMott as the fun-but-dangerous Hugh Morrus. In 2002, the former United States Champion's career took a serious turn when he began training the Superstars of tomorrow on *Tough Enough*. Under his given name, DeMott used fear as his chief teaching technique. His most noteworthy pupils were Matt Cappotelli and John Morrison.

DeMott's in-ring success paled in comparison to the heights he reached as Hugh Morrus. After tearing through many of *SmackDown*'s Superstars, as well as Rikishi, in early 2003, he found himself most often appearing on *Velocity*. After several months, he transitioned from the ring to the announce booth, calling *Velocity* action alongside *Tough Enough* alum Josh Mathews.

Bill Miller

HT 6'6"	**WT** 290lbs.	**FROM** Fremont, Ohio

SIGNATURE MOVE Backbreaker

TITLE HISTORY United States Tag Team Championship

YEARS ACTIVE (1960-1969) (1970-1979) (1980-1989) (1990-1999) (2000-PRESENT)

Before entering the world of sports-entertainment in 1952, this Ohio State Buckeyes alumnus won two Big Ten conference amateur titles. He was also was a letterman in track and football and a member of the 1950 Rose Bowl team. A licensed veterinarian and member of the United States Navy, Dr. Bill Miller started his rounds in the AWA and NWA promotions.

In 1964 the doctor debuted in the World Wide Wrestling Federation and tested his skills against the world's fiercest ring animals, monsters and giants. Often seen in singles and tag team action, he won the U.S. Tag Team Championship, along with his brother Dan, in August, 1965 when they beat the team of Cowboy Bill Watts and Gorilla Monsoon. Miller left the company in 1976 and retired from competition shortly thereafter. In 1997 the Navy veteran passed away. That same year he was inducted into the Hall of Fame of his beloved alma-mater, Ohio State.

Billy & Chuck

With their matching headbands, boy-band entrance theme, and touchy-feely affection for each other, the relationship between Billy & Chuck often appeared to go beyond

MEMBERS Billy Gunn, Chuck Palumbo

COMBINED WEIGHT 535 lbs.

TITLE HISTORY World Tag Team Champions

YEARS ACTIVE (1960-1969) (1970-1979) (1980-1989) (1990-1999) (2000-PRESENT)

simple tag team partners. With their personal stylist, Rico, in their corner, the duo became two-time World Tag Team Champions.

In September 2002, Chuck presented Billy with a gorgeous ring and asked Billy to be his partner for life. Billy excitedly agreed and the news began to dominate national news. It wasn't long before Billy & Chuck were featured on such major outlets as *The Today Show* and *The New York Times*.

By the time the commitment ceremony rolled around, Billy developed a case of cold feet. Just moments before the actual ceremony took place, the duo put a halt to it and claimed their entire union was nothing but a publicity stunt.

Following the shocking revelation, Billy & Chuck soon went their separate ways. While both have enjoyed some measure of success, neither has been able to recreate the same notoriety they enjoyed as the controversial Billy & Chuck.

Billy Gunn

HT 6'3"	**WT** 260 lbs.	**YEARS ACTIVE** (1960-1969) (1970-1979) (1980-1989) (1990-1999) (2000-PRESENT)

FROM Austin, Texas   **SIGNATURE MOVE** The Fame-asser

TITLE HISTORY World Tag Team Champion, Intercontinental Champion, Hardcore Champion

World Wrestling Entertainment first saw Billy Gunn in 1993 as part of the Smokin' Gunns. Together with his brother Bart, the team held the World Tag Team Championship three times. After the Smokin' Gunns parted ways, he teamed with "Road Dogg" Jesse James in the New Age Outlaws.

After five World Tag Team Championship reigns and time spent as part of D-Generation X, Billy focused on his singles career. Known as "Mr. Ass," he became a Hardcore Champion for the first time in 1999. Three months later, he defeated X-Pac to become *King of the Ring*. On November 23, 2000, Gunn defeated Eddie Guerrero for the Intercontinental Championship.

After briefly reforming the New Age Outlaws and rejoining DX, Billy found a new partner in Chuck Palumbo. Billy & Chuck became one of the most controversial teams in sports-entertainment history, as evidenced by their commitment ceremony, but also tasted success once again as WWE Tag Team Champions.

In 2003 Billy returned to the singles ranks and drove female fans wild as the ever-popular "Mr. Ass." In November 2004, Gunn's tenure with WWE came to an end. "Mr. Ass" will forever be remembered as a skilled and versatile performer who held 10 Tag Team titles.

Billy Jack Haynes

| **HT** 6'3" | **WT** 246 lbs. | **FROM** Portland, Oregon |

SIGNATURE MOVE Full Nelson

YEARS ACTIVE  1960-1969 1970-1979 **1980-1989** 1990-1999 2000 PRESENT

The pride of Portland, Billy Jack Haynes began his in-ring career in 1982. Over the next few years, he developed a fan following in the Portland, Florida, Mid-Atlantic, and World Class territories. Haynes possessed immense power and an impressive array of mat wrestling moves.

Haynes debuted in WWE in 1986 and was an immediate hit with audiences around the country. His impressive start made him a contender for the Intercontinental Championship, and his matches with Randy "Macho Man" Savage got the attention of the WWE Championship Committee. He is remembered for a violent confrontation with Hercules in a Battle of the Full Nelson Match at *WrestleMania III*.

In 1988, he teamed with fellow Oregonian Ken Patera and battled teams such as Demolition and the Heenan Family. Billy Jack Haynes will be remembered as one of the true masters of the Full Nelson and one of WWE's greatest heroes of the 1980s.

Billy the Kid

YEARS ACTIVE 1960-1969 **1970-1979** 1980-1989 1970-1979 2000 PRESENT

Named after the infamous American outlaw, Billy the Kid was one of the South's most renowned midget wrestlers of the 1970s. Clad in a 10-gallon hat and scruffy beard, his cowboy persona helped solidify his status as one of the division's premier attractions.

For much of 1972, Billy the Kid formed a popular tag team with Wee Wee Wilson. In December, they teamed with Darling Dagmar to turn back Little Buiser, Diamond Lil & Johnny Reb in a memorable six-man tag team match. The bout proved to be one of the last times Billy the Kid and Wee Wee Wilson worked as a team, as they soon found themselves engaged in a bitter rivalry.

Billy Kidman

| **HT** 5'10" | **WT** 195 lbs. | **FROM** Allentown, Pennsylvania |

SIGNATURE MOVE Shooting Star Press

TITLE HISTORY WWE Tag Team Champion, Cruiserweight Champion

YEARS ACTIVE  1960-1969 1970-1979 1980-1989 1990-1999 **2000 PRESENT**

If you passed Billy Kidman in the street, you might not recognize him as a skilled sports-entertainer. He's not overly large, doesn't really wear flashy clothes and isn't very boisterous. In the ring, however, his talents are undeniable. The often underrated Kidman came to WWE following the promotion's acquisition of WCW in 2001. He made a strong first impression, upending Gregory Helms to claim the Cruiserweight Championship in his debut match. The win served as a sign of things to come for Kidman, who went on to capture the title three more times in WWE.

In July 2004, Kidman teamed with Paul London to defeat The Dudley Boys for the WWE Tag Team Championship. It appeared as though things couldn't be going any better for the high-flying Superstar. However, when his signature Shooting Star Press nearly ended the career of Chavo Guerrero, feelings of extreme guilt beset Kidman. It wasn't long before he couldn't bring himself to execute his most powerful weapon. A dejected Kidman even walked away from a September 2004 title defense, leaving his partner to fend for himself.

Kidman later blamed the fans for forcing him to become a more vicious in-ring competitor. The accusations immediately turned fans against the longtime favorite. Since leaving the promotion, Kidman has competed on independent cards and began training the Superstars of tomorrow.

Billy White Wolf

| **HT** 6' | **WT** 245 lbs. | **FROM** Oklahoma |

SIGNATURE MOVE Indian Deathlock

TITLE HISTORY World Tag Team Champion

YEARS ACTIVE 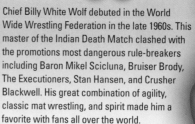 1960-1969 **1970-1979** 1980-1989 1990-1999 2000 PRESENT

Chief Billy White Wolf debuted in the World Wide Wrestling Federation in the late 1960s. This master of the Indian Death Match clashed with the promotions most dangerous rule-breakers including Baron Mikel Scicluna, Bruiser Brody, The Executioners, Stan Hansen, and Crusher Blackwell. His great combination of agility, classic mat wrestling, and spirit made him a favorite with fans all over the world.

White Wolf's virtuous path brought him together with another ring great, Chief Jay Strongbow. On December 7, 1976 White Wolf and Strongbow defeated The Executioners, and Nikolai Volkoff & Tor Kamata in a three team tournament for the vacant World Tag Team Championships. The Native Americans held the ultimate tag team prize for eight months until White Wolf suffered a career-ending injury. While his career ended prematurely, Chief Billy White Wolf will always be remembered as a hero to fans all over the world and a pioneer in the sport.

Black Bart 🇺🇸

HT 6'4" **WT** 350 lbs. **FROM** Pampa, Texas

SIGNATURE MOVE Flying Leg Drop

YEARS ACTIVE   1960-1969 1970-1979 **1980-1989** 1990-1999 2000-PRESENT

A tough-as-nails Texan, Black Bart left a lasting impression on his opposition literally, as it wasn't uncommon to see him his opponents using his trademark "BB" branding iron. Prior to his brief WWE stint in 1989, Black Bart gained notoriety competing in the Southern territories of the United States with his tag team parter, Ron Bass. The duo carried their successful union from state to state before ultimately going their separate ways in 1985.

As a singles competitor, perhaps Black Bart's biggest victory came in September 1986 when he defeated Chris Adams for the World Class Championship Wrestling title. Unfortunately for Bart, however, he lost the title one month later to Kevin Von Erich.

The Blackjacks 🇺🇸

MEMBERS Blackjack Mulligan, Blackjack Lanza

TOTAL COMBINED WEIGHT 585 lbs.

TITLE HISTORY World Tag Team Champions

YEARS ACTIVE 1960-1969 **1970-1979 1980-1989** 1990-1999 2000-PRESENT

A couple of rough and tumble Texans, Blackjack Mulligan & Blackjack Lanza broke nearly every rule in the book on their way to the WWE Hall of Fame.

The Blackjacks first teamed with each other in the early 1970s. Clad in their signature cowboy hats, leather vests, and black gloves, Mulligan & Lanza captured tag team championships in the World Wrestling Association and National Wrestling Alliance before bringing their game to WWE in the mid-1970s.

The Blackjacks enjoyed a nearly three-month World Tag Team Championship reign in 1975. After losing the titles in November, Mulligan & Lanza failed to reach the same heights, but their amazing legacy would be recreated two decades later.

In 1996, Barry Windham, the son of Blackjack Mulligan, teamed with Blackjack Lanza's nephew, Justin "Hawk" Bradshaw, to form The New Blackjacks. In appearance, the tag team looked identical to the original tandem. Unfortunately, that's where the similarities stopped. After failing to properly represent the legend of the original Blackjacks, Windham & Bradshaw went their separate ways.

In 2006, Blackjack Mulligan & Blackjack Lanza were given the ultimate honor when their efforts in the tag team ranks landed them in the WWE Hall of Fame.

Blackjack Mulligan 🇺🇸

HT 6'9" **WT** 300 lbs. **FROM** Eagle Pass, Texas

SIGNATURE MOVE The Claw

TITLE HISTORY World Tag Team Champion

YEARS ACTIVE   1960-1969 **1970-1979 1980-1989** 1990-1999 2000-PRESENT

Sports-entertainment was introduced to one of its fiercest competitors in the early 1970s. A former Marine and NFL player, Blackjack Mulligan was a merciless force throughout the United States and after graduating from Verne Gagne's wrestling school, he formed a team with Blackjack Lanza. With their black handle-bar mustaches, black ring attire and black hearts, they were reminiscent of outlaws from the Wild West. In 1975, they arrived in WWE with Capt. Lou Albano as their manager. During Mulligan's time in WWE, he fought the likes of Bruno Sammartino, Pedro Morales, Haystacks Calhoun, and Andre The Giant. That November, he outlasted 19 other competitors and won a $10,000 Battle Royal.

After a brief hiatus, Blackjack returned to WWE in 1983 and soon became a fan favorite. Mulligan's beat 'em and leave 'em style was so popular with WWE audiences that he hosted his own talk show segment *Blackjack's Barbeque* in 1985. Mulligan continued his winning ways until he left the company in 1987. His legacy lived on through his sons Barry and Kendall Windham. On April 1, 2006, Mulligan was inducted into the WWE Hall of Fame.

Blu Brothers 🇺🇸

MEMBERS Jacob, Eli **TOTAL COMBINED WEIGHT** 640 lbs.

YEARS ACTIVE   1960-1969 1970-1979 1980-1989 **1990-1999** 2000-PRESENT

Identical twins from the mountains of Appalachia, Jacob & Eli Blu were led to WWE by their Uncle Zebekiah. Their long, flowing hair and bushy beards certainly provided for an unorthodox appearance; but when the bell rang, the Blu Brothers proved to possess a traditional powerhouses approach to tag team wrestling.

Making their WWE debut in January 1995, Jacob & Eli used their identical appearances to confuse opponents, officials and onlookers. Their dastardly tricks, coupled with their immense power, guided them to many victories. After three months of impressing WWE officials, Jacob & Eli earned a spot on the *WrestleMania XI* card. The twin brothers headed into the event with a great deal of momentum, but were unable to stop The Allied Powers, Lex Luger & British Bulldog.

The Blu Brothers' WWE careers cooled after their *WrestleMania* loss. After failing to defeat The Smoking Gunns at *SummerSlam 1995*, Jacob & Eli made a quiet exit from WWE.

Blue Meanie

HT 6'1" **WT** 323 lbs.

FROM Atlantic City, New Jersey

SIGNATURE MOVE

Meaniesault

YEARS ACTIVE

Following a comedic ECW career, Blue Meanie made his WWE debut in late 1998. Originally a member of Al Snow's JOB Squad, the blue-haired Superstar proved to be equally entertaining inside WWE rings.

In early 1999, Meanie resumed the hilarious impersonations that made him so popular in ECW. As Bluedust, he battled Goldust at *St. Valentine's Day Massacre*. Meanie failed in his quest to defeat the original 'Dust, but managed to entertain thousands along the way.

After a five-year absence from WWE, Blue Meanie returned at *One Night Stand* in June 2005 with the rest of the Blue World Order. After a few more appearances, including a win over JBL on *SmackDown*, the Blue Meanie left WWE.

BOB BACKLUND

HT 6'1" **WT** 234 lbs.

FROM Princeton, Minnesota

SIGNATURE MOVE Crossface Chickenwing

YEARS ACTIVE

TITLE HISTORY WWE Champion, World Tag Team Champion

It was always easy to cheer for Bob Backlund during the late 1970s and early 1980s. His boy-next-door looks made him impossible to dislike, while his superior athleticism solidified his lofty in-ring status. Backlund's second stint with WWE, however, was a completely different story. With age, he became more maniacal. By the mid-1990s, he was borderline insane, which makes the Bob Backlund story even more fascinating.

Backlund first made a name for himself within wrestling circles while competing at North Dakota State University, where he captured the NCAA Division II heavyweight wrestling championship. Shortly after college, the successful amateur wrestler took his game to the pro ranks, debuting for his home state's American Wrestling Association (AWA) in 1974. For the next several years, Backlund bounced between various wrestling regions.

THE WWE COMES CALLING

In the spring of 1977, Backlund received the opportunity of a lifetime when Vincent J. McMahon called to offer him a shot with WWE. He quickly accepted the opportunity, packed his bags and left his small-town life in Minnesota for the bright lights of New York City and WWE. With Arnold Skaaland as his manager, Backlund became an instant hit with WWE fans. His All-American persona gave audiences somebody they could look up to; and within months of his arrival, he was catapulted to the top of the card.

" THAT'S MISTER BACKLUND! "

After several unsuccessful attempts to capture the WWE Championship, Backlund finally dethroned "Superstar" Billy Graham in February 1978 despite the champion's leg being on the ropes during the count. His reign will forever go down in history as one of the greatest of all time, lasting nearly six years (second only to Bruno Sammartino's nearly eight-year reign).

In search of more gold, Backlund teamed with Pedro Morales to defeat the Wild Samoans for the World Tag Team Championship at Shea Stadium in August 1980. Unfortunately for Backlund, he was forced to vacate the title due to a WWE rule at the time that prohibited a Superstar from holding more than one championship at any given time.

Backlund's epic WWE Championship reign came to a controversial end in December 1983. While defending against The Iron Sheik, Backlund found himself locked in the challenger's dreaded Camel Clutch. Refusing to submit, he suffered in the submission move for an extended period of time. Finally, in an attempt to prevent permanent damage, manager Arnold Skaaland threw in the towel for Backlund. The popular former champion later suggested that his reign should never have ceased, due to the fact that he didn't give up. The protest proved ineffective and Backlund quickly left WWE soon after.

A NEW ERA, AND A NEW ATTITUDE

Nearly one decade after vanishing from the sports-entertainment world, Mr. Backlund made a shocking return to WWE in 1992. In his early 40s at the time, WWE fans didn't expect much success from the aging Superstar. They were wrong.

The 1990s version of Bob Backlund proved to be much different from the boy-next-door champion everybody loved in the 1970s and 80s. This Bob Backlund was a rage-filled, middle-aged maniac who quickly drew the ire of fans with his endless rants and overly verbose vocabulary. Inside the ring, however, he was just as dangerous as ever.

In November 1994, the aging Backlund defied the odds when he defeated Bret Hart for the WWE Championship at *Survivor Series*. Ironically, his second reign began the same way his first one ended when Hart's mother threw in the towel, signifying the end of her son's reign.

Backlund's second run as WWE Champion failed to mirror the success of his first. A mere three days after capturing the title, he was defeated by Diesel in a match that lasted only eight seconds.

The WWE record books will forever recognize Backlund's second reign as one of the shortest of all time. Despite the loss to Diesel, however, his brief time atop WWE capped off one of the most successful returns in sports-entertainment history. It also put a fitting exclamation point on a career that will be remembered as one of the greatest of all time.

"Cowboy" Bobby Duncum was drafted by the St. Louis Cardinals of the NFL and made his ring debut in 1971. Running into Duncum was like running into a brick wall. The only thing longer than his mean streak was his list of fallen opponents. After victories, Duncum stayed in the ring and attacked his already battered foe adding insult to injury. The Cowboy did things his way, on his terms and if someone didn't like it, they'd get a fist straight to the jaw.

In 1974, Bobby Duncum arrived in WWE and immediately made his presence known when he won a 20-man over-the-top-rope battle royal. He had a series of bloodbaths with Bruno Sammartino, including a Texas Death Match at the Boston Garden with Gorilla Monsoon as special guest referee. After leaving the company in 1975, Duncum won several regional territories titles in the NWA.

In 1979, the Cowboy returned to WWE and was led to the ring by the Grand Wizard, focusing on eliminating then-WWE Champion Bob Backlund. In 1982 the Cowboy from Austin left WWE for good.

BOBBY "THE BRAIN" HEENAN

" A FRIEND IN NEED IS A PEST. "

Bobby Heenan is arguably one of the most gifted minds in the history of sports-entertainment. Heenan was a revolutionary manager to the greatest legends the industry has ever seen. In addition, he was a fearless broadcast journalist who reported the stories that fit his personal agenda. His direction was simple, "Listen to me, you go straight to the top. Don't, you're never heard from again." Strong words from a Weasel!

The first time Bobby Heenan walked into the Indianapolis Coliseum for a wrestling event, he knew what he wanted to do with the rest of his life. Forced to leave school in the seventh grade to care for his family, Bobby Heenan took a job in the profession he loved, selling programs. He made his pro debut in 1965 and in the early 1970s, he appeared as "Pretty Boy" Heenan. When he managed the duo of "Crippler" Ray Stevens and Nick Bockwinkel, he announced that he should be refered to as "The Brain."

While wreaking havoc through Minneapolis, Heenan accumulated a collection of outlaws known as "The Heenan Family." The founding members consisted of multiple AWA Champion Bockwinkel, Stevens, Bobby Duncum, Sr., Dick Warren, and Blackjack Lanza. In 1984, the manager extraordinaire debuted in WWE and immediately began his quest to rid sports-entertainment of its most beloved heroes. Heenan's first client was Big John Studd. The massive giant was the cornerstone of Heenan's Family and set his sights on Andre the Giant. As Heenan expanded his strategic assembly of WWE's most feared figures, Superstars were often victim to baseless attacks by the likes of Studd, King Kong Bundy, Ken Patera, and "Mr. Wonderful" Paul Orndorff. During this time, "The Brain" unflaggingly strategized to destroy Hulkamania and employed any tactics in hopes of dethroning the then-World Champion. Heenan's propensity to hit-and-run during matches and interviews earned him the infamous alias "Weasel," which was chanted wherever he went.

In 1986, "The Brain" expanded his resume and became a broadcast journalist alongside Gorilla Monsoon. As he warmly referred to his audience as "humanoids," the two future WWE Hall of Famers worked together on Prime Time Wrestling, Wrestling Challenge, and several pay-per-view events.

HT 5'10" **WT** 242 lbs. **FROM** Beverly Hills, California

Due to his weasel-like ways, the Heenan Family had a constantly changing roster through the decade and he often paid the piper for his dastardly ways. "The Brain's" conniving ways bore their sweetest fruit when he persuaded Andre the Giant to turn his back on best friend Hulk Hogan for a WWE Championship match at *WrestleMania III*. Despite his inability to taste championship gold at the Pontiac Silverdome, Heenan continued to recruit talent from all over the world. The year 1989 proved to be an exemplary one for Heenan as he saw his first title in WWE at *WrestleMania V* when "Ravishing" Rick Rude defeated Ultimate Warrior for the Intercontinental title. Success continued when Heenan entered the talk show arena with *The Bobby Heenan Show*. He managed two teams to the World Tag Team Championship in 1989, as the Brain Busters defeated Demolition in July, and The Colossal Connection defeated Demolition in December.

The 1990s saw Heenan become the "Perfect" manager when he led Mr. Perfect to the Intercontinental Championship. Heenan was also instrumental in bringing in multiple time NWA and WCW Champion "Nature Boy" Ric Flair to the company and substantiated Flair's claim that he was the "real" World Champion. Arguably the greatest free-agent acquisition in sports-entertainment history, Flair won the WWE Championship twice with Heenan as a key adviser. As *Monday Night Raw* burst on to cable television, Heenan did anything he could to get on the air. On December 6, 1993, Heenan was given his WWE exit when then-President Gorilla Monsoon tossed him and his belongs out into the cold for good.

Heenan's schedule stayed full. He served as a color commentator for WCW, and he made his Hollywood debut in 1995's *Timemaster* alongside acting legend Noriyuku "Pat" Morita and Michelle Williams. On April 3, 1997 then-Indianapolis Mayor Steve Goldberg declared it "Bobby Heenan Day" throughout the city. Heenan joined fellow WWE Hall of Famer "Mene" Gene Okerlund to call the action at *Wrestlemania X-7*'s Gimmick Battle Royal. On March 13, 2004, Bobby Heenan's unparalleled career was honored when he was inducted into the WWE Hall of Fame the night before *WrestleMania XX*.

Bobby Lashley 🇺🇸

HT 6'3" **WT** 273 lbs.

FROM Colorado Springs, Colorado

SIGNATURE MOVE The Dominator

TITLE HISTORY

United States Champion, ECW Champion

YEARS ACTIVE | 1960 1969 | 1970 1979 | 1980 1989 | 1990 1999 | 2000 PRESENT

A product of the United States Army, Bobby Lashley is a three-time National Amateur Wrestling Champion, a four-time All-American, a two-time Armed Forces Champion, and a Silver Medalist in the 2002 Military World Championships. In September 2005, Bobby debuted on *SmackDown*. Lashley's power and amateur background served him well as he met opponents like Big Vito, Simon Dean, William Regal, and Val Venis. Bobby appeared at *WrestleMania 22* in a Money In the Bank Ladder Match. In 2006, he became ECW Champion after surviving the Extreme Elimination Chamber at *December to Dismember*. Bobby reached the pinnacle of his career at *WrestleMania 23* when he was Donald Trump's representative in *"The Battle of The Billionaires"* and fans saw Mr. McMahon get his head shaved when he beat Umaga. When he lost the ECW Championship under questionable circumstances, he regained it at *One Night Stand* in a Street Fight.

BOBO BRAZIL

| HT | 6'6" | WT | 270 lbs. | FROM | Benton Harbor, Michigan |

| SIGNATURE MOVE | Coco Butt | YEARS ACTIVE | 1960 1969 | 1970 1979 | 1980 1989 | 1960 1969 | 2000 PRESENT |

The legend of Bobo Brazil goes well beyond wins and losses. As a black man competing during a turbulent time in America, Brazil showed amazing grace while overcoming racial stereotypes and barriers. Along the way, he became recognized as sports-entertainment's Jackie Robinson and one of the industry's most influential figures.

Originally named Boo Boo Brazil, the Michigan native made his professional debut in 1951 and competed in the Detroit area. It wasn't until a printing error billed him Bobo that fans began to recognize Brazil under his now-famous name.

It was common practice during this time for African-American competitors to be booked against each other. With that, he spent much of his career battling the likes of Ernie Ladd and Thunderbolt Patterson. However, Brazil's in-ring arsenal, highlighted by the "Coco Butt" head butt, eventually proved to be too valuable for promoters to limit. As a result, he finally battled such legendary opponents as Killer Kowalski and Freddie Blassie. Brazil's fans eventually demanded to see more and more of their hero. His popularity finally forced many promoters to book him in dream matches against several other popular Superstars of the time, such as Andre the Giant and Bruno Sammartino.

After leaving WWE in the late 1960s, Brazil went on to compete throughout Los Angeles, Detroit, and Japan among other locales. During this time, he engaged in a bloody rivalry with The Sheik that saw Brazil capture a version of the United States Championship (not the current WWE title). When Brazil returned to WWE in 1976, the promotion actually announced him as the U.S. Champion, despite the fact that it was not a WWE-recognized title. The act was an enormous sign of respect for the sports-entertainment pioneer.

Bobo Brazil's remarkable career was honored with induction into the WWE Hall of Fame in 1994. The ceremony recognized his amazing in-ring conquests, as well as his tireless civil rights efforts that helped paved the way for those who followed.

THE BODY SHOP

Even after injuries sidelined Jesse "The Body" Ventura's in-ring career, the charismatic Superstar remained a pivotal personality on WWE television. In addition to assuming color commentating responsibilities on such shows as *All-Star Wrestling*, Ventura hosted his own interview segment called *The Body Shop*.

Using a makeshift gym as a set, Ventura welcomed WWE's most hated Superstars to *The Body Shop*. Week after week, the likes of Randy "Macho Man" Savage and Bobby Heenan appeared to spew their oft-unpopular opinions, as Ventura sat back and agreed with every word.

In late 1985, "Magnificent" Don Muraco assumed hosting duties of *The Body Shop*. Despite having a new host, the interviews remained equally biased toward WWE's villains. One of *The Body Shop*'s most memorable moments saw Freddie Blassie shock the world when he revealed he had sold half of his stable of Superstars to WWE newcomer, the "Doctor of Style" Slick.

The Bodydonnas

MEMBERS Skip, Zip

COMBINED WEIGHT 455 lbs.

YEARS ACTIVE

TITLE HISTORY

World Tag Team Champions

These fitness gurus made their WWE debut in May 1995. Skip, alongside his manager, Sunny, issued a challenge to everyone to get off their butts and get into shape. Skip performed jumping jacks and pushups during his contests. While he started in singles action, he was soon joined by his fraternal twin brother, Zip. The Bodydonnas trio was complete and ready to whip WWE into shape.

While Sunny made hearts race outside the ring, the Bodydonnas did their damage inside of it. With some help from their manager, Skip & Zip reached the pinnacle when they won a World Tag Team Championship Tournament at *WrestleMania XII*. Unfortunately for the exercise fiends, they lost the titles to the Godwinns, and Sunny followed the gold. The Bodydonnas tried to fill the empty position with a new manager, Kloudy, but this association was short-lived.

The fitness fanatics disbanded in 1996 and went their separate ways. The Bodydonnas will be remembered for their fitness vignettes as much as their seamless teamwork in the ring. The message from their manager summed it up best, "You've seen the rest, now see the best."

Bolo Mongol

YEARS ACTIVE

HT 6'3" **WT** 291 lbs. **FROM** Mongolia

Geto & Bepo Mongol terrorized the tag team ranks during the late 1960s and early 1970s. Collectively known as The Mongols, their unorthodox style led them to countless victories, including a reign as WWE's International Tag Team Champions. After more than one year with the titles, The Mongols lost the gold to Bruno Sammartino & Dominic DeNucci in June 1971.

The loss failed to set The Mongols back much, as they quickly worked their way back into the win column, but then a freak injury sidelined Bepo. Many thought the injury meant the end of The Mongols, but Geto quickly replaced his partner with the equally unorthodox Bolo Mongol.

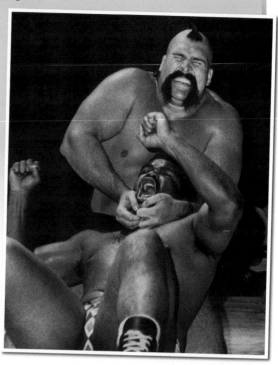

Bolo had the signature Mongol look, complete with horns of hair on an otherwise bald head. Together, Bolo & Geto briefly kept the legend of The Mongols alive in the Pittsburgh territory, as well as Japan. Shortly after the new Mongols debuted, Bolo broke away from Geto to form his own identity.

The Bolsheviks

YEARS ACTIVE

MEMBERS Nikolai Volkoff, Boris Zhukov **COMBINED WEIGHT** 604 lbs.

These two powerful Superstars joined forces in the name of Mother Russia in the spring of 1988. These men were determined to spark a revolution, with WWE as their battleground. To the disgust of fans and opponents all over the globe, the two came to the ring waiving the Soviet flag and sang the Russian National Anthem before each match.

Nikolai Volkoff & Boris Zhukov specialized in crushing double-team moves and underhanded tactics in their matches. Heading into *SummerSlam 1988*, the Russians were set for a collision with the Powers of Pain. After a string of strong performances, Volkoff & Zhukov earned a match against the Hart Foundation at *WrestleMania VI*. Unfortunately for the Soviets, they were defeated in 19 seconds in front of a capacity SkyDome crowd.

Soon after the loss, the bond that held The Bolsheviks together was irrevocably broken. Volkoff & Zhukov battled across the United States and for the first time in his career, Nikolai Volkoff was a fan favorite. Boris Zhukov remained one of the most hated villains until his departure from WWE in 1991.

Boogeyman

HT 6'2" **WT** 260 lbs.

FROM The Bottomless Pit

SIGNATURE MOVE Boogeyslam

YEARS ACTIVE   1960-1969 1970-1979 1980-1989 1990-1999 2000-PRESENT

Some of the toughest men to walk the planet are found in WWE, but when the lights go out they all fear the Boogeyman. Hailing from The Bottomless Pit, Boogeyman first started spooking the WWE roster in October 2005. Despite his unbelievably creepy appearance, he managed to be a tough man to find. Hiding in various backstage locales, Boogeyman would only pop out to frighten fellow Superstars with a disturbing rendition of a classic nursery rhyme.

Boogeyman's in-ring debut came at the expense of Simon Dean on a December 2005 edition of *SmackDown*. After pummeling Dean within moments of the opening bell, Boogeyman went on to spook nearly the entire *SmackDown* roster, including former WWE Champion John "Bradshaw" Layfield. At the 2006 *Royal Rumble*, Boogeyman made quick work of JBL, finishing him off with his patented Pump-Handle Slam. After the match, Boogeyman celebrated his first pay-per-view victory with a mouthful of live worms.

After turning back one former World Champion, Boogeyman focused his sinister sights on yet another past titleholder. On the grand stage of *WrestleMania 22*, he defeated the mighty King Booker, but not before planting a worm-filled kiss on Queen Sharmell. Boogeyman's destructive athleticism in the ring, coupled with his unparalleled ability to get inside a man's head, has undoubtedly caused a few Superstars to sleep with the lights on.

BOOKER T

HT 6'3" **WT** 253 lbs. **FROM** Houston, Texas

SIGNATURE MOVE Book End, Scissor Kick

TITLE HISTORY World Heavyweight Champion, Intercontinental Champion, Hardcore Champion, World Tag Team Champion

YEARS ACTIVE    1960-1969 1970-1979 1980-1989 1990-1999 2000-PRESENT

Before this five-time WCW Champion was a king, Booker T was arguably the most celebrated tag team competitor in the history of the industry. A ten-time co-holder of the WCW World Tag Team Championship with his brother Stevie Ray as a member of Harlem Heat, the duo dominated the WCW tag team scene in the 1990s. Booker then became a top singles competitor and ended the historic last episode of *WCW Monday Nitro* as WCW Champion. In the weeks that followed WWE's purchase of its one-time rival, Booker T invaded WWE when he attacked Stone Cold Steve Austin at *King of the Ring*. Booker then participated in the first ever WCW match to be held on WWE programming when he defended his WCW Championship on *Monday Night Raw* against Buff Bagwell. Booker became a key member of The Alliance as they attempted to overthrow WWE. He won the World Tag Team Championship on Nov. 1, 2001 when he & Test defeated The Rock & Chris Jericho on *SmackDown*.

Perhaps Booker's finest moment came when he defeated Rey Mysterio for the World Heavyweight Championship at *The Great American Bash 2006*. For Booker, it was validation that his dominance in WCW could translate over to WWE. He further drove home that point when he won a Champion of Champions Match at *No Mercy 2006*, defeating the reigning WWE Champion, John Cena, and the ECW Champion, Big Show. Few Superstars have matched the success of this exciting performer who, over the course of his career, has held over 30 championships. In the air or on the mat, few can match the fight, athleticism, and charisma of Booker T. Now can you dig that, sucka?

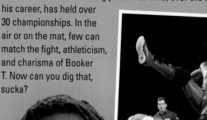

Booker T & Goldust

COMBINED WEIGHT 523 lbs.

TITLE HISTORY

World Tag Team Champions

YEARS ACTIVE   1960-1969 1970-1979 1980-1989 1990-1999 2000-PRESENT

One of the more unlikely tag team pairings in recent memory, these two Superstars came together in 2002 on *Raw* thanks to Goldust showing Booker T they could form a great duo. They were able to blend their different ring styles to create an incredible chemistry. They were also a part of some of the funniest segments in *Raw* history and hosted their own segment "Booker T & Goldust At The Movies."

On December 15, 2002, they won a Fatal-Four Way Elimination Match for the World Tag Team Championship but lost the titles to Lance Storm & William Regal on *Raw*. After failed attempts to win back the gold, the team split, but the two Superstars remained allies.

Boris Malenko

YEARS ACTIVE | 1960 1969 | 1970 1979 | 1980 1989 | 1960 1969 | 2000 PRESENT

HT 5'10" **WT** 220 lbs. **FROM** Moscow, Russia **SIGNATURE MOVE** Russian Sickle

With the "Red Scare" still lingering in the United States, Boris Malenko used his Russian ancestry to strike fear into both opponents and fans. A master antagonist, Malenko could draw more hatred from audiences than any other Superstar of his time.

Malenko was much more than an ire-inspiring Russian; he was also a brilliant competitor inside the ring. In fact, his amazing abilities earned him the nicknames "The Great Malenko" and "Professor Malenko." Despite possessing superior in-ring skills, however, Malenko was not above cheating to earn a victory. It wasn't uncommon to see him biting or jabbing the eyes of an opponent in an attempt to gain the upper hand.

In May 1967, Malenko defeated Wahoo McDaniel to capture the National Wrestling Alliance Florida Heavyweight Championship. It was his first of 11 NWA titles, including seven reigns as the Florida Brass Knuckles Champion. Malenko passed away in 1994, but he left behind an amazing legacy, which includes two sons who also competed in the ring, Joe and Dean Malenko.

Boris Zhukov

YEARS ACTIVE | 1960 1969 | 1970 1979 | 1980 1989 | 1990 1999 | 2000 PRESENT

HT 6'2 **WT** 275 lbs. **FROM** Siberia, Russia **SIGNATURE MOVE** Flying Clothesline

Boris Zhukov first appeared in World Class Championship Wrestling in 1983 and toured the territories of the Southeastern United States of America. Boris traveled to the AWA in 1985, where he made a name for himself squaring off against foes like Sgt. Slaughter and Jimmy "Superfly" Snuka.

In 1987, the formidable Russian came to WWE and immediately teamed with Nikolai Volkoff to form the Bolsheviks. The two powerhouses were managed by the "Doctor of Style" Slick and were serious threats for the World Tag Team Championship. Boris was also commended for his habits when he won "Best Personal Hygiene" at the 1987 Slammy Awards. Boris returned to singles action after he and Volkoff split until he left WWE in 1991.

Since then, Boris has continued to appear on independent cards all over the world. Fans will never forget the name Boris Zhukov, or the pain he brought opponents throughout his career.

BRA & PANTIES MATCH

The name of this match alone whips male fans into a chaotic frenzy. In this match, the participating WWE Divas begin in the match in their usual ring attire. The winner of the match is the first Diva to strip her opponent down to her bra and panties.

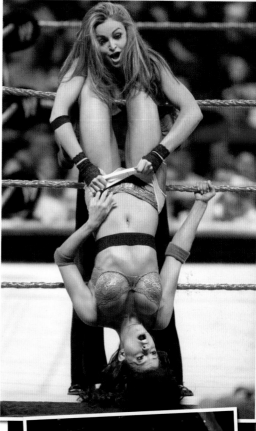

Brady Boone

| HT | 5'10" | WT | 220 lbs. |

| FROM | Oregon City, Oregon |

| SIGNATURE MOVE | Moonsault |

Hailing from the state of Oregon, Brady Boone was recognized as one of the top high school gymnasts in the United States before embarking on his sports-entertainment career. In the late 1980s he debuted in WWE displaying his high flying, aerial style as seen on such programs as *Wrestling Challenge* and *Wrestling Spotlight*. During this time reports circulated around wrestling that he also donned a mask as the Battle Kat. However, that was never confirmed.

As his in-ring career came to a close, Boone was hired by WCW to serve as a referee. Sadly, on December 18, 1998 Brady Boone's life suddenly ended when he was killed in an automobile accident in Orlando. His high-flying legacy will always be remembered and admired by true mat fans all over the globe.

Brain Busters

| MEMBERS | Arn Anderson, Tully Blanchard | COMBINED WEIGHT | 475 lbs. |

| TITLE HISTORY | World Tag Team Champions |

As founding members of the legendary Four Horsemen, Arn Anderson & Tully Blanchard created historic reputations that preceded their WWE debut. Once they arrived in WWE, their impressive teamwork went a long way toward proving they were as good as everybody believed.

Trading in manager J.J. Dillon for Bobby "The Brain" Heenan, the two-time NWA Tag Team Champions made their way to WWE in 1988. Billed as the Brain Busters (playing off their manager's nickname), Anderson & Blanchard made quick work of WWE's top teams, including The Rockers at *Saturday Night's Main Event* and Strike Force at *WrestleMania V*. Despite their impressive record, it took the team more than seven months to receive their first high-profile World Tag Team Championship opportunity.

In May 1989, the Brain Busters challenged Demolition for the tag titles on *Saturday Night's Main Event*. Anderson & Blanchard walked away with the disqualification victory but not the championship. Two months later, they finished the job when they beat Demolition in a two-out-of-three falls match. With the titles in their possession, the Brain Busters were finally considered a part of WWE's upper echelon of Superstars.

The Brain Busters left WWE in late 1989. While their stay in the promotion was brief, Anderson & Blanchard used the time to prove to a national audience that they were one of the most intelligent and technically sound tag teams of the 1980s.

Brakkus

| HT | 6'0" | WT | 275 lbs. | FROM | Germany | SIGNATURE MOVE | Powerslam |

This powerhouse and former professional bodybuilder came to WWE in 1996. Brakkus was a relentless rule-breaker and wanted not only to beat his opponents, but to break them. He met Superstars like Dr. X, the Sultan, Rockabilly, the Jackyl, and Jeff Jarrett. In February 1998, he appeared at Extreme Championship Wrestling's *CyberSlam* and fought Tazz for the ECW Television title. Later that year, he competed in the Brawl For All Tournament, losing in disappointing fashion to Savio Vega. After the loss, Brakkus returned to Europe and has not been seen in WWE since.

BRET "HIT MAN" HART

| HT | 6' | WT | 235 lbs. |

FROM Calgary, Alberta, Canada

SIGNATURE MOVE Sharpshooter

YEARS ACTIVE 1960-1969 · 1970-1979 · 1980-1989 · 1990-1999 · 2000-PRESENT

TITLE HISTORY WWE Champion, World Tag Team Champion, Intercontinental Champion

HALL OF FAME 2006

> ## THE BEST THERE IS. THE BEST THERE WAS. THE BEST THERE EVER WILL BE.

Born into wrestling royalty, Bret Hart was destined to make his living inside the ring. His father, Stu, a top competitor, was also well-known for training many of the biggest names in sports-entertainment. Some of Bret's earliest memories include sitting in the family basement watching his father physically dissect men half his age and twice his size. Bret started building his reputation while competing in his father's Stampede Wrestling promotion. He quickly became one of Calgary's top draws and caught the eye of Vince McMahon. In 1984, rather than trying to lure Bret over to WWE, McMahon simply bought Stampede Wrestling and the rights to its competitors, including Bret.

THE HART FOUNDATION AND WORLD CHAMPIONSHIPS

Bret's career didn't immediately take off south of the border, but he soon teamed with Jim "The Anvil" Neidhart and success soon followed. Dubbed the Hart Foundation, the duo possessed the perfect combination of technical ability and pure power. With Jimmy Hart as their manager, the Hart Foundation captured the World Tag Team Championship on two separate occasions.

After losing the World Tag Team Championship to the Nasty Boys at *WrestleMania VII*, Bret leapt into singles competition. In a matter of months, he won his first major singles title, defeating Mr. Perfect for the Intercontinental Championship at *SummerSlam 1991*. Bret would go on to capture the Intercontinental Championship one more time before setting his sights on the WWE Championship.

On October, 12, 1992, Bret won his first of five WWE Championships. Bret's title reign was derailed at *WrestleMania IX* by Yokozuna. In typical Bret Hart fashion, he refused to let the loss ruin him. More determined than ever, he turned back Razor Ramon, Mr. Perfect, and Bam Bam Bigelow all in one evening to be crowned the 1993 *King of the Ring*.

With every major championship and a *King of the Ring* victory on his resumé, Bret had little left to prove, however he refused to rest on his legendary reputation. Intent on regaining sports-entertainment's ultimate prize, Bret was declared a co-winner of the 1994 *Royal Rumble*. The victory earned him another opportunity at the WWE Championship, which he capitalized on at *WrestleMania X*, defeating Yokozuna to reclaim the title.

TROUBLE IN THE FAMILY

Bret Hart will always be remembered as one of the greatest champions in WWE history, but one of his most memorable rivalries revolved around more than titles. In 1994, the Harts were a family in crisis. The normally tight-knit clan was nearly torn apart when Bret's younger brother, Owen, attacked the "Hit Man" in a jealous rage. The rivalry resulted in some of the most emotionally-charged encounters to ever take place within a WWE ring. Owen was never able to wrest the WWE Championship away from Bret, but his *WrestleMania X* victory over his older brother went a long way in his attempt to get out from under his legendary shadow.

Unfortunately, Bret's final WWE match is widely recognized as one of the most infamous moments in sports-entertainment history. As a result of what is now commonly referred to as the "Montreal Incident", Bret Hart and Vince McMahon engaged in a bitter war of words that lasted several years Bret went to compete in WCW, where he captured the promotion's heavyweight title. McMahon's and Hart's differences couldn't stop the "Hit Man" from being honored as one of sports-entertainment's greatest when he was inducted into the WWE Hall of Fame in 2006.

Bret Hart's Submission Match with Stone Cold Steve Austin at WrestleMania 13 was his last WrestleMania appearance.

The Brian Kendrick

HT	5'8"	WT	184 lbs.	SIGNATURE MOVE	Sliced Bread No. 2

FROM	Venice, California	YEARS ACTIVE	1960-1969 1970-1979 1980-1989 1990-1999 2000-PRESENT

TITLE HISTORY WWE Tag Team Champion, World Tag Team Champion

A graduate of the Shawn Michaels Wrestling Academy, Brian Kendrick entered WWE with the proper fundamentals, a high threshold for pain, and the charismatic flair that only HBK could teach. In 2003, Brian debuted in WWE and wowed crowds with his aerial moves and speed. He soon found a tag team partner in fellow high-flyer Paul London. In early 2004, Kendrick left WWE to hone his skills overseas.

In September 2005, he returned to WWE and took aim at sports-entertainment's premier figures. Stronger, faster, and tougher, Kendrick reunited with London and the two thrilled audiences. On May 21, 2006, they defeated MNM for the WWE Tag Team Championship. Kendrick & London held the titles for an unprecedented 334 days. In June 2007, the team was drafted to *Raw* and focused on getting to the top. During a tour of South Africa, they defeated Lance Cade & Trevor Murdoch to capture the World Tag Team Championship. Though they lost the belts three days later, they are one of the few teams to hold both championships.

At the 2008 Supplemental Draft, Kendrick was sent back to *SmackDown* and unveiled a side of himself fans never thought they'd see. With a new attitude, wardrobe, and bodyguard named Ezekiel, "The" Brian Kendrick displayed sneaky rule-breaker tactics and new dance moves. To know what "The" Brian Kendrick is going to do next, one must watch "The" Brian Kendrick. After all, he's the man with the plan.

Brie & Nikki Bella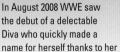

HT	5'6"	FROM	Scottsdale, Arizona

YEARS ACTIVE	1960-1969 1970-1979 1980-1989 1990-1999 2000-PRESENT

In August 2008 WWE saw the debut of a delectable Diva who quickly made a name for herself thanks to her moves on her way to the ring and dizzying ones in it. Brie Bella bested two-time Women's Champion Victoria in her first match on SmackDown and proved it was not beginner's luck when she pinned WWE's Black Widow the next week for the second straight time. A few weeks after her debut, Natalya and Victoria uncovered the fact that Brie had a twin sister, named Nikki, who would switch places with her during matches. Even though the twins lost their underhanded advantage they didn't allow it to slow down their quest for glory in the ring. As they continue to come into their own, the Divas Division on *SmackDown* best beware of these rising stars.

Brian Pillman

HT	6'0"	WT	227 lbs.	FROM	Cincinnati, Ohio

YEARS ACTIVE	1960-1969 1970-1979 1980-1989 1990-1999 2000-PRESENT

A former member of the Cincinnati Bengals, Brian Pillman turned to wrestling in 1986. No longer restricted by the shoulder pads and helmet, the unpredictable Superstar could unleash the real man lurking inside. The result: sports-entertainment's most notorious "Loose Cannon."

Armed with the training he received from Stu Hart, Pillman made his debut in Canada's Stampede Wrestling. Within a few short years, he cemented himself as one of the industry's premiere high flyers, which caught the attention of WCW. As a member of WCW, Pillman used his acrobatic attack to claim two Light Heavyweight Championships and the WCW Tag Team Championship.

It wasn't until Pillman made his way to WWE in 1996 that fans began to see the true "Loose Cannon." Despite being sidelined with a severe ankle injury, Pillman managed to shock audiences with his unpredictable behavior.

Filled with an uncontrollable rage, he engaged in a memorable rivalry with the bizarre Goldust. Unfortunately, Pillman unexpectedly passed away soon after in Minnesota. His tragic death took away one of sports-entertainment's most colorful personalities.

Brisco Brothers

WWE Hall of Fame 2008

MEMBERS	Gerald, Jack	COMBINED WEIGHT	461 lbs.

YEARS ACTIVE	1960-1969 1970-1979 1980-1989 1960-1969 2000-PRESENT

Throughout sports-entertainment's rich history, there have been several famous brother tag team combinations. While they are all exceptional in their own right, Jack & Gerald Brisco are a cut above. The elder brother, Jack, was a stand-out amateur wrestler at Oklahoma State and is one of only three men to hold the NCAA Wrestling and NWA Championships. He made his pro debut in 1965 and went on to worldwide stardom. Gerald, like his brother Jack, knew success in the amateur ranks and won several AAU Tournaments. He was also a stand-out at Oklahoma State. Trained by brother Jack, Gerald debuted in 1968 and went on to hold many titles throughout the NWA.

As a team during the 1970s, they displayed poetic continuity and superior ring strategy. Their dominance was shown in the ring as well as in their standing offer to any misguided challengers, "C'mon down! You know where the gold is!"

In 1984, the Briscos made their much-anticipated WWE debut and did not disappoint. They raised the bar for tag team competition before retiring from the ring. Jack returned to Tampa, FL and expanded their famous "Brisco Brothers Body Shop." Gerald became a confidant to Vince McMahon and during the late 1990s often appeared on television beside the Chairman with fellow associate Pat Patterson.

In March 2008, the Brisco Brothers reached the pinnacle of sports-entertainment when they were inducted in to WWE Hall of Fame. As individuals, they are two of the most decorated figures in all of sports-entertainment. Together, the Brisco Brothers are icons who epitomized the word "team" and are eternally revered as consummate professionals.

"THE BRITISH BULLDOG" DAVEY BOY SMITH

| HT | 5'11" | WT | 260 lbs. | FROM | Manchester, England | SIGNATURE MOVE | Powerslam | YEARS ACTIVE | 1960-1969 | 1970-1979 | 1980-1989 | 1990-1999 | 2000-PRESENT |

TITLE HISTORY World Tag Team Champion, European Champion, Intercontinental Champion, Hardcore Champion

WWE audiences first saw Davey Boy Smith in 1985 alongside his cousin, the Dynamite Kid. Together, they formed a revolutionary tag team, the British Bulldogs. They amazed audiences with their in-ring acrobatics and fluid teamwork. They won the World Tag Team Championship at *WrestleMania 2,* defeating the Dream Team (Brutus Beefcake & Greg Valentine). After a nine-month title reign they lost the titles in controversial fashion to the Hart Foundation.

In 1990, the protégé of mat legend Stu Hart returned as a singles wrestler and referred to himself as the "British Bulldog." Sporting the Union Jack, his blend of power, agility, and aerial moves made him a top attraction in North America and Europe. He faced his brother-in-law, Bret "Hit Man" Hart, in the main event of *SummerSlam 1992* for the Intercontinental Championship. In front of over 80,000 fans at Wembley Stadium, the British Bulldog emerged victorious in arguably the greatest match of his career.

After a disappointing loss to Shawn Michaels on a November episode of *Saturday Night's Main Event,* he left WWE, but returned in 1993 to form the Allied Powers with Lex Luger.

After turning on his American ally, the Bulldog joined Camp Cornette. While teamed with another brother-in-law, Owen Hart, the duo won the World Tag Team Championship from the Smoking Gunns at *In Your House: Mind Games* in 1996. The Bulldog then took a bite out of the history books on February 26, 1997 in Berlin, Germany when he defeated Owen Hart in the tournament finals to crown the first European Champion. In late 1997, he joined Bret Hart, Owen Hart, Jim Neidhart, and Brian Pillman in the ever-dangerous Hart Foundation. After the infamous "Montreal Incident" where Shawn Michaels defeated Bret Hart amid high controversy at *Survivor Series 1997,* Bulldog followed Bret and Neidhart to WCW in 1998. After leaving the organization, Bulldog returned to WWE in August 1999 and tangled with main event Superstars The Rock, Triple H, Mankind, and Big Show. Sadly in 2002, Davey Boy Smith passed away.

BRITISH BULLDOGS

| | YEARS ACTIVE | 1960-1969 | 1970-1979 | 1980-1989 | 1990-1999 | 2000-PRESENT |

| **MEMBERS** | Davey Boy Smith, Dynamite Kid | **COMBINED WEIGHT** | 471 lbs. | **TITLE HISTORY** | World Tag Team Champions |

Behind the perfect combination of speed and power, the British Bulldogs became one of the most popular tag teams of their time. Originally competing in promotions throughout Canada and Japan, Dynamite Kid & Davey Boy Smith jumped to WWE in the mid-1980s and quickly gained tag-team success, as well as the hearts of the fans.

Shortly after making their WWE debut, the British Bulldogs, behind the tutelage of Capt. Lou Albano and rocker Ozzy Osbourne, defeated the Dream Team (Greg Valentine & Brutus Beefcake) for the World Tag Team Championship at *WrestleMania 2.* The popular duo maintained a strong hold on the titles for nine months before losing them to the Hart Foundation in January 1987. The match proved very costly, as some questionable officiating by Danny Davis also led to Dynamite Kid suffering serious injury.

Following the loss, the Bulldogs took some time off to rehab Dynamite Kid's injuries. When they returned, they immediately set their sights on gaining revenge on Davis. Teaming with Tito Santana, the Bulldogs sought vengeance at *WrestleMania III* when they battled Davis & the Hart Foundation. Unfortunately, the match didn't go in their favor, as the dastardly Davis weaseled his way to a win.

The Bulldog's popularity reached new heights when they added mascot Matilda to the team. The lovable bulldog accompanied Dynamite Kid & Davey Boy Smith to ringside for all their matches and quickly became a fan favorite. Her popularity eventually drew ire of the Islanders, who dognapped the adorable pooch.

The Islanders' distasteful act lead the Bulldogs to another Six-Man Tag Team Match when they partnered with fellow animal lover Koko B. Ware to battle the dognappers and their manager Bobby Heenan at *WrestleMania IV.* Much like their *WrestleMania III* match, the Bulldogs were unable to secure victory.

The Bulldogs struggled to get back on track following the *WrestleMania IV* loss, and disappeared from the WWE scene by 1989. Despite the losses they experienced late in their tenure, Dynamite Kid & Davey Boy Smith used a unique blend of quickness and strength to build an impressive legacy that is still admired today.

Brock Lesnar 🇺🇸

| HT | 6'3" | WT | 295 lbs. | SIGNATURE MOVE | F5 |

| FROM | Minneapolis, Minnesota | TITLE HISTORY | WWE Champion |

| YEARS ACTIVE | 1960 1969 | 1970 1979 | 1980 1989 | 1990 1999 | 2000 PRESENT |

When Brock Lesnar entered WWE, he brought with him a championship amateur career and an overwhelming physique. The impressive combination caused many to believe they were looking at "The Next Big Thing." Over the course of his WWE career, Lesnar proved those predictions to be correct.

Under the tutelage of Paul Heyman, Lesnar made an immediate impact upon his 2002 debut. A mere three months into his career, he defeated Rob Van Dam to win the prestigious *King of the Ring* tournament. Two months after that, he beat The Rock for the WWE Championship. In short, Lesnar accomplished more in half a year than most Superstars do in an entire career.

Over the next two years, Lesnar continued to shine, especially against Undertaker. At *No Mercy 2002*, he defeated the "Deadman" inside the demonic Hell in a Cell. At the following year's event, Lesnar beat Undertaker in a Biker Chain Match. He even last eliminated the "Deadman" to win the 2003 *Royal Rumble*. With his victory in the *Rumble*, Lesnar earned the opportunity to challenge Kurt Angle for the WWE Championship at *WrestleMania XIX*. With visions of making it big in the NFL, Lesnar left WWE in 2004. While fans never got to see him succeed on the gridiron, nobody will ever forget the impact Lesnar made in the ring during his brief WWE tenure.

Brooke 🇺🇸

| HT | 5'4" | FROM | Houston, Texas |

| YEARS ACTIVE | 1960 1969 | 1970 1979 | 1980 1989 | 1990 1999 | 2000 PRESENT |

In 2006, Brooke saw the WWE Diva Search as her ticket to the big time. WWE, on the other hand, did not. She was cut from the competition just prior to the final eight hopefuls being announced.

Despite being eliminated, the aspiring Diva made a solid impression on WWE officials, who offered her a spot in their developmental program. After just a few months of training, the beautiful brunette made it to the big time when she debuted on *ECW* in January 2007. As a member of Extreme Exposé, Brooke performed seductive dance routines alongside Kelly Kelly and Layla. The threesome electrified male audiences and caught the eye of recording artist Timbaland, who placed the girls in his music video, "Throw it on Me".

The Brood

| YEARS ACTIVE | 1960 1969 | 1970 1979 | 1980 1989 | 1990 1999 | 2000 PRESENT |

| MEMBERS | David Heath (formerly known as Gangrel), Edge & Christian, Matt & Jeff Hardy |

In 1998, a mystical force appeared in World Wrestling Entertainment. Led by David Heath, known in WWE as Gangrel, Edge & Christian often entered into WWE events rising from underground surrounded by a circle of flames. They crept to the ring as their leader sipped blood from his chalice and spit it out at the crowd. They often participated in bizarre rituals, intimidating and frightening the weak.

Opponents were viewed as enemies from another world and often victims to their bloodbaths, which occurred when the lights in the arena went out and a red light appeared. When the light came back the victim was laying in the ring covered in blood. In early 1999, they joined Undertaker's Ministry of Darkness.

The Brood left Undertaker's faction and battled the Hardy Boys. During one match, the brothers and their manager were doused in blood. As Edge & Christian grew as a tag team, they removed themselves from their leader's influence. For a brief period of time, David Heath recruited Matt & Jeff Hardy, forming a New Brood, but it broke apart when the Hardys acquired a new manager. Both Edge & Christian and the Hardy Boys became two of WWE's most successful tag teams. David Heath faded from the scene until his 2007 return to at WWE's *Raw 15th Anniversary* special.

The Brooklyn Brawler 🇺🇸

| HT | 6'0" | WT | 248 lbs. | SIGNATURE MOVE | Sidewalk Smash |

| FROM | Brooklyn, New York | YEARS ACTIVE | 1960 1969 | 1970 1979 | 1980 1989 | 1990 1999 | 2000 PRESENT |

From the rough streets of Brooklyn, New York, this Superstar was brought into WWE by Bobby Heenan. During a 1989 episode of *Prime Time Wrestling*, the Brooklyn Brawler made his presence felt when he jumped the Red Rooster and handed him a five boroughs beat-down.

The man from the County of Kings had a short-lived partnership with another New York City native, Bad News Brown. The Brawler also battled with Koko B. Ware after the fans voted for the two Superstars to lock up for Coliseum Video's *Fan Favorites* video cassette release.

The Brooklyn Brawler continued his street-fighting ways into the 1990s. He appeared on WWE television for the remainder of the decade and developed a reputation for showing up whenever he felt someone needed to get roughed up. You never knew when the Brawler would appear on *Raw*, *Smackdown* or *ECW* and take his rough-housing tactics to the next big Superstar.

Brother Love

Dressed in a white suit, the red-faced Brother Love claimed to preach the good word of love to WWE audiences of the late 1980s and early 1990s. The sight of him invoked thoughts of scandalous televangelists; despite nearly being booed out of every arena, he constantly used his annoying catchphrase to tell people how he felt: "I love you!"

Brother Love is best known for hosting a weekly interview segment appropriately named *The Brother Love Show*. He used the segment to verbally attack popular Superstars of the time. His long list of dissatisfied guests includes Hulk Hogan, Brutus Beefcake, and Dusty Rhodes.

While Brother Love's antics on *The Brother Love Show* are widely chronicled by WWE historians, it's a lesser-known fact that might just be the preacher's ultimate career highlight. Amazingly, it was Brother Love, not Paul Bearer, who first introduced WWE audiences to Undertaker at *Survivor Series 1990*. He went on to manage the "Deadman" through February 1991, at which time he sold the future WWE Hall of Famer's contract to Bearer.

The Brothers of Destruction

MEMBERS	Undertaker, Kane	COMBINED WEIGHT	628 lbs.

TITLE HISTORY	World Tag Team Champions, WCW Tag Team Champions

YEARS ACTIVE	1960-1969	1970-1979	1980-1989	1990-1999	2000-PRESENT

When WWE first saw Undertaker and his half-brother in the ring, the two were bitter rivals and combatants in some of the most dangerous contests World Wrestling Entertainment has ever known.

An early glimpse of what they could be as a united force was visible at the 2001 *Royal Rumble*. Enter the Brothers of Destruction. The powerful moves they used as individuals were more deadly as double-team maneuvers. With their immense power, they crushed anyone who got in their way. The duo joined forces again in February and they defeated Rikishi & Haku in a First Blood Match on *SmackDown*.

During their battles with Alliance members Diamond Dallas Page and Kanyon, they became the first team ever to unify the WWE and WCW Tag Team titles in a Steel Cage Match at *SummerSlam 2001*. Over the years, they have both reformed and reopened old battle wounds depending on where their path of destruction leads them.

Since they are family, they do tend to fight from time to time. However, history (and stretchers) have shown the worst beatings one could receive is when these brothers join forces. When you face the Brothers of Destruction, winning becomes a secondary concern to survival.

THE BROTHER LOVE SHOW

Despite its host professing an annoying level of affection for everybody, love certainly was not in the air at *The Brother Love Show*. Hosted by the red-faced Brother Love, the weekly interview segment debuted in 1988 and provided a platform for WWE's most controversial Superstars to voice their unpopular opinions. Much like *Piper's Pit* before it, *The Brother Love Show* served as the scene of some of WWE's most memorable moments.

In 1990, Earthquake brutally attacked Hulk Hogan at *The Brother Love Show*. The onslaught was so severe that it ignited one of the hottest rivalries of the summer. "The Hulkster" later gained revenge when he defeated Earthquake at *SummerSlam*.

The following year, Brother Love used his show to announce he was too busy bringing the message of love to the fans to properly continue managing Undertaker. He then introduced the world to the "Deadman's" new guiding light, Paul Bearer. Together, Undertaker and Bearer went on to become one of the most successful Superstar-manager combinations ever.

In a truly fateful moment in the history of *The Brother Love Show*, the host welcomed Ultimate Warrior to the set in March 1991. At the time, Warrior was preparing for his Retirement Match against Randy Savage at *WrestleMania VII*. As a warm-up, Warrior decided to start sending people into retirement right then and there. He proceeded to destroy *The Brother Love Show* set, officially marking the end of the interview segment.

Bruiser Brody

HT	6'8"	WT	283 lbs.	SIGNATURE MOVE	Knee Drop

FROM	Santa Fe, New Mexico	YEARS ACTIVE	1960-1969	1970-1979	1980-1989	1990-1999	2000-PRESENT

Known for his wild hair, big bushy beard and bulging eyes, Bruiser Brody was a madman in the truest sense of the word. After 15 unpredictable years in the ring, the brawler earned the reputation as one of the toughest of his time, but instead will be remembered best by his tragic passing.

After making his professional debut in 1973, Brody became known as a bit of a nomad. Bouncing around from promotion to promotion, he never stayed in one place for very long. During his brief stints in WWE, WCCW, AWA and the NWA, among other places, he took part in memorable battles against Andre the Giant, Abdullah the Butcher, Dick the Bruiser and the Von Erichs.

Internationally, Brody was seen as a legend, especially in Puerto Rico. Unfortunately, the Puerto Rican ring would be the last he would ever compete in. In July 1988, Frank "Bruiser Brody" Goodish was stabbed to death in a locker room shower. Brody's impact and frenetic ring style live on in the memories of all who witnessed his mayhem.

BRUNO SAMMARTINO

HT 5'10" **WT** 265 lbs. **FROM** Abbruzi, Italy **SIGNATURE MOVE** Bearhug **YEARS ACTIVE**   1960/1969 1970/1979 1980/1989 1990/1999 2000 PRESENT

TITLE HISTORY WWE Champion; United States Tag Team Champion

He graced the covers of countless magazines, was a mainstream cultural icon, and holds the record of 211 consecutive Madison Square Garden sell-outs. Over the course of his heralded career, he was WWE Champion a combined 13 years. He is professional wrestling's quintessential ambassador, and to this day, fans can still hear the chants of his name in the hallowed grounds of the arenas and stadiums where he once so gallantly fought.

Bruno could adjust to the style of any opponent. He could be a brawler, a classic mat wrestler, or use his surprising quickness and power to defeat opponents.

Born into a respected family in October 1935, Bruno Sammartino grew up as one of seven siblings. As a boy, he played soccer and excelled in both Greco-Roman and freestyle wrestling. When Bruno set foot on Ellis Island in 1951, he was 16 years old and barely 90 pounds. He was often bullied at school and heckled for not speaking English. Determined to put an end to the harassment, Bruno began an exhausting weightlifting regiment at his local YMCA. He stunned experienced lifters with his natural gifts of strength and endurance. By 18, he weighed 257 lbs. In 1959, Sammartino set world records by lifting 569 lbs. in the bench-press, 715 lbs. in the squat and 700 lbs. in the deadlift. People pleaded with him to join United States Olympic team, but Bruno's love of weight training was not for a gold medal, it was to prepare him for his career in professional wrestling.

Almost instantly, he accumulated legions of devoted fans. Before he knew it, he was in Washington D.C. to meet the president of the Capitol Wrestling Corporation, Vincent J. McMahon, his business partner, Joseph Raymond "Toots" Mondt, and Willie Gilzenberg. Within six months, he was in the main event at Madison Square Garden when he teamed with Antonino "Argentina" Rocca. Despite early success, Bruno was frustrated with certain aspects of the business and took a break from the ring.

A NEW CHAMPION GAINS GOLDEN GUIDANCE

In February 1963, Bruno returned to Vince J. McMahon and his newly named World Wide Wrestling Federation, whose champion was "Nature Boy" Buddy Rogers. After Bruno's impressive showings, many believed the "Nature Boy" and "Italian Strongman" were on an inevitable collision course. On May 17, 1963, the two met in front of a sell-out Madison Square Garden crowd. In an unbelievable turn of events, Sammartino forced Rogers to submit in just 48 seconds to become the new WWE Champion.

With the most prestigious championship in the world around his waist, Bruno needed a trusted advisor to assist in the guidance of his career. "Golden Boy" Arnold Skaaland answered the call and remained with Sammartino almost 20 years. Along the way, Bruno amassed an amazing following that eclipsed all who came before him. In fact, Bruno hosted his own radio show in New York City where he played songs from his prized personal record collection.

Bruno traveled tirelessly, carrying the WWE Championship with pride. In August 1968, he ventured to Japan for a series of "Champion vs. Champion" best two-out-of-three falls matches against *puroresu* legend, Shohei "Giant" Baba. Bruno also teamed with former foe Skull Murphy and took on Baba with fellow Rikidozan protégé Antonio Inoki. Of all his challengers during the late 1960s, no one was more vicious than Killer Kowalski. The bouts between these men were not showcases of technical ring skill or displays of power, they were epic blood-soaked battles. In 1969, the two combatants had a match that ended in pure bedlam in the main event of the only wrestling card in the history of Fenway Park in Boston.

Even though he was known as a singles Superstar, Bruno was also an excellent tag team competitor. On July 26, 1967, he teamed with Spiros Arion to defeat The Sicilians for the United States Tag Team Championship. Unfortunately, due to Sammartino's responsibilities as WWE Champion, he was forced to relinquish the titles. To the delight of fans everywhere, this was not the only time Bruno held tag team gold. He won the International Tag Team Championship on December 8, 1969 with Gotham City's Battman, when the duo toppled Prof. Toru Tanaka & Mitsu Arakawa. Bruno continued to appear in tag bouts throughout his career with friends such as Bobo Brazil, Andre the Giant, Chief Jay Strongbow, Pedro Morales, and former enemy turned ally Gorilla Monsoon.

A RECORD REIGN ENDS

On January 18, 1971, "The Russian Bear" Ivan Koloff shocked the world when he defeated Sammartino at Madison Square Garden to win the WWE Championship. Bruno's record-setting reign of seven-years, eight months and one day was over. His return to the ring in 1972 began in Los Angeles, where he made a special appearance and won a 22-man Battle Royal. On September 30, 1972, at the original Showdown At Shea, Sammartino met friend, and then-champion Pedro Morales in a classic 1 hour, 18 minute contest made more incredible because it was contested on a rain-slicked mat. Despite the treacherous conditions, the showdown is considered one of the greatest, technically sound wrestling matches of all time. The match ended in a draw due to Shea Stadium's curfew.

In 1973, Bruno returned to WWE to standing ovations throughout the region. On December 10, Sammartino made history when he became the first two-time WWE Champion as he defeated Stan "The Man" Stasiak. Due to the prestige Sammartino brought to wrestling's richest prize, rule-breakers from far and wide traveled to WWE in search of fame and fortune. The treacherous trio of The Grand Wizard and future WWE Hall of Famers, Capt. Lou Albano, and "Classy" Freddie Blassie continued to recruit new contenders from all corners of the Earth to dethrone Sammartino. As the dishonorable threesome learned time-and-time again, the power and heart of Sammartino was too much for the wretched henchman they employed.

Sammartino's fame expanded during the 1970s, as he was featured on the *Famous Sports Legends* television program hosted by future Major League Baseball Hall of Famer, Johnny Bench. He also appeared on the NBC network late-night talk show *Tomorrow with Tom Snyder.*

Appearances on major national broadcasts encouraged more Superstars to set their sights set on the champion. In 1976, Ken Patera arrived in WWE and he was one of the few opponents who matched the strength and grappling technique of the champion. Fred Blassie brought in Stan "The Lariat" Hansen. During their championship match on April 26, Hansen broke Sammartino's neck with his dreaded Lariat clothesline. Driven by revenge, Bruno returned weeks later against doctor's orders to defeat Hansen at the second Showdown from Shea event.

On April 30, 1977, Bruno once again was the victim of in-ring controversy. In his title defense against "Superstar" Billy Graham, the self-proclaimed "Tower of Power" pinned Sammartino with his feet on the top rope for added (and illegal) leverage. The referee never saw it and awarded the title to Graham. Despite rematches, Sammartino couldn't regain what many felt was rightfully his. Bruno soon entered semi-retirement, where fans saw him travel the country in singles and tag team matches.

THE STUDENT TURNS ON THE TEACHER

Still the adored heroic figure, Bruno made the transition from the ring to the broadcast booth. Serving as color commentator on *Championship Wrestling* with Vince K. McMahon, Bruno once again was a fixture on WWE programming. In 1980, Bruno agreed to once again lace up his boots for a good-will, 15-minute exhibition contest with his former pupil, Larry Zbyszko. The match was a traditional exchange of holds and maneuvers until Zbyszko became frustrated with his mentor's effective counters and refusal to push the attack himself. The issue came to a boiling point as Sammartino inadvertently knocked Zbyszko out of the ring. When Bruno held the rope open for Larry to re-enter the ring, Zbyszko brutally attacked his teacher in a fit of rage, hitting him three times in the head with a ringside chair.

A Steel Cage Match was signed for the historic Showdown At Shea III. Bruno told his broadcast partner Vince McMahon in front of a live studio audience, "I'm going to destroy Larry Zbyzsko." Though the match was a violent clash and both men's bodies were battered, Sammartino's resolve made him unstoppable. When it was all said and done, Sammartino walked through the cage door and proved he was indeed the master.

In 1984, Bruno decided to help guide the WWE career of his son, David. It didn't take long for the new generation of Superstars to challenge Bruno in hopes of making a name for themselves. The first contenders were "Rowdy" Roddy Piper and "Cowboy" Bob Orton. Bruno also had heated exchanges with Randy "Macho Man" Savage after his attack on Ricky Steamboat. As Sammartino gave fans a locker room report, Savage taunted both Steamboat and Sammartino. At his wit's end, Sammartino attacked Savage and had to be restrained.

The matches between Bruno and the then-Intercontinental Champion were so fierce, the score could only be settled in a Steel Cage with each man having a tag team partner. Bruno warned WWE officials and his fans that these matches were going to be brutal. He enlisted the help of Tito Santana to combat the attacks of Savage & "Adorable" Adrian Adonis. Bruno's last WWE match was when he teamed with then-WWE Champion Hulk Hogan. To fans, this was a dream team of professional wrestling's best from its past, present, and future as the two mega-heroes met the enormous pair of King Kong Bundy & One Man Gang. After their victory, Bruno continued his expert commentary alongside Vince McMahon until he left WWE in March 1988.

BRUTUS BEEFCAKE

HT 6'4" **WT** 272 lbs. **FROM** San Francisco, California

SIGNATURE MOVE Sleeper Hold

TITLE HISTORY World Tag Team Champion

YEARS ACTIVE 1960-1969 1970-1979 **1980-1989** 1990-1999 2000-PRESENT

This extraordinary athlete debuted in 1984, managed by "Luscious" Johnny Valiant. This hated rule breaker loved to strut and display his physical prowess in the ring, using a high knee to put away opponents. As fans chanted "Fruitcake," he formed the vaunted Dream Team with Greg Valentine. The arrogant pair won the World Tag Team Championship on August 24, 1985 when they defeated the U.S. Express. They held the titles until they were defeated by the British Bulldogs in a fast-paced thriller at *WrestleMania 2*. After the team disbanded at *Wrestlemania III*, audiences were introduced to WWE's new barber, and "Adorable" Adrian Adonis was the first customer.

With exciting new ring music, new ring attire, and steel shears, fans went wild as Brutus "The Barber" Beefcake took out opponents with his dreaded sleeper hold. Once they went to sleep, Brutus started struttin' and cuttin'. An intense rivalry with the Honky Tonk Man led to an Intercontinental Championship Match at the inaugural *SummerSlam*. Sadly, Brutus never made the match, as "Outlaw" Ron Bass attacked him days before the event.

He eventually returned and, as the Mega-Powers exploded, "the Barber" came to the aid of Hulk Hogan. The two longtime friends battled Randy "Macho Man" Savage & Zeus in the *SummerSlam 1989* main event. In 1990, Brutus nearly lost his life in a parasailing accident. He received emergency surgery that lasted over seven hours. Eight titanium plates, 32 screws, 100 feet of steel wire, and a reconstructed skull later, the surgery's success was a miracle of medicine. He was told he'd never walk again but after months of physical rehabilitation, he returned to WWE and launched his talk show, *The Barber Shop*. When he was back at full strength, he formed the Mega-Maniacs with Hulk Hogan.

Today, Beefcake is the general manager at one of the largest gyms in New England and still makes select appearances on the independent circuit. Brutus' life is one of courage, commitment and desire. This legend is one of WWE's most beloved heroes, and he has left his mark on the heads of opponents and in the hearts of fans.

Brute Bernard

HT 6'2" **WT** 250 lbs.

FROM

Montreal, Quebec, Canada

TITLE HISTORY

United States Tag Team Champion

YEARS ACTIVE 1960-1969 1970-1979 1980-1989 1960-1969 2000-PRESENT

A true Canadian wild man, Brute Bernard featured an uncontrollable, untamed ring style. Despite his unruly attitude, he always managed to find a tag team partner. In fact, many consider him to be one of the finest tag team wrestlers of his time.

The biggest win of Bernard's WWE career came in May 1963 when he teamed with Skull Murphy to defeat The Great Scott & Buddy Austin for the United States Tag Team Championship, the predecessor to today's World Tag Team Championship. The duo held the titles for six long months before finally being upended by Gorilla Monsoon & Killer Kowalski. In addition to his union with Murphy, Bernard also formed successful tag teams with Larry Hamilton, The Angel, Jay York, and Mike Paidousis.

Buddy Landell

HT 6' **WT** 220 lbs.

FROM Knoxville, Tennessee

SIGNATURE MOVE

Figure-Four Leglock

YEARS ACTIVE 1960-1969 1970-1979 1980-1989 1990-1999 2000-PRESENT

Since 1979, Buddy Landell has traveled throughout the United States to become one of the ring's toughest and most accomplished veterans. In the mid 1980s, Landell became notorious throughout Tennessee and Jim Crockett Promotions. He continued to appear on independent cards through the early 1990s and saw success in Smoky Mountain Wrestling.

In December 1995, Landell debuted in WWE at *In Your House* against Ahmed Johnson. Over the next six years, Landell appeared sporadically for WWE in matches against Bob Holly, Matt Hardy, Bret "Hit Man" Hart, Edge, the Godfather, and Triple H. He still makes appearances on the independent scene to show "he's still got it."

Buddy Rogers (see page 52)

Buddy Rose

HT	6'1"	WT	271 lbs.	FROM	Las Vegas, Nevada

SIGNATURE MOVE Las Vegas Jackpot

YEARS ACTIVE 1960-1969 · 1970-1979 · 1980-1989 · 1990-1999 · 2000-PRESENT

Shortly after making his 1973 debut, "Playboy" Buddy Rose was seen as one of the brightest up-and-coming stars of his time. Fast forward two decades and he was still competing in the ring, but by this time, Rose was universally scoffed for letting his figure grow to unhealthy proportions.

The young Rose was never short on arrogance. Born with a platinum spoon in his mouth, according to manager the Grand Wizard, Rose was afforded the finest things in life, including limousines and private jets. In the ring, however, he was anything but a preppy snob. In fact, his brutality made him one of the most feared Superstars of the early 1980s, and eventually led to a series of WWE Championship opportunities against Bob Backlund.

Over time, Rose began to gain a considerable amount of weight. With each pound he packed on, the less intimidating he became. By the end of his career, he was relegated to comedy sketches. His most infamous scene portrayed him as the star of an infomercial for the Blow Away diet system. According to Blow Away, losing weight was a breeze. Rose's figure told another story.

Bull Buchanan

HT	6'7"	WT	296 lbs.	FROM	Cobb County, Georgia

SIGNATURE MOVE Scissors Kick

TITLE HISTORY World Tag Team Champion

YEARS ACTIVE 1960-1969 · 1970-1979 · 1980-1989 · 1990-1999 · 2000-PRESENT

A former prison guard, Bull Buchanan built his tough exterior while maintaining order in Georgia's most notorious penitentiaries. When pushing around hardened criminals became mundane for the near 300 pounder, he turned to the rough rings of WWE in 2000.

Originally the tag team partner of fellow prison guard Big Boss Man, Buchanan finally found the challenge he was looking for. The duo's brief time together was highlighted with many big wins, including a victory over The Godfather & D-Lo Brown at *WrestleMania 2000*.

Shortly after *WrestleMania*, Buchanan joined Steven Richards' Right to Censor campaign. Trading in his nightstick for a shirt and tie, the massive Superstar became a force in the tag ranks with partner The Goodfather. The converted tandem held the World Tag Team Championship for one month in late 2000.

B

Bull Nakano

YEARS ACTIVE 1960-1969 · 1970-1979 · 1980-1989 · 1990-1999 · 2000-PRESENT

HT	5'7"	FROM	Kawaguchi, Japan	SIGNATURE MOVE	Guillotine Legdrop

TITLE HISTORY Women's Champion

A professional in Japan since the age of 15, Bull Nakano was a Women's Junior Champion in All-Japan Pro Wrestling. Her fame reached America and in March 1986 she debuted in World Wrestling Entertainment alongside the legendary Dump Masamoto.

In 1994, Nakano returned to WWE to win the only title that eluded her for her entire career. She battled with Alundra Blayze and in front of over 45,000 fans at Tokyo's Egg Dome, Nakano defeated Alundra to become WWE Women's Champion. She held the title for over four months until losing it back to Blayze. Nakano left WWE in 1995 and briefly appeared in WCW until she retired in 1997.

Bull Nakano will be forever remembered as one of the greatest female competitors of all time. Her dominance in the ring was a testament to her commitment to harnessing her talent to the utmost.

Bull Ortega

HT	5'11"	WT	300 lbs.

YEARS ACTIVE  1960-1969 · 1970-1979 · 1980-1989 · 1960-1969 · 2000-PRESENT

This pillar of power caught the eye of fan and foe alike during his 1966 WWE debut. After emerging victorious in a series of handicap matches, Bull Ortega was considered a serious WWE Championship contender. His offense was built around power and submission moves, but Bull Ortega also possessed deceptive speed.

When circumstances called for it, Bull Ortega joined forces with fellow rule-breakers of the era including Luke Graham, Bulldog Brower, Prof. Toru Tanaka, Tank Morgan, and Baron Mikel Scicluna. Bull Ortega's toughest challenge came in the form of then-WWE Champion, Bruno Sammartino. Though he tried often, Ortega failed to defeat Sammartino for the title.

BUDDY ROGERS

HT	6'	WT	235 lbs	FROM	Camden, New Jersey

SIGNATURE MOVE	Figure-Four Leglock	YEARS ACTIVE	1960-1969 · 1970-1979 · 1980-1989 · 1990-1999 · 2000-PRESENT

TITLE HISTORY	WWE Champion, United States Tag Team Champion

Being a WWE Superstar is an honor reserved for the world's most amazing athletes. Of these honored men, only a select few ever gain entry into the prestigious fraternity of WWE Champions. The brotherhood boasts such great names as Triple H, Ric Flair, and Superstar Billy Graham. While these men earned immortality, there was one man who blazed the trail they rode to greatness: "Nature Boy" Buddy Rogers.

Rogers' first career choice was that of a police officer. While enforcing the law proved to be an honorable profession, he yearned for the spotlight. With no professional experience to his credit, Rogers confronted New Jersey wrestling promoters Ray and Frank Hanley and demanded an opportunity to prove himself in the ring. Impressed by the youngster's aggressive behavior, they offered him twenty dollars and a match on the following evening's card. On July 4, 1939, Rogers made his debut with an easy victory.

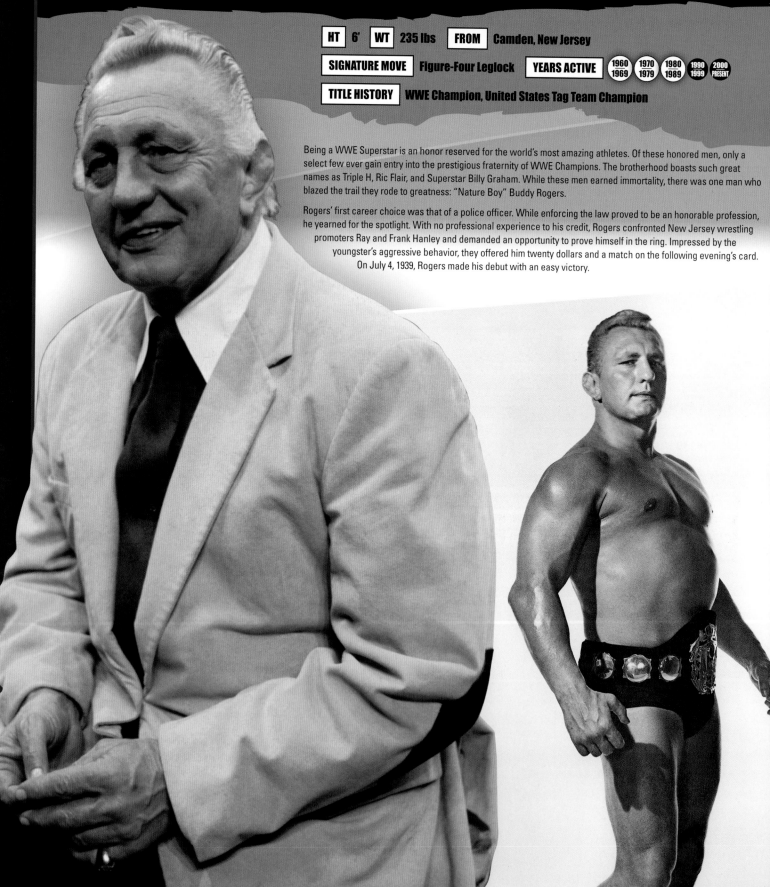

" THE NATURE BOY "

Despite his conceited persona, Rogers had an amazing ability to fill arenas, especially after winning the NWA Championship. This proved to be huge for Capitol Wrestling, who controlled Rogers' schedule. Over the next two years, McMahon and Mondt sold out Madison Square Garden countless times behind Rogers' huge drawing power.

Rogers' lack of title defenses outside of the Northeast didn't sit well with the other NWA promoters. Eventually, the NWA collectively decided that having Rogers defend the title almost exclusively in the Northeast was bad for business. As a result of the decision, they contacted Lou Thesz to try to unseat Rogers. This caused a certain degree of conflict between Capitol Wrestling and the NWA, who eventually got their way when Thesz toppled Rogers for the title in Toronto on January 14, 1963.

THE BIRTH OF WWE

Following the match, McMahon and Mondt refused to recognize the controversial title change, claiming that a championship cannot change hands during a one-fall match (a common rule at the time). To further illustrate their point, McMahon and Mondt withdrew Capitol Wrestling from the NWA to form their own wrestling promotion called the World Wide Wrestling Federation, which today's fans know as WWE.

In April 1963, McMahon and Mondt's new promotion was born with their hand-picked Superstar, Buddy Rogers, leading the way as champion. Fans instantly took to the new wrestling promotion, thanks in large part to the credibility Rogers brought as champion. While he held the championship for less than one month before making way for Bruno Sammartino, the "Nature Boy" truly blazed the trail for all the future WWE Champions that followed.

A NEW GENERATION

Following the loss to Sammartino, Rogers quietly took a step back from his wrestling career to address his failing health. In the late- 1970s, he reemerged in the Mid-Atlantic wrestling territory to confront a young Ric Flair, who also claimed to be the "Nature Boy." Unfortunately for Rogers, he was unable to keep up with the younger Flair, as he fell to the future 16-time World Champion in July 1978.

In the early-1980s, Rogers made a brief return to WWE to manage the career of Jimmy "Superfly" Snuka. On rare occasions, he would even lace up his boots to compete with Snuka in tag action. However, after suffering a broken hip in a match against Capt. Lou Albano & Ray Stevens, the original "Nature Boy" decided his competitive days were finished.

The great Buddy Rogers passed away on July 6, 1992, due to complications from a heart attack and multiple strokes. Rogers received the ultimate honor when he was posthumously inducted into the WWE Hall of Fame by then-WWE Champion Bret Hart in June 1994. The induction was a fitting honor to a man who was the first to hold the prestigious title known today as the WWE Championship.

"NATURE BOY" EARNS GOLD

Rogers' early years in the ring were spent competing under several names, but in Texas in 1944 he settled on the name Buddy Rogers and added the nickname, "Nature Boy." With the new name came a new look and attitude, which included an arrogant air, blonde hair, tanned muscles, and a deliberately cocky strut. Decades later, the legendary Ric Flair patterned his entire persona after Rogers, right down to the signature figure-four leglock.

The new Rogers turned heads as he began to compile an impressive record. Shortly after becoming "Nature Boy," he carried his newfound success straight to the National Wrestling Alliance Texas Heavyweight Championship.

On January 1, 1950, "The Nature Boy" added to his legacy when he defeated Johnny Valentine in the finals of a tournament to crown the first-ever NWA United States Champion. He went on to hold the title for an unprecedented 11 years.

TERRITORIAL CONFLICT

As was normally the case in those days, Rogers bounced around from territory to territory, mainly working in the United States' Midwestern region. When he made trips to the Northeast, however, Rogers worked for Jack Pfefer until the promoter left the territory. With Pfefer out of the New York wrestling scene, Rogers was left without a Northeast promoter. The powerhouse promoting tandem of Vincent J. McMahon and Toots Mondt moved quickly to sign Rogers to Capitol Wrestling Corporation.

Shortly after aligning with Capitol Wrestling, Rogers captured the NWA Championship when he defeated Pat O'Connor in front of a record crowd at Chicago's Comiskey Park on June 30, 1961. After the victory the cocky Rogers grabbed the microphone and proclaimed, "to a nicer guy, it couldn't happen." It was this type of egotistical display that made the "Nature Boy" one of the most hated Superstars by both the fans and his fellow competitors.

When his in-ring career ended, Buddy Rogers went on to host a popular interview segment called Rogers' Corner.

Bull Ramos

| HT | 6' | WT | 350 lbs. |

| FROM | Houston, Texas |

YEARS ACTIVE

"Apache" Bull Ramos was a proud Native American who put his wrestling skills on display all over the world. In addition to finding great success in American rings, Ramos used his massive size to dominate opponents in Korea, Australia, and Japan.

As a member of WWE, Ramos earned the unique distinction of competing in the old Madison Square Garden's final show, as well as the new Garden's first show. He successfully turned back Antonio Pugliese in the old Garden, but came up short in the new arena, losing to WWE Champion Bruno Sammartino.

After failing in several attempts to dethrone Sammartino, Ramos headed west where he was able to capture the NWA Pacific Northwest Tag Team Championship with WWE Hall of Famer Jesse Ventura.

Bulldog Brower

YEARS ACTIVE

| HT | 5'8" | WT | 270 lbs. | FROM | Hamilton, Ontario, Canada |

| SIGNATURE MOVE | The Brower Lock |

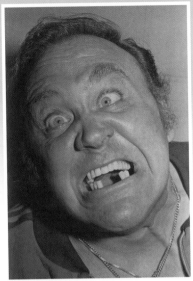

This former chiropractic student started in Stampede Wrestling. Bulldog Brower was infamous all over the world as a one man riot in the ring. At one point he even tangled with Terrible Ted, the wrestling bear and body slammed the gargantuan Haystacks Calhoun! Often led to the ring by Lou Albano, Brower fought with Superstars throughout the mid 1960s and 1970s. Bower was known for his battles for the WWE Championship against Bruno Sammartino. Later in the decade he came within seconds of beating then-WWE Champion Bob Backlund.

Brower retired from active competition in 1988. On September 15, 1997 he passed away after complications following hip surgery. Bulldog Brower was as feared as anyone who ever laced up a pair of boots and is regarded as one of the original terrors of sports-entertainment. In the time since his death both fans and his fellow Superstars have reminisced on his classic battles, terrorizing ring presence, and chilling interviews.

BUNKHOUSE BRAWL

Known as an Extreme Rules or Hardcore Match by today's WWE fans, the Bunkhouse Brawl is a no-holds-barred battle between warring Superstars. Unlike traditional matches, the use of weapons is not only legal, but extremely encouraged.

The Bunkhouse Brawl gained fleeting fame in WCW, who used the match as their answer to WWE's Hardcore Matches. At *Fall Brawl 2000*, Mike Awesome defeated Jeff Jarrett in a Bunkhouse Brawl after, of all people, actor Gary Coleman nailed Jarrett with a guitar. Later that year, Jarrett teamed with the Harris Brothers to defeat the Filthy Animals in a Bunkhouse Brawl at *Starrcade*.

BURIED ALIVE MATCH

This terrifying, career-altering match was introduced at *In Your House* where Undertaker squared off against Mankind. This is a sadistic match where brutal beatings are prerequisites for victory. The object of this bout is to throw your opponent into a six-foot deep grave. Once they are in, the Superstar must then bury their opponent under dirt.

Undertaker has fought in all of the Buried Alive matches, including the first ever shown on network television when Undertaker & Big Show teamed against the Rock 'N' Sock Connection on *SmackDown*. One of the most famous Buried Alive matches was at the 2003 *Survivor Series*, when Undertaker lost to Mr. McMahon. As a result, the "Deadman" was missing from the WWE for months until *WrestleMania XX*.

Bushwhackers

| **MEMBERS** | Butch, Luke | **COMBINED WEIGHT** | 498 lbs. |

| **YEARS ACTIVE** | 1960 1969 | 1970 1979 | 1980 1989 | 1990 1999 | 2000 PRESENT |

Luke and Butch traveled to World Wrestling Entertainment by way of New Zealand in December 1988. As they came to the ring, they licked the heads of their adoring fans and affectionately yelled in their ears. Despised by opponents, the Bushwhackers made an immediate impact on the tag team ranks as they scored victories over the Bolsheviks, the Rougeaus, Brain Busters, and Powers of Pain.

Their unorthodox ring style combined primitive roughhousing with sophisticated tag team tactics. The duo used a wide array of double-team moves, including the devastating Double Gutbuster. The Bushwhackers also displayed an ability to fight any form of opponent, as shown in their battles with Rhythm & Blues, the Orient Express, Money Inc., and the Natural Disasters.

The Bushwhacker lifestyle was contagious and even caught the interest of "Mean" Gene Okerlund who traveled to New Zealand to conduct a special profile on the tandem. The team's meager accommodations in the outback initially made Gene reluctant to continue, but once he had their fresh Bushwhacker Buzzard off the grill he returned in traditional Bushwhacker garb of a black tank-top and camouflage pants and had to be carried away to return the States.

Luke & Butch are WWE Legends and one of the most beloved tag teams in sports-entertainment history. They are remembered as a fun-loving duo who took on all challengers and were masters of the unexpected.

Butterbean

| **HT** | 5'11" | **WT** | 316 lbs. | **FROM** | Jasper, Alabama |

| **YEARS ACTIVE** | 1960 1969 | 1970 1979 | 1980 1989 | 1990 1999 | 2000 PRESENT |

A famous Toughman contest winner, boxer, and mixed martial-artist, Butterbean began boxing professionally in 1994. His loyal fan following grew and he made his first WWE appearance in 1997 when he defeated Marc Mero at *In Your House: Degeneration-X*. He returned in 1999 to win the Brawl For All Match against Bart Gunn at *WrestleMania XV*. Today, Butterbean continues to compete in organizations all over the world for boxing and mixed martial-arts.

Butch Reed

| **HT** | 6'2" | **WT** | 255 lbs. | **FROM** | Kansas City, Missouri |

| **YEARS ACTIVE** | 1960 1969 | 1970 1979 | 1980 1989 | 1990 1999 | 2000 PRESENT |

Originally a football player by trade, Butch Reed jumped to wrestling in 1978. While most footballers find it difficult to make the transition to the ring, Reed picked up his new craft quickly, resulting in many claiming he was a "natural."

Reed's early days were spent competing in the Mid-South territory, but when he came up short in a Loser Leaves Town Match, the athletic Superstar was forced to find a new home. It didn't take long for Reed to land on his feet, as WWE officials had been watching him from afar and jumped at the opportunity to bring him in to the company.

With manager Slick by his side, Reed debuted in WWE in 1986 with a new look. He dyed his hair blonde, adopted "The Natural" nickname and developed an arrogant attitude. In the ring, though, he was still the same dominant force.

Reed's first big WWE win came at the expense of Koko B. Ware at *WrestleMania III*. The victory eventually landed Reed a series of Intercontinental Championship matches against Ricky Steamboat. Reed was ultimately unsuccessful in capturing the title, but didn't let that deter him from being a force in WWE. Later than year, he teamed with One Man Gang to sneak attack "Superstar" Billy Graham. The savage beating forced Graham into permanent retirement.

Reed left WWE in 1988, but would resurface in WCW as Ron Simmons' partner in the powerful tag team Doom, which won the WCW Tag Team Championship.

Buzz Sawyer

| **HT** | 5'9" | **WT** | 240 lbs. | **FROM** | St. Petersburg, Florida |

| **YEARS ACTIVE** | 1960 1969 | 1970 1979 | 1980 1989 | 1990 1999 | 2000 PRESENT |

Always the first to remind fans of his greatness, Buzz Sawyer certainly never suffered from any self-esteem issues. Luckily for Sawyer, he was, as legendary announcer Gordon Solie put it, double-tough, making it easy for him to back up his boastful comments.

Sawyer's WWE career only consisted of a handful of matches, but outside of WWE, the man known as "Mad Dog" attained great success in many of the nation's southern territories, including Georgia Championship Wrestling and the Texas-based World Class Championship Wrestling.

While in Georgia, Sawyer turned back Tommy Rich to claim the NWA National Heavyweight Championship in May 1982. His time in the Lone Star State was highlighted by a lengthy reign as Texas Heavyweight Champion, which he captured from Brian Adias in July 1986. Over the course of his career, Sawyer engaged in memorable rivalries with some of the sport's greatest, including the Von Erichs, the Four Horsemen, and Ronnie Garvin.

bWo (Blue World Order)

MEMBERS Big Stevie Cool, The Blue Guy, Hollywood Nova

YEARS ACTIVE 1960-1969 1970-1979 1980-1989 1990-1999 **2000 PRESENT**

During the height of the New World Order's popularity, a band of misfits joined forces to parody the powerful WCW faction in ECW. Known as the Blue World Order, each Superstar assumed the identity of an nWo member. As expected, the bWo garnered more laughs than victories, but that didn't stop them from hilariously mocking the nWo each week while brashly declaring, "We're taking over!"

Eight years after the bWo disbanded, the faction made an unexpected return at *ECW One Night Stand* in 2005. This time, the group found themselves right in the middle of all the hullabaloo. The bWo later earned a spot on *SmackDown* and an appearance at *The Great American Bash*.

Unfortunately for the bWo, their reunion tour did not last. One month into their run, Big Stevie Cool, The Blue Guy, and Hollywood Nova disbanded again.

Camp Cornette

MEMBERS Vader, Owen Hart, British Bulldog

YEARS ACTIVE 1960-1969 1970-1979 1980-1989 **1990-1999** 2000 PRESENT

Loudmouth manager Jim Cornette's quest to dominate WWE during the mid-to-late 1990s largely depended on the success of three men: Vader, Owen Hart and British Bulldog. Collectively known as Camp Cornette, the trio was assembled with hopes of catapulting Cornette's managerial career to the WWE Championship, a status he formerly held while working with Yokozuna.

As the largest Superstar in the stable, Vader seemed the logical choice to bring the title to Cornette. After teaming with Hart & Bulldog to flatten WWE Champion Shawn Michaels and his partners, Sid & Ahmed Johnson, Vader was awarded a title opportunity against HBK.

Unfortunately for Camp Cornette, a WWE Championship reign was not in the cards, as Michaels defeated Vader at *SummerSlam 1996*. Both Hart and Bulldog also competed on the *SummerSlam* card; however, Cornette was too busy working with Vader to pay much attention to his other Superstars. The manager's disregard for their success eventually led to the demise of Camp Cornette.

The Cabinet

MEMBERS JBL, Orlando Jordan, the Basham Brothers, Amy Weber

TITLE HISTORY WWE Championship, United States Championship, WWE Tag Team Championship

YEARS ACTIVE 1960-1969 1970-1979 1980-1989 1990-1999 **2000 PRESENT**

Shortly after John "Bradshaw" Layfield won the WWE Championship at *The Great American Bash 2004*, he employed Superstars to protect his interests and do his bidding inside and outside of the ring. The group operated like a corporation, with each member having a title and responsibilities. Orlando Jordan, the United States Champion, was the Chief of Staff. Doug & Danny Basham were the Secretaries of Defense and held the WWE Tag Team Championship. Amy Weber was the Image Consultant.

The group was defined by their brash behavior and the Longhorn pose, which was in homage to their leader. They bullied the *SmackDown* roster and clashed with the brand's top Superstars and even clashed with ECW's Blue World Order. The Cabinet disbanded in the summer of 2005 when injuries forced JBL to take a break from in-ring competition.

CANADIAN HEAVYWEIGHT CHAMPIONSHIP

The Canadian Heavyweight Championship was introduced in the summer of 1985 as World Wrestling Entertainment expanded its global reach into the provinces of Canada. The championship was awarded to Dino Bravo on August 1, 1985. Dino Bravo went on to defend the championship all over Canada during its brief existence. On January 6, 1986, the Canadian Heavyweight Championship was retired as Dino Bravo choose to concentrate on becoming WWE Champion.

Can-Am Connection

MEMBERS Rick Martel, Tom Zenk

COMBINED WEIGHT 471 lbs.

YEARS ACTIVE

 1960-1969 | 1970-1979 | **1980-1989** | 1990-1999 | 2000 PRESENT

Take one of the top grapplers from Canada and add one of Minnesota's best athletes and you get the high-flying duo known as the Can-Am Connection. Rick Martel & Tom Zenk debuted in WWE in 1987 and became almost instant championship contenders after an impressive victory at *WrestleMania III* against the Magnificent Muraco & "Cowboy" Bob Orton.

The Can-Am Connection eventually earned a shot at the World Tag Team Championship. However, then-champions, the Hart Foundation, took out Zenk before the match started. Zenk never fully recovered from his injuries and disappeared from WWE. Martel, seeking revenge for the heinous action, recruited Tito Santana and the pair competed under the name Strike Force. The Can-Am Connection enjoyed unprecedented success during their brief time together. Fans to this day wonder what might have been had the duo remained together.

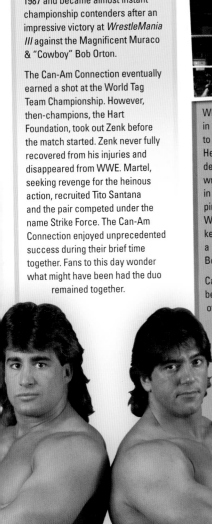

CANDICE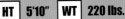

HT 5'7" **FROM** Milwaukee, Wisconsin

SIGNATURE MOVE Candywrapper

TITLE HISTORY Women's Champion

YEARS ACTIVE 1960-1969 | 1970-1979 | 1980-1989 | 1990-1999 | **2000 PRESENT**

When Candice Michelle arrived in WWE in 2004, very few insiders expected her to be anything more than just a pretty face. Hearing the whispers, the determined Diva dedicated herself to proving her detractors wrong. Within three years of stepping foot in a ring for the first time, she reached the pinnacle of her profession, capturing the Women's Championship. She managed to keep the pretty face along the way, becoming a *Playboy* cover girl and star of several Super Bowl commercials.

Candice's WWE career nearly came to an end before it ever began. After failing to make the finals of the 2004 Diva Search, it appeared as though the beautiful brunette was at a career crossroads. Fortunately, WWE officials saw something they liked in her and offered a contract. At first, Candice's limited wrestling ability restricted her to non-competitive roles. While she enjoyed the attention she was garnering, Candice realized she was beginning to be regarded simply as eye candy.

Behind countless hours of training she undertook from former Four Horsemen enforcer Arn Anderson, Candice became a legitimate threat in the Women's Division by 2007. On June 24, she proved her worth when she defeated Melina for the coveted Women's Championship at *Vengeance*. The win capped off Candice's amazing evolution into a dominant female force in the ring.

All the while Candice has maintained an unmatched level of sensuality that eventually landed her on the cover of *Playboy*. On top of all this, Candice is also recognized as the controversially popular girl in the Go Daddy Super Bowl ads. Through it all, however, Candice's first love remains the wrestling ring, where she continues to battle and look good doing it.

Carlito

HT 5'10" **WT** 220 lbs.

FROM The Caribbean

SIGNATURE MOVE The Backstabber

TITLE HISTORY Intercontinental Champion, United States Champion, WWE Tag Team Championship

YEARS ACTIVE 1960-1969 | 1970-1979 | 1980-1989 | 1990-1999 | **2000 PRESENT**

This brash second-generation Superstar had an unbelievable debut in November 2004 when he beat John Cena for the United States Championship on *SmackDown*. Carlito warned everyone that he spits in the face of people who don't want to be cool. Unfortunately for his opponents, many Superstars fail to live up to his definition of cool. The year 2005 saw the debut of his talk segment *Carlito's Cabana*, where he disrespected guests and fans on a frequent basis.

After the Draft Lottery, Carlito brought his cool demeanor to *Raw* and again made an incredible debut when he beat Shelton Benjamin for the Intercontinental Championship. Though he lost it later in the year to "Nature Boy" Ric Flair, this bad apple remained a serious threat to any WWE Champion. He also had time to kick it with the ladies as he developed a romance with Torrie Wilson.

In 2008, he returned to *SmackDown* and formed a team with his brother, Primo. Another amazing athlete, the duo proved that two Colons are more dangerous than one when they bested Curt Hawkins & Zack Ryder for the WWE Tag Team Championship.

CARLITO'S CABANA

Decked out in beach chairs, buckets of apples and oversized sun umbrellas, *Carlito's Cabana* certainly appears to be a cool place. That is, until its host opens his mouth.

Claiming to be the authority on all things cool, Carlito started hosting his own interview segment in April 2005. Unfortunately for fans, this means the arrogant Superstar from the Caribbean now had the platform to pontificate on his own greatness.

When he isn't bragging, Carlito actually welcomes some of WWE's biggest names to his set. Hulk Hogan's appearance on the Fourth of July 2005 led to one of the biggest matches of Carlito's career. After Kurt Angle interrupted the segment, a tag team encounter was signed pitting Carlito & Angle against Hogan & Shawn Michaels. Unfortunately for Carlito, his team came up short, but he will forever have the memory of competing alongside three of the greatest Superstars to ever lace a pair of boots. Other notable guests of *Carlito's Cabana* include Mr. McMahon, Eddie Guerrero and *Piper's Pit* host "Rowdy" Roddy Piper.

Carlos Colon

| YEARS ACTIVE | 1960 1969 | 1970 1979 | 1980 1989 | 1990 1999 | 2000 PRESENT |

| HT | 5'10" | WT | 246 lbs. | FROM | Santa Isabel, Puerto Rico |

Puerto Rican fans recognize Carlos Colon as the founder and star of the World Wrestling Council promotion. While his in-ring dominance certainly leaves an impressive legacy, the legend of Carlos Colon amazingly continues to grow each time his two sons enter a WWE ring.

After spending the late 1960s competing in the Northeast territories of the United States, Colon retreated to his native Puerto Rico, where he became an iconic figure. Colon briefly competed in WWE during the early 1990s. The only high-profile account of his tenure was his participation in the 1993 *Royal Rumble*. Colon managed to eliminate Damien Damento from the contest before being tossed out by Yokozuna. Colon's greatest contributions to WWE would come more than 10 years later when his son Carlito made his WWE debut, followed by another son, Primo Colon.

Charlie Haas

| YEARS ACTIVE | 1960 1969 | 1970 1979 | 1980 1989 | 1990 1999 | 2000 PRESENT |

| HT | 6'2" | WT | 242 lbs. | FROM | Edmond, Oklahoma |

| SIGNATURE MOVE | Haas of Pain | TITLE HISTORY | WWE Tag Team Champion |

As a former two-time Big East amateur wrestling champion at Seton Hall University, Charlie Haas possesses technical grappling mastery that few can match. The result has been a successful WWE career, highlighted by several reigns atop the tag team division.

Haas made his debut on Dec. 26, 2002. Along with partner Shelton Benjamin, he was introduced as a member of Team Angle. His main responsibility was to ensure then-WWE Champion Kurt Angle would hold on to his title. Along the way, however, Haas & Benjamin won some gold of their own, defeating Los Guerreros for the WWE Tag Team Championship in February 2003.

The duo of Haas & Benjamin, who dubbed themselves the "World's Greatest Tag Team," were forced to go their separate ways in March 2004 when the WWE Draft sent Benjamin to *Raw*. The separation didn't stop Haas from seeking another WWE Tag Team Championship. Shortly after the draft, Haas formed an odd-but-successful team with the eccentric Rico. With Miss Jackie by their side, Haas & Rico defeated Rikishi & Scotty 2 Hotty for the titles in April 2004.

Haas was released from WWE in July 2005. He spent the next several months competing on the independent circuit, hoping to get the opportunity to compete in WWE again. On April 17, 2006, he got that chance when he made his surprise return to the ring, defeating former partner Benjamin.

Chavo Guerrero 🇺🇸

YEARS ACTIVE 1960–1969 · 1970–1979 · 1980–1989 · **1990–1999** · **2000 PRESENT**

HT 5'9" **WT** 215 lbs. **FROM** El Paso, Texas **SIGNATURE MOVE** Frog Splash

TITLE HISTORY Cruiserweight Champion, WWE Tag Team Champion, ECW Champion

This third-generation Superstar is a member of wrestling royalty as the Guerrero name is synonymous with success, power, and adulation since sports-entertainment's earliest days. He was introduced to American audiences during his days in WCW. Chavo then introduced himself to WWE in 2001 as a member of The Alliance.

A childhood dream came true in November 2002 when he and his uncle, Eddie Guerrero, became WWE Tag Team Champions. Since his uncle's passing in 2005, Chavo has dedicated every match to Eddie's memory and uses his Frog Splash as a tribute to him. Over the next few years, he continued to wear different prizes and battled with a variety of Superstars as one of WWE's notorious figures. The "Mexican Warrior" kicked off 2008 as the ECW Champion as he defeated CM Punk in a No Disqualification affair.

Chavo Guerrero remains one of sports-entertainment's premier performers. His legacy grows as he continues to take his family name into the 21st Century and honors his late uncle with every match.

Chavo Guerrero, Sr. 🇺🇸

YEARS ACTIVE 1960–1969 · **1970–1979** · **1980–1989** · **1990–1999** · **2000 PRESENT**

HT 5'11" **WT** 229 lbs. **FROM** El Paso, Texas **TITLE HISTORY** Cruiserweight Champion

As the oldest son of wrestling great Gory Guerrero, Chavo Guerrero, Sr. was responsible for ushering in his family's second generation of Superstars, which also included Mando, Hector, and Eddie Guerrero.

A legend in Los Angeles, Chavo captured the territory's Americas Heavyweight Championship a record 15 times during the 1970s and early 1980s. His record-breaking number of title reigns came at the expense of such great names as Ernie Ladd, Roddy Piper, and Pat Patterson. He also claimed tag team gold with his father and brother Hector, among others.

In 2004, Chavo arrived in WWE alongside his son, Chavo Guerrero. Affectionately referred to as "Chavo Classic" during this time, he mainly served as a mentor to his son. However, in May 2004, the elder Guerrero was uncharacteristically placed in a Triple Threat Match against his boy and Spike Dudley. In a shocking turn of events, Chavo Classic capitalized on a bizarre set of circumstances to defeat the younger Guerrero for the Cruiserweight Championship. He lost the title to Rey Mysterio one month later.

Cherry 🇺🇸

HT 5'6"

FROM The Other Side Of The Tracks

YEARS ACTIVE 1960–1969 · 1970–1979 · 1980–1989 · 1990–1999 · **2000 PRESENT**

This sweetheart roller-skated into World Wrestling Entertainment in January 2007. On the arm of her boyfriend, Deuce, and her brother, Domino, this bubble-gum chewing babe was at ringside always ready to help her guys to win.

Her team ended the record-breaking reign of Brian Kendrick & Paul London, earning the WWE Tag Team Championship in the process. Eventually, the Diva traded in her roller skates for wrestling boots as she took on Victoria, Natayla, and Michelle McCool. Unfortunately for Cherry, this venture into competition with the start of a fan following led to her being dumped by Deuce & Domino in favor of Maryse. Before it was all said and done, Cherry defeated Maryse on *SmackDown*.

In August 2008, Cherry returned to her side of the tracks and left WWE. There may be other girls around, but none that can turn heads like Cherry.

CHIEF JAY STRONGBOW

| HT | 6'2" | WT | 247 lbs. | FROM | Pawhuska, Oklahoma | SIGNATURE MOVE | Tomahawk Chop |

| TITLE HISTORY | World Tag Team Champion | YEARS ACTIVE | 1960 1969 | 1970 1979 | 1980 1989 | 1990 1999 | 2000 PRESENT |

This future WWE Hall of Famer's career began in 1947. Throughout the 1950s and 1960s, he was one of the brightest stars in the NWA and held several singles and tag team titles around the southeastern United States. In 1970, Chief Jay Strongbow debuted in WWE and became an instant hero with his colorful Indian ring attire and high-flying attacks. The Chief fought rule-breakers such as Prof. Toru Tanaka, Waldo Von Erich, Ivan Koloff, Pampero Firpo, Tarzan Tyler, Crusher Verdu, George "The Animal" Steele, Killer Kowalski, Eddie Graham, The Sheik, Johnny Rodz, and Blackjack Mulligan.

With each Tomahawk Chop, Strongbow's popularity rose. In May 1972, he won his first of four World Tag Team Championships as he and Sonny King defeated Baron Mike Scicluna & King Curtis Iaukea. Although Strongbow & King only held the title for one month, Chief loved being a part of a team and thrived on the fierce competition. Strongbow captured his second tag team championship in 1976 when he formed an alliance with fellow Native American warrior Chief Billy White Wolf. Their title reign was suddenly cut short when White Wolf suffered a career-ending neck injury at the hands of Ken Patera. Strongbow sought to avenge his partner's heartless attack. Back in singles action, Strongbow locked up with Stan "The Man" Stasiak, Tor Kamata, Spiros Arion, Baron Von Raschke, Mr. Fuji, and the Valiant Brothers.

Strongbow's violent battles against WWE's most vicious villains continued, and in 1979, he waged war on Greg "The Hammer" Valentine. After Valentine broke Strongbow's leg, the Chief came back with a vengeance and settled their score in an Indian Strap Match at Madison Square Garden. In 1980, Strongbow took a brief hiatus from WWE and toured Puerto Rico. He was then brought into Georgia Championship Wrestling and joined another great, Chief Wahoo McDaniel. Strongbow returned to WWE in 1982 and formed another great tag team. This time, the men were bonded by blood. Along with his brother, Jules, the pair from Pawhuska, Oklahoma defeated Mr. Fuji & Mr. Saito for the titles on June 28th. The Strongbows lost and regained the titles from Fuji & Saito later that year before they finally succumbed to the Wild Samoans in 1983. Strongbow's remarkable popularity brought him to Hollywood, when he appeared in 1984's *Micki & Maude,* starring Dudley Moore.

The Chief retired from full-time action in 1985 and became a high-ranking member of the WWE front-office. Fans saw him return to television in 1994 when he mentored newcomer Tatanka in the young Native American's rivalry against Irwin R. Schyster. The relationship between the two Native Americans was so strong Chief gave Tatanka a sacred head dress in recognition of his WWE success. That June, Strongbow's unbelievable six-decade career was honored as Tatanka inducted him into the WWE Hall of Fame. Shortly thereafter, Strongbow put the world of sports-entertainment behind him and relocated to Georgia where he still lives today.

Chief Jay Strongbow is warmly remembered as one of the most beloved figures in WWE history. Many consider him the greatest Native American to ever step into the ring and not one with which to trifle. Strongbow was a hero in whom all WWE fans could believe. All hail the Chief!

Chief Jay Strongbow & Chief Billy White Wolf

| **COMBINED WEIGHT** | 500 lbs. | **YEARS ACTIVE** | 1960-1969 | 1970-1979 | 1980-1989 | 1970-1979 | 2000-PRESENT |

TITLE HISTORY World Tag Team Champions

In 1976, these two Native American icons decided it was time to team up and face the World Wide Wrestling Federation as a unified force. Once together in the ring, Chief Jay Strongbow and Chief Billy White Wolf became instant contenders for the World Tag Team Championship. On December 7, 1976, the Chiefs defeated Nikolai Volkoff & Tor Kamata and the Executioners in a three-team tournament for the vacant World Tag Team Championships. They held the titles for eight months. However, just when they looked unstoppable, Billy White Wolf suffered a career-ending injury courtesy of Ken Patera. As a result, White Wolf was forced to vacate his half of the championship and retire.

As a team, Chief Jay Strongbow and Chief Billy White Wolf are always mentioned when the greatest teams of all-time are discussed. They will forever be remembered as an inspiration to Native Americans everywhere.

Chief White Owl

| **HT** | 5'10" | **WT** | 230 lbs. |

FROM Cherokee, North Carolina

SIGNATURE MOVE Tomahawk Chop

| **YEARS ACTIVE** 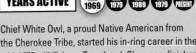 | 1960-1969 | 1970-1979 | 1980-1989 | 1970-1979 | 2000-PRESENT |

Chief White Owl, a proud Native American from the Cherokee Tribe, started his in-ring career in the mid-1950s. Utilizing a Tomahawk Chop as a finisher, his early career was highlighted by runs in several different territories, including Montreal, Florida, Pittsburgh and even the Bahamas.

After making a name for himself in promotions worldwide, Chief White Owl briefly joined WWE, where he gained notoriety teaming with fellow Native Americans Wahoo McDaniel and Chief Big Heart. Madison Square Garden was the site of his greatest WWE victory, as he teamed with Big Heart to defeat Smasher Sloan & Waldo Von Erich in May 1965.

After leaving WWE, Chief White Owl went on to compete in Detroit before eventually landing with the Buffalo-based National Wrestling Federation.

CHRIS BENOIT

| **HT** | 5'11 | **WT** | 229 lbs. | **FROM** | Edmonton, Alberta Canada | **SIGNATURE MOVE** | Crippler Crossface |

TITLE HISTORY Intercontinental Champion, World Tag Team Champion, World Heavyweight Champion, United States Heavyweight Champion

| **YEARS ACTIVE** | 1960-1969 | 1970-1979 | 1980-1989 | 1990-1999 | 2000-PRESENT |

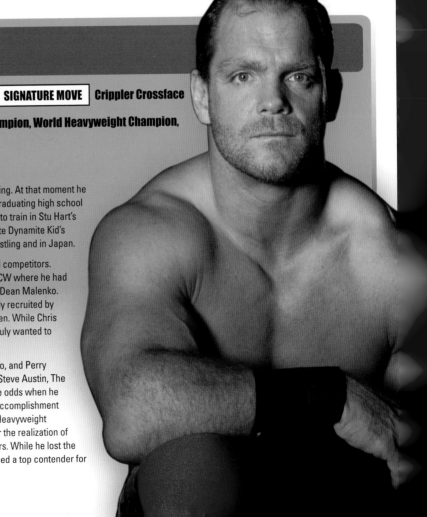

When Chris Benoit was twelve years old he saw the Dynamite Kid perform in the ring. At that moment he dedicated himself to building his body for a career in sports entertainment. After graduating high school in 1985, Chris pursued his dream and every week drove almost two-hundred miles to train in Stu Hart's famous Dungeon. Benoit worked tirelessly to learn this sacred art form and emulate Dynamite Kid's mannerisms and moves. Shortly thereafter he debuted in Calgary's Stampede Wrestling and in Japan.

By the early 1990s Benoit had a reputation as one of the world's greatest technical competitors. After he won Japan's prestigious Super J-Cup Tournament in 1994, he arrived in ECW where he had many memorable matches and held the ECW World Tag Team Championship with Dean Malenko. In October 1995 Benoit signed with World Championship Wrestling and was quickly recruited by future WWE Hall of Famer "Nature Boy" Ric Flair for a revival of The Four Horsemen. While Chris eventually held every championship the company had to offer, he knew what he truly wanted to achieve in sports-entertainment was unattainable in WCW.

In January 2000, he made a radical debut alongside Eddie Guerrero, Dean Malenko, and Perry Saturn. In WWE Benoit competed against many of the best, including Stone Cold Steve Austin, The Rock, Undertaker, Kurt Angle, Chris Jericho, and Batista. In 2004, Benoit defied the odds when he bested twenty-nine other Superstars to win the *Royal Rumble*. This monumental accomplishment led him to fulfilling his destiny at *WrestleMania XX*, when he captured the World Heavyweight Championship in a Triple Threat Match versus Triple H and Shawn Michaels. After the realization of an eighteen-year dream, Benoit defended his championship against all challengers. While he lost the prestigious prize nine months later to Randy Orton at *SummerSlam*, Benoit remained a top contender for many of WWE's renowned championships.

CHRIS JERICHO

HT 6' **WT** 226 lbs. **FROM** Manhasset, New York **SIGNATURE MOVE** Codebreaker, Walls of Jericho, Lionsault

TITLE HISTORY WWE Champion, World Heavyweight Champion, Intercontinental Champion, World Tag Team Champion, European Champion, Hardcore Champion

Among the many things Chris Jericho knows how to do well is make a memorable first impression. His 1999 debut, which saw him revealed as the Superstar behind the mysterious Y2J millennium countdown, remains one of the most brilliant entrances of all time. Believe it or not, Jericho managed to out-do himself when he re-debuted in 2007 as the savior behind a cryptic binary code.

The importance of Jericho's original debut was heightened by the fact that he came over from WCW during the height of the Monday Night Wars. Making an instant impact, he captured the Intercontinental Championship just four months into his tenure. The victory proved to be the first of many title reigns for Y2J.

Following the championship win, Jericho's charisma and athleticism placed him in the center of many memorable WWE moments, including a Triple Threat Match at *WrestleMania 2000* that saw both the Intercontinental and European championships defended. However, Jericho's greatest moment came in December 2001 when he defeated both The Rock and Stone Cold Steve Austin in one night to become the Undisputed WWE Champion.

The WWE Championship victory was the culmination of a lifelong dream for Jericho. Despite having his name permanently etched into the history books, he was far from done building his legacy. In the years that followed, Y2J's innovative offense earned him inclusion into some of WWE's biggest matches, including an epic encounter against Shawn Michaels at *WrestleMania XIX* and the groundbreaking *WrestleMania 21* Money in the Bank Ladder Match.

Jericho's WWE career came to an abrupt halt when he lost a "You're Fired" Match to John Cena in August 2005. With his WWE days seemingly behind him, the self-proclaimed "Ayatollah of Rock 'n' Rolla" released three rock albums with his band Fozzy. He also concentrated on acting and penned his autobiography, *A Lion's Tale: Around the World in Spandex*.

Two years after leaving WWE, Jericho made a highly-publicized return to save the fans from Randy Orton's WWE Championship reign. While he wasn't able to wrest the title away from Orton, Y2J did use his patented Codebreaker to capture the Intercontinental Championship for a record eighth time. He again reached the pinnacle of his profession when he won a Championship Scramble Match at *Unforgiven 2008* to earn the World Heavyweight Championship.

Chris Masters

HT 6'4" **WT** 275 lbs. **FROM** Los Angeles, California

SIGNATURE MOVE Masterlock

YEARS ACTIVE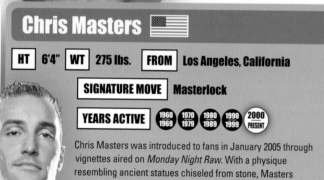

Chris Masters was introduced to fans in January 2005 through vignettes aired on *Monday Night Raw*. With a physique resembling ancient statues chiseled from stone, Masters dominated opponents with a variety of power moves and his version of the full nelson that took the debilitating submission move to all-new heights. Masters began the "Masterlock Challenge," which was open to all WWE Superstars. He offered $1,000 to anyone who could break the hold. The dollar amount grew each week. At its height, the Masterlock Challenge was worth $20,000.

Although the Master Lock was broken on a few occasions, Masters cited outside interference and the challenge continued for months. It was officially broken by then-ECW Champion Bobby Lashley. During the June 2007 Draft, Masters was selected to *SmackDown*, where he appeared until he departed WWE in November 2007.

Chris Tolos

HT 6' **WT** 220 lbs. **FROM** Hamilton, Ontario, Canada

TITLE HISTORY United States Tag Team Champion

YEARS ACTIVE

Decades after dominating the tag team scene in the 1950s and 1960s, Chris and John Tolos are still considered one of the greatest duos to ever come out of Canada. Known as The Canadian Wrecking Crew, the brothers captured titles all over North American wrestling territories, including Florida, Detroit, and Toronto.

While in WWE, Chris, the older of the two brothers, helped lead the team to the United States Tag Team Championship. They defeated Hall of Famers Gorilla Monsoon & Killer Kowalski for the titles in December 1963. Though primarily a tag team competitor, Chris, also known as "The Body", had a memorable 1968 rivalry with Mike DiBiase, father of WWE legend, Ted DiBiase.

Christian 🇨🇦

| HT | 6'1" | WT | 224 lbs. | YEARS ACTIVE | 1960-1969 | 1970-1979 | 1980-1989 | 1990-1999 | 2000-PRESENT |

SIGNATURE MOVE Unprettier **FROM** Toronto, Ontario, Canada

TITLE HISTORY Intercontinental Champion, World Tag Team Champion, Light Heavyweight Champion, European Champion, Hardcore Champion

Over the course of his seven-year WWE career, Christian transformed from a brooding introvert into one of the most charismatic personalities in recent memory. Along the way, despite never performing like a true fan favorite, he adopted a strong following of admirers he affectionately called his "peeps."

Christian found recurring success in the tag team ranks. Over and over, he captured the World Tag Team Championship, nine times in total (seven with Edge, one with Lance Storm, one with Chris Jericho). During this time, his participation in the earliest TLC Matches helped revolution tag team competition.

On his own, the self-proclaimed "Captain Charisma" was equally successful. In addition to becoming a three-time Intercontinental Champion, he also proudly held the now-defunct European, Hardcore, and Light Heavyweight titles. Toward the end of his WWE stay, Christian started to come into his own as a main event Superstar. With his "Problem Solver," Tyson Tomko, by his side, he engaged in a rivalry against WWE Champion John Cena in 2005. It culminated with a main event match at *Vengeance*, but will probably more be remembered for the amusing freestyle raps Christian performed.

Christian's WWE contract expired in October 2005. Despite not being contractually obligated to compete, he took part in two November shows so that his "peeps" could see him one more time.

Christy Hemme 🇺🇸

| HT | 5'5" | FROM | Los Angeles, California |

SIGNATURE MOVE Standing Split-legged Leg Drop

YEARS ACTIVE 1960-1969 | 1970-1979 | 1980-1989 | 1990-1999 | 2000-PRESENT

Christy Hemme's life changed forever when she was selected over 7,000 women to become the first *Raw Diva Search* Winner. Christy's first taste of how life as a Diva would go was when she faced runner-up Carmella DeCesare in a Lingerie Pillow Fight at *Taboo Tuesday*.

Hemme became special guest ring announcer and timekeeper for some of WWE's biggest matches, and was also training for the ring with Lita. In April 2005, Christy landed on the cover of *Playboy*. The issue's success rubbed some of her fellow Divas the wrong way and she soon stood across the ring from her most vocal critic, Trish Stratus, at *WrestleMania 21*. Christy lost to the Women's Champion that night, but found some success while battling the likes of Victoria and Melina, before Hemme left World Wrestling Entertainment in December 2005.

Christopher Nowinski 🇺🇸

| HT | 6'5" | WT | 270 lbs. | FROM | Watertown, Massachusettes |

SIGNATURE MOVE Honor Roll

TITLE HISTORY Hardcore Champion

YEARS ACTIVE 1960-1969 | 1970-1979 | 1980-1989 | 1990-1999 | 2000-PRESENT

Christopher Nowinski is brilliant, and he's not afraid to remind you of it, either. The self-absorbed Harvard graduate first began annoying fans in 2001 as a cast member on *Tough Enough*. Nowinski failed to win the competition, but impressed officials enough to earn a WWE contract. As a member of the WWE roster, Nowinski's holier-than-thou attitude made him tough to like, but his abilities in the ring were undeniable.

By the end of his rookie campaign, Nowinski had scored major victories over his trainer, Al Snow, and *Tough Enough* champion Maven. Unfortunately, however, his promising career came to an abrupt halt when he retired due to post-concussion syndrome. Despite no longer being active in the ring, Nowinski remained a valuable part of the organization, serving as a political correspondent for Smackdown Your Vote!

Chuck Palumbo 🇺🇸

| HT | 6'7" | WT | 280 lbs. | FROM | San Diego, California |

SIGNATURE MOVE Full Throttle

TITLE HISTORY World Tag Team Champion

YEARS ACTIVE 1960-1969 | 1970-1979 | 1980-1989 | 1990-1999 | 2000-PRESENT

Chuck Palumbo's WWE career is the story of two completely different Superstars. After Palumbo & Sean O'Haire lost the WCW Tag Team Championship in 2001, Palumbo found his career going nowhere fast. With nothing to lose, he formed a union with tag team specialist Billy Gunn. The result: the most controversial pairing in sports-entertainment history.

Billy & Chuck enjoyed two World Tag Team Championship reigns, but it was the flamboyant tandem's commitment ceremony that attracted the highest levels of national attention. Moments before officially becoming partners for life, though, Billy & Chuck revealed that the entire event was a hoax. The team split up soon after. Three years later, Palumbo returned with a persona that more closely resembled his identity outside the ring. When not competing, he has a passion for building custom motorcycles. The thrill-seeking Palumbo has carried that obsession into the arena, riding a steel horse to the ring prior to his matches.

Chuck Tanner

YEARS ACTIVE

1960 1969 1970 1979 **1980 1989** 1990 1999 2000 PRESENT

Chuck Tanner's tattoo-covered arms certainly helped him look the part of a successful Superstar. The truth is, however, the only thing Tanner was good at in the ring was making his competition look impressive. During the early 1980s, despite failing to garner any success, Tanner continually stepped into the ring to challenge the likes of the Iron Sheik, Don Muraco, and "Mr. Wonderful" Paul Orndorff. Each time, he was met with the same fate: Defeat. Today, Tanner's unimpressive won-loss record puts him alongside some of history's most unsuccessful Superstars, including Brooklyn Brawler, Frankie Williams, and Barry Horowitz.

CHYNA

HT 5'10 **FROM** Londonderry, New Hampshire

TITLE HISTORY Women's Champion, Intercontinental Champion

YEARS ACTIVE 1960 1969 1970 1979 1980 1989 **1990 1999** 2000 PRESENT

After her days in the Peace Corps, Chyna undertook grueling days of training at Killer Kowalski's Pro Wrestling School. At the time, no one thought they were witnessing the development of one of the most ground-breaking figures in sports-entertainment history. She was first seen on WWE programming coming from the crowd to assist Hunter-Hearst Helmsley and became the famous enforcer for D-Generation X.

As Chyna broke away from the notorious faction her character became more defined and her star grew brighter as she became the first-ever female competitor in the *Royal Rumble*. In the ring, Chyna became known as "The 9th Wonder of The World." She made history at *No Mercy 1999* when she beat Jeff Jarrett to be crowned the first female Intercontinental Champion in World Wrestling Entertainment history!

The spotlight on her grew as she was a presenter at The MTV Movie Awards, released her own fitness video, and appeared on the television show *3rd Rock From The Sun*. In November of 2000 she made a splash as the covergirl of *Playboy* magazine and broke all sales records previously held by the publication. In January of 2001 her remarkable life story hit print as her autobiography, *If They Only Knew* attacked the NY Times Bestseller list. Two months later she fulfilled another dream when she beat Ivory for the Women's Championship at *WrestleMania X-7*. Shortly thereafter, she was the host of *Robot Wars: Extreme Warriors*.

Since parting ways with WWE in November of 2001, she has remained in the public eye. Though her days in the ring appear to be behind her, the world will never forget her contributions to sports-entertainment as a Superstar, pop-culture figure and a woman. In her prime, she was an unstoppable force who opened a new realm for WWE Divas.

Clarence Mason

YEARS ACTIVE

1960 1969 1970 1979 1980 1989 **1990 1999** 2000 PRESENT

One of the most litigious human beings to ever practice law, Clarence Mason debuted on WWE television as the attorney for James E. Cornette. Mason made his presence immediately felt as he was able to regain the tag team titles lost the previous night at *In Your House* since Owen Hart, the Superstar pinned, was not recognized as a title holder in the match. Mason then contested every decision made that was not in the best interest of his clients and threatened lawsuits whenever possible. Mason was also known for hand delivering subpoenas to Superstars.

After his tenure with Camp Cornette he focused on the career of Crush. Mason soon guided the Nation of Domination until the group disbanded in the late 1990s. Mason then left WWE and opened his own law practice in south Florida. As he himself proclaimed, "Don't worry, Clarence Mason is on the scene, and justice will be served..." Mason will be forever remembered as one of the most controversial figures of the 1990s.

CM Punk

| **HT** | 6'1" | **WT** | 222 lbs. | **FROM** | Chicago, Illinois |

SIGNATURE MOVE G.T.S. (Go To Sleep)

TITLE HISTORY ECW Champion, World Heavyweight Champion, World Tag Team Champion

YEARS ACTIVE (1960 1969) (1970 1979) (1980 1989) (1990 1999) (**2000 PRESENT**)

The Straight-Edge Superstar first developed a cult following on the independent wrestling scene. CM Punk incorporated various fighting styles from all over the world and melded it into one lethal fighting style with several types of weaponry. Punk professes a life focused on strength of self and personal development free of drugs, alcohol, or tobacco. The ink on his arms are insight into where this man has been and where he's going.

At the 2006 *Survivor Series,* he emerged from Team DX a true Superstar. In 2007 he climbed to the top of The Land of Extreme when he defeated John Morrison for the ECW Championship. At *Wrestlemania XXIV,* he became "Mr. Money In The Bank" and cashed in his opportunity at his *Raw* debut and beat Edge to become World Heavyweight Champion.

CM Punk derives strength from his discipline as an individual whose life is completely free of negative outside influences. He gets his rush from WWE competition. Punk brings down the house every time he steps in the ring and he's only going to become stronger as he gains experience. What he's accomplished in his short WWE tenure is more than many could ever imagine, and he has a bright future ahead.

The Cobra

| **HT** | 5'10" | **WT** | 224 lbs. | **FROM** | Uganda |

TITLE HISTORY Junior Heavyweight Champion

YEARS ACTIVE (1960 1969) (1970 1979) (**1980 1989**) (1990 1999) (2000 PRESENT)

Like many other masked Superstars of the 1980s, the Cobra was lightning quick with a strong aerial assault. Unlike his veiled counterparts, the Cobra was quite a sharp-dressed man. The custom-made sports coat he wore to the ring went a long way in setting him apart from his masked colleagues.

One of the Cobra's first tastes of championship gold came in November 1983 when he defeated Davey Boy Smith for the National Wrestling Alliance Junior Heavyweight Championship. Ironically, he also defeated Smith's future British Bulldogs tag team partner, Dynamite Kid, for the WWE Junior Heavyweight Championship one year later.

The Cobra held the Junior Heavyweight Championship for five months before losing to Hiro Saito in Hiroshima, Japan. He eventually regained the title two months later, but was forced to vacate it when WWE discontinued recognizing the championship in October 1985.

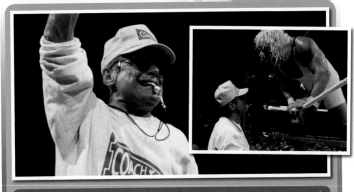

The Coach

YEARS ACTIVE (1960 1969) (1970 1979) (1980 1989) (**1990 1999**) (2000 PRESENT)

After a making a career of bringing professional athletes across all sports to unprecedented heights, The Coach brought his combination of intellect and training techniques to WWE in 1991. The core of his belief system was simple: Win! Win! Win! However, it extended to underhanded tactics and rule-breaking where Coach could be heard yelling at ringside, "Discipline! Break their legs, smash their faces. The only people I want with me are winners!" His desire for victory also translated to him getting involved in the action when a referee's attention was diverted.

On an episode of *The Funeral Parlor,* Bobby Heenan introduced The Coach as the new manager of then-Intercontinental Champion, Mr. Perfect. Heenan said he was retiring from managing to pursue broadcasting full-time. Under new management, Perfect thrived and proved that The Coach's strategies could, would, and did cross over to WWE. The Coach decided to expand his talent pool and brought the Beverly Brothers into WWE. The Coach took his whistle and departed the company later that same year. The Coach is remembered as one of the most intense and physical managers ever.

Cody Rhodes

| **HT** | 6'1" | **WT** | 219 lbs. | **FROM** | Charlotte, North Carolina |

TITLE HISTORY World Tag Team Champion

YEARS ACTIVE (1960 1969) (1970 1979) (1980 1989) (1990 1999) (**2000 PRESENT**)

Growing up the son of the legendary "American Dream" Dusty Rhodes, Cody Rhodes was taught that there was a certain route one had to take to become a successful WWE Superstar. According to the elder Rhodes, a young upstart had to be patient while paying his dues in low-profile matches. Well, Cody Rhodes isn't patient.

"When you're this good, you don't pay dues," claimed a cocky Cody Rhodes after turning his back on his former mentor, Hardcore Holly. Rhodes saw Holly as a dinosaur who was good for nothing other than holding him back. Instead, the newcomer chose to align himself with another young and dynamic Superstar, Ted DiBiase.

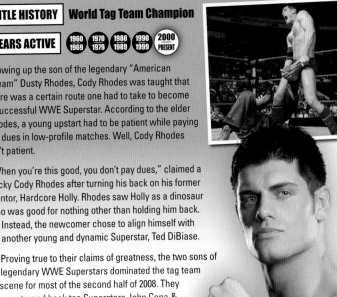

Proving true to their claims of greatness, the two sons of legendary WWE Superstars dominated the tag team scene for most of the second half of 2008. They even turned back top Superstars John Cena & Batista to claim their second World Tag Team Championship reign.

With an entire career ahead of him, there's no telling the heights Rhodes will eventually reach, but if you ask him, the cocky Superstar will tell you he'll be every bit as good as his Hall of Fame father.

Col. Mustafa

HT 6' **WT** 263 lbs. **FROM** Iraq **SIGNATURE MOVE** Camel Clutch

In 1991, the United States was in the midst of the Gulf War and WWE was under its own attack by one-time hero, Sgt. Slaughter. On March 30, 1991, Mustafa became the third member of Slaughter's despicable Triangle of Terror and showed his powerful, ruthless tactics in the ring.

During his campaign of terror in WWE, Mustafa attacked Superstars such as Undertaker, Big Boss Man, Koko B. Ware, "Hacksaw" Jim Duggan, and Bret "Hit Man" Hart. Mustafa was then part of the famous "Match Made In Hell" at *SummerSlam 1991* where he and cohorts Gen. Adnan and Sgt. Slaughter took on Hulk Hogan & Ultimate Warrior. By May 1992, Mustafa returned to the Middle East.

Colin Delaney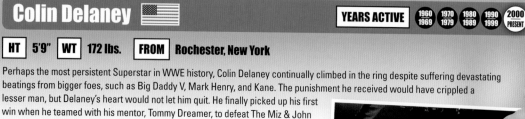

HT 5'9" **WT** 172 lbs. **FROM** Rochester, New York

Perhaps the most persistent Superstar in WWE history, Colin Delaney continually climbed in the ring despite suffering devastating beatings from bigger foes, such as Big Daddy V, Mark Henry, and Kane. The punishment he received would have crippled a lesser man, but Delaney's heart would not let him quit. He finally picked up his first win when he teamed with his mentor, Tommy Dreamer, to defeat The Miz & John Morrison in February 2008.

Despite the victory, Delaney had yet to be offered a full-time contract. He finally earned his spot on the roster after defeating ECW general manager Armando Estrada in May. With job security in his back pocket, Delaney revealed his true colors when he turned on Dreamer at *The Great American Bash*. Dreamer eventually got his revenge, however, defeating his protégé in an Extreme Rules Match in August. Delaney left ECW a few days later.

The Colossal Connection

MEMBERS Andre The Giant, Haku **COMBINED WEIGHT** 852 lbs. **TITLE HISTORY** World Tag Team Champions

In 1989, Bobby Heenan unveiled his Colossal Connection at *Survivor Series*. They manhandled their opponents, and just weeks later, conquered Demolition to earn the World Tag Team Championship. During that time in WWE history, it was unheard of for Ax & Smash to be dominated in that fashion.

As champions, they were virtually unstoppable. As they entered a new decade, their stranglehold on the titles appeared to have no end in sight. However, after a botched double-team move led to Demolition regaining the tag titles at *WrestleMania VI*, "The Brain" lost his wits. After a slap in the face from his manager, Andre cleared the ring of his former family members, and the Colossal Connection was gone forever.

Despite a brief partnership, the Colossal Connection gave a glimpse of what can happen when two monsters are brought together by an individual obsessed with fame, power, and championships. If they hadn't self-destructed, there's no telling when the campaign of destruction would have ended.

Corporal Kirschner

A former member of the 82nd Airborne division of the U.S. Army, Corporal Kirschner fought for the American way inside and outside the ring. Prior to entering WWE, Kirschner developed

HT 6'2" **WT** 263 lbs. **FROM** Fort Bragg, North Carolina **SIGNATURE MOVE** Corporal Clutch

a military style of combat while serving in the armed forces. When he debuted in 1985, he transferred that style into many rivalries with foreign Superstars, most notably Nikolai Volkoff. In fact, it was against the Russian powerhouse that Kirschner picked up his biggest win, besting Volkoff in a Flag Match at *WrestleMania 2*.

Unfortunately for Kirschner, victories were few and far between after *WrestleMania 2*. Following only moderate success against the likes of the Iron Sheik and "Adorable" Adrian Adonis, the Corporal turned his sights to the tag scene, teaming up with Danny Spivey. The duo, however, failed to make waves in the tag team division. Kirschner left WWE shortly after. Despite Kirschner's short stay in WWE, longtime fans will always look back at his tenure with great fondness, as it was difficult not to cheer for the tough serviceman who carried Old Glory to the ring.

THE CORPORATION

MEMBERS | Mr. McMahon, Shane McMahon, The Rock, Big Show, Big Boss Man, Ken Shamrock, Kane, Triple H, Chyna, Test, Shawn Michaels, Gerald Brisco, Pat Patterson, Sgt. Slaughter, Pete Gas, Rodney, Joey Abs

Leading up to *Survivor Series 1998*, Mr. McMahon began to surround himself with his own entourage of former Superstars, which consisted of Sgt. Slaughter, Gerald Brisco, and Pat Patterson. The group had some influence, largely due to McMahon's powerful position within WWE, but lacked any real Superstar power. That all changed at *Survivor Series* when Mr. McMahon and his son Shane helped The Rock capture the WWE Championship, thus marking the official start of The Corporation.

With The Rock in the fold, The Corporation became an enticing destination for WWE Superstars with championship aspirations. They knew that with Mr. McMahon making the calls, they would be set up for instant greatness. Just as many predicted, The Corporation owned all the major titles in WWE by year's end (The Rock was WWE Champion, Ken Shamrock was Intercontinental Champion, and Big Boss Man & Shamrock were World Tag Team Champions).

Though dominant in their rivalries with Stone Cold Steve Austin, Mankind, and D-Generation X, The Corporation enjoyed only a brief existence. The beginning of the end came in April 1999 when Shane assumed leadership responsibilities after claiming his father had his priorities mixed up. According to the younger McMahon, Vince cared more about combating Undertaker's obsession with Shane's sister Stephanie than he did The Corporation. From that point, the male McMahons engaged in a bitter rivalry that eventually resulted in Shane merging his Corporation with Undertaker's Ministry of Darkness. The result was one super faction called The Corporate Ministry.

"COWBOY" BOB ORTON

| HT | 6'1" | WT | 242 lbs. | FROM | Kansas City, Kansas | SIGNATURE MOVE | Superplex |

YEARS ACTIVE | 1960-1969 | 1970-1979 | 1980-1989 | 1990-1999 | **2000-PRESENT**

"Cowboy" Bob Orton first appeared in WWE in 1982 managed by the Grand Wizard. He had battles against then-WWE Champion Bob Backlund. Orton returned to the NWA and made headlines when he and Dick Slater accepted $25,000 from Harley Race to end the career of "Nature Boy" Ric Flair.

The man credited with inventing the Superplex returned to WWE in the spring of 1984 to become bodyguard to "Rowdy" Roddy Piper. After his left forearm was broken in a match, Orton continued to compete with a cast. This was often the subject of controversy, as "Cowboy" was accused of using it as a weapon well after the injury had healed. Though Orton was not an active participant at the original *WrestleMania*, no one made a bigger impact in the outcome of the match. As the corner man for "Hot Rod" and "Mr. Wonderful" Paul Orndorff, Orton attempted to hit Mr. T with the cast, but he missed and struck Orndorff instead, helping give Hulk Hogan & Mr. T the victory. Orton continued to back Piper through his *WrestleMania 2* boxing match against Mr. T, but when Piper changed his ways, Orton swore his allegiance to "Adorable" Adrian Adonis. The "Ace" also formed a successful tag team with the Magnificent Muraco with Mr. Fuji as their manager.

Orton remained active in a limited capacity for the remainder of the decade and began training his son, Randy, for a career in sports-entertainment. In February 2005, it was announced that "Ace's" heralded career would be honored with induction into the WWE Hall of Fame. During this time, he returned to WWE to manage his son in his rivalry against Undertaker.

"Cowboy" Bob Orton comes from one of the greatest families in professional wrestling history. One of the first Superstars to utilize the ropes for a finishing maneuver, Orton was an innovative technician in the ring and a hated villain. The Orton family legacy moves well into the 21st century with his son, Randy. To those who oppose them, it feels like the "Age of Orton" is entering its eighth decade.

Cowboy Lang 🇨🇦

YEARS ACTIVE 1960 1969 · 1970 1979 · 1980 1989 · 1990 1999 · 2000 PRESENT

HT 4' **WT** 109 lbs. **FROM** Calgary, Alberta, Canada

For more than 30 years, Cowboy Lang was considered one of the world's premiere midget wrestlers. Debuting in the mid-1960s at just 16 years old, Lang charged to the ring in his signature cowboy hat and boots.

Over the course of his successful career, Lang performed on some of the biggest cards of his time, including the American Wrestling Association's (AWA) WrestleRock on April 20, 1986. On that night, Lang teamed with Little Mr. T to defeat Lord Littlebrook & Little Tokyo.

Throughout Lang's career, Little Tokyo proved to be one of his most bitter rivals. The foes spent much of the early 1980s battling over the National Wrestling Alliance World Midget Championship, which they traded on two separate occasions.

Crash Holly 🇺🇸

YEARS ACTIVE 1960 1969 · 1970 1979 · 1980 1989 · 1990 1999 · 2000 PRESENT

HT 5'10" **WT** Over 400 lbs. (alleged) **FROM** Mobile, Alabama **SIGNATURE MOVE** The Crash Course

TITLE HISTORY Hardcore Champion, European Champion, Light Heavyweight Champion, World Tag Team Champion

Crash Holly could not be deterred from joining his cousin, Hardcore Holly, in WWE. He was also adamant about competing amongst sports-entertainment's greatest heavyweights. In 1999, Crash debuted on *Raw* and brought a scale with him to the ring to force opponents to prove they measured up. While he and his cousin often argued, they proved to be a formidable team when they could agree on the target of a famous Holly beatdown. This was no more evident then when they won the World Tag Team Championship from the Rock 'N' Sock Connection.

In 2000, he joined the Hardcore Division, and over the next three years became known as the Houdini of Hardcore. Crash wore the Hardcore Championship on over 20 occasions. Later in the year, he was accompanied to the ring by his cousin, Molly, and occassionally reformed his team with Hardcore Holly. Crash later added more trophies to his mantle when he won the Light Heavyweight title, and in 2001, he captured the European Championship. Crash continued to get in the face of all challengers no matter their size or reputation until he left the company in June 2003.

Sadly, in November 2003, Crash Holly passed away. He entertained millions with his performances in the ring and touched even more with his heart.

Cruiserweight Championship (see page 70)

Crush 🇺🇸

YEARS ACTIVE 1960 1969 · 1970 1979 · 1980 1989 · 1990 1999 · 2000 PRESENT

HT 6'6" **WT** 315 lbs. **FROM** Konai, Hawaii

SIGNATURE MOVE The Skull Crush

In 1992, World Wrestling Entertainment was greeted by a happy man from the Hawaiian Islands with massive power named Kona Crush. Soon after his debut, he shortened his name to Crush and did exactly that to his opponents. He met Doink at *WrestleMania IX*, where audiences saw two Doinks attack Crush. After this match, his attitude changed and he fell under the dangerous influence of Mr. Fuji. Now using the heart punch to finish opponents, he attacked his former friend, Randy "Macho Man" Savage. The battles between the two raged on until their Falls Count Anywhere Match at *WrestleMania X*.

Crush returned to WWE in 1996. He was first a member of the Nation of Domination, but later formed the Disciples of the Apocalypse faction with Chainz, Skull & 8-Ball. After he left WWE, he competed in WCW and Japan but a spinal injury forced him into retirement. Tragically, in August 2007, he passed away. Whether he was beloved or booed, this powerhouse was one of WWE's biggest Superstars of the 1990s.

Crusher Verdu 🇺🇸

| HT | 5'10" | WT | 275 lbs. | FROM | Columbus, Ohio |

SIGNATURE MOVE Bear Hug

YEARS ACTIVE 1960-1969 1970-1979 1980-1989 1990-1999 2000-PRESENT

Known as "The Spanish Hercules", Crusher Verdu was an amateur wrestling champion and regarded as a powerhouse across Europe and the territories of the National Wrestling Alliance (NWA). When he entered the World Wide Wrestling Federation, Superstars were placed on alert. Managed by the likes of Tony Angelo and Capt. Lou Albano, he stopped at nothing to reach the top. Verdu was driven to dethrone champion Bruno Sammartino, but never managed to beat the Italian Strongman.

Crusher Verdu retired from the ring in the early 1980s. To this day, when ring experts talk about all-time strongmen, "The Spanish Hercules" Crusher Verdu always makes the list!

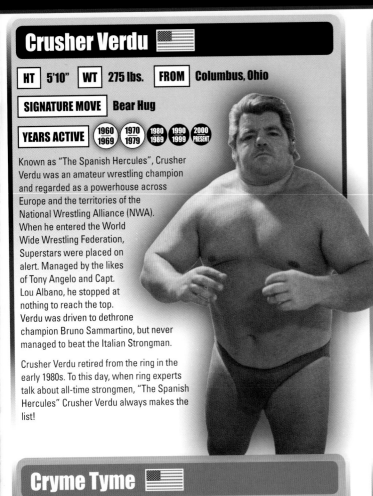

Crybaby Cannon 🇨🇦

| FROM | Montreal, Quebec, Canada |

YEARS ACTIVE 1960-1969 1970-1979 1980-1989 1990-1999 2000-PRESENT

At 360 pounds, George "Crybaby" Cannon was a mountain of a man. Prior to his days inside the ring, Cannon parlayed his massive size into a successful football career, playing for the Canadian Football League's Regina Roughriders.

While his massive frame helped him earn many wins, Cannon gained most of his notoriety from being a manager. In addition to guiding the careers of the Mongols, he also managed the famed tag team the Fabulous Kangaroos. In 1983, Cannon struck a deal with Vince McMahon to help bring WWE to Detroit. This was just the beginning of WWE's national, and eventual global, dominance of the sports-entertainment scene.

Cryme Tyme 🇺🇸

| MEMBERS | Shad, JTG | COMBINED WEIGHT | 530 lbs. |

YEARS ACTIVE 1960-1969 1970-1979 1980-1989 1990-1999 2000-PRESENT

In an attempt to entertain WWE audiences, Cryme Tyme proudly performs over-the-top parodies of the typical societal stereotypes they have encountered during their lives, including stealing cars, televisions, wallets, and more.

In the ring, however, it's all business for Cryme Tyme. Using the perfect combination of speed and power, JTG & Shad can hang with WWE's best teams, as evidenced by their debut victory over Spirit Squad in October 2006. Their momentum carried over into their first pay-per-view match where they stole a win from the Highlanders, Lance Cade & Trevor Murdoch and Charlie Haas & Viscera at *Cyber Sunday*.

Cryme Tyme began a six-month hiatus from WWE in September 2007. Upon returning to the company in 2008, however, JTG & Shad picked up right where they left off, stealing other people's "money, money, yeah, yeah." They even found themselves alongside John Cena during his war against JBL.

Curt Hawkins & Zach Ryder 🇺🇸

| COMBINED WEIGHT | 435 lbs. |

TITLE HISTORY WWE Tag Team Champions

YEARS ACTIVE 1960-1969 1970-1979 1980-1989 1990-1999 2000-PRESENT

After garnering only minor victories as the Major Brothers, Curt Hawkins & Zack Ryder toughened their image after aligning themselves with Edge in December 2007. The result: Major success in the tag-team ranks.

As members of the "Rated-R Superstar's" La Familia faction, the Edge look-alikes began to come into their own on *SmackDown*. After turning back the brand's top tag teams, including Jesse & Festus and Finlay & Hornswoggle, Hawkins & Ryder dethroned WWE Tag Team Champions The Miz & John Morrison at *The Great American Bash 2008*. The talented New York natives defended the titles for more than two months before being upended by brothers Carlito & Primo in September 2008.

CRUISERWEIGHT CHAMPIONSHIP

The WWE Cruiserweight Championship originated in World Championship Wrestling (WCW) in 1991. The title was designed to recognize sports-entertainment's top cruiserweights. However, the Cruiserweight Championship was forced to overcome several lofty obstacles early its existence before finally achieving its level of prominence in WWE.

Less than one year after its inception, the Cruiserweight Championship was stripped from an injured Brad Armstrong, which resulted in a four-year hiatus. After the title made its return in 1996, cruiserweights like Dean Malenko and Rey Mysterio wowed audiences while rebuilding the championship's reputation.

WWE fans began to familiarize themselves with the Cruiserweight Championship in 2001 when Shane McMahon purchased WCW.

1991

OCT 27 — Chattanooga, TN — Brian Pillman defeats Richard Morton
In the finals of a tournament to crown the first-ever Cruiserweight Champion, Brian Pillman defeats Richard Morton.

DEC 25 — Atlanta, GA — Jushin Liger defeats Brian Pillman

1992

FEB 29 — Milwaukee, WI — Brian Pillman defeats Jushin Liger

JUNE 20 — Augusta, GA — Scotty Flamingo defeats Brian Pillman

JULY 05 — Atlanta, GA — Brad Armstrong defeats Scotty Flamingo

1997

JAN 22 — Milwaukee, WI — Dean Malenko defeats Ultimo Dragon

FEB 24 — San Francisco, CA — Syxx defeats Dean Malenko

JUNE 28 — Los Angeles, CA — Chris Jericho defeats Syxx

JULY 28 — Charleston, WV — Alex Wright defeats Chris Jericho

AUG 12 — Colorado Springs, CO — Chris Jericho defeats Alex Wright

SEPT 14 — Winston-Salem, NC — Eddie Guerrero defeats Chris Jericho

OCT 26 — Las Vegas, NV — Rey Mysterio defeats Eddie Guerrero

1999

MAR 15 — Cincinnati, OH — Rey Mysterio defeats Billy Kidman

JUN 14 — Baltimore, MD — Chris Jericho defeats Dean Malenko

AUG 08 — Sturgis, SD — Juventud Guerrera defeats Chris Jericho

SEPT 14 — Greenville, SC — Billy Kidman defeats Juventud Guerrera

NOV 16 — Wichita, KS — Juventud Guerrera defeats Billy Kidman

NOV 22 — Auburn Hills, MI — Billy Kidman defeats Juventud Guerrera

NOV 21 — Toronto, Ontario — Evan Karagias defeats Disco Inferno

DEC 19 — Washington, DC — Madusa defeats Evan Karagias

2000

JAN 16 — Cincinnati, OH — Oklahoma defeats Madusa
Oklahoma was forced to vacate the Cruiserweight Championship after exceeding the weight limit.

FEB 20 — San Francisco, CA — The Artist defeats Lash LeRoux
The Artist beat Lash LeRoux in the finals of a tournament to crown a new Cruiserweight Champion.

MAY 15 — Biloxi, MS — Crowbar and Daffney defeat Chris Candido
Crowbar and Daffney beat Chris Candido and Tammy Sytch in a Mixed Tag Team Match to become co-holders of the Cruiserweight Championship.

MAY 22 — Grand Rapids, MI — Daffney defeats Crowbar

JUNE 06 — Knoxville, TN — Lt. Loco defeats Daffney
Lt. Loco won a Triple Threat Match that included Disco Inferno and then-champion Daffney.

JULY 31 — Cincinnati, OH — Lance Storm defeats Lt. Loco

AUG 14 — Kelowna, B.C. — Elix Skipper awarded Cruiserweight Championship by Lance Storm.

2001

MAR 18 — Jacksonville, FL — Shane Helms defeats Chavo Guerrero

JULY 05 — Tacoma, WA — Billy Kidman defeats Shane Helms

JULY 30 — Philadelphia, PA — X-Pac defeats Billy Kidman and unifies the Light Heavyweight and Cruiserweight Championships.

OCT 11 — Moline, IL — Billy Kidman defeats X-Pac

OCT 22 — Kansas City, MO — Tajiri defeats Billy Kidman

MAY 16 — Montreal, Quebec — The Hurricane defeats Tajiri
The Hurricane pinned Tajiri in a Triple Threat Match that also included Billy Kidman.

JUNE 23 — Columbus, OH — Jamie Noble defeats The Hurricane

NOV 17 — New York, NY — Billy Kidman defeats Jamie Noble

FEB 23 — Montreal, Quebec — Matt Hardy defeats Billy Kidman

2003

JUN 05 — Anaheim, CA — Rey Mysterio defeats Matt Hardy

SEPT 25 — Philadelphia, PA — Tajiri defeats Rey Mysterio

MAY 06 — Tucson, AZ — Jacqueline defeats Chavo Guerrero

MAY 16 — Los Angeles, CA — Chavo Guerrero defeats Jacqueline

MAY 20 — Las Vegas, NV — Chavo Classic defeats Chavo Guerrero
Chavo Classic pinned Chavo Guerrero in a Triple Threat Match that also included Spike Dudley.

JUNE 17 — Chicago, IL — Rey Mysterio defeats Chavo Classic

JULY 29 — Cincinnati, OH — Spike Dudley defeats Rey Mysterio

DEC 12 — Atlanta, GA — Funaki defeats Spike Dudley

OCT 09 — Houston, TX — Juventud defeats Nunzio

NOV 15 — Rome, Italy — Nunzio defeats Juventud

NOV 26 — Sheffield, England — Juventud defeats Nunzio

DEC 19 — Providence, RI — Kid Kash defeats Juventud

2006

JAN 29 — Miami, FL — Gregory Helms defeats Funaki
Gregory Helms pinned Funaki in a Cruiserweight Invitational Match that also included Paul London, Jamie Noble, Nunzio, and then-champion Kid Kash.

2007

FEB 18 — Los Angeles, CA
Chavo Guerrero defeats Jimmy Wang Yang
Chavo Guerrero pinned Jimmy Wang Yang in a Cruiserweight Open that also included Daivari, Funaki, Shannon Moore, Scotty 2 Hotty, Jamie Noble, and then-champion Gregory Helms.

JULY 23 — San Jose, CA
Hornswoggle defeats Jamie Noble
Hornswoggle pinned Jamie Noble in a Cruiserweight Open that included Shannon Moore, Jimmy Wang Yang, Funaki, and then-champion Chavo Guerrero.

2005

FEB 20 — Pittsburgh, PA
Chavo Guerrero defeats Paul London
Chavo Guerrero last eliminated Paul London from an Elimination Match that also included Akio, Spike Dudley, Shannon Moore, and then-champion Funaki.

MAR 31 — Houston, TX
Paul London wins Cruiserweight Championship
Paul London last eliminated Billy Kidman from an 8-man Battle Royal that also included Funaki, Akio, Nunzio, Scotty 2 Hotty, Spike Dudley, and then-champion Chavo Guerrero.

AUG 06 — Bridgeport, CT
Nunzio defeats Paul London

2004

JAN 01 — Washington, DC
Rey Mysterio defeats Tajiri

FEB 15 — San Francisco, CA
Chavo Guerrero defeats Rey Mysterio

2002

APR 04 — Rochester, NY
Billy Kidman defeats Tajiri

APR 21 — Kansas City, MO
Tajiri defeats Billy Kidman

OCT 02 — San Francisco, CA
Mike Sanders defeats Elix Skipper
Mike Sanders and Kevin Nash beat Elix Skipper in a Handicap Match.

DEC 04 — Lincoln, NE
Chavo Guerrero defeats Mike Sanders

MAR 30 — Baltimore, MD
Billy Kidman defeats The Artist

MAR 31 — Pittsburgh, PA
The Artist defeats Billy Kidman

APR 16 — Chicago, IL
Chris Candido wins Cruiserweight Championship
Chris Candido outlasted Juventud Guerrera, Shannon Moore, Crowbar, Lash LeRoux, and The Artist to become the new titleholder.

APR 19 — Gainesville, FL
Psicosis defeats Rey Mysterio
Psicosis won a Fatal Four Way Match that also included Blitzkreig, Juventud Guerrera, and then-champion Rey Mysterio.

APR 26 — Fargo, ND
Rey Mysterio defeats Psicosis

AUG 19 — Lubbock, TX
Lenny Lane defeats Rey Mysterio

WCW strips Lenny Lane of the Cruiserweight Championship.

OCT 04 — Kansas City, MO
Psicosis is awarded Cruiserweight Championship

OCT 04 — Kansas City, MO
Disco Inferno defeats Psicosis

...injury forces ...ad Armstrong ...vacate the Cruiserweight Championship in September 1992.

1996

MAR 20 — Nagoya, Japan
...hinjiro Otani defeats ...ris Benoit
...injiro Otani beat Chris ...it in the finals of ...tournament to crown ...new Cruiserweight ...hampion.

MAY 02 — Orlando, FL
...ean Malenko defeats ...hinjiro Otani

JULY 08 — Orlando, FL
...ey Mysterio defeats ...ean Malenko

OCT 27 — Las Vegas, NV
Dean Malenko defeats Rey Mysterio

DEC 29 — Nashville, TN
...ltimo Dragon defeats ...ean Malenko

NOV 10 — Memphis, TN
Eddie Guerrero defeats Rey Mysterio

DEC 29 — Baltimore, MD
Ultimo Dragon defeats Eddie Guerrero

1998

JAN 06 — Daytona Beach, FL
Juventud Guerrera defeats Ultimo Dragon

JAN 15 — Lakeland, FL
Rey Mysterio defeats Juventud Guerrera

JAN 24 — Dayton, OH
Chris Jericho defeats Rey Mysterio

MAY 17 — Worcester, MA
Dean Malenko defeats Chris Jericho

Dean Malenko was forced to vacate the championship because he wore a mask to the ring when he won the right to face Chris Jericho for the title.

THE CUTTING EDGE

In 2005, Edge joined a fraternity of noted WWE loudmouths when he was given his own interview segment, *The Cutting Edge*. Just like "Rowdy" Roddy Piper, Jesse Ventura, Adrian Adonis, and Brother Love before him, the "Rated-R Superstar" uses his time with the microphone to incite fans with his unpopular opinions. In March 2006, *The Cutting Edge* turned hardcore when Edge welcomed Mick Foley to a special *Saturday Night's Main Event* edition of the segment. With just weeks before their *WrestleMania 22* Hardcore Match, each Superstar pulled out all the stops in an attempt to gain valuable momentum. In the years that followed, Edge has used *The Cutting Edge* to assault numerous other fan favorites, including Kane and CM Punk.

CYBER SUNDAY

TABOO TUESDAY

Known as *Taboo Tuesday* for its first two years, *Cyber Sunday* gives WWE fans the opportunity to vote on virtually every aspect of the event.

October 19, 2004
Milwaukee, WI - Bradley Center

Main Event: Randy Orton vs. "Nature Boy" Ric Flair, Steel Cage Match

November 01, 2005
San Diego, CA - iPayOne Center

Main Event: World Heavyweight Champion John Cena vs. Shawn Michaels vs. Kurt Angle in a Triple Threat Match

November 05, 2006
Cincinnati, OH - U.S. Bank Arena

Main Event: World Heavyweight Champion King Booker vs. WWE Champion John Cena vs. ECW Champion Big Show, Triple Threat Match

October 28, 2007
Washington, DC - Verizon Center

Main Event: World Heavyweight Champion Batista vs. Undertaker

October 26, 2008
Phoenix, AZ - US Airways Center

Main Event: World Heavyweight Champion Chris Jericho vs. Batista, Stone Cold Steve Austin as the special guest referee

---

Daivari 🇺🇸

YEARS ACTIVE 1960 1969 | 1970 1979 | 1980 1989 | 1990 1999 | **2000 PRESENT**

HT 5'10" **WT** 206 lbs. **FROM** Detroit, Michigan

Detroit native Daivari accused his fellow countrymen of racist activity toward him and other Arab-Americans. Clearly, his sentiments did not sit well with the melting pot of WWE fans, but that didn't stop him from continually spewing his unpopular opinions.

In the ring, Daivari's early days looked bright, especially after defeating Shawn Michaels in his singles debut in April 2005. When his partner, Muhammad Hassan, left WWE later that summer, his career was knocked off track and never fully recovered. Following Hassan's departure, Daivari focused mainly on managing. His list of clients included Kurt Angle, Mark Henry, and The Great Khali.

Damien Demento

YEARS ACTIVE 1960 1969 | 1970 1979 | 1980 1989 | **1990 1999** | 2000 PRESENT

HT 6'3" **WT** 269 lbs. **FROM** The Outer Reaches of Your Mind

SIGNATURE MOVE Jumping Knee Drop

Demento and his odd forms of behavior inhabited WWE for the first time in October 1992. He prowled the ring, all the while speaking aloud to the voices speaking to him in his head. Demento disturbed all who watched him and battled the likes of Virgil, Bob Backlund, Tatanka, and Tito Santana.

Despite Demento's peculiar persona, audiences became curious about what he would do next. In the ring, he saw continued success, which led him to the main event of the first ever *Monday Night Raw* against Undertaker. By the summer of 1994, Damian Demento left WWE.

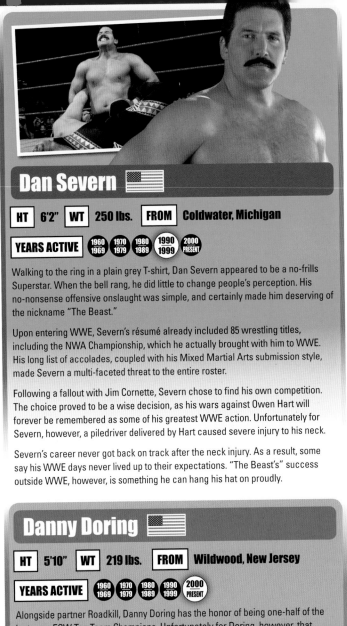

Dan Severn

| HT | 6'2" | WT | 250 lbs. | FROM | Coldwater, Michigan |

YEARS ACTIVE 1960-1969 1970-1979 1980-1989 **1990-1999** 2000-PRESENT

Walking to the ring in a plain grey T-shirt, Dan Severn appeared to be a no-frills Superstar. When the bell rang, he did little to change people's perception. His no-nonsense offensive onslaught was simple, and certainly made him deserving of the nickname "The Beast."

Upon entering WWE, Severn's résumé already included 85 wrestling titles, including the NWA Championship, which he actually brought with him to WWE. His long list of accolades, coupled with his Mixed Martial Arts submission style, made Severn a multi-faceted threat to the entire roster.

Following a fallout with Jim Cornette, Severn chose to find his own competition. The choice proved to be a wise decision, as his wars against Owen Hart will forever be remembered as some of his greatest WWE action. Unfortunately for Severn, however, a piledriver delivered by Hart caused severe injury to his neck.

Severn's career never got back on track after the neck injury. As a result, some say his WWE days never lived up to their expectations. "The Beast's" success outside WWE, however, is something he can hang his hat on proudly.

Danny Doring

| HT | 5'10" | WT | 219 lbs. | FROM | Wildwood, New Jersey |

YEARS ACTIVE 1960-1969 1970-1979 1980-1989 1990-1999 **2000-PRESENT**

Alongside partner Roadkill, Danny Doring has the honor of being one-half of the last-ever ECW Tag Team Champions. Unfortunately for Doring, however, that accolade failed to result in any WWE success. In fact, his entire WWE career only amounted to a handful of matches, none of which he won.

During 2004 and 2005, Doring made a few unsuccessful appearances on *Heat* and *Velocity*. Despite his losing record, he was awarded a contract to compete on WWE's reborn ECW brand. After losses to Mike Knox, Rob Van Dam, and CM Punk, Doring was released from his contract in December 2006.

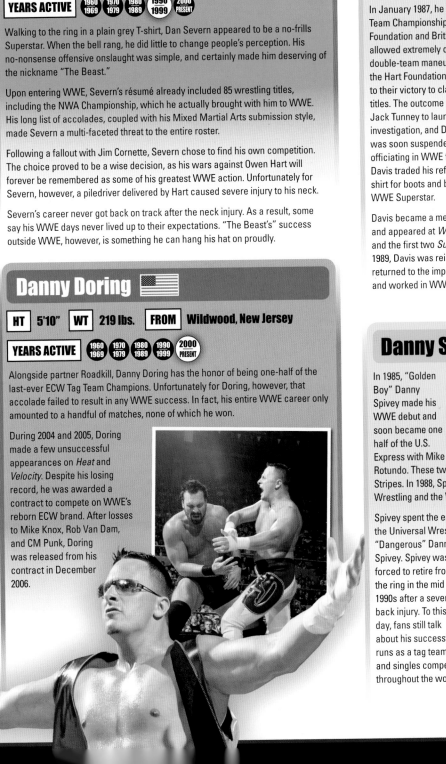

Danny Davis

| HT | 6' | WT | 180 lbs. | FROM | Dover, New Hampshire |

| **SIGNATURE MOVE** | Boston Crab |

YEARS ACTIVE 1960-1969 1970-1979 **1980-1989** 1990-1999 2000-PRESENT

WWE audiences were introduced to Davis in the early 1980s as a referee. However, people uncovered a disturbing trend as Davis was seemingly becoming tolerant of rule-breaking tactics. Alleged offenses included making fast counts, not enforcing basic rules and turning a blind eye to the questionable activities.

In January 1987, he officiated the World Tag Team Championship Match between the Hart Foundation and British Bulldogs. Davis allowed extremely questionable double-team maneuvers from the Hart Foundation, which led to their victory to claim the titles. The outcome prompted Jack Tunney to launch an investigation, and Davis was soon suspended from officiating in WWE for life. Davis traded his referee's shirt for boots and became a WWE Superstar.

Davis became a member of the Hart Foundation and appeared at *WrestleMania III* and *IV* and the first two *Survivor Series* events. In 1989, Davis was reinstated as an official. He returned to the impartial ways of his early career and worked in WWE rings until the mid-1990s.

Danny Spivey

In 1985, "Golden Boy" Danny Spivey made his WWE debut and soon became one half of the U.S. Express with Mike Rotundo.

| HT | 6'8" | WT | 280 lbs. | FROM | Tampa, Florida |

| **SIGNATURE MOVE** | Bulldog |

YEARS ACTIVE 1960-1969 1970-1979 **1980-1989** 1990-1999 2000-PRESENT

These two fan favorites came to the ring waving the Stars & Stripes. In 1988, Spivey left the company and toured with All-Japan Pro Wrestling and the World Wrestling Council in Puerto Rico.

Spivey spent the early 1990s in WCW, All-Japan Pro Wrestling and the Universal Wrestling Federation, where he was often known as "Dangerous" Danny Spivey. Spivey was forced to retire from the ring in the mid 1990s after a severe back injury. To this day, fans still talk about his successful runs as a tag team and singles competitor throughout the world.

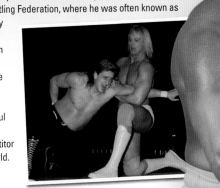

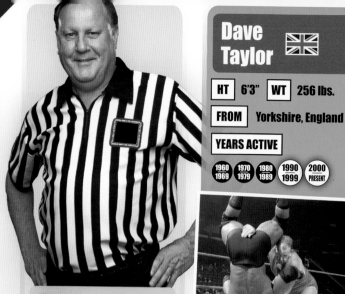

Dave Hebner 🇺🇸

Dave Hebner first appeared in WWE in the mid-1980s. He developed a reputation as an excellent referee and was involved in one of the most controversial moments in sports-entertainment on February 5, 1988. In the *WrestleMania III* WWE Championship rematch on *The Main Event,* it was revealed after the match's controversial ending that "Million Dollar Man" Ted DiBiase paid someone to undergo plastic surgery to look like Hebner and ensure that Hulk Hogan did not leave Market Square Arena in Indianapolis as WWE Champion.

Hebner continued to be one of WWE's top officiators, unafraid to get involved in the action to uphold the rules until he became a member of WWE's front office. In 2005, Dave Hebner and World Wrestling Entertainment parted ways. He will always be remembered as one of the best referees of all time, able to handle any type of match and any number of participants.

Dave Taylor 🇬🇧

HT 6'3" **WT** 256 lbs.

FROM Yorkshire, England

YEARS ACTIVE

1960-1969 · 1970-1979 · 1980-1989 · **1990-1999** · 2000-PRESENT

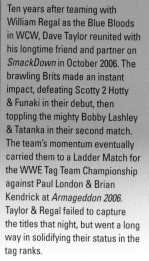

Ten years after teaming with William Regal as the Blue Bloods in WCW, Dave Taylor reunited with his longtime friend and partner on *SmackDown* in October 2006. The brawling Brits made an instant impact, defeating Scotty 2 Hotty & Funaki in their debut, then toppling the mighty Bobby Lashley & Tatanka in their second match. The team's momentum eventually carried them to a Ladder Match for the WWE Tag Team Championship against Paul London & Brian Kendrick at *Armageddon 2006.* Taylor & Regal failed to capture the titles that night, but went a long way in solidifying their status in the tag ranks.

After the 2007 WWE Draft forced the successful British tandem to go their separate ways, Taylor briefly teamed with Paul Burchill before serving as Drew McIntyre's mentor.

David Sammartino 🇺🇸

HT 5'8" **WT** 252 lbs.

FROM Pittsburgh, Pennsylvania

SIGNATURE MOVE
Figure-Four Leg Lock

YEARS ACTIVE

1960-1969 · 1970-1979 · **1980-1989** · 1990-1999 · 2000-PRESENT

The son of former WWE Champion and all-time great Bruno Sammartino, young David dreamed about creating his own path to stardom. He began his career under the name Bruno Sammartino, Jr., but soon decided to adopt his birth name. In 1984, David entered WWE and pinned Jerry Valiant during his television debut. David enjoyed some success and competed at the first *WrestleMania* against Brutus Beefcake.

In the summer of 1986, David left WWE and briefly appeared in the AWA. For the remainder of the 1980s, he traveled independent promotions throughout the United States. In 1990, he was part of the short-lived UWF and, in 1996, he was part of the WCW Cruiserweight Division. Today, David is retired from the ring and has a successful personal training business in Georgia, where he resides with his family.

Dawn Marie 🇺🇸

HT 5'7"

FROM Rahway, New Jersey

YEARS ACTIVE

1960-1969 · 1970-1979 · 1980-1989 · 1990-1999 · **2000-PRESENT**

The ring has seen its share of seductive women, but never before has a Diva used sex as a weapon as effectively, or lethally, as Dawn Marie. Over the course of her career, the manipulative brunette seduced countless male targets, both young and old.

Dawn Marie's greatest romantic exploit came in October 2002 when she fell for Al Wilson, the father of fellow Diva Torrie Wilson. Despite being half Wilson's age, Dawn Marie engaged in a passionate relationship with Torrie's father, which did not sit well with Torrie. After just weeks together, the two lovebirds agreed to become husband and wife.

Dressed in nothing but their very revealing underwear, the couple was married in January 2003. Unfortunately, the wedding was one of the last times anybody would see Al Wilson alive, as Dawn Marie proved to be too much woman for him. His heart eventually gave out and he died on their honeymoon.

Proving a leopard never changes her spots, Dawn Marie was back at it the following year when her affair with Charlie Haas effectively ended his engagement to Miss Jackie. Luckily for all the WWE Superstars (and their fathers), the seductive Diva left WWE shortly thereafter.

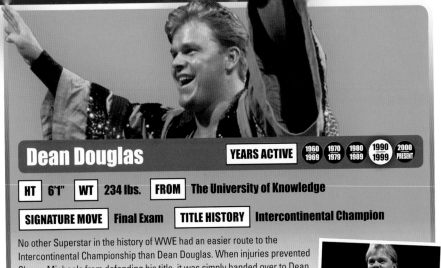

Dean Douglas

| | | | | | | YEARS ACTIVE | 1960 1969 | 1970 1979 | 1980 1989 | **1990 1999** | 2000 PRESENT |

| **HT** 6'1" | **WT** 234 lbs. | **FROM** The University of Knowledge |

| **SIGNATURE MOVE** Final Exam | **TITLE HISTORY** Intercontinental Champion |

No other Superstar in the history of WWE had an easier route to the Intercontinental Championship than Dean Douglas. When injuries prevented Shawn Michaels from defending his title, it was simply handed over to Dean Douglas. Without even breaking a sweat, Douglas celebrated becoming the new Intercontinental Champion.

The celebration, however, didn't last long. Within moments of being awarded the title, Douglas was forced to defend it against Razor Ramon, who promptly defeated him and took the title. Despite owning one of the least impressive Intercontinental Championship reigns in WWE history, the arrogant Douglas believed he had something he could teach all his fellow Superstars. Watching from his satellite classroom, he would grade the action he saw in the ring. Douglas proved to be a tough man to impress, as he never gave a favorable review. Some of the more notable Superstars Douglas offered failing grades to include 1-2-3 Kid, Barry Horowitz, and Shawn Michaels.

Dean Ho

| **FROM** Hawaii |

| **SIGNATURE MOVE** The Full Nelson |

| **TITLE HISTORY** World Tag Team Champion |

| **YEARS ACTIVE** | **1960 1969** | **1970 1979** | 1980 1989 | 1990 1999 | 2000 PRESENT |

This happy Hawaiian was a bodybuilder who won the "Mr. Hawaiian Islands" championship in 1956. In 1962, Dean Ho made his ring debut in the Pacific Northwest Wrestling territory and for the next decade Ho appeared all over the Pacific Northwest and Hawaii.

In 1973, Dean debuted in WWE and tested his skills against the best and brightest. Dean Ho's in-ring style combined martial arts, grappling abilities, and aerial moves. He formed a popular tag team with Tony Garea and the duo went on to hold the World Tag Team Championship for close to six months. Dean continued to appear on WWE until 1976. He then traveled portions of Georgia, San Francisco, and then returned to Vancouver and Portland in the Northwest. He decided to hang up his boots in December 1983.

Today, the happy Hawaiian lives in Vancouver, British Columbia and owns a highly touted gourmet catering business. Dean Ho is recognized for all his in-ring accomplishments and versatility as well as a persona that influenced countless others that set foot in the ring after him.

Dean Malenko

| **HT** 5'10 | **WT** 212 lbs. | **FROM** Tampa, Florida |

| **SIGNATURE MOVE** Texas Cloverleaf |

| **TITLE HISTORY** Light Heavyweight Champion |

| **YEARS ACTIVE** | 1960 1969 | 1970 1979 | 1980 1989 | **1990 1999** | **2000 PRESENT** |

Trained by his famous father, "Professor" Boris Malenko, Dean first consistently appeared on American television during his days with ECW, earning a reputation as a peerless technical competitor. In 1995, "The Man Of 1,000 Holds" moved on to WCW, where he held many championships.

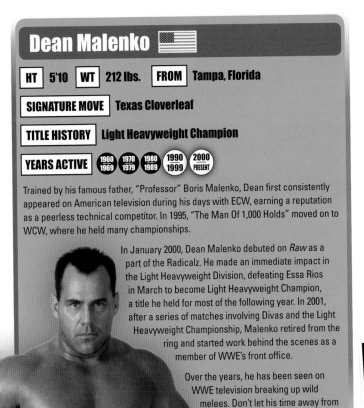

In January 2000, Dean Malenko debuted on *Raw* as a part of the Radicalz. He made an immediate impact in the Light Heavyweight Division, defeating Essa Rios in March to become Light Heavyweight Champion, a title he held for most of the following year. In 2001, after a series of matches involving Divas and the Light Heavyweight Championship, Malenko retired from the ring and started work behind the scenes as a member of WWE's front office.

Over the years, he has been seen on WWE television breaking up wild melees. Don't let his time away from the ring fool you. He stays in ring shape and, if a Superstar goes too far during one of these wild brawls, they'll get taken down in the blink of an eye.

Debra

| | | **YEARS ACTIVE** | 1960 1969 | 1970 1979 | 1980 1989 | **1990 1999** | **2000 PRESENT** |

| **HT** 5'5" | **FROM** Tuscaloosa, Alabama |

| **TITLE HISTORY** Women's Champion |

A former beauty pageant queen, Debra brought her award-winning looks to WCW in 1996. Alongside her then-husband Steve McMichael, the curvy blonde was originally seen as nothing more than eye candy. By the end of her career, however, she earned a reputation as one of the most powerful females of her time.

After a few years by McMichael's side, Debra jumped to WWE in 1998. At first glance, she gave the impression of a no-nonsense businesswoman. However, once she broke out of her shell, Debra revealed herself as quite an exhibitionist. In fact, it wasn't uncommon to see her remove her suits in an attempt to help her man at the time, Jeff Jarrett, pick up wins. This tactic also led to Jerry Lawler's famous "puppies" catchphrase.

As a competitor, Debra didn't quite have the skills of a Fabulous Moolah, but that didn't stop her from capturing the Women's Championship, albeit on a technicality. In May 1999, Sable had disrobed Debra in an

Evening Gown Match, thus winning the encounter. Commissioner Shawn Michaels saw things a bit differently, though. In his eyes, the winner should be the Diva left wearing nothing but her underwear. As a result, he reversed the decision and awarded the match and Women's Championship to Debra.

Debra was so inspired by HBK's leadership that night that she later went on to become Lieutenant Commissioner, thus proving herself as one of the most powerful females of her time.

DECEMBER TO DISMEMBER

December to Dismember was an ECW-exclusive pay-per-view that took place on December 3, 2006 at the James Brown Arena in Augusta, Georgia. The event included ECW veterans Tommy Dreamer, Balls Mahoney, and the FBI and other top Superstars like the Hardys, MNM, and Elijah Burke.

The main event was a bloody Extreme Elimination Chamber Match that locked ECW Champion Big Show, Bobby Lashley, Rob Van Dam, Hardcore Holly, Test, and CM Punk in the sadistic chamber. Bobby Lashley survived the extreme encounter (and Big Show's barbed wire bat!) to claim the ECW Title.

DEMOLITION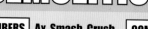

MEMBERS Ax, Smash, Crush   **COMBINED WEIGHT** 978 lbs.

TITLE HISTORY World Tag Team Champions

YEARS ACTIVE 1960-1969 1970-1979 1980-1989 1990-1999 2000-PRESENT

Originally looked upon by many as a cheap Road Warriors rip off, Demolition could have easily folded under the weight of the naysayers. Instead, they combined their intimidating appearance with an aggressive in-ring style to dominate the WWE tag team scene for five years.

Clad in studded leather and colorful face paint, Ax & Smash made their WWE debut in 1987. With Mr. Fuji as their manager, Demolition destroyed their early competition, which consisted of some of the most popular tag teams of the time, including the British Bulldogs, Young Stallions, and Killer Bees.

The following year, Demolition carried their dominance into *WrestleMania IV* where they defeated Strike Force for the World Tag Team Championship. Behind the devastation of their Decapitation finisher, Ax and Smash held the titles for a record-breaking sixteen months.

In the midst of Demolition's epic World Tag Team Championship reign, the conniving Mr. Fuji turned his back on his clients to join forces with the Powers of Pain. Empathetic fans everywhere began to see Ax & Smash in a new light. Almost overnight, Demolition was transformed into the most popular tag team in WWE.

Demolition's dominance grew throughout 1990 when they added Crush as the team's third member. Younger and stronger, Crush served as the muscles for the already-forceful tag team. On several occasions, he also stepped in to help Smash through team's third reign as World Tag Team Champions.

By 1991, the trio began to fade, making way for such tag teams as the Nasty Boys and Road Warriors. Their final high-profile match came in a losing effort when they fell to international sensations Genichiro Tenryu & Koji Kitao at *WrestleMania VII*.

To this day, fans look back at Demolition's dominance over WWE as one of the most impressive displays in the history of tag team wrestling. Not bad for a team who were originally looked upon as copycats.

Deuce & Domino

COMBINED WEIGHT 730 lbs.

TITLE HISTORY

WWE Tag Team Champions

YEARS ACTIVE

   1960-1969 1970-1979 1980-1989 1990-1999 2000-PRESENT

Deuce & Domino made their WWE debut in 2007, claiming to be the biggest attraction in all of the past, present, and future. Led to the ring by Domino's sister, Cherry, the duo considered themselves God's gift to women.

Deuce & Domino shocked the world when they defeated Brian Kendrick & Paul London for the WWE Tag Team Championship. They held the titles for four months, eventually losing to the combination of MVP & Matt Hardy. Cracks in the team began to show when Cherry started to run around with Michelle McCool. Deuce & Domino kicked her to the curb in favor of Maryse. Unfortunately for fans of these throwbacks, a lost match prompted a brawl between the pair, ending their partnership in the process. In August 2008, Domino left WWE and Deuce tried his hand at singles competition.

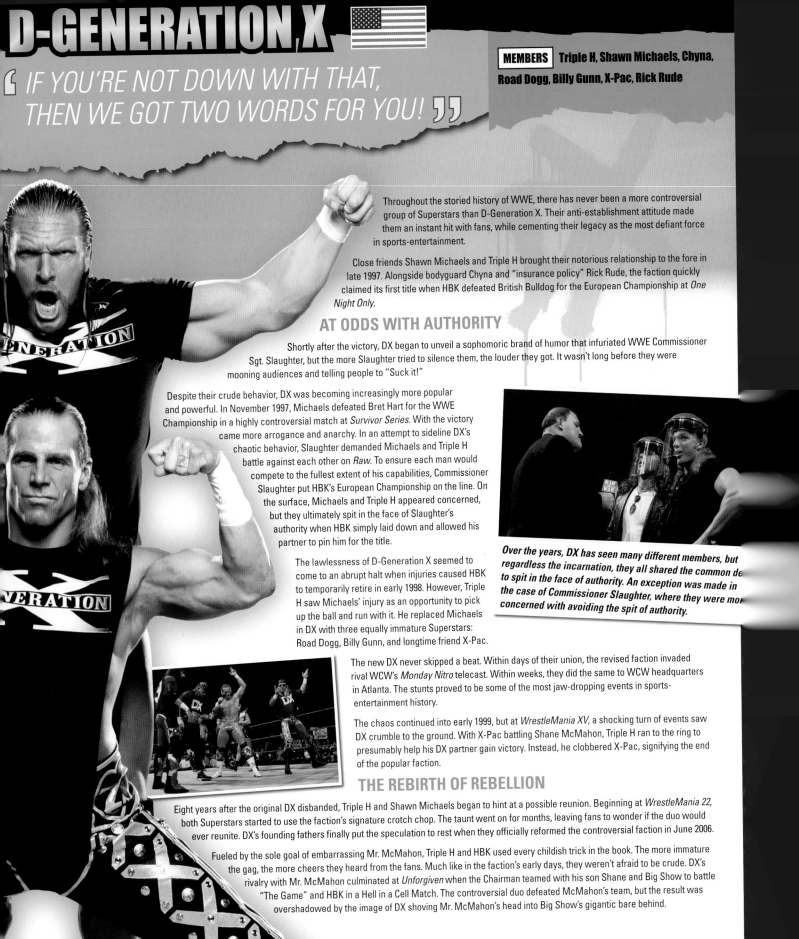

D-GENERATION X

" IF YOU'RE NOT DOWN WITH THAT, THEN WE GOT TWO WORDS FOR YOU! "

MEMBERS | Triple H, Shawn Michaels, Chyna, Road Dogg, Billy Gunn, X-Pac, Rick Rude

Throughout the storied history of WWE, there has never been a more controversial group of Superstars than D-Generation X. Their anti-establishment attitude made them an instant hit with fans, while cementing their legacy as the most defiant force in sports-entertainment.

Close friends Shawn Michaels and Triple H brought their notorious relationship to the fore in late 1997. Alongside bodyguard Chyna and "insurance policy" Rick Rude, the faction quickly claimed its first title when HBK defeated British Bulldog for the European Championship at *One Night Only*.

AT ODDS WITH AUTHORITY

Shortly after the victory, DX began to unveil a sophomoric brand of humor that infuriated WWE Commissioner Sgt. Slaughter, but the more Slaughter tried to silence them, the louder they got. It wasn't long before they were mooning audiences and telling people to "Suck it!"

Despite their crude behavior, DX was becoming increasingly more popular and powerful. In November 1997, Michaels defeated Bret Hart for the WWE Championship in a highly controversial match at *Survivor Series*. With the victory came more arrogance and anarchy. In an attempt to sideline DX's chaotic behavior, Slaughter demanded Michaels and Triple H battle against each other on *Raw*. To ensure each man would compete to the fullest extent of his capabilities, Commissioner Slaughter put HBK's European Championship on the line. On the surface, Michaels and Triple H appeared concerned, but they ultimately spit in the face of Slaughter's authority when HBK simply laid down and allowed his partner to pin him for the title.

The lawlessness of D-Generation X seemed to come to an abrupt halt when injuries caused HBK to temporarily retire in early 1998. However, Triple H saw Michaels' injury as an opportunity to pick up the ball and run with it. He replaced Michaels in DX with three equally immature Superstars: Road Dogg, Billy Gunn, and longtime friend X-Pac.

Over the years, DX has seen many different members, but regardless the incarnation, they all shared the common de to spit in the face of authority. An exception was made in the case of Commissioner Slaughter, where they were mor concerned with avoiding the spit of authority.

The new DX never skipped a beat. Within days of their union, the revised faction invaded rival WCW's *Monday Nitro* telecast. Within weeks, they did the same to WCW headquarters in Atlanta. The stunts proved to be some of the most jaw-dropping events in sports-entertainment history.

The chaos continued into early 1999, but at *WrestleMania XV*, a shocking turn of events saw DX crumble to the ground. With X-Pac battling Shane McMahon, Triple H ran to the ring to presumably help his DX partner gain victory. Instead, he clobbered X-Pac, signifying the end of the popular faction.

THE REBIRTH OF REBELLION

Eight years after the original DX disbanded, Triple H and Shawn Michaels began to hint at a possible reunion. Beginning at *WrestleMania 22*, both Superstars started to use the faction's signature crotch chop. The taunt went on for months, leaving fans to wonder if the duo would ever reunite. DX's founding fathers finally put the speculation to rest when they officially reformed the controversial faction in June 2006.

Fueled by the sole goal of embarrassing Mr. McMahon, Triple H and HBK used every childish trick in the book. The more immature the gag, the more cheers they heard from the fans. Much like in the faction's early days, they weren't afraid to be crude. DX's rivalry with Mr. McMahon culminated at *Unforgiven* when the Chairman teamed with his son Shane and Big Show to battle "The Game" and HBK in a Hell in a Cell Match. The controversial duo defeated McMahon's team, but the result was overshadowed by the image of DX shoving Mr. McMahon's head into Big Show's gigantic bare behind.

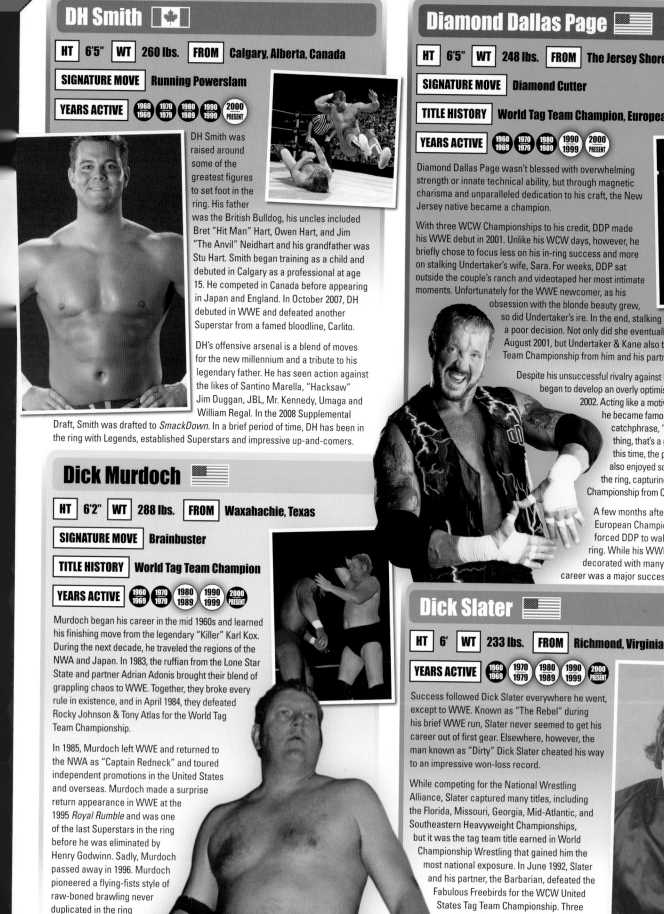

DH Smith 🇨🇦

| HT | 6'5" | WT | 260 lbs. | FROM | Calgary, Alberta, Canada |

SIGNATURE MOVE Running Powerslam

YEARS ACTIVE (1960-1969) (1970-1979) (1980-1989) (1990-1999) **(2000 PRESENT)**

DH Smith was raised around some of the greatest figures to set foot in the ring. His father was the British Bulldog, his uncles included Bret "Hit Man" Hart, Owen Hart, and Jim "The Anvil" Neidhart and his grandfather was Stu Hart. Smith began training as a child and debuted in Calgary as a professional at age 15. He competed in Canada before appearing in Japan and England. In October 2007, DH debuted in WWE and defeated another Superstar from a famed bloodline, Carlito.

DH's offensive arsenal is a blend of moves for the new millennium and a tribute to his legendary father. He has seen action against the likes of Santino Marella, "Hacksaw" Jim Duggan, JBL, Mr. Kennedy, Umaga and William Regal. In the 2008 Supplemental Draft, Smith was drafted to *SmackDown.* In a brief period of time, DH has been in the ring with Legends, established Superstars and impressive up-and-comers.

Dick Murdoch 🇺🇸

| HT | 6'2" | WT | 288 lbs. | FROM | Waxahachie, Texas |

SIGNATURE MOVE Brainbuster

TITLE HISTORY World Tag Team Champion

YEARS ACTIVE (1960-1969) (1970-1979) (1980-1989) (1990-1999) (2000 PRESENT)

Murdoch began his career in the mid 1960s and learned his finishing move from the legendary "Killer" Karl Kox. During the next decade, he traveled the regions of the NWA and Japan. In 1983, the ruffian from the Lone Star State and partner Adrian Adonis brought their blend of grappling chaos to WWE. Together, they broke every rule in existence, and in April 1984, they defeated Rocky Johnson & Tony Atlas for the World Tag Team Championship.

In 1985, Murdoch left WWE and returned to the NWA as "Captain Redneck" and toured independent promotions in the United States and overseas. Murdoch made a surprise return appearance in WWE at the 1995 *Royal Rumble* and was one of the last Superstars in the ring before he was eliminated by Henry Godwinn. Sadly, Murdoch passed away in 1996. Murdoch pioneered a flying-fists style of raw-boned brawling never duplicated in the ring before or since.

Diamond Dallas Page 🇺🇸

| HT | 6'5" | WT | 248 lbs. | FROM | The Jersey Shore |

SIGNATURE MOVE Diamond Cutter

TITLE HISTORY World Tag Team Champion, European Champion

YEARS ACTIVE (1960-1969) (1970-1979) (1980-1989) (1990-1999) **(2000 PRESENT)**

Diamond Dallas Page wasn't blessed with overwhelming strength or innate technical ability, but through magnetic charisma and unparalleled dedication to his craft, the New Jersey native became a champion.

With three WCW Championships to his credit, DDP made his WWE debut in 2001. Unlike his WCW days, however, he briefly chose to focus less on his in-ring success and more on stalking Undertaker's wife, Sara. For weeks, DDP sat outside the couple's ranch and videotaped her most intimate moments. Unfortunately for the WWE newcomer, as his obsession with the blonde beauty grew, so did Undertaker's ire. In the end, stalking Sara proved to be a poor decision. Not only did she eventually defeat DDP in August 2001, but Undertaker & Kane also took the World Tag Team Championship from him and his partner, Kanyon.

Despite his unsuccessful rivalry against Undertaker, DDP began to develop an overly optimistic attitude in 2002. Acting like a motivational speaker, he became famous for his cheerful catchphrase, "that's not a bad thing, that's a good thing." During this time, the positive Page also enjoyed some success in the ring, capturing the European Championship from Christian in January.

A few months after winning the European Championship, injury forced DDP to walk away from the ring. While his WWE days were not decorated with many highlights, his career was a major success.

Dick Slater 🇺🇸

| HT | 6' | WT | 233 lbs. | FROM | Richmond, Virginia |

YEARS ACTIVE (1960-1969) (1970-1979) (1980-1989) (1990-1999) (2000 PRESENT)

Success followed Dick Slater everywhere he went, except to WWE. Known as "The Rebel" during his brief WWE run, Slater never seemed to get his career out of first gear. Elsewhere, however, the man known as "Dirty" Dick Slater cheated his way to an impressive won-loss record.

While competing for the National Wrestling Alliance, Slater captured many titles, including the Florida, Missouri, Georgia, Mid-Atlantic, and Southeastern Heavyweight Championships, but it was the tag team title earned in World Championship Wrestling that gained him the most national exposure. In June 1992, Slater and his partner, the Barbarian, defeated the Fabulous Freebirds for the WCW United States Tag Team Championship. Three years later, he teamed with the rugged Bunkhouse Buck to take the WCW Tag Team Championship from Harlem Heat.

Dick the Bruiser

After spending the early 1950s as a member of the Green Bay Packers, Dick the Bruiser made the jump to wrestling in 1954. His affinity for breaking bones immediately earned him the reputation as "The World's Most Dangerous Wrestler." The lofty status went straight to his head, as the egotistical tough guy was often heard saying, "There isn't a man alive I can't lick."

HT	6'1"	WT	261 lbs.	FROM	Reno, Nevada

SIGNATURE MOVE Top Rope Knee Drop

YEARS ACTIVE 1960–1969 1970–1979 1980–1989 1990–1999 2000 PRESENT

Dick the Bruiser is most recognized for his efforts as a wrestler and promoter of the Indianapolis-based World Wrestling Association. While there, he became one of the game's greatest tag team competitors, capturing the promotion's tag titles 14 times with the likes of The Crusher, Bill Miller, and the legendary Bruno Sammartino.

In 1971, Dick the Bruiser found himself on the wrong side of one of history's most significant matches. With The Sheik as his partner, he came up short against Tarzan Tyler & Luke Graham in a match to declare the first-ever World Tag Team Champions in WWE history. Undeterred by the loss, The Bruiser went on to capture eight more tag team championships over the next 15 years.

While Dick the Bruiser is best remembered for being a noted tough man, many fail to credit him with one of the wittiest comments of all time. According to legend, The Bruiser is the first person to call Bobby Heenan "The Weasel." Decades later, Heenan still gets taunted by the derogatory nickname.

The Dicks

MEMBERS	Chad Dick, James Dick

COMBINED WEIGHT	430 lbs.

YEARS ACTIVE 1960–1969 1970–1979 1980–1989 1990–1999 2000 PRESENT

Clad in Chippendales outfits and carrying mirrors to the ring, Chad & James Dicks' pre-match ritual saw them strip down to their ring attire to what they believed was the delight of female fans.

Upon their debut in late 2005, the egotistical tandem scored a few big victories. It wasn't long before the WWE caught up to them, which resulted in a series of losses. In February 2006, the Dicks came up short in handicap action against Boogeyman. They were released from WWE immediately after.

DIESEL

YEARS ACTIVE 1960–1969 1970–1979 1980–1989 1990–1999 2000 PRESENT

HT	6'10"	WT	328 lbs.	FROM	Detroit, Michigan	SIGNATURE MOVE	Jacknife Powerbomb

TITLE HISTORY WWE Champion, Intercontinental Champion, World Tag Team Champion

This giant began his WWE career in 1993 as the bodyguard of Shawn Michaels. At the 1994 *Royal Rumble*, WWE Superstars felt the force of diesel power when he eliminated seven men in under 18 minutes. That night showed that "Big Daddy Cool" was on his way to stardom.

On April 13, 1994, Diesel won his first major title when he defeated Razor Ramon for the Intercontinental Championship. While still champion, he teamed up with Shawn Michaels to capture the World Tag Team titles. He lost the Intercontinental Championship to Razor in a rematch at *SummerSlam* when Shawn Michaels' "Sweet Chin Music" was out of tune. Tensions grew between the partners, and it boiled up at *Survivor Series* when the two could no longer coexist and forfeited the World Tag Team Championship.

On November 26, 1994, Diesel made history when he replaced an injured Bret "Hit Man" Hart and defeated Bob Backlund in eight seconds to become WWE Champion. "Big Daddy Cool's" championship reign lasted almost one full year and gave the title a stability it had not known since the days of Hulk Hogan and Randy "Macho Man" Savage.

Diesel reconnected with his friend Shawn Michaels after an attack by Sycho Sid. They joined forces as "The Dudes With Attitudes," and the duo enjoyed another World Tag Team Championship reign. Diesel continued to dominate in singles action until he met Undertaker at *WrestleMania XII*.

In 1996, Diesel left WWE and arrived on the set of *WCW Monday Nitro* under his real name, Kevin Nash. He formed with Outsiders with close friend Scott Hall, and the pair swore to take down WCW. Along with Hulk Hogan, they created the New World Order (nWo), and stayed with the company until 2001.

Kevin Nash returned to WWE in February 2002, recreating the nWo with Hogan and Hall. After recovering from a severe injury, Nash returned as his own man in April 2003 to save old friend Shawn Michaels from a beating courtesy of Triple H, Chris Jericho, and Ric Flair. This led to many battles with former friend Triple H, including a Hell In A Cell Match at *Bad Blood*. Kevin Nash's last WWE match was at *SummerSlam 2003* in the Elimination Chamber.

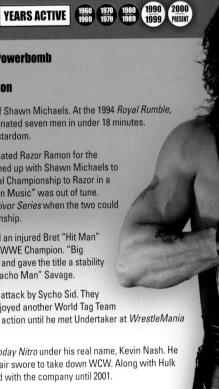

Diesel & Shawn Michaels

COMBINED WEIGHT	550 lbs.	YEARS ACTIVE	1960-1969	1970-1979	1980-1989	**1990-1999**	2000-PRESENT

TITLE HISTORY	World Tag Team Champions

Diesel and Michaels first joined forces in 1993 when Michaels, then the Intercontinental Champion, hired Diesel as his bodyguard. Diesel played a major role in the success of "The Heartbreak Kid" and soon ventured into the ring to compete. On August 28, 1994, they defeated the Headshrinkers to win the World Tag Team Championship. Unfortunately, after HBK inadvertently tagged Diesel with Sweet Chin Music during their 1994 *Survivor Series* match, the duo parted ways and forfeited the championship.

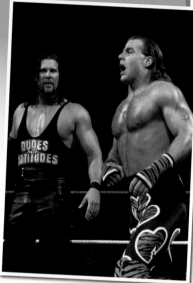

They reunited in 1995 as "Two Dudes With Attitudes." Diesel was WWE Champion and Michaels held the Intercontinental title. In a match against Owen Hart & Yokozuna at *In Your House* included the stipulation that if "Big Daddy Cool" or HBK were pinned, the Superstar who pinned him would win that title. If Michaels or Diesel scored a pin, they would become new World Tag Team Champions. Michaels & Diesel won the match but because of a loophole discovered by attorney Clarence Mason, they were forced to relinquish the titles. WWE's favorite team split again in late 1995. They reunited briefly in 2002 when Diesel, now using his real name Kevin Nash, returned to WWE.

Dino Bravo

HT	6'	WT	248 lbs.	YEARS ACTIVE	1960-1969	**1970-1979**	1980-1989	1990-1999	2000-PRESENT

FROM	Montreal, Quebec, Canada	SIGNATURE MOVE	Side Suplex

TITLE HISTORY	World Tag Team Championship, Canadian Heavyweight Champion

Trained by Canadian legend Gino Brito, Dino Bravo began his in-ring career in 1970 and formed a popular tag team with his mentor, known as the Italian Connection. In 1978, Dino debuted in WWE and soon won the World Tag Team Championship with Dominic DeNucci. After a three month reign with the titles, Bravo competed in singles competitions before he left the company in 1979. After a seven-year absence, Bravo returned to WWE and became the bleached blond associate of the Dream Team. He also joined forces with Greg Valentine in the New Dream Team.

For the remainder of his career, Bravo battled the biggest names in WWE both by himself and with the Canadian Earthquake. In the spring of 1992, he retired from active competition and opened a training school. Sadly, in March 1993, this Canadian legend died at his Montreal home. Whether he was a fan favorite or rule-breaker, Dino Bravo is remembered as one of the most powerful men in WWE history.

Dink The Clown

HT	4'	WT	95 lbs.

FROM	Parts Unknown	SIGNATURE MOVE	Cannonball

YEARS ACTIVE	1960-1969	1970-1979	1980-1989	**1990-1999**	2000-PRESENT

Presented as a gift to Doink the Clown, this sidekick packed quite a punch when called upon. Dink rarely left the side of Doink during the clown's days in WWE and gave splitting headaches to referees and opposing Superstars alike.

Dink joined his fellow clown in action against Bam Bam Bigelow & Luna Vachon. The four battled at *WrestleMania X* and from there the mischievous clowns took their act to the 1994 *Survivor Series*. In one of the most chaotic contests in WWE history, Dink teamed with Doink, Pink & Wink against Jerry "The King" Lawler and Queazy, Sleazy & Cheezy in a mixed tag team match. Dink followed his larger counterpart and exited WWE in 1995.

The Disciples of Apocalypse

MEMBERS	Crush, Chainz, Skull, 8-Ball

YEARS ACTIVE	1960-1969	1970-1979	1980-1989	**1990-1999**	2000-PRESENT

After being fired from the Nation of Domination, Crush formed a biker gang of Superstars he called the Disciples of Apocalypse. According to the former Nation member, DOA was a true brotherhood of Superstars who lived, rode, and fought together.

Fans expected greatness from Crush, Chainz, Skull & 8-Ball after they made their impressive debut in June 1997, but by the end of the year, Crush had left WWE and Chainz went on to pursue a singles career, leaving Skull & 8-Ball as the sole members of the faction.

As a tag team, Skull & 8-Ball engaged in an intense rivalry against the Legion of Doom. During this time, longtime LOD manager Paul Ellering actually turned on his team to join forces with DOA. The move will forever be remembered as one of the most shocking moments in tag team history.

With Ellering by their side, Skull & 8-Ball were able to turn back LOD at *Fully Loaded 1998*. Later that year, however, Droz teamed with LOD to get the ultimate measure of revenge on DOA & Ellering, defeating the trio at *Judgment Day*.

DIVAS CHAMPIONSHIP

Despite being just as athletic in the ring, *SmackDown*'s Divas spent years watching from the sidelines as *Raw*'s women competed over the Women's Championship. In the summer of 2008, *SmackDown* general manager Vickie Guerrero finally stood up for her brand when she introduced the Divas Championship. Michelle McCool etched her name in the history books as the first-ever Divas Champion when she defeated Natalya in a tournament final at *The Great American Bash 2008.*

2008

JULY 20 Uniondale, NY

Michelle McCool defeats Natalya

In the finals of a tournament to crown the first-ever Divas Champion, Michelle McCool defeated Natalya.

DEC 20 Toronto, ON

Maryse defeats Michelle McCool

D-Lo Brown

| HT | 6'3" | WT | 268 lbs. | FROM | Chicago, Illinois |

| **TITLE HISTORY** | European Champion, Intercontinental Champion |

| **YEARS ACTIVE** | 1960–1969 | 1970–1979 | 1980–1989 | 1990–1999 | 2000–PRESENT |

In 1997, Brown debuted in WWE as a member of the Nation of Domination, but he had a falling out with its leaders, first Faarooq, and then The Rock. Amidst the turmoil within the ranks of the Nation, D-Lo defeated Triple H for the European Championship at *Fully Loaded 1998* and became the first Superstar to hold the European and Intercontinental Championships concurrently.

After a brief partnership with the Godfather, D-Lo partnered with former Headbanger Chaz in 2000 and formed Lo Down with their manager, Tiger Ali Singh. Later in 2002, D-Lo acquired the managerial services of Theodore R. Long and became part of his Thuggin' and Buggin' Enterprises, a group to fight the oppression within WWE. Soon after, D-Lo and WWE went their separate ways.

For the next four years, D-Lo competed on the independent scene and toured Japan. In June 2008, he returned to WWE. As D-Lo likes to say, "Chumps better recognize and become down with the Brown!"

Doink

| **YEARS ACTIVE** | 1960–1969 | 1970–1979 | 1980–1989 | 1990–1999 | 2000–PRESENT |

| HT | 5'10" | WT | 243 lbs. | FROM | Parts Unknown |

| **SIGNATURE MOVE** | The Whoopie Cushion |

In late 1992, this clown brought his circus act to WWE. His mean-spirited pranks both in and out of the ring made him a prime target of competitors and audiences alike. At *WrestleMania IX,* he attacked Crush with the aid of an imposter, adding confusion to his cruel antics. Doink could not contain the joy he received by making others miserable.

After an incident with Jerry "The King" Lawler, fans began to embrace Doink, who displayed a softer side. His pranks brought out laughter from audiences and he introduced a sidekick, named Dink. The two battled Bam Bam Bigelow & Luna Vachon at *WrestleMania X.* At that year's *Survivor Series,* he assembled a crew of Dink, Wink, and Pink to battle Lawler's team of Queazy, Cheesy, and Sleazy. Although his appearances became less frequent, he still makes unexpected arrivals. Although fans and Superstars didn't always appreciate his brand of humor, he always kept his opponents in stitches.

Dok Hendrix

Put a microphone in front of Dok Hendrix and he could talk for hours. Amazingly, the only thing that was louder than this boisterous WWE announcer was his neon-colored suits. The energetic Hendrix began his WWE announcing career in 1995. His high-octane style propelled him to become a regular on such weekly WWE shows as *Superstars* and *Action Zone.* Hendrix even assumed color commentator duties for several pay-per-view matches.

In addition to sitting at the announcer table, Hendrix also served as WWE's main interviewer, a role made famous years earlier by WWE Hall of Famer "Mean" Gene Okerlund. Hendrix's most famous interview occurred at the 1996 *King of the Ring* when he held the microphone for Stone Cold Steve Austin's now famous "Austin 3:16" rant.

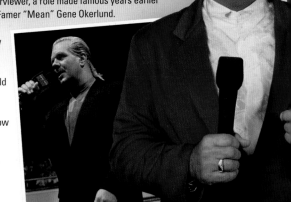

Dominic DeNucci

HT	6'3"	WT	245 lbs.	FROM	Pittsburgh, Pennsylvania

SIGNATURE MOVE	Airplane Spin

YEARS ACTIVE 1960-1969 1970-1979 1980-1989 1990-1999 2000-PRESENT

TITLE HISTORY	International Tag Team Champion, World Tag Team Champion

DeNucci debuted in WWE in 1965. Fans cheered his mat skills and strength, as he fought for all that was honorable. DeNucci won his first major title in 1971 when he teamed with Bruno Sammartino to defeat the Mongols and capture the International Tag Team Championship. In 1975, he teamed with Victor Rivera to win the World Tag Team Championship. DeNucci earned a third reign with the World Tag Team titles in 1978, partnering with Dino Bravo.

In the mid-1980s, DeNucci retired from the ring. He opened a wrestling school in Freedom, Pennsylvania and trained the likes of hardcore legend Mick Foley, former ECW Champion Shane Douglas, and former WCW referee Brian Hildebrand.

Dominic DeNucci & Dino Bravo

COMBINED WEIGHT	593 lbs.	

TITLE HISTORY	World Tag Team Champions

YEARS ACTIVE 1960-1969 1970-1979 1980-1989 1990-1999 2000-PRESENT

The team of Dominic DeNucci & Dino Bravo quickly rose through the tag team division's ranks as fans appreciated their blend of teamwork, agility, and strength. On March 14, 1978 they bested the terrors from Japan, Prof. Toru Tanaka & Mr. Fuji, to become World Tag Team Champions. Their championship reign ended when they lost the titles to the Yukon Lumberjacks on June 26, 1978. Both men continued to compete, but the pair was never able to recapture the tag team championship.

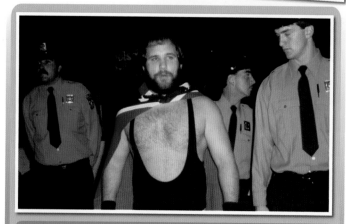

Don Kernodle

HT	6'1"	WT	290 lbs.	FROM	Burlington, North Carolina

YEARS ACTIVE 1960-1969 1970-1979 1980-1989 1990-1999 2000-PRESENT

As part of the legendary Sgt. Slaughter's Cobra Corps faction, Don Kernodle's early years were filled with a great education and many victories. Known then as Pvt. Don Kernodle, the North Carolinian used what he learned from Slaughter to rise to the top of the National Wrestling Alliance tag team ranks with partner Pvt. Jim Nelson.

In 1983, Kernodle began a successful union with "Cowboy" Bob Orton, before ultimately turning his back on the United States to align himself with hated Russian Ivan Koloff. In May 1984, Kernodle & Koloff captured the NWA Mid-Atlantic Tag Team Championship.

In addition to wrestling, Kernodle's resume features a role in the 1978 motion picture *Paradise Alley*. He appropriately played a wrestler, alongside other Superstars such as Dick Murdoch, Ted DiBiase, and Ray Stevens.

Don Leo Jonathan

HT	6'6"	WT	300 lbs.	FROM	Salt Lake City, Utah

YEARS ACTIVE 1960-1969 1970-1979 1980-1989 1990-1999 2000-PRESENT

Decades before high-flying action became the rage in sports-entertainment, Don Leo Jonathan was mesmerizing opponents with standing dropkicks, backflips, and even lofty leaps over the top rope. What made Jonathan's cat-like agility even more jaw-dropping was the fact that he was the size of a small tree at 6'6" and 300 pounds.

Over the course of his 30-year career, Jonathan competed all over the globe, including Europe, Canada, South Africa, Australia, and Japan. Known as "the Mormon Giant," Jonathan enjoyed his greatest notoriety in the early 1970s while battling another colossal figure, Andre the Giant. In addition, Jonathan found great success competing in the tag team division with such partners as Jimmy Snuka, Haystacks Calhoun, and Rocky Johnson.

DON MURACO

| HT | 6'3" | WT | 275 lbs. | FROM | Sunset Beach, Hawaii | TITLE HISTORY | Intercontinental Champion |

One of the most hated Superstars of the 1980s, Don Muraco was often showered with chants of "beach bum" while on his way to the ring. Once the bell rang, however, he proved to be anything but a bum. His technical mastery carried him to a Hall of Fame career, which was highlighted by two lengthy reigns as Intercontinental Champion.

Managed by the Grand Wizard, Muraco entered WWE in 1980. Dubbed "The Magnificent One," the cocky Superstar drew the fans' rage when he defeated the immensely popular Pedro Morales for the Intercontinental Championship in June 1981. Coincidentally, Morales was also the victim of Muraco's second Intercontinental Championship win in January 1983.

Muraco's second reign, which lasted a little more than one year, will forever be remembered by a title defense that many consider the greatest in Intercontinental Championship history. In October 1983, Muraco turned back challenger Jimmy "Superfly" Snuka in a grueling Madison Square Garden Steel Cage encounter. The result of the match, however, remains an afterthought. Instead, fans fondly recall Snuka executing his death-defying Superfly Splash from the top of the towering cage onto Muraco. Many Superstars credit the sight of Snuka flying through the air as their inspiration to enter sports-entertainment.

Muraco finally lost his title to Tito Santana in February 1984. Following the loss, "The Magnificent One" ascended to the top of the card, unsuccessfully challenging Hulk Hogan for the WWE Championship on several occasions. In 1987, Muraco took on the managerial services of fellow Hall of Famer "Superstar" Billy Graham. With a newly chiseled physique, Muraco worked his way into the good graces of the fans.

The new-look Muraco competed in the main event of the first-ever *Survivor Series* before disappearing from WWE in 1988. Eight years later, he returned to the WWE scene to induct longtime rival Jimmy Snuka in the WWE Hall of Fame. Muraco's successes were later recognized with his own induction in 2004.

Don Muraco & "Cowboy" Bob Orton

| COMBINED WEIGHT | 512 lbs. |

The devious Mr. Fuji used his resources to bring together the Magnificent Muraco and "Cowboy" Bob Orton in 1987. A tag team expert in his own right, Mr. Fuji taught both men the finer arts to tag team competition and how to sink to new lows to achieve victory.

Muraco & Orton were more than eager to display their new techniques, and along with Fuji, all three became quite efficient at brandishing a cane. Their rivalry with the Can-Am Connection culminated at the historic *WrestleMania III*. Although the rule-breakers didn't win, the largest live indoor audience in history watched them proudly show why they became one of the most abhorred tandems in WWE. The team continued to torment opponents and break the rules until the duo turned on each other in August.

Dory Funk, Jr.

| HT | 6'2" | WT | 240 lbs. | FROM | The Double Cross Ranch |

| SIGNATURE MOVE | Spinning Toe Hold |

This second-generation competitor made his debut in 1963 after receiving training from his famous father. In 1968, Dory, Jr. plied his trade in the NWA, where he enjoyed the second-longest reign as NWA Champion in history. During his travels, he invented the Texas Clover Leaf submission hold and Funk Forearm Uppercut.

In 1986, Dory ventured to WWE under his nickname, Hoss. He and brother Terry branded the logo of the Double Cross Ranch into the flesh of their beaten opponents. They engaged in a memorable rivalry with the Junkyard Dog that culminated in a Funk victory at *WrestleMania 2*. In 1994, the brothers moved to ECW. In 1996, Dory returned to WWE at the *Royal Rumble* and proved he could still put up a fierce fight.

In 1997, Dory opened the the Funkin' Conservatory to train future stars. Graduates of the school include the Hardy Boys, Edge, and Mickie James. After a heralded five-decade career, Dory Funk, Jr. is one of the most distinguished, respected, and celebrated figures of all time.

Doug Gilbert

HT	6'	**WT**	240 lbs.	**FROM**	Lexington, Tennessee	

SIGNATURE MOVE Piledriver

YEARS ACTIVE

Following in the footsteps of his father, Tommy, and brother, "Hot Stuff" Eddie Gilbert, "Dangerous" Doug Gilbert debuted in 1986.

Throughout the late 1980s and early 1990s, Doug competed in the United States, Puerto Rico and the NWA. As Doug's travels continued, he became well-versed in the hardcore style. In 1993, Doug was a member of the USWA and appeared on cards with several WWE Superstars. In 1996, Doug won a *Royal Rumble*-style match in Memphis. The winner of the match earned a spot in the *WWE Royal Rumble* weeks later in Fresno, CA.

Today, Doug still competes in the U.S., Puerto Rico and Japan. He has kept the Gilbert family name alive inside the ring and has added to its legacy.

The Dream Team

MEMBERS	Greg Valentine, Brutus Beefcake, Dino Bravo
COMBINED WEIGHT	520 lbs.
TITLE HISTORY	World Tag Team Champions

YEARS ACTIVE

The Dream Team consisted of an established, rugged second-generation Superstar and two-time Intercontinental Champion in Greg "The Hammer" Valentine, and a brash, powerful athlete in Brutus Beefcake whose strength was only second to his vanity. Managed by "Luscious" Johnny Valiant, this pair was considered championship contenders almost instantly. Valiant did an amazing job of bringing the two Superstars together and meshing their unique styles. The despised Beefcake and Valentine reached the top when they defeated the U.S. Express for the World Tag Team Championship on August 24, 1985 at the Philadelphia Spectrum.

The Dream Team broke every rule in the book to maintain a stranglehold on the titles. The duo enjoyed an almost seven-month reign as World Tag Team Champions until they faced the British Bulldogs at *WrestleMania 2*. While they continued to be threats within the tag team division, an associate was soon added in Canadian strongman Dino Bravo. Despite a win at *WrestleMania III* against the Rougeau Brothers, dissention within their ranks overflowed and Beefcake was left by himself in the ring. As Bravo became the new member of group, they were appropriately named the New Dream Team. Later that night Beefcake officially became a fan favorite as the "Barber" in him came out.

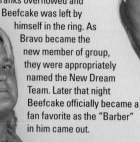

"Dr. D" David Schultz

HT	6'6"	**WT**	267 lbs.	**FROM**	Nashville, Tennessee

SIGNATURE MOVE Flying Corkscrew Elbow

YEARS ACTIVE

Before his assault on the ranks of World Wrestling Entertainment, David Schultz was one of the most feared men in wrestling territories across North America. To Dr. D, matches were not contests to determine which opponent was the better

man, they were personal wars where everything was on the line and no tactic was off-limits.

In 1984, Dr. D prescribed his form of pain in the WWE and aligned himself with "Rowdy" Roddy Piper, "Mr. Wonderful" Paul Orndorff, and "Cowboy" Bob Orton. As his reputation as one of the most dangerous men in WWE grew, his tenure with the company ended abruptly after a celebrated run-in with a news journalist turned physical while conducting a feature story on professional wrestling. "Dr. D" David Schultz will always be considered one of the ring's most dangerous figures who was always ready for a fight.

Droz   **YEARS ACTIVE**

HT	6'4"	**WT**	270 lbs.	**FROM**	Mays Landing, New Jersey

SIGNATURE MOVE New Jersey Naptime

In the early 1990s, Darren Drozdov was one of the top NCAA Football players in the United States. After a stint in the NFL, he trained for a life in the ring. After a short stay in ECW, Droz entered WWE in 1998 and caught the attention of Vince McMahon when he learned Droz could vomit on command. Droz's in-ring abilities caught the eye of the the Legion of Doom. When Droz donned spiked shoulder pads for the first time, a childhood dream was fulfilled. When the LOD went their separate ways, Droz formed an alliance with fellow pierced Superstar Albert.

Tragically on October 5, 1999, Droz suffered a career ending injury in a match that has confined him to a wheelchair. Droz continues to contribute to WWE through his commentaries on WWE. com and in print. Droz remains the fun-loving individual who is loved by all who know him and he is determined to one day walk again.

Dude Love & Stone Cold Steve Austin

COMBINED WEIGHT 552 lbs.

TITLE HISTORY

World Tag Team Champions

YEARS ACTIVE

1960-1969 | 1970-1979 | 1980-1989 | **1990-1999** | 2000-PRESENT

When injuries to Shawn Michaels prematurely ended the World Tag Team Championship reign of Stone Cold Steve Austin & HBK, the "Texas Rattlesnake" was able to choose a new partner when he battled Owen Hart & British Bulldog in a match to crown the new titlists. Mankind volunteered to be Stone Cold's new teammate, but Austin claimed he was better off by himself than with the deranged freak.

When the match began, Stone Cold planned on going into battle at a disadvantage, but much to his surprise, Mick Foley's fun-loving alter ego came to the ring to even the sides. The unlikely duo defeated Hart & Bulldog for the gold and went on to hold the titles for close to two months before a severe neck injury sidelined Stone Cold.

THE DUDLEY BOYS

MEMBERS D-Von, Bubba Ray **COMBINED WEIGHT** 565 lbs.

TITLE HISTORY World Tag Team Champions

YEARS ACTIVE 1960-1969 | 1970-1979 | 1980-1989 | 1990-1999 | **2000-PRESENT**

Few teams revolutionized tag team wrestling more than the Dudley Boys, and none have achieved more success. In fact, they are the only tandem in sports-entertainment history to capture the ECW, WCW, and World tag titles. Half-brothers D-Von & Bubba Ray Dudley first made a name for themselves competing in ECW during the late 1990s. While there, they earned a reputation as a hardcore powerhouse, as well as a record eight reigns with the promotion's tag titles.

In 1999, The Dudley Boys took their success to WWE where they gained instant national recognition. Within months, they were World Tag Team Champions. Furthermore, D-Von & Bubba Ray were painfully introducing a new brand of hardcore competition to WWE. The Dudley Boys' penchant for driving opponents through wooden tables via the Dudley Death Drop paved the way for several groundbreaking matches. At the 2000 *Royal Rumble*, D-Von & Bubba Ray battled the Hardy Boys in the first-ever Tag Team Tables Match. The popularity of the carnage eventually raised the stakes to even more dangerous encounters. Later that year, they took part in the first-ever Tables, Ladders & Chairs Match against Edge & Christian and the Hardy Boys at *SummerSlam*. The same three teams battled in an epic TLC encore at *WrestleMania X-Seven*. Both matches were won by Edge & Christian.

D-Von & Bubba Ray added to their already-historic resume when they defeated Matt & Jeff Hardy for the WCW Tag Team Championship in October 2001. They would later unify the WCW and WWE World Tag Team Championships when they defeated the Hardy Boys again at *Survivor Series*.

The unthinkable occurred in 2002 when the WWE Draft separated D-Von & Bubba Ray. On their own, the half-brothers failed to replicate the success they gained as a team. Luckily, their solo efforts only lasted eight months before they shockingly reunited at *Survivor Series*.

Together again, The Dudley Boys picked up right where they left off. By the time their WWE careers had ended, D-Von & Bubba Ray collected nine tag team championship reigns, as well as a legacy second to none.

Duke "The Dumpster" Droese

HT 6'6" **WT** 305 lbs.

FROM Mount Trashmore, Florida

YEARS ACTIVE

1960-1969 | 1970-1979 | 1980-1989 | **1990-1999** | 2000-PRESENT

When it comes to taking out the trash, few Superstars did it with as much enthusiasm as Duke "The Dumpster" Droese. Originally a sanitation engineer by trade, Droese made the transition from his garbage route to the ring with one goal in mind: ridding WWE of its trash.

According to Droese, the Superstar with the most stink on him was Hunter Hearst-Helmsley, and it was against Helmsley that Droese picked up the biggest victory of his career. With the coveted No. 30 spot in the 1996 *Royal Rumble* on the line, Droese defeated the Greenwich blue blood via reverse decision.

Unfortunately for Droese, Helmsley went on to have one of the greatest careers of all time, while the sanitation engineer soon found himself back on his garbage route. Droese did, however, manage to make a brief but memorable return to the ring in 2001 when he competed in *WrestleMania X-Seven*'s Gimmick Battle Royal, which was ultimately won by former WWE Champion the Iron Sheik.

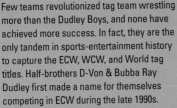

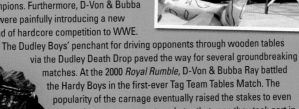

"THE AMERICAN DREAM" DUSTY RHODES

| **HT** 6'2" | **WT** 275 lbs. | **FROM** Austin, Texas | **SIGNATURE MOVE** Bionic Elbow |

YEARS ACTIVE  1960-1969 1970-1979 1980-1989 1990-1999 2000-PRESENT

The son of a plumber, Dusty Rhodes suffered from the crippling disease osteomyelitis, a bone affliction that prevented him from walking as a boy. As a man of the people, he possessed tremendous drive, courage and charisma that combined to make him 275 pounds of blue-eyed soul who captivated an entire nation.

In September 1977, "The American Dream" came to WWE and waged war against then-WWE Champion "Superstar" Billy Graham. Their matches sold out Madison Square Garden and culminated in a Texas Bullrope Match. Dusty left and went on to great success in Florida and the Carolinas region, enjoying three reigns as NWA Champion. His epic struggle against the Four Horsemen in the mid-1980s is widely considered one of the greatest rivalries of all time.

In 1990, Rhodes returned to WWE as the blue-collar worker for the common man. In polka-dotted ring trunks with his valet Sapphire, his popularity reached its greatest heights as he engaged in bitter rivalries

with the Big Boss Man, "Macho King" Randy Savage, and "Million-Dollar Man" Ted DiBiase. In the early 1990s, Dusty returned to WCW as a broadcaster. In 2000, he made a brief stop in ECW.

In 2005, he returned to WWE working behind the scenes. Even after five decades, he isn't afraid to step in the ring and show today's competitors how to mix it up, as witnessed at the 2006 *Survivor Series* when he teamed with Ric Flair, Sgt. Slaughter & Ron Simmons.

He's wined and dined with kings and queens, and he's slept in alleys and dined on pork and beans. Dusty Rhodes was the true working man's champion. As his son Cody said as he inducted Dusty into the WWE Hall of Fame in 2007, "He didn't need a 'Pit' or a 'Parlor,' all he needed was a mic." Dusty Rhodes has truly lived life at the end of a lightning bolt.

Dusty Wolfe

| **HT** 5'11" | **WT** 215 lbs. |

FROM San Antonio, Texas

SIGNATURE MOVE Spinning Toe Hold

YEARS ACTIVE 1960-1969 1970-1979 1980-1989 1990-1999 2000-PRESENT

Wolfe started his career in his hometown of San Antonio. In 1984, he decided it was time to travel to territories in Kansas City, Memphis, Florida, and the Von Erich's World Class region. From there, Wolfe traveled to Puerto Rico and Hawaii, becoming skilled in various ring styles.

Dusty Wolfe debuted in WWE in 1987 and quickly became a staple on its televised programs. He traded blows with the likes of Jake Roberts, "Ravishing" Rick Rude, "Hacksaw" Jim Duggan, the Blue Blazer, and the Junkyard Dog. In 1993, Wolfe left WWE and resumed his independent promotion travels in Puerto Rico, South Africa and Japan until 1996. For the next two years, he appeared in WCW before he resumed his mat career on the independent circuit.

A dream that began at 18 years of age turned into a 20-plus year career. When asked to summarize his career, Wolfe was once quoted as saying, "Getting in the ring was a privilege."

Dynamite Kid

YEARS ACTIVE 1960-1969 1970-1979 1980-1989 1990-1999 2000-PRESENT

| **HT** 5'9" | **WT** 225 lbs. | **FROM** Manchester, England | **SIGNATURE MOVE** Flying Headbutt |

TITLE HISTORY World Tag Team Champion, Junior Heavyweight Champion

Faster than greased lighting, as tough and technically sound as anyone to lace up a pair of boots, Dynamite Kid did it all in the ring. Dynamite Kid's innovative offensive moves influenced everyone who saw him in action.

Bruce Hart brought the Dynamite Kid to Stampede Wrestling after watching him in action in the late 1970s. In the early 1980s, Dynamite Kid was a top contender for the WWE Junior Heavyweight Championship. In his Madison Square Garden debut in 1982, he faced then-champion Tiger Mask. The bouts between the pair made headlines all over the world. Dynamite Kid eventually captured the Junior Heavyweight crown in February, 1984 when he defeated the Cobra.

Later that year, Dynamite Kid joined with Davey Boy Smith to form the British Bulldogs. With Lou Albano in their corner, they claimed the World Tag Team Championship at *WrestleMania 2*. After losing the titles to the Hart Foundation, the Bulldogs left WWE in November 1988.

Dynamite Kid retired from active competition in 1991, and released his autobiography titled *Pure Dynamite* in 1999. Dynamite Kid will be remembered as one of the most innovative, and possibly the greatest pound-for-pound, Superstars of all-time.

Earl Hebner

For close to 20 years, Earl Hebner served as the third man in the ring for some of WWE's biggest matches. He was also behind many of the promotion's most controversial moments.

In February 1988, Dave Hebner was assigned the WWE Championship Match between Hulk Hogan and Andre the Giant. Prior to the match, Ted DiBiase paid Earl to have plastic surgery to look more like his brother. DiBiase then locked Dave in a backstage room and sent Earl to call the match. In the end, evil Earl proved to be under DiBiase's influence, as he called the match in Andre's favor, thus ending Hogan's four-year reign at the top.

Nearly 10 years later, Earl was at the center of controversy again when he prematurely called for the bell during the WWE Championship Match between Shawn Michaels and Bret Hart. The controversial call ended the match, which is now commonly referred to as the Montreal Incident, and Hart's championship reign.

Earl Maynard

HT 5'11" **WT** 240 lbs.

FROM Barbados

SIGNATURE MOVE Headbutt

YEARS ACTIVE 1960 1969 · 1970 1979 · 1980 1989 · 1990 1999 · 2000 PRESENT

As a boy growing up in Barbados, Earl Maynard had visions of greatness. Already a top bodybuilder, and member of the British Air Force, he wrestled as a means of staying in peak physical condition.

For two decades he pulled double-duty as a Superstar in both sports-entertainment and body building. While in the World Wide Wrestling Federation, Maynard collided with the likes of Baron Mikel Scicluna, Johnny Rodz, and Gorilla Monsoon.

In 1968, Earl added another element to his already versatile persona and made his silver screen debut in the feature film *Melinda*. He continued to appear in films for many years, and today he is a film producer/director. He's viewed as a legend in both the ring and bodybuilding circles.

Earthquake

YEARS ACTIVE 1960 1969 · 1970 1979 · 1980 1989 · 1990 1999 · 2000 PRESENT

HT 6'7" **WT** 468 lbs. **FROM** Vancouver, British Columbia, Canada

SIGNATURE MOVE Earthquake Splash **TITLE HISTORY** World Tag Team Champion

With more than 450 pounds tacked to his enormous frame, Earthquake made arenas shake and Superstars tremble every time he walked the aisle. Behind the threat of his ring-rattling Earthquake Splash finisher, the massive Superstar was a perennial contender for every WWE title.

Disguised as a fan, Earthquake made his WWE debut in November 1989 when Jimmy Hart pulled him out of the audience to sit on Ultimate Warrior's back as the Superstar attempted pushups. Once in the ring, Earthquake revealed his allegiance to Hart by squashing the unexpected Warrior. From that point on, the oversized Superstar proved himself as one of WWE's most dangerous competitors. His assaults were so severe, in fact, that many of his opponents were forced to leave the ring on a stretcher.

Earthquake quickly reached main event status after attacking Hulk Hogan on an edition of *The Brother Love Show*. The assault left the Hulkster's ribs severely injured and made Earthquake the target of the fans' hatred worldwide. Their rivalry culminated at *SummerSlam 1990* where Hogan earned a countout victory over the big man.

The following year, Earthquake teamed with Typhoon to form the colossal tag team known as the Natural Disasters. Together, they defeated Money Inc. to capture the World Tag Team Championship in July 1992.

The East-West Connection

MEMBERS
Adrian Adonis, Jesse "The Body" Ventura

COMBINED WEIGHT 580 lbs.

YEARS ACTIVE 1960 1969 · 1970 1979 · 1980 1989 · 1990 1999 · 2000 PRESENT

This team first formed in the late 1970s in Verne Gagne's AWA. Noticed by "Classy" Freddie Blassie, Adonis & Ventura were brought to WWE in 1981. With Blassie in their corner, they became prime-time players in WWE. Whether contending for the World Tag Team titles, or as individuals for the WWE Championship, the East-West Connection could beat anyone from any direction.

A combination of injuries and different goals led to their separation, although they remained close allies. Ventura went on to become one of the greatest color commentators ever and a 2004 WWE Hall of Fame inductee. Adonis transformed into one of WWE's most versatile and gifted performers. The legendary East-West Connection should always be included in a discussion of influential tag teams. Whether you approved of their practices or not, you can't deny their success.

DEBUT 2006

ECW CHAMPIONSHIP

The original ECW, a grassroots independent promotion that became a phenomenon in the Eastern United States, helped redefine sports-entertainment into what it is today. Housed in Philadelphia's ECW Arena, which was actually a bingo hall, Paul Heyman and Tod Gordon created a fertile breeding ground for many of the Superstars who are household names today. Caught in the crossfire between WWE and WCW during the infamous Monday Night Wars, ECW lost key talent to the larger promotions and struggled financially, eventually going out of business in 2001.

WWE acquired the assets to ECW in 2003. In 2005 under the WWE banner, the brand was gloriously resurrected at *ECW One Night Stand*, which was a tremendous success. One year later, ECW returned and became WWE's third active brand, and the brand has flourished, once again serving as a proving ground of many of today's young Superstars.

When the ECW brand was relaunched in June, 2006, Paul Heyman awarded the championship to Rob Van Dam, who was also the reigning WWE Champion. Since then, some of the biggest names in sports-entertainment have fought tenaciously to hold the title.

2006

JAN 13 Trenton, NJ
Rob Van Dam is named ECW Champion

JULY 04 Philadelphia, PA
Big Show defeats Rob Van Dam

While the figures and settings may have changed, the force behind ECW remains the same. Superstars like ECW Original Tommy Dreamer, John Morrison, The Miz, Chavo Guerrero, Matt Hardy, Mark Henry, and Elijah Burke strive for hardcore supremacy with every bit of intensity that their predecessors.

DEC 03 Lowell, MA
Bobby Lashley defeats Big Show
Bobby Lashley pinned Big Show in an Extreme Elimination Chamber Match that also included Rob Van Dam, CM Punk, Test, and Hardcore Holly

2007

APR 29 Atlanta, GA
Mr. McMahon defeats Bobby Lashley

JUNE 03 Jacksonville, FL
Bobby Lashley defeats Mr. McMahon

On June 11, Bobby Lashley is stripped of the title when he is drafted to *Raw*.

JUNE 25 Houston, TX
John Morrison defeats CM Punk

SEP 01 Cincinnait, OH
CM Punk defeats John Morrison

2008

JAN 22 Charlottesville, VA
Chavo Guerrero defeats CM Punk

MAR 30 Orlando, FL
Kane defeats Chavo Guerrero

JUNE 29 Dallas, TX
Mark Henry defeats Kane

SEP 07 Cleveland, OH
Matt Hardy becomes ECW Champion
Matt Hardy pinned the Miz in a Championship Scramble Match that also included Mark Henry, Finlay, and Chavo Guerrero.

Eddie Gilbert

| **HT** 5'10" | **WT** 222 lbs. | **FROM** Lexington, Tennessee |

SIGNATURE MOVE Hot Shot

YEARS ACTIVE

Proudly nicknamed "Hot Stuff," Eddie Gilbert certainly had a high opinion of his in-ring abilities. Coming from the popular Gilbert wrestling family, he had every right to be a little cocky. Growing up, Eddie and brother Doug learned the business firsthand from their father, Tennessee wrestling great Tommy Gilbert.

Despite being remembered as one the South's greatest competitors, Gilbert's brief WWE career never really took off. He gained some notoriety as a protégé to WWE Champion Bob Backlund. The relationship, however, was short-lived and Gilbert soon returned to the South.

Gilbert owns the distinction of being involved in the first-ever NWA pay-per-view match. Teaming with Larry Zbyszko & Rick Steiner, he battled Sting, Michael Hayes & Jimmy Garvin at *Starrcade 1987*. Over the next several years, Gilbert gained the reputation of coming up big when it counted, including several times against Jerry "The King" Lawler when the United States Wrestling Association Unified World Heavyweight Championship was on the line.

Eddie Graham

| **HT** 5'11" | **WT** 215 lbs. | **FROM** Tampa, Florida |

TITLE HISTORY United States Tag Team Champion

YEARS ACTIVE

WWE's national spotlight never really shined on Eddie Graham, but that doesn't mean he wasn't one of the most influential personalities of his time. Over the course of his 30-year career, Graham became known as a skilled competitor and brilliant promoter.

Early in his career, Graham teamed with his brother, Jerry, to capture the United States Tag Team Championship four times while competing in Vincent J. McMahon's Capitol Wrestling. The success led to great notoriety in the Northeast, but it wasn't until he moved to Florida in 1960 that Graham really began to come into his own.

By 1968, Graham had become a legend in Florida, but when a locker room window fell on his head, he was forced to sit on the sidelines for 15 months. Unable to compete, Graham still managed to make waves when he took over responsibilities of Championship Wrestling from Florida. As promoter of the popular territory, Graham built an impressive roster, which included such legends as Dusty Rhodes, Dory Funk, Jr., and Bruiser Brody.

Graham's power continued to grow in 1976 when he was elected president of the National Wrestling Alliance. While in office, he helped create the first-ever World title unification match, which pit NWA Champion Harley Race against WWE Champion "Superstar" Billy Graham. Health reasons forced Graham to step down from his post in 1978, officially marking the end of one of the most influential careers of his time.

HALL OF FAME 2008

EDDIE GUERRERO

"LATINO HEAT"

HT	5'8"	WT	220 lbs.

FROM El Paso, Texas

SIGNATURE MOVE Frog Splash, Lasso from El Paso

TITLE HISTORY WWE Champion, WWE Tag Team Champion, Intercontinental Champion, United States Champion, European Champion

YEARS ACTIVE 1960-1969 1970-1979 1980-1989 **1990-1999** **2000-PRESENT**

The story of Eddie Guerrero is one of inspiration and heartbreak. After personal demons cost the second-generation Superstar his career and family, he dedicated himself to becoming clean and returning to society. The inspirational Guerrero eventually defeated his demons and returned to greatness. Tragically, however, Eddie Guerrero was taken from this world shortly after clawing his way back to the top of sports-entertainment.

SECOND GENERATION SUPERSTAR

As the son of influential Mexican wrestler Gory Guerrero, Eddie grew up in and around the business. From an early age, it was clear his passion was sports-entertainment. He spent most of his time in the family's wrestling ring, which was situated in the backyard. Before his fifth birthday, he was already delivering dropkicks to his older brothers.

Once he became old enough, Guerrero started competing professionally in Mexico and Japan. It wasn't until he began working for Extreme Championship Wrestling in 1995 that he gained any true exposure in the United States. While in ECW, Guerrero captured the Television Championship on two occasions, but it was classic matches against Dean Malenko that caught the eye of World Championship Wrestling (WCW) officials.

While things were going great for Guerrero inside the ring, his personal life was in severe jeopardy. In 1999, an impaired Guerrero nearly killed himself in a violent car wreck. Fortunately, Guerrero lived, but he failed to address the demons that were invading his life. In 2000, Guerrero moved to WWE where he gained instant notoriety as Chyna's fun-loving boyfriend. Affectionately referred to as "Latino Heat," Guerrero won the European and Intercontinental Championships within his first year with the company. Guerrero's in-ring success couldn't help fend off his personal demons. Addiction again caught up with him. This time, it cost him his wife and his job. He had hit rock bottom.

TURNING AROUND HIS LIFE

Rather than slipping further into addiction, Guerrero used his recent woes to help drive him. He eventually crushed his demons, won back his wife and was given a second chance with WWE. The WWE fans welcomed back the new Eddie Guerrero with open arms. Much like his first stint with the company, he compiled an impressive list of championships. In addition to becoming a four-time WWE Tag Team Champion (twice with his nephew Chavo, once with Tajiri, once with Rey Mysterio), Guerrero had the honor of bringing the United States Championship back to prominence in 2003.

Guerrero's greatest in-ring conquest came in February 2004 when he defeated Brock Lesnar for the WWE Championship at *No Way Out*. The victory brought Guerrero full circle and completed his quest for redemption. As WWE Champion, Guerrero earned the ultimate opportunity of defending his title at *WrestleMania XX* at the famed Madison Square Garden. In the world of sports-entertainment, there is no greater honor. Guerrero seized the opportunity, defeating Kurt Angle to retain the title.

Guerrero's inspirational WWE Championship reign came to an end when John "Bradshaw" Layfield defeated him in a Texas Bull Rope Match at *The Great American Bash* in June 2004. Undeterred by the loss, Guerrero, as he had done so many times before, fought to regain his lofty status. By late 2005, he had solidified himself as a legitimate threat for the World Heavyweight Championship.

A TRAGIC END

On November 13, 2005, Eddie Guerrero was found dead in his hotel room in Minneapolis. He was thirty-eight. In the days that followed, the entire wrestling world publicly mourned the tragic loss of an inspirational human being. In 2006, Guerrero took his rightful place in wrestling history when he was posthumously inducted into the WWE Hall of Fame. The night's celebration was proof that the great memories of Eddie Guerrero will live on forever.

Superstars gather in tribute to Eddie Guerrero.

Eddie Guerrero celebrating his victory over Brock Lesnar.

EDGE 🍁

YEARS ACTIVE | 1960-1969 | 1970-1979 | 1980-1989 | **1990-1999** | **2000-PRESENT**

HT 6'5" **WT** 250 lbs. **FROM** Toronto, Canada **SIGNATURE MOVE** Spear

TITLE HISTORY WWE Champion, World Heavyweight Champion, Intercontinental Champion, United States Champion, World Tag Team Champion

After he experienced "The Ultimate Challenge" at *WrestleMania VI* from a seat in Toronto's SkyDome and saw his hero Hulk Hogan battle Ultimate Warrior, Edge swore to one day headline a *WrestleMania*. After winning an essay writing contest in the *Toronto Star*, he received free wrestling training by Sweet Daddy Siki and Ron Hutchinson at Sully's Gym. Edge made his WWE debut in 1998. He first started to shine as part of a tag team during the WWE's "Attitude" Era. Along with Christian, Edge was a part of the one of the most famous tag teams in sports-entertainment history. He was involved in some of the most brutal matches the world has ever seen. Edge & Christian won their first World Tag Team Championship in the Tables, Ladders & Chairs Match at *WrestleMania 2000*.

When Edge & Christian split, Edge established himself as a singles star after he won the 2001 *King of the Ring*. On the July 4, 2002 episode of *SmackDown*, he teamed with childhood idol Hulk Hogan and captured the World Tag Team Championship.

In November 2004, his autobiography, *Adam Copeland on Edge*, was released. It was a huge hit among WWE fans. Edge etched his name in the history books once again in 2005 when he competed in the inaugural "Money In The Bank" Ladder Match at *WrestleMania 21*. After the Elimination Chamber at *New Year's Revolution 2006*, Edge cashed in his Money in the Bank clause to face John Cena and speared his way to his first WWE Championship. Since then, sports-entertainment's quintessential opportunist hasn't looked back.

Throughout his awesome career he's suffered a torn ACL, ruptured labra, a broken neck, a fractured skull, and countless stitches. After over a decade in WWE, the "Rated-R Superstar" has become recognized as one of its most detested and decorated figures. He has proven over and over again that he will go to any lengths to achieve what he wants, when he wants. He is one of the most talented, ruthless, and resilient competitors WWE has ever known.

While Edge has been involved in a great number of rivalries, perhaps none was more personal than his clashes with Matt Hardy over his relationship with Lita.

EDGE & CHRISTIAN 🍁

YEARS ACTIVE | 1960-1969 | 1970-1979 | 1980-1989 | **1990-1999** | **2000-PRESENT**

COMBINED WEIGHT 470 lbs. **TITLE HISTORY** World Tag Team Champions

Despite seven reigns atop the tag team division (and reeking of awesomeness) Edge & Christian were never very well liked by WWE audiences, but that didn't stop them from giving back to the fans. "For the benefit of those with flash photography," the two would say, "we'll strike a five-second pose for you."

With their oversized sunglasses and corny catchphrases, Edge & Christian would always manage to get a reluctant laugh out of the fans who loved to hate them. In the ring, however, their offensive onslaught was no joke. They first began to open eyes as a unit when they competed against Matt & Jeff Hardy in the Terri Invitational Tournament in 1999. The best-of-five series culminated in a Ladder Match, which proved to be a precursor for the innovative action the team would display in the years that followed.

Edge & Christian captured their first World Tag Team Championship by turning back the Dudley Boys and the Hardy Boys at *WrestleMania 2000*. The encounter, which was dubbed a Triangle Ladder Match, ultimately featured both tables and chairs as weapons. The popularity of the destruction witnessed in the now-famous match eventually led to the creation of the Tables, Ladders & Chairs (TLC) Match. Over the next year, Edge & Christian proved themselves masters of the TLC Match, defeating the Dudleys and Hardys at *SummerSlam* and *WrestleMania X-Seven*.

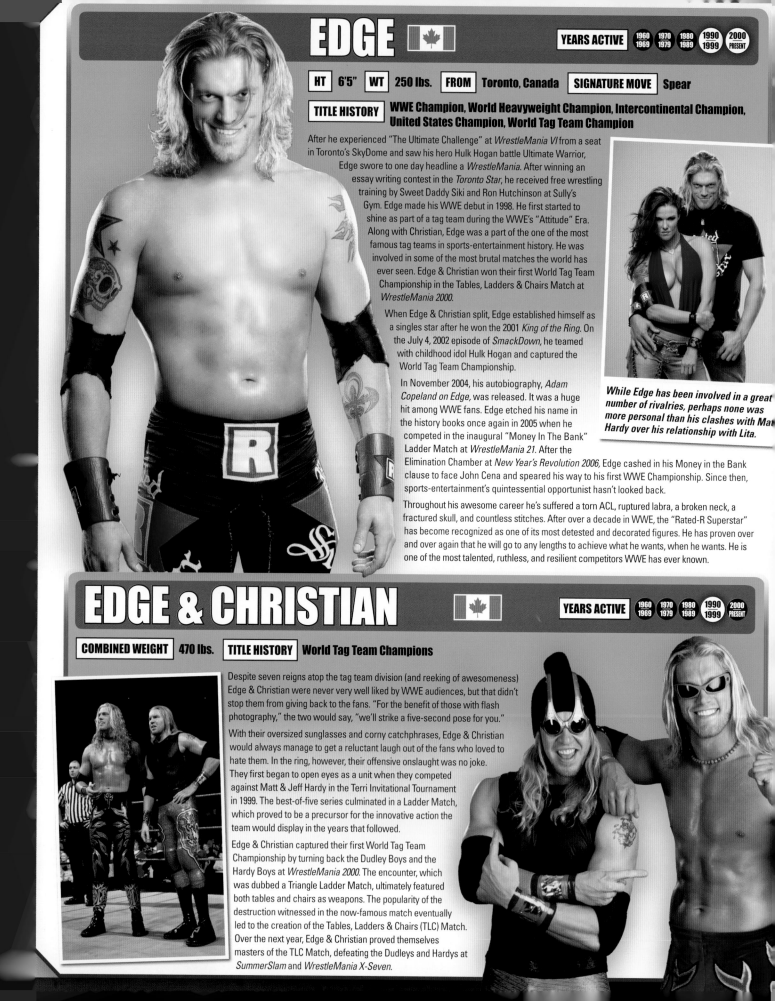

Edouard Carpentier 🇨🇦

| HT | 5'10" | WT | 228 lbs. |

FROM Montreal, Quebec, Canada

SIGNATURE MOVE Flying Head Scissors

YEARS ACTIVE   1960-1969 1970-1979 1980-1989 1990-1999 2000-PRESENT

Many WWE fans recognize Edouard Carpentier as the host of the company's French broadcast of WWE programming during the 1980s, but it was his awe-inspiring arsenal of high-flying ring action that endeared him to fans decades prior.

Dubbed "the Flying Frenchman", Carpentier's aerial assault left opponents' heads spinning. His acrobatic style eventually lead him to a reign as National Wrestling Alliance (NWA) Champion. He defeated the legendary Lou Thesz for the title in June 1957; his reign was marred by controversy when the NWA later failed to recognized the victory after Carpentier's manager left the promotion. The incident will forever be remembered as one of the most controversial moments in the NWA's history.

El Olympico 🇲🇽

| HT | 5'9" | WT | 234 lbs. |

FROM Mexico City, Mexico

SIGNATURE MOVE Flying Cross Body

YEARS ACTIVE   1960-1969 1970-1979 1980-1989 1990-1999 2000-PRESENT

This high-flying masked man began his career in his homeland of Mexico and arrived in the World Wide Wrestling Federation in 1972. He became an instant fan-favorite with his mixture of high flying maneuvers and submission holds. El Olympico showcased his skills in front of a packed Shea Stadium at the 1972 Showdown At Shea as he defeated Chuck O'Connor.

The man from South of the border stood opposite side of the ring from greats including Dory Funk, Sr., Terry Funk, Greg "The Hammer" Valentine and Mr. Fuji. By the end of the 1970s, El Olympico returned to Mexico, but this virtuoso of *lucha libre* will always be fondly remembered as someone who upheld the tradition of Mexican wrestling no matter where the fight took him.

EIGHT-MAN TAG MATCH

This type of match consists of eight total participants, with four competitors to a team. Historically, this match takes place when some or all those involved have scores to settle. It can be held in different variations including standard tag team rules, where two participants are in the ring and must tag in and out, one pinfall for victory. Alternately, elimination rules can be applied where the odds become stacked in the favor of one team as fast as a referee's three-count. An Eight-Man Tag Match can also employ Texas Tornado rules where all eight Superstars are in the ring fighting at once though this happens rarely.

Elijah Burke 🇺🇸

YEARS ACTIVE   1960-1969 1970-1979 1980-1989 1990-1999 2000-PRESENT

| HT | 6'1" | WT | 235 lbs. | **FROM** | Jacksonville, Florida |

SIGNATURE MOVE The Elijah Express

Elijah Burke is a naturally gifted athlete who has won several tough man contests across the Eastern seaboard of the U.S. He also boasts an amateur boxing record of 103-1, with 102 KOs.

Elijah first appeared on *SmackDown* in July 2006. In November, he joined the ranks of ECW, where he disrespected the original ECW establishment: Rob Van Dam, Sabu, Tommy Dreamer, and the Sandman. The "Paragon of Virtue" formed a faction called the New Breed to battle the ECW Originals at *WrestleMania 23*. Time will tell how far this Superstar will go within WWE. However, it's important to understand that he will not allow anyone to stand in his way. A warning to any challengers: If you cross his path, you will feel the force of the Elijah Experience.

ELIMINATION CHAMBER

Created by *Raw* general manager Eric Bischoff in 2002, the Elimination Chamber combines elements from *Royal Rumble*, *Survivor Series*, and *War Games* matches into one steel structure. Designed with the sole intention of punishing the human body, the Chamber consists of two miles of chain, 10 tons of steel and is a gigantic 36 feet in diameter.

An Elimination Chamber Match starts with two Superstars in the ring. After a predetermined length of time, a new Superstar is released from his pod in the Chamber and enters the battle. This continues until six Superstars enter the match. Eliminations can only occur via pinfall or submission. After five Superstars are eliminated, the last man standing is declared the victor.

The inaugural Elimination Chamber Match took place at *Survivor Series 2002*. Triple H walked into the encounter as World Heavyweight Champion. By night's end, however, he had spilled buckets of blood, lost his title and was about to embark on a 48-hour stay in the hospital. A battered Shawn Michaels was declared the winner of the match, which also included Booker T, Rob Van Dam, Chris Jericho, and Kane.

Over the next several years, the danger of the match caused the Elimination Chamber to be used very sparingly. As a result, only a handful of Superstars can stake claim to a victory inside the steel structure, including John Cena, Undertaker, and Triple H.

ELIMINATION MATCH

An Elimination Match is either a tag team match or a match with any number of participants in which once a competitor is pinned, he or she is no longer part of the match. Sometimes when a Superstar is pinned in a tag match, it forces that person's partner to leave the ring area as well. This style of match became famous at *Survivor Series* where teams strived to survive. In the early 1990s, a Three Way Dance (much like a Triple Threat Match in WWE) became popular in Extreme Championship Wrestling. The first fall would eliminate a competitor, at which point the match became a traditional one-fall contest between the two remaining combatants. A variation is the Fatal Four Way Match, where four participants are in the ring at the same time and, on occasion, uses the same rules as the Three-Way Dance.

ELIZABETH

Decades after making her WWE debut, Elizabeth's impact is still being felt today. Appropriately dubbed the "First Lady of Sports-Entertainment," her gentle-yet-influential contributions helped pave the way for all the females that followed.

In 1985, WWE newcomer Randy "Macho Man" Savage set out on a search to find a manager. Nearly every personality with a manager's license threw his hat in the ring. In the end, Savage unveiled the beautiful Miss Elizabeth as his choice. Over the next seven years, Savage and Elizabeth's very public rollercoaster relationship provided fans with a soap-opera type romance never before seen in WWE.

Upon her debut, both fans and Superstars were smitten by her innocent smile and impeccable style. The admiration she received, however, didn't sit well with Savage. The jealous Superstar continually took his frustrations out on his harmless manager, despite the fact that she never acted on anybody's advances.

The always-classy Elizabeth took Savage's verbal attacks in stride. Instead of simply walking away, she stood by her man and helped guide him to greatness. In 1988, Elizabeth achieved the ultimate goal when she managed Savage to the WWE Championship at *WrestleMania IV*. The win made Elizabeth the first female to manage a WWE Champion.

Elizabeth's relationship with Savage reached its boiling point in 1989 when her friendship with Hulk Hogan sent Macho Man into a jealous rage. The couple split soon after, sending Elizabeth into a more private lifestyle and Savage into a working relationship with Sensational Sherri.

In 1991, after Savage lost a Retirement Match to Ultimate Warrior at *WrestleMania VII*, Elizabeth reemerged to save her man from an attacking Sherri. Following the save, Elizabeth and Savage shared a loving embrace that drew tears of happiness from nearly everybody watching. The couple celebrated their love later that year when they married at *SummerSlam 1991*. The smile on Elizabeth's face told the entire story of a beautiful woman who finally found happiness in WWE.

ERIC BISCHOFF

HT 5'10" **WT** 195 lbs. **FROM** Detroit, Michigan

Eric Bischoff began his sports-entertainment career in August 1987 in the syndication and sales department for Verne Gagne's American Wrestling Association (AWA). He made the transition from behind the desk to behind the microphone and joined the long line of famous AWA announcers. In 1991, Eric Bischoff moved to World Championship Wrestling (WCW), where he began a complete overhaul of a fledgling division of Turner Broadcasting.

After he launched *WCW Monday Nitro* live in 1995, the face of sports-entertainment changed and The Monday Night Wars began. He signed major stars away from WWE, made innovations in how the product was presented, acquired talent from ECW, and is credited for the creation of the nWo. Under Eric Bischoff's direction, WCW went from a perennial also-ran to an over $300 million dollar sports-entertainment and broadcasting front-runner that won the ratings war 84 weeks in a row. When he left the company in 1999, he did so as the president of Turner/Time Warner's WCW Division.

Bischoff once again made sports-entertainment history in 2002 when he was introduced by Mr. McMahon as the new General Manager of *Raw*. No one in their wildest dreams thought this controversial figure, who tried to put McMahon out of business, would walk onto *Raw* and embrace the WWE Chairman, then join forces with him.

As General Manager, Eric pushed his personal agenda and maintained his special gift of making enemies wherever he went. In 2006, his autobiography, *Controversy Creates Cash*, was released and sky-rocketed to *The New York Times Bestseller List*.

Despite the fact that Mr. Bischoff is likely not on top of many "most popular" lists, his achievements, business contributions, and successes are indisputable. Sports-entertainment would not be where it is today without the drive, and commitment Eric Bischoff has displayed in his over 20-plus years in the sports-entertainment industry.

ERNIE LADD

Hall of Fame 1995

HT 6'9" **WT** 320 lbs. **FROM** New Orleans, Lousiana

Ernie "The Big Cat" Ladd was a two-sport athlete before being a two-sport athlete was vogue. After being selected by the San Diego Chargers in the 1961 American Football League draft, Ladd called the gridiron home for eight grueling seasons. During this time, he played in three AFL Championship Games, winning titles in 1963 with the Chargers and 1967 with the Kansas City Chiefs.

While still an active member of the AFL, Ladd took part in a publicity stunt that saw him answer the challenge of several Los Angeles wrestlers. He went into the encounter assuming he would mop the floor with the smaller competition. Instead, they proved their dominance over Ladd, which eventually fueled the fire within "The Big Cat" to learn the craft of wrestling.

Ladd began wrestling in the Los Angeles area during AFL off-seasons. Behind the name he already built for himself on the field, he became an instant hit, as fans loved to hate the arrogant footballer-turned-wrestler.

Ladd landed in WWE in 1968. Guided by legendary manager the Grand Wizard, he became a perennial challenger for the promotion's top prize. When he wasn't trying to claim the WWE Championship from Bruno Sammartino, he was engaging in memorable rivalries with fellow big men Andre the Giant, Gorilla Monsoon, and Haystacks Calhoun.

When his in-ring career came to a close, Ladd remained a part of the wrestling community as a manager and color commentator. His most notable time behind the mic saw him call a portion of the action at *WrestleMania 2*.

In 1981, the San Diego Chargers recognized Ladd as a gridiron great when they inducted him into their Hall of Fame. His in-ring accomplishments were later honored when he was enshrined in the WWE Hall of Fame in 1995.

Essa Rios 🇲🇽

| HT | 5'10" | WT | 215 lbs. | FROM | Guadalajara, Mexico |

SIGNATURE MOVE Moonsault

TITLE HISTORY Light Heavyweight Championship

YEARS ACTIVE 1960-1969 · 1970-1979 · 1980-1989 · 1990-1999 · **2000 PRESENT**

In February 2000, Essa Rios debuted on *Sunday Night Heat* accompanied by his valet, Lita. He was a highly regarded competitor and was immediately given a shot at Gillberg's Light Heavyweight Championship, which he won in under a minute. He didn't hold the title for long, though, and became increasingly angered by mounting losses. After losing a match, his frustration boiled over and he turned on Lita, attacking her until the Hardy Boys came to her rescue. In 2001, Essa Rios left WWE and returned to Mexico. Since then, he has appeared in various promotions throughout his homeland and the United States.

Eugene 🇺🇸

| HT | 6'1" | WT | 225 lbs. | FROM | Louisville, Kentucky |

SIGNATURE MOVE Special versions of other Superstar's moves

TITLE HISTORY World Tag Team Champion

YEARS ACTIVE 1960-1969 · 1970-1979 · 1980-1989 · 1990-1999 · **2000 PRESENT**

When Eugene first arrived on the WWE scene in April 2004, nobody would have predicted he'd become a future World Tag Team Champion. As the special-needs nephew of *Raw* General Manager Eric Bischoff, Eugene was seen by many as a non-threat. When the bell rang, Eugene proved to be a wrestling savant.

Using moves he learned while watching his favorite Superstars years earlier, Eugene was able to catch opponents off guard en route to an impressive early career. In addition to his expansive repertoire of moves, Eugene also possessed incredible strength.

Despite being a special Superstar, Eugene managed to earn major pay-per-view matches against the industry's greatest stars, including contests against Triple H and Kurt Angle on back-to-back *SummerSlam* cards. However, it was his teaming with William Regal that garnered the most success. In November 2004, the duo defeated La Resistance and Tajiri & Rhyno on *Raw* to capture the coveted World Tag Team Championship.

EUROPEAN CHAMPIONSHIP

Introduced to WWE audiences in February 1997, the European Championship was widely recognized as a stepping-stone to great many of its holders went on to capture World Championships lat careers, including Triple H, Kurt Angle, and Eddie Guerrero.

After defeating Owen Hart in a tournament final, the British Bulldo recognized as the first-ever European Champion. His reign laste than 200 days, longer than any other European Champion in histo title was eventually vacated in July 2002 when Rob Van Dam def Hardy to unify the European and Intercontinental Championships

1997

FEB 26 Berlin, Germany

British Bulldog defeats Owen Hart

In the finals of a tournament to crown the first-ever European Champion, British Bulldog defeated Owen Hart.

SEPT 20 Birmingham, England

Shawn Michaels defeats British Bulldog

DEC 22 Lowell, MA

Triple H defeats Shawn Michaels

1998

JAN 22 Davis, CA

Owen Hart defeats Goldust

Owen Hart beat Goldust, who was dressed as then-champion Triple H, to win the European Championship. Despite Triple H not officially being involved in the match, Commissioner Sgt. Slaughter allowed the decision to stand.

MAR 16 Phoenix, AZ

Triple H defeats Owen Hart

JULY 20 Binghamton, NY

D-Lo Brown defeats Triple H

SEPT 21 Sacramento, CA

X-Pac defeats D-Lo Brown

OCT 05 East Lansing, MI

D-Lo Brown defeats X-Pac

OCT 18 Chicago, IL

X-Pac defeats D-Lo Brown

1999

FEB 15 Birmingham, AL

Shane McMahon defeats X-Pac

Shane McMahon and Kane defeated X-Pac and Triple H when McMahon pinned X-Pac. Pre-match stipulations stated that if anybody pinned X-Pac, that man would be awarded the European Championship.

JUNE 21 Memphis, TN

Mideon becomes European Champion

Mideon was declared European Champion after he found the title in Shane McMahon's bag.

JULY 25 Buffalo, NY

D-Lo Brown defeats Mideon

AUG 22 Minneapolis, MN

Jeff Jarrett defeats D-Lo Brown

AUG 23 Ames, IA

Mark Henry becomes European Champion

Jeff Jarrett awarded the European Championship to Mark Henry after he helped Jarrett defeat D-Lo Brown one night earlier.

SEPT 26 Charlotte, NC

D-Lo Brown defeats Mark Henry

OCT 28 Springfield, MA

British Bulldog defeats D-Lo Brown

DEC 12 Fort Lauderdale, F

Val Venis defeats British Bulldog

Val Venis pinned British Bulldog to win the European Championship in a Triple Threat Match that also included D'Lo Brown.

2000

FEB 10 Austin, TX

Kurt Angle defeats Val Venis

APR 02 Anaheim, CA

Chris Jericho defeats Chris Benoit

Chris Jericho pinned Chris Benoit to win the European Championship in a Triple Threat Match that also included then-champion Kurt Angle.

APR 03	Los Angeles, CA	APR 01	Houston, TX	MAR 21	Ottawa, Ontario
Eddie Guerrero defeats Chris Jericho		Eddie Guerrero defeats Test		William Regal defeats Diamond Dallas Page	
JULY 23	Dallas, TX	APR 26	Denver, CO	APR 08	Phoenix, AZ
Perry Saturn defeats Eddie Guerrero		Matt Hardy defeats Eddie Guerrero		Spike Dudley defeats William Regal	
AUG 31	Fayetteville, NC	AUG 27	Grand Rapids, MI	MAY 06	Hartford, CT
Al Snow defeats Perry Saturn		The Hurricane defeats Matt Hardy		William Regal defeats Spike Dudley	
OCT 16	Detroit, MI	OCT 22	Kansas City, MO	JULY 08	Philadelphia, PA
William Regal defeats Al Snow		Bradshaw defeats The Hurricane		Jeff Hardy defeats William Regal	
DEC 02	Sheffield, England	NOV 01	Cincinnati, OH		
Crash Holly defeats William Regal		Christian defeats Bradshaw		Rob Van Dam defeated Jeff Hardy on July 21, 2002 to unify the European and Intercontinental Championships.	

DEC 04	East Rutherford, NJ
William Regal defeats Crash Holly	

2002

JAN 31	Norfolk, VA
Diamond Dallas Page defeats Christian	

2001

JAN 22	Lafayette, LA
Test defeats William Regal	

Evan Bourne 🇺🇸

HT	5'9"	WT	183 lbs.	FROM	St. Louis, Missouri

SIGNATURE MOVE Shooting Star Press

YEARS ACTIVE 1960-1969 1970-1979 1980-1989 1990-1999 **2000 PRESENT**

Evan Bourne idolized the likes of Rey Mysterio, Dean Malenko, Bret Hart, and Eddie Guerrero. Evan also displayed a taste for hardcore as he also admired the brutal stylings of ECW Originals Rob Van Dam, Sabu, and Tazz. Determined to bring something unique to sports-entertainment, Evan traveled the world and incorporated the techniques he learned from everywhere he competed. In June 2008, Evan arrived in ECW and amazed audiences with his array of high-flying maneuvers.

This man lives by a formula he has created that will ensure his WWE success for years to come: take one-third positive attitude, one-third technical brilliance, and three-thirds aerial magic and you get the Bourne Combination. Opposing Superstars can't say they haven't been warned.

Eve 🇺🇸

FROM	Los Angeles, California

YEARS ACTIVE 1960-1969 1970-1979 1980-1989 1990-1999 **2000 PRESENT**

This vision of beauty from the City of Angels is no stranger to the entertainment industry. A professional dancer well-versed in several styles, she was a member of the NBA's Los Angeles Clippers Spirit Dancers. Her moves were also featured on television programs like ABC's *Show Me the Money!*, *Days of our Lives*, and Damon Wayans' *The Underground*.

Her unrelenting desire for excellence drove her to enter and win the 2007 Diva Search. On Feb. 1, 2008, she debuted on *SmackDown* and conducted an interview with Batista. While Eve is regarded as one of the sexiest women on television, she's also an intellectual person who enjoys philosophical debates. Eve is a passionate advocate for various causes and known for her dedication to charitable work. This Latin Diva is well on her way to doing big things in WWE.

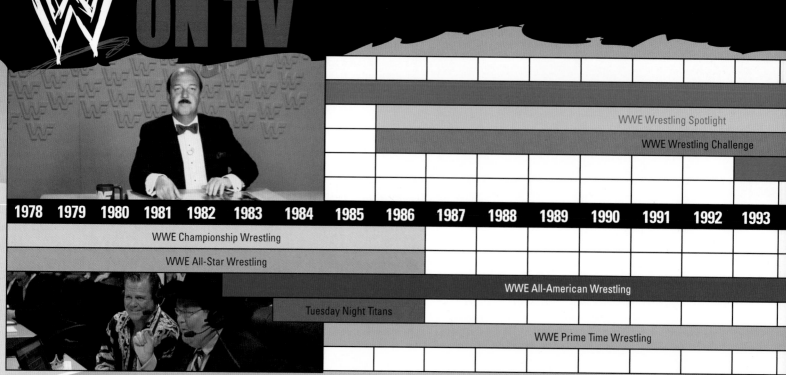

												WWE Wrestling Spotlight			
									WWE Wrestling Challenge						
1978	1979	1980	1981	1982	1983	1984	1985	1986	1987	1988	1989	1990	1991	1992	1993
WWE Championship Wrestling															
WWE All-Star Wrestling															
								WWE All-American Wrestling							
					Tuesday Night Titans										
							WWE Prime Time Wrestling								

WWE CHAMPIONSHIP WRESTLING

Years Broadcast: 1978 - 1986

Championship Wrestling was the first-ever nationally syndicated WWE television program. With Vince McMahon as the voice of the program, the show featured in-ring action from promotion's top stars.

WWE ALL-STAR WRESTLING

Years Broadcast: Mid-1970s - 1986

Featuring matches between the era's top Superstars and lesser-known competitors, *All-Star Wrestling* was not all that different from other sports-entertainment shows of its time. Very often, however, *All-Star Wrestling* also served as a home for big announcements. In January 1984, Gene Okerlund broke the news that Hulk Hogan was named the No. 1 contender for the WWE Championship. He later went on the defeat the Iron Sheik for the title and become one of the greatest champions in WWE history.

Years Broadcast: 1983 - 1994

Airing on the USA Network, *All-American Wrestling* featured exclusive WWE action during its first several years of existence. As the 1990s rolled around, however, the show served mainly as a vehicle to show highlights from the past week of WWE action.

TUESDAY NIGHT TITANS

Years Broadcast: 1984 - 1986

See page 315

Years Broadcast: 1985 - 1993

A weekly two-hour show hosted mainly by Bobby Heenan and Gorilla Monsoon, *Prime Time Wrestling* featured matches from arenas across the country. In 1991, the show's format was slightly altered to include a live studio audience. By the end of the year, however, the show changed again. This time, it featured roundtable discussions lead by Vince McMahon.

Years Broadcast: 1985 - PRESENT

See page 195

Years Broadcast: 1986 - 1995

A weekly syndicated show, *Wrestling Spotlight* served dual purposes by recapping recent WWE action and featuring exclusive matches. The show was hosted from a studio Sean Mooney and Sherri Martel, among others.

Years Broadcast: 1986 - 1996

Wrestling Challenge was a weekly syndicated show hosted at various times by Gorilla Monsoon, Tony Schiavone, Jim Ross, Bobby Heenan, and Stan Lane, among others. For much of its existence, the show featured exclusive matches. However, in the mid-1990s, *Wrestling Challenge* became a highlight show hosted by Dok Hendrix and Mr. Perfect.

Years Broadcast: 1993 - PRESENT

See page 242

WWE MANIA

Years Broadcast: 1993 - 1997

During the mid-to-late 1990s, the USA Network's weekend programming included *WWE Mania*, a weekly highlight show hosted by Todd Pettengill and Stephanie Wiand.

WWE SUNDAY NIGHT SLAM

Years Broadcast: 1994 - 1995

Much like the popular *Free For All* program, *Sunday Night Slam* previewed the action fans could expect to see on WWE's monthly pay-per-views.

WWE ACTION ZONE

Years Broadcast: 1994 - 1996

The earliest days of *Action Zone* featured exclusive in-ring competition from WWE's top Superstars, including Bret Hart defending the WWE Championship against Owen Hart on the show's premiere episode. By the end of its second year, however, *Action Zone* became a highlight show hosted by Todd Pettengill and Dok Hendrix.

WWE FREE FOR ALL

Years Broadcast: 1996 - 1998

During the mid-to-late 1990s *Free For All* counted down the final thirty minutes before the start of each monthly pay-per-view. In addition to recapping the stories that lead up to the event, *Free For All* also featured exclusive live matches. The most notable *Free For All* match saw the Bodydonnas topple the Godwinns for the World Tag Team Championship just minutes before the official start of *WrestleMania XII*.

Years Broadcast: 1996 - 2001

Hosted by Todd Pettengill and Sunny (and later Michael Cole) *Livewire* was originally a live call-in show where fans were given the opportunity to interact with their favorite Superstars. Towards the end of the show's existence, it dropped its interactivity in favor of highlights.

Years Broadcast: 1997 - 1999

The edgy content found on *Shotgun Saturday Night* epitomized WWE's popular Attitude Era. Emanating from nightclubs rather than arenas, the show featured some of the 1990s most controversial moments.

Years Broadcast: 1998 – 2008

Heat saw many different looks and feels over the course of its ten-year existence. The show's formats included matches and interviews, music videos, recapping events, and previews of upcoming pay-per-views.

Timeline of WWE programming (1994–2008):

Program	1994	1995	1996	1997	1998	1999	2000	2001	2002	2003	2004	2005	2006	2007	2008
WWE Action Zone	██	██	██	██											
WWE Shotgun Saturday Night					██	██	██								
WWE Excess								██	██						
WWE 24/7 Classics On Demand											██	██	██	██	██
Main Event	██	██	██	██	██										
WWE Livewire			██	██	██	██	██	██							
WWE Bottom Line									██	██	██	██			
WWE Madison Square Garden Classics													██	██	██
WWE Velocity									██	██	██	██	██		
Monday Night Raw	██	██	██	██	██	██	██	██	██	██	██	██	██		
WWE Jakked						██	██	██	██						
WWE A.M.Raw												██	██	██	██
Tough Enough									██	██	██	██			
WWE Vintage Collection															██
WWE Sunday Night Slam	██														
WWE Free For All		██	██	██	██										
WWE Metal						██	██	██	██						
WWE Experience											██	██			
ECW													██	██	██
SmackDown						██	██	██	██	██	██	██	██	██	██
WWE Heat	██	██	██	██	██	██	██	██	██	██	██	██	██	██	██
Confidential									██	██	██	██	██		
Afterburn									██	██	██	██	██		

Years Broadcast: 1999 - PRESENT

See page 280

Years Broadcast: 1999 - 2002

Airing Saturday afternoons in syndication, *Metal* featured in-ring WWE action. Kevin Kelly and Dr. Tom Prichard called the matches from ringside.

Years Broadcast: 1999 - 2002

Airing Saturday nights in syndication, *Jakked* featured in-ring WWE action. Over the course of the show's history, matches were called by Michael Cole, Michael Hayes, and Jonathan Coachman.

Years Broadcast: 2001 - 2002

Telecast live from WWE studios in Connecticut, *Excess* was touted as the premier show for TNN's Slammin' Saturday Night lineup of programming. The show's format featured two hours of highlights and interviews, as well as the opportunity for fans to call in and talk to their favorite Superstars.

Years Broadcast: 2001 - 2004

See page 311

Years Broadcast: 2002 - 2004

Hosted by "Mean" Gene Okerlund, *Confidential* was known for pulling the curtain back to allow fans see inside the sports-entertainment industry. The show touched on topics previously considered taboo, including the truth behind the Montreal Incident and Stone Cold Steve Austin's highly-publicized departure from WWE in 2002.

Years Broadcast: 2002 - 2005

A weekend syndication show, *AfterBurn* highlighted the past week's high points from *SmackDown* and *Velocity*, including matches and interviews.

Years Broadcast: 2002 - 2005

A weekly syndicated magazine show, *Bottom Line* looked back at the week that was on *Monday Night Raw* and *Heat*. Marc Loyd served as the show's main host; Jonathan Coachman and Todd Grisham also briefly held the honors.

Years Broadcast: 2002 – 2006

Much like *Heat* did for *Raw*, *Velocity* served as platform to highlight the recent action on *SmackDown*, as well as feature exclusive matches involving the brand's Superstars. In 2005, the show moved from television screens to computer monitors when it began streaming over WWE.com.

Years Broadcast: 2004 - Present

Hosted by Todd Grisham and Ivory, *The WWE Experience* was a one-hour kid-friendly recap of the week that was in WWE. The show also took viewers behind the scenes to see the Superstars' favorite activities outside the ring.

Years Broadcast: 2004 - Present

As the name suggests, *24/7 Classics On Demand* is WWE's video on demand subscription service. It features approximately forty hours of new programming each month, pulling memorable events in sports-entertainment history from its gigantic library, which includes action from WCW, AWA, ECW, WCCW and other promotions.

Years Broadcast: 2005 - Present

A.M. Raw condenses the most recent two hours of *Monday Night Raw* into a fast-paced sixty minutes of action. The highlight show also features a continuous ticker at the bottom of the screen where fans can catch up on the latest WWE news and test their knowledge with trivia and fun facts.

Years Broadcast: 2006 - PRESENT

See page 88

WWE MADISON SQUARE GARDEN CLASSICS

Years Broadcast: 2006 - Present

Airing Wednesday nights on the MSG Network, *Madison Square Garden Classics* looks back at the greatest matches to ever take place in the "World's Most Famous Arena."

WWE VINTAGE COLLECTION

Years Broadcast: 2008 – Present

Hosted by "Mean" Gene Okerlund, *Vintage Collection* is an overseas sensation and features classic matches from WWE's expansive library.

EVOLUTION

MEMBERS "Nature Boy" Ric Flair, Triple H, Batista, Randy Orton

TITLE HISTORY World Heavyweight Champion, World Tag Team Champions, Intercontinental Champion

If you combined the greatest in-ring competitor of all-time, the present "King of Kings" and two bright, young Superstars, you would have Evolution. In 2003, "Nature Boy" Ric Flair, Triple H, Batista and third-generation Superstar Randy Orton formed a group that represented the evolution of sports-entertainment. This villainous group was led by Triple H, and with Ric Flair his second-in-command, the men used their experience and knowledge to their advantage. During its existence, this group butted heads with Superstars of all types such as Shawn Michaels, Goldberg, Rob Van Dam, Mick Foley, Edge, and the Dudley Boys.

Evolution reached its apex when all four members held WWE championships. Triple H was the World Heavyweight Champion, Flair and Batista were World Tag Team Champions and Orton was the Intercontinental Champion. When Randy Orton won the World Heavyweight Championship in August 2004, he was unceremoniously removed from the group. Batista later won the 2005 *Royal Rumble* and decided to challenge for Triple H's World Heavyweight Championship at *WrestleMania 21*, where the "Animal" won the title. At *WWE Homecoming*, a returning Triple H turned on Flair and Evolution disbanded. On the *Raw 15th Anniversary*, this famous group had a reunion that saw Triple H, Ric Flair, & Batista team up for a six-man match. Randy Orton refused to rejoin his former stablemates, he opposed them with Edge & Umaga.

Evolution was about success, domination, and women. Since the group dissolved in 2005, "Nature Boy" Ric Flair was inducted into the WWE Hall of Fame, Triple H temporarily reformed D-Generation X and continues to wear a king's crown. Batista and Randy Orton have each held world championships on multiple occasions.

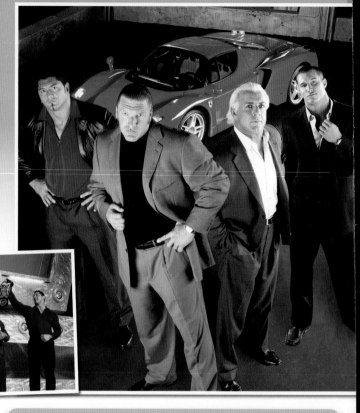

Executioner

FROM Parts Unknown

After several grueling months of trying, Undertaker was finally on the verge of ridding WWE of his arch nemesis, Mankind, at *In Your House: Buried Alive*. However, before he could complete the job, a mysterious masked man attacked Undertaker from behind with a steel shovel. The masked monster, who was later revealed to be Paul Bearer's hired assassin known as the Executioner, then proceeded to bury the "Deadman" under six feet of soil.

Miraculously, Undertaker survived the burial and challenged the Executioner to a match at *In Your House: It's Time* in December 1996. Under "Armageddon Rules," Undertaker Tombstoned his way to victory. The Executioner was gone from WWE soon after.

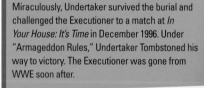

The Executioners

MEMBERS Executioner No. 1, Executioner No. 2, Executioner No. 3

COMBINED WEIGHT 758 lbs.

TITLE HISTORY World Tag Team Champions

Very little is known about The Executioners other than they were complete terrors in the ring. Hiding their faces with masks and replacing their names with numbers, Executioner No. 1 & Executioner No. 2 instilled the fear of the unknown into WWE in the mid-1970s.

In May 1976, The Executioners, who were managed by Capt. Lou Albano, reached the top of the tag division when they defeated Louis Cerdan & Tony Parisi for the World Tag Team Championship in Philadelphia. The mysterious duo held the titles for seven months before controversy caused them to lose the gold. By this time, the tag team had welcomed a third member into the fold, appropriately named Executioner No. 3. The new member participated in a title defense against Billy White Wolf & Chief Jay Strongbow. At the time, this was an illegal practice in WWE, resulting in The Executioners being stripped of the titles.

Extreme Exposé

MEMBERS	Kelly Kelly, Layla, Brooke

| YEARS ACTIVE | 1960-1969 | 1970-1979 | 1980-1989 | 1990-1999 | **2000 PRESENT** |

The heart of this dance group and its extreme beginnings began as Kelly Kelly started her career in sports-entertainment in 2006 as part of ECW. In January 2007, Kelly returned to ECW and promised the Exposé would be back but that now she was bringing friends. The trio of Kelly, 2006 Diva Search winner Layla and Brooke danced in the ring with moves so hot the ring almost melted during their performances.

That August, the three Divas brought the extreme to *FHM* and appeared in an exclusive online pictorial that drove web traffic off the charts. Unfortunately for its devout followers, dissention amongst the Exposé members set in when chick magnet The Miz appeared on the ECW scene. The group dissolved for good after Brooke parted ways with WWE. Kelly Kelly and Layla settled their differences in the ring.

Ezekiel Jackson

HT	6'4"	WT	305 lbs.	FROM	Harlem, New York

| YEARS ACTIVE | 1960-1969 | 1970-1979 | 1980-1989 | 1990-1999 | **2000 PRESENT** |

When "The" Brian Kendrick needed an associate with muscle, he turned to Ezekiel Jackson. The massive Jackson made his WWE debut alongside Kendrick in July 2008. From that point on, it was clear that his intimidating presence was going to go a long way in helping the smaller Kendrick climb the WWE ladder.

Prior to entering WWE, Jackson spent his formative years navigating the tough streets of Harlem, New York. While there, he wasn't afraid to use his immense size to get what he wanted. While he has only been in WWE a short period of time, it looks like he plans to utilize the same philosophy when dealing with his fellow Superstars.

EXTREME RULES MATCH

From the days of the original ECW in which every match was waged in this manner, Extreme Rules kick the rules of a traditional match to the curb. There are no disqualifications and no countouts. However, unless specified before the bell rings, the outcome of the match must be decided inside the ring.

Fabulous Freebirds

MEMBERS	Michael Hayes, Terry Gordy, Buddy Roberts

COMBINED WEIGHT	765 lbs.

| YEARS ACTIVE | 1960-1969 | 1970-1979 | **1980-1989** | 1990-1999 | 2000 PRESENT |

Michael "P.S." Hayes, Terry "Bam Bam" Gordy, and Buddy "Jack" Roberts truly were ahead of their time. Known as the Fabulous Freebirds, the threesome created a never-before-seen level of showmanship that is often emulated by today's Superstars. When it came to getting dirty, the Freebirds owned a gang-like mentality that could carry them through the toughest of wars.

While their WWE stay only lasted a few weeks, the Freebirds gained great success in other promotions throughout the United States. During the threesome's 1980s heyday, they held titles in the NWA, World Class, and UWF, among other territories.

In 1982, the Freebirds made history when they became the first-ever World Class Six-Man Tag Team Champions. Over the next six years, the trio engaged in one of the bloodiest rivalries of all time when they battled the Von Erichs for the titles. In all, the rivals traded the titles 10 times.

Outside the ring, the Freebirds gained the reputation as drinkers, rabble rousers, and even singers. At the height of the Rock 'n' Wrestling craze, Hayes became the first Superstar to record his own entrance theme, "Badstreet USA."

FABULOUS MOOLAH 🇺🇸

| HT | 5'5" | FROM | Columbia, South Carolina | SIGNATURE MOVE | The Backbreaker |

In 1949, fans saw a lovely valet in a leopard-skin skirt named Slave Girl Moolah. This vixen turned heads as she led the likes of "Nature Boy" Buddy Rogers to the ring. She was later trained by the most dominant female star of her generation, Mildred Burke. Now known as the Fabulous Moolah, she climbed the championship ladder, and in 1956, outlasted 12 other ladies to win the vacant Women's Championship. When she raised her arms in triumph with the championship, she took the first step toward an unprecedented 28-year championship dynasty. Her fame was immeasurable, as close friends Elvis Presley and Jerry Lee Lewis often attended her matches.

Moolah was unstoppable as she traveled the globe and defended her title. In 1972, her legend grew when she and Vince J. McMahon successfully lifted the ban that prohibited women from wrestling at Madison Square Garden. That September, she successfully defended her prize at the first-ever Showdown At Shea event against Debbie Johnson.

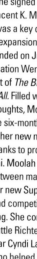

DECADES OF DOMINATION

As The Fabulous One entered her fourth decade in the ring, a new era was dawning. In 1983, she signed an exclusive agreement with Vincent K. McMahon and her Women's title was a key component to WWE's national expansion. Moolah's historic title reign ended on July 23, 1984, when she met sensation Wendi Richter on MTV's broadcast of *The Brawl To End It All*. Filled with vengeful thoughts, Moolah ended the six-month reign of her new nemesis thanks to protégé, Lelani Kai. Moolah split time between managing her new Superstar and competing in the ring. She continued to battle Richter and pop star Cyndi Lauper,

At the height of the "Attitude" Era, Moolah returned to WWE programming with friend Mae Young.

who helped launch the "Rock N' Wrestling Connection." Moolah regained her championship by deceptive means on November 25, 1985. Richter was signed to defend the title against the unknown Spider Lady. A hush fell over Madison Square Garden when the masked arachnid pinned their heroine. Fans were aghast when an enraged Richter ripped off Spider's mask and revealed it was Moolah. With the coveted prize around her waist, Moolah enjoyed a third title reign.

Moolah added another chapter to the WWE history books at *WrestleMania III* when she became the "Queen of WWE" as she accompanied "King" Harley Race and manager Bobby Heenan to the ring. Her championship campaign came to an end at the Sam Houston Coliseum on July 24, 1987, when she lost the gold to protégé "Sensational" Sherri Martel. That November, Moolah captained her team of Rockin' Robin, Velvet McIntyre & The Jumping Bomb Angels to victory in the inaugural *Survivor Series* over Martel, Lelani Kai, Judy Martin, Donna Christanello & Dawn Marie. As the year came to an end, Moolah disappeared from WWE.

In 1995, Moolah took her rightful place among the immortals as the first woman inducted into the WWE Hall of Fame. She shocked the world on October 17, 1999, when she returned to the ring in her 70s and defeated Ivory to capture her fourth Women's Championship, 43 years after she won her first Women's title. This unbelievable accomplishment made her the oldest champion in the history of sports-entertainment.

The Fabulous Kangaroos 🇦🇺

MEMBERS

Al Costello, Roy Heffernan, Don Kent

TITLE HISTORY

United States Tag Team Champions

YEARS ACTIVE

| 1960–1969 | 1970–1979 | 1980–1989 | 1990–1999 | 2000 PRESENT |

Many historians consider the original Fabulous Kangaroos, Al Costello & Roy Heffernan, to be the duo responsible for putting tag team competition on the map. Managed by Wild Red Berry, The Fabulous Kangaroos made their debut in the late 1950s. The Australian tandem quickly endeared themselves to New York City crowds by tossing boomerangs into the audience.

Costello & Heffernan enjoyed three runs as WWE United States Tag Team Champions. Their final reign proved to be their most successful, as the Kangaroos maintained a firm grip on the titles for more than one year before finally losing to Johnny Valentine & Bob Ellis in January 1962. Shortly after the loss, Costello & Heffernan left WWE to work in various other United States territories, as well as Canada. The Fabulous Kangaroos did make a brief return in the early 1970s. This time, however, Heffernan was replaced by Don Kent.

TITLE HISTORY Women's Champion

The spotlight continued to follow Moolah and in 2002 she authored her autobiography, *The Fabulous Moolah: First Goddess of the Squared Circle*. In September 2003, she became the first octogenarian to compete in a WWE ring when she defeated Victoria on her 80th birthday during *Monday Night Raw*. Over the next few years, she continued to appear on WWE programming, events, and pay-per-views. In 2004, she was prominently featured in the film documentary, *Lipstick and Dynamite* about the golden age of women's wrestling and was a guest on *The Tonight Show with Jay Leno*.

The Fabulous Moolah passed away on November 2, 2007 at the age of 84. Moolah will always be synonymous with success and is regarded as the undisputed icon of women's wrestling. This pioneer of sports-entertainment's period of domination as Woman's Champion is unmatched by any figure, in any sport, male or female.

The Fabulous Rougeau Brothers 🇨🇦

HALL OF FAME 1995

MEMBERS

Jacques Rougeau, Raymond Rougeau

COMBINED WEIGHT 472 lbs.

YEARS ACTIVE

1960-1969 | 1970-1979 | 1980-1989 | 1990-1999 | 2000 PRESENT

Trained by their legendary father, brothers Jacques & Raymond were fixtures of the Montreal wrestling scene in the 1970s. The Fabulous Rougeau Brothers made their WWE debut in February 1986 and caught the eye of audiences from the opening bell with quick tags and smooth double-team moves.

In what was originally scheduled as a friendly exhibition match between top title contenders, the Rougeaus resorted to cheating to attain victory over the Killer Bees. The once-honorable Rougeaus became condescending and smarmy and they mocked the United States. To make matters worse, their new manager, Jimmy Hart, still had the Hart Foundation's contract and gave a percentage of their earnings to the Rougeaus as performance bonuses. In 1989, the Rougeaus engaged in a series of matches against the Rockers, which lead to a six-man clash at *SummerSlam*.

In 1990, Raymond was forced to retire due to injuries and became a broadcaster on WWE French television up until 1998. Jacques returned to the company in 1993 as part of the Quebecers. Today, Raymond is a popular politician in Canada and Jacques runs a successful regional promotion and training academy in Montreal.

Farmer Pete

YEARS ACTIVE **1960 1969** | **1970 1979** | **1980 1989** | **1990 1999** | **2000 PRESENT**

With his torn jeans, ragged hat and lucky horseshoe placed around his neck, Farmer Pete certainly looked as tough he spent plenty of time in the fields, which is surprising seeing as he dedicated much of his life to the ring.

A legend in Canada, the midget wrestler spent decades competing in the Ontario territory. When he wrestled in the United States, he worked in numerous regions, most notably Georgia. During the early 1950s, the Peach State was the site of Pete's memorable rivalries with Sky Low Low and Irish Jackie.

FBI (Full Blooded Italians)

MEMBERS Nunzio, Chuck Palumbo, Johnny Stamboli, Tony Mamaluke, Trinity

YEARS ACTIVE **1960 1969** | **1970 1979** | **1980 1989** | **1990 1999** | **2000 PRESENT**

A former member of ECW's Full Blooded Italians faction, Nunzio resurrected the group in WWE in 2003. With Chuck Palumbo and Johnny Stamboli also in the fold, the FBI, complete with every Italian stereotype, got off to a brilliant start when they whacked Nathan Jones just minutes before the start of *WrestleMania XIX*. Unfortunately for the FBI, that's where their highlights stopped.

In the following months, Nunzio, Palumbo & Stamboli fell to the likes of Billy Kidman, Booker T and an up-and-coming John Cena. By the end of 2004, the Italian trio quietly went their separate ways, but left behind a legacy WWE fans would rather "fuhgetabout." When ECW was revived by WWE in 2006, Nunzio briefly teamed again with Tony Mamaluke, with Trinity at their side.

Fatu **YEARS ACTIVE** **1960 1969** | **1970 1979** | **1980 1989** | **1990 1999** | **2000 PRESENT**

HT 6'1" **WT** 282 lbs. **FROM** The Isle of Samoa

SIGNATURE MOVE Monster Splash

TITLE HISTORY World Tag Team Champion

First seen by most in the World Class region, Fatu was one half of the Samoan Swat Team with Samu. Under the tutelage of Paul E. Dangerously, they battled the likes of the Midnight Express, Doom, the Road Warriors, and the Steiner Brothers as contenders for the WCW Tag Team Championship.

Samu and Fatu debuted in WWE in August 1992 as the feared Headshrinkers. The team reached the top of the mountain in April 1994 when they became World Tag Team Champions. The team disbanded in early 1995, but Fatu returned to WWE months later alone as a positive influence to fans everywhere against villains like Waylon Mercy, British Bulldog, Owen Hart, Hunter Hearst-Helmsley, Vader, and King Kong Bundy. By April 1996, Fatu left WWE.

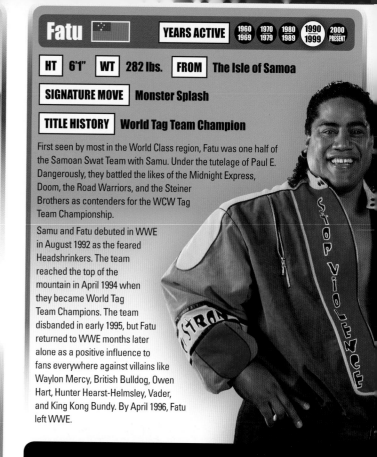

FINISHER MATCH

On very rare occasions, Superstars have mustered up enough energy to kick out of a pin despite being hit with an opponent's signature finishing move. As a result, the match must continue. In a Finisher Match, however, there is no pinning and no kicking out. Once a Superstar delivers his finishing move, or a pre-determined move stipulated before the bell rings, the match is officially over and that man is declared the winner.

While rare, there have been a few memorable Finisher Matches in WWE history. In September 1999, Mr. McMahon forced Triple H to compete against the mighty Big Show in a match that could only be ended when one Superstar delivered a chokeslam to the other. The match naturally favored Big Show, who not only used the chokeslam as his regular finisher, but also had a considerable size advantage over "The Game." In the end, it was Big Show lifting Triple H by the neck and slamming him down to the canvas.

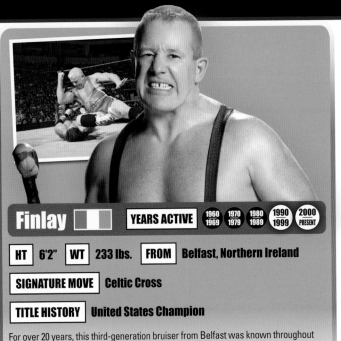

Finlay

YEARS ACTIVE	1960-1969	1970-1979	1980-1989	**1990-1999**	**2000 PRESENT**

HT 6'2" **WT** 233 lbs. **FROM** Belfast, Northern Ireland

SIGNATURE MOVE Celtic Cross

TITLE HISTORY United States Champion

For over 20 years, this third-generation bruiser from Belfast was known throughout Europe and Asia as one of the ring's most brutal competitors. He held 16 major championships before coming to the United States in 1996 as a member of WCW. In January 2006, Finlay debuted on *SmackDown* and put WWE on notice that he loved to fight. With the help of his shillelagh, Finlay quickly established himself as the most vicious Superstar within the brand.

During his first year in WWE, Finlay managed to capture the United States Championship with an assist from Hornswoggle and his shillelagh. Recently, Finlay admitted that he was Hornswoggle's father. In 2008, Finlay and Hornswoggle were drafted into the ranks of ECW and immediately felt at home in the Land of Extreme. Regardless of the fans' feelings toward him and his son, one thing is certain when you meet Finlay in the ring: You are in for the fight of your life!

FIRST BLOOD MATCH

F

Few matches in sports-entertainment history are as twisted and perverse as the First Blood Match. There are no pinfalls, countouts, submissions, or disqualifications. The first Superstar to successfully draw blood from his foe is declared the winner.

The most infamous First Blood Match in WWE history pitted WWE Champion Stone Cold Steve Austin against Kane at the 1998 *King of the Ring*. Kane, with his face obscured by his mask, was awarded the victory after Undertaker busted open Stone Cold with a chair. The referee failed to see the "Deadman's" interference and awarded the decision and WWE Championship to Kane.

More recently, John Cena defeated John "Bradshaw" Layfield in a First Blood Match at the 2008 *One Night Stand* pay-per-view when he wrapped a steel chain around JBL's neck, causing the self-proclaimed "Wrestling God" to spit up blood.

FLAG MATCH

When national pride is on the line, there is only one way for two Superstars to best settle the score: a Flag Match.

With each Superstar's flag hoisted high above opposite ringposts, the goal is to ascend to the top rope and capture your flag before the opposition can do the same. While it sounds simple, Flag Matches are notoriously more difficult than the rules imply, as the emotionally charged battles are oftentimes fueled by an extreme sense of patriotism.

In July 1997, Canada's famed Maple Leaf and America's Old Glory occupied opposite sides of the ring for one of the most memorable Flag Matches in *Raw* history. Bret Hart, Owen Hart, & British Bulldog represented Canada, while Dude Love, Undertaker, & Stone Cold Steve Austin defended the United States. In the end, it was Bret capturing the Canadian flag for the win, thanks to a little help from "Loose Cannon" Brian Pillman.

Flash Funk

HT 5'11" **WT** 243 lbs. **FROM** Philadelphia, Pennsylvania

SIGNATURE MOVE Funky Flash Splash

YEARS ACTIVE	1960-1969	1970-1979	1980-1989	**1990-1999**	**2000 PRESENT**

This veteran of WCW and ECW made his WWE debut at the 1996 *Survivor Series* as a member of Team Yokozuna. As he made his way to the ring accompanied by the Funkettes, the sell-out Madison Square Garden crowd realized that this Superstar was unique. His aerial attacks were felt by many Superstars, including Hunter Hearst-Helmsley, Owen Hart, Mankind, and Kane. In the spring of 1998, Flash Funk left WWE and split his time between ECW and Japan. He continued his journeys until 2006, when he briefly returned to WWE. Although Flash Funk and WWE parted ways again, he returned during the *Raw* 15th Anniversary broadcast and competed in the 15 Years of *Raw* Battle Royal.

The funk phenomenon continues to appear all over the world and he still flawlessly executes his version of the 450 Splash, known as the Funky Flash Splash. His days as a WWE Superstar are fondly remembered as Flash Funk was so funky, he showed everyone how to get up and boogie down!

THE FLOWER SHOP

When Adrian Adonis traded in his leather jacket for pink tights and eye makeup, he also increased his already legendary reputation as one of history's most antagonizing loudmouths. Rather than try to silence the opinionated Superstar (a move many fans would have applauded), WWE took the opposite approach by giving him his own interview segment.

Serving as a replacement for *Piper's Pit*, *The Flower Shop* debuted in 1986 with Adonis as the host. Each week, the "Adorable One" welcomed the likes of Paul Orndorff, Hillbilly Jim, and Hercules to his set, which he decorated with hundreds of flowers and plants. Much like the *Pit* before it, *The Flower Shop* served as a platform for the host to berate the fans' favorite Superstars and stroke the egos of the rulebreakers.

When Piper finally returned to WWE in August 1986, an inevitable showdown between *The Flower Shop* and *Piper's Pit* took place. During the unique segment, Roddy Piper verbally assaulted Adonis and his new bodyguard, "Cowboy" Bob Orton. While Piper's words were powerful, they were nothing compared to the beatdown he received at the hands of Adonis & Orton. The following week, Piper retaliated by destroying *The Flower Shop* with a baseball bat. The actions ultimately resulted in a Hair vs. Hair Match at *WrestleMania III*. Piper won the encounter and Adonis had his trademark golden locks shaved clean.

FOUR CORNERS MATCH

While a Four Corners Match features four Superstars (or teams) competing in one match, the rules state that only two Superstars can wrestle at one time. The others must remain outside the ring and wait to be tagged into the action.

The unique rules force Superstars to tag out only when they absolutely need a breather. If a Superstar is not one of the two competitors competing in the ring, there is a good chance he will be an inactive bystander while the match's deciding fall occurs.

In 2002, Billy & Chuck put their World Tag Team Championship on the line in a Four Corners Match at *WrestleMania X8*. The rules heavily favored the crowning of new champions, but in the end, Billy & Chuck fended off the Hardy Boys, APA and the Dudley Boys to retain their titles.

One champion who was not as lucky was Lita. In November 2002, she lost her Women's Championship to Ivory when defending in a Four Corners Match also featuring Trish Stratus and Jacqueline.

Frankie Williams 🇺🇸

YEARS ACTIVE	1960 1969	1970 1979	1980 1989	1990 1999	2000 PRESENT

HT 5'9" **WT** 239 lbs. **FROM** Columbus, Ohio

This rugged competitor from the midwestern United States came to WWE in 1976. In one of his first matches, he took on "Nature Boy" Ric Flair at Madison Square Garden. This set the tone for a career of locking up with some of the greatest individuals in sports-entertainment.

For the next decade, Williams made it tough on opponents like Ken Patera, Baron Von Raschke, Spiros Arion, Ivan Koloff, Bulldog Brower, Nikolai Volkoff, Ernie Ladd, and Greg Valentine. Williams' highest profile battle came in March 1984 when he was a guest on *Piper's Pit* and was attacked by the "Hot Rod." This led to Williams being assaulted by Piper after defending his pride and honor. In 1991, Frankie Williams passed away after a battle with cancer. He will warmly be remembered as a fan favorite who fought with the heart of a lion and never gave up in the ring, no matter who opposed him.

FREDDIE BLASSIE

"PENCIL-NECK GEEK."

HT	5'10"	WT	220 lbs.

FROM St. Louis, Missouri

YEARS ACTIVE 1960–1969 1970–1979 1980–1989 1990–1999 2000 PRESENT

HALL OF FAME 1994

F

Freddie Blassie was a trusted member of the WWE family for more than 30 years. While the fans loved to hate him, everybody who knew him simply loved him.

Born in February 1918, Blassie grew up in St. Louis, where he initially developed his love for wrestling. After getting his feet wet competing in carnivals, he started working for several Midwest and Northeast promoters. While in the Northeast, he briefly wrestled for Jess McMahon, grandfather of WWE Chairman Vince McMahon.

THE CLASSY VETERAN

Blassie's budding wrestling career was temporarily derailed when the United States Navy called him to serve in World War II. After the war, in an attempt to capitalize on his Naval experience, he returned to the ring as "Sailor" Fred Blassie. The sailor persona didn't take off the way Blassie had hoped, as he seemed to garner more boos from the fans than his rule-breaking opponents. In what would prove to be a wise move, Blassie embraced their hatred. He ditched his sailor's cap, dyed his hair blonde and began insulting the fans. The result: "Classy" Freddie Blassie, one of the most hated Superstars of all time.

The ire Blassie drew from the fans is legendary and may never be duplicated. After being stabbed by angry fans more than 20 times and having acid thrown on him, he was eventually forced to travel with full security forces at all times.

WORLDWIDE NOTORIETY

Throughout the 1950s, Blassie captured numerous championships while competing in the country's Southeast territories. He moved to Los Angeles in 1960, where he duplicated his success by capturing the World Wrestling Association Heavyweight Championship on four occasions. During this time, Blassie competed in a legendary battle with Japanese wrestler Rikidozan. According to legend, Blassie bloodied Rikidozan so badly that it caused several elderly Japanese fans to suffer heart attacks.

The popularity of the bloodbath earned Blassie an opportunity at Bruno Sammartino's WWE Championship in 1964. Unfortunately, Blassie's penchant for breaking the rules cost him the match. Several years later, he unsuccessfully challenged Pedro Morales for the WWE Championship as well.

Blassie's in-ring career began to slow down by the mid-1970s. Despite not being able to compete in the ring, he yearned to remain a part of the wrestling community. That's when Vincent J. McMahon hired Blassie to be a manager. He spent the next 13 years developing one of the most successful managerial careers in sports-entertainment history.

In September 1977, he guided Mr. Fuji & Professor Tanaka to the World Tag Team Championship. A few years later, he had the distinction of introducing a young Hulk Hogan to WWE audiences. Blassie's greatest success came while managing The Iron Sheik. In December 1983, he was in Sheik's corner when the Iranian Superstar ended Bob Backlund's nearly six-year WWE Championship reign. The victory proved to be the biggest of any Blassie protégé.

In March 1985, Blassie became a part of history when he lead Nikolai Volkoff & The Iron Sheik to the first-ever title change in *WrestleMania* history. In traditional Blassie fashion, he used his cane to help his duo turn back the U.S. Express for the World Tag Team Championship at the inaugural *WrestleMania*.

The following year, Blassie sold half interest in his stable of Superstars to managing newcomer Slick. Shortly after that, he decided to retire, awarding the "Doctor of Style" full control of his men.

Using his infamous cane as a weapon, Blassie lead many great Superstars to WWE prominence.

When Blassie hung up his cane for good, the wrestling world lost one of its greatest entertainers. Despite their dislike for him, fans everywhere began to miss the days when legendary "Classy" Freddie Blassie would call them "pencil-neck geeks!"

Freddy Joe Floyd

| HT | 6'1" | WT | 235 lbs. |

FROM Bowlegs, Oklahoma

YEARS ACTIVE

1960 1969 · 1970 1979 · 1980 1989 · **1990 1999** · 2000 PRESENT

Freddy Joe Floyd was a Southern boy trying to make good in the world of sports-entertainment. When he finally broke into WWE in the mid-1990s, he became an overnight sensation in his small hometown of Bowlegs, Oklahoma. Unfortunately, the admiration of his hometown did not equate to wins for Floyd. Week after week, Bowlegs residents would huddle around a small television only to watch their hero continually fall to the likes of Vader, Billy Gunn, and the deranged Mankind.

The unrelenting Floyd kept battling, despite his unimpressive record. His perseverance finally paid off when he scored a count-out victory over Triple H, thanks in large part to interference by Mr. Perfect. When Floyd's singles career failed to take off, he tried his hand at tag team competition. With fellow journeyman Barry Horowitz by his side, the Southerner suffered a similar fate. By mid-1997, he had left WWE to return to Bowlegs.

Frenchy Martin

| HT | 6'2" | WT | 240 lbs. |

FROM Quebec City, Quebec, Canada

SIGNATURE MOVE Knee Drop

YEARS ACTIVE

1960 1969 · **1970 1979** · **1980 1989** · 1990 1999 · 2000 PRESENT

Frenchy Martin started his in-ring career in 1971 in Quebec, but soon traveled west to Stu Hart's Stampede Wrestling. From there, he found success in Puerto Rico and Japan in singles and tag team action. In 1986, Frenchy moved south to WWE.

After success as a competitor, Martin decided to share his wealth of knowledge as a manager, beginning in 1987 with "Canadian Strongman" Dino Bravo. Martin guided Bravo to championship contention and launched an anti-American campaign that revolved around the slogan, "USA Is Not Okay." Frenchy was also known to assist his client with a punch or kick when necessary. As he entered his third decade in sports-entertainment, he changed jobs and became a popular color commentator for WWE's French programming.

Today, Frenchy Martin trains budding Superstars in Canada. He will always remembered as one of sports-entertainment's most dangerous figures.

Friar Ferguson

| HT | 6'1" | WT | 385 lbs. |

YEARS ACTIVE

1960 1969 · 1970 1979 · 1980 1989 · **1990 1999** · 2000 PRESENT

Unlike most men of the cloth, Friar Ferguson enjoyed inflicting pain on people. He loved it so much, in fact, that he oftentimes broke out into dance whenever he felled an opponent. His love for brutality wasn't the only characteristic that set him apart from his fellow religious servants. Unlike most friars, Ferguson completely ignored his vow of poverty, spending staggering amounts of money at the buffet line. At nearly 400 pounds, he was one of the largest Superstars of his time.

After only a few weeks, Ferguson disappeared from WWE, presumably to return to a life of preaching the good word.

FULLYLOADED

Fully Loaded was a short-lived annual pay-per-view that began as an *In Your House* event, but was eventually replaced by *Vengeance*.

July 26, 1998

Fresno, CA - Selland Arena

Main Event: World Tag Team Champions Kane & Mankind vs. Undertaker & Stone Cold Steve Austin

July 25, 1999

Buffalo, NY - Marine Midland Arena

Main Event: WWE Champion Stone Cold Steve Austin vs. Undertaker, First Blood Match

July 23, 2000

Dallas, TX - Reunion Arena

Main Event: WWE Champion The Rock vs. Chris Benoit

Funaki 🇯🇵

YEARS ACTIVE | 1960-1969 | 1970-1979 | 1980-1989 | **1990-1999** | **2000-PRESENT**

HT 5'7" **WT** 180 lbs. **FROM** Japan

SIGNATURE MOVE Rising Sun

TITLE HISTORY Cruiserweight Champion, Hardcore Champion

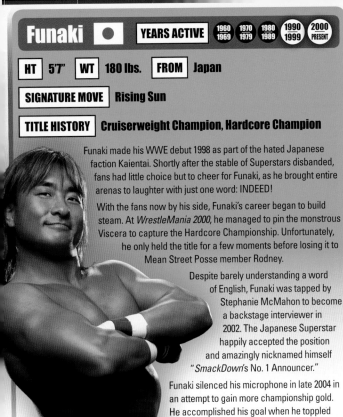

Funaki made his WWE debut 1998 as part of the hated Japanese faction Kaientai. Shortly after the stable of Superstars disbanded, fans had little choice but to cheer for Funaki, as he brought entire arenas to laughter with just one word: INDEED!

With the fans now by his side, Funaki's career began to build steam. At *WrestleMania 2000*, he managed to pin the monstrous Viscera to capture the Hardcore Championship. Unfortunately, he only held the title for a few moments before losing it to Mean Street Posse member Rodney.

Despite barely understanding a word of English, Funaki was tapped by Stephanie McMahon to become a backstage interviewer in 2002. The Japanese Superstar happily accepted the position and amazingly nicknamed himself "*SmackDown*'s No. 1 Announcer."

Funaki silenced his microphone in late 2004 in an attempt to gain more championship gold. He accomplished his goal when he toppled titleholder Spike Dudley at *Armageddon* to capture the Cruiserweight Championship. He held the title for two months before losing it to Chavo Guerrero.

THE FUNERAL PARLOR

Hosted by Paul Bearer, *The Funeral Parlor* was the most frightening talk show segment in WWE history. From its debut in 1991, *The Funeral Parlor* lured the enemies of Undertaker and Paul Bearer into its dark chamber. The show was specifically intended to give people a glimpse into the world of Undertaker and his morbid keeper. During its time on the air WWE Superstars, Legends, and Hall of Famers made their way through it. Although some have still not returned…

The Funk Brothers 🇺🇸

YEARS ACTIVE | 1960-1969 | 1970-1979 | **1980-1989** | 1990-1999 | 2000-PRESENT

MEMBERS Terry, Dory, Jimmy Jack **COMBINED WEIGHT** 587 lbs.

When it comes to being the roughest, toughest, meanest, and most technically gifted Superstars to compete in the ring, you'll be hard pressed to find many greater than the Funk Brothers. In 1985, Terry and Dory Funk were hired by Jimmy Hart and brought into WWE. The Amarillo ruffians obliged the "Mouth of the South" and administered beatings to dozens of Superstars over the next year, and branded their fallen foes with the Double-Cross Ranch logo.

While the Funks battled the likes of Ricky Steamboat, the British Bulldogs, Hulk Hogan, Pedro Morales, and Paul Orndorff, their battles against Junkyard Dog remains one of the most violent times in WWE history and culminated in a tag team match at *WrestleMania 2*.

By summer of 1986, Terry left WWE, while Dory continued to appear briefly alongside younger brother, Jimmy Jack, before returning to the NWA and Japan. In the early 1990s, Terry and Dory appeared in ECW and cemented their iconic status throughout Asia.

Fuzzy Cupid 🇺🇸

HT 4' **WT** 86 lbs.

FROM Newport, Rhode Island

YEARS ACTIVE | **1960-1969** | 1970-1979 | 1980-1989 | 1990-1999 | 2000-PRESENT

When he was a young adult, Leon Stap took a trip to Texas that would forever change his life. While there, he attended a live wrestling event and immediately became amazed by the level of athleticism displayed by the midget wrestlers. He quickly sought out the show's promoter, asking him how he could get into wrestling. The promoter sent Stap to Detroit for training, and the rest is midget wrestling history.

After learning the ropes, Stap debuted in 1952 as Fuzzy Cupid. Although midget wrestling was extremely popular at this time, Cupid was one of the most unpopular Superstars in his division, as there wasn't a rule he wouldn't break.

Cupid earned his greatest success competing as a tag team with famed midget competitor Sky Low Low. Together, they ruled the Canadian midget tag team scene of the mid-1960s. Cupid & Sky Low Low also engaged in a short but memorable WWE rivalry with Tiny Tim & Pancho Lopez.

Gail Kim 🇨🇦

| HT | 5'4" | FROM | Toronto, Ontario, Canada |

| SIGNATURE MOVE | Top-rope Hurricanrana |

| TITLE HISTORY | Women's Championship |

| YEARS ACTIVE | 1960-1969 | 1970-1979 | 1980-1989 | 1990-1999 | **2000 PRESENT** |

She walked to the ring in sleek, long leather coats and sunglasses. Inside the ring, she used a mix of lucha libre, Japanese, and Canadian grappling styles along with a variety of unique submission holds that left opponents broken and battered.

After vignettes aired on *Monday Night Raw*, this Maple-Leaf minx burst onto the WWE scene and made history in her debut in June 2003. She won the Women's Championship when she defeated seven other Divas in an over-the-top rope Battle Royal. Gail lost the belt to the persistent Molly Holly one month later on *Raw*. She spent the majority of the next year trying to regain the title, but was unsuccesful.

Gama Singh 🇮🇳

| HT | 5'10" | WT | 225 lbs. | FROM | Punjabi, India |

| SIGNATURE MOVE | Camel Clutch |

| YEARS ACTIVE | 1960-1969 | 1970-1979 | **1980-1989** | 1990-1999 | 2000 PRESENT |

Born in India, Gama Singh never fully achieved a solid reputation in the United States. He did, however, become a major draw for WWE during the promotion's international tours of the early-to-mid 1980s. Wrestling fans in such places as Australia, Kuwait, and Dubai came out in droves every time Singh was advertised to compete. His chief competition during this time was Roddy Piper. He also had many memorable battles with Don Muraco and "Cowboy" Bob Orton. When not competing in WWE, Singh became very successful working for Stu Hart's Stampede Wrestling in Calgary.

David Heath — Known in WWE as Gangrel

| YEARS ACTIVE | 1960-1969 | 1970-1979 | 1980-1989 | **1990-1999** | 2000 PRESENT |

| HT | 6'1" | WT | 250 lbs. | FROM | The Other Side of Darkness | SIGNATURE MOVE | Blood Bath |

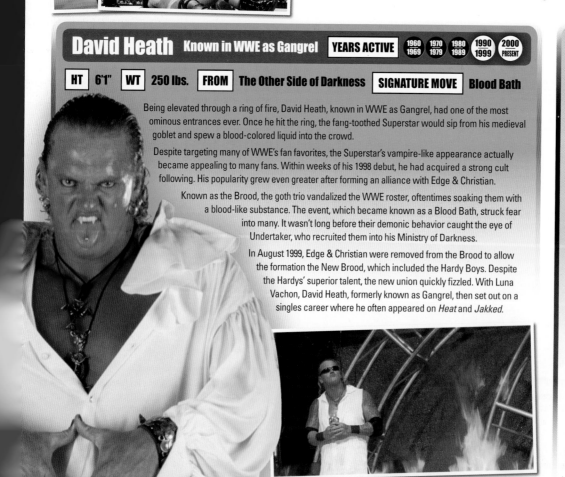

Being elevated through a ring of fire, David Heath, known in WWE as Gangrel, had one of the most ominous entrances ever. Once he hit the ring, the fang-toothed Superstar would sip from his medieval goblet and spew a blood-colored liquid into the crowd.

Despite targeting many of WWE's fan favorites, the Superstar's vampire-like appearance actually became appealing to many fans. Within weeks of his 1998 debut, he had acquired a strong cult following. His popularity grew even greater after forming an alliance with Edge & Christian.

Known as the Brood, the goth trio vandalized the WWE roster, oftentimes soaking them with a blood-like substance. The event, which became known as a Blood Bath, struck fear into many. It wasn't long before their demonic behavior caught the eye of Undertaker, who recruited them into his Ministry of Darkness.

In August 1999, Edge & Christian were removed from the Brood to allow the formation the New Brood, which included the Hardy Boys. Despite the Hardys' superior talent, the new union quickly fizzled. With Luna Vachon, David Heath, formerly known as Gangrel, then set out on a singles career where he often appeared on *Heat* and *Jakked*.

Gary Michael Cappetta

As a child, Gary Michael Cappetta admired the work of ring announcers Jimmy Lennon, Sr., Buddy Wagner, and "Friendly" Bob Freed. At a WWE show in 1974, Cappetta volunteered to be the ring announcer that evening. Once his voice traveled throughout the arena, WWE knew they had their man for events in the New Jersey, Delaware, and Pennsylvania areas.

The advent of cable television and home video resulted in Cappetta being the first wrestling ring announcer who enjoyed an international following. He continued to announce the biggest matches in the world until his departure from WWE in 1985. In 1989, he accepted an offer from WCW and appeared at all their major events. Since he was fluent in Spanish, Gary also commentated on WCW's Spanish telecasts before retiring in May 1995.

Capetta became a teacher, but still followed the industry he loved. He began work on his personal reflections from experiences in sports-entertainment and penned the autobiography *Bodyslams: Memoirs of a Wrestling Pitchman* to critical and commercial acclaim. The response was so great Cappetta adapted the work into a one-man stage show titled *Bodyslams & Beyond*.

Gavin Spears

HT	6'3"	**WT**	225 lbs.	**FROM**	Niagara Falls, Ontario, Canada

SIGNATURE MOVE Running Death Valley Driver

YEARS ACTIVE 1960-1969 1970-1979 1980-1989 1990-1999 **2000 PRESENT**

This Superstar is a man on a mission to prove he is the next in a long line of distinguished grapplers from the Great White North. Gavin Spears is accustomed to being the best at whatever endeavors he pursues. A top hockey player for over a decade, Spears decided to leave the rink and enter the ring following boyhood idols like "Ravishing" Rick Rude, "The Model" Rick Martel, Mr. Perfect, and "Nature Boy" Ric Flair.

In August 2008, Spears debuted in WWE and announced he was the "Crown jewel of ECW's New Superstar Initiative." Spears feels his time in ECW will show, beyond a shadow of a doubt, that there is everyone else in WWE and then there is Gavin Spears. Audiences and Superstars are strongly encouraged to study him, they may learn something.

Gene Kiniski

HT	6'4"	**WT**	270 lbs.	**FROM**	Edmonton, Alberta, Canada

SIGNATURE MOVE Backbreaker

TITLE HISTORY United States Tag Team Champion

YEARS ACTIVE 1960-1969 1970-1979 1980-1989 1990-1999 2000 PRESENT

One of the greatest athletes to ever come out of Canada, Gene Kiniski excelled in the Canadian Football League before turning down National Football League offers, choosing instead a life in the ring. Armed with the training he received from Tony Morelli and the legendary Dory Funk, Sr., Kiniski debuted in 1953. Within two years, he was challenging Lou Thesz for the NWA Championship. Still relatively green, Kiniski failed to wrest the title away from Thesz, but the two Superstars would meet again more than 10 years later.

In 1961, Kiniski defeated Verne Gagne to capture the AWA Championship. The victory gave him his first World title and opened the doors to several WWE Championship opportunities against Bruno Sammartino. At one point in 1964, Kiniski actually believed he defeated Sammartino for the title and left Madison Square Garden with the WWE Championship belt. Kiniski, though not the rightful champion, kept the title in his possession for nearly one month before losing to Sammartino in a rematch.

More than a decade after failing in his initial attempts to gain the NWA Championship, Kiniski beat the legendary Thesz for the title in January 1966. He held the championship for more than three years before being upended by Dory Funk, Jr. At the time of his defeat, Kiniski owned the second longest reign in NWA history, thus proving himself as one of the greatest competitors of all time.

GENE OKERLUND

"Mean" Gene Okerlund is arguably the most recognizable interviewer in the history of the ring. Over the course of his 30 years in wrestling, his pull-no-punches approach to interviewing resulted in revealing answers from the game's greatest, including Andre the Giant, Ric Flair and Hulk Hogan.

Okerlund's first big break came in the early 1970s, when he was tapped to serve as a temporary interviewer in the AWA. His line of questioning, however, was so impressive that he soon earned a full-time role behind the mic. While there, he interviewed many future WWE stars, such as Hulk Hogan and Bobby Heenan. It was during this period when Jesse Ventura gave him the moniker, "Mean" Gene, which took root and lasts to this day.

In 1984, Okerlund made the jump to WWE. It's here that he proved his esteemed place in ring lore. He also proved to be quite the vocalist, as it was his singing of the national anthem that kicked off the inaugural *WrestleMania*.

After nine years of asking WWE Superstars the tough questions, Okerlund headed to WCW in 1993. As a member of WCW's announce team, he served as the promotion's backstage interviewer during the height of the "Monday Night Wars."

In April 2006, Okerlund was recognized as one of the greatest voices in WWE history when he was inducted into the WWE Hall of Fame by his close friend Hulk Hogan.

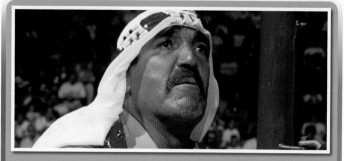

General Adnan

HT 6' **WT** 245 lbs. **FROM** Iraq

YEARS ACTIVE 1960-1969 1970-1979 1980-1989 **1990-1999** 2000-PRESENT

With the Gulf War foremost in the mind of every American, Iraqi sympathizer Sgt. Slaughter introduced WWE audiences to General Adnan in 1991. Striking an eerie resemblance to Saddam Hussein, Adnan was brought in to serve as Sgt. Slaughter's commanding officer. According to Slaughter, Adnan was a great military mind from a great military power, Iraq.

The defining moment of Adnan's WWE career saw the Iraqi holding a Hulk Hogan T-shirt while Sgt. Slaughter set it on fire. The blaze incited fans nationwide, as they recognized the Hulkster as the definitive American hero. In the ultimate sign of disrespect, Adnan simply laughed as the shirt went up in flames.

In addition to acting as manager, Adnan also competed in the ring alongside Col. Mustafa and Slaughter. Known as The Triangle of Terror, Adnan, Mustafa & Slaughter headlined *SummerSlam 1991* when they battled Hulk Hogan & Ultimate Warrior. Dubbed "A Match Made in Hell", Hogan & Warrior turned back The Triangle in a thrilling main event. Afterward, Adnan & Mustafa publicly blamed Slaughter for the loss, marking the official end of The Triangle.

Genichiro Tenryu

HT 6'1" **WT** 260 lbs. **FROM** Katsuyama City, Japan

SIGNATURE MOVE Northern Lights Bomb

YEARS ACTIVE 1960-1969 1970-1979 1980-1989 **1990-1999** 2000-PRESENT

Genichiro Tenryu was a renowned sumo wrestler before he embarked on his career in sports-entertainment. In the early 1990s, Tenryu made several WWE appearances. His first official showing was at *WrestleMania VII* when he and partner Koji Katao annihilated Demolition in less than five minutes. The next battle was in his homeland during the SWS/WWE series of co-promoted supershows. On the first night, he pinned Randy "Macho Man" Savage in front of a capacity crowd at the Tokyo Dome. One week later, he joined forces with Hulk Hogan in a battle against the Legion of Doom.

Tenryu competed in the 1993 and 1994 *Royal Rumble* before returning to his homeland. Genichiro Tenryu is regarded as one of the best competitors to emerge from Japan and is among a small group of men in the history of *puroresu* to hold pinfall victories over both Antonio Inoki and Shohei "Giant" Baba.

"Gentleman" Jerry Valiant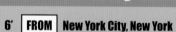

HT 6' **FROM** New York City, New York **SIGNATURE MOVE** Sleeper

TITLE HISTORY World Tag Team Champion **YEARS ACTIVE** 1960-1969 **1970-1979** **1980-1989** 1990-1999 2000-PRESENT

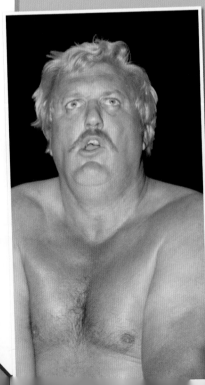

"Gentleman" Jerry Valiant debuted in February 1979 as the third brother of the famous Valiant family. Often accompanied to the ring by brother Jimmy and managed by Capt. Lou Albano, the "Gentleman" was dangerous on his own or teaming with his brothers. The Valiants were so hated that fans often attacked them before, during and after their matches. Often, they had great trouble leaving the venue at which they appeared.

One month into his WWE tenure, Jerry and brother Johhny bested Tony Garea & Larry Zbyszko to etch the Valiant name in the annuls of the WWE as World Tag Team Champions. They held the titles for more than seven months before losing them to Tito Santana & Ivan Putski. In 1980, the Valiants went their own way in the world of sports-entertainment. The big city slicker returned to WWE in singles action in 1983 and remained a despised Superstar until he departed the company in 1986.

George South

HT 6'2" **WT** 240 lbs.

FROM Atlanta, Georgia

SIGNATURE MOVE The Claw Hold

YEARS ACTIVE

1960-1969 1970-1979 **1980-1989** 1990-1999 2000-PRESENT

A fixture of Jim Crockett Promotions in the early and mid 1980s, George South later plied his trade in the World Wrestling Federation and continued his rule-breaking ways against opponents like Ricky Steamboat, the British Bulldogs, Koko B. Ware, Jake Roberts, Tito Santana, and the Junkyard Dog.

Today, George appears on the independent circuit and has his own wrestling school training prospective stars of tomorrow. Regardless of the year, fans never know when he's going to step through the ropes and bring an opponent to his limit.

GEORGE "THE ANIMAL" STEELE

G

HT	6'1"	WT	275 lbs.

FROM Detroit, Michigan

SIGNATURE MOVE The Flying Hammerlock

YEARS ACTIVE 1960-1969 | 1970-1979 | 1980-1989 | 1990-1999 | 2000-PRESENT

Since its inception in 1963, WWE has been home to some of the most bizarre individuals to walk the earth. However, no one has proved to be more peculiar than WWE Hall of Famer George "The Animal" Steele. With his hirsute body, green tongue, and voracious appetite for turnbuckles, Steele's vicious assaults made him of one professional wrestling's most despised figures.

In the summer of 1968, this uncontrollable maniac debuted in WWE. To the horror of audiences, Steele attacked the likes of Eduard Carpentier, "Golden Boy" Arnold Skaaland, High Chief Peter Maivia and Chief Jay Strongbow. "The Animal's" most violent rivalry was with WWE Champion Bruno Sammartino. Steele stopped at nothing to maim the champion and rip away the prized title from him. No type of match settled the war as the two collided in Lumberjack, Stretcher, and Steel Cage matches and further, their Texas Death Match had to be officiated by boxing legend Joe Louis. For the entire decade "The Animal" was one of the most serious threats to the championship reigns of Sammartino, Pedro Morales, and Bob Backlund. Though his unorthodox behavior and bizarre outbursts frightened those around him, his Flying Hammerlock was a feared submission hold and could break an opponent's arm or separate a shoulder within seconds.

Steele's multitude of illegal tactics included unending biting fits, blatant chokes, scratching, clawing, and eye-rakes. George was also dubbed "The Master of the Foreign Object" as he had a propensity of hiding a foreign object somewhere on his person and accosted his opponents when the referee's attention was diverted. During this terror-filled time in history, Steele was guided by "Classy" Freddie Blassie, the Grand Wizard, Mr. Fuji, and "Luscious" Johnny Valiant. George surprised the world in 1984 when he returned to WWE. After being abandoned by partners Iron Sheik and Nikolai Volkoff on *Saturday Night's Main Event,* Steele heard roars from the crowd alongside a re-hired Capt. Lou Albano. Despite being as unpredictable as ever, he became one of wrestling's most beloved figures.

GREEN TONGUE-TIED IN LOVE

In 1986 "The Animal" was in the middle of an intense, yet puzzling love triangle with then-Intercontinental Champion Randy "Macho Man" Savage and his manager, the lovely Miss Elizabeth. Steele and Savage clashed at *WrestleMania 2* and continued their violent encounters throughout WWE in a classic tale of "Beauty and The Beast." Instead of winning championship gold, George was more focused on carrying Miss Elizabeth in his arms and spending time with her. "The Animal" remained a nuisance to the "Macho Man" at *WrestleMania III* when he helped Ricky Steamboat beat Savage for the Intercontinental Championship. George continued to rip turnbuckles and opponents into the latter part of the 1980s. To add to his already perplexing persona, George was joined at ringside by friend and confidant, the puppet known as "Mine." Soon after, Steele disappeared from the WWE.

In 1994, George invaded Hollywood when he debuted in acclaimed director Tim Burton's Oscar-winning film, *Ed Wood*. Then, in typical "Animal" fashion, George astonished fans when he returned to WWE during the "Attitude Era" as a member of The Oddities.

The lore of George Steele becomes greater as time goes on. He is one of the most adored characters in the history of professional wrestling and an individual who entertained legions of fans wherever he went. What was truly remarkable about his legendary career was once eyes were on him, audiences were captivated by him, and he didn't have to say one word. The wrestling world was never the same upon his entry or exit, and he'll always be one of the ring's most unique figures.

In 1995, George Steele's 40-year career and countless contributions were celebrated as he was inducted into the WWE Hall of Fame.

George Wells 🇺🇸

HT 6'3" **WT** 243 lbs.

FROM Oakland, California

YEARS ACTIVE

(1960 1969) (1970 1979) (**1980 1989**) (1990 1999) (2000 PRESENT)

An accomplished football player, George Wells was drafted by the Dallas Cowboys before taking his game to the Canadian Football League. After nearly a decade on the gridiron, he entered the wrestling arena, where he would later become famous for his run-in with Jake Roberts' famous snake.

After Roberts defeated Wells at *WrestleMania 2*, Jake's snake wrapped itself around the former footballer's neck. The force of the attack caused Wells to foam from the mouth and fans worldwide to hide their eyes in fear. Wells' brief stay in WWE ended quickly after.

Giant Gonzales 🇦🇷

YEARS ACTIVE (1960 1969) (1970 1979) (1980 1989) (**1990 1999**) (2000 PRESENT)

HT 8' **WT** 460 lbs. **FROM** Argentina **SIGNATURE MOVE** Chokeslam

At a towering 8-feet tall, Giant Gonzales was one of the most impressive individuals to ever enter a WWE ring. Making his debut in January 1993, he immediately set his sights on Undertaker and eliminated him from the *Royal Rumble*. The move laid the foundation for a rivalry that lasted the length of Gonzales's WWE career.

At *WrestleMania IX*, the bitter feelings between the two giants nearly came to a premature end when Gonzales attacked Undertaker with a cloth soaked in chloroform. With Undertaker rendered motionless, many onlookers began to fear the worst. Miraculously, Undertaker rose to his feet and cleared the ring of his nemesis.

Following his assault on Undertaker, Gonzales tried to finish the job at *SummerSlam 1993* when he battled the "Deadman" in a Rest in Peace Match. Like *WrestleMania*, however, the result favored Undertaker. After the match, a frustrated Gonzales hit his smarmy manager, Harvey Wippleman, with his signature chokeslam. The attack immediately put the giant in the good graces of the fans. He didn't have long to enjoy it, though, as Gonzales was gone from WWE soon thereafter.

Gillberg 🇺🇸

YEARS ACTIVE (1960 1969) (1970 1979) (1980 1989) (**1990 1999**) (**2000 PRESENT**)

HT 6' **WT** 227 lbs. **FROM** Atlanta, Georgia **SIGNATURE MOVE** The Jackhammer

TITLE HISTORY Light Heavyweight Champion

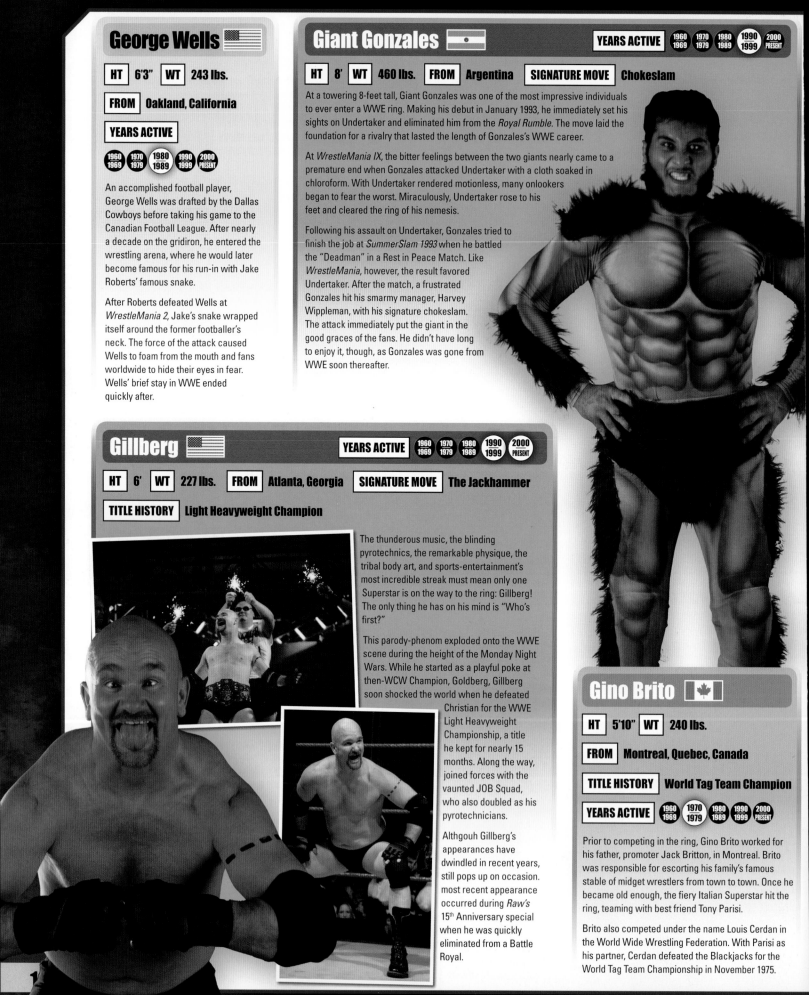

The thunderous music, the blinding pyrotechnics, the remarkable physique, the tribal body art, and sports-entertainment's most incredible streak must mean only one Superstar is on the way to the ring: Gillberg! The only thing he has on his mind is "Who's first?"

This parody-phenom exploded onto the WWE scene during the height of the Monday Night Wars. While he started as a playful poke at then-WCW Champion, Goldberg, Gillberg soon shocked the world when he defeated Christian for the WWE Light Heavyweight Championship, a title he kept for nearly 15 months. Along the way, joined forces with the vaunted JOB Squad, who also doubled as his pyrotechnicians.

Althgouh Gillberg's appearances have dwindled in recent years, still pops up on occasion. most recent appearance occurred during *Raw's* 15th Anniversary special when he was quickly eliminated from a Battle Royal.

Gino Brito 🇨🇦

HT 5'10" **WT** 240 lbs.

FROM Montreal, Quebec, Canada

TITLE HISTORY World Tag Team Champion

YEARS ACTIVE (1960 1969) (**1970 1979**) (1980 1989) (1990 1999) (2000 PRESENT)

Prior to competing in the ring, Gino Brito worked for his father, promoter Jack Britton, in Montreal. Brito was responsible for escorting his family's famous stable of midget wrestlers from town to town. Once he became old enough, the fiery Italian Superstar hit the ring, teaming with best friend Tony Parisi.

Brito also competed under the name Louis Cerdan in the World Wide Wrestling Federation. With Parisi as his partner, Cerdan defeated the Blackjacks for the World Tag Team Championship in November 1975.

The Glamour Girls

MEMBERS Judy Martin, Leilani Kai | **TITLE HISTORY** Women's Tag Team Champions

YEARS ACTIVE 1960/1969 1970/1979 **1980/1989** 1990/1999 2000/PRESENT

With long blonde hair and glittery gold tights, Judy Martin & Leilani Kai claimed to bring glamour to the Women's Division in the mid-to-late 1980s. They also brought winning. The egotistical duo, appropriately named The Glamour Girls, will be remembered as the only two-time WWE Women's Tag Team Champions.

Martin & Kai picked up their first tag titles in August 1985 at the expense of Velvet McIntyre & Desiree Peterson. With manager Jimmy Hart leading the way, The Glamour Girls held a firm grasp on the gold until January 1988 when the Jumping Bomb Angels upset them at the inaugural *Royal Rumble*.

After reclaiming the titles from the Jumping Bomb Angels in Japan, Martin & Kai returned to the United States, where they successfully defended the titles until the titles became defunct in 1989.

The Gobbledy Gooker

YEARS ACTIVE 1960/1969 1970/1979 1980/1989 **1990/1999** 2000/PRESENT

At the 1990 *Survivor Series*, there was a giant egg outside the Hartford Civic Center and "Mean" Gene Okerlund was determined to find out its contents. The weeks of speculation ended when the egg hatched and the Gobbledy Gooker emerged. Once in the ring, this agile cross between a human and a turkey shook a leg with dance moves, forward rolls, and flips over the ropes.

The Gobbledy Gooker quietly vanished after its initial appearance, but just when the world thought it was safe from this avian anomaly, the Goobledy Gooker's feathered fury appeared at *WrestleMania X-7*'s Gimmick Battle Royal. Unfortuantely, it was among the first contestants eliminated.

The Godfather

YEARS ACTIVE 1960/1969 1970/1979 1980/1989 1990/1999 **2000/PRESENT**

HT 6'6" | **WT** 320 lbs. | **FROM** The Red Light District | **SIGNATURE MOVE** Pimp Drop, Ho Train

TITLE HISTORY Intercontinental Champion, World Tag Team Champion

WWE's popular "Attitude" Era was defined by the promotion's persistence to push the envelope. During this time, and while many Superstars were controversial, no Superstar ruffled more feathers than The Godfather.

A noted pimp, The Godfather was accompanied to the ring by a long line of scantily clad women he affectionately referred to as his "Ho Train." Despite being surrounded by miles of shapely curves, he somehow was under the impression that "pimpin' ain't easy."

In the ring, the normally fun-loving Superstar was all business. He defeated the likes of Faarooq, Marc Mero, and Viscera on his way to becoming a legitimate threat to the Intercontinental Championship, which he captured when he defeated Goldust in April 1999. He went on to defend the title for six weeks before Jeff Jarrett upended him on an episode of *Raw*.

The Godfather's "Ho Train" was briefly derailed when he joined Steven Richards' Right to Censor crusade in 2000. While he did manage to claim the World Tag Team Championship under the RTC banner, fans couldn't come to grips with a WWE sans their favorite pimp. Luckily for everybody, The Godfather came to his senses and once again began keeping company with his lovely ladies in 2002.

The Godwinns 🇺🇸

MEMBERS Phineas I., Henry O.

COMBINED WEIGHT 573 lbs.

TITLE HISTORY

World Tag Team Champions

YEARS ACTIVE   1960-1969 | 1970-1979 | 1980-1989 | 1990-1999 | 2000-PRESENT

These hog farmers brought their bucket of slop to WWE from Arkansas in the mid-1990s. Managed by Hillbilly Jim, Phineas and Henry brought the fighting style from the back of the barn into the ring. The good ol' boys scuffled with the likes of the Bodydonnas, the Smokin' Gunns, and the New Rockers and finished off opponents with the Slop Drop.

In April 1996, they became World Tag Team Champions, but their reign lasted a single week. During a match against the Legion of Doom, Henry was hit with a Doomsday Device that resulted in a serious injury. That incident sparked a new attitude in the Godwinns. They dismissed Hillbilly Jim and attacked opponents with slop buckets. At *In Your House: Badd Blood*, they defeated the Headbangers for a second run at the WWE Tag Team Championship, but fell in defeat two days later to Hawk & Animal.

Despite two titles reigns that were among the shortest in WWE history, the Godwinns are remembered for bringing their unique wrestling style to matches.

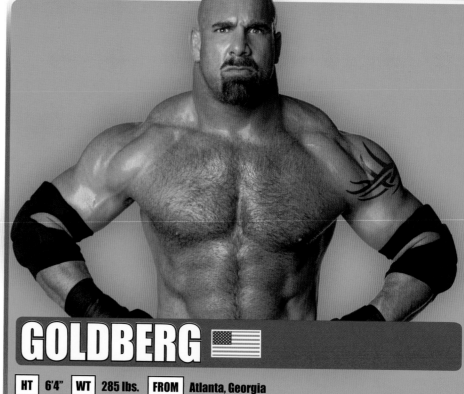

GOLDBERG 🇺🇸

HT 6'4" **WT** 285 lbs. **FROM** Atlanta, Georgia

SIGNATURE MOVE Jackhammer **TITLE HISTORY** World Heavyweight Champion

YEARS ACTIVE   1960-1969 | 1970-1979 | 1980-1989 | 1990-1999 | 2000-PRESENT

A former member of the NFL's Atlanta Falcons, Goldberg turned to professional wrestling in 1997. What followed was the single most impressive rookie campaign in sports-entertainment history. With no experience and limited ability, Goldberg used his immense size to rack up an improbable 173-0 record. With each passing victory, the newcomer confidently questioned, "Who's next?"

Goldberg's early WCW days saw him pick up wins over seasoned veterans such as Raven and Perry Saturn. It wasn't long before his impressive Jackhammer finisher started shooting him up the rankings. By the end of his first year in sports-entertainment, the undefeated Goldberg had captured the prestigious United States Championship.

Goldberg put his unbelievable streak on the line against Hollywood Hogan's WCW Championship on a July 1998 edition of *WCW Monday Nitro*. The dream continued for Goldberg that night, as he defeated the legendary Hulkster for the title. He went on to defend the championship for five months before losing both the title and his undefeated streak to Kevin Nash at *Starrcade 1998*.

WWE fans finally got their first glimpse of Goldberg when he made his highly anticipated debut with the company in March 2003. Much like his early days in WCW, his impact was immediate. The Rock, Chris Jericho, and Christian were just a few of the high-profile names that fell to Goldberg.

By July, Goldberg had his sights set on claiming the World Heavyweight Championship. Unlike his first WCW Championship victory, however, then-champion Triple H wasn't going to go down easy. To ensure he would continue to hold the gold, "The Game" had his Evolution stablemates watching his back.

After a few failed attempts at getting through Evolution, Goldberg put his career on the line against Triple H's title at *Unforgiven 2003*. In the end, it was Goldberg who walked away with the title. Unfortunately for the new champion, he failed to recreate the same magic he made while holding the WCW Championship.

In his final match of what many might term a disappointing WWE career, Goldberg defeated Brock Lesnar at *WrestleMania XX*. Afterwards, guest referee Stone Cold Steve Austin delivered Stunners to both Goldberg and Lesnar. It was the last WWE fans saw of either man.

The Golden Terror

Despite the mystery surrounding The Golden Terror's career, records can accurately prove that he competed during the 1960s. He had a brief WWE stay that saw him fall to WWE Champion Bruno Sammartino on several different occasions. In addition to Sammartino, The Golden Terror's unimpressive won-loss record was also marred by Arnold Skaaland, Bobo Brazil, and Chief Wahoo McDaniel, among others.

After competing in WWE, The Golden Terror moved his mysterious mat game to Georgia where he formed regular tag teams with Butcher Vachon and George Harris. According to record books, The Golden Terror's time in Georgia was equally unsuccessful as his WWE days.

Goldust

HT 6'6" **WT** 260 lbs. **FROM** Hollywood, California **SIGNATURE MOVE** Curtain Call

TITLE HISTORY Intercontinental Champion, World Tag Team Champion, Hardcore Champion

Dressed in gold from head to toe, Goldust resembled an award statue more than he did a Superstar, which is fitting considering his fondness for quoting classic movies. What he loved more than the silver screen was a good game of psychological warfare. Playing off the homophobic fears of opponents, Goldust oftentimes made suggestive advances toward his foes, leaving them vulnerable for him to land his signature Curtain Call finisher.

While Goldust's showmanship was unparalleled, his in-ring skills were even greater. After all, he is the son of the great Dusty Rhodes. Within months of his debut, Goldust used his natural ability, as well as some mind games, to defeat Razor Ramon for the Intercontinental Championship. It was his first of three reigns with the prestigious title.

In late 1997, a confused Goldust left his "director" Marlena to become, believe it or not, an even more bizarre Superstar referred to as The Artist Formerly Known as Goldust. With Luna Vachon by his side,  he engaged in a brief rivalry with Marc Mero and Sable before finally coming to his senses and returning to the Goldust persona that made him so successful.

Back in gold, Goldust spent the next several years struggling to regain the greatness of his early WWE days. In 2002, he finally returned to championship form when he teamed with Booker T to capture the World Tag Team Championship.

Goon

HT 6'1" **WT** 250 lbs. **FROM** Duluth, Minnesota

Extended stays in the penalty box for slashing and high-sticking deemed the Goon too rough for the sport of hockey. After getting kicked off every team he played for, he finally took his brutal style of competition to the one place that welcomed rough-housing: WWE.

Clad in a complete hockey uniform, including skate-like boots, the Goon used hockey-style checks to put his opponents on ice. At *WrestleMania X-Seven*, he competed in the biggest match of his career when he participated in the famed Gimmick Battle Royal. Six years later, he returned to WWE to be a part of another Battle Royal during *Raw's* 15th Anniversary Special.

GORILLA MONSOON

HT 6'7" **WT** 401 lbs.

TITLE HISTORY

United States Tag Team Champion

YEARS ACTIVE 1960-1969 1970-1979 1980-1989 1990-1999 2000 PRESENT

Some fans may only recognize Gorilla Monsoon by the legendary words he spoke while announcing WWE action during the 1980s and 1990s. Lines such as "he's unloading the heavy artillery" and "the irresistible force meets the immovable object" made him a lovable legend, but it was his brute force in the ring decades prior that made him one of the most hated Superstars of his time.

Before entering the pro ranks, Gorilla Monsoon excelled as an amateur wrestler at Ithaca University. In fact, his accomplishments landed him induction into the school's Athletic Hall of Fame in 1973. After a successful collegiate career, Monsoon made the leap to the pros, defeating Pauncho Lopez in his 1959 debut. From that moment, it was clear the oversized savage would be a force to be reckoned with in the ring.

WWE TITLE RUNS

In November 1963, Monsoon claimed his first WWE title when he teamed with Killer Kowalski to wrest the United States Tag Team Championship from Skull Murphy & Brute Bernard. Just days after the victory, Monsoon challenged Bruno Sammartino for the WWE Championship at Madison Square Garden. The now-famous encounter went to a 90-minute draw. Both Superstars later cited the match as the toughest of their respective careers.

The rule-breaking tandem of Monsoon & Kowalski lost their tag titles to the Tolos Brothers in December 1963. Monsoon eventually reclaimed gold, however, when he teamed with Bill Watts to defeat Gene Kiniski & Waldo Von Erich in April 1965.

On a fateful night in 1969, Monsoon made the unlikely transition to one of wrestling's most-beloved figures when he found himself on the receiving end of a brutal attack at the hands of the hated Sheik. Former rival Bruno Sammartino ran to Monsoon's aid, signifying to the crowd that it was acceptable to cheer for the big man. As a fan favorite, Monsoon spent the rest of his legendary career battling the likes of "Superstar" Billy Graham and Ernie Ladd.

The most highly publicized event of Monsoon's career took place in 1976 when an arrogant Muhammad Ali tried to steal the spotlight from the wrestling action in the ring. Upset with the antics, Monsoon lifted Ali up into his signature airplane spin and dropped him to the ground. The move was front-page news across the nation.

A NEW LIFE JUST OUTSIDE THE RING

After more than 20 years in the ring, Monsoon's competitive career came to an end when he lost a Retirement Match to Ken Patera in 1980. While the loss marked the end of a successful in-ring career for Monsoon, it also sparked the beginning of the next chapter of the big man's legendary story.

In 1982, WWE's new owner Vince McMahon (who actually bought a fraction of the company from Monsoon, among others) put the retired Superstar behind the announcers' table. In the years that followed, Monsoon's voice became synonymous with WWE's biggest matches. In addition to calling the action at the first-ever *WrestleMania*, Monsoon and his partner Jesse "The Body" Ventura were behind the mic for the epic *WresltleMania III* encounter between Andre the Giant and Hulk Hogan.

In later years, Monsoon formed one of history's most popular announcing tandems when he teamed with Bobby Heenan.

In 1994, Monsoon received the ultimate honor when he was inducted into the WWE Hall of Fame. However, unlike most Hall of Famers, he didn't retreat back into retirement. Monsoon stayed active behind the microphone before finally elevating his status to that of WWE President, a role he held for two years.

Monsoon made his final WWE appearance in 1999 when he served as a ringside judge as boxer Butterbean battled Bart Gunn in a Brawl For All Match at *WrestleMania XV*. The emotional ovation he received by the WWE fans in Philadelphia that night capped off an amazing career that may never be duplicated.

Robert "Gorilla Monsoon" Marella passed away later that year at the age of 62. He will forever be remembered as a true gentle giant who did it all in the world of sports-entertainment.

GRAND WIZARD

YEARS ACTIVE 1960 1969 1970 1979 1980 1989 1990 1999 2000 PRESENT

As a radio disc jockey in the 1960s, the Grand Wizard flipped phrases with the speed of an auctioneer and the eloquence of a beat poet. His sports-entertainment career began in Detroit's "Big Time Wrestling" promotion as he managed The Sheik. He became one of the first managers to physically insert himself into contests on his client's behalf.

Clad in a mish-mash of spangled attire, including a turban and wrap-around sunglasses, the Grand Wizard ominously walked to the ring with the presence of a giant. The mere sight of this man incited near riots throughout the northeastern United States. He possessed a vocabulary like no other and frightened all who listened to him. He could weave words into images of destruction, punctuated by the pain delivered by the ruthless men in his employ.

He made an instant impact on the WWE as his first protégé, Stan Stasiak ended the historic WWE Championship reign of Pedro Morales in 1973. The Wizard put professional wrestling's richest prize around the waist of another one of his henchman in 1977 when "Superstar" Billy Graham defeated Bruno Sammartino. He also managed greats such as Pat Patterson, Ken Patera, and the Magnificent Muraco to the Intercontinental Championship.

He guided other notable figures, including Killer Kowalski, Mr. Fuji, "Big Cat" Ernie Ladd, Greg Valentine, and "Cowboy" Bob Orton. He often conspired with "Classy" Freddie Blassie and Capt. Lou Albano to rid WWE of its greatest heroes. The Grand Wizard was always quick to remind the public, "It's hard to be humble when you're great!"

Sadly, on Oct. 12, 1983, this innovative sports-entertainment figure died after a heart attack. The Grand Wizard's immeasurable influence on the world of professional wrestling was finally put into perspective when he was posthumously inducted in the WWE Hall of Fame in 1995.

THE GREAT AMERICAN BASH

June 27, 2004

Norfolk, VA - Norfolk Scope

Main Event: Undertaker vs. The Dudley Boyz, Handicap Match

July 24, 2005

Buffalo, NY - HSBC Arena

Main Event: World Heavyweight Champion Batista vs. JBL

July 22, 2007

San Jose, CA - HP Pavilion

Main Event: WWE Champion John Cena vs. Bobby Lashley

July 20, 2008

Uniondale, NY - Nassau Coliseum

Main Event: WWE Champion Triple H vs. Edge

The Great Kabuki

| HT | 5'10" | WT | 240 lbs. | FROM | Singapore |

SIGNATURE MOVE Thrust Kick

YEARS ACTIVE 1960 1969 1970 1979 1980 1989 1990 1999 2000 PRESENT

This martial-arts expert arrived in the United States in the 1970s. Long black hair and paint in the design of an ancient Japanese warrior combined to shroud the scarred features of his face, which was disfigured in his youth by hot coals. During his time in America, he appeared throughout the NWA and was the first to spit a secret green mist at his opponents.

In the early 1990s, Kabuki appeared on the famed co-promoted SWS/WWE supercards throughout Japan. At the behest of Mr. Fuji, the legendary mercenary made his sole WWE appearance at the 1994 *Royal Rumble* to take out Lex Luger. Despite his attacks, Kabuki was eventually eliminated by Luger, the eventual co-winner of the event with Bret Hart. He soon

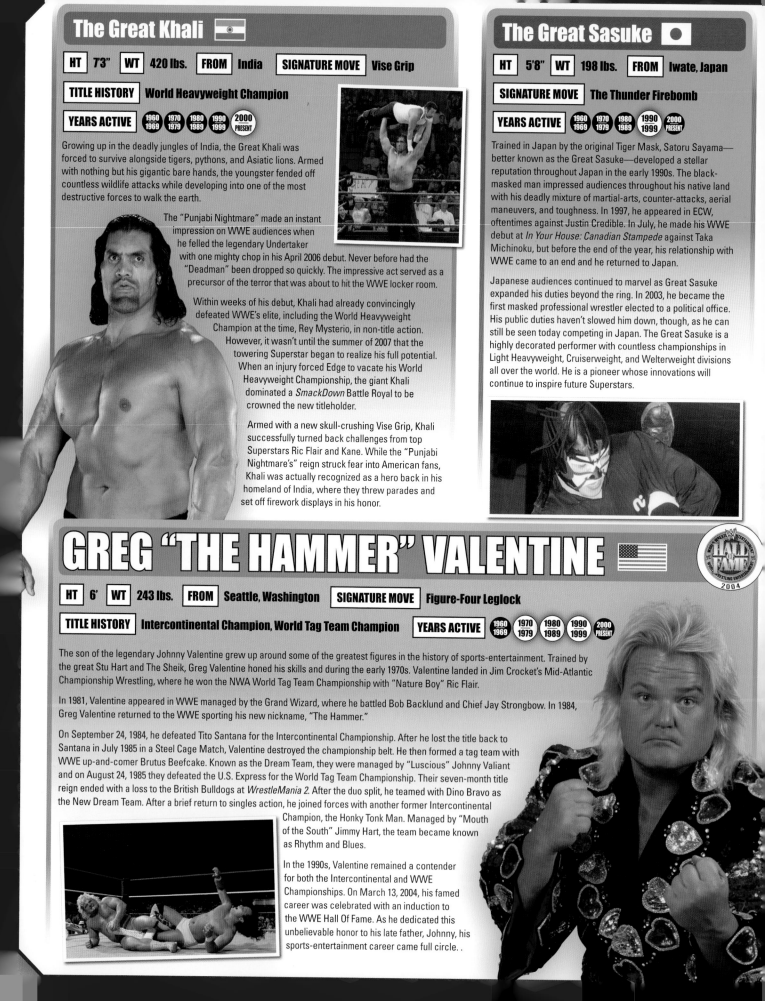

The Great Khali 🇮🇳

| HT | 7'3" | WT | 420 lbs. | FROM | India | SIGNATURE MOVE | Vise Grip |

TITLE HISTORY World Heavyweight Champion

YEARS ACTIVE (1960-1969) (1970-1979) (1980-1989) (1990-1999) **2000 PRESENT**

Growing up in the deadly jungles of India, the Great Khali was forced to survive alongside tigers, pythons, and Asiatic lions. Armed with nothing but his gigantic bare hands, the youngster fended off countless wildlife attacks while developing into one of the most destructive forces to walk the earth.

The "Punjabi Nightmare" made an instant impression on WWE audiences when he felled the legendary Undertaker with one mighty chop in his April 2006 debut. Never before had the "Deadman" been dropped so quickly. The impressive act served as a precursor of the terror that was about to hit the WWE locker room.

Within weeks of his debut, Khali had already convincingly defeated WWE's elite, including the World Heavyweight Champion at the time, Rey Mysterio, in non-title action. However, it wasn't until the summer of 2007 that the towering Superstar began to realize his full potential. When an injury forced Edge to vacate his World Heavyweight Championship, the giant Khali dominated a *SmackDown* Battle Royal to be crowned the new titleholder.

Armed with a new skull-crushing Vise Grip, Khali successfully turned back challenges from top Superstars Ric Flair and Kane. While the "Punjabi Nightmare's" reign struck fear into American fans, Khali was actually recognized as a hero back in his homeland of India, where they threw parades and set off firework displays in his honor.

The Great Sasuke 🇯🇵

| HT | 5'8" | WT | 198 lbs. | FROM | Iwate, Japan |

| SIGNATURE MOVE | The Thunder Firebomb |

YEARS ACTIVE (1960-1969) (1970-1979) (1980-1989) **1990-1999** (2000 PRESENT)

Trained in Japan by the original Tiger Mask, Satoru Sayama—better known as the Great Sasuke—developed a stellar reputation throughout Japan in the early 1990s. The black-masked man impressed audiences throughout his native land with his deadly mixture of martial-arts, counter-attacks, aerial maneuvers, and toughness. In 1997, he appeared in ECW, oftentimes against Justin Credible. In July, he made his WWE debut at *In Your House: Canadian Stampede* against Taka Michinoku, but before the end of the year, his relationship with WWE came to an end and he returned to Japan.

Japanese audiences continued to marvel as Great Sasuke expanded his duties beyond the ring. In 2003, he became the first masked professional wrestler elected to a political office. His public duties haven't slowed him down, though, as he can still be seen today competing in Japan. The Great Sasuke is a highly decorated performer with countless championships in Light Heavyweight, Cruiserweight, and Welterweight divisions all over the world. He is a pioneer whose innovations will continue to inspire future Superstars.

GREG "THE HAMMER" VALENTINE 🇺🇸

HALL OF FAME 2004

| HT | 6' | WT | 243 lbs. | FROM | Seattle, Washington | SIGNATURE MOVE | Figure-Four Leglock |

TITLE HISTORY Intercontinental Champion, World Tag Team Champion   **YEARS ACTIVE** (1960-1969) **1970-1979** **1980-1989** **1990-1999** **2000 PRESENT**

The son of the legendary Johnny Valentine grew up around some of the greatest figures in the history of sports-entertainment. Trained by the great Stu Hart and The Sheik, Greg Valentine honed his skills and during the early 1970s, Valentine landed in Jim Crocket's Mid-Atlantic Championship Wrestling, where he won the NWA World Tag Team Championship with "Nature Boy" Ric Flair.

In 1981, Valentine appeared in WWE managed by the Grand Wizard, where he battled Bob Backlund and Chief Jay Strongbow. In 1984, Greg Valentine returned to the WWE sporting his new nickname, "The Hammer."

On September 24, 1984, he defeated Tito Santana for the Intercontinental Championship. After he lost the title back to Santana in July 1985 in a Steel Cage Match, Valentine destroyed the championship belt. He then formed a tag team with WWE up-and-comer Brutus Beefcake. Known as the Dream Team, they were managed by "Luscious" Johnny Valiant and on August 24, 1985 they defeated the U.S. Express for the World Tag Team Championship. Their seven-month title reign ended with a loss to the British Bulldogs at *WrestleMania 2*. After the duo split, he teamed with Dino Bravo as the New Dream Team. After a brief return to singles action, he joined forces with another former Intercontinental Champion, the Honky Tonk Man. Managed by "Mouth of the South" Jimmy Hart, the team became known as Rhythm and Blues.

In the 1990s, Valentine remained a contender for both the Intercontinental and WWE Championships. On March 13, 2004, his famed career was celebrated with an induction to the WWE Hall Of Fame. As he dedicated this unbelievable honor to his late father, Johnny, his sports-entertainment career came full circle. .

Guillotine Gordon

HT **6'** WT **260 lbs.**

SIGNATURE MOVE **Piledriver**

YEARS ACTIVE

1960 1969 | 1970 1979 | 1980 1989 | 1990 1999 | 2000 PRESENT

Through the early to mid-1960s, Guillotine Gordon received attention for taking rule-breaking to all-new lows in Georgia. In 1965, he brought his cut-and-slash style to WWE and made it difficult for anyone to prosper while he was in the ring.

A famous powerhouse and brawler, he battled the top Superstars of the era, including Angelo Savoldi, Smasher Sloan, Bulldog Brower, Spiros Arion, and Carlos Colon. As his reputation grew and his regard for rules lessened, Gordon earned a shot at then-WWE Champion Bruno Sammartino in brawls throughout the Northeast.

In 1969, Guillotine Gordon left WWE and returned to the territories of the National Wrestling Alliance (NWA). Although it's been almost 40 years since he brutalized opponents in a WWE ring, his rule-breaking ways inspired new Superstars who were looking to take the quick and easy path to cheap victories.

Gunner Scott

HT **6'** WT **230 lbs.** FROM **Tulsa, Oklahoma** SIGNATURE MOVE **The Crowbar**

YEARS ACTIVE 1960 1969 | 1970 1979 | 1980 1989 | 1990 1999 | **2000 PRESENT**

In April 2006, Gunner Scott shocked the sports-entertainment world when he defeated Booker T in his *SmackDown* debut. Gunner continued to taste success in bouts against Simon Dean, Finlay, Orlando Jordan, Gregory Helms, and Sylvester Terkay. His version of the dangerous fujiwara armbar, known as the Crowbar, showed he could mix it up in any situation versus virtually any opponent.

As Gunner's star was on the rise it suddenly burned out that June. After a match with Mr. Kennedy, The Great Khali planted Scott with a double choke throw and Daivari stuffed the young hopeful inside a body bag. That was the last anyone ever saw of Gunner Scott.

"Hacksaw" Jim Duggan (see page 120)

The Gymini

MEMBERS **Jesse, Jake** COMBINED WEIGHT **608 lbs.**

YEARS ACTIVE 1960 1969 | 1970 1979 | 1980 1989 | 1990 1999 | **2000 PRESENT**

In January 2006, fitness guru Simon Dean introduced the world to two massive twins collectively known as the Gymini. For months, the only thing known about the tandem was their colossal size. After several victories on *SmackDown* and *Velocity*, the identical duo finally revealed themselves as Jesse & Jake. Despite the revelation, opponents and commentators still couldn't tell the two Superstars apart.

Luckily, confused onlookers didn't need to struggle with their identity for long. In May, just four months after their debut, The Gymini made their final WWE televised appearance.

Haiti Kid

YEARS ACTIVE 1960 1969 | 1970 1979 | **1980 1989** | 1990 1999 | 2000 PRESENT

Haiti Kid's contributions to midget wrestling earned him great respect from Superstars of all sizes. In fact, many of the larger Superstars from the 1980s considered Haiti Kid a close friend, including Hillbilly Jim and Mr. T.

Prior to *WrestleMania 2*, however, Kid's alliance with Mr. T actually caused him great humiliation. Attempting to get under T's skin, "Rowdy" Roddy Piper abducted Kid and proceeded to cut his hair into a Mohawk. Afterward, Mr. T demanded that his little friend be in his corner at *WrestleMania 2* when he gained revenge on Piper.

The following year, Kid found himself in the center of one of the most infamous *WrestleMania* moments ever. With Hillbilly Jim & Little Beaver as his partners, he stepped in the ring to face King Kong Bundy, Lord Littlebrook & Little Tokyo. Unfortunately, when things started going poorly for Bundy, the big man took out his aggression on the smaller Beaver. At that point, Kid, along with the two other midgets and Hillbilly Jim, came to Beaver's aid. The image of friends and foes banding together to help Little Beaver will forever be remembered as an amazing *WrestleMania* memory.

"HACKSAW" JIM DUGGAN

| HT | 6'3" | WT | 240 lbs. | FROM | Glens Falls, New York | SIGNATURE MOVE | Three Point Stance Clothesline |

YEARS ACTIVE 1960-1969 1970-1979 **1980-1989** **1990-1999** **2000-PRESENT**

Above all else, "Hacksaw" Jim Duggan certainly knows how to withstand the test of time. The patriotic Superstar has an amazing thirty years of experience behind him, yet he still shows no sign of ever letting up.

After nearly ten years of competing in various smaller promotions, Duggan debuted in WWE in January 1987. He made his first major statement at *WrestleMania III*, attacking the Iron Sheik & Nikolai Volkoff during the singing of the Russian National Anthem. The act solidified Duggan's status as one of America's most patriotic Superstars. He even taped a small American flag to his signature 2x4.

The following year, Duggan made history when he last eliminated One Man Gang to win the first-ever *Royal Rumble* Match. The popularity of the event led WWE to creating an entire pay-per-view around the match the following January. One year later, Duggan claimed the *King of the Ring* crown from Haku. Again, the popular event would later become an annual pay-per-view extravaganza.

Behind the power of his devastating three-point stance clothesline, Duggan earned an opportunity at American turncoat Sgt. Slaughter's WWE Championship in 1991. Despite having Hulk Hogan in his corner, Duggan was unable to unseat the champ, but did earn a disqualification victory.

In 1994, Duggan jumped to WCW where he had a measure of success. While impressive, his greatest victory during his WCW stay came in 1998 when he defeated kidney cancer. The brave Duggan credits early detection, the grace of God, and a superior medical team for saving his life.

With a new outlook on life, Duggan returned to WWE in 2005. Despite his best competitive days being far behind him, he still manages to extract thunderous ovations from the fans every time he hits the ring. Win, lose or draw, you can bet "Hacksaw" will entertain the fans with his signature "Hoooooooo!"

Haku

YEARS ACTIVE 1960-1969 1970-1979 **1980-1989** **1990-1999** **2000-PRESENT**

| HT | 6'1" | WT | 275 lbs. | FROM | Isle of Tonga |

| SIGNATURE MOVE | Savate Kick |

| TITLE HISTORY | World Tag Team Champion |

This rugged Polynesian powerhouse was trained in sumo wrestling and many different martial-arts styles. WWE audiences first saw him in the mid 1980s as King Tonga. He made history on June 15, 1986, when he slammed Big John Studd during his "$15,000 Body Slam Challenge." He soon became known as Haku and joined with Tama to form the tag team combination known as The Islanders. During their match against the Can-Am Connection, they fell under the influence of Bobby "The Brain" Heenan and became rule-breakers.

After the team parted ways, Haku remained a member of the Heenan Family and one of WWE's most feared men. In June 1988, the coronation of Haku was witnessed by all after he defeated "King" Harley Race. When he joined Andre the Giant as the Colossal Connection, the two dominated the tag team scene. They defeated Demolition on December 13, 1989 to become World Tag Team Champions. While they parted ways after their *WrestleMania VI* loss, Haku remained in WWE and briefly formed a team with the Barbarian. In late 1992 Haku left WWE.

In the mid 1990s, he appeared in WCW where he reunited with the Barbarian and formed the Faces of Fear. In 2001, Haku was announced as a contestant for the *Royal Rumble*. In early 2002, Haku left WWE and returned to the independent scene in the U.S. and Japan.

Hakushi

| HT | 5"11" | WT | 238 lbs. | FROM | Japan |

YEARS ACTIVE 1960-1969 1970-1979 1980-1989 **1990-1999** **2000-PRESENT**

Well respected in his homeland of Japan for his innovative offense, Hakushi unleashed his unique in-ring style on WWE in 1995. With his skin covered in Japanese script from head to toe, he certainly drew the attention of fans. It was his combination of superior martial arts skills and amazing agility, however, that caught the eyes of his competition.

After impressive showings against then-unknown rookie Matt Hardy and Ricky Santana, Hakushi was catapulted into a high-profile rivalry against Bret "Hit Man" Hart. Against one of WWE's best, Hakushi certainly impressed many despite coming up short at *In Your House* in May 1995.

Undeterred by the loss, Hakushi used his lightning-quick speed to upend the equally-fast 1-2-3 Kid at *SummerSlam 1995*. Initially, the win looked like the launching pad he needed to climb the WWE ranks. Inexplicably, however, he became involved with perennial loser Barry Horowitz. Hakushi's career never recovered.

In 1996, Hakushi became victimized by Justin "Hawk" Bradshaw's branding iron. Greatly embarrassed by the situation, the Japanese Superstar never showed his face in WWE again.

HANDICAP MATCH

This contest goes back to the beginning of WWE and is any match where one Superstar or one team of Superstars square-off against a team with a greater amount of Superstars on it. Depending on the stipulation, usually these bouts follow the rules of a traditional tag team match, where two participants are in the ring and in order for a team member to be brought into the match they must be tagged in.

Handicap matches were originally reserved for giants and powerhouses like Haystacks Calhoun, Bruno Sammartino, King Kong Bundy, Gorilla Monsoon, Big John Studd, and Andre The Giant to display dominance. In recent years, they have become popular to put a Superstar in a precarious position to threaten the reign of a champion or to make life miserable for certain Superstars.

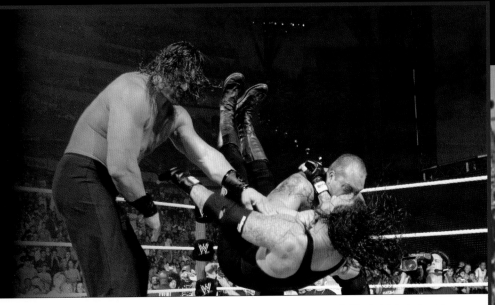

The Hangman

| HT | 6'3" | WT | 292 lbs. | FROM | Matane, Quebec, Canada | SIGNATURE MOVE | Bearhug |

YEARS ACTIVE 1960-1969 | 1970-1979 | 1980-1989 | 1990-1999 | 2000-PRESENT

After his first several matches, reports of this Canadian's vicious actions in the ring and his post-match treatment of defeated foes spread quickly across the globe. Dressed head-to-toe in black, the Hangman was prepared to take his rope to the United States after a brief tour of Japan.

In the late 1970s, he debuted in WWE with manager "Classy" Freddie Blassie in his corner. The Hangman sent chills through arenas, as he was known to hang defeated opponents over the top rope with his noose pulled tight around their necks. After defeating Rene Goulet at Showdown at Shea 1980, the Hangman became a serious contender for the WWE Championship held by Bob Backlund at the time.

By 1982, the Hangman left WWE and spread terror throughout promotions all over the world. In 1986, the Hangman hung up his boots and returned to Canada. To this day, the feelings of dread left in his wake linger in all the arenas he visited.

Hans Mortier

| HT | 5'11" | WT | 250 lbs. | FROM | Nuremberg, Germany |

SIGNATURE MOVE The Full Nelson

YEARS ACTIVE 1960-1969 | 1970-1979 | 1980-1989 | 1990-1999 | 2000-PRESENT

Hans Mortier was a world-class bodybuilder before he entered the ring and was known by many as "The Great." A former European Champion, Mortier and his "unbreakable" full nelson arrived in WWE in 1968. Led to the ring by "Wild" Red Berry, he became an immediate threat to the title reign of then-WWE Champion, Bruno Sammartino. Mortier also teamed with his brother Max to wreak havoc on opposing tandems. His bouts for wrestling's richest prize against Sammartino were so physical the rivalry had to be settled in a Texas Death Match in Philadelphia. Hans Mortier will go down in wrestling lore as one of the most hated villains and biggest threats to Sammartino's WWE Championship.

Hans Schmidt

| HT | 6'4" | WT | 250 lbs. | FROM | Munich, Germany |

YEARS ACTIVE 1960-1969 | 1970-1979 | 1980-1989 | 1990-1999 | 2000-PRESENT

Few Superstars attracted more hatred from the fans than Hans Schmidt. Known as the Teuton Terror, he stepped to the ring wearing a German World War II helmet, which enraged American audiences. Schmidt's brute, powerhouse ring style struck instant fear into his opponents. His complete disregard for the rules made it nearly impossible for referees to maintain order in his matches.

Schmidt captured several titles while competing for the National Wrestling Alliance (NWA). However, he was never able to score the big one, as his attempts to topple NWA Champion Lou Thesz fell short.

HARDCORE CHAMPIONSHIP

The Hardcore Championship not only broke all the rules, it took the rules and smashed them into thousands of little pieces. Ironically, that was the same concept behind the Hardcore Championship belt—an old WWE Championship belt that was broken into little pieces then taped back together.

The concept of the Hardcore Championship was unique as it catered to no-holds-barred style of wrestling that was becoming increasingly popular in the late 1990s. In a Hardcore Championship title defense, anything and everything was legal, including the use of weapons and competing in locations outside the traditional arena. As the title started to take on a life of its own, so did its lack of rules. It wasn't long before the Hardcore Championship was being defended under 24/7 rules, meaning any Superstar could challenge the champion at any time of the day, as long as he (or she) had a referee with him (or her). The 24/7 rules resulted in an exorbitant amount of title changes. In fact, over its lifespan, which lasted less than four years, the Hardcore Championship changed hands more than 200 times!

The Hardcore Championship became defunct in August 2002, when Rob Van Dam defeated Tommy Dreamer to unify it with the Intercontinental Championship.

1998

NOV 02 — Houston, TX
Mr. McMahon awards Mankind the Hardcore Championship, crowning him the first-ever titleholder.

NOV 30 — Baltimore, MD
Big Boss Man defeats Mankind

DEC 15 — Spokane, WA
Road Dogg defeats Big Boss Man

Injury forced Road Dogg to vacate the Hardcore Championship in February 1999.

1999

FEB 14 — Memphis, TN
Hardcore Holly defeats Al Snow

MAR 15 — San Jose, CA
Billy Gunn defeats Hardcore Holly

2000

JAN 17 — New Haven, CT
Test defeats Big Boss Man

FEB 22 — Nashville, TN
Crash Holly defeats Test

The 24/7 rule was instituted during Crash Holly's reign.

MAR 13 — Newark, NJ
Pete Gas defeats Crash Holly
Crash Holly defeats Pete Gas

APR 02 — Anaheim, CA
Tazz defeats Crash Holly
Viscera defeats Tazz
Funaki defeats Viscera
Rodney defeats Funaki
Joey Abs defeats Rodney
Thrasher defeats Joey Abs
Pete Gas defeats Thrasher
Tazz defeats Pete Gas
Crash Holly defeats Tazz
Hardcore Holly defeats Crash Holly

JUN 19 — Nashville, TN
Gerald Brisco defeats Crash Holly
Pat Patterson defeats Gerald Brisco

JUNE 25 — Boston, MA
Crash Holly defeats Pat Patterson

JUNE 27 — Hartford, CT
Steve Blackman defeats Crash Holly

JULY 02 — Tampa, FL
Crash Holly defeats Steve Blackman
Steve Blackman defeats Crash Holly

AUG 22 — Lafayette, LA
Shane McMahon defeats Steve Blackman

AUG 27 — Raleigh, NC
Steve Blackman defeats Shane McMahon

SEPT 24 — Philadelphia, PA
Crash Holly defeats Steve Blackman

FEB 11 — Boston, MA
Hardcore Holly defeats Raven
Al Snow defeats Hardcore Holly
Raven defeats Al Snow

FEB 17 — Cedar Falls, IA
Steve Blackman defeats Raven
Raven defeats Steve Blackman

FEB 18 — Cape Girardeau, MO
Steve Blackman defeats Raven
Raven defeats Steve Blackman

FEB 25 — Las Vegas, NV
Billy Gunn defeats Raven
Raven defeats Billy Gunn
Big Show defeats Raven

FEB 25 — Las Vegas, NV
Billy Gunn defeats Raven
Raven defeats Billy Gunn
Big Show defeats Raven

MAR 19 — Albany, NY
Raven defeats Big Show

AUG 19 — San Jose, CA
Rob Van Dam defeats Jeff Hardy

SEPT 10 — San Antonio, TX
Kurt Angle defeats Rob Van Dam
Rob Van Dam defeats Kurt Angle

DEC 09 — San Diego, CA
Undertaker defeats Rob Van Dam

2002

FEB 05 — Los Angeles, CA
Maven defeats Undertaker

FEB 26 — Boston, MA
Goldust defeats Maven

MAR 11 — Detroit, MI
Al Snow defeats Goldust

APR 14 — Abilene, TX
William Regal defeats Bubba Ray Dudley
Spike Dudley defeats William Regal
Goldust defeats Spike Dudley
Bubba Ray Dudley defeats Goldust

APR 15 — College Station, TX
Raven defeats Bubba Ray Dudley
Tommy Dreamer defeats Raven
Stevie Richards defeats Tommy Dreamer
Bubba Ray Dudley defeats Stevie Richards

APR 19 — Uniondale, NY
Goldust defeats Bubba Ray Dudley
Raven defeats Goldust
Bubba Ray Dudley defeats Raven

APR 20 — Des Moines, IA
Goldust defeats Bubba Ray Dudley
Raven defeats Goldust
Bubba Ray Dudley defeats Raven

MAY 06 — Hartford, CT
Bubba Ray Dudley defeats Stevie Richards
Raven defeats Bubba Ray Dudley
Justin Credible defeats Raven
Crash Holly defeats Justin Credible
Trish Stratus defeats Crash Holly
Stevie Richards defeats Trish Stratus

MAY 25 — Winnipeg, Manitoba
Tommy Dreamer defeats Stevie Richards
Raven defeats Tommy Dreamer
Stevie Richards defeats Raven

MAY 26 — Red Deer, Saskatchewan
Tommy Dreamer defeats Stevie Richards
Raven defeats Tommy Dreamer
Stevie Richards defeats Raven

MAY 27 — Edmonton, Alberta
Terri defeats Stevie Richards
Stevie Richards defeats Terri

JUNE 30 — Uncasville, CT
Raven defeats Bradshaw
Crash Holly defeats Raven
Stevie Richards defeats Crash Holly
Bradshaw defeats Stevie Richards

JULY 06 — Frederick, MD
Stevie Richards defeats Bradshaw
Crash Holly defeats Stevie Richards
Christopher Nowinski defeats Crash Holly
Bradshaw defeats Christopher Nowinski

JULY 07 — Wildwood, NJ
Stevie Richards defeats Bradshaw
Crash Holly defeats Stevie Richards
Christopher Nowinski defeats Crash Holly
Bradshaw defeats Christopher Nowinski

JULY 12 — Lakeland, FL
Justin Credible defeats Bradshaw
Spike Dudley defeats Justin Credible
Big Show defeats Spike Dudley

JULY 28 — Columbia, SC
Raven defeats Bradshaw
Justin Credible defeats Raven
Shawn Stasiak defeats Justin Credible
Bradshaw defeats Shawn Stasiak

JULY 29 — Greensboro, NC
Jeff Hardy defeats Bradshaw
Johnny Stamboli defeats Jeff Hardy
Tommy Dreamer defeats Johnny Stamboli

AUG 03 — Miami, FL
Bradshaw defeats Tommy Dreamer
Tommy Dreamer defeats Bradshaw

AUG 04 — Pittsburgh, PA
Bradshaw defeats Tommy Dreamer
Tommy Dreamer defeats Bradshaw

AUG 09 — Kelowna, British Columbia
Shawn Stasiak defeats Tommy Dreamer
Stevie Richards defeats Shawn Stasiak
Tommy Dreamer defeats

AUG 10 — Kamloops, British Columbia: Shawn Stasiak defeats Tommy Dreamer / Stevie Richards defeats Shawn Stasiak / Tommy Dreamer defeats Stevie Richards

AUG 11 — Vancouver, British Columbia: Shawn Stasiak defeats Tommy Dreamer / Stevie Richards defeats Shawn Stasiak / Tommy Dreamer defeats Stevie Richards

AUG 17 — Terre Haute, IN: Raven defeats Tommy Dreamer / Shawn Stasiak defeats Raven / Tommy Dreamer defeats Shawn Stasiak

AUG 18 — Evansville, IN: Shawn Stasiak defeats Tommy Dreamer / Stevie Richards defeats Shawn Stasiak / Tommy Dreamer defeats Stevie Richards

AUG 19 — Norfolk, VA: Bradshaw defeats Tommy Dreamer / Crash Holly defeats Bradshaw / Tommy Dreamer defeats Crash Holly

AUG 26 — New York, NY: Rob Van Dam defeats Tommy Dreamer / Rob Van Dam beats Tommy Dreamer to unify the Hardcore and Intercontinental Championships.

JULY 13 — Daytona Beach, FL: Justin Credible defeats Bradshaw / Shawn Stasiak defeats Justin Credible / Bradshaw defeats Shawn Stasiak

JULY 14 — Bethlehem, PA: Justin Credible defeats Bradshaw / Shawn Stasiak defeats Justin Credible / Bradshaw defeats Shawn Stasiak

JULY 15 — East Rutherford, NJ: Johnny Stamboli defeats Bradshaw / Bradshaw defeats Johnny Stamboli

JULY 26 — Houston, TX: Raven defeats Bradshaw / Justin Credible defeats Raven / Shawn Stasiak defeats Justin Credible / Bradshaw defeats Shawn Stasiak

JULY 27 — San Antonio, TX: Raven defeats Bradshaw / Justin Credible defeats Raven / Shawn Stasiak defeats Justin Credible / Bradshaw defeats Shawn Stasiak

JULY 28 — Columbia, SC: Raven defeats Bradshaw / Justin Credible defeats Raven / Shawn Stasiak defeats Justin Credible / Bradshaw defeats Shawn Stasiak

JUNE 02 — New Orleans, LA: Tommy Dreamer defeats Stevie Richards / Raven defeats Tommy Dreamer / Stevie Richards defeats Raven

JUNE 03 — Dallas, TX: Bradshaw defeats Stevie Richards

JUNE 22 — Cincinnati, OH: Raven defeats Bradshaw / Spike Dudley defeats Raven / Shawn Stasiak defeats Spike Dudley / Bradshaw defeats Shawn Stasiak

JUNE 28 — Washington, DC: Shawn Stasiak defeats Bradshaw / Spike Dudley defeats Shawn Stasiak / Stevie Richards defeats Spike Dudley / Bradshaw defeats Stevie Richards

JUNE 29 — New York, NY: Shawn Stasiak defeats Bradshaw / Spike Dudley defeats Shawn Stasiak / Stevie Richards defeats Spike Dudley / Bradshaw defeats Stevie Richards

APR 29 — Buffalo, NY: Stevie Richards defeats Bubba Ray Dudley

MAY 01 — Cologne, Germany: Tommy Dreamer defeats Stevie Richards / Goldust defeats Tommy Dreamer / Stevie Richards defeats Goldust

MAY 02 — Glasgow, Scotland: Shawn Stasiak defeats Stevie Richards / Justin Credible defeats Shawn Stasiak / Crash Holly defeats Justin Credible / Stevie Richards defeats Crash Holly / Shawn Stasiak defeats Stevie Richards / Stevie Richards defeats Shawn Stasiak

MAY 03 — Birmingham, England: Crash Holly defeats Stevie Richards / Stevie Richards defeats Crash Holly

MAY 04 — London, England: Booker T defeats Stevie Richards / Crash Holly defeats Booker T / Booker T defeats Crash Holly / Stevie Richards defeats Booker T

MAR 12 — Cleveland, OH: Maven defeats Al Snow

MAR 17 — Toronto, Ontario: Spike Dudley defeats Maven

MAR 17 — Toronto, Ontario: The Hurricane defeats Spike Dudley / Mighty Molly defeats The Hurricane / Christian defeats Mighty Molly / Maven defeats Christian

MAR 26 — Philadelphia, PA: Raven defeats Maven

APR 01 — Albany, NY: Bubba Ray Dudley defeats Raven

APR 07 — Denver, CO: William Regal defeats Bubba Ray Dudley / Goldust defeats William Regal / Raven defeats Goldust / Bubba Ray Dudley defeats Raven

APR 13 — Odessa, TX: William Regal defeats Bubba Ray Dudley / Spike Dudley defeats William Regal / Goldust defeats Spike Dudley / Bubba Ray Dudley defeats Goldust

APR 01 — Houston, TX: Kane defeats Raven

APR 17 — Nashville, TN: Rhyno defeats Kane

MAY 21 — San Jose, CA: Big Show defeats Rhyno

MAY 28 — Calgary, Alberta: Chris Jericho defeats Big Show / Rhyno defeats Chris Jericho

JUNE 12 — Baltimore, MD: Test defeats Rhyno

JUNE 25 — New York, NY: Rhyno defeats Test / Mike Awesome defeats Rhyno

JULY 10 — Birmingham, AL: Jeff Hardy defeats Mike Awesome

JULY 22 — Cleveland, OH: Rob Van Dam defeats Jeff Hardy

AUG 13 — Chicago, IL: Jeff Hardy defeats Rob Van Dam

SEPT 24 — Philadelphia, PA: Perry Saturn defeats Crash Holly

DEC 22 — Chattanooga, TN: Crash Holly defeats Tazz

2001

JAN 22 — Lafayette, LA: Raven defeats Steve Blackman / Al Snow defeats Raven / Raven defeats Al Snow

FEB 03 — Greensboro, NC: K-Kwick defeats Raven / Crash Holly defeats K-Kwick / Raven defeats Crash Holly

FEB 04 — Columbia, SC: K-Kwick defeats Raven / Crash Holly defeats K-Kwick / Raven defeats Crash Holly

FEB 06 — North Charleston, SC: Hardcore Holly defeats Raven / Raven defeats Hardcore Holly

FEB 10 — St. Paul, MN: Hardcore Holly defeats Raven / Raven defeats Hardcore Holly

APR 03 — Los Angeles, CA: Crash Holly defeats Hardcore Holly

APR 11 — Tampa, FL: Perry Saturn defeats Crash Holly / Tazz defeats Perry Saturn / Crash Holly defeats Tazz

APR 24 — Raleigh, NC: Matt Hardy defeats Crash Holly

APR 25 — Charlotte, NC: Crash Holly defeats Matt Hardy

MAY 06 — London, England: British Bulldog defeats Crash Holly

MAY 09 — New Haven, CT: Crash Holly defeats British Bulldog

MAY 15 — Cleveland, OH: Crash Holly defeats British Bulldog

JUN 06 — Detroit, MI: Godfather's Ho defeats Crash Holly / Crash Holly defeats Godfather's Ho

JUN 13 — St. Louis, MO: Gerald Brisco defeats Crash Holly / Crash Holly defeats Gerald Brisco

MAR 28 — Philadelphia, PA: Hardcore Holly defeats Billy Gunn

APR 25 — Providence, RI: Al Snow defeats Hardcore Holly

JULY 25 — Buffalo, NY: Big Boss Man defeats Al Snow

AUG 22 — Minneapolis, MN: Al Snow defeats Big Boss Man

AUG 24 — Kansas City, MO: Big Boss Man defeats Al Snow

SEPT 07 — Albany, NY: British Bulldog defeats Big Boss Man

SEPT 07 — Albany, NY: After beating Big Boss Man for the Hardcore Championship, British Bulldog gives the title to Al Snow.

OCT 12 — Birmingham, AL: Big Boss Man defeats Al Snow

Hardcore Holly

HT	6'	WT	235 lbs.

FROM Mobile, Alabama

SIGNATURE MOVE Alabama Slam

TITLE HISTORY

World Tag Team Champion,
Hardcore Champion

YEARS ACTIVE	1960 1969	1970 1979	1980 1989	1990 1999	2000 PRESENT

Few Superstars can boast as lengthy a WWE career as Bob "Hardcore" Holly. With 15 years to his credit, he has seen it all, from the New Generation to the "Attitude" Era to the WCW Invasion. While many things have changed over the course of his career, there has always been one constant: Bob Holly is Hardcore.

The tough-as-nails Superstar earned his "Hardcore" moniker during the height of the Hardcore Division's popularity. Known for having no mercy in the ring, Holly brutalized his opponents on his way to six Hardcore Championship reigns. While the title is now dormant, the "Alabama Slammer" still competes like the title is on the line.

Over the years, Holly's hard-hitting ring style has also translated to success in the tag team ranks. A three-time World Tag Team Champion, he has captured the titles with partners 1-2-3 Kid, Crash Holly, and Cody Rhodes.

In 2001, the normally gruff Holly took a hiatus from the ring to teach WWE hopefuls on *Tough Enough.* Using tough love as his primary teaching tool, Holly molded several future Superstars.

Over the course of his WWE career, Hardcore Holly has seen and done it all. Unfortunately for the rest of the WWE locker room, he shows no sign of slowing down any time soon.

THE HARDY BOYS

Matt & Jeff Hardy became wrestling fanatics after they watched *WrestleMania IV*. As teenagers, they trained to wrestle on a trampoline and soon promoted their own wrestling shows at area high schools, outdoor fairs, and armories under their company name, OMEGA. This budding promotion also featured fellow future Superstars Gregory Helms and Joey Mercury. The Hardys did anything to be involved with the wrestling business and their dream was to one day be World Tag Team Champions.

Matt & Jeff made their WWE debut in 1994 and were soon seen on *Monday Night Raw* against the WWE's top talent. In the late 1990s they began to be noticed for their agility, teamwork, and resilience. Matt was the ring general who could beat you from the air or the ground. Jeff was the enigmatic figure and aerial daredevil who at any time, and from anywhere, could put away an opponent. Their boyhood dream became reality when they defeated the APA for the World Tag Team Championship. To some, this would be the end, but for the Hardys, it was only the beginning.

In April 1999, the Hardy Boys acquired the guidance of the legendary Michael "P.S." Hayes, known at the time as Dok Hendrix.

The Hardys met with opponents who shared their desire to push the tag team division to the forefront of WWE. At *No Mercy 1999,* they had the first-ever tag team Ladder Match against Edge & Christian. At *WrestleMania 2000*, they met both Edge & Christian and the Dudley Boys in a Triple Threat Ladder Match. Months later at *SummerSlam,* the three teams squared off in the first-ever Tables, Ladders and Chairs (TLC) Match. During this time, the Hardys also added a third risk-taker to their group, Lita. The trio was inseparable and became known as Team Xtreme.

Hardy

After years together, the Hardys went their own way to fulfill their individual dreams. In 2006, they reunited as part of Team DX at the *Survivor Series*. Amazingly, they won the World Tag Team Championship for the seventh time in 2007.

Today, they enjoy distinguished singles careers, but the Hardys are revered as true innovators of sports-entertainment and credited for taking tag team competition to new heights. WWE fans hold out hope at every event that they will see a reunion of the exciting tandem that when together, defy all laws of physics.

COMBINED WEIGHT 461 lbs.

TITLE HISTORY

World Tag Team Champions, WCW World Tag Team Champions

"TEAM XTREME"

JEFF HARDY

Harley Race

HT 6'1" **WT** 253 lbs.

FROM Kansas City, Missouri

SIGNATURE MOVE Fisherman Suplex

YEARS ACTIVE	1960 1969	1970 1979	1980 1989	1990 1999	2000 PRESENT

Harley Race is the rare type of man who comes out of the womb ready to battle. He debuted in the ring as a teenager in the 1960s and formed a team with Larry "The Ax" Hennig. In 1967, Race authored an article in an issue of *Wrestling Revue* magazine titled "Why We Are The Greatest." The two parted ways toward the end of the decade and focused on singles careers.

During the 1970s and early 1980s, Race was the NWA's most commanding figure and held the NWA Championship eight times. Race's fame was so great he was even recognized by WWE and battled in historic unification matches with then-champions "Superstar" Billy Graham and Bob Backlund.

In 1986, he debuted in WWE with his impressive list of credentials and won an early version of the *King of the Ring* tournament. Now known as "King" Harley Race, he became a leading member of the Heenan Family and battled against Ricky "The Dragon" Steamboat, Hillbilly Jim, Tito Santana, Junkyard Dog, and Hulk Hogan. After he suffered an injury in a match against Hogan, he lost his crown to Haku.

In 2004, Harley's iconic career was immortalized as he became a member of the WWE Hall of Fame on the eve of *WrestleMania XX*. With his intense interview style and rugged, technical presence in the ring, Harley Race will go down in history as one of the toughest men to ever walk the Earth.

THE HART FOUNDATION

MEMBERS 🇨🇦 🇺🇸 🇬🇧

YEARS ACTIVE (1960 1969) (1970 1979) (1980 1989) (1990 1999) (2000 PRESENT)

Bret "Hit Man" Hart, Jim "The Anvil" Neidhart, Owen Hart, Davey Boy Smith, Brian Pillman

TITLE HISTORY

WWE Champion, World Tag Team Champions, Intercontinental Champion, European Champion

To fully appreciate the Hart Foundation's impact on sports-entertainment, you must travel through two decades of WWE action to examine its different incarnations.

Originally a tag team, the Hart Foundation debuted as a rule-breaking tandem in the mid-1980s. Bret "Hit Man" Hart provided the team's quickness and technical skill, while Jim "the Anvil" Neidhart served as the muscle. The duo, which was managed by Jimmy "Mouth of the South" Hart, enjoyed two World Tag Team Championship reigns. In January 1987, they defeated the British Bulldogs for their first. Three years later, they downed Demolition to reclaim the titles.

By the end of 1990, it was becoming evident that the "Hit Man" was destined for singles success. Following a loss to the Nasty Boys at *WrestleMania VII*, the Hart Foundation split and Bret went on to achieve legendary status as a singles competitor.

Seven years later, Hart & Neidhart reunited to wage war against the United States. This time, however, they welcomed Owen Hart, Davey Boy Smith, and Brian Pillman into the faction, bringing the Hart Foundation's membership up to five.

The new Hart Foundation, which was lead by then-WWE Champion Bret Hart, arrogantly waved Canadian and British flags, while denouncing the supposed immoral values of the United States. Their actions clearly infuriated American fans, but made the Hart Foundation heroes in Canada, which was the site of their greatest victory.

In front of a capacity crowd in Calgary's Saddledome, the Hart Foundation defeated Stone Cold Steve Austin, the Legion of Doom, Goldust & Ken Shamrock when Owen rolled up Stone Cold for the win. The Canadian crowd enthusiastically cheered their heroes, as numerous members of the Hart family celebrated in the ring.

Harvey Wippleman 🇺🇸

FROM Walls, Mississippi

TITLE HISTORY Women's Champion

YEARS ACTIVE (1960 1969) (1970 1979) (1980 1989) (1990 1999) (2000 PRESENT)

Despite being short in stature, Harvey Wippleman has guided some of sports-entertainment's biggest Superstars. His list of oversized clients includes Sid Justice, Giant Gonzales, Kamala, Adam Bomb, and even big Bertha Faye.

Wippleman's managerial prowess lead his protégés to many high-profile encounters, including major *WrestleMania* matches. In the main event of *WrestleMania VIII*, he guided Sid Justice to a controversial disqualification loss to Hulk Hogan. One year later, at *WrestleMania IX*, Wippleman lead the near 8-foot Giant Gonzales into battle against Undertaker.

Despite building a stable of some of the biggest horses in the game, Wippleman always had trouble winning titles for his clients. Then he met love interest Bertha Faye. Wippleman guided his girlfriend's career from the trailer park all the way up to the Women's Championship in 1995. The title was the only one Wippleman ever captured during his days as a WWE manager.

Five years after managing a Women's Champion, Wippleman actually won the title himself. Disguised as a female named Hervina, he defeated the Kat in a Lumberjill Snow Bunny Match.

HAYSTACKS CALHOUN

YEARS ACTIVE 1960-1969 1970-1979 1980-1989 1990-1999 2000-PRESENT

| HT | 6'4" | WT | 601 lbs. | FROM | Morgan's Corner, Arkansas |

SIGNATURE MOVE Big Splash

TITLE HISTORY World Tag Team Champion

Recognized by many as sports-entertainment's first giant, Haystacks Calhoun made his professional debut in the 1950s. His battles with fellow colossus, the over 700 pound Happy Humphrey gave new meaning to the phrase "when worlds collide." Crushing his way into the 1960s Calhoun was revered as a legend of the ring with his trademark beard, overalls and horse shoe around his neck.

In 1964 this happy behemoth debuted in World Wrestling Entertainment and became one of the most popular figures throughout the Northeast. Calhoun promised all "There are going to be a lot of pancakes around here before I get finished."

"'Stacks" formed a formidable team with Bobo Brazil and the duo were top contenders for the U.S. Tag Team Championship. By August 1965 Calhoun left the company and toured the United States and Canada. He returned to WWE in 1968 and picked up where he left off as one of the most popular Superstars in the region. In May, 1973 Calhoun & Tony Garea defeated Mr. Fuji & Pro. Toru Tanaka and became World Tag Team Champions.

Haystacks continued to amaze WWE audiences through 1979. In the 1980s he battled diabetes but sadly lost his battle in December 1989. Haystacks Calhoun's influence can still be felt today and he'll always be warmly remembered as one of the ring's most beloved heros and most sought after attractions.

The Headbangers

YEARS ACTIVE 1960-1969 1970-1979 1980-1989 1990-1999 2000-PRESENT

MEMBERS Mosh, Thrasher **COMBINED WEIGHT** 492 lbs.

TITLE HISTORY World Tag Team Champions

Mosh & Thrasher made their debut in 1997, sporting kilts (they claimed real men wore skirts) and black face paint. The team combined speed and power to soften up their opponents, then finished them off with their signature Stage Dive move.

Their career reached its peak during *In Your House: Ground Zero* in a Fatal Four Way Elimination Match. After Dude Love and "Stone Cold" Steve Austin forfeited the World Tag Team Championships, Mosh & Thrasher outlasted the Godwinns, Legion of Doom and the Hart Foundation with an assist from a Stunner courtesy of "Stone Cold" Steve Austin. They held the titles for close to one month before a disappointing loss to the Godwinns at *In Your House: Badd Blood*. By late 2000, the metalheads parted ways and pursued individual careers within WWE. At times they entered what would be temporary partnerships, but couldn't duplicate their past successes. By 2001, both had left WWE to compete in other promotions.

The Headshrinkers

YEARS ACTIVE 1960-1969 1970-1979 1980-1989 1990-1999 2000-PRESENT

Samu & Fatu are proud members of a long line of savage Samoan Superstars to terrorize WWE. Collectively known as The Headshrinkers, the duo displayed a dangerous combination of size, agility and ferocity on their way to becoming one of the most feared tag teams of the mid-1990s.

MEMBERS Samu, Fatu, Sionne **TITLE HISTORY** World Tag Team Champions

Success didn't come quickly for The Headshrinkers. Managed by Afa, the tandem struggled to make a name for themselves during their first year with WWE. After competing in many non-descript matches against the likes of High Energy and the Steiner Brothers, the savage unit employed the services of legendary manager Capt. Lou Albano. The move proved to be the spark the team needed to succeed.

With the "Manager of Champions" leading the way, The Headshrinkers quickly became top contenders in the tag team division. In April 1994, they shot to the top when they defeated The Quebecers for the World Tag Team Championship. Over the course of the next four months, Samu & Fatu turned back all comers, including the Smoking Gunns and Yokozuna & Crush. Unfortunately for The Headshrinkers, their impressive reign was unexpectedly derailed when Shawn Michaels & Diesel defeated them in August.

Following the loss, a frustrated Samu left WWE. The massive Sionne briefly filled the vacancy, but the new version of The Headshrinkers simply could not recreate the magic. Fatu & Sionne split soon after.

The Heart Throbs

MEMBERS	Antonio, Romeo

YEARS ACTIVE

These heartbreakers entered WWE in 2005 and were so sexy they almost didn't know what to do with themselves. Antonio and Romeo wrapped up the attenion of the ladies in the audience with their charisma, and placed feathered boas around choice females to invite the ladies to dance in the ring with them after victories.

The Heart Throbs battled for tag team gold against the likes of William Regal & Tajiri, the Hurricane & Rosey, Lance Cade & Trevor Murdoch, Big Show & Kane, and Snitsky & Tomko. They also teamed with Victoria in intense mixed tag matches. In February 2006, the two self-proclaimed Don Juans left WWE.

The Heavenly Bodies

MEMBERS	"Gigolo" Jimmy DelRay, Tom Pritchard
COMBINED WEIGHT	460 lbs.

YEARS ACTIVE

In 1993, smooth operators "Gigolo" Jimmy DelRay & Tom Pritchard came to WWE by way of Smoky Mountain Wrestling. Fans knew that with manager James E. Cornette in their corner, the duo would be a well-oiled machine with an innate mean streak.

DelRay & Pritchard defeated team after team and soon confronted the Smokin' Gunns and the Steiner Brothers. They demanded—and received—a shot at the World Tag Team Championship at *SummerSlam 1993*. Although the encounter ended with a defeat, the Heavenly Bodies captured the Smoky Mountain Tag Team Championship a few months later at *Survivor Series*. For the early portion of 1994, they appeared on WWE programming with the Smoky Mountain titles. In August 1995, DelRay & Pritchard left WWE and briefly ventured over to ECW. In 1996, however, the team went their separate ways.

The Heenan Family

MEMBERS	Andre the Giant, Big John Studd, King Kong Bundy, Ken Patera, The Missing Link, Adrian Adonis, Paul Orndorff, Harley Race, Hercules, The Barbarian, Rick Rude, Haku, Tama, Brook-lyn Brawler, Mr. Perfect, Red Rooster, Arn Anderson, Tully Blanchard

YEARS ACTIVE

Though not related by blood, members of Bobby "The Brain" Heenan's stable of Superstars were so close he referred to them as family, The Heenan Family. The impressive ensemble traces its roots back to the early 1970s and the AWA. As a manager in the Minneapolis-based promotion, Heenan guided the careers of the territory's top names, including Nick Bockwinkel and "Cowboy" Bob Orton.

In 1984, Heenan moved to WWE, where he introduced his family approach to managing to his earliest clients, Ken Patera and Big John Studd. Within months of their union, Heenan had Studd challenging Hulk Hogan for the WWE Championship. Studd's main-event status caught the eye of many other Superstars who began to knock on Heenan's door. Before long, the manager's list of clients grew to epic proportions. Superstars such as King Kong Bundy and Harley Race were all clamoring to sign with Heenan.

The Family's biggest acquisition came in 1987 when Andre the Giant joined. Landing the massive Superstar proved to be a major coup for Heenan, who parlayed the signing into one of the biggest matches of all time: Hogan vs. Andre at *WrestleMania III*.

While Andre was unable to bring the WWE Championship to The Heenan Family, he did later team with Haku to claim the World Tag Team Championship. Heenan lead the Brain Busters to the same accolade in 1989. He also managed Rick Rude and Mr. Perfect to the Intercontinental Championship.

Heidenreich

HT	6'7"	WT	285 lbs.
FROM	New Orleans, Lousiana		

SIGNATURE MOVE

Cobra Clutch

TITLE HISTORY

WWE Tag Team Champion

YEARS ACTIVE

Heidenreich's size certainly intimidated opponents, but it was the uncertainty of what was going on in his crazed head that truly scared Superstars. With tattoos spread over his chiseled frame, Heidenreich was known for reciting cryptic poetry before attacking. Even more unnerving was the fact that nobody was safe from him, as Heidenreich was known to assault Superstars, announcers, and even fans.

In October 2004, Heidenreich cost Undertaker an opportunity at reclaiming the WWE Championship. Over the next several months, the Superstars faced off in several high-profile encounters. Unfortunately for Heidenreich, Undertaker bested him every bout, including a Casket Match at the 2005 *Royal Rumble*.

After failing to derail Undertaker, Heidenreich took a more fan-friendly approach to life. His poems, which he called "disasterpieces," softened in content, and he even began making friends with young WWE fans. The new-and-improved Heidenreich also began forming friendships with fellow Superstars, including Road Warrior Animal. Together, the duo defeated MNM to capture the WWE Tag Team Championship in July 2005.

HELL IN A CELL

For over a decade, Hell In A Cell has been considered the most dangerous match in all of sports-entertainment. Victory can only be achieved by pinfall or submission, but that victory can seem empty after feeling the brunt of the enclosed structure. This contest is one where the participants, regardless of the outcome, do not exit in the same condition in which they entered.

The Cell was unveiled in October 1997 at the *In Your House: Badd Blood* pay-per-view. That evening, Undertaker and Shawn Michaels gave the world a brutal look at what was to come and what all future participants should fear. Audiences will forever have the image of Michaels crashing through the Spanish announce table, and Undertaker catapulting HBK face-first into the steel.

As the years went on and WWE rivalries grew in hostility, the 20-foot steel enclosure required a redesign. In September 2006, at *Unforgiven*, the newly constructed 30 x 30, 3,500 square feet of steel beams and remorseless steel mesh was unveiled. Its first combatants were D-Generation X facing Mr. McMahon, Shane McMahon, & Big Show in the only Hell in a Cell Handicap Match to date. Superstars such as Undertaker and Triple H have become synonymous with this dangerous match, and perhaps the most famous bout was in 1998 when Undertaker launched Mankind off the top of the cage onto the Spanish announce table. Later in the match, Undertaker chokeslammed Mankind through the roof of the cage to the ring below.

This match type has a hellish history that will only intensify in the future. WWE Superstars know its dangers, but at the same time know that surviving the frightening structure can create an undeniable legacy that will last for generations.

Hercules

YEARS ACTIVE | 1960 1969 | 1970 1979 | **1980 1989** | **1990 1999** | 2000 PRESENT

| **HT** 6'1" | **WT** 270 lbs. | **FROM** Tampa, Florida | **SIGNATURE MOVE** The Human Torture Rack |

This stoic pillar of power came to World Wrestling Entertainment in 1986 managed by "Classy" Freddie Blassie. The strength of Hercules led him to numerous victories in a matter of minutes. He soon came to the ring with a steel chain around his neck which added intimidation to an already imposing figure. When his contract was acquired by Bobby "The Brain" Heenan, Hercules was more dangerous then ever.

He battled Billy Jack Haynes in a violent "Full Nelson Challenge" at *WrestleMania III*. At *WrestleMania IV*, Hercules was pitted against Ultimate Warrior. Hercules' rivalries with WWE's heroes continued until he became a victim of a plot himself in 1988 when Heenan tried to sell him to "Million-Dollar Man" Ted DiBiase. With the fans behind him, Hercules battled Earthquake, Greg Valentine, and Mr. Perfect. At the end 1990, Hercules formed the villainous Power & Glory with Paul Roma, managed by the "Doctor of Style" Slick. While they made for a formidable team, they separated after a series of disappointing defeats.

Hercules and WWE parted ways in 1991. He was seen through the decade in various promotions both in the United States and Japan displaying his raw power. Sadly, in March 2004, he passed away. This WWE Legend was one of the strongest and most intense competitors ever to ply his trade inside the ring.

Hercules Ayala

| **HT** 6'1" | **WT** 265 lbs. |

FROM Puerto Rico

YEARS ACTIVE

1960 1969 | **1970 1979** | 1980 1989 | 1990 1999 | 2000 PRESENT

As a child on the tropical island of Puerto Rico, Hercules Ayala loved professional wrestling and his idol was island star, Hurricane Castillo. In his early 20s Ayala relocated to Boston, where he met WWE's Angelo Savoldi. Ayala then landed in the World Wide Wrestling Federation shortly after his professional debut in 1971.

Ayala showed his skills and power all over the world. In Canada, Ayala was called "The Strongest Man In Wrestling" and ran roughshod through Stu Hart's Stampede territory where he tangled with Dynamite Kid, Davey Boy Smith, Harley Race, and Bret "Hit Man" Hart. Ayala left the Stampede territory for a return to Puerto Rico one year before Vince McMahon took over the region's wrestling activities from his father, Vincent J. McMahon.

High Energy 🇺🇸 🇨🇦

MEMBERS "The Rocket" Owen Hart, "The Birdman" Koko B. Ware

COMBINED WEIGHT 456 lbs.

YEARS ACTIVE 1960-1969 1970-1979 1980-1989 **1990-1999** 2000-PRESENT

In 1992, Owen Hart and Koko B. Ware combined their abilities and threw fashion sense out the window. Decked out in fluorescent pants and checkered suspenders, the duo used speed and frequent tags to build momentum and dominate opponents.

High Energy took to the air in bouts against the best teams in WWE at the time, including the Headshrinkers and then-World Tag Team Champions, Money Inc. Unfortunately, just as High Energy was taking off, Owen Hart was sidelined with a serious knee injury. By the time he returned and was ready to once again take flight, Koko B. Ware was off flying high for other promotions. Fans of the colorful duo wish their partnership would have lasted longer, as the excitement they brought to WWE was unparalleled.

The Highlanders 🏴󠁧󠁢󠁳󠁣󠁴󠁿

YEARS ACTIVE 1960-1969 1970-1979 1980-1989 1990-1999 **2000-PRESENT**

MEMBERS Rory McAllister, Robbie McAllister **FROM** Oban, Scotland

COMBINED WEIGHT 470 lbs.

Rory & Robbie McAllister left their homes in the rugged Scottish Highlands in search of tag team gold. Since arriving in the United States in July 2006, however, they haven't had the easiest time adjusting to the American way of life.

When not attempting to figure out such technological advancements as a television or cell phone, the Highlanders are often found fending off WWE's top tag teams. Utilizing the Scot Drop, the fighting cousins have picked up victories over Spirit Squad, Lance Cade & Trevor Murdoch, and Paul London & Brian Kendrick.

Much like WWE Hall of Famer and fellow Scotsman "Rowdy" Roddy Piper, Rory & Robbie sported traditional plaid kilts to the ring. Many Americans scoffed at the sight of men in the pleated skirt-like garment, but the Highlanders enjoyed much success during their time in WWE.

HIGHLIGHT REEL

Chris Jericho is rarely at a loss for words, as evidenced by his reoccurring interview segment, *The Highlight Reel*. Debuting on *Raw* in April 2003, *The Highlight Reel* was Y2J's "cooler and more entertaining" answer to *Piper's Pit*, which had resurfaced on *SmackDown* earlier in the month.

Kicking the segment off with a bang, Jericho welcomed Goldberg as his first-ever guest on *The Highlight Reel*. Fresh off his WWE in-ring debut against The Rock, Goldberg fielded several hard-hitting questions from Y2J, including queries about why the former WCW Champion refused to compete against Jericho while both were employed by the now-defunct organization. The pull-no-punches approach to interviewing laid the groundwork for what would go on to become one of the most entertaining interview segments in WWE history.

Shortly after *The Highlight Reel*'s debut, Y2J introduced his "obscenely and obesely expensive" Jeritron 5000, which was later renamed the Jeritron 3000 and Jeritron 6000 in HD, among other names. For the first several years of the segment's existence, the Jeritron 5000 served simply as a screen to showcase highlights. However, in June 2008, that all changed when Y2J drove Shawn Michaels' head through the plasma screen. The move nearly blinded HBK and successfully launched a bitter five-month rivalry between the two Superstars.

One month after destroying the Jeritron 5000 with Michaels' head, Jericho shelved *The Highlight Reel*, claiming he no longer wanted to be seen as the fans' party host for the new millennium.

THE HILLBILLIES

YEARS ACTIVE 1960-1969 1970-1979 **1980-1989** 1990-1999 2000-PRESENT

MEMBERS Hillbilly Jim, Uncle Elmer, Cousin Luke, Cousin Junior

Now don't go messin' with these country boys! Formed by Hillbilly Jim in 1985, the Hillbillies came to WWE to even the odds in Hillbilly Jim's battles against the Heenan Family, Jesse Ventura, "Rowdy" Roddy Piper, "Cowboy" Bob Orton and Mr. Fuji and many others. Jim's relatives were a huge hit with audiences as Elmer, Luke, and later, Junior, battled in both singles and tag team action.

In one of the most touching moments in WWE history, Uncle Elmer was married on *Saturday Night's Main Event* despite the crude attempts by Piper to interrupt the ceremony. The reception was a star-studded event that included a poem recited by "Leapin'" Lanny Poffo and a surprise appearance from Tiny Tim.

By 1986, the cousins went back to the farm and Hillbilly Jim remained with the company. The Hillbillies will forever be remembered for putting smiles on the faces of fans wherever they traveled and weren't afraid to put a beating on no good vermin either.

Hillbilly Jim

YEARS ACTIVE 1960-1969 1970-1979 **1980-1989** 1990-1999 2000-PRESENT

HT 6'7" **WT** 285 lbs. **FROM** Mudlick, Kentucky

SIGNATURE MOVE Bear Hug

At 6'7", it's hard not to notice Hillbilly Jim, especially when he's sitting in the front row. In late 1984, "Rowdy" Roddy Piper spotted the towering fan at a WWE Live Event and asked him to come on *Piper's Pit*. The arrogant Hot Rod mocked Jim's big bushy beard and denim overalls, but eventually offered to train him for a WWE career. Jim, despite wanting to start a ring career, declined the offer and chose to learn from Hulk Hogan instead.

After several weeks of training, the Kentucky native made his in-ring debut, defeating veteran Terry Gibbs with an impressive bear hug. The win marked the beginning of a long love affair between the fans and Hillbilly Jim. Audiences loved the country boy so much, in fact, that they began demanding more of him. Unable to keep up with the lofty demands, Hillbilly Jim introduced his equally lovable family members Uncle Elmer, Cousin Luke, and Cousin Junior.

At *WrestleMania III*, Hillbilly Jim competed in the biggest match of his career when he teamed with midget wrestlers Little Beaver & Haiti Kid to battle King Kong Bundy and his pint-sized pals, Lord Littlebrook & Little Tokyo. The match was marred by controversy when the gigantic Bundy attacked Little Beaver. The sight of Hillbilly Jim carrying his limp little friend from the ring that night remains one of *WrestleMania*'s most memorable images.

Hisashi Shinma

YEARS ACTIVE 1960-1969 **1970-1979** **1980-1989** 1990-1999 2000-PRESENT

A known figure for years within the world of Japanese *puroresu*, Hisashi Shinma began his tenure as WWE President in 1978. He set a tone of no nonsense leadership while making important strides to expand WWE's reach internationally. Shinma was instrumental in building many of the supercards that featured WWE Superstars and the best from New Japan Pro Wrestling, including the famous match that pit Muhammad Ali against Antonio Inoki. Hisashi was commonly seen at ringside impeccably dressed, making sure that WWE contests were filled with fighting spirit and its rules were always upheld.

Mr. Shinma honored the position with his wisdom, dignity and respect until 1984, when he was succeeded by Jack Tunney. Hisashi Shinma will be heralded as the man who upheld the standards of WWE at all costs, no matter what the circumstances were or what public pressures existed at the time.

The Holly Cousins

MEMBERS Crash, Hardcore, Molly

COMBINED WEIGHT Over 800 lbs. (allegedly)

TITLE HISTORY World Tag Team Champions

YEARS ACTIVE 1970-1979 1970-1979 1980-1989 1990-1999 2000-PRESENT

At first, Crash and Hardcore Holly constantly bickered about who was tougher, even when they were paired together in tag team matches. Calling themselves the "Superheavyweights," they insisted on competing only with the giants of sports-entertainment since they claimed a combined weight of allegedly over 800 lbs. Crash brought a scale to the ring with him to ensure that opponents measured up to the Superheavyweights' lofty standards.

In October 1998, Crash and Hardcore Holly defeated the dysfunctional Rock 'N' Sock Connection to win the World Tag Team Championship. After losing the title a month later, Crash and Hardcore remained top title contenders and even won a 16-team Battle Royal. In 2000, the beautiful and talented Molly Holly entered WWE and stepped right into the family business. At *WrestleMania 2000,* Crash and Hardcore fought one another in addition to 11 other Superstars in a Hardcore Battle Royal.

While all three cousins went on to hold different titles during their respective stays in WWE, many fans would argue that this trio made the most magic when they appeared as a family.

HONKY TONK MAN

HT 6'1" **WT** 243 lbs. **FROM** Memphis, Tennessee

SIGNATURE MOVE Shake, Rattle, and Roll **TITLE HISTORY** Intercontinental Champion

YEARS ACTIVE 1960-1969 1970-1979 1980-1989 1990-1999 2000-PRESENT

Many consider the Honky Tonk Man to be one of the greatest Superstars of the 1980s, including the Honky Tonk Man himself. Taking arrogance to a whole new level, it wasn't uncommon to hear the guitar-wielding Superstar remind audiences, "I'm cool, I'm cocky, I'm bad." Unfortunately for all the Honky Tonk Man detractors out there, of which there were plenty, he was everything he claimed to be.

With long sideburns and slicked-back hair, Honky Tonk Man rode into WWE in a pink Cadillac in 1986. Upon arriving, the Elvis look-alike expected to be showered with admiration. Instead, the fans vehemently despised the cocky newcomer. The boos, however, never deterred the Honky Tonk Man from succeeding in the ring. Alongside his manager "Colonel" Jimmy Hart, he set out on an impressive string of victories over WWE's most-noted Superstars, including his first big-name victim Jake Roberts at *WrestleMania III.*

Shortly after *WrestleMania,* the Honky Tonk Man defeated Ricky Steamboat for the Intercontinental Championship in Buffalo, New York. The win proved historic, as he went on to hold the title for nearly fifteen months, longer than any other Superstar in history.

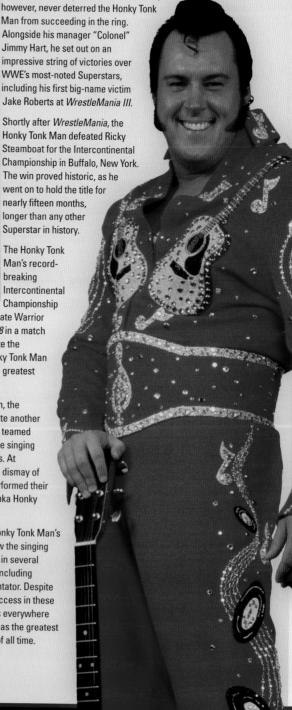

The Honky Tonk Man's record-breaking Intercontinental Championship reign came to an abrupt halt when Ultimate Warrior dethroned the titlist at *SummerSlam 1988* in a match that lasted a mere thirty seconds. Despite the humiliating loss, many consider the Honky Tonk Man to be exactly what he claimed to be: The greatest Intercontinental Champion of all-time.

Following his record-breaking reign, the Honky Tonk Man set out to create another record—a musical record. He teamed with Greg Valentine to form the singing duo known as Rhythm & Blues. At *WrestleMania VI,* much to the dismay of the sold-out SkyDome, they performed their single "Hunka, Hunka, Hunka Honky Love."

The twilight of the Honky Tonk Man's legendary career saw the singing Superstar contribute in several different capacities, including manager and commentator. Despite achieving moderate success in these new roles, however, fans everywhere will always remember him as the greatest Intercontinental Champion of all time.

Hornswoggle

HT	4'4"	**WT**	135 lbs.	**FROM**	Ireland

SIGNATURE MOVE Tadpole Splash

TITLE HISTORY Cruiserweight Champion

YEARS ACTIVE (1960 1969) (1970 1979) (1980 1989) (1990 1999) (2000 PRESENT)

For a man so small in stature, Hornswoggle sure knows how to cause a huge commotion. Once revealed to be the illegitimate son of WWE Chairman Mr. McMahon, the pint-sized Superstar had the entire wrestling world buzzing over his newfound power. After only five months as a member of the McMahon family, JBL revealed the little guy was actually the son of Finlay.

The attention Hornswoggle garnered as a member of the McMahon family was not all that foreign to him. As a small person, he's used to people staring at him, especially when he's beating Superstars twice his size in the ring. That's right, the little Hornswoggle owns victories over such Superstars as Carlito and Jamie Noble. He even turned back five of *SmackDown's* top names to capture the Cruiserweight Championship in July 2007. The victory put Hornswoggle on the same list with history's greatest cruiserweights.

Despite gaining great fame in the ring, Hornswoggle considers his father's safety his main priority. Each time Finlay hits the ring, the feisty Hornswoggle is always right behind him ready to offer a helping hand, whether it's whacking an opponent with a shillelagh or delivering his signature Tadpole Splash.

HOWARD FINKEL

FROM New York, New York	**YEARS ACTIVE**	(1960 1969) (1970 1979) (1980 1989) (1990 1999) (2000 PRESENT)

Howard Finkel began his career in the early 1970's as an usher at the New Haven Coliseum. After he persuaded his boss to contact WWE about holding events there he met Vince McMahon, and by 1976 he was the ring announcer during WWE events at the venue. In 1979, Finkel became a full-time WWE employee and the first staff member of Titan Sports, hired by Vince and Linda McMahon.

As the company entered its critical phase of national expansion, Finkel was selected as the lead ring announcer during a time where WWE needed its own voice. Howard Finkel was heard everywhere—television programs such as *Championship Wrestling, Tuesday Night Titans,* and *Saturday Night's Main Event.*

Finkel also appeared at untelevised stadium shows, pay-per-view events, and provided voice-overs for live event advertisements. WWE was a global entity and Howard Finkel's distinctive delivery was recognized by fans in preparation of the incredible happenings that took place. Into the 1990s, fans and colleagues bestowed him the nickname "The Fink," and at *WrestleMania IX,* he was introduced as "Finkus Maximus." From 1993 to 1997, he was the ring announcer for the company's flagship program, *Monday Night Raw.*

Towards the late 1990s, Howard took on a lighter schedule and announced for live events while branching out to co-host the Internet program *WWE Byte This.* In August 2002, he entered into a dispute with up-and-coming ring announcer Lilian Garcia which turned physical. Unfortunately for "The Fink," he came up on the short end of the stick in an Evening Gown/Tuxedo Match for the right to be the *Raw* ring announcer.

Today, Finkel works in a behind-the-scenes role for the company, hosts the popular "Out Think The Fink" segment on WWE.com and announces the Hall of Fame inductees at *WrestleMania.* Howard Finkel is a unique figure within WWE and a ring announcing icon. His remarkable three-decade career is a true testament to the passion he has for sports-entertainment. He has given millions of fans memories that they will carry for their rest of their lives.

HULK HOGAN

HT	67"	WT	303 lbs.	FROM	Venice Beach, California	YEARS ACTIVE	1960–1969	1970–1979	1980–1989	1990–1999	2000–PRESENT

SIGNATURE MOVES	Atomic Leg Drop	TITLE HISTORY	WWE Champion, World Tag Team Champion

Hulk Hogan, the most recognizable icon of professional wrestling, came from humble beginnings. During high school he had two passions: music and wrestling. He played in a string of bands within the bustling Tampa music scene. When he wasn't on stage, he was running to arenas to see his favorite stars of the ring. Once he saw "Superstar" Billy Graham jump on the middle turnbuckle and hit a double-bicep pose, the young Hogan knew his place was in the ring. One night after a concert he met the Briscos and soon introduced himself to Mike Graham. Graham arranged for Hogan to train with Japanese grappling master, Hiro Matsuda. After eighteen months of training he toured the Alabama, Pensacola, and Memphis territories.

AN EARLY TASTE OF MAINSTREAM POPULARITY

In 1978, Hulk Hogan debuted in the World Wide Wrestling Federation managed by "Classy" Freddie Blassie. Despite his questionable ways, he connected with the crowd at the 1980 Showdown At Shea when he met Andre the Giant in a wild bout. Against the wishes of Vince J. McMahon, Hogan left the company and appeared in *Rocky III* as "Thunderlips."

Hulk drifted to the AWA and though he resumed his rule-breaking ways, he quickly became a top contender to the AWA Championship. Hulk also traveled to Japan and defeated *puroresu* legend Antonio Inoki to become the first-ever IWGP Heavyweight Champion.

HULKAMANIA RUNS WILD

Hulk Hogan returned to WWE in January 1984 and aided Bob Backlund against the Wild Samoans and Lou Albano. With the fans now behind him, Hulk was ready to catapult to the top of the ladder. Later that month, he replaced an injured Backlund and defeated the Iron Sheik for the WWE Championship. That night, dubbed "Super Monday," saw the birth of the most powerful force in the universe. Commentator Gorilla Monsoon perfectly proclaimed, "Hulkamania is here!"

The Hulkster became the voice of an entire generation. Hogan professed the importance of truth, training, saying your prayers, and eating your vitamins. By 1985, Hulk was splashed all over the mainstream media as he appeared on the *A-Team* and hosted *Saturday Night Live*.

The company's licensing and merchandising took the world by storm, spearheaded by the red and yellow of Hulkamania. The Hulkster had his own books, action figures, clothing line, workout set, vitamin pack, and an animated series titled *Hulk Hogan's Rock 'n' Wrestling*.

His success didn't sit well with Roddy Piper. In the main event of the first *WrestleMania*, Hogan and his partner, Mr. T, had Jimmy Snuka in their corner, while Piper had Paul Orndorff as his partner and "Cowboy" Bob Orton in their corner. Boxing legend Muhammad Ali was brought in as the special guest referee. The event was such a success that Hogan graced the April 29, 1985 issue of *Sports Illustrated*.

During a 1986 episode of *Saturday Night's Main Event* Hogan became the victim of a three-man attack by Don Muraco, Heenan, and King Kong Bundy. Despite missing than a month with broken ribs, and ignoring doctor's orders, Hogan defeated Bundy in a Steel Cage Match at *WrestleMania 2*.

"WHATCHA GONNA DO WHEN HULKAMANIA RUNS WILD ON YOU?"

WRESTLEMANIA III AND A MILLION DOLLAR THREAT

A giant threat to Hulk Hogan's career came from an unexpected source. Andre the Giant appeared on *Piper's Pit* with Bobby Heenan, and challenged Hogan to a WWE Championship match at *WrestleMania III*. Over 93,000 fans were on hand as the world's two most recognizable figures stood in the center of the ring. During the match, Hulk Hogan did the unthinkable and hoisted the 500-pound Andre the Giant and bodyslammed him. After Hulk Hogan's victory, which ended Andre's fifteen year undefeated streak, Hulkamaniacs all over the world rose to their feet in triumph.

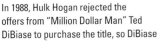

In 1988, Hulk Hogan rejected the offers from "Million Dollar Man" Ted DiBiase to purchase the title, so DiBiase allied with Andre the Giant and Bobby Heenan. They plotted to dethrone the Hulkster during a nationally televised episode of *The Main Event* through subterfuge. With the plot uncovered, WWE president Jack Tunney declared the title vacant and that a new champion would be crowned in a tournament at *WrestleMania IV*. The quarterfinals match between Hogan and Andre ended in a double disqualification, so neither man was eligible to win the tournament.

THE RISE AND FALL OF THE MEGA POWERS

In the tournament finals, Hulk Hogan aided former foe, Randy "Macho Man" Savage against the "Million Dollar Man." The two Superstars became inseparable and soon *Hulkamania* and *"Macho Madness"* merged into the Mega Powers. Over the summer the Mega-Powers battled against Andre the Giant and Ted DiBiase, leading to clashes at the main event of the first *SummerSlam* and the 1988 *Survivor Series*.

Unfortunately, during *The Main Event* a series of misunderstandings between Hogan and Savage lead to the Macho Man slapping Hogan. After the match, the disagreement escalated and Macho Man blindsided Hulk Hogan. His former partner ignited the fuse that would lead to a colossal explosion at *WrestleMania V* where Hulk Hogan reclaimed the WWE Championship.

NO HOLDS BARRED

On June 2, 1989, the movie *No Holds Barred* opened and Hulk Hogan was the main attraction. The success of the picture led to a dispute with co-star Zeus. After a series of attacks on the Champion, Hulk Hogan and Brutus Beefcake defeated Zeus and Randy Savage at *SummerSlam '89*.

In the next decade, Hulk continued to star in feature films and commercials. After the Hulkster defeated Savage on *The Main Event* with special guest referee Buster Douglas, he moved on to other title contenders. At the 1990 *Royal Rumble* fate brought the two largest personas in the WWE nose-to-nose in the middle of the ring. The even exchange between Hogan and Ultimate Warrior had everyone on their feet. Even after the WWE Champion won his first *Royal Rumble*, the question remained if the two Superstars met, who would win? WWE answered the call and signed a *Title Vs. Title* bout for the main event of *WrestleMania VI*.

Even though Hogan lost the WWE Championship to Ultimate Warrior that night, he exited with the grace of a true champion. He even joined Ultimate Warrior in victory at the 1990 *Survivor Series*, and in the *Match Made in Hell* at *SummerSlam '91*. Hogan went on to hold the WWE Championship three more times, and win a second *Royal Rumble* before leaving WWE to concentrate on raising his family and a movie career.

WCW AND THE nWo

In June 1994, Hogan was lured back to sports-entertainment by WCW. In July, he defeated Ric Flair to become WCW Champion. Despite holding the title on six separate occasions, his WCW tenure is remembered more for the shocking turn at *Bash At The Beach* in 1996, where Hogan revealed himself as the mystery partner of the Outsiders, Scott Hall and Kevin Nash.

As he turned his back on millions of Hulkamaniacs worldwide, "Hollywood" Hulk Hogan declared that the fans could "stick it" and formed the New World Order (nWo) with Hall and Nash.

After the 2002 *Royal Rumble*, the nWo were brought into WWE by Vince McMahon. The nWo's involvement in WWE reached its peak at *WrestleMania X-8*, Hogan's first appearance at the event in nine years, as Hollywood Hogan faced The Rock in a match labled *Icon vs. Icon*. Following that classic showdown, Hogan and The Rock shook hands and battled Scott Hall and Kevin Nash, who had turned their backs on Hogan.

RETURN TO THE RED AND YELLOW

Hulk removed the nWo attire and returned to the ring in the red and yellow of Hulkamania. With Hulkamania reinvigorated, the Hulkster found himself across the ring at *Backlash* from "The Game" Triple H. After a wild battle Hogan captured his sixth WWE Championship. Though the Hulkster lost the title to Undertaker at *Judgment Day*, he added a new prize to his collection when he won the World Tag Team Championship with Edge. Later in the year his autobiography titled *Hollywood Hulk Hogan* landed atop the New York Times Bestseller list. The next year he headlined *WrestleMania XIX* in a street fight against Mr. McMahon.

After being inducted in the Hall Of Fame at *WrestleMania 21*, Hulk saved Eugene from Muhammed Hassan and Daivari. Hogan was recruited by Shawn Michaels to eradicate the duo. On an episode of *Monday Night Raw,* Michaels suddenly turned on Hogan after they beat Kurt Angle & Carlito. HBK mocked sports-entertainment's most beloved figure, but Hulk Hogan had the last laugh and defeated the "Showstopper" in their *Legend vs. Icon* Match at *SummerSlam*.

In April 2005, Hulk Hogan's career was honored at the Hall Of Fame ceremony, where he was inducted by Sylvester Stallone.

Hogan also appeared at the *Raw Homecoming* in October 2005, battled Randy Orton at *SummerSlam 2006*, and saved Hornswoggle in 2008 from The Great Khali at the *Raw 15th Anniversary* broadcast.

The Hurricane 🇺🇸

HT 6' **WT** 215 lbs.

FROM Raleigh, North Carolina

SIGNATURE MOVE Eye of the Hurricane

TITLE HISTORY Cruiserweight Champion, European Champion, Hardcore Champion, World Tag Team Champion

YEARS ACTIVE 1960-1969 1970-1979 1980-1989 1990-1999 2000 PRESENT

"Stand back, there's a Hurricane coming through!"

The WWE's favorite superhero, The Hurricane, appeared shortly after the WCW Invasion of 2001. He often appeared backstage dressed in a suit and glasses as a mild-mannered beat reporter for the Daily Globe.

He was drafted to *SmackDown* in 2002 and captured the Cruiserweight Championship shortly afterward in a Triple Threat Match. Later that year, he arrived on *Raw* and formed an unlikely, yet successful, team with Kane. The Hurricane's powers continued to serve him well when on the March 10, 2003 edition of *Raw* he pinned The Rock. He enjoyed a successful association with Superhero-in-Training Rosey, and their Super-sidekick Stacey, which lead to a World Tag Team Championship reign.

Hurricane Helms 🇺🇸

YEARS ACTIVE 1960-1969 1970-1979 1980-1989 1990-1999 2000 PRESENT

HT 6' **WT** 215 lbs. **FROM** Raleigh, North Carolina

SIGNATURE MOVE Shining Wizard

TITLE HISTORY Cruiserweight Champion, World Tag Team Champion, European Champion, Hardcore Champion

It took years, but the Hurricane Helms fans see on WWE television each week is the same Gregory Helms that walks the streets of his hometown of Raleigh, North Carolina. No masks. No gimmicks. Just one cocky Superstar intent on ruling the wrestling world.

In January 2006, Helms jumped to *SmackDown* and immediately captured the Cruiserweight Championship. His reign, which saw him best such top contenders such as Matt Hardy, Jamie Noble, and Super Crazy, is widely recognized as the greatest of all-time. When it was all said and done, Helms held the title for a record thirteen months, twice the length of the second longest reign.

Prior to WWE, Helms also proved his worth while competing in WCW. In fact, he was the Cruiserweight Champion at the time WWE purchased WCW. In the conversation of the great Cruiserweights of all time, Helms is not only included, but just may be at the top of the list.

"I QUIT" MATCH

No match puts a WWE Superstar's pride to the test more than an "I Quit" Match. As the name suggests, the goal is to beat your opponent so badly that he says the embarrassing words "I quit," thus admitting his inferiority.

The first mainstream "I Quit" Match in WWE history pitted Bret "Hit Man" Hart against Bob Backlund at *WrestleMania XI*. With "Rowdy" Roddy Piper serving as special referee, Hart added insult to injury when he forced Backlund to quit using his own Crossface Chicken Wing.

Following *WrestleMania XI*, the "I Quit" Match was shelved for nearly four years. When it finally returned, however, it produced one of history's most vicious matches. With the WWE Championship on the line at the 1999 *Royal Rumble*, The Rock handcuffed Mankind's hands behind his back. He then proceeded to smash the champ's head with more than 10 brutal steel chair shots. The force of the shots rendered Mankind unconscious, but The Rock fooled everybody by playing audio of his opponent saying "I quit" over the arena loudspeakers. As a result, The Rock walked away with the WWE Championship.

WWE's only intergender "I Quit" Match put Stephanie McMahon up against her own father at *No Mercy 2003*. Holding nothing back, Mr. McMahon went at his daughter as if she was Big Show or Kane. In the end, Stephanie's mother couldn't bear to watch any longer and threw the towel in on her daughter's behalf.

IN YOUR HOUSE

1995

IN YOUR HOUSE 1

MAY 14 Syracuse, NY

Onondaga War Memorial

Main Event: WWE Champion Diesel vs. Sycho Sid

IN YOUR HOUSE 2: THE LUMBERJACKS

JULY 23 Nashville, TN

Nashville Municipal Auditorium

Main Event: WWE Champion Diesel vs. Sycho Sid, Lumberjack Match

IN YOUR HOUSE 3: TRIPLE HEADER

SEP 24 Saginaw, MI

Saginaw Civic Center

Main Event: WWE Champion Diesel & Intercontinental Champion Shawn Michaels vs. British Bulldog & Yokozuna

IN YOUR HOUSE 4: GREAT WHITE NORTH

OCT 22 Winnipeg, Manitoba, Canada

Winnipeg Arena

Main Event: WWE Champion Diesel vs. British Bulldog

IN YOUR HOUSE 5: SEASON'S BEATINGS

DEC 17 Hershey, PA

Hersheypark Arena

Main Event: WWE Champion Bret "Hit Man" Hart vs. British Bulldog

1996

IN YOUR HOUSE 6: RAGE IN THE CAGE

FEB 16 Louisville, KY

Louisville Gardens

Main Event: WWE Champion Bret "Hit Man" Hart vs. Diesel, Steel Cage Match

IN YOUR HOUSE 7: GOOD FRIENDS, BETTER ENEMIES

APR 28 Omaha, NE

Omaha Civic Center

Main Event: WWE Champion Shawn Michaels vs. Diesel, No Holds Barred Match

IN YOUR HOUSE 8: BEWARE OF DOG

MAY 26 Florence, SC

Florence Civic Center

Main Event: WWE Champion Shawn Michaels vs. British Bulldog

MAY 28 North Charleston, SC

North Charleston Coliseum

Main Event: Intercontinental Champion Goldust vs. Undertaker, Casket Match

IN YOUR HOUSE 9: INTERNATIONAL INCIDENT

JULY 21 Vancouver, BC

General Motors Place

Main Event: WWE Champion Shawn Michaels, Intercontinental Champion Ahmed Johnson & Sycho Sid vs. Vader, Owen Hart & British Bulldog

IN YOUR HOUSE 10: MIND GAMES

SEP 22 Philadelphia, PA

CoreStates Center

Main Event: WWE Champion Shawn Michaels vs. Mankind

IN YOUR HOUSE 11: BURIED ALIVE

OCT 20 Indianapolis, IN

Market Square Arena

Main Event: Undertaker vs. Mankind, Buried Alive Match

IN YOUR HOUSE 12: IT'S TIME

DEC 15 West Palm Beach, FL

West Palm Beach Auditorium

Main Event: WWE Champion Sycho Sid vs. Bret "Hit Man" Hart

1997

IN YOUR HOUSE 13: FINAL FOUR

FEB 16 Chattanooga, TN

UTC Arena

Main Event: Bret " Hit Man" Hart vs. Undertaker vs. Stone Cold Steve Austin vs. Vader, Vacant WWE Championship Four Corners Elimination Match

IN YOUR HOUSE 14: REVENGE OF UNDERTAKER

APR 26 Rochester, NY

War Memorial Auditorium

Main Event: WWE Champion Undertaker vs. Mankind

IN YOUR HOUSE 15: A COLD DAY IN HELL

MAY 11 Richmond, VA

Richmond Coliseum

Main Event: WWE Champion Undertaker vs. Stone Cold Steve Austin

IN YOUR HOUSE 16: CANADIAN STAMPEDE

JULY 06 Calgary, Alberta, Canada

Saddledome

Main Event: Bret "Hit Man" Hart, Jim Neidhart, Brian Pillman, Owen Hart & British Bulldog vs. Stone Cold Steve Austin, Goldust, Ken Shamrock & Legion of Doom

IN YOUR HOUSE 17: GROUND ZERO

SEP 07 Louisville, KY

Louisville Gardens

Main Event: Shawn Michaels vs. Undertaker

IN YOUR HOUSE 18: BADD BLOOD

OCT 05 St. Louis, MO

Kiel Center

Main Event: Shawn Michaels vs. Undertaker, Hell in a Cell Match

IN YOUR HOUSE 19: DEGENERATION-X

DEC 07 Springfield, MA

Springfield Civic Center

Main Event: WWE Champion Shawn Michaels vs. Ken Shamrock

1998

IN YOUR HOUSE 20: NO WAY OUT OF TEXAS

FEB 15 Houston, TX

Compaq Center

Main Event: Stone Cold Steve Austin, Cactus Jack, Chainsaw Charlie & Owen Hart vs. Triple H, Billy Gunn, Road Dogg & Savio Vega

IN YOUR HOUSE 21: UNFORGIVEN

APR 26 Greensboro, NC

Greensboro Coliseum

Main Event: WWE Champion Stone Cold Steve Austin vs. Dude Love

IN YOUR HOUSE 22: OVER THE EDGE

MAY 31 Milwaukee, WI

Wisconsin Center Arena

Main Event: WWE Champion Stone Cold Steve Austin vs. Dude Love, No Disqualification Falls Count Anywhere Match, Mr. McMahon as special guest referee

IN YOUR HOUSE 23: FULLY LOADED

JULY 26 Fresno, CA

Selland Arena

Main Event: World Tag Team Champions Kane & Mankind vs. Undertaker & Stone Cold Steve Austin

IN YOUR HOUSE 24: BREAKDOWN

SEP 27 Hamilton, Ontario, Canada

Copps Coliseum

Main Event: WWE Champion Stone Cold Steve Austin vs. Undertaker vs. Kane, Triple Threat Match

IN YOUR HOUSE 25: JUDGMENT DAY

OCT 18 Rosemont, IL

Rosemont Horizon

Main Event: Kane vs. Undertaker, Vacant WWE Championship Match, Stone Cold Steve Austin as special guest referee

IN YOUR HOUSE 26: ROCK BOTTOM

DEC 13 Vancouver, British Columbia, Canada

General Motors Place

Main Event: Stone Cold Steve Austin vs. Undertaker, Buried Alive Match

1999

IN YOUR HOUSE 27: ST. VALENTINE'S DAY MASSACRE

FEB 14 Memphis, TN

The Pyramid

Main Event: Stone Cold Steve Austin vs. Mr. McMahon, Steel Cage Match

IN YOUR HOUSE 28: BACKLASH

APR 25 Providence, RI

Providence Civic Center

Main Event: WWE Champion Stone Cold Steve Austin vs. The Rock, Shane McMahon as special guest referee

INTERCONTINENTAL CHAMPIONSHIP

After unifying the North and South American Championships in September 1979, Pat Patterson was recognized as the first-ever Intercontinental Champion. Patterson's impressive resumé prior to becom[...] Intercontinental Champion gave the title instant credibility. However, nobody could have predicted that the Intercontinental Championship would eventually become one of the most prestigious titles in sports-entertainment history.

Over the next several decades, many future Hall of Famers went on to prove their greatness with the Intercontinental Championship strapped around their waist, including Greg "The Hammer" Valentin[...] Mr. Perfect, and "Rowdy" Roddy Piper. Several others used the title to propel themselves to World Championship reigns, including Shawn Michaels, Stone Cold Steve Austin, and The Rock.

1979

SEPT 09 — Rio de Janeiro
Pat Patterson becomes Intercontinental Champion

After winning a tournament in Rio de Janeiro, Pat Patterson unified the North and South American Championships to become the first-ever Intercontinental Champion.

1980

APR 21 — New York, NY
Ken Patera defeats Pat Patterson

DEC 08 — New York, NY
Pedro Morales defeats Ken Patera

1981

JUNE 20 — Philadelphia, PA
Don Muraco defeats Pedro Morales

1987

MAR 29 — Pontiac, MI
Ricky Steamboat defeats Randy Savage

JUNE 02 — Buffalo, NY
Honky Tonk Man defeats Ricky Steamboat

1988

AUG 29 — New York, NY
Ultimate Warrior defeats Honky Tonk Man

1989

APR 02 — Atlantic City, NJ
Rick Rude defeats Ultimate Warrior

JAN 19 — Albany, NY
Roddy Piper defeats The Mountie

APR 05 — Indianapolis, IN
Bret Hart defeats Roddy Piper

AUG 29 — London, England
British Bulldog defeats Bret Hart

OCT 27 — Terre Haute, IN
Shawn Michaels defeats British Bulldog

1993

MAY 17 — New York, NY
Marty Jannetty defeats Shawn Michaels

JUNE 06 — Albany, NY
Shawn Michaels defeats Marty Jannetty

After failing to defend the Intercontinental Championship within 30 days, Shawn Michaels was stripped of the title.

MAY 22 — Trois-Rivieres, Quebec
Jeff Jarrett defeats Razor Ramon

JULY 23 — Nashville, TN
Shawn Michaels defeats Jeff Jarrett

Injuries forced Shawn Michaels to relinquish the Intercontinental Championship on October 22, 1995.

OCT 22 — Winnipeg, Manitoba
Dean Douglas is awarded Intercontinental Championship

OCT 22 — Winnipeg, Manitoba
Razor Ramon defeats Dean Douglas

1996

JAN 21 — Fresno, CA
Goldust defeats Razor Ramon

Goldust was stripped of the Intercontinental Championship after a title defense against Savio Vega ended in controversy.

AUG 03 — East Rutherford, NJ
Stone Cold Steve Austin defeats Owen Hart

Shortly after winning the Intercontinental Championship, injuries forced Stone Cold Steve Austin to relinquish the title.

OCT 05 — St. Louis, MO
Owen Hart defeats Faarooq in the finals of a tournament to crown a new Intercontinental Champion

NOV 09 — Montreal, Quebec
Stone Cold Steve Austin defeats Owen Hart

DEC 08 — Portland, ME
The Rock becomes Intercontinental Champion

The Rock was awarded the Intercontinental Championship after Stone Cold Steve Austin forfeited the title.

MAY 31 — Moline, IL
Jeff Jarrett defeats The Godfather

JULY 24 — Toronto, Ontario
Edge defeats Jeff Jarrett

JULY 25 — Buffalo, NY
Jeff Jarrett defeats Edge

JULY 26 — Dayton, OH
D-Lo Brown defeats Jeff Jarrett

AUG 22 — Minneapolis, MN
Jeff Jarrett defeats D-Lo Brown

OCT 17 — Cleveland, OH
Chyna defeats Jeff Jarrett

MAY 08 — Uniondale, NY
Chris Benoit defeats Chris Jericho

JUNE 22 — Memphis, TN
Rikishi defeats Chris Benoit

JULY 06 — Ft. Lauderdale, FL
Val Venis defeats Rikishi

AUG 27 — Raleigh, NC
Chyna defeats Trish Stratus

Chyna & Eddie Guerrero battled Val Venis & Trish Stratus in a Mixed-Tag Team Match, where the winner of the match would be declared Intercontinental Champion. Chyna pinned Stratus to win the title.

SEPT 03 — Knoxville, TN
Eddie Guerrero defeats Chyna

Eddie Guerrero pinned Chyna to become Intercontinental Champion in a Triple Threat Match that also included Kurt Angle.

2002

JAN 20 — Atlanta, GA
William Regal defeats Edge

AUG 19 — San Jose, CA
Edge defeats Lance Storm

SEPT 23 — Pittsburgh, PA
Christian defeats Edge

OCT 21 — St. Louis, MO
Edge defeats Christian

NOV 05 — Uniondale, NY
Test defeats Edge

NOV 18 — Greensboro, NC
Edge defeats Test

Edge pinned Test to unify the Intercontinental and United States Championships.

2003

MAY 18 — Charlotte, N[...]
Christian wins the Intercontinental Championship

Christian last eliminated Booker T in a Battle Royal to crown the new Intercontinental Champion.

JULY 07 — Montreal, Quebec
Booker T defeats Christian

AUG 10 — Des Moines, IA
Christian defeats Booker T

SEPT 29 — Chicago, IL
Rob Van Dam defeats Christian

OCT 27 — Fayetteville, NC
Chris Jericho defeats Rob Van Dam

OCT 27 — Fayetteville, NC
Rob Van Dam defeats Chris Jericho

138

1983
- NOV 23 — New York, NY — Pedro Morales defeats Don Muraco

1984
- JAN 22 — New York, NY — Don Muraco defeats Pedro Morales

1985
- FEB 11 — Boston, MA — Tito Santana defeats Don Muraco
- SEPT 24 — London, Ontario — Greg Valentine defeats Tito Santana

1986
- JULY 06 — Baltimore, MD — Tito Santana defeats Greg Valentine
- FEB 08 — Boston, MA — Randy Savage defeats Tito Santana

1990
- AUG 28 — East Rutherford, NJ — Ultimate Warrior defeats Rick Rude
- Ultimate Warrior vacated the Intercontinental Championship shortly after defeating Hulk Hogan for the WWE Championship in April 1990.

1991
- APR 23 — Austin, TX — Mr. Perfect defeats Tito Santana in the finals of a tournament to crown a new Intercontinental Champion.
- AUG 27 — Philadelphia, PA — Texas Tornado defeats Mr. Perfect
- NOV 19 — Rochester, NY — Mr. Perfect defeats Texas Tornado

1992
- AUG 26 — New York, NY — Bret Hart defeats Mr. Perfect
- JAN 17 — Springfield, MA — The Mountie defeats Bret Hart

1994
- SEPT 27 — New Haven, CT — Razor Ramon defeats The Model
- After being the last two Superstars standing in a Battle Royal, Razor Ramon and The Model squared off to crown a new Intercontinental Champion.

1995
- APR 13 — Rochester, NY — Diesel defeats Razor Ramon
- AUG 29 — Chicago, IL — Razor Ramon defeats Diesel
- JAN 22 — Tampa, FL — Jeff Jarrett defeats Razor Ramon
- Jeff Jarrett was stripped of the Intercontinental Championship on April 26, 1995 after a title defense against Bob Holly ended in controversy.
- APR 26 — Moline, IL — Jeff Jarrett defeats Bob Holly to reclaim the vacated title
- MAY 19 — Montreal, Quebec — Razor Ramon defeats Jeff Jarrett

1996
- APR 01 — San Bernardino, CA — Goldust defeats Savio Vega to reclaim the vacant title.
- JUNE 23 — Milwaukee, WI — Ahmed Johnson defeats Goldust
- Injuries forced Ahmed Johnson to relinquish the Intercontinental Championship on August 12, 1996.

1997
- FEB 13 — Lowell, MA — Rocky Maivia defeats Hunter Hearst Helmsley
- APR 28 — Omaha, NE — Owen Hart defeats Rocky Maivia
- SEPT 23 — Hershey, PA — Marc Mero defeats Faarooq in the finals of a tournament to crown a new intercontinental Champion
- OCT 21 — Fort Wayne, IN — Hunter Hearst Helmsley defeats Marc Mero

1998
- AUG 30 — New York, NY — Triple H defeats The Rock
- Injuries forced Triple H to relinquish the Intercontinental Championship on October 9, 1998.
- OCT 12 — Uniondale, NY — Ken Shamrock defeats X-Pac in the finals of a tournament to crown a new Intercontinental Champion

1999
- FEB 14 — Memphis, TN — Val Venis defeats Ken Shamrock
- MAR 15 — San Jose, CA — Road Dogg defeats Val Venis
- MAR 29 — East Rutherford, NJ — Goldust defeats Road Dogg
- APR 12 — Detroit, MI — The Godfather defeats Goldust

2000
- DEC 12 — Sunrise, FL — Chris Jericho defeats Chyna
- Chris Jericho and Chyna were declared co-Intercontinental Champions on January 3, 2000, after a match between the two ended in a double pinfall.
- JAN 23 — New York, NY — Chris Jericho defeats Chyna. Chris Jericho pinned Chyna to become undisputed Intercontinental Champion in Triple Threat Match that also included Hardcore Holly.
- FEB 27 — Hartford, CT — Kurt Angle defeats Chris Jericho
- APR 02 — Anaheim, CA — Chris Benoit defeats Chris Jericho. Chris Benoit pinned Chris Jericho to win the Intercontinental Championship in a Triple Threat Match that also included then-champion Kurt Angle.
- MAY 04 — Richmond, VA — Chris Jericho defeats Chris Benoit

2001
- NOV 23 — Sunrise, FL — Billy Gunn defeats Eddie Guerrero
- DEC 10 — Birmingham, AL — Chris Benoit defeats Billy Gunn
- JAN 21 — New Orleans, LA — Chris Jericho defeats Chris Benoit
- APR 05 — Oklahoma City, OK — Triple H defeats Chris Jericho
- APR 12 — Philadelphia, PA — Jeff Hardy defeats Triple H
- APR 16 — Knoxville, TN — Triple H defeats Jeff Hardy
- MAY 20 — Sacramento, CA — Kane defeats Triple H
- JUNE 28 — New York, NY — Albert defeats Kane
- JULY 23 — Buffalo, NY — Lance Storm defeats Albert

2004
- DEC 14 — Orlando, FL — Randy Orton defeats Rob Van Dam
- MAR 17 — Toronto, Ontario — Rob Van Dam defeats William Regal
- APR 21 — Kansas City, MO — Eddie Guerrero defeats Rob Van Dam
- MAY 27 — Edmonton, Alberta — Rob Van Dam defeats Eddie Guerrero
- JULY 29 — Greensboro, NC — Chris Benoit defeats Rob Van Dam
- AUG 25 — Uniondale, NY — Rob Van Dam defeats Chris Benoit
- SEPT 16 — Denver, CO — Chris Jericho defeats Rob Van Dam
- SEPT 30 — Houston, TX — Kane defeats Chris Jericho
- OCT 20 — Little Rock, AR — Triple H defeats Kane
- With his victory over Kane, Triple H unified the World Heavyweight Championship with the Intercontinental Championship. The Intercontinental Title remained inactive until May 2003.
- JULY 11 — Hartford, CT — Edge defeats Randy Orton
- Injuries forced Edge to relinquish the Championship on September 6.
- SEPT 12 — Portland, OR — Chris Jericho defeats Christian. Chris Jericho defeated Christian in a Ladder Match to crown a new Intercontinental Champion.
- OCT 19 — Milwaukee, WI — Shelton Benjamin defeats Chris Jericho

2005
- JUNE 21 — Phoenix, AZ — Carlito defeats Shelton Benjamin
- SEPT 19 — Oklahoma City, OK — Ric Flair defeats Carlito

continued on next page

2006

FEB 20 Trenton, NJ

Shelton Benjamin defeats Ric Flair

APR 30 Lexington, KY

Rob Van Dam defeats Shelton Benjamin

MAY 15 Lubbock, TX

Shelton Benjamin defeats Rob Van Dam

Shelton Benjamin, Chris Masters & Triple H battled John Cena & Rob Van Dam in a 3-on-2 Handicap Texas Tornado Match. Pre-match stipulations stated that if any member of Benjamin's team defeated Cena or Rob Van Dam, they would win that Superstar's title.

JUN 25 Charlotte, NC

Johnny Nitro defeats Shelton Benjamin

Johnny Nitro pinned Shelton Benjamin to become Intercontinental Champion in a Triple Threat Match that also included Carlito.

2007

FEB 19 Bakersfield, CA

Umaga defeats Jeff Hardy

APR 16 Milan, Italy

Santino Marella defeats Umaga

JULY 02 Dallas, TX

Umaga defeats Santino Marella

SEPT 03 Columbus, OH

Jeff Hardy defeats Umaga

OCT 02 Topeka, KS

Jeff Hardy defeats Johnny Nitro

NOV 06 Columbus, OH

Johnny Nitro defeats Jeff Hardy

NOV 13 Manchester, England

Jeff Hardy defeats Johnny Nitro

2008

MAR 10 Milwaukee, WI

Chris Jericho defeats Jeff Hardy

JUNE 06 Dallas, TX

Kofi Kingston defeats Chris Jericho

AUG 18 Indianapolis, IN

Santino Marella becomes Intercontinetnal Champion

In an intergender Winner Takes All Match, Santino Marella & Beth Phoenix defeated Kofi Kingston & Mickie James.

NOV 10 Manchester, England

William Regal defeats Santino Marella

International Tag Team Championship

This tag team championship was the precursor to the most prestigious prize in all of tag team wrestling, the World Tag Team Championship.

1969

JUNE 01 Osaka, Japan

Prof. Toru Tanaka & Mitsu Arakawa win a tournament to be crowned the first World Wide Wrestling Federation International Tag Team Champions.

DEC 08 New York, NY

Bruno Sammartino & Battman defeat Prof. Toru Tanaka & Mitsu Arakawa

On Dember 12, Victor Rivera replaces Bruno Sammartino as co-holder of the title due to Sammartino's obligations as World Heavyweight Champion.

1970

JUNE 15 New York, NY

The Mongols defeat Victor Rivera & Battman in a Best 2-out-of-3 Falls Match to win the titles

In 1971, The Mongols disappeared from the World Wide Wrestling Federation and took the International Tag Team Championship belts with them. The International Tag Team Championship was considered vacated due to inactivity and would remain so for more than a decade. The World Wide Wrestling Federation crowned Luke Graham & Tarzan Tyler as World Tag Team Champions at the end of a June 3, 1971 tournament. The duo met and defeated The Mongols on November 12, voiding any claim the Mongols had to the championship.

1985

MAY 24 Kobe, Japan

Tatsumi Fujinami & Kengo Kimura defeat Adrian Adonis & Dick Murdoch in the tournament finals to crown new champions. The titles were almost exclusively defended in Japan for the remainder of the year before being retired.

Irish Jackie

YEARS ACTIVE

Prior to entering WWE, midget wrestler Irish Jackie struggled to make it big while competing in Southern wrestling territories. For much of the 1950s, he fell to the likes of Little Beaver and Pee Wee James. After moving north to WWE in the 1960s, Irish Jackie began to find his winning ways. He wowed northern audiences alongside his new partner the Jamaica Kid. The famed Boston Garden was the scene of many of the team's victories over rivals Sky Low Low and Little Brutus. Irish Jackie also had many remarkable battles against Sonny Boy Cassidy in the late 1960s.

"Iron" Mike Sharpe

YEARS ACTIVE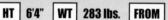

HT 6'4" **WT** 283 lbs. **FROM** Hamilton, Ontario, Canada **SIGNATURE MOVE** Forearm Smash

A second-generation Superstar, "Iron" Mike Sharpe was a rough and tough customer who proclaimed himself "Canada's Greatest Athlete." He was first seen by WWE audiences in the early 1980s managed by Lou Albano.

During the mid-1980s, Sharpe traveled through Canada and Japan before returning to WWE programming. Sharpe always attributed his success to himself, but others attributed it to the controversial black armpad that covered his right forearm.

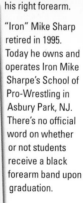

"Iron" Mike Sharp retired in 1995. Today he owns and operates Iron Mike Sharpe's School of Pro-Wrestling in Asbury Park, NJ. There's no official word on whether or not students receive a black forearm band upon graduation.

IRON SHEIK

"IRAN NUMBER ONE! IRON SHEIK NUMBER ONE!"

HT 6' **WT** 258 lbs.

FROM Tehran, Iran

SIGNATURE MOVE Camel Clutch

YEARS ACTIVE 1960–1969 1970–1979 1980–1989 1990–1999 2000–PRESENT

TITLE HISTORY WWE Champion, World Tag Team Champion

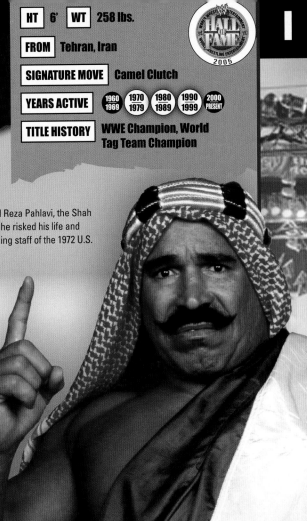

The Iron Sheik is remembered as one of the most loathed villains in the history of the ring. His mixture of technical ring skill, charisma, and athleticism brought terror to WWE and its fans to heights that may never be seen again. Whether he was in singles or tag team competition, one word can be used to describe the Iron Sheik: dangerous.

As a member of the Iranian Army, this man became a national wrestling champion and later the bodyguard for Mohammed Reza Pahlavi, the Shah of Iran. He was an alternate on the 1968 Iranian Olympic wrestling team and a two-time Asian freestyle champion. In 1970, he risked his life and defected to the United States, where he won several AAU Championships. His impressive credentials led him to the coaching staff of the 1972 U.S. Olympic team, and, in 1973, he was trained for a career in the ring by Verne Gagne.

In 1979, the Iron Sheik entered WWE swinging his Persian Clubs. In his Madison Square Garden debut, he won a 20-man over-the-top-rope battle royal and earned a WWE Championship Match in that night's main event against Bob Backlund. After that bout, he tied-up with the likes of Bruno Sammartino, Antonio Inoki, Ted DiBiase, Dominic DeNucci, Chief Jay Strongbow, Gorilla Monsoon, and Tito Santana. He left WWE in 1980 and toured the Southeastern territories of the NWA. While he toured the United States and exuded anti-American rhetoric, the terror from Tehran became known as a cold blooded rule-breaker, a premier ring technician and "The Master of the Suplex."

AT ODDS WITH AMERICA'S CHAMPIONS

In the fall of 1983, the Iron Sheik, with "Classy" Freddie Blassie as his manager, returned to WWE. Sheik waved the flag of his home nation as he shouted, "Iran Number One!"

The Iron Sheik attacked the company's most beloved heroes with his controversial loaded boot and forced them to submit with his dangerous Camel Clutch. On December 26, 1983, Sheik won the WWE Championship amidst a sea of controversy when Bob Backlund's manager, Arnold Skaaland, threw in the towel as the injured champion was trapped in the Camel Clutch. However, his title reign would be short lived. Replacing an injured Backlund, Hulk Hogan defeated Sheik for the WWE Championship on January 23, 1984, at Madison Square Garden. Despite the loss, the Iron Sheik was part of the match that catapulted professional wrestling into the age of sports-entertainment. Enraged in defeat, the Sheik started a war with another American hero, Sgt. Slaughter. These bloody battles spread across America and came to a head at the "World's Most Famous Arena." On June 16, 1984, Sheik and Slaughter used Madison Square Garden as their battlefield in a legendary Boot Camp Match that gave new meaning to the word "violence."

The Iron Sheik entered the tag team division and formed an alliance with Nikolai Volkoff. With the Freddy Blassie at ringside, the duo became World Tag Team Champions when they defeated the U.S. Express at the first-ever *WrestleMania*. Though Sheik & Volkoff lost the titles back to Windham & Rotundo that June in Poughkeepsie, they remained a lethal team.

The Iron Sheik returned to singles action and fought to the finals of the first-ever *King Of The Ring* tournament against the Magnificent Muraco. At *WrestleMania III*, he and Volkoff reunited with new manager Slick and fought the Killer Bees in a melee that was interrupted by "Hacksaw" Jim Duggan.

In 1997, the man from Tehran returned to WWE as the manager of the Sultan. He then came back at *WrestleMania X-Seven* and won the over-the-top-rope Gimmick Battle Royal, but not before reigniting his rivalry with Sgt. Slaughter. The night before *WrestleMania 21*, the Iron Sheik was inducted into the WWE Hall of Fame. Today, the Sheik tours the world attending autograph conventions and training sessions.

THE IRON SHEIK & NIKOLAI VOLKOFF

COMBINED WEIGHT	571 lbs.	TITLE HISTORY	World Tag Team Champions	YEARS ACTIVE	1960 1969	1970 1979	**1980 1989**	1990 1999	2000 PRESENT

Separately, the Iron Sheik and Nikolai Volkoff were quite a force to be reckoned with in the ring. Together they were nearly unstoppable. Both members of "Classy" Freddie Blassie's stable of Superstars, the Iron Sheik & Nikolai Volkoff began teaming with each other in 1984. The foreign rule-breakers instantly became recognized as the time's most-hated tag team. The fans learned to loathe them even more when Volkoff demanded arenas all across the United States stand for the singing of the Russian national anthem. When Volkoff was done serenading the fans, The Iron Sheik would famously remind everybody, "Russia, number one. Iran, number one, U.S.A., pooey!"

At the inaugural *WrestleMania* in 1985, the Iron Sheik & Nikolai Volkoff used some help from their manager's infamous cane to defeat the U.S. Express for the World Tag Team Championship. The victory marked the first-ever title change in *WrestleMania* history. The duo held the titles for nearly three months before Mike Rotundo & Barry Windham reclaimed the gold in Poughkeepsie, New York.

Following the loss, the Iron Sheik & Nikolai Volkoff temporarily set out on singles careers, which was highlighted by the big Russian's patriotic rivalry with American hero Corporal Kirschner.

By 1987, Blassie had sold interest in his stable of Superstars to "The Doctor of Style" Slick. The new manager reunited the Iron Sheik & Nikolai Volkoff for a brief run that saw the foreigners defeat The Killer Bees at *WrestleMania III*. Slick eventually aligned Volkoff with fellow Russian Boris Zhukov to form the Bolsheviks. The move effectively marked the end of the successful tag team. Both the Iron Sheik and Nikolai Volkoff were honored with induction into the WWE Hall of Fame in 2005.

IRWIN R. SCHYSTER

				YEARS ACTIVE	1960 1969	1970 1979	1980 1989	**1990 1999**	2000 PRESENT

HT	6'3"	WT	248 lbs.	FROM	Washington D.C.	SIGNATURE MOVE	The Write-off	TITLE HISTORY	World Tag Team Champion

In 1991, World Wrestling Entertainment was antagonized by one Mr. Irwin R. Schyster, commonly known as I.R.S. He accused everyone of being worthless tax cheats and reminded everyone of their duty to pay their taxes to the United States government. While his lengthy diatribes upheld the United States tax laws, he had no problem whatsoever in breaking the rules of WWE during his matches.

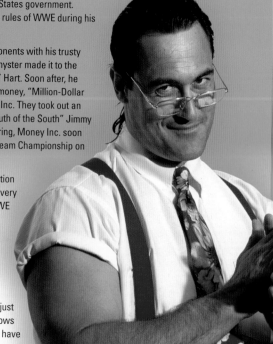

This technically sound competitor was not afraid to wallop opponents with his trusty briefcase, which he insisted on having with him at all times. Schyster made it to the finals of the 1991 *King of the Ring*, where he met Bret "Hit Man" Hart. Soon after, he joined forces with another Superstar who was infatuated with money, "Million-Dollar Man" Ted DiBiase. As a tag team, they were known as Money, Inc. They took out an insurance policy and acquired the managerial services of "Mouth of the South" Jimmy Hart. As one of the the most cunning duos ever to set foot in a ring, Money Inc. soon had their first taste of WWE gold after winning the World Tag Team Championship on February 2, 1992.

When the team parted ways, I.R.S. returned to singles competition and was one of the early fixtures of *Monday Night Raw*. With every match, he proved why he was a top contender for both the WWE Championship and Intercontinental Championship. In 1994, he joined the ranks of the Million Dollar Corporation. Schyster knew no boundries as he interfered in Undertaker's matches and repossessed sacred grave sites until their match at the 1995 *Royal Rumble*.

During his WWE tenure, Irwin R. Schyster was one of the company's top talents and a versatile Superstar who could adjust to any opponent's fighting style. When he appears today, it shows that no matter what time of year it is, or how much money you have in the bank, you're never safe from the tax man.

The Islanders

| MEMBERS | Haku, Tama | COMBINED WEIGHT | 501 lbs. |

Haku & Tama wanted to achieve success through dedication, hard work, and honesty. They displayed these traits throughout their matches in the mid-1980s. After *WrestleMania III* they were signed to compete against the popular Can-Am Connection. What was supposed to be a contest between sportsman turned into a vicious attack as Haku & Tama became clients of Bobby Heenan and his family. With a newfound aggression, they ruthlessly took aim at anyone pointed out by Bobby Heenan. They showed their true devotion to "the Brain" when they dognapped Matilda, the mascot of the British Bulldogs. The Bulldogs, along with Koko B. Ware, punished the transgression at *WrestleMania IV*. The abduction went as one of the most heartless acts in WWE history.

The Islanders soon went separate ways. Tama left WWE in April 1988. Haku soon became "King" Haku and reigned as a World Tag Team Champion as a part of the Colossal Connection.

Isaac Yankem DDS

HT	6'10"	WT	300 lbs.
FROM	Decatur, Illinois
SIGNATURE MOVE	DDS

YEARS ACTIVE 1960-1969 1970-1979 1980-1989 **1990-1999** 2000-PRESENT

Isaac Yankem was one of the least liked Superstars in WWE history. Despite his lack of popularity, however, the evil dentist claimed to be a walking public service announcement. According to Yankem, he let his teeth deteriorate to show the "rotten-teethed idiots" what can happen if they don't practice oral hygiene. The message didn't connect with the fans of WWE, but the malodorous effect it had on his opponents was brilliant.

Jerry Lawler introduced Yankem to WWE audiences in the summer of 1995. As "The King's" personal dentist, Yankem's sole purpose was to extract pain (and teeth) from Lawler's prime rival, Bret Hart. When Yankem and Hart finally squared off at *SummerSlam 1995*, a victory was not the dentist's prime objective. Instead, Yankem set out to permanently end Hart's career. He nearly accomplished his goal when he wrapped Hart's neck between two ring ropes. Luckily for Bret, WWE officials broke up the horrifying scene before permanent damage could be done.

The Italian Stallion

| HT | 6'3" | WT | 260 lbs. | FROM | Naples, Italy | SIGNATURE MOVE | Powerslam |

A storied amateur athlete, the Italian Stallion immigrated to the United States from Naples, Italy. He entered sports-entertainment in 1983 and spent his formative years in Jim Crockett Promotions. During his time there, he appeared at the first Jim Crockett, Sr. Memorial Cup Tag Team Tournament in 1986, as well as *Clash of Champions IV*.

In 1990, the Stallion wanted to test his mettle against WWE's Superstars. He appeared on broadcasts of *Wrestling Challenge* facing the Honky Tonk Man, Shawn Michaels, and Greg Valentine.

In 1995, Stallion left WWE and spent time among independent promotions in the Southeastern part of the United States. After returning to his adopted home in North Carolina, he opened a training school with George South. Noted alumni from their academy include R-Truth and Jeff and Matt Hardy.

ITEM ON A POLE MATCH

The Item on a Pole Match adds a level of brutality to already dangerous WWE matches, as it legalizes the use of weaponry. The match features a pre-selected weapon, usually a nightstick or pair of brass knuckles, hanging above one of the top turnbuckles. The first Superstar to reach the weapon can legally use it to inflict pain on his opponent.

At No Way Out 2002, Edge and William Regal battled it out in a bloody Brass Knuckles on a Pole Match. Regal won the encounter to retain his Intercontinental Championship.

The normally brutal match turned sexy in August 2006 when Candice and Torrie Wilson competed in a Paddle on a Pole Match. Candice was the first to retrieve the paddle, but rather than using it on Torrie, she handed it to her opponent and asked to be spanked.

IVAN KOLOFF

YEARS ACTIVE 1960-1969 · 1970-1979 · 1980-1989 · 1990-1999 · 2000-PRESENT

HT 6'1" **WT** 298 lbs. **FROM** Moscow, Russia **SIGNATURE MOVE** Bearhug **TITLE HISTORY** WWE Champion

At a time when tension between the United States and Soviet Union was at its height, Russian powerhouse Ivan Koloff proved to be the ultimate threat to American wrestling fans' in-ring heroes. Known as "The Russian Bear," Koloff joined WWE in 1970, under the tutelage of manager Lou Albano. The sight of him struck communistic fears into American fans, but it was his dreaded bear hug and knee drop that frightened the WWE locker room.

Within months of Koloff's debut, fans had their greatest fear realized when "the Russian Bear" handily defeated their champion of nearly eight years, Bruno Sammartino. A stunned Madison Square Garden crowd watched in disbelief as their hero's shoulders were pinned to the mat for seemingly the longest three seconds in sports-entertainment history. After the match, the ring announcer refused to announce Koloff as the winner, fearing a riot might ensue.

A mere three weeks into his shocking championship reign, Koloff crossed paths with a hungry Pedro Morales. Much to the fans' delight, Morales beat Koloff for the WWE Championship, marking the end of the most terrifying title reign to date.

Shortly after the loss, Koloff disappeared from the WWE scene, only to return periodically during the 1970s and 1980s to challenge Sammartino and Bob Backlund. When he wasn't making rare WWE appearances, "the Russian Bear" was gaining tag team notoriety in the Mid-Atlantic territory. His impressive list of partners includes Ray Stevens, Krusher Khruschev, Dick Murdoch, and nephew Nikita Koloff.

At age fifty, Koloff took his game to the budding Eastern Championship Wrestling. His popular past and memorable matches with Jimmy Snuka and Sandman helped the promotion build the foundation for what would later be recognized as the hardcore powerhouse Extreme Championship Wrestling.

IVAN PUTSKI

YEARS ACTIVE

| HT | 5'10" | WT | 245 lbs. | FROM | Krakow, Poland | SIGNATURE MOVE | The Polish Hammer | TITLE HISTORY | World Tag Team Champion |

In 1976, World Wrestling Entertainment was introduced to the phenomenon known as "Polish Power." As a former professional body builder, Ivan Putski possessed great strength and a fire that burned to rid WWE of its questionable elements. He was the first Polish Superstar and with his success and charisma became one of the top names in WWE. He took the fight to individuals such as Crusher Blackwell, Bruiser Brody, Stan Hansen, Ivan Koloff, Spiros Arion, and Baron Mikel Scicluna. Putski's feats of strength continued to garner attention and he competed in the 1978 World's Strongest Man Competition. As his following grew, Putski began to speak more English to his legion of fans, sang his favorite Polish songs and professed the importance of "Polish Power" after his matches.

On October 22, 1979, Putski teamed Tito Santana to defeat Johnny & Jerry Valiant to win the World Tag Team Championship. The duo complemented each other perfectly and held the belts for months before losing to the Wild Samoans. As "Polish Power" entered the 1980s, he remained a huge star.

In 1995, Ivan took his rightful place amongst sports-entertainment's elite when he was enshrined in the WWE Hall of Fame. "Polish Power" made his triumphant return to WWE television in 1997 when he appeared alongside his son Scott on *Monday Night Raw* and tangled with Jerry Lawler and Brian Christopher.

Ivan Putski is one of professional wrestling's most admired individuals whose fame transcended ethnicities and broke down geographic barriers. For this, everyone loves "Polish Power!"

Ivory

YEARS ACTIVE

| HT | 5'5" | FROM | Seattle, Washington | SIGNATURE MOVE | Poison Ivy |

| TITLE HISTORY | Women's Champion |

If someone wants excellent ring skills, a fabulous physique, and a mean streak that turns smiles into frowns, look no further than this former WWE Diva. She first appeared on WWE programming in 1999 as the Valentine's Day gift from D-Lo Brown to tag team partner Mark Henry. Trained by Mexican legend Mondo Guerrero, it didn't take Ivory long to challenge the Divas in the ring.

After capturing the Women's Championship on an episode of *Monday Night Raw*, she participated in the first-ever Women's Hardcore match against Tori. She held the prized championship for four months before suffering a loss to Fabulous Moolah at *No Mercy*.

Something in Ivory snapped after the loss that caused her to join the Right To Censor. Her clothing now consisted of ankle-length skirts, a button-down white shirt, modest black heels and her hair worn up in a tightly wrapped bun. She enjoyed success as part of the group, winning the Women's Championship two more times.

After the Right to Censor disbanded, Ivory became a trainer on the second season of *WWE Tough Enough,* then traded in her ring gear for a microphone as the co-host of the now-defunct *WWE Experience.*

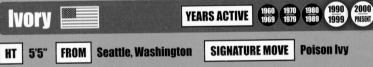

Jack Swagger

| HT | 6'4" | WT | 263 lbs. | FROM | Perry, Oklahoma |

| YEARS ACTIVE |

The charismatic Jack Swagger caught the eye of ECW general manager Theodore Long in September 2008 and the GM signed the self-proclaimed "All American American" as a part of his New Superstar Initiative. The move proved to be just the break that Swagger needed, as he hasn't looked back since making his impressive debut.

Swagger's cocky smile and arrogant strut make him tough to cheer for, but fans can't help but appreciate his confidence. After only weeks in the promotion, Swagger stood up to ECW legend Tommy Dreamer. With guts like that, it's only a matter of time before Swagger is sporting gold around his waist.

JACK TUNNEY

He wasn't a muscle man. He didn't possess cat-like quickness, and he never owned a devastating offensive arsenal. Despite these perceived shortcomings, Jack Tunney was one of the most feared men in all of sports-entertainment during the 1980s and 1990s.

As WWE President, Tunney was one of the most respected authoritative figures of his time. Usually ruling from afar, unlike many of today's leaders, he only showed up when matters became too heavy for his referees to police. This style of leadership proved to be fruitful, as his tenure saw few controversies. When things did get ugly, however, you could safely bet Tunney would mete out punishment with an iron fist.

To this day, many of Tunney's decisions are looked back upon with great fondness. In 1986, the WWE President was forced to make a difficult decision when one of his top draws, Andre the Giant, failed to show at several of his contracted appearances. Seeing Andre's absence as an insult to the paying fans, Tunney suspended the popular "Eighth Wonder of the World" from competitive action. A few months later, Tunney made a similar ruling when he suspended rogue official Danny Davis for life, following the referee's blatant bias towards rule breakers.

Perhaps Tunney's toughest decision came when a series of controversial matches between Hulk Hogan and Undertaker forced the President to vacate the WWE Championship in 1991. The ruling eventually lead to the WWE Championship being on the line at the 1992 *Royal Rumble*, which was won by Ric Flair.

As is normally the case with any administration, Tunney's time in office did see some controversial rulings. When Bret Hart and Lex Luger were simultaneously last eliminated from the 1994 *Royal Rumble*, rather than sending the two Superstars into the ring to declare a definitive winner, Tunney announced them as co-winners. He then ruled that both men would receive an opportunity at the WWE Championship at *WrestleMania X*, but not before confusing everybody with talk of a coin toss, "suitable competition" and guest referees.

Despite the rare miscue, Tunney's time in office will forever be looked upon as time when Superstars actually feared their boss and lawlessness was unacceptable.

Jackie Gayda

HT	5'7"	**FROM**	Cleveland, Ohio

SIGNATURE MOVE	Neckbreaker

YEARS ACTIVE	1960 1969	1970 1979	1980 1989	1990 1999	2000 PRESENT

Jackie Gayda's determination, strength, and in-ring ability led to her becoming the co-winner of the second season of *Tough Enough*. Before she knew it, Miss Jackie was strutting her stuff on *Raw* and *SmackDown* with the most beautiful and dangerous females in all of sports-entertainment.

In 2003, she added valet to her resumé when she began to accompany Rico to the ring, and later in her career she managed Rico & Charlie Haas to the WWE Tag Team Championship. Jackie became fond of interfering on her team's behalf, so they fought in mixed tag matches. On her own, she locked up with Trish Stratus and Lita and became a contender for the Women's Championship. At *WrestleMania XX*, she partnered with Stacy Keibler against Torrie Wilson & Sable in a Playboy Evening Gown Match. Jackie left WWE in June 2005 and spent a brief time on the independent scene before retiring from the ring.

Jacqueline

HT	5'3"	**FROM**	Dallas, Texas

TITLE HISTORY	Women's Champion, Cruiserweight Champion

YEARS ACTIVE	1960 1969	1970 1979	1980 1989	1990 1999	2000 PRESENT

Over the course of her WWE career, Jacqueline had the unique distinction of being equally successful against both male and female Superstars. In fact, her impressive record against the men of WWE actually carried her to the male-dominated Cruiserweight Championship. The bombshell from Dallas defeated Chavo Guerrero in May 2004 to become the only woman in WWE history to ever hold the gold.

Jacqueline's Cruiserweight Championship proved to be the final highlight of her brilliant six-year WWE run. It also served as a golden bookend to a career that took off after capturing the Women's Championship mere months after making her debut.

The period between Jacqueline's high-profile debut and ground-breaking finale was filled with one memorable moment after another. The feisty Diva will forever be remembered for her involvement in the all-female faction Pretty Mean Sisters. Affectionately referred to as P.M.S., Jacqueline, alongside Terri and Ryan Shamrock, preyed on the male Superstars of WWE, usually making them their love slaves. The list of their conquests includes D-Lo Brown and Mark Henry.

" IF YOU KEEP PLAYING WITH SNAKES, SOON YOU'LL GET BIT.

HT 6'6"	**WT** 249 lbs.
FROM	Stone Mountain, Georgia
SIGNATURE MOVE	The DDT
YEARS ACTIVE	1960-1969 · 1970-1979 · 1980-1989 · 1990-1999 · 2000-PRESENT

The son of the legendary Grizzly Smith, Jake Roberts' career in professional wrestling began in Louisiana as a referee. He traveled throughout the Southeastern United States and Calgary's Stampede Wrestling, gaining the reputation of being a superior technician and ring psychologist. Along the way, he invented one of the most lethal moves in the history of sports-entertainment, the DDT.

Jake "the Snake" Roberts debuted in WWE in 1986 alongside his python, Damien, who was often restless inside his burlap sack during Jake's matches. After a DDT, Jake often brought out Damien and dropped the snake on his fallen opponents.

From the start of his WWE career, Jake was often at the center of intense rivalries. In one of his first matches, Jake delivered a DDT to Ricky "the Dragon" Steamboat on concrete during *Saturday Night's Main Event*. The assault left Steamboat unconscious and sparked a bitter rivalry that lead to a Snake Pit Match at *The Big Event* in Toronto.

Jake Roberts quickly became known for cryptic interviews that sent chills down the spines of all of saw them. His speaking acumen convinced WWE to give him his own talk show segment which he called *The Snake Pit*. During an episode of *The Snake Pit*, Jake was attacked by the Honky Tonk Man, who smashed a guitar over Jake's head. The heinous action lead to a match at *WrestleMania III*. His victory there changed the attitude of fans, and suddenly capacity crowds were calling for Jake's signature DDT.

Jake shook up the early days of the married life of Randy Savage and Elizabeth. He presented the couple with a king cobra who leapt up and bit the "Macho Man."

Jake was featured at *WrestleMania* for the next several years, incluing a match against Andre the Giant at *WrestleMania V* and a Blindfold Match against Rick "the Model" Martel at *WrestleMania VII* after Roberts was blinded by Martel's signature cologne, Arrogance.

GETTING PERSONAL

The intesity of those rivalries could not compare to the emotions generated by personal attacks against those closest to Jake. "Ravishing" Rick Rude would often select a female fan from the audience for a post-match kiss. One night, he picked Jake's wife, who refused to participate. After a slap and a shove, Jake arrived to defend his wife. Roberts and Rude engaged in a brutal war that lasted several months and was exacerbated each time Rude's wrestling trunks bore a likeness of Roberts' wife.

Damien was the target of another Superstar who tried to attack Jake by proxy. The behemoth Earthquake crushed Damien while Jake watched helplessly, tangled in the ring ropes. After the loss of his snake, Roberts went back home to Stone Mountain, Georgia. When Roberts finally returned, he unveiled a monstrous python he called Lucifer.

After revealing that Lucifer was Damien's older brother, a demonic-looking Roberts boldly claimed his new snake was the devil himself. Coincidentally, Roberts began to display a darker persona after the debut of Lucifer. His return to the darkside was just as mysterious as his sudden disappearance from WWE after his *Wrestlemania VIII* match against Undertaker.

"The Snake" spent the next few years in seclusion, but returned at the *Royal Rumble*. While Jake struck fear into the hearts of a new generation, he met his match in Stone Cold Steve Austin at the *King Of The Ring* finals. Austin's victory gave rise to the era of Stone Cold and arguably sports-entertainment's most famous chapter and verse, "Austin 3:16."

Jake again vanished from WWE in 1997, and rumors swirled as to his whereabouts. Jake made an incredible return on the March 14, 2005 episode of *Monday Night Raw* and warned "Legend Killer" Randy Orton about the fear one feels when facing Undertaker at *WrestleMania*. That November, WWE released the retrospective DVD titled, *Jake The Snake Roberts: Pick Your Poison* to sate the public's ravenous apetite for the history of the man whose methods changed the face of sports-entertainment.

Jamaica Kid

HT 4'4" **WT** 94 lbs.

FROM Jamaica

SIGNATURE MOVE Jumping Headbutt

YEARS ACTIVE

1960-1969 1970-1979 1980-1989 1990-1999 2000-PRESENT

An outstanding export from the island of the Greater Antilles, Jamaica Kid arrived in the World Wide Wrestling Federation in the summer of 1964. For over a decade he was a mainstay with a jumping headbutt that stopped most of his foes dead in their tracks. His matches were filled with action and entertained audiences wherever he appeared.

Jamaica's battles with the likes of Sky Low Low, Fuzzy Cupid, Billy the Kid, Farmer Pete, Little Brutus, Frenchy Lamont, Pee Wee Adams and Dirty Morgan helped put the midget division on the map. He had a steady array of tag team partners that included Little Beaver, Tiny Tim, Irish Jackie, Sonny Boy Cassidy, Pancho Lopez, Cowboy Bradley, and Little Louie. These bouts were as unpredictable and exciting as anything ever seen in the ring.

James Dudley

HALL OF FAME 1994

Although he spent more time behind the scenes than in front of capacity crowds, James Dudley was one of the most important and influential men in sports-entertainment history. WWE Chairman Vince K. McMahon once said, "Had there been no James Dudley, the WWE possibly wouldn't exist as it does today."

Before he played an integral role in the success of WWE, James Dudley was a catcher for the Baltimore Elite Giants of the Negro League. When his playing days ended, he looked toward a career that matched the thrill of being on the baseball diamond. In the early 1940s, he started as an employee of Jess McMahon and ultimately became a trusted associate of Vincent J. McMahon. History was made in 1956 when Vince, Sr. appointed Dudley manager of Turner Arena in Washington, D.C., making Dudley the first African-American to run a major arena in the United States.

Dudley's keen business acumen allowed Vince McMahon to concentrate on growing his business to other areas. As WWE's reach expanded, Dudley's job responsibilities continued to grow. By 1980, he retired and became a valued consultant to Vince K. McMahon. In 1994, Dudley was included in the first full-class of sports-entertainment immortals in the WWE Hall of Fame.

On June 1, 2004, Dudley passed away at the age of 93. He was more than a valued employee to several generations of McMahons. He was a cherished friend and made a lasting impact on everyone around him.

Jazz

HT 5'4" **FROM** New Orleans, Lousiana

TITLE HISTORY Women's Champion

YEARS ACTIVE 1960-1969 1970-1979 1980-1989 1990-1999 2000-PRESENT

With washboard abs and muscles on top of muscles, Jazz was one of WWE's most-feared Divas between 2001 and 2004. The tattooed powerhouse debuted on one of WWE's biggest stages when she competed in a Six-Pack Challenge at the 2001 *Survivor Series*. The encounter whet her appetite for championship glory, and in February 2002, she defeated Trish Stratus for the Women's Championship.

After a successful championship stint, Jazz took on Theodore Long as her manager. With Long leading her career, Jazz was able to upend Stratus a second time for the title at *Backlash 2003*. She held the championship for two months before losing it to Gail Kim in a Divas Battle Royal. Jazz left WWE a few months later.

Jazz returned in June 2006 when she represented ECW in a match against Women's Champion Mickie James. Jazz came up short in her attempt to topple James, and was never seen on WWE television again.

Jamie Noble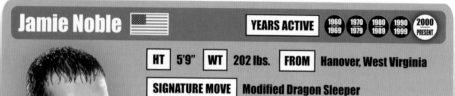

YEARS ACTIVE 1960-1969 1970-1979 1980-1989 1990-1999 2000-PRESENT

HT 5'9" **WT** 202 lbs. **FROM** Hanover, West Virginia

SIGNATURE MOVE Modified Dragon Sleeper

TITLE HISTORY Cruiserweight Champion

Jamie Noble is the exact opposite of many of the country boys that have competed in World Wrestling Entertainment since its inception. Raised in the trailer parks of West Virginia, Noble will do anything in his matches to get what he wants.

He won his first Cruiserweight Championship from The Hurricane at the 2002 *King of the Ring* and enjoyed an almost five-month title reign. After a one year hiatus, Noble returned as part of the short-lived team, the Pitbulls. While on *SmackDown,* he fought the likes of Rey Mysterio, Jimmy Wang Yang, Shannon Moore, and Hornswoggle. He began hearing cheers from the crowd when he came to the aid of Diva Michelle McCool to protect her from Chuck Palumbo.

Noble has become known for his impulsive and unpredictable behavior from week-to-week. Regardless of where he appears or what his demeanor is, he always has one thing on his mind: championships.

Jean Pierre LaFitte

| HT | 6'1" | WT | 235 lbs. | FROM | New Orleans, Louisiana |

YEARS ACTIVE 1960–1969 1970–1979 1980–1989 **1990–1999** 2000–PRESENT

An ancestor of the infamous LaFitte family of pirates, Jean Pierre LaFitte made his WWE debut in 1995. His goal was to exact revenge on the United States, starting with WWE Superstars, for the Embargo Act of 1807 that forced his family out of New Orleans.

With a patch over his right eye, LaFitte showed all of the characteristics of an evil pirate, including thievery. His most-noted victim was Bret Hart, from who he stole his signature leather jacket and sunglasses. Unfortunately for LaFitte, Hart gained revenge when he defeated him at *In Your House* in September 1995. LaFitte left WWE shortly after the loss.

Jeff Jarrett

| HT | 6' | WT | 230 lbs. | FROM | Nashville, Tennessee |

SIGNATURE MOVE Figure-Four Leglock

TITLE HISTORY Intercontinental Champion, World Tag Team Champion

YEARS ACTIVE 1960–1969 1970–1979 1980–1989 **1990–1999** 2000–PRESENT

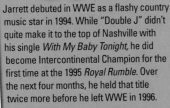

Jarrett debuted in WWE as a flashy country music star in 1994. While "Double J" didn't quite make it to the top of Nashville with his single *With My Baby Tonight,* he did become Intercontinental Champion for the first time at the 1995 *Royal Rumble.* Over the next four months, he held that title twice more before he left WWE in 1996.

Jarrett then appeared in WCW and became a United States Champion as well as member of the famed Four Horsemen. In 1997, he returned to WWE where he ditched the country-western scene and lived by the motto/warning, "Don't Piss Me Off." As he returned to Intercontinental glory, he reunited with longtime associate Debra. With her considerable assets added to his formidable arsenal, Jeff then formed a well-known tandem with Owen Hart. On January 25, 1999, they became World Tag Team Champions. He also had memorable battles against Chyna, who defeated him in a "Good Housekeeping Match" for the Intercontinental prize at *No Mercy.* Jarrett parted ways with WWE again and returned to WCW where he proclaimed himself "The Chosen One." He remained with the organization, where he became WCW Champion, until it closed in March 2001.

Jeff Hardy **YEARS ACTIVE** 1960–1969 1970–1979 1980–1989 **1990–1999** 2000–PRESENT

| HT | 6'1" | WT | 225 lbs. | FROM | Cameron, North Carolina |

SIGNATURE MOVE Swanton Bomb

TITLE HISTORY Intercontinental Champion, World Tag Team Champion, European Champion, Light Heavyweight Champion, Hardcore Champion, WWE Champion

Ten years ago, if you asked somebody if Jeff Hardy would still be competing today, the answer would probably be "no." While his high-flying style of offense certainly excites audiences, his kamikaze attacks oftentimes leave people wondering how much longer he can continue damaging his body. Miraculously, the ultimate risk taker has defied the odds and avoided serious injury to become one of WWE's most popular Superstars.

Alongside his brother Matt, Jeff first began making a name for himself in 1998. Known as the Hardy Boys, Jeff & Matt spent the next few years redefining the art of tag team competition. Their battles with the Dudley Boys and Edge & Christian, particularly their TLC Matches, featured truly groundbreaking action that today's tag teams strive to recreate.

On his own, Hardy has proven to be a true artist. Using the ring as his canvas, Hardy has executed his awe-inspiring Swanton Bomb to create the ultimate portrait of success. A multiple-time Intercontinental Champion, Hardy finally rose to main-event status in 2008 when he challenged Randy Orton for the WWE Championship at the *Royal Rumble.* Jeff Hardy finally reached the top of the mountain in December, 2008 when he pinned Edge during a Triple Threat Match at *Armageddon.* Now that he's at the top, there's no telling how this daredevil plans on coming down.

Jeff Jarrett & Owen Hart

The most successful tag teams historically combine opposing styles in an effort to form the most well-rounded unit possible. Jeff Jarrett & Owen Hart, on the other hand, fused their similar styles into one technically sound team. The rare pairing proved fruitful, as they owned the tag scene during their brief time together. Of course, it didn't hurt that they had the bosomy Debra by their side, either.

COMBINED WEIGHT 457 lbs.

TITLE HISTORY World Tag Team Champions

YEARS ACTIVE 1960–1969 1970–1979 1980–1989 **1990–1999** 2000–PRESENT

The former Intercontinental Champions began teaming together in late 1998. During this time, Hart was going through a bit of an identity crisis, which resulted in him occasionally donning his Blue Blazer mask. Claiming to be a superhero, Hart believed his true identity was concealed, but in reality, the entire world knew it was him under the mask, especially when the Blazer would team with Jeff Jarrett (Hart's tag team partner).

After teaming with Jarrett as the Blue Blazer for several tag team matches, Hart dropped his masked persona to defeat Big Boss Man & Ken Shamrock for the World Tag Team Championship in January 1999. The crafty combination of Jarrett & Hart went on an impressive winning streak that saw them topple such teams as the Public Enemy and Legion of Doom during their four-month reign.

After losing the titles in April, Hart reverted back to his Blue Blazer persona, but that didn't stop him from conveniently showing up by the side of Jarrett.

Jerry Graham

HT 5'10" **WT** 245 lbs. **FROM** Phoenix, Arizona **TITLE HISTORY** United States Tag Team Champion

A member of the famed Graham family, Dr. Jerry Graham was a noted troublemaker in and out of the ring. When the madman wasn't wreaking havoc with brothers Crazy Luke, Eddie, and "Superstar" Billy Graham in the ring, he was butting heads with law enforcement all over the nation.

Graham won tag team titles in six different promotions over the course of his career. His first taste of success came in 1955 when he teamed with Don McIntyre to topple Bill & Fred Blassie for the Georgia version of the NWA Tag Team Championship. Over the next 20 years, Graham formed championship teams with Abdullah the Butcher, Jim Wright, and brother Eddie. He even captured the WWE United States Tag Team titles with brother Luke in June 1964.

While Graham's main source of fame came from his action in between the ropes, his run-ins with the law are simply legendary. Following the passing of his mother, Graham broke into the morgue to steal her corpse. In doing so, he assaulted several morgue workers and security. A few years later, the police picked him up after he was seen shooting the lights out at a Utah house of worship. According to legend, Graham maintained his outlaw-like attitude even while spending his final days in hospice.

JERRY "THE KING" LAWLER

HT 6' **WT** 243 lbs. **FROM** Memphis, Tennessee **SIGNATURE MOVE** Piledriver **YEARS ACTIVE** 1960-1969 1970-1979 1980-1989 1990-1999 2000-PRESENT

Jerry Lawler first became involved with professional wrestling when his caricutures were discovered by famous announcer Lance Russell. Trained by "Fabulous" Jackie Fargo, Lawler went on to become a legend in the Mid-South and Memphis territories during the 1970s and 1980s. His most well-known rivalry actually began outside of the ring. In the early 1980s, the war of words between Lawler and Andy Kaufman became mainstream news when as guests on *The David Letterman Show*, Lawler slapped Kaufman out of his chair and sent the Hollywood star into an obscenity-laced tirade. The rivalry was recreated by Hollywood in 1999, as "The King" made his silver-screen debut in *Man On The Moon*, a movie based on Kaufman's life.

Though he held numerous regional championships, his shining moment in the ring came on May 9, 1988 when he beat Curt Hennig for the AWA Championship. Lawler later unified the title when he defeated legend Kerry Von Erich for his World Class Championship.

In 1993, Lawler debuted in WWE as an announcer. Lawler has been a long-time announcer for *Monday Night Raw* and along with partner Jim Ross, has changed the face of television broadcasting. He also enjoyed his own talk show segment appropriately called, *The King's Court*. His outspoken attitude as a commentator lead to heated matches with Bret "Hit Man" Hart. This war raged on until their "Kiss My Foot" Match at the 1995 *King of the Ring*.

Lawler also garnered media attention when he took aim at an entire promotion during ECW's first invasion of WWE. Lawler's crown continued to shine in 2002 when his autobiography titled, *It's Good To Be King… Sometimes* became one of the best-selling WWE books of all-time.

In 2007, his unbelievable career was celebrated as friend William Shatner inducted him into the WWE Hall of Fame. Jerry Lawler has been one of the top figures in sports-entertainment for almost 40 years. Whether he is in the ring dropping a fist from the middle rope, or behind the broadcast booth eagerly volunteering to help the Divas, he has entertained millions all over the world with this wit, creativity, and charisma.

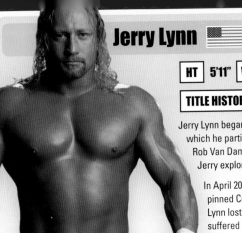

Jerry Lynn 🇺🇸

YEARS ACTIVE	1960-1969	1970-1979	**1980-1989**	**1990-1999**	**2000 PRESENT**

HT	5'11"	**WT**	212 lbs.	**FROM**	Minneapolis, Minnesota	**SIGNATURE MOVE**	Cradle Piledriver

TITLE HISTORY Light Heavyweight Champion

Jerry Lynn began his career in the late 1980s and, as his reputation began to grow, he made appearances in WCW and WWE during which he participated in the Light Heavyweight Championship tournament. Lynn's next stop was ECW and a slew of matches with Rob Van Dam that were considered classics amongst the ECW faithful. In the weeks and months that followed ECW's closure, Jerry explored his options and felt he needed to prove himself where the world would be watching.

In April 2001, Lynn returned to WWE and had his debut match on *Sunday Night Heat*. In his return, the former ECW Champion pinned Crash Holly and won the prized Light Heavyweight championship that eluded him four years prior. Unfortunately, Lynn lost the title a little over one month later to a driven Jeff Hardy. Lynn renewed his rivalry against Rob Van Dam, but he suffered a torn patella and parted ways with the company in February 2002.

Jesse & Festus 🇺🇸

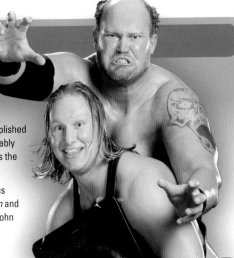

YEARS ACTIVE	1960-1969	1970-1979	1980-1989	1990-1999	**2000 PRESENT**

COMBINED WEIGHT 501 lbs.

Much like the legendary Hillbilly Jim before them, Jesse & Festus are a couple of country boys you don't go messin' with. Jesse, the brains of the operation, brings to the ring an accomplished amateur background, while Festus, the team's brawn, inexplicably transforms from a gentle giant into a beast every time he hears the ring bell sound.

After making their WWE debut in October 2007, Jesse & Festus have made short work of many of the top units in *SmackDown* and ECW, including then-WWE Tag Team Champions The Miz & John Morrison in non-title action in early 2008.

JESSE "THE BODY" VENTURA

HALL OF FAME 2004

HT	6'2"	**WT**	245 lbs.	**FROM**	Brooklyn Park, Minnesota		

YEARS ACTIVE	1960-1969	**1970-1979**	**1980-1989**	**1990-1999**	**2000 PRESENT**

🇺🇸 *"Win if you can. Lose if you must. But always cheat."*

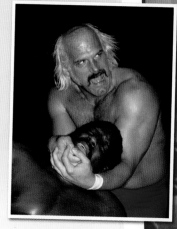

Luckily for residents of Minnesota, Jesse Ventura didn't employ his famous phrase while serving as their governor. He did, however, live by the motto during his days in the ring. After a successful stint with the American Wrestling Association (AWA), Ventura, whose impressive build earned him the nickname "The Body," entered WWE in the early 1980s. As a member of the East-West Connection tag team (with Adrian Adonis), he nearly claimed the World Tag Team Championship on several occasions.

Ventura's colorful singles career mirrored his tag days, as he came close to claiming the WWE Championship from Bob Backlund, but was never able to seal the deal. A second opportunity at the title came Ventura's way when he was scheduled to challenge Hulk Hogan in 1984. Unfortunately, health issues prevented Ventura from taking part in the match. He later retired to the broadcast booth.

As a commentator, Ventura sat ringside for some of WWE's biggest matches, including the *WrestleMania III* encounter between Hogan and Andre the Giant. Just like his days in the ring, Ventura pulled no punches when it came to voicing his opinions. This bold attitude served as the perfect complement to his legendary partner Gorilla Monsoon's more direct approach to announcing.

Blessed with a magnetic personality, Ventura made the natural progression into Hollywood in 1987. His list of credits include box-office hits *Predator*, *The Running Man*, and *Demolition Man*. Ventura's career took an unexpected turn in 1990 when he won the race for mayor of Brooklyn Park, Minnesota. Eight years later, he rose all the way up to the office of governor, where he was affectionately known as Jesse "The Governing Body" Ventura.

In 2004, Ventura's accomplishments in and out of the ring were honored when he was inducted into the WWE Hall of Fame.

Jillian

HT 5'6"	**FROM** Los Angeles, California	**SIGNATURE MOVE** The High Note

YEARS ACTIVE 1960-1969 | 1970-1979 | 1980-1989 | 1990-1999 | **2000 PRESENT**

This Diva first appeared in late 2005 as a "fixer" for MNM. She was later seen at the side of business mogul John "Bradshaw" Layfield. Within a short period, Jillian made it clear that if she was at ringside, then she would make her presence felt and her voice heard.

At *No Way Out* in 2007, Jillian proudly made her WWE singing debut and though her lead vocals were greeted by a chorus of boos, she was motivated to become the greatest pop recording artist on the planet. In the ring, she became a top contender for the Women's Championship. In December 2007, she released her debut album titled, *A Jingle With Jillian*. This collection of her favorite Christmas tunes was a hit with fans. Jillian continues to steam up television sets on *Raw* with her in-ring skills as well as setting new standards of audio quality singing her entrance theme "Sliced Bread" on her way to the ring.

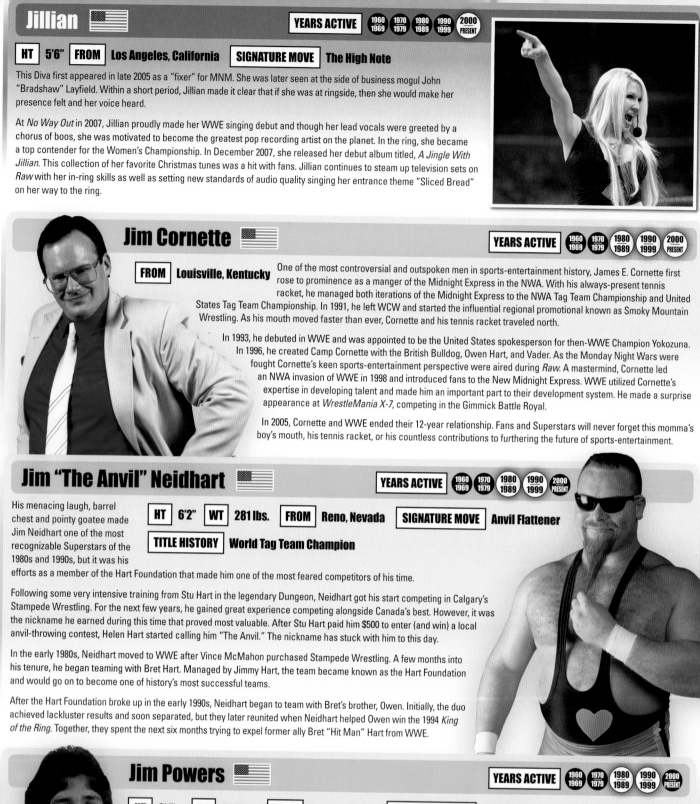

Jim Cornette

YEARS ACTIVE 1960-1969 | 1970-1979 | 1980-1989 | 1990-1999 | 2000 PRESENT

FROM Louisville, Kentucky

One of the most controversial and outspoken men in sports-entertainment history, James E. Cornette first rose to prominence as a manger of the Midnight Express in the NWA. With his always-present tennis racket, he managed both iterations of the Midnight Express to the NWA Tag Team Championship and United States Tag Team Championship. In 1991, he left WCW and started the influential regional promotional known as Smoky Mountain Wrestling. As his mouth moved faster than ever, Cornette and his tennis racket traveled north.

In 1993, he debuted in WWE and was appointed to be the United States spokesperson for then-WWE Champion Yokozuna. In 1996, he created Camp Cornette with the British Bulldog, Owen Hart, and Vader. As the Monday Night Wars were fought Cornette's keen sports-entertainment perspective were aired during *Raw*. A mastermind, Cornette led an NWA invasion of WWE in 1998 and introduced fans to the New Midnight Express. WWE utilized Cornette's expertise in developing talent and made him an important part to their development system. He made a surprise appearance at *WrestleMania X-7*, competing in the Gimmick Battle Royal.

In 2005, Cornette and WWE ended their 12-year relationship. Fans and Superstars will never forget this momma's boy's mouth, his tennis racket, or his countless contributions to furthering the future of sports-entertainment.

Jim "The Anvil" Neidhart

YEARS ACTIVE 1960-1969 | 1970-1979 | 1980-1989 | 1990-1999 | 2000 PRESENT

His menacing laugh, barrel chest and pointy goatee made Jim Neidhart one of the most recognizable Superstars of the 1980s and 1990s, but it was his

HT 6'2"	**WT** 281 lbs.	**FROM** Reno, Nevada	**SIGNATURE MOVE** Anvil Flattener
TITLE HISTORY World Tag Team Champion			

efforts as a member of the Hart Foundation that made him one of the most feared competitors of his time.

Following some very intensive training from Stu Hart in the legendary Dungeon, Neidhart got his start competing in Calgary's Stampede Wrestling. For the next few years, he gained great experience competing alongside Canada's best. However, it was the nickname he earned during this time that proved most valuable. After Stu Hart paid him $500 to enter (and win) a local anvil-throwing contest, Helen Hart started calling him "The Anvil." The nickname has stuck with him to this day.

In the early 1980s, Neidhart moved to WWE after Vince McMahon purchased Stampede Wrestling. A few months into his tenure, he began teaming with Bret Hart. Managed by Jimmy Hart, the team became known as the Hart Foundation and would go on to become one of history's most successful teams.

After the Hart Foundation broke up in the early 1990s, Neidhart began to team with Bret's brother, Owen. Initially, the duo achieved lackluster results and soon separated, but they later reunited when Neidhart helped Owen win the 1994 *King of the Ring*. Together, they spent the next six months trying to expel former ally Bret "Hit Man" Hart from WWE.

Jim Powers

YEARS ACTIVE 1960-1969 | 1970-1979 | 1980-1989 | 1990-1999 | 2000 PRESENT

HT 6'1"	**WT** 235 lbs.	**FROM** New York City	**SIGNATURE MOVE** Powerslam

Trained by Big John Studd, Jim Powers made his WWE debut in 1984. With his good looks and physique, Powers was an instant hit with the women in the WWE audience. He was quickly recognized as an outstanding competitor who excited crowds all over the world. He first took to the mat as a singles competitor, but started to search for a partner as 1986 came to a close.

In March 1987, Jim Powers & Paul Roma formed the Young Stallions. The duo's theme song *Crank It Up* prepared the audience for their fast-paced, high-flying style that featured quick tags and thrilling double-team maneuvers. Unfortunately, the team's inability to capture the World Tag Team Championship by 1989 resulted in a bad split. Powers resumed his singles career and appeared at WWE events up until 1994 before leaving for WCW, where he wrapped up his career in sports-entertainment.

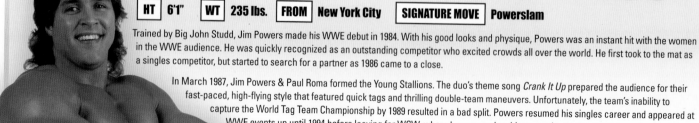

JIM ROSS

" *IT'S GOING TO BE A SLOBBERKNOCKER!* "

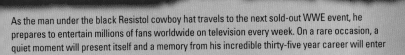

FROM Westville, Oklahoma

YEARS ACTIVE 1960-1969 1970-1979 1980-1989 1990-1999 2000-PRESENT

As the man under the black Resistol cowboy hat travels to the next sold-out WWE event, he prepares to entertain millions of fans worldwide on television every week. On a rare occasion, a quiet moment will present itself and a memory from his incredible thirty-five year career will enter into his mind.

Jim Ross grew up idolizing men like his father, John Wayne, and Mickey Mantle. His excursion into sports-entertainment began in 1974 working for LeRoy McGuirk. The 22 year old was not only the driver for the legendary, legally blind promoter, but also a referee who maintained order in the Tulsa territory. From there Jim worked for "Cowboy" Bill Watts and became the voice for Mid-South Wrestling and its Power Pro television program, which later became the Universal Wrestling Federation. As the UWF was purchased by Jim Crockett Promotions, Ross became the lead play-by-play announcer for the National Wrestling Alliance. Corporate buyouts in the 1980s continued when Ted Turner purchased the business from the Crocketts and launched World Championship Wrestling (WCW). Jim's body of work grew when he became nationally recognized as the voice of the NFL's Atlanta Falcons. All the while, he worked to get to the big time and become internationally known.

After a nineteen year journey Jim Ross made it to sports-entertainment's premiere entity and debuted at *WrestleMania IX*. Alongside Randy "Macho Man" Savage and Bobby Heenan, Ross called the action at the "World's Largest Toga Party." His broadcast duties expanded in 1994 when he was the host of WWE Radio and heard on *Monday Night Raw, Action Zone,* and *Shotgun Saturday Night.*

In 1997, Ross became one-half of what would be a future WWE Hall of Fame broadcast team, as he and Jerry Lawler were the voices of *Monday Night Raw.* The voice of Jim Ross and his partner chronicled the conflict that became known as "The Monday Night Wars." More times than not, if an important moment took place in the ring, the good ol' boy from Oklahoma made the call. During his famed career, Jim at times has had to reluctantly leave the broadcast booth and knock the taste out of someone's mouth to the pleasure of WWE audiences. During this era, J.R.'s fame led him to the silver screen in 1999 when he appeared in the critically acclaimed *Man on the Moon.* As J.R. continued to broaden the scope of announcing as the voice of *Monday Night Raw,* he brought his many talents to the world of publishing in 2003 when he penned his top-selling cookbook titled, *True Ringside Tales, BBQ, and Down-Home Recipes.*

Jim Ross is considered an esteemed authority on the history of sports-entertainment and one of the most inventive broadcast personalities ever. In 2007, Ross traveled to the world of higher learning and gave lectures at MIT about the global phenomenon of professional wrestling. Days later, Ross entered the chamber of immortals as he was inducted into the WWE Hall of Fame. Later, based on the resounding success of his barbecue product line he opened "J.R.'s Family Bar-B-Q Restaurants" in his home state of Oklahoma.

"Business is about to pick up here."

After the 2008 Draft, Ross brought his Hall of Fame voice to *SmackDown* and brings that big game feel to every broadcast. Over time, prominent figures have given their own commentary regarding "The Voice of WWE." Triple H said, "There is no else I'd rather have call my match than Jim Ross." WWE Hall of Famer "Nature Boy" Ric Flair added, "A lot of people are good, few are great. Jim Ross is great." Perhaps no words ring truer than those of Stone Cold Steve Austin, "Jim Ross is the best ever, end of story."

Jim Ross is a WWE institution and is the soundtrack to the greatest moments in sports-entertainment history. He was blessed with the unique gift to paint wonderful murals of imagery with speech. Every week on WWE television and on monthly pay-per-views, WWE fans are fortunate enough to hear his priceless works of art, one piece truly more valuable than the next.

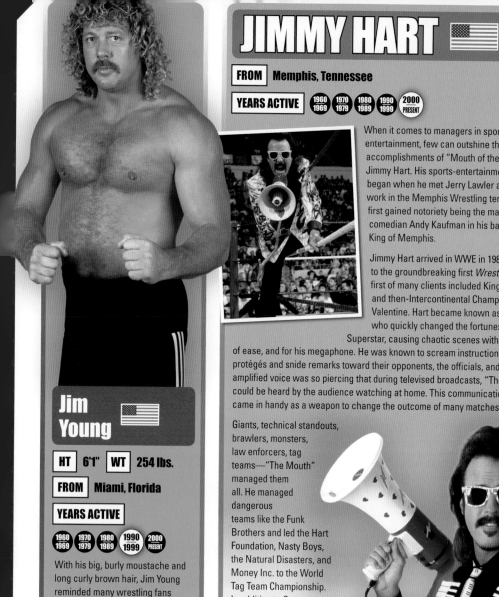

JIMMY HART

FROM Memphis, Tennessee

YEARS ACTIVE 1960-1969 1970-1979 1980-1989 1990-1999 **2000 PRESENT**

When it comes to managers in sports-entertainment, few can outshine the accomplishments of "Mouth of the South" Jimmy Hart. His sports-entertainment career began when he met Jerry Lawler and started work in the Memphis Wrestling territory. He first gained notoriety being the manager for the comedian Andy Kaufman in his battles with the King of Memphis.

Jimmy Hart arrived in WWE in 1985 just prior to the groundbreaking first *WrestleMania*. His first of many clients included King Kong Bundy and then-Intercontinental Champion, Greg Valentine. Hart became known as a manager who quickly changed the fortunes of a given Superstar, causing chaotic scenes with the greatest of ease, and for his megaphone. He was known to scream instructions to his protégés and snide remarks toward their opponents, the officials, and fans. Hart's amplified voice was so piercing that during televised broadcasts, "The Mouth" could be heard by the audience watching at home. This communication piece also came in handy as a weapon to change the outcome of many matches.

Giants, technical standouts, brawlers, monsters, law enforcers, tag teams—"The Mouth" managed them all. He managed dangerous teams like the Funk Brothers and led the Hart Foundation, Nasty Boys, the Natural Disasters, and Money Inc. to the World Tag Team Championship. In addition to Greg Valentine, Jimmy also managed the Honky Tonk Man and the Mountie to the Intercontinental Championship. Jimmy's managerial genius extended to the Women's ranks as he managed the Glamour Girls to the WWE Women's Tag Team Championship. He capped off his WWE career in style in 1993 when he managed Hulk Hogan to his fifth WWE Championship.

In 1994, Jimmy took his megaphone South and landed in WCW with his close friend, Hulk Hogan. During his time in WCW, he continued to write entrance themes as well as perform invaluable duties behind the scenes.

In 2005, the "Mouth of the South's" exceptional career was honored as he was inducted into the WWE Hall of Fame. This unforgettable figure still appears for WWE and is one of the most loved characters in the history of sports-entertainment.

Jim Young

HT 6'1" **WT** 254 lbs.

FROM Miami, Florida

YEARS ACTIVE 1960-1969 1970-1979 1980-1989 **1990 1999** 2000 PRESENT

With his big, burly moustache and long curly brown hair, Jim Young reminded many wrestling fans of Magnum T.A. Unfortunately, Young's appearance is the only characteristic he shared with the NWA legend. During his WWE tenure of the early-to-mid 1980s, Young lost more often than not. The Superstars who regularly bettered their record against the Florida native included Don Muraco, Big John Studd, The Missing Link, and "Dr. D" David Schultz.

Jimmy Jack Funk

HT 6' **WT** 242 lbs.

FROM Amarillo, Texas

SIGNATURE MOVE Bulldog

YEARS ACTIVE 1960-1969 1970-1979 1980-1989 **1990 1999** 2000 PRESENT

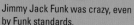

Jimmy Jack Funk was crazy, even by Funk standards.

For decades, fans feared the wild Funk brothers. Hailing from Amarillo, Texas, Terry and Hoss made a career out of their maniacal in-ring actions. Little did anybody know, however, that there was a younger Funk back home at the Double Cross Ranch that was even crazier. In 1986, Terry and Hoss finally introduced WWE audiences to Jimmy Jack, their uncontrollable and unpredictable brother.

Managed by Jimmy Hart, Jimmy Jack kept with the Funk ways by wearing a cowboy hat and boots to the ring. In addition to this classic Funk garb, he also sported a mask over his eyes and noose around his neck.

According to the Funks, Jimmy Jack was an amazing amateur wrestler who only missed competing in the Olympics because of the American boycott of the Moscow Games in 1980. Unfortunately for Jimmy Jack, his supposed amateur success never equated to wins in a WWE ring, as he frequently fell short in matches against the likes of Blackjack Mulligan and Hillbilly Jim.

JIMMY "SUPERFLY" SNUKA

YEARS ACTIVE 1960 1970 1980 1990 2000
1969 1979 1989 1999 PRESENT

HT 5'10" **WT** 235 lbs. **FROM** The Fiji Islands

SIGNATURE MOVE Superfly Splash

No nickname in sports-entertainment history has been more appropriately assigned than "Superfly." Gliding through the sky, Jimmy Snuka used his aerial theatrics to amaze audiences and inspire countless future Superstars.

As a young boy growing up on the islands of Fiji, Snuka perfected his Superfly Splash by diving off cliffs. In 1969, he took his awe-inspiring leap to Hawaii where he made his professional debut. Not long after his first match, Snuka moved to the mainland and began competing in the Pacific Northwest.

In the late 1970s, Snuka traveled to the Mid-Atlantic territory where news of his gravity-defying Superfly Splash began to circulate around the United States. Fans nationwide wanted to witness the move firsthand. They finally got the opportunity in 1982 when Snuka signed on with WWE.

FLYING HIGH IN THE WWE

Within weeks of his debut, Snuka soared straight to main events. Behind manager Capt. Lou Albano, the savage newcomer earned several opportunities at Bob Backlund's WWE Championship. Their most notable encounter took place at Madison Square Garden. With the WWE Championship within reach, Snuka climbed to the top of the 15-foot steel cage and dove straight down toward Backlund's body. Unfortunately for Snuka, the champion narrowly escaped the Superfly Splash. The stunt cost Snuka the match, but remains one of the most memorable moments of all time.

After Albano failed to deliver the championship to Snuka, the high-flying Superstar began to take the advice of the legendary Buddy Rogers, who told "Superfly" that his manager was stealing from him. Snuka immediately fired Albano and took Rogers on as his new manager. The move ignited one of the most brutal rivalries of the 1980s. Looking for revenge, Albano sent his new protégé, Ray Stevens, after Snuka. The two Superstars bled buckets over the course of their intense rivalry.

In 1983, Snuka focused his attention on attaining the Intercontinental Championship from Don Muraco. Much like his quest for the WWE Championship, Snuka's road to glory went through a Steel Cage Match. This time, "Superfly" landed his breathtaking leap from the top of the steel structure. Unfortunately, the match had already ended in Muraco's favor at the time of aerial assault. While Snuka failed to pry the Intercontinental Championship away that night, he did successfully inspire a young Mick Foley who was watching from the third row. In his 1999 autobiography, *Have a Nice Day!*, Foley called the leap, "The most impressive sight I've ever seen."

PIPER'S PIT AMBUSH

Snuka's amazing Superfly Splash from the top of the cage instantly made him WWE's most popular Superstar, which naturally made him the target of the time's least popular competitor, "Rowdy" Roddy Piper. In 1984, the loudmouth Scot invited the soft-spoken Snuka to be a guest on *Piper's Pit.* "Superfly" obliged, but was prepared to be the object of a verbal assault, as was usually the case when fan favorites visited the *Pit.* Instead, Snuka was brutally attacked by a coconut-wielding Piper. The mugging was so vicious that the two Superstars actually tore the *Piper's Pit* set to the ground. Decades later, the attack is widely acknowledged as the most infamous moment in *Piper's Pit* history.

Following the incident, Snuka volunteered to be in the corner of Hulk Hogan & Mr. T when they battled Piper & Paul Orndorff in the main event of the first-ever *WrestleMania.* After the event, "Superfly" made appearances in other territories (he was the first champion recognized by the group that would one day become Extreme Championship Wrestling) and with WWE before entering into semi-retirement in 1994.

Snuka's sports-entertainment accomplishments were recognized by WWE when they inducted him into the Hall of Fame in 1996. On the night following the ceremony, "Superfly" donned his leopard-print trunks for one of his final leaps through the MSG skies.

155

Jimmy Wang Yang

| HT | 5'9" | WT | 206 lbs. |

| FROM | Austell, Georgia |

| SIGNATURE MOVE | Corkscrew 450 Splash |

| YEARS ACTIVE | 1960 1969 | 1970 1979 | 1980 1989 | 1990 1999 | **2000 PRESENT** |

In August 2006, this newcomer appeared on *SmackDown* and showed he's not the one to ask where to find good Chinese food. Jimmy Wang Yang could not be more proud of his affinity for anything country. With a fusion of martial-arts and good old fashioned Southern rough-housing, Jimmy Wang Yang has become one of the premier Cruiserweights in the world.

The black cowboy-hat wearing Superstar continues to be a fan favorite in WWE. He comes to the ring to the sounds of knee-slappin' country tunes, and has faced off against the best Cruiserweights in WWE, including Gregory Helms, Chavo Guerrero, Jamie Noble, and Kenny Dykstra.

He may not be a stereotypical redneck, but Jimmy Wang Yang breaks stereotypes every time he steps out his front door, and opponents every time he steps in the ring.

J.O.B. SQUAD

| YEARS ACTIVE | 1960 1969 | 1970 1979 | 1980 1989 | **1990 1999** | 2000 PRESENT |

| MEMBERS | Al Snow, Hardcore Holly, Scorpio, Gillberg, Blue Meanie |

Headed by Al Snow, the J.O.B. Squad banded together in 1998 after coming to the realization that they weren't getting a proper exposure in a high-profile storyline. They accepted their spots on the roster, and even developed the catchphrase "pin me, pay me," meaning they would put up with losing, just as long as they were paid.

Ironically, shortly after coming together, each member of the J.O.B. Squad began to experience great success. In fact, during their brief stay together, the J.O.B. Squad captured three championships; Gillberg became Light Heavyweight Champion and both Al Snow and Hardcore Holly won the Hardcore Championship.

Joey Abs

| YEARS ACTIVE | 1960 1969 | 1970 1979 | 1980 1989 | **1990 1999** | 2000 PRESENT |

| HT | 6'3" | WT | 277 lbs. | FROM | Greenwich, Connecticut |

| TITLE HISTORY | Hardcore Champion |

When the Mean Street Posse walked the affluent streets of Greenwich, Connecticut, they made their fellow sweater-vest-wearing neighbors tremble in fear. When they appeared in WWE in 1999, however, they failed to induce the same trepidation. Instead, the WWE simply looked down upon them as Shane McMahon's bratty friends. At least that's how they saw Pete Gas and Rodney. Joey Abs was a different story.

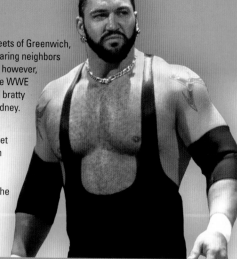

As the biggest and baddest member of the Mean Street Posse, Abs picked up significantly more victories than his stablemates, but that wasn't really saying much, considering their lackluster won-loss record. Abs did, however, manage to permanently etch his name into the WWE records book when he captured the Hardcore Championship at *WrestleMania 2000*. In typical Mean Street Posse fashion, he lost the gold only seconds after capturing it.

Joey Maggs

| YEARS ACTIVE | 1960 1969 | 1970 1979 | 1980 1989 | 1990 1999 | 2000 PRESENT |

| HT | 6' | WT | 235 lbs. | FROM | Baltimore, Maryland |

Joey Maggs was never the biggest Superstar on the card, but what he lacked in size, he made up for in quickness. Dubbed "Jumping" Joey Maggs, the Superstar from Baltimore used his speed to bounce around the ring and dizzy his opponents.

People began to take notice of Maggs while he was competing in the United States Wrestling Association. Maggs soon left for the bright lights of WCW, once earning a shot at Steve Austin's WCW Television Championship at *Clash of the Champions* in 1992. Through the rest of the 1990s, he joined WWE, appearing on the television shows *Prime Time Wrestling* and *Monday Night Raw*.

JOEY STYLES

YEARS ACTIVE · 1960-1969 · 1970-1979 · 1980-1989 · **1990-1999** · **2000 PRESENT**

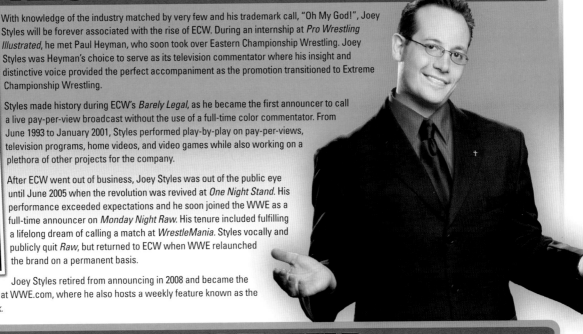

With knowledge of the industry matched by very few and his trademark call, "Oh My God!", Joey Styles will be forever associated with the rise of ECW. During an internship at *Pro Wrestling Illustrated*, he met Paul Heyman, who soon took over Eastern Championship Wrestling. Joey Styles was Heyman's choice to serve as its television commentator where his insight and distinctive voice provided the perfect accompaniment as the promotion transitioned to Extreme Championship Wrestling.

Styles made history during ECW's *Barely Legal*, as he became the first announcer to call a live pay-per-view broadcast without the use of a full-time color commentator. From June 1993 to January 2001, Styles performed play-by-play on pay-per-views, television programs, home videos, and video games while also working on a plethora of other projects for the company.

After ECW went out of business, Joey Styles was out of the public eye until June 2005 when the revolution was revived at *One Night Stand*. His performance exceeded expectations and he soon joined the WWE as a full-time announcer on *Monday Night Raw*. His tenure included fulfilling a lifelong dream of calling a match at *WrestleMania*. Styles vocally and publicly quit *Raw*, but returned to ECW when WWE relaunched the brand on a permanent basis.

Joey Styles retired from announcing in 2008 and became the Director of Digital Media Content at WWE.com, where he also hosts a weekly feature known as the *Oh My God! Moment of the Week*.

JOHN "BRADSHAW" LAYFIELD

YEARS ACTIVE · 1960-1969 · 1970-1979 · 1980-1989 · 1990-1999 · **2000 PRESENT**

HT	6'6"	**WT**	290 lbs.	**FROM**	New York, New York	**SIGNATURE MOVE**	Clothesline from Hell

TITLE HISTORY	WWE Champion, World Tag Team Champion, United States Champion, European Champion, Hardcore Champion

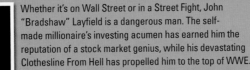

Whether it's on Wall Street or in a Street Fight, John "Bradshaw" Layfield is a dangerous man. The self-made millionaire's investing acumen has earned him the reputation of a stock market genius, while his devastating Clothesline From Hell has propelled him to the top of WWE.

Following a brief professional football career, JBL invested his attention on entering sports-entertainment. After a few years competing on the independent circuit, he made the leap to WWE. Over the next eight years, he proved himself as one of the toughest Superstars around. However, it wasn't until he began to publicize his impressive portfolio in March 2004 that he gained greatness.

Claiming to be a great American, the new JBL focused his energies on many of the United States' political matters, including illegal immigrants. His bold statements drew the attention of then-WWE Champion Eddie Guerrero. The two Superstars quickly engaged in a memorable rivalry that saw JBL claim the WWE Championship from Guerrero in June 2004.

Despite holding the WWE Championship, JBL sought even more power. To ensure he would have complete control over *SmackDown*, he formed a strong cabinet of Superstars around him. With Chief of Staff Orlando Jordan and Secretaries of Defense Danny & Doug Basham by his side, JBL went on to become the longest-reigning WWE Champion in *SmackDown* history.

In May 2006, JBL's in-ring career seemingly came to an end when a defeat at the hands of Rey Mysterio forced him into early retirement. Instead of retreating back to Wall Street after the loss, he donned a headset and became *SmackDown's* color commentator, alongside play-by-play man Michael Cole. JBL remained a fixture at the announce booth until Chris Jericho lured him out of retirement in December 2007.

Back in the ring, the self-proclaimed "Wrestling God" picked up right where he left off. He even managed to gain a level of retribution from the man who took his WWE Championship from him when he defeated John Cena in a New York City Parking Lot Brawl at *The Great American Bash* in July 2008.

JOHN CENA

| HT | 6'1" | WT | 240 lbs. | FROM | West Newbury, Massachusetts | YEARS ACTIVE | 1960-1969 | 1970-1979 | 1980-1989 | 1990-1999 | 2000-PRESENT |

| SIGNATURE MOVES | The FU, STFU | TITLE HISTORY | WWE Champion, United States Champion, World Tag Team Champion, World Heavyweight Champion |

John Cena's fight to be his own person started in suburban West Newbury, Massachusettes. As a hip-hop fanatic, a young Cena was often jumped by neighborhood kids who preferred a more alternative rock lifestyle. When he hit the gym at age 15, his former attackers suddenly disappeared. While a Division III All-American offensive lineman at Springfield College, John also earned a degree in Exercise Physiology. After a brief stint working at a gym, John decided to pursue the profession of childhood idols Shawn Michaels, Ultimate Warrior, and Hulk Hogan.

By 2002, he made his debut on *SmackDown*. Cena's first taste of a WWE title came after a display of superhuman strength when he hit Big Show with an FU, earning the United States Championship at *WrestleMania XX*. From that point, the "Doctor of Thuganomics" did big things, and while his freestyle rap verses entertained his growing legion of fans, he preferred to settle things in the ring.

At *WrestleMania 21*, John beat JBL for the WWE Championship. As he proudly announced, "The Champ is here," John displayed his new spinning WWE Championship belt and showed that the championship doesn't make the man, but the man makes the championship. That May, he officially entered the rap game and released his album, *You Can't See Me*, which debuted at No. 15 on the *Billboard* charts. The record exceeded all expectations and has sold over 500,000 copies to date.

Cena proved he was the prototypical competitor when he defeated JBL once and for all in a barbaric "I Quit" Match at *Judgment Day* 2005. Days later, Cena again brought audiences to their feet when he was announced as the first draft pick selected to to *Monday Night Raw* by then-General Manager Eric Bischoff. Shortly thereafter, one of his dreams came true when he teamed with his boyhood heroes, Shawn Michaels and Hulk Hogan, in six-man tag action. Cena proudly represented WWE all over the world.

" HUSTLE. LOYALTY. RESPECT. "

In 2006, his year started in disappointing fashion. He survived The Elimination Chamber, but Edge cashed in his Money In The Bank clause and defeated Cena to become the WWE Champion. Weeks later, John won back his title from Edge at the *Royal Rumble.* Cena then showed how extreme he could be at ECW's *One Night Stand,* but due to interference from Edge, the champ lost his title to Rob Van Dam. The war raged on between the Chain Gang leader and "Rated-R Superstar" and culminated in a Tables, Ladders & Chairs Match in Edge's hometown of Toronto, Canada. Cena, however, reclaimed what was his when he performed an FU off a 16-foot ladder and put Edge through two tables.

John Cena displayed his versatility again on October 13, 2006, when he entered the world of Hollywood and starred in **The Marine.**

In his third straight *WrestleMania* main event, he successfully defended his WWE Championship against Shawn Michaels in front of over 80,000 fans at Detroit's Ford Field.

His next challenger was a former World Champion and a self-described "Legend Killer." Randy Orton was named the No. 1 Contender, but "The Champ" tore his right pectoral tendon during an assault from Orton. Cena underwent successful surgery and was told he required up to one year of rehabilitation. Forced to surrender the WWE Championship, John's resolve was tested as he began intense physical therapy. In vintage Cena fashion, he made an unannounced return at the 2008 *Royal Rumble.* With the fans at a fever pitch, he eliminated Triple H and was well on his way to another *WrestleMania* main event.

In a relatively brief period of time, John Cena has become one of the greatest Superstars in the history of World Wrestling Entertainment. The man who is a fearless warrior from bell-to-bell is a multi-faceted entertainment figure who elevates everyone around him. WWE Chairman Vince McMahon once said, "John Cena was born to be WWE Champion." This general of the Chain Gang fearlessly leads his army against all challengers.

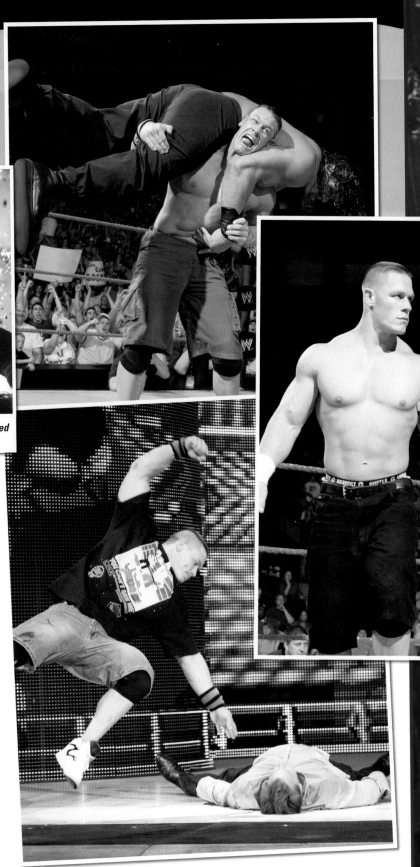

John Morrison

HT 6'2" **WT** 219 lbs. **FROM** Los Angeles, California **SIGNATURE MOVE** Snapshot, Moonlight Drive

TITLE HISTORY ECW Champion, WWE Tag Team Champion, Intercontinental Champion

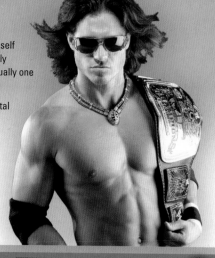

John Morrison's arrogant attitude certainly makes him tough to like. Just don't tell him that; his warped impression of himself has him believing the earth is covered with Morrison Followers (or MoFos, as he calls them) who eagerly await the weekly installments of *The Dirt Sheet*. Despite his over-inflated sense of self worth, the self-proclaimed "Shaman of Sexy" is actually one of the most talented athletes on the WWE roster.

Ever since Morrison's *SmackDown* debut in April 2005, gold seems to gravitate to his waist. A multiple-time Intercontinental and WWE Tag Team Champion, the cocky Superstar certainly has the résumé to back up his boastful claims. However, it wasn't until he was drafted to ECW in June 2007 that Morrison truly took his game to the next level.

Within one week of his arrival on the extreme brand, the self-appointed "Tuesday Night Delight" defeated CM Punk for the vacant ECW Championship. Over the next several months, Morrison defeated Punk time and time again before the challenger finally defeated him in September.

In typical Morrison fashion, he wasn't without gold for long. In November, he teamed with then-rival The Miz to capture the WWE Tag Team Championship from Matt Hardy & MVP. After the victory, the two conceited Superstars realized they had more in common than originally thought and went on to enjoy a lengthy eight-month reign.

John Morrison & The Miz

COMBINED WEIGHT 439 lbs. **TITLE HISTORY** WWE Tag Team Champions

John Morrison & The Miz might just be the most self-centered tag team in sports-entertainment history. Respectively known as "The Shaman of Sexy" and "The Chick Magnet", Morrison & Miz's larger-than-life egos draw instant ire from audiences. Unfortunately for the fans who love to hate them, the arrogant tandem is as good as they are narcissistic.

In November 2007, the egotistical Superstars took full advantage of the *SmackDown/ECW* working agreement, which allowed talent to cross from brand to brand, when they jumped to the Friday night show to upend Matt Hardy & Montel Vontavious Porter for the WWE Tag Team Championship. After the win, Morrison & Miz successfully defended the titles against both rosters of Superstars, including Jesse & Festus, CM Punk & Kane and the father-son duo of Finlay & Hornswoggle at *Night of Champions* in June 2008.

While incredibly successful in the ring, Morrison & Miz are even more known for their popular WWE.com web cast, *The Dirt Sheet*. Airing weekly, the duo uses the show to poke fun at their most recent competition.

John Tolos

HT 6'2" **WT** 240 lbs. **FROM** Hamilton, Ontario, Canada

SIGNATURE MOVE Knuckle Corkscrew

TITLE HISTORY United States Tag Team Champion

"Golden Greek" John Tolos was one of the biggest stars in all of sports-entertainment. At one time he held five territory Championships simultaneously and appeared on television wearing all the belts. He and his brother Chris, known as the Canadian Wrecking Crew, dissected opponents and won tag team championships wherever they traveled. On December 28, 1963 they defeated Killer Kowalski & Gorilla Monsoon for the United States Tag Team Championship. John Tolos was also a major contender to the WWE Championship held at the time by Bruno Sammartino.

Whether he appeared in tag team matches with his brother Chris, or in singles competition, the "Golden Greek" helped change the face of wrestling. His villainous ways continue to influence rule-breakers all over the world. His famous proclamation can still be heard today: "The only way to spell wrestling is T-O-L-O-S!"

Johnny DeFazio

FROM Pittsburgh, Pennsylvania

TITLE HISTORY

Junior Heavyweight Champion, International Tag Team Champion

A native of Pittsburgh, "Jumpin'" Johnny DeFazio started his career competing for his hometown's Studio Wrestling promotion in the 1960s. While he enjoyed great success in Pittsburgh, DeFazio will forever be remembered for being WWE's first-ever Junior Heavyweight Champion. He went on to win the now-defunct title four times, a record that will never be broken.

In addition to his four runs as Junior Heavyweight Champion, DeFazio went on to form several winning tag teams, including unions with Ace Freeman and Geto Mongol, but it was his teaming with Bepo Mongol that garnered the most success. DeFazio & Bepo defeated Luke Graham & Tarzan Tyler in New York City for the International Tag Team Championship in December 1971. Prior to retiring in the mid-1980s, DeFazio engaged in many brutal battles with rivals Sgt. Slaughter and Bobby Duncum.

Johnny Polo

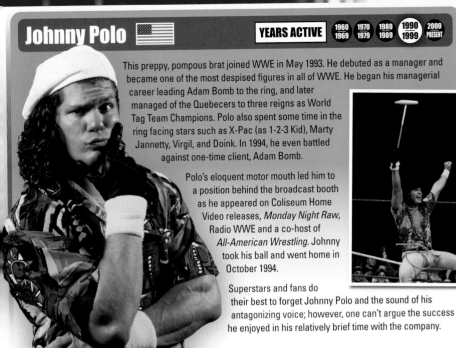

This preppy, pompous brat joined WWE in May 1993. He debuted as a manager and became one of the most despised figures in all of WWE. He began his managerial career leading Adam Bomb to the ring, and later managed of the Quebecers to three reigns as World Tag Team Champions. Polo also spent some time in the ring facing stars such as X-Pac (as 1-2-3 Kid), Marty Jannetty, Virgil, and Doink. In 1994, he even battled against one-time client, Adam Bomb.

Polo's eloquent motor mouth led him to a position behind the broadcast booth as he appeared on Coliseum Home Video releases, *Monday Night Raw*, Radio WWE and a co-host of *All-American Wrestling*. Johnny took his ball and went home in October 1994.

Superstars and fans do their best to forget Johnny Polo and the sound of his antagonizing voice; however, one can't argue the success he enjoyed in his relatively brief time with the company.

Johnny Powers

HT 6'4" **WT** 265 lbs.

FROM Hamilton, Ontario, Canada

SIGNATURE MOVE Powerlock

YEARS ACTIVE 1960-1969 **1970-1979** 1980-1989 1990-1999 2000 PRESENT

On more than one occasion, Johnny Powers came within milliseconds from dethroning longtime WWE Champion Bruno Sammartino. Had things played out just a little differently, fans today would look back at Powers' career as one of the greatest ever. Instead, Powers now has little to show for his brief WWE stay.

Powers used the Powerlock (a version of the figure four leglock) to turn back opponents in many northern wrestling territories. He defeated the legendary Freddie Blassie and Johnny Valentine to gain championships on two separate occasions.

Johnny Rodz

HALL OF FAME 1996

HT 5'8" **WT** 239 lbs. **FROM** New York, New York **SIGNATURE MOVE** Falling Headbutt

Widely recognized as the hardest working man in sports-entertainment, "The Unpredictable" Johnny Rodz used his undying passion to compete to earn the respect of his peers. Unfortunately for Rodz, however, his hard work rarely resulted in victories, as the New York City native lost more matches than he won.

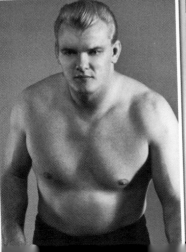

Despite his unenviable won-loss record, Rodz earned the ultimate honor of being inducted into the WWE Hall of Fame in 1996. Brooklyn Brawler, a fellow New Yorker who also lost more matches than he won, inducted Rodz during an emotional ceremony in the Big Apple.

After retiring from the ring in the mid-1980s, Rodz began training the Superstars of tomorrow. Using the gritty Gleason's Gym as a training facility, Rodz harnassed his unorthodox style to teach aspiring competitors respect for the game. Many of his pupils went on to enjoy high-profile WWE careers, including Tommy Dreamer, Tazz, and Matt Striker.

Johnny Valentine

HT 6'4" **WT** 255 lbs. **FROM** Seattle, Washington **SIGNATURE MOVE** Atomic Skull Crusher

TITLE HISTORY United States Tag Team Champion

With tanned skin, sculpted frame, and bleached-blonde hair, Johnny Valentine certainly had the look of a successful professional wrestler. Calling himself "Handsome," Valentine's arrogant attitude made him one of the most hated men in wrestling for close to three decades.

Valentine started competing in Argentina in 1947, but soon afterward, he was back in the United States where he began to build one of the game's greatest legacies. With more than fifty different National Wrestling Alliance titles to his credit, few can match his success in the ring.

In July 1975, Valentine defeated Harley Race for the United States Championship. Well into his third decade of competition, the victory proved Valentine as a timeless talent with plenty of fight left in him. Unfortunately, a mere three months after capturing the title, Johnny Valentine's life would tragically change forever when he was involved in a plane crash. The impact from the accident, which also involved Ric Flair, David Crockett, Tim Woods, and Bob Bruggers, left Valentine partially paralyzed.

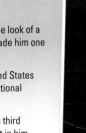

No longer able to compete in the ring, Valentine watched from the sidelines with great pride as his son, Greg Valentine, carried the family name throughout his Hall of Fame career.

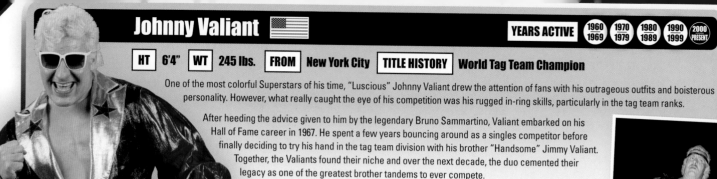

Johnny Valiant 🇺🇸

YEARS ACTIVE ⬤1960 1969 ⬤1970 1979 ⬤1980 1989 ⬤1990 1999 ⬤2000 PRESENT

HT 6'4" **WT** 245 lbs. **FROM** New York City **TITLE HISTORY** World Tag Team Champion

One of the most colorful Superstars of his time, "Luscious" Johnny Valiant drew the attention of fans with his outrageous outfits and boisterous personality. However, what really caught the eye of his competition was his rugged in-ring skills, particularly in the tag team ranks.

After heeding the advice given to him by the legendary Bruno Sammartino, Valiant embarked on his Hall of Fame career in 1967. He spent a few years bouncing around as a singles competitor before finally deciding to try his hand in the tag team division with his brother "Handsome" Jimmy Valiant. Together, the Valiants found their niche and over the next decade, the duo cemented their legacy as one of the greatest brother tandems to ever compete.

In May 1974, the Valiant Brothers defeated Tony Garea & Don Ho in Hamburg, Pennsylvania, to capture the coveted World Tag Team Championship. For more than a year, the flamboyant combination successfully defended the titles before finally being upended by Victor Rivera & Dominic DeNucci. At the time, their reign was recognized as the longest in WWE tag team history. Following his in-ring career, Valiant turned his efforts toward managing. After a brief stint guiding the career of a young Hulk Hogan in the AWA, "Lucious" Johnny jumped back to WWE, where he led Brutus Beefcake & Greg Valentine to the World Tag Team Championship.

Jonathan Coachman 🇺🇸

YEARS ACTIVE ⬤1960 1969 ⬤1970 1979 ⬤1980 1989 ⬤1990 1999 ⬤2000 PRESENT

In 2000, Jonathan Coachman became a regular member of the WWE broadcast team as he conducted backstage interviews and wrap-up segments. Coachman was an energetic young reporter who often entertained WWE fans with his antics during interviews. His segments with The Rock became immensely popular as the "Brahma Bull" often forced him to sing, dance, and smile for the camera after multiple insults.

Coachman worked his way into announcing duties, first on *Sunday Night Heat* with Al Snow, then in 2005 Coachman became a full-time *Raw* announcer alongside Jim Ross and Jerry Lawler. He also co-hosted the first-ever WWE Diva Search and "CoachCast" on WWE.com. Coachman also found time to compete in the ring, including appearances at *Backlash 2004* and *Taboo Tuesday* in 2005.

After first serving as an executive assistant to the McMahon family, Coachman traded general manager duties with William Regal from August to October of 2007. Coach's final role with WWE was as a part of the *SmackDown* annouce team with Michael Cole. Jonathan Coachman departed WWE on amicable terms in spring 2008 to allow him to focus on his other sports broadcast interests.

Jos LeDuc 🇨🇦

YEARS ACTIVE ⬤1960 1969 ⬤1970 1979 ⬤1980 1989 ⬤1990 1999 ⬤2000 PRESENT

HT 6'1" **WT** 280 lbs. **FROM** Godbout, Quebec, Canada

SIGNATURE MOVE One-armed Backbreaker

During an interview, Jos LeDuc once said, "When I'm breathing, I make things happen…" This was a concise summation of what turned into a storied four decade career. Trained in Judo, Jos LeDuc received his degree in ring arts from Calgary's Stu Hart. In the early 1970s the lumberjack appeared on World Wide Wrestling Federation cards in singles action, and in tags with brother, Paul, as well as other partners. During this time LeDuc also sparked a bloody rivalry against Bruno Sammartino over the WWE Championship.

In 1988 he re-emerged in WWE under the guidance of Frenchy Martin. He also appeared in Hulk Hogan's 1989 film *No Holds Barred* and continued to destroy opponents until his retirement in 1995. While visiting family in 1999, this wrestling legend passed away due to complications from diabetes. Jos LeDuc created his own path to stardom and will always be regarded as one of the most feared, and wild Superstars to set foot in the ring.

Jose Estrada 🇺🇸

FROM Brooklyn, New York

TITLE HISTORY Junior Heavyweight Champion

YEARS ACTIVE ⬤1960 1969 ⬤1970 1979 ⬤1980 1989 ⬤1990 1999 ⬤2000 PRESENT

While competing in the United States, the proud Puerto Rican Jose Estrada called Brooklyn home. His WWE career was highlighted by a three-day Junior Heavyweight Championship reign in January 1978. Estrada captured the title by defeating Tony Garea on January 20. Three days later, he lost the title to Japanese star Tatsumi Fujinami. Estrada was never able to reclaim the prize.

Much of Estrada's WWE in-ring action took place inside the famed Madison Square Garden. It was there that he engaged in many encounters against the likes of Greg Gagne and Outback Jack. Estrada also owns the dubious distinction of falling to the legendary Kerry Von Erich in the fabled Texan's MSG debut.

Back in his native Puerto Rico, Estrada honed his craft competing for the World Wrestling Council. Estrada is also the father of former WWE Superstar Jose Estrada, Jr.

Jose Lothario

HT 5'7" **WT** 245 lbs.

FROM San Antonio, Texas

YEARS ACTIVE

1960-1969 1970-1979 1980-1989 1990-1999 2000-PRESENT

Jose Lothario debuted in the ring during the mid 1960s. Lothario became a hero to millions throughout the southern United States in the territories of the NWA and in Mexico. He also spent time in successful tag teams with Dory Funk, Jr., Mil Mascaras, Chief Wahoo McDaniel, Eddie Graham, Ivan Putski, and Rocky Johnson.

Many WWE fans saw him for the first time in August 1987 at the retirement show for legendary promoter Paul Boesch. Jose was in the corner of Tito Santana & Mil Mascaras. In 1996, he appeared in WWE as the manager to his protégé, Shawn Michaels, in his quest for the WWE Championship. Lothario also teamed with his star pupil against members of Camp Cornette. He even stepped into the ring with James E. Cornette at *In Your House: Mind Games*.

By early 1997, Jose returned to San Antonio and shared his love of the action in the ring with students. Lothario will be remembered as a hero in the ring and an excellent teacher.

Jose Luis Rivera

HT 6'3" **WT** 231 lbs.

FROM Puerto Rico

SIGNATURE MOVE Boston Crab

YEARS ACTIVE

1960-1969 1970-1979 1980-1989 1990-1999 2000-PRESENT

Jose Luis Rivera came from a long line of Latin grapplers and graced the WWE from 1984 until 1990. With a background including boxing, Jose rarely hesitated to resort to fisticuffs when necessary. During a 1986 episode of *Piper's Pit*, Roddy Piper expressed doubt in Rivera's abilities in the ring and mocked his Spanish accent. Although Jose was unable to best the loudmouth and his bodyguard, both of them discovered that Jose Luis Rivera had an unwaivering will and an excess of courage.

During his six-year career in WWE, Jose Luis Rivera's actions in the ring left everyone from Puerto Rico with a feeling of pride due in part to his toughness and fighting spirit.

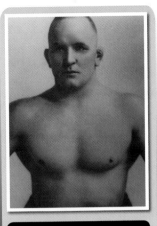

Joseph Raymond "Toots" Mondt

A young Joe Mondt subscribed to a wrestling correspondence course offered by the renowned "Farmer" Burns and honed his "hooking" skills, which is the ability to apply crippling submission holds. Mondt became part of a traveling show and was discovered by the man whose correspondence course led him to the sport and gave him his nickname, "Toots."

Professional wrestling changed forever in 1919 when Mondt met promoter Billy Sandow and legendary grappler Ed "Strangler" Lewis. This triumvirate became known as the Gold Dust Trio. "Toots" had a vision to change the way professional wrestling, as a product, was presented to the public. To make it more entertaining, he introduced "Slam Bang Western Wrestling" which was a style that mixed kicking, strikes, and various forms of contact to generate more excitement. He developed the concept of time limit matches and a package wrestling show that was a program with rivalries between participants with "good guys" and "bad guys."

By the end of the 1940s, "Toots" had positioned himself as the undisputed czar of wrestling in the Northeast section of the United States. In the 1950s, Mondt's stranglehold on the Northeast was contested by a promoter with strong ties to the television industry, Vincent J. McMahon. At the same time McMahon courted Mondt's top attraction, Antonino "Argentina" Rocca.

The two former rivals soon became allies and they broke away from the NWA to form the WWE in 1963. By 1969, a number of health issues forced Toots to retire. On June 11, 1976, Mondt passed away at age 82.

Joy Giovani

HT 5'4"

FROM Boston, Massachusetts

YEARS ACTIVE

1960-1969 1970-1979 1980-1989 1990-1999 2000-PRESENT

Joy Giovanni's curvaceous frame first caught the attention of the WWE Universe in 2004 when the Boston native competed in the $250,000 *Raw* Diva Search. She failed to win the competition, but WWE officials recognized the power of her healing hands and hired her to be a massage therapist later that year.

Shortly after her hiring, Joy and her close friend, Big Show, engaged in a rivalry with fellow Diva Search contestant Amy Weber and JBL. Things turned disturbing when Weber and JBL kidnapped Joy, tied her up, gagged her and left her in the trunk of a limo. The emotional kidnapping failed to derail Joy. The following month, at *No Way Out*, she won the 2005 Rookie Diva of the Year contest, turning back Michelle McCool, Rochelle, and Lauren. Unfortunately, the *No Way Out* victory failed to catapult Joy's career. She left WWE a few months later.

Judgment DAY

♀
October 18, 1998
Rosemont, IL - Rosemont Horizon
Main Event: Kane vs. Undertaker, Vacant WWE Championship Match, Stone Cold Steve Austin as special guest referee

♀
May 21, 2000
Louisville, KY - Freedom Hall
Main Event: WWE Champion The Rock vs. Triple H, 60-Minute Iron Man Match

May 20, 2001
Sacramento, CA - Arco Arena
Main Event: WWE Champion Stone Cold Steve Austin vs. Undertaker, No Holds Barred Match

May 19, 2002
Nashville, TN - Gaylord Entertainment Center
Main Event: WWE Champion Hulk Hogan vs. Undertaker

May 18, 2003
Charlotte, NC - Charlotte Coliseum
Main Event: WWE Champion Brock Lesnar vs. Big Show, Stretcher Match

May 16, 2004
Los Angeles, CA - STAPLES Center
Main Event: WWE Champion Eddie Guerrero vs. JBL

May 22, 2005
Minneapolis, MN - Target Center
Main Event: WWE Champion John Cena vs. JBL, "I Quit" Match

May 21, 2006
Phoenix, AZ - US Airways Center
Main Event: World Heavyweight Champion Rey Mysterio vs. JBL

May 20, 2007
St. Louis, MO - Scottrade Center
Main Event: WWE Champion John Cena vs. The Great Khali

May 18, 2008
Omaha, NE - Qwest Center
Main Event: WWE Champion Triple H vs. Randy Orton, Steel Cage Match

---

Judy Grable

YEARS ACTIVE 1960-1969 1970-1979 1980-1989 1990-1999 2000-PRESENT

HT 5'4" **WT** 175 lbs. **FROM** Bremerton, Washington
SIGNATURE MOVE Dropkick

Judy Grable was one of sports-entertainment's first sex symbols. Debuting in 1938, the fair-haired femme excited male audiences decades before blonde bombshells such as Torrie Wilson and Trish Stratus. Unlike Torrie and Trish, however, Grable spent most of her career as a noted rule breaker, which incited most fans.

Grable's greatest rivalry came against the Fabulous Moolah. The two women spent nearly a decade battling each other. Their most memorable encounter came in 1956 when Moolah defeated Grable in the finals of a tournament to crown the first-ever Women's Champion. Moolah went on to hold the title for nearly thirty years.

Grable retired from the ring shortly after her 1956 loss to Moolah. Despite never capturing the WWE Women's Championship, she will forever be remembered as one of the true trailblazers of female wrestling.

Judy Martin

YEARS ACTIVE 1960-1969 1970-1979 1980-1989 1990-1999 2000-PRESENT

HT 5'6" **SIGNATURE MOVE** Powerbomb **TITLE HISTORY** Women's Tag Team Champion

One of the toughest women to enter WWE, Judy Martin first appeared in WWE in 1979 seen in singles and tag team action. She became regular partners with Leilani Kai and fought the likes of Donna Christianello, Joyce Grable, Desiree Peterson, and Fabulous Moolah.

During the mid-1980s, Martin became a threat to the title reign of then Women's Champion Wendi Richter. In 1987, she reunited with Kai to form the Glamour Girls and with Jimmy Hart in their corner, the team won the Women's Tag Team Championship. Martin remained a contender for the singles title until she left the company in 1989.

The Jumping Bomb Angels

YEARS ACTIVE 1960-1969 1970-1979 1980-1989 1990-1999 2000-PRESENT

MEMBERS Noriyo Tateno, Itsuki Yamazaki **COMBINED WEIGHT** 242 lbs.

TITLE HISTORY Women's World Tag Team Champions

Just as summer 1987 got underway, Noriyo Tateno & Itsuki Yamazaki came to WWE and heated up the Women's Division. Once the bell rang, the Jumping Bomb Angels used fast tags, quick countermoves, and impressive acrobatics that all translated into high-power offense.

As members of Fabulous Moolah's team at the first *Survivor Series,* they emerged the sole survivors. At the 1988 *Royal Rumble,* they captured tag team gold in a thrilling two-out-of-three falls bout. As they proudly defended the titles, Tateno & Yamazaki became heroes to female fans across the United States and the world. After their title reign came to an end, the duo went their separate ways.

While they were together, they lifted fans to their feet and dropped opponents to the canvas on all four corners of the Earth. In the process, they changed the face of women's wrestling forever.

JUNIOR HEAVYWEIGHT CHAMPIONSHIP

The now-defunct Junior Heavyweight Championship was a precursor to the more recent Cruiserweight Championship. Designed to recognize the achievements of Superstars 220 lbs. and under, names like Black Tiger, Tiger Mask, and Dynamite Kid all enjoyed reigns as Junior Heavyweight Champion. The lighter Superstars thrilled audiences with their quick-paced action until 1985 when the title was vacated.

Early records of the championship offer conflicting reports but between 1967 and 1972, the title was traded multiple times between Johnny De Fazio and Jackie Nichols. The championship was inactive from De Fazio's retirement in 1972 until 1978.

1978

JAN 20 — Uniondale, NY
Carlos Estrada defeats Tony Garea

JAN 23 — New York, NY
Tatsumi Fujinami defeats Jose Estrada

1979

OCT 02 — Osaka, Japan
Ryuma Go defeats Tatsumi Fujinami

OCT 04 — Tokyo, Japan
Tatsumi Fujinami defeats Ryuma Go

Tatsumi Fujinami vacated the Junior Heavyweight Championship in December 1981 after entering the heavyweight division.

1982

JAN 01 — Tokyo, Japan
Tiger Mask defeats Dynamite Kid
Tiger Mask beat Dynamite Kid in a match to crown a new Junior Heavyweight Champion.

Injury forced Tiger Mask to vacate the title in April 1982.

MAY 06 — Fukuoka, Japan
Black Tiger defeats Gran Hamada
Black Tiger beat Gran Hamada in a match to crown a new Junior Heavyweight Champion.

MAY 26 — Osaka, Japan
Tiger Mask defeats Black Tiger

Injury forced Tiger Mask to vacate the Junior Heavyweight Championship on April 3, 1983.

1983

JUNE 13 — Mexico City, Mexico
Tiger Mask defeats Fishman
Tiger Mask beat Fishman in a match to crown a new Junior Heavyweight Champion.

Tiger Mask vacated the title after retiring in August 1983.

1984

FEB 07 — Tokyo, Japan
Dynamite Kid defeats The Cobra
Dynamite Kid beat The Cobra in a match to crown a new Junior Heavyweight Champion.

Dynamite Kid vacated the title in November 1984.

DEC 28 — New York, NY
The Cobra defeats Black Tiger
The Cobra beat Black Tiger in a match to crown a new Junior Heavyweight Champion.

1985

MAY 20 — Hiroshima, Japan
Hiro Saito defeats The Cobra

JULY 20 — Osaka, Japan
The Cobra defeats Hiro Saito

JUNKYARD DOG

YEARS ACTIVE 1960–1969 | 1970–1979 | 1980–1989 | 1990–1999 | 2000–PRESENT

HALL OF FAME 2004

| HT | 6'3" | WT | 280 lbs. | FROM | Charlotte, North Carolina | SIGNATURE MOVE | Powerslam |

In 1984, Junkyard Dog became an instant star in WWE. As WWE entered its phase of national expansion, JYD was featured in toy and merchandise lines and even sang his own hit entrance theme, *Grab Them Cakes*. Whether it was his rolling headbutt or his patented powerslam, opponents knew Junkyard Dog's bite was just as bad as his bark.

Junkyard Dog appealed to fans of all ages and walks of life, and he brought children from the audience in the ring to dance with him. JYD's battles with the Funks, Adrian Adonis, "Rowdy" Roddy Piper, "Cowboy" Bob Orton and the Magnificent Muraco were all of epic proportions. None of those battles were as personal as his rivalry against "King" Harley Race as they fought tooth-and-nail at *WrestleMania III*. Junkyard Dog continued to bring fans to a fever pitch and met "Ravishing" Rick Rude at the very first *SummerSlam* at Madison Square Garden. Regrettably, the Dog and WWE parted ways in November 1988.

Before the end of the year, he returned to his home area and WCW. Soon after, he left the company and competed on the independent scene through the mid 1990s. In May 1998, he was honored as a hardcore legend at ECW's *Wrestlepalooza* and once again ruled the ring as fans chanted his name. Tragically, just weeks later, he was involved in a fatal one-car accident while driving home from his daughter's high school graduation.

On March 14, 2004, Junkyard Dog's extraordinary career came full circle as he was posthumously inducted into the WWE Hall of Fame the night before *WrestleMania XX*. With his daughter LaToya on hand to accept the honor, she told touching stories of how her father loved his fans and WWE. No matter where in the world that Junkyard Dog appeared, one thing was for sure: fans of all ages, color, and creeds were going to be on their feet as one raucous force as their hero rocked the ring.

Just Joe 🍁

HT 6'4" **WT** 252 lbs. **FROM** Toronto, Ontario, Canada

YEARS ACTIVE 1960-1969 1970-1979 1980-1989 1990-1999 **2000 PRESENT**

During the latter half of 2000, a mysterious man began to appear backstage at WWE events. When the Superstars asked him who he was, he simply told them that he was Joe, Just Joe. The man with no last name was an unpopular presence backstage. He was always stirring the pot, telling people that others were talking trash about them. On the rare occasion when Joe stepped into the ring, he proved to be just as unsuccessful as he was unpopular. He routinely lost to the likes of Essa Rios, Steve Blackman, and even Brooklyn Brawler. By 2001, Joe had quietly disappeared from WWE.

Justin Credible 🇺🇸

HT 6' **WT** 225 lbs. **FROM** Ozone Park, New York **SIGNATURE MOVE** That's Incredible

TITLE HISTORY Hardcore Champion

YEARS ACTIVE 1960-1969 1970-1979 1980-1989 1990-1999 **2000 PRESENT**

This ego-maniac came to the original ECW with a chip on his shoulder and a Singapore cane in his hand. His finishing manuever, "That's Incredible" was a spinning Tombstone Piledriver that planted his opponent's head on the mat and brought him much success in the world of sports-entertainment. He formed "The Impact Players" with Lance Storm and proceeded to hold multiple titles in ECW before leaving the company in 2001.

After joining WWE, Justin Credible became a member of X-Factor, then joined the ECW/WCW Alliance. Before he left the company in 2003, he captured the Hardcore Championship on several, albeit brief, occassions. Justin returned to WWE in 2006 as part of the new ECW and tangled with CM Punk before he parted ways with the company in September of that same year.

Justin "Hawk" Bradshaw 🇺🇸

HT 6'6" **WT** 309 lbs. **FROM** Roscoe, Texas **SIGNATURE MOVE** Lariat Clothesline

YEARS ACTIVE 1960-1969 1970-1979 1980-1989 **1990-1999** 2000 PRESENT

During his WWE debut in 1996, Justin "Hawk" Bradshaw immediately reminded audiences of past rugged Texans Dick Murdoch and Stan Hansen. Like the Lone Star State Superstars before him, his nasty demeanor and immense size made him an instant threat in the WWE locker room.

After defeating a foe, Bradshaw oftentimes used his personalized JB branding iron to mark and embarrass his victim. In fact, Hakushi was so embarrassed after being branded in March 1996 that he never showed his face in WWE again. One week later, Fatu fell victim to the branding iron just moments before being flattened by Bradshaw's signature lariat clothesline in a match that lasted only eight seconds. With his manager Zebekiah Blu by his side, Bradshaw dominated WWE rings through the beginning of 1997. He later went on to form the New Blackjacks with Barry Windham.

Justin Roberts 🇺🇸

Justin Roberts realized at a young age that entertaining groups of people came naturally to him. As a child growing up in the Windy City, he loved watching WWE and dreamed of one day being under the bright lights himself.

When he was 16, Justin started out working for local wrestling events and became comfortable in front of various size crowds. After he graduated from the University of Arizona, Roberts auditioned for WWE and began his sports-entertainment career in 2002 filling in during Raw and SmackDown events. Two years later, he found himself a full-time member of WWE. Fast forward to present day, and Roberts is the ring announcer on SmackDown living his dream every week.

Justin Roberts has become one of the most recognizable voices in sports-entertainment. It will be exciting to see where he goes from here and where his determination and talents take him.

Kaientai

YEARS ACTIVE 1960-1969 1970-1979 1980-1989 **1990-1999** 2000-PRESENT

MEMBERS Taka Michinoku, Funaki, Mens Teioh, Dick Togo, Yamaguchi-San

Funaki, Mens Teioh, and Dick Togo were first introduced to American audiences when they attacked Taka Michinoku in March 1998. Managed by Yamaguchi-San, the group known as Kaientai wowed fans with their rapid-fire offensive onslaught.

Shortly after Kaientai's debut, it was learned that Yamaguchi-San's wife was having an affair with Val Venis. This lead to one of the most infamous moments in WWE history, as Yamaguchi-San threatened revenge, telling Venis, "I choppy choppy your pee pee." The following week, Venis tagged with Michinoku to battle Kaientai. During the match, however, Michinoku turned on his partner and helped Yamaguchi attempt to make good on his promise. Luckily for Venis, Yamaguchi-San's aim wasn't very good.

With Michinoku in the fold, Kaientai became even more dangerous. Although short in stature, the faction boasted huge levels of confidence. Unfortunately, the promising Japanese faction didn't last long as Teioh, Togo, and Yamaguchi-San left WWE in late 1998. Their departure left Michinoku and Funaki as the lone members of the faction. The pair wasted little time showing WWE audiences the true meaning of EVIL. INDEED!

Kama Mustafa

YEARS ACTIVE 1960-1969 1970-1979 1980-1989 **1990-1999** 2000-PRESENT

HT 6'6" **WT** 320 lbs. **SIGNATURE MOVE** Turning Side Slam

Originally known as the "Supreme Fighting Machine" of Ted DiBiase's Million Dollar Corporation, this enforcer met Undertaker in a Casket Match at *SummerSlam 1995*. In early 1997, Kama became a member of the Nation of Domination where his vicious fighting style aided the Nation in their battles against the Legion of Doom, Ken Shamrock, Ahmed Johnson, the Disciples of the Apocalypse, Los Boriquas, and D-Generation X.

During 1998, the Nation of Domination's leadership changed hands and Kama decided to part ways with the militant faction.

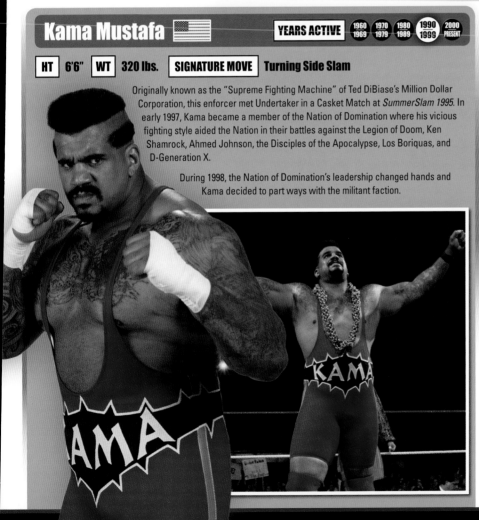

Kamala The Ugandan Giant

HT 6'7" **WT** 380 lbs. **FROM** Uganda

SIGNATURE MOVE Big Splash

YEARS ACTIVE 1960-1969 1970-1979 **1980-1989** 1990-1999 2000-PRESENT

Hailing from the Ugandan jungle, Kamala is recognized as one of history's most frightening Superstars. Believe it or not, his overwhelming size might not have been his scariest trait. Some Superstars are on record as saying they feared most the inability to read his simple mind.

Lead to the ring by his handler Kim Chee, the Ugandan Giant never seemingly possessed the intellect required to communicate with fellow Superstars or referees. Instead, he let his savage beatings do the talking. His impressive list of victims eventually put him in line for a series of WWE Championship opportunities against Hulk Hogan in 1986 and 1987. The big man failed to capitalize on the opportunities and left WWE soon after.

In 1992, Kamala re-emerged from the dark jungles of Uganda. This time, he was recruited by Harvey Wippleman to take down Undertaker. Like so many before him, the Ugandan Giant was unable to defeat the "Deadman." After losing to Undertaker in WWE's first-ever Casket Match (known then as a Coffin Match), Kamala became the target of inhumane abuse from his handlers. Luckily, Reverend Slick was there to save the giant. For the remainder of Kamala's career, Slick chose to treat him as a man, not a savage. Unfortunately, the new approach didn't result in many wins.

KANE

| HT | 7' | WT | 323 lbs. | FROM | Parts Unknown | SIGNATURE MOVE | Chokeslam, Tombstone Piledriver |

TITLE HISTORY — WWE Champion, ECW Champion, Intercontinental Champion, World Tag Team Champion, Hardcore Champion

Nobody has had a tougher road to WWE superstardom than Kane. Once believed to be dead, the "Big Red Monster" had to overcome many obstacles just to get to WWE. Once there, he unleashed years of internal pain, en route to one of the most unbelievable careers ever. WWE first laid eyes on Kane in October 1997 when he tore the door off *Badd Blood's* Hell in a Cell to confront his half-brother, Undertaker. For years, the "Phenom" assumed Kane had perished in a fire that also claimed the lives of Undertaker's mother and father. The look on the "Phenom's" face as he stared into Kane's eyes told a story of utter disbelief. Reality came crashing down quickly, however, as Kane victimized Undertaker with a crushing Tombstone piledriver.

At *WrestleMania XIV*, Kane and Undertaker squared off in their first official match. The encounter marked the first of many emotional battles between the half-brothers. They even competed in Inferno Matches, which saw Kane set ablaze, just as he was when he was young. Miraculously, the warring brothers have occasionally found it within themselves to operate as a team. With Undertaker by his side, Kane captured the World Tag Team Championship twice. He's also won tag titles with Big Show, Rob Van Dam and Mankind, among others.

Kane's greatest victory came at the 1998 *King of the Ring* where he defeated Stone Cold Steve Austin for the WWE Championship in a controversial First Blood Match. Unfortunately for the "Big Red Monster," he lost the prestigious title to Stone Cold the following night. The emotional scarring Kane suffered following the horrific fire of his childhood caused him to hide behind a mysterious mask. Using the disguise as a psychological crutch, Kane was able to stuff his pain deep inside, while focusing his efforts on terrorizing WWE. In June 2003, however, a loss to Triple H caused the "Big Red Monster" to face the world unmasked. No longer hiding behind the mask, Kane proved to be even more emotionally unstable. The troubled Superstar went on a path of unthinkable destruction, highlighted by setting Jim Ross on fire and electrocuting Shane McMahon. In the ring, he remained equally imposing, winning the ECW Championship in March 2008.

Kane & X-Pac

| COMBINED WEIGHT | 535 lbs. | TITLE HISTORY | World Tag Team Champions |

These two Superstars were at somewhat of a crossroads when they joined forces in 1999. X-Pac provided high-flying offense and educated feet to the group, while Kane's raw power and intimidating demeanor kept opponents on their heels. With the energetic X-Pac, Kane's personality evolved. He learned what it was like to have a heart, to feel joy and to feel pain. He also began to speak with the use of a mechanical voice box. This gave "the Big Red Monster" a unique charisma and soon Cupid's arrow struck and his new girlfriend Tori began to lead Kane and X-Pac to the ring.

The two became World Tag Team Champions for the first time on March 30, 1999. They enjoyed a second title reign but split in October when X-Pac turned on his friend and stole Tori with a little help from D-Generation X.

Karl Gotch

| HT | 6'1" | WT | 245 lbs. | FROM | Germany | SIGNATURE MOVE | German Suplex |

TITLE HISTORY — World Tag Team Champion

A bona fide tough man, Karl Gotch began his amateur wrestling career in Hamburg, Germany, at the ripe age of 9. He perfected his craft over the next 15 years, resulting in a spot in the 1948 Olympics in London. Following the Olympic games, Gotch turned to the pro circuit, spending much of his early days competing in Europe.

In 1959, Gotch brought his skills to the United States. According to legend, many U.S. promoters feared booking him due to his overly aggressive style in the ring. Even the great "Nature Boy" Buddy Rogers supposedly feared stepping in the ring with Gotch. When he did convince promoters to use him, Gotch proved to be almost unstoppable in the ring. In 1961, he captured his first major singles title when he defeated Don Leo Jonathan for the Ohio version of the AWA Championship. He held the title for two years before finally losing to the legendary Lou Thesz.

Gotch's WWE career was fleeting, but did result in a championship reign. In December 1971, the mighty German teamed with Rene Goulet to become the second World Tag Team Champions in WWE history.

Karl Gotch & Rene Goulet

YEARS ACTIVE | 1960 1969 | **1970 1979** | 1980 1989 | 1990 1999 | 2000 PRESENT

COMBINED WEIGHT 465 lbs. | **TITLE HISTORY** World Tag Team Champions

Karl Gotch & Rene Goulet were considered two of the most skilled technical competitors of their time. Despite their similar styles, the duo only competed as a team for a brief period during the early 1970s.

A former Olympian, Gotch brought his amazing amateur background to the team, while Goulet was recognized for his sound submission style. In December 1971, they ended the six-month World Tag Team Championship reign of Tarzan Tyler & Luke Graham. Gotch & Goulet held the titles for two months before being upended by Baron Mikel Sicluna & King Curtis in Philadelphia.

Shortly after losing the World Tag Team Championship, Gotch & Goulet went their separate ways. Gotch took his craft to Japan, where he became known as "The God of Professional Wrestling." Goulet continued competing for WWE, where he wrestled on many historic cards, including *The Brawl to End it All* in July 1984.

Karl Von Hess

HT 5'10" | **WT** 220 lbs.

FROM Germany

SIGNATURE MOVE The Claw

YEARS ACTIVE | 1960 1969 | 1970 1979 | 1980 1989 | 1990 1999 | 2000 PRESENT

During the mid-1950s, this vile Nazi sympathizer caused near riots whenever he appeared in Vincent J. McMahon's Capitol Wrestling Company. In 1963, Hess continued the tradition in World Wrestling Entertainment. This incredible physical specimen battled the best Superstars of the era, including "Golden Boy" Arnold Skaaland, and Antonino "Argentina" Rocca.

Von Hess quickly became known as the worst type of villain and reminded audiences of a darker period in the world's history. By the late 1960s he left the world of sports-entertainment to the joy of all who saw him compete, or fell victim to his brutal attacks.

Katie Vick

Many WWE Superstars have used head games to gain the psychological advantage over an opponent. Triple H took this tactic to the extreme when he accused Kane of murder in October 2002. According to "The Game," Kane killed a girl named Katie Vick after the car he was driving swerved off the road. To make matters worse, "The Game" claimed Kane took physical advantage of Vick afterward that same night.

With hopes of putting the entire ordeal behind him, Kane admitted to being behind the wheel the night Vick died, but the "Big Red Monster" claimed it was an accident. With everything out in the open, the saga should have gone away. However, Triple H took the heinous exploit to an unimaginable level when he presented a mock video of the girl's wake.

The disgusting display remains one of the most controversial moments in WWE history. While it offended many, the ploy was successful in getting inside Kane's head. At *No Mercy 2002*, "The Game" defeated Kane to unify the Intercontinental and World Heavyweight Championships.

Katie Lea Burchill

YEARS ACTIVE | 1960 1969 | 1970 1979 | 1980 1989 | 1990 1999 | **2000 PRESENT**

FROM Chelsea, England

As the little sister to Paul Burchill, Katie Lea loves nothing more than to see her "most brutal, most vicious, most beautiful" brother destroy his competition. In fact, the Diva seems to get an inexplicable pleasure from watching Paul inflict pain.

In the ring, Katie Lea is no stranger to punishment. Claiming to be the recipient of "good genes," the beautiful Brit has proven to be a dominant force against both men and women. In addition to impressive showings against Mickie James and Kelly Kelly, Katie Lea owns a victory over the extreme luchador Super Crazy.

KC James & Idol Stevens

| **COMBINED WEIGHT** | 470 lbs. | **YEARS ACTIVE** | 1960-1969 | 1970-1979 | 1980-1989 | 1990-1999 | 2000 PRESENT |

For a few months in 2006, KC James & Idol Stevens were the hottest tag team on *SmackDown*. Managed by Michelle McCool, the young tandem defeated Scotty 2 Hotty & Funaki in their August debut. The momentum of their initial victory carried James & Stevens to a shocking non-title win over WWE Tag Team Champions Paul London & Brian Kendrick a few days later.

With a victory over the WWE Tag Team Champions to their credit, James & Stevens became an overnight success. Over the next few weeks, their wins started to mount, and at *No Mercy 2006* they were awarded an opportunity at London & Kendrick's titles. James & Stevens came up short in their attempt to claim the gold. Shortly after the pay-per-view loss, the duo disappeared just as quickly as they exploded onto the scene.

Kelly Kelly

| **YEARS ACTIVE** | 1960-1969 | 1970-1979 | 1980-1989 | 1990-1999 | 2000 PRESENT |

| **FROM** | Jacksonville, Florida |

Kelly Kelly has never been afraid of showing off her assets. After debuting in ECW in June 2006, the beautiful blonde gained instant popularity with her *Kelly's Expose* segment. Unfortunately, her then-boyfriend, Mike Knox, failed to see the fun and constantly interrupted Kelly.

After an ugly breakup with Knox, Kelly briefly performed as a member of Extreme Expose, a dancing trio that also included ECW Divas Layla and Brooke. More recently, Kelly has chosen to focus her efforts on an in-ring career. In a matter of mere months, she has evolved into one of the most improved females on the roster. Some of her most impressive victories have come at the expense of the considerably stronger Beth Phoenix.

Ken Patera

| **YEARS ACTIVE** | 1960-1969 | 1970-1979 | 1980-1989 | 1990-1999 | 2000 PRESENT |

| **HT** | 6'1" | **WT** | 267 lbs. | **FROM** | Portland, Oregon | **SIGNATURE MOVE** | Full Nelson |

| **TITLE HISTORY** | Intercontinental Champion |

Ken Patera was a world-class powerlifter who won four gold medals at the 1971 Pan-Am Games and a bronze medal at the 1972 Olympics. After training with Verne Gagne, Patera debuted for the AWA in 1973 and quickly became one of its most dangerous rule-breakers.

Patera came to World Wrestling Entertainment in 1977 and stalked then-champion Bruno Sammartino. That year he competed in several of the World's Strongest Man Competitions and ended the career of Chief Billy White Wolf with his swinging neckbreaker. Patera was voted "Most Hated Wrestler" by *Pro Wrestling Illustrated*. In 1980, he defeated Pat Patterson to become the second Intercontinental Champion. His motto was "Win if you can, lose if you must, but always cheat."

After a hiatus from WWE, he returned in 1987 as an Olympic hero determined to rid the world of his former manager, Bobby Heenan. Coliseum Video released *The Ken Patera Story* in 1988, but Patera left WWE shortly afterward. Ken Patera will always be remembered as one of sports-entertainment's most decorated and powerful performers. Whether a dastardly rule-breaker or determined American hero he entertained fans everywhere.

Ken Shamrock

| **YEARS ACTIVE** | 1960-1969 | 1970-1979 | 1980-1989 | 1990-1999 | 2000 PRESENT |

| **HT** | 6'1" | **WT** | 243 lbs. | **FROM** | Sacramento, California | **SIGNATURE MOVE** | Ankle Lock |

| **TITLE HISTORY** | Intercontinental Champion, World Tag Team Champion |

Over the past 15 years, many men have attempted a jump to WWE from the world of mixed martial arts. Only one man, however, was able to do it with great success. That would be "The World's Most Dangerous Man," Ken Shamrock.

Shamrock's first role in WWE was that of special guest referee for Stone Cold Steve Austin's epic "I Quit" Match against Bret "Hit Man" Hart at *WrestleMania 13*. Following *WrestleMania*, Shamrock made his own in-ring debut, destroying Vernon White. The convincing victory introduced the MMA legend as a legitimate threat in WWE.

In June 1998, Shamrock achieved his first major WWE accolade when he defeated The Rock to win the prestigious *King of the Ring* tournament. Later that year, he used the ankle lock to breeze through yet another tournament. This time, the prize was the coveted Intercontinental Championship. With the Intercontinental Championship in his possession, Shamrock eyed even more gold. Teaming with fellow Corporation member Big Boss Man, he accomplished his goal when the duo defeated the New Age Outlaws for the World Tag Team Championship in December 1998. After less than three years in WWE, Shamrock left to restart his MMA career. While his sports-entertainment tenure was brief, it certainly proved memorable.

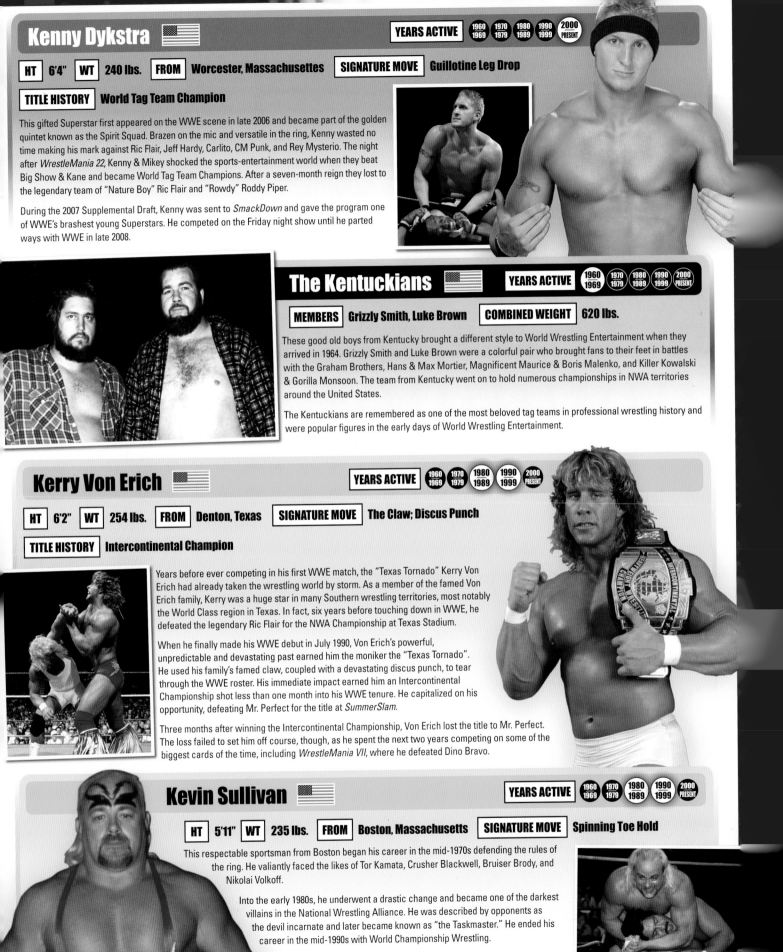

Kenny Dykstra

HT 6'4"	**WT** 240 lbs.	**FROM** Worcester, Massachusetts	**SIGNATURE MOVE**	Guillotine Leg Drop

YEARS ACTIVE 1960–1969 | 1970–1979 | 1980–1989 | 1990–1999 | 2000–PRESENT

TITLE HISTORY World Tag Team Champion

This gifted Superstar first appeared on the WWE scene in late 2006 and became part of the golden quintet known as the Spirit Squad. Brazen on the mic and versatile in the ring, Kenny wasted no time making his mark against Ric Flair, Jeff Hardy, Carlito, CM Punk, and Rey Mysterio. The night after *WrestleMania 22*, Kenny & Mikey shocked the sports-entertainment world when they beat Big Show & Kane and became World Tag Team Champions. After a seven-month reign they lost to the legendary team of "Nature Boy" Ric Flair and "Rowdy" Roddy Piper.

During the 2007 Supplemental Draft, Kenny was sent to *SmackDown* and gave the program one of WWE's brashest young Superstars. He competed on the Friday night show until he parted ways with WWE in late 2008.

The Kentuckians

YEARS ACTIVE 1960–1969 | 1970–1979 | 1980–1989 | 1990–1999 | 2000–PRESENT

MEMBERS Grizzly Smith, Luke Brown   **COMBINED WEIGHT** 620 lbs.

These good old boys from Kentucky brought a different style to World Wrestling Entertainment when they arrived in 1964. Grizzly Smith and Luke Brown were a colorful pair who brought fans to their feet in battles with the Graham Brothers, Hans & Max Mortier, Magnificent Maurice & Boris Malenko, and Killer Kowalski & Gorilla Monsoon. The team from Kentucky went on to hold numerous championships in NWA territories around the United States.

The Kentuckians are remembered as one of the most beloved tag teams in professional wrestling history and were popular figures in the early days of World Wrestling Entertainment.

Kerry Von Erich

YEARS ACTIVE 1960–1969 | 1970–1979 | 1980–1989 | 1990–1999 | 2000–PRESENT

HT 6'2"	**WT** 254 lbs.	**FROM** Denton, Texas	**SIGNATURE MOVE**	The Claw; Discus Punch

TITLE HISTORY Intercontinental Champion

Years before ever competing in his first WWE match, the "Texas Tornado" Kerry Von Erich had already taken the wrestling world by storm. As a member of the famed Von Erich family, Kerry was a huge star in many Southern wrestling territories, most notably the World Class region in Texas. In fact, six years before touching down in WWE, he defeated the legendary Ric Flair for the NWA Championship at Texas Stadium.

When he finally made his WWE debut in July 1990, Von Erich's powerful, unpredictable and devastating past earned him the moniker the "Texas Tornado". He used his family's famed claw, coupled with a devastating discus punch, to tear through the WWE roster. His immediate impact earned him an Intercontinental Championship shot less than one month into his WWE tenure. He capitalized on his opportunity, defeating Mr. Perfect for the title at *SummerSlam*.

Three months after winning the Intercontinental Championship, Von Erich lost the title to Mr. Perfect. The loss failed to set him off course, though, as he spent the next two years competing on some of the biggest cards of the time, including *WrestleMania VII*, where he defeated Dino Bravo.

Kevin Sullivan

YEARS ACTIVE 1960–1969 | 1970–1979 | 1980–1989 | 1990–1999 | 2000–PRESENT

HT 5'11"	**WT** 235 lbs.	**FROM** Boston, Massachusetts	**SIGNATURE MOVE** Spinning Toe Hold

This respectable sportsman from Boston began his career in the mid-1970s defending the rules of the ring. He valiantly faced the likes of Tor Kamata, Crusher Blackwell, Bruiser Brody, and Nikolai Volkoff.

Into the early 1980s, he underwent a drastic change and became one of the darkest villains in the National Wrestling Alliance. He was described by opponents as the devil incarnate and later became known as "the Taskmaster." He ended his career in the mid-1990s with World Championship Wrestling.

Kevin Thorn

YEARS ACTIVE 1960-1969 1970-1979 1980-1989 1990-1999 2000 PRESENT

HT 6'3" **WT** 270 lbs. **SIGNATURE MOVE** Original Sin Modified Neckbreaker

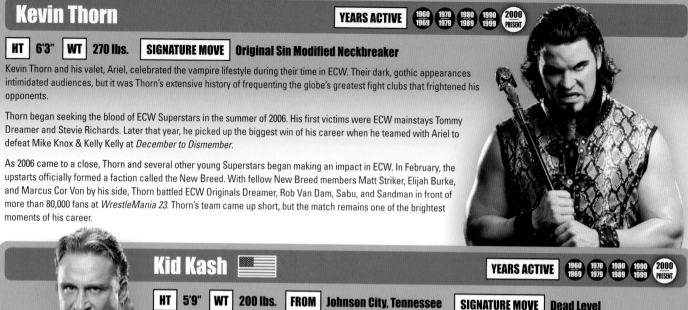

Kevin Thorn and his valet, Ariel, celebrated the vampire lifestyle during their time in ECW. Their dark, gothic appearances intimidated audiences, but it was Thorn's extensive history of frequenting the globe's greatest fight clubs that frightened his opponents.

Thorn began seeking the blood of ECW Superstars in the summer of 2006. His first victims were ECW mainstays Tommy Dreamer and Stevie Richards. Later that year, he picked up the biggest win of his career when he teamed with Ariel to defeat Mike Knox & Kelly Kelly at *December to Dismember*.

As 2006 came to a close, Thorn and several other young Superstars began making an impact in ECW. In February, the upstarts officially formed a faction called the New Breed. With fellow New Breed members Matt Striker, Elijah Burke, and Marcus Cor Von by his side, Thorn battled ECW Originals Dreamer, Rob Van Dam, Sabu, and Sandman in front of more than 80,000 fans at *WrestleMania 23*. Thorn's team came up short, but the match remains one of the brightest moments of his career.

Kid Kash

YEARS ACTIVE 1960-1969 1970-1979 1980-1989 1990-1999 2000 PRESENT

HT 5'9" **WT** 200 lbs. **FROM** Johnson City, Tennessee **SIGNATURE MOVE** Dead Level

TITLE HISTORY Cruiserweight Champion

A former Television Champion in the old ECW, Kid Kash jumped to WWE in June 2005. In his debut match on *Heat*, the cruiserweight came up short against the lightning-quick Tajiri. The loss proved costly to Kash, who failed to see any more time on WWE television for several months.

Shortly after re-emerging on the WWE scene, Kash began to make quick work of *SmackDown's* top cruiserweights, including Paul London, Scotty 2 Hotty, and Super Crazy. At *Armageddon 2005*, he defeated Juventud for the Cruiserweight Championship.

Following his reign as Cruiserweight Champion, Kash briefly teamed with Jamie Noble. Collectively known as the Pit Bulls, Kash & Noble displayed an unorthodox style that oftentimes saw them bite their opponents.

The Killer Bees

YEARS ACTIVE 1960-1969 1970-1979 1980-1989 1990-1999 2000 PRESENT

MEMBERS B. Brian Blair, Jumpin' Jim Brunzell **COMBINED WEIGHT** 465 lbs.

The Killer Bees buzzed into WWE in 1985 and took the tag team division on an exciting ride. The Bees used outstanding teamwork and high-flying manuevers to establish themselves as one of the top teams in all of World Wrestling Entertainment.

When opponents would come at the duo with under-handed tricks, the Killer Bees would often resort to "masked confusion" where they would don matching masks and switch places in the ring without making tags. At the inaugural *Survivor Series* the Bees and Young Stallions were the survivors of their tag team match.

The team split up when B. Brian Blair left the company, with Jumpin' Jim departing shortly thereafter. Fans will always remember the Killer Bees for their exciting matches, high-energy, and innovations to tag team wrestling.

Killer Khan

YEARS ACTIVE 1960-1969 1970-1979 1980-1989 1990-1999 2000 PRESENT

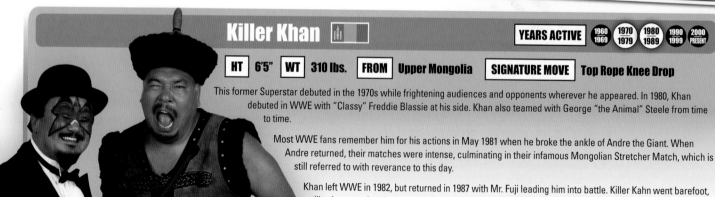

HT 6'5" **WT** 310 lbs. **FROM** Upper Mongolia **SIGNATURE MOVE** Top Rope Knee Drop

This former Superstar debuted in the 1970s while frightening audiences and opponents wherever he appeared. In 1980, Khan debuted in WWE with "Classy" Freddie Blassie at his side. Khan also teamed with George "the Animal" Steele from time to time.

Most WWE fans remember him for his actions in May 1981 when he broke the ankle of Andre the Giant. When Andre returned, their matches were intense, culminating in their infamous Mongolian Stretcher Match, which is still referred to with reverance to this day.

Khan left WWE in 1982, but returned in 1987 with Mr. Fuji leading him into battle. Killer Kahn went barefoot, utilized a sumo-inspired pre-match ritual and spewed green mist into the eyes of his opponents. In 1988, he returned to Mongolia and today resides in Japan. Memories of Killer Kahn and his violent acts in the ring will continue to haunt fans and Superstars for decades to come.

KILLER KOWALSKI

| HT | 6'7" | WT | 280 lbs. | FROM | Windsor, Ontario, Canada |

| SIGNATURE MOVE | Stomach Claw | TITLE HISTORY | United States Tag Team Champion |

This remarkable athlete made his professional in-ring debut in 1947 as Tarzan Kowalski. Over the next seven years, he captured several regional singles and tag team titles in multiple NWA territories. In 1950, he defeated the Texas Tag Team Champions in a handicap match by himself! In January 1953, Kowalski made history when he appeared in the first match televised in Canada.

After an incident involving Kowalski left his opponent short one ear, he became the most despised man in all of professional wrestling. The fans' anger was so intense that he required police escorts to and from the ring to ensure his safety. In 1957, he arrived in Vince McMahon Sr.'s Capitol Wrestling Corporation and displayed his bloodthirsty tendencies. Kowalski returned in 1963 and began a relentless pursuit of the WWE Championship. He became one of the greatest threats to Bruno Sammartino's reign. That November, he formed one of the most dominating teams in WWE history with Gorilla Monsoon. The two monsters beat Skull Murphy & Brute Bernard to become United States Tag Team Champions. Kowalski also traveled to Japan and had a series of matches with Shoehi "Giant" Baba that were televised throughout the entire country.

Kowalski worked sparodically with the McMahon-led company over the following years and, in 1974, he concluded his battles against Bruno Sammartino in a Texas Death Match. In 1976, Kowalski and Big John Studd concealed their identities and competed as the Executioners.

In 1977, this legend retired from active competition and opened "Killer Kowalski's School of Professional Wrestling." For the first time in decades, he was able to show people his passions outside the ring. He became a philanthropist working for children with special needs as well as a renowned photographer. In 2001, he published a collection of his photos.

In 1996, he was inducted by one of his pupils, Triple H, into the WWE Hall of Fame. Kowalski was honored again in 2007 when he was inducted into the National Polish-American Sports Hall of Fame. On August 30, 2008, Kowalski passed away at 81. Killer Kowalski was one of the true pioneers of professional wrestling, and one of its first mainstream celebrities.

Kim Chee

An expert handler of wild animals, this masked man's identity became a topic of conversation when he arrived in WWE in 1986. As part of the contingent that came with Kamala "the Ugandan Giant" to the ring, Kim Chee was the only individual that could communicate with Kamala and curtail his behavior. Given his unique talents, he was an invaluable asset to managers who wanted the giant as part of their stable of WWE Superstars.

Kim Chee was also willing to interfere in a match on Kamala's behalf if it was deemed necessary. Though they have spent periods of time apart, history has shown that if you see Kim Chee, Kamala is not too far behind. The identity and origin of this individual remains a mystery that will probably remain unsolved.

King Curtis Iaukea

| HT | 6'3" | WT | 290 lbs. | FROM | Honolulu, Hawaii | SIGNATURE MOVE | Splash |

| TITLE HISTORY | World Tag Team Champion |

King Curtis Iaukea began his illustrious professional wrestling career in the early 1960s, competing mainly for promotions in Australia and his home state of Hawaii. Despite his blatant disregard for the rules and his unkempt appearance, audiences in both locales accepted him with great fondness.

The mighty Hawaiian didn't spend much time in WWE, but he did manage to gain great success during his brief stint with the promotion. In February 1972, Iaukea teamed with Baron Mikel Scicluna to defeat Karl Gotch & Rene Goulet for the World Tag Team Championship. With Lou Albano as their manager, Iaukea & Scicluna held the titles for more than three months before being dethroned by Chief Jay Strongbow & Sonny King.

Using a flattening splash to finish off his foes, Iaukea eventually compiled enough victories to earn a shot at the coveted WWE Championship, held at the time by Pedro Morales. Unfortunately, the King was unable to unseat Morales and left WWE soon after.

KING KONG BUNDY

HT 6'4" **WT** 458 lbs. **FROM** Atlantic City, New Jersey

SIGNATURE MOVE Avalanche Splash **YEARS ACTIVE** 1960-1969 1970-1979 **1980-1989** **1990-1999** **2000-PRESENT**

The rules of the ring are simple. To defeat your opponent via pinfall, you must keep his shoulders on the mat for three seconds. Unless, of course, you're King Kong Bundy. The massive Bundy pummeled his opponents so severely that he demanded referees count all the way up to five. The stunt was the ultimate slap in the face of his foes and went a long way in intimidating future competition.

Originally managed by Jimmy Hart, Bundy used the inaugural *WrestleMania* as the site of his first commanding victory. In a matter of a mere nine seconds, the man appropriately dubbed "the Walking Condominium," crushed veteran S.D. Jones. The victory opened the eyes of everybody associated with WWE, including Bobby Heenan, who acquired Bundy from Hart shortly after *WrestleMania*.

Under Heenan's tutelage, Bundy set his sights on ridding WWE of Hulk Hogan. He nearly accomplished his goal when he ambushed Hulk Hogan on *Saturday Night's Main Event* in December 1985. With help from Don Muraco, Bundy delivered several rib-crushing splashes that almost ended Hogan's career. The Hulkster eventually recovered and put his WWE Championship on the line against Bundy in a Steel Cage Match at *WrestleMania 2*. The match, which Hogan won, is still *WrestleMania's* only steel cage main event.

Bundy's string of memorable *WrestleMania* moments continued the following year when he nearly splattered Little Beaver all over the canvas. Luckily, the other competitors involved in the match saved Beaver from a certain demise.

Following the events of *WrestleMania III*, Bundy took a six-year hiatus from WWE. When he returned however, he found himself involved in yet another high-profile *WrestleMania* encounter. In 1995, Bundy attempted to become the first Superstar to put a blemish on Undertaker's legendary *WrestleMania* winning streak. Unfortunately for the big man, he went the way of so many other greats that have unsuccessfully tried to bury the "Deadman." Bundy disappeared shortly after *WrestleMania XI*, marking the end of an imposing WWE career.

King Kong Bundy & Big John Studd

COMBINED WEIGHT 822 lbs.

YEARS ACTIVE 1960-1969 1970-1979 **1980-1989** 1990-1999 2000-PRESENT

Paired up in 1985 by Bobby Heenan, this colossal combination's first target was the only Superstar larger than them, Andre the Giant. In August 1985, Bundy interfered in Studd's singles match against Andre. The unwarranted attack left the Eighth Wonder of the World with an injured sternum and set the stage for a lengthy rivalry. Unfortunately for Bundy & Studd, Andre proved his superiority by beating the team numerous times with various partners, including Hulk Hogan, Hillbilly Jim, and Junkyard Dog.

In 1986, Bundy & Studd got back on the winning track, turning back smaller teams such as the Killer Bees. However, just when momentum seemed to be on their side, Andre derailed them again. Disguised as a masked Superstar called Giant Machine, Andre picked up where he left off, making Bundy & Studd's life miserable. Studd left WWE the following year, marking the end of the gigantic tag team.

KING of the RING

King of the Ring began as a one night, single-elimination tournament in 1985. In 1993, King of the Ring became a yearly pay-per-view event which featured the tournament of the same name. After 2002, the tournament was put on hiatus for a few years. It was revived in 2006 on *SmackDown* but the tournament took place over a month instead of a single day. In 2008, *Raw* hosted a one night tournament but Superstars from *SmackDown* and *ECW* were invited to participate.

PAY-PER-VIEW EVENTS

June 13, 1993
Dayton, OH - Nutter Center

Main Event: Bret "Hit Man" Hart vs. Bam Bam Bigelow, King of the Ring finals

June 19, 1994
Baltimore, MD - Baltimore Arena

Main Event: "Rowdy" Roddy Piper vs. Jerry "the King" Lawler

June 25, 1995
Philadelphia, PA - The Spectrum

Main Event: WWE Champion Diesel & Bam Bam Bigelow vs. Tatanka & Sycho Sid

June 23, 1996
Milwaukee, WI - MECCA Arena

Main Event: WWE Champion Shawn Michaels vs. British Bulldog, Mr. Perfect as special guest referee

June 8, 1997
Providence, RI - Providence Civic Center

Main Event: WWE Champion Undertaker vs. Faarooq

June 28, 1998
Pittsburgh, PA - The Civic Arena

Main Event: WWE Champion Stone Cold Steve Austin vs. Kane, First Blood Match

June 27, 1999
Greensboro, NC - Greensboro Coliseum

Main Event: Shane McMahon & Mr. McMahon vs. Stone Cold Steve Austin, Ladder Match

June 25, 2000
Boston, MA - FleetCenter

Main Event: WWE Champion Triple H, Shane McMahon & Mr. McMahon vs. The Rock, Kane & Undertaker

June 24, 2001
East Rutherford, NJ - Continental Airlines Arena

Main Event: WWE Champion Stone Cold Steve Austin vs. Chris Benoit vs. Chris Jericho, Triple Threat Match

June 23, 2002
Columbus, OH - Nationwide Arena

Main Event: WWE Champion Undertaker vs. Triple H

KING OF THE RING CHRONOLOGY

1985: Don Muraco
1986: Harley Race
1987: Randy Savage
1988: Ted DiBiase
1989: Tito Santana
1990: No Tournament

1991: Bret "Hit Man" Hart
1992: No Tournament
1993: Bret "Hit Man" Hart
1994: Owen Hart
1995: Mabel

1996: Stone Cold Steve Austin
1997: Hunter Hearst-Helmsley
1998: Ken Shamrock
1999: Billy Gunn
2000: Kurt Angle

2001: Edge
2002: Brock Lesnar
2003: No Tournament
2004: No Tournament
2005: No Tournament

2006: Booker T
2007: No Tournament
2008: William Regal

THE KLIQ

MEMBERS Shawn Michaels, Diesel, Razor Ramon, Triple H, X-Pac

Although never acknowledged as a legitimate on-air faction, the Kliq was perhaps one of the most powerful WWE forces during the mid-1990s. Comprised of Shawn Michaels, Diesel, Razor Ramon, Triple H, and X-Pac (as 1-2-3 Kid), the Kliq was a group that used their popularity and power to make demands from WWE's top decision makers.

The Kliq made their first public appearance at Madison Square Garden in 1996. With Diesel and Ramon about to leave WWE for rival WCW, members of the backstage faction joined in an unscheduled heartfelt embrace in the middle of the ring. The move, which is commonly referred to as the "Curtain Call," infuriated Vince McMahon. Years later, the Kliq's "Curtain Call" remains one of sports-entertainment's most controversial moments.

Klondike Bill

HT 6' **WT** 365 lbs.

FROM Kodiak Island, Alaska

SIGNATURE MOVE Bear Hug

YEARS ACTIVE 1960 1969 1970 1979 1980 1989 1990 1999 2000 PRESENT

After a successful amateur wrestling career, Bill Solowekyo turned to Stu Hart's legendary Dungeon to prepare him for the pro ranks. After amazing the hard-to-impress Hart with his toughness, Solowekyo donned a pair of worn blue jeans, tied a tattered white rope around his waist and adopted the name Klondike Bill. The rest is Canadian wrestling history.

Billed from Kodiak Island, Alaska, Klondike Bill amazed crowds throughout Canada with his superhuman strength and his firm bear hug finisher and was a threat to nearly every champion. Shockingly, however, Klondike Bill only captured one crown while competing in Canada.

Klondike Bill also brought his game to the United States where he was equally feared. While competing in the United States, he enjoyed two National Wrestling Alliance Tag Team Championship reigns with partners Nelson Royal and Luke Brown.

Kofi Kingston

HT 6' **WT** 218 lbs. **FROM** Jamaica **SIGNATURE MOVE** Trouble In Paradise

TITLE HISTORY Intercontinental Champion

Named after the capital of his island nation home, Kofi Kingston burst onto the WWE scene in January 2008. He was an instant standout with his unique abilities, wide smile, and Jamaican vernacular; this fan favorite brought the fury of the Caribbean Sea to opponents like Elijah Burke, Shelton Benjamin, Big Daddy V, Matt Striker, and Kenny Dykstra.

In June, Kofi was drafted to *Raw* and in his first match on the brand, Kofi brought WWE gold to the tropics when he defeated Chris Jericho for the Intercontinental Championship at *Night of Champions*. Kingston is heralded as a master of forward momentum and one of WWE's most promising Superstars. This "Jamaican Sensation" has given Monday nights a fresh wave of excitement and brings the colors of his home country with him as he captivates audiences all over the world.

Koko B. Ware

| HT | 5'7" | WT | 228 lbs. | FROM | Union City, Tennessee |

SIGNATURE MOVE Ghostbuster

YEARS ACTIVE

Starting in 1986, competitors in WWE were dazzled by the high-flying attacks of Koko B. Ware. With the help of his macaw, Frankie, he taught fans all over the world how to do the "Birdman" dance. In the ring, Koko B. Ware dazed opponents with his unmatched flying dropkick, then finished off matches with his version of a brainbuster, known as the Ghostbuster

Koko and Frankie were immortalized in 1987 when they became part of the famed WWE action-figure line from LJN Toys. That year he also sang the lead on the title track to WWE's platinum-selling album *Piledriver*. Koko joined forces with Owen Hart to form High-Energy in 1992. That next year Koko was again part of history when he had the first-ever match on *Monday Night Raw* against Yokozuna. Koko left World Wrestling Entertainment in 1994. After more than a decade away from WWE television he appeared in the Legends Ceremony at the October 2005 *WWE Raw Homecoming* and weeks later returned to the ring on *Heat* against Rob Conway.

Kronik

YEARS ACTIVE 1960 1969 | 1970 1979 | 1980 1989 | 1990 1999 | 2000 PRESENT

| MEMBERS | Brian Adams, Bryan Clark | COMBINED WEIGHT | 573 lbs. |

When Steven Richards began to verbally assault Undertaker in September 2001, fans everywhere assumed the former Right To Censor leader had lost his mind. In reality, however, he was simply luring in Undertaker so that his newest acquisition, Kronik, could attack from behind.

Shortly after their debut, Kronik, which consisted of former WCW Tag Team Champions Brian Adams & Bryan Clark, targeted Undertaker once again. This time, they cost Undertaker & Kane the World Tag Team Championship. At *Unforgiven 2001*, the Brothers of Destruction finally gained revenge when they decisively defeated Kronik in tag action. A few days later, Adams & Clark were released from WWE. In all, their WWE tenure lasted less than one month.

KURT ANGLE

YEARS ACTIVE 1960 1969 | 1970 1979 | 1980 1989 | 1990 1999 | 2000 PRESENT

| HT | 6' | WT | 250 lbs. | FROM | Pittsburgh, Pennsylvania | **SIGNATURE MOVE** | Ankle Lock |

TITLE HISTORY European Champion, Intercontinental Champion, Hardcore Champion, World Tag Team Champion, WWE Champion, World Heavyweight Champion, WCW Champion, United States Champion

From the day he was born, Kurt Angle's life was about proving that he was the absolute best in whatever he did. Years of dedication resulted in a gold medal in freestyle wrestling at the 1996 Summer Games. Kurt decided to enter sports-entertainment and he knew that if he was to succeed, he needed to take a serious approach. After Angle graduated from the world-renowned Funkin' Conservatory, he debuted in World Wrestling Entertainment in 2000.

In February, he defeated Val Venis for the European Championship on *SmackDown* and days later defeated Chris Jericho for the Intercontinental Title at *No Way Out*. In October, he defeated The Rock at *No Mercy* for his first WWE Championship. Angle showed he was for real when he defeated Stone Cold Steve Austin, The Rock, Undertaker, Triple H, and Rikishi in a Hell in a Cell Match at *Armageddon*.

In 2001, Angle's incredible achievements continued as he won the *King of the Ring* tournament, penned his autobiography, *It's True, It's True*, and was inducted into the National Amateur Wrestling Hall of Fame. Over the next five years, Kurt had famous battles against the likes of Chris Jericho, Shawn Michaels, John Cena, Rey Mysterio, Eddie Guerrero, Hulk Hogan, and "Nature Boy" Ric Flair.

After being on both *Raw* and *SmackDown* brands, Angle was drafted to ECW in the spring of 2006 and defeated Randy Orton at *One Night Stand*. Kurt Angle is one of the most decorated athletes in the history of sports-entertainment. His list of victories reads like a Who's Who of legends. No one will ever likely match his intensity, integrity, and intelligence. He can make you tap out from any position within seconds. Oh, it's true!

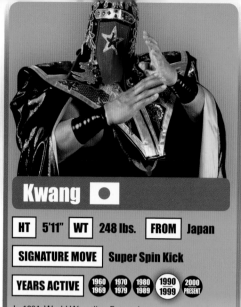

Kwang

| HT | 5'11" | WT | 248 lbs. | FROM | Japan |

SIGNATURE MOVE Super Spin Kick

YEARS ACTIVE 1960–1969 1970–1979 1980–1989 **1990–1999** 2000–PRESENT

In 1994, World Wrestling Entertainment was infiltrated by a martial-arts expert named Kwang. Managed by Harvey Whippleman, Kwang was known for his disregard for rules, and for using a mysterious Asian mist that was often used to blind opponents.

During his time in WWE, Kwang battled the likes of Undertaker, Lex Luger, Tatanka, 1-2-3 Kid, and Bret "Hit Man" Hart. At one point Kwang formed a dangerous alliance with another Superstar well-versed in several martial-arts styles, Hakushi. By the middle of 1995 Kwang left WWE and has not been seen on television since.

La Resistance

YEARS ACTIVE 1960–1969 1970–1979 1980–1989 1990–1999 **2000–PRESENT**

MEMBERS Sylvain Grenier, Rene Dupree, Robert Conway **COMBINED WEIGHT** 727 lbs.

FROM Quebec, Canada **TITLE HISTORY** World Tag Team Champions

For a little more than two years, the French Canadian combination of Sylvain Grenier, Rene Dupree & Robert Conway dominated the WWE tag team scene. Dubbed La Resistance, Grenier & Dupree immediately opened eyes when they attacked Scott Steiner during their April 2003 debut. Less than two months later, they had the World Tag Team Championship strapped around their waists. Using a whiplash side slam finisher known as the Au Revoir, La Resistance turned back all comers. However, they needed a little help from an American to get past the Dudley Boys. At *SummerSlam 2003*, the faction's newest member, turncoat Robert Conway, attacked D-Von & Bubba Ray, allowing La Resistance to pick up the win.

In the months that followed, the three-man faction utilized their numbers advantage to succeed in WWE's competitive tag team ranks. With Conway in the fold, La Resistance appeared unstoppable until Dupree was unexpectedly drafted to *SmackDown* in March 2004.

With Grenier & Conway holding down the fort, many insiders predicted doom for La Resistance. However, the new duo proved to be even more successful than the original, earning three more championship reigns.

LADDER MATCH

122

...d the first-ever televised

The Ladder Match is designed to reveal what lengths, or in this case heights, a Superstar is willing to go to get what he wants. With an item (usually a championship belt) hanging from the arena ceiling, the goal is to climb the ladder and claim the item before your opponent. The first Superstar to grab the item is declared the winner.

Oftentimes, the ladder serves as much more than just a climbing device. It's not uncommon to see a Superstar swing the metal object into his opponent's body. More aerial Superstars also use the top of the ladder as a jumping-off point, which results in some of the most breath-taking offense ever witnessed.

According to legend, the Ladder Match was conceived in Canada in the early 1970s. The match wasn't seen by WWE fans until Shawn Michaels and Bret Hart battled over the Intercontinental Championship in 1992.

The first WWE Championship Ladder Match didn't occur until 1999 when Mankind put his title on the line against The Rock. Using some help from Big Show, The Rock successfully climbed the ladder first to reclaim the WWE Championship.

At the 1999 *King of the Ring*, Shane & Mr. McMahon battled Stone Cold Steve Austin in the first WWE Ladder Match that did not feature a title hanging from the ceiling. Instead, the three men fought for ownership of WWE, which was ultimately won by the McMahons.

The Money in the Bank Ladder Match has grown into one of WWE's most popular annual events. First taking place at *WrestleMania 21*, Edge held back five other Superstars to claim the briefcase and a World Championship opportunity. The Rated-R Superstar cashed in his title shot at *New Year's Revolution 2006*, defeating John Cena for the WWE Championship. In the years that followed, Rob Van Dam and CM Punk have successfully parlayed their Money in the Bank victories into World Championship reigns.

Lance Cade 🇺🇸

| YEARS ACTIVE | 1960-1969 | 1970-1979 | 1980-1989 | 1990-1999 | **2000 PRESENT** |

| **HT** | 6'5" | **WT** | 262 lbs. | **FROM** | Nashville, Tennessee | **TITLE HISTORY** | World Tag Team Champion |

Lance Cade received his first big break in September 2005 and the proud Southerner took full advantage of the opportunity. Teaming with Trevor Murdoch, the duo defeated The Hurricane & Rosey in their first *Raw* match. A few weeks later, they used the momentum from that win to capture the World Tag Team Championship. The rugged Southerners held the titles for close to two months before losing to Big Show & Kane. After the loss, Cade & Murdoch chose to split amicably, an amazing feat considering tag teams rarely break on good terms.

On his own, Cade struggled to find his way. After six long months of non-descript matches, he finally chose to reform his union with Murdoch. The decision to reunite proved advantageous, as two more championship reigns soon followed. After an uncharacteristic losing streak plagued the team in May 2008, Cade took out his frustrations on Murdoch, officially marking the end of the successful tandem. Cade's second attempt at singles success got off to a much more positive start. Rather than sitting back and waiting for the spotlight to come to him, Cade went out and grabbed it for himself. After wisely forming a working relationship with Chris Jericho, Cade has positioned himself in the mix alongside such legends as Shawn Michaels and Triple H.

Lance Cade & Trevor Murdoch 🇺🇸

| YEARS ACTIVE | 1960-1969 | 1970-1979 | 1980-1989 | 1990-1999 | **2000 PRESENT** |

| **COMBINED WEIGHT** | 501 lbs. | **TITLE HISTORY** | World Tag Team Champions |

This cowboy and truck driving tough guy used a blend of down-home fightin' and power to quickly make an impact *Raw*. Shortly after their debut, everyone learned that Cade was trained by Shawn Michaels while Murdoch was trained by Harley Race.

The two captured the World Tag Team Championship from The Hurricane & Rosey at *Unforgiven 2005*. Shortly after their title loss to Big Show & Kane at *Taboo Tuesday* they parted ways to focus on singles careers. They reformed in 2007 for the *Raw* tag team Battle Royal, showing a new regard for sportsmanship. They went on to hold the tag team titles facing teams like the Hardys, Paul London & Brian Kendrick, and Hardcore Holly & Cody Rhodes. Their relationship slowly unraveled, ultimately leading to Lance Cade turning on his longtime partner in early 2008.

Lance Cassidy 🇺🇸

| YEARS ACTIVE | 1960-1969 | 1970-1979 | 1980-1989 | **1990-1999** | 2000 PRESENT |

| **HT** | 6'1" | **WT** | 232 lbs. | **FROM** | Texas | **SIGNATURE MOVE** | Top Rope Clothesline |

Over the course of sports-entertainment, there have been many cowboys who have made the successful transition to the ring. Names such as Dick Murdoch, Blackjack Mulligan, and Terry Funk immediately come to mind. Lance Cassidy may never appear on that legendary list, but in late 1992, the gun-slinging Cassidy used his patented top-rope clothesline to earn victories over Terry Taylor, Brooklyn Brawler and Skinner. Unfortunately, that's where Cassidy's success stopped. By 1993, only a few months into his WWE career, he left the rigors of the ring to return to his ranch.

Lance Storm 🇨🇦

| YEARS ACTIVE | 1960-1969 | 1970-1979 | 1980-1989 | **1990-1999** | **2000 PRESENT** |

| **HT** | 6' | **WT** | 231 lbs. | **FROM** | Calgary...Alberta, Canada | **SIGNATURE MOVE** | Canadian Crab |

| **TITLE HISTORY** | Intercontinental Champion, World Tag Team Champion |

A graduate of Stu Hart's Dungeon, Lance Storm first made waves in Canada and Japan before he arrived in Smokey Mountain Wrestling, where he teamed with Chris Jericho as the Thrillseekers. He soon moved to ECW and formed the Impact Players with Justin Credible. He didn't claim to be the whole show, just the best part of it. In June 2000, Storm went to World Championship Wrestling and held multiple titles shortly after making his debut. Fans were treated to a preview of what was to come in WWE after Storm renamed each belt to suit a Canadian champion.

Storm landed in WWE in 2001, first as part of the Alliance, then as part of the hated Un-Americans group with Christian, Test, and William Regal. Storm enjoyed a few Tag Team Championship reigns with his Un-American partners, but ultimately the group split after a string of losses.

His last match for WWE was at the first *One Night Stand* against former partner Chris Jericho. He officially retired from active ring competition in 2007. Today this technically gifted athlete trains prospects for a career in the ring at the Storm Wrestling Academy.

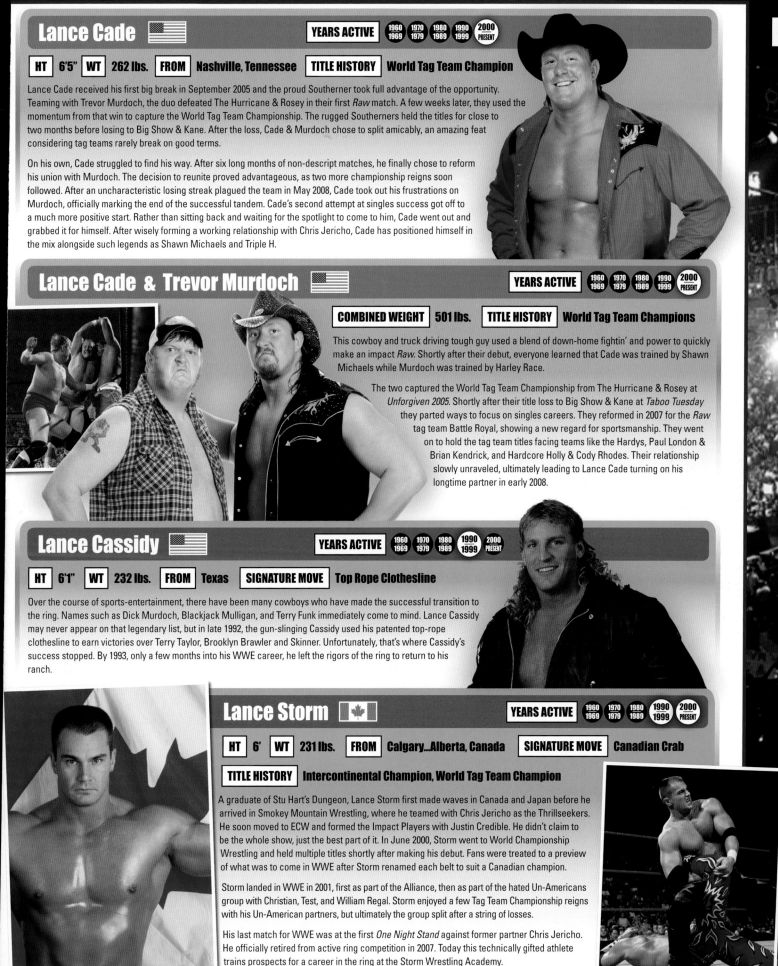

FAN SIGNS

Outside of The Rock facing Mankind at *Halftime Heat*, WWE events are never complete without fans. These days, part of the WWE fan experience is boldly sharing your opinion on a store-bought piece of poster board covered in permanent marker. Fan signs started to make appearances as WWE blanketed the world with its television programming in the 1980s. When *Monday Night Raw* started to air, the phenomenon exploded to what is seen today at each WWE event. From proclamations of support for a favored Superstar to shocking statements that straddle the line of good taste, WWE fans are never afraid to show the world what's on their minds.

Lanny Poffo

YEARS ACTIVE

| HT | 6' | WT | 236 lbs. | FROM | Downers Grove, Illinois | SIGNATURE MOVE | Honor Roll |

Lanny Poffo has the unique distinction of being one of the WWE's most-admired Superstars, as well as one of the most despised. Affectionately known as "Leaping" Lanny, Poffo amazed audiences with his high-flying ability. Many credit him for introducing the moonsault to American arenas in the mid-1980s. Additionally, Poffo's arsenal of aerial attacks included a breathtaking backflip off the top rope, which some consider a precursor to today's Swanton Bomb.

Poffo complemented his remarkable wrestling talent with an aptitude for writing poetry. Prior to each match, he would recite one of his witty limericks before throwing Frisbees out to the crowd. Poffo's rhymes made him one of the most-beloved Superstars of his time.

In 1989, Poffo's poetry began to take a hurtful twist. The once fun-loving Superstar started to use his words to verbally attack the fans and their favorites, such as Hulk Hogan. Claiming to possess superior intellect, Poffo renamed himself the Genius. He would go on to become one of the most hated Superstars of his time.

Larry "The Axe" Hennig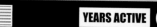

YEARS ACTIVE

| HT | 6'1" | WT | 275 lbs. | FROM | Robbinsdale, Minnesota |

More recent WWE fans might only recognize Larry "the Axe" Hennig as the father of Mr. Perfect. Longtime fans know him as one of the toughest Superstars of the 1960s and 1970s. Following a championship high school wrestling career, Hennig was awarded a scholarship to compete at the University of Minnesota. Although he never cashed in on his full scholarship, he used the opportunity to develop impeccable amateur skills, which he later brought to the professional ranks.

Debuting in the early 1960s, Hennig quickly established himself as a tag-team specialist. His earliest partners were Duke Hoffman and The Viking; both pairings resulted in title reigns. However, it wasn't until he formed a union with the legendary Harley Race that Hennig truly began to be recognized as a legitimate ring warrior. The duo won their first tag titles (AWA) in 1965. Over the next two years, the powerhouse team would go on to claim three more reigns in two separate promotions. An unfortunate knee injury knocked Hennig out of action in 1967, thereby marking the end of the momentum he gained while teaming with Race.

Late in his career, Hennig experienced the greatest thrill a wrestling father could imagine when he teamed with his son, WWE Hall of Famer Curt Hennig, to capture the NWA Pacific Northwest Tag Team Championship.

Larry Sharpe

YEARS ACTIVE

| FROM | New Jersey |

Larry Sharpe joined WWE in 1974 after a successful amateur wrestling career, which ultimately resulted in an induction into the New Jersey College Hall of Fame. However, Sharpe was unable to reclaim the magic he created on the amateur level. He then went on to look for success in other wrestling promotions, including Stampede Wrestling. While a member of Stu Hart's Stampede promotion, Sharpe captured the International Tag Team Championship with his partner Ripper Collins.

Despite moderate success in the ring, Sharpe is most known for training many of the sport's top names, including Big Show, Bam Bam Bigelow, and Kevin Von Erich.

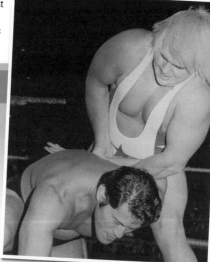

Larry Zybyzko

| HT | 5'9" | WT | 233 lbs. | FROM | Pittsburgh, Pennsylvania | SIGNATURE MOVE | Piledriver |

| TITLE HISTORY | World Tag Tam Champion | **YEARS ACTIVE**  |

After growing up as a close family friend of Bruno Sammartino, Larry Zbyzko became his protégé in 1972. Audiences loved his excellent technical skills and sportsmanship, and the fire he displayed when getting back at an opponent for breaking the rules. Zybyzko left the WWE breifly, but returned in 1976. In 1978, he teamed with Tony Garea to become World Tag Team Champions in 1978.

At the end of the decade, Zybyzko's frustration as being known chiefly as Sammartino's pupil boiled over, and he attacked his teacher during a technical exhibition. The attack lead to a Steel Cage Match at the 1980 Showdown At Shea. The attack is remembered as one of the most shocking acts of betrayal in sports-entertainment. He soon left WWE but excelled at every stop he made, from the AWA to WCW. After retiring from active competition, he became an announcer for WCW until it closed its doors in 2001.

Layla

HT	5'3"

YEARS ACTIVE

 1960 1969 1970 1979 1980 1989 1990 1999 2000 PRESENT

This fiery WWE Diva was a dancer for the NBA's Miami Heat before she won the 2006 *Diva Search*. She made her first WWE appearance at *SummerSlam,* where she joined other Divas in a playful spank-fest in the locker room shower. Layla then brought her unreal appeal to *SmackDown* before she joined ECW. In ECW, Layla joined Kelly Kelly and Brooke to form the tantalizing Extreme Exposé. After the trio acrimoniously dissolved their partnership, Layla was drafted to *Raw* during the 2008 Supplemental Draft.

Since her WWE debut, Layla has experienced mainstream attention including features in *King, JET, Smooth* and *FHM* in addition to appearing on *Family Feud* and *Project Runway*. In April 2008, she was also a featured trainer on *Celebrity Fit Club Boot Camp*. The spunky Diva believes everything happens for a reason and that you should always follow your instincts.

LEGION OF DOOM

MEMBERS	Hawk, Animal	COMBINED WEIGHT	530 lbs.

TITLE HISTORY World Tag Team Champions

YEARS ACTIVE 1960 1969 1970 1979 1980 1989 1990 1999 2000 PRESENT

The Legion of Doom snacked on danger and dined on death for nearly two decades. Along the way, the face-painted Superstars earned a reputation as history's most influential tag team.

Hawk & Animal first came together in 1983 as part of "Precious" Paul Ellering's nine-man stable, the Legion of Doom. The duo's dominance eventually earned them sole ownership of the L.O.D. name. Behind the power of their devastating Doomsday Device—a clothesline delivered by Hawk to a battered opponent sitting on Animal's shoulders—L.O.D. became a world-renowned force before first setting their feet in a WWE ring in 1990.

L.O.D. made an immediate impact upon their arrival, helping the Hart Foundation capture the World Tag Team Championship from Demolition. Over the course of the next year, Hawk & Animal made quick work of such teams as Power & Glory and the Orient Express. Their dominance eventually lead them past the Nasty Boys at *SummerSlam 1991*, earning the duo their first taste of the World Tag Team Championship.

Hawk & Animal quietly left WWE in 1992, only to make a shocking return five years later. Many feared the 1997 version of L.O.D. were too long in the tooth to compete with the promotion's younger teams. They quickly put those fears to rest when they defeated the Godwinns to reclaim the World Tag Team Championship. They held the titles for nearly two months before losing them to the up-and-coming New Age Outlaws.

Following the loss, Hawk & Animal slightly reinvented themselves as L.O.D. 2000. Led by the lovely Sunny, the recharged duo picked up their final major victory when they won the *WrestleMania XIV* Tag Team Battle Royal.

The Legion of Doom that fans recognized as the greatest tag team of all time came to a tragic end when Michael "Hawk" Hegstrand passed away in October 2003. Since that time, Animal has attempted to recreate the magic he made with Hawk, including a WWE Tag Team Championship reign with Heidenreich, but there is only one duo that can make entire arenas stand up in unison and scream, "Oh, what a rush!"

Leilani Kai

HT	5'7"	FROM	Hawaii

SIGNATURE MOVE

Aloha Splash

TITLE HISTORY

Women's Champion,
Women's Tag Team Champion

YEARS ACTIVE

1960 1969 1970 1979 1980 1989 1990 1999 2000 PRESENT

Competitors don't come much tougher than this woman from Hawaii. Trained by Fabulous Moolah, she began her career in local promotions in the mid-1970s. In 1977, she joined WWE and became an instant contender for the championship held by her teacher.

In 1985, she beat Wendi Richter at *The War To Settle The Score* for the Women's Championship. Shortly after her loss to Richter at *WrestleMania*, Kai formed a team with another Moolah protégé, Judy Martin. Known as the Glamour Girls, Kai and Martin defeated Velvet McIntyre & Desiree Peterson in a wild championship bout in Cairo, Egypt. When they returned to America, they found a new manager in "Mouth of the South" Jimmy Hart. The Girls traded title reigns with the Jumping Bomb Angels until retiring as the champions in 1989. Leilani left WWE, but returned briefly in 1994. She competed in World Championship Wrestling until the late 1990s, and today she remains active in the independent scene all over the world.

Lena Yada

| HT | 5'4" | FROM | Honolulu, Hawaii |

YEARS ACTIVE (1960-1969) (1970-1979) (1980-1989) (1990-1999) (2000 PRESENT)

WWE fans best recognize Lena Yada as the 2007 Diva Search contestant who now serves as a backstage interviewer for ECW. The self-proclaimed "Asian Sensation" has been in the public eye long before trying her hand at sports-entertainment.

In addition to competing as a professional surfer, Lena has assembled an impressive acting resume. Her movie credits include a role in the box-office hit *I Now Pronounce You Chuck & Larry*. She also landed an appearance on the popular *Baywatch* parody, *Son of the Beach*. A fitness fanatic, Lena has also used her toned frame to open eyes in many swimsuit competitions.

Les Thornton

| HT | 5'9" | WT | 225 lbs. | FROM | Manchester, England |

YEARS ACTIVE (1960-1969) (1970-1979) (1980-1989) (1990-1999) (2000 PRESENT)

WWE record books are not filled with Les Thornton accomplishments, but that doesn't mean he wasn't a success in the ring. Prior to defining himself as a tough-as-nails Superstar from England, Thornton excelled as a boxer in the British Navy, as well as a professional rugby player. After making his sports-entertainment debut in the late 1950s, Thornton toured the globe, earning the respect of foreign fans. Beirut, New Zealand, Germany and Australia are just a few of the territories he dominated before venturing to North America.

When Thornton arrived in Canada, he began competing for Stu Hart's Stampede Wrestling promotion. While there, he captured the North American Heavyweight Championship twice. Thornton didn't compete for WWE until the latter days of his career. During the infancy of WWE's global dominance, the organization recognized Thornton as a Superstar with great international influence. WWE quickly made Thornton a focal point of its overseas tours of the mid-1980s.

LEX LUGER

YEARS ACTIVE (1960-1969) (1970-1979) (1980-1989) (1990-1999) (2000 PRESENT)

| HT | 6'6" | WT | 275 lbs. | FROM | Chicago, Illinois | SIGNATURE MOVE | Running Forearm; Human Torture Rack |

After a series of injuries forced him to leave pro football, Lex Luger trained with Hiro Matsuda to learn the art of the ring. Following a celebrated stint in WCW, WWE fans first saw Lex Luger as part of the World Bodybuilding Federation. Luger was officially unveiled at the 1993 *Royal Rumble* as "the Narcissist." He became one of the most hated Superstars in WWE, as before each match he posed in front of full-body mirrors.

That summer, Luger shocked the world on America's birthday. After numerous Superstars and professional athletes failed to slam then-WWE Champion Yokozuna, Luger flew in via helicopter onto the deck of the USS Intrepid to answer the call. In a Herculean display of strength, Luger lifted and slammed the 600-plus pound champion. As everyone in attendance rejoiced, the days of "the Narcissist" were gone and WWE's "American Original" had arrived.

Covered in the red, white and blue of the USA, Luger embarked on the "Lex Express," a nationwide bus tour during which he campaigned for a shot at the WWE Championship. Millions of fans from far and wide answered the call to support him. Lex received a shot at Yokozuna's title at *SummerSlam 1993*, but Luger won by countout and the title remained with the giant sumo. Luger wasn't done with Yokozuna, however. Luger and Bret "Hit Man" Hart were declared co-winners of the 1994 *Royal Rumble*. They both had a chance to capture the WWE Championship from Yokozuna at *WrestleMania X*. Unfortunately, the title wasn't in the cards for Lex, as Hart defeated Yokozuna for the title.

He went on to form a popular team with the British Bulldog, dubbed the Allied Powers. The duo faced off against the Million-Dollar Corporation and were considered top contenders for the World Tag Team Championship. In September 1995, Lex suddenly left WWE, making a shocking appearance on the initial episode of *WCW Monday Nitro,* which was widely acknowledged as the first major salvo of the Monday Night War.

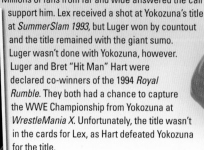

LIGHT HEAVYWEIGHT CHAMPIONSHIP

The now-defunct Light Heavyweight championship was initially awarded in 1997 at a tournament during the *In Your House: Degeneration X* Pay Per View. Eight of the greatest Light Heavyweights in the world competed. Taka Michinoku, Brian Christopher, Super Loco, and Águila were among the participants. During its existence the Light Heavyweight Championship changed hands 13 times, totaling 11 different champions including Christian, Jeff Hardy, Dean Malenko, X-Pac, and Taijiri.

1997

DEC 07 — Springfield, MA

Taka Michinoku defeats Brian Christopher in the finals of the Light Heavyweight tournament

1998

OCT 18 — Rosemont, IL

Christian defeats Taka Michinoku

NOV 19 — Columbus, OH

Gillberg defeats Christian

2000

FEB 10 — Austin, TX

Essa Rios defeats Gillberg

MAR 13 — East Rutherford, NJ

Dean Malenko defeats Essa Rios

APR 17 — State College, PA

Scotty 2 Hotty defeats Dean Malenko

APR 27 — Charlotte, NC

Dean Malenko defeats Scotty 2 Hotty

2001

MAR 15 — Anaheim, CA

Crash Holly defeats Dean Malenko

APR 29 — Chicago, IL

Jerry Lynn defeats Crash Holly

JUNE 07 — Grand Forks, ND

Jeff Hardy defeats Jerry Lynn

JUNE 25 — New York, NY

X-Pac defeats Jeff Hardy

AUG 06 — Anaheim, CA

Taijiri defeats X-Pac

AUG 19 — San Jose, CA

X-Pac defeats Taijiri

The title was abandoned in 2001 when WWE put the WCW/ECW Alliance out of business. The WCW Cruiserweight Championship was then adopted as the WWE Cruiserweight Championship.

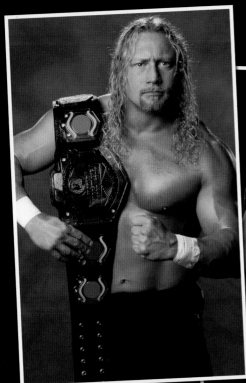

Lilian Garcia

With nearly a decade of experience, Lilian Garcia has provided the ring introductions for some of sports-entertainment's most historic matches. Along the way, her melodious tone has become synonymous with the success of WWE's flagship program, *Monday Night Raw*.

In addition to announcing, Lilian is an accomplished vocalist. Prior to each *Raw*, the beautiful Diva shows off her talents with an emotional rendition of *The Star-Spangled Banner*. She has also opened up for many professional sports teams, including the New York Jets and Phoenix Suns. The popularity of her amazing voice eventually lead to the production of her own album, *¡Quiero Vivir!*, which was released in October 2007.

With all this talent, it was only a matter of time before a Superstar made a pass at her. In May 2005, the inevitable occurred when the mighty Viscera proclaimed his love for the ring announcer. On the surface, Lilian and Big Vis didn't look like the prototypical couple; but inside, they shared a deep connection, or so Lilian thought. In June, a smitten Lilian proposed marriage to her man. She was ultimately heartbroken when he chose to be with the Godfather's ladies rather than marry her.

With Viscera a distant memory, Lilian draws the attention of male fans worldwide when she poses for *WWE Magazine's* annual swimsuit edition each summer.

LINDA McMAHON

Born in New Bern, North Carolina, Linda Marie Edwards was a Southern belle like no other. She was a member of the Girl Scouts of America, an honor student who enjoyed sports, and a member of her church choir. One day after service, she met a young Vince McMahon and it was love at first sight. When the two wed in 1966, Vince promised her two things, "I'll always love you, and there will never be a dull moment." Vince quickly learned that was going to be a two-way street.

After she graduated from East Carolina University, the McMahons moved to Washington, DC. In 1979, Linda and Vince relocated to Massachusetts and created Titan Sports. After purchasing the Cape Cod Coliseum, they promoted various events, from professional wrestling to rock concerts and professional hockey. In 1980, they incorporated Titan Sports, and in 1982, bought Capitol Wrestling Corporation from Vince's father. Linda and Vince gave World Wrestling Entertainment the opportunity to be seen beyond the geographic region of the Northeast and marketed it as the premier form of entertainment.

Their revolutionary approach helped cultivate WWE's broader appeal, which led to syndication and later national and international television contracts. The McMahons ran these activities concurrently with new branding and trademarking initiatives that put World Wrestling Entertainment in a class by itself.

Linda negotiated and implemented WWE's first-ever licensing contract with then-industry leading toy company LJN to produce a line of action figures. Today, that product line is considered a classic within the toy business and is sought after by collectors. She also managed the development of WWE publications and in the beginning wrote a majority of the articles. This foresight, drive, and success were a harbinger of the multi-million dollar revenue streams that Linda would go on to create for the company. In 1993, she became President of WWE and in 1997, was made its Chief Executive Officer. Under Linda's leadership, the company continued to prosper. In October 1999, WWE undertook a successful initial public offering and today trades on the New York Stock Exchange.

During the "Attitude" Era, WWE programming became a family affair. As her husband and two children, Shane and Stephanie, ran roughshod throughout the company, Linda was often the sensible voice of reason who upheld the honor of World Wrestling Entertainment and kept the family in line. Although at times it was a struggle to maintain order, she always achieved her goal.

In addition to her brilliant business accomplishments and performance in front of the camera, Linda has been instrumental in nurturing WWE's community and charitable pursuits.

She spearheaded the creation of WWE's Get R.E.A.L. educational programs, as well as the company's nationwide *WrestleMania* Reading Challenge. She also led the development of WWE's Smackdown Your Vote! with partners including the League of Women Voters, the National Association of Secretaries of State, and the Harvard Institute of Politics.

In recognition for her work over the past 20 years to support children, the Make-A-Wish Foundation awarded WWE its highest honor, the Chris Grecius Award in 2004. In honor of the company's efforts for over two decades, Linda was appointed to the Make-A-Wish Foundation of America National Advisory Council in 2005. She is also a major supporter of The Starlight Foundation and the USO. In addition, Linda served as the Honorary Corporate Chair of the Multiple Myeloma Research Foundation and on the Governor's Council for the World Special Olympics. Linda continues to be a visionary in the world of philanthropy and business.

In 2007, she was named one of Multichannel News' Wonder Woman award recipients, recognizing her accomplishments with WWE and as a leader in the U.S. cable television industry. Today, Linda oversees and guides the strategic direction of World Wrestling Entertainment's content and products that are distributed on a global basis via broadcast, syndication and cable television, publications, mobile phones, and the Internet. Other key businesses areas include licensing, merchandising, home video, e-commerce, and catalog sales.

For over three decades, the work of Linda McMahon has been a critical component to the success of a company that was once run out of a basement with a staff of two. Now it is an integrated, multi-billion dollar, publicly traded media giant. While the McMahon family all shares a sense of pride when it comes to World Wrestling Entertainment, Linda McMahon continues to be the power behind the throne.

LITA

HT 5'6" **FROM** Sanford, North Carolina **SIGNATURE MOVE** Litacanrana

TITLE HISTORY Women's Champion

When Lita first arrived in WWE, she became instantly recognizable by her fiery red hair, gigantic shoulder tattoo, and high-flying ring presence. By the time she left, however, Lita was widely known for her lewd actions and questionable behavior.

Lita joined WWE in 2000 and quickly made a name for herself as the valet of Essa Rios. However, when jealousy drove a wedge between the two, she shifted her allegiances to the Hardy Boys. Known as Team Xtreme, the threesome went on to wow crowds with their acrobatic offense for nearly five years. During this period, Lita also developed a romantic relationship with Matt Hardy.

As an in-ring competitor, Lita enjoyed four reigns as Women's Champion. Her first came at the expense of Stephanie McMahon-Helmsley in August 2000. The match, which was officiated over by The Rock, was the first *Raw* main event to feature competition from the Women's Division.

Lita's meteoric rise to the top came crashing down in 2002 when she suffered a neck injury while shooting scenes for FOX's *Dark Angel*. The injury proved so severe that major surgery was required, which forced Lita out of action for a year and a half.

In 2004, Lita became the object of Kane's sadistic desires. When she refused to give in to his advances, he began tormenting her boyfriend, Matt Hardy. Fearing for Matt's wellbeing, Lita eventually caved in to Kane's demands as a way to halt the monster's constant attacks. However, this was just the first of two indiscretions she hoped Matt would never discover.

The following year, Lita began a romantic relationship with Edge while she was still involved with Matt. When it became public, the three Superstars engaged in the ugliest love triangle in sports-entertainment history. To make matters worse for the broken-hearted Matt, Lita and Edge continually flaunted their love for the entire world to see. They even engaged in a highly publicized celebration following Edge's WWE Championship victory in January 2006.

Lita left WWE following a loss to Mickie James at *Survivor Series* 2006. It was a bittersweet moment for the Diva, as she was finally given the opportunity to keep her private life out of the spotlight.

Little Boogeyman

FROM The Bottomless Pit **SIGNATURE MOVE** Pump Handle Slam

YEARS ACTIVE 1960-1969 1970-1979 1980-1989 1990-1999 **2000 PRESENT**

This little worm eater appeared in WWE alongside his larger counterpart in 2007 during the Boogeyman's rivalry with Finlay. "Little Boogey" was brought to the world of sports-entertainment to counter the presence of Hornswoggle. As the two beings from the Bottomless Pit battled Ireland's toughest sons, the shorter version showed he was just as disgusting and just as dangerous in the ring.

History has shown that the Superstars of WWE are never safe as long as the Boogeyman is around. Where he dwells, this frightening miniature sidekick is somewhere close.

Little Beaver

HT 4'6" **WT** 60 lbs. **FROM** Quebec, Canada

SIGNATURE MOVE Dropkick

YEARS ACTIVE 1960-1969 1970-1979 1980-1989 1990-1999 **2000 PRESENT**

In 1948, Little Beaver made his debut, sporting a mohawk and a full-length headdress. He became one of the most popular Superstars in the world and in 1963 he joined WWE. His battles with rival Sky Low Low made headlines in wrestling publications everywhere. In September 1972, Little Beaver teamed with Little Louie against Sonny Boy Hayes and Pee Wee Adams at the first-ever Showdown At Shea.

The highest and lowest points of his career may have come in the same night. At *WrestleMania III* he teamed with Hillbilly Jim & Haiti Kid in a mixed tag against King Kong Bundy, Lord Littlebrook & Little Tokyo but received an elbow drop from King Kong Bundy. Little Beaver never competed again. In December 1996, Little Beaver passed away at 61 years old.

Little Brutus

YEARS ACTIVE

1960 1969 · **1970 1979** · **1980 1989** · **1990 1999** · **2000 PRESENT**

Little Brutus competed in WWE's Northeast territory during midget wrestling's surge in popularity in the 1960s. During this time, he wrestled mainly as a tag team competitor, alongside Sky Low Low, Billy the Kid, and Butch Cassidy. Chief rival Jamaica Kid normally upended the bearded Brutus during these encounters. In October 1969, Brutus gained the ultimate revenge when he defeated Jamaica Kid in one-on-one action in Boston.

After his in-ring career came to a close, Little Brutus turned to training future midget wrestlers. His most noted pupil was Dink the Clown.

Little Tokyo

YEARS ACTIVE **1960 1969** · **1970 1979** · **1980 1989** · **1990 1999** · **2000 PRESENT**

HT 4'7" **WT** 45 lbs. **FROM** Tokyo, Japan **SIGNATURE MOVE** Flying Chop

One of the most successful midget stars of the ring during the 1970s and 1980s, Little Tokyo took WWE by storm in 1975 and performed in packed arenas all over the northeast section of the United States.

Over the years Tokyo developed an intense rivalry with Cowboy Lang over who was the best midget wrestler in the world. As sports-entertainment grew, Little Tokyo was there to do his part, appearing at *WrestleMania III* in the mixed tag match with King Kong Bundy & Lord Littlebrook to square-off against Hillbilly Jim, Little Beaver & Haiti Kid.

Few Superstars in any era of any physical stature enjoyed the years of success that Little Tokyo did. He is remembered fondly as a gifted performer who stood the test of time.

Lo Down

YEARS ACTIVE **1960 1969** · **1970 1979** · **1980 1989** · **1990 1999** · **2000 PRESENT**

MEMBERS D-Lo Brown, Chaz **COMBINED WEIGHT** 511 lbs.

Prior to 2000, both D-Lo Brown and Chaz enjoyed championship-caliber WWE careers. When they decided to unite as Lo Down in July 2000, fans everywhere assumed the same level of success would follow the talented tandem. It didn't.

Shortly after forming Lo Down, D-Lo & Chaz employed the managerial services of Tiger Ali Singh. The duo began to dress like their manager, complete with turbans. Their won-loss record also resembled that of Singh's, which wasn't very impressive.

Lo Down's biggest win came at the expense of Kaientai. Competing on *Heat*, D-Lo & Chaz turned back the Japanese duo to earn a spot in the 2001 *Royal Rumble*. They never made it to the *Royal Rumble* and, instead, comedian Drew Carey took their spot.

Lord Alfred Hayes

YEARS ACTIVE **1960 1969** · **1970 1979** · **1980 1989** · **1990 1999** · **2000 PRESENT**

HT 5'9" **WT** 238 lbs. **FROM** Windermere, England **SIGNATURE MOVE** London Bridge

When he debuted in WWE in 1982, he was retired from active competition. In his earlier years, Lord Alfred Hayes was known throughout Europe, Japan, and parts of the National Wrestling Alliance as a dangerous grappler and crafty champion.

WWE audiences first saw the Lord as Vince McMahon's partner in crime on the hit talk show *Tuesday Night Titans*. From there Alfred's pleasant demeanor became regularly seen on WWE programming as he became a backstage interview correspondent, introductory announcer, and color commentator. As WWE's business expanded their home video business exploded and Lord Alfred was a major part of several of the products released during that time. Hayes continued his excellent work into the 1990s as he was seen on early episodes of *Monday Night Raw*. In 1995, Alfred and WWE parted ways after a successful partnership that lasted over a decade.

He retired from sports-entertainment and quietly enjoyed the fruits of his labor in his adopted home state of Texas. Sadly, in July 2005 this WWE legend passed away at his home. Lord Alfred Hayes spent decades as one of the top figures in sports-entertainment, whether it was in the ring or behind the microphone.

Lord Littlebrook 🇬🇧

| HT | 4'4" | WT | 108 lbs. | FROM | London, England |

Hailing from London, England, Lord Littlebrook possessed many of the same noble qualities today's fans see in William Regal, only much less annoying. Complete with his monocle and plaid jacket, this small-stature wrestler looked every bit the part of a proper Englishman.

While competing in the United States, Littlebrook managed to capture the NWA World Midget Championship in 1966. He also garnered much attention during his days in the AWA. However, it was his *WrestleMania III* match that will always remain Littlebrook's ultimate highlight. Teaming with Little Tokyo & King Kong Bundy, he took on Hillbilly Jim and his friends, Haiti Kid & Little Beaver. In the end, Littlebrook's team lost via disqualification when Bundy inexplicably attacked Beaver.

After his in-ring career came to an end, Littlebrook worked as a manager and trainer. His most noted pupil, Butch Reed, also competed at *WrestleMania III*.

Los Boricuas 🇵🇷

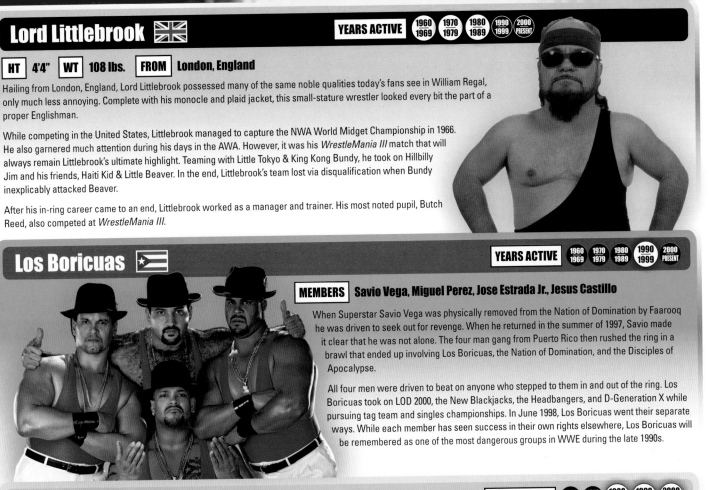

| MEMBERS | Savio Vega, Miguel Perez, Jose Estrada Jr., Jesus Castillo |

When Superstar Savio Vega was physically removed from the Nation of Domination by Faarooq he was driven to seek out for revenge. When he returned in the summer of 1997, Savio made it clear that he was not alone. The four man gang from Puerto Rico then rushed the ring in a brawl that ended up involving Los Boricuas, the Nation of Domination, and the Disciples of Apocalypse.

All four men were driven to beat on anyone who stepped to them in and out of the ring. Los Boricuas took on LOD 2000, the New Blackjacks, the Headbangers, and D-Generation X while pursuing tag team and singles championships. In June 1998, Los Boricuas went their separate ways. While each member has seen success in their own rights elsewhere, Los Boricuas will be remembered as one of the most dangerous groups in WWE during the late 1990s.

Los Conquistadors

Men underneath gold masks entered World Wrestling Entertainment in 1987. They were conquerors of the ring in other parts of the world but traveled to WWE to face the best tag teams in the world. Their disregard for the rules did not win them any fans and in most instances it did not help win matches either. Their win/loss record was not a true indicator of their abilities in the ring and they were always considered a dangerous tag team.

The Conquistadors gave a glimpse of their old world form at the inaugural *Survivor Series* when they were the last team fighting for victory. Though they went down in a losing effort, that impressive showing kept them in the World Tag Team Title hunt.

Since their departure in the late 1980s the masked men have made sporadic appearances in WWE, even as recently as 2003. Both fans and Superstars alike have questioned whether or not these recent appearances are the originals or other Superstars assuming the golden identities for nefarious purposes.

Los Guerreros 🇺🇸

| MEMBERS | Eddie Guerrero, Chavo Guerrero | COMBINED WEIGHT | 441 lbs. | FROM | El Paso, Texas | TITLE HISTORY | WWE Tag Team Champions |

They lie. They cheat. They steal. Despite their immoral qualities, Los Guerreros were one of the most popular tag teams of their time.

Eddie Guerrero started teaming with his nephew, Chavo, during the summer of 2002. After cheating their way to victory over many of *SmackDown*'s finest tag teams, they were entered into a tournament to crown the first-ever WWE Tag Team Champions. Unfortunately, Los Guerreros fell short in the semifinals.

Eddie & Chavo rebounded from the defeat. Only one month after the loss, they found themselves on top of the tag team mountain when they won a Triple Threat Match to capture the titles at *Survivor Series 2002*. They went on to hold the gold for three months before losing to Shelton Benjamin & Charlie Haas.

The dastardly uncle-nephew combination enjoyed one more reign atop the tag division before Chavo brutally attacked Eddie in January 2004, signifying the end of the adored Los Guerreros. After the breakup, both Guerreros went on to lie, cheat, and steal their way to great singles success.

LOU ALBANO

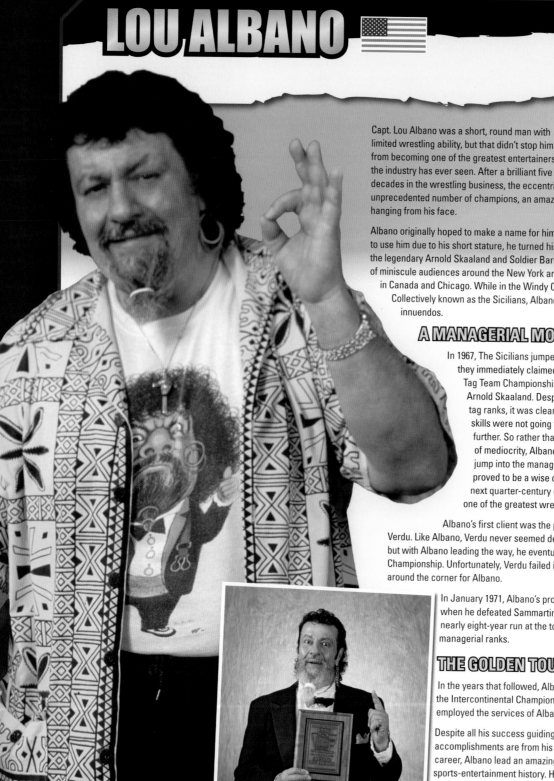

HT	5'10"	WT	350 lbs.

FROM Carmel, New York

TITLE HISTORY United States Tag Team Champion

YEARS ACTIVE 1960-1969 1970-1979 1980-1989 1990-1999 2000-PRESENT

Capt. Lou Albano was a short, round man with limited wrestling ability, but that didn't stop him from becoming one of the greatest entertainers the industry has ever seen. After a brilliant five decades in the wrestling business, the eccentric Albano will forever be remembered for managing an unprecedented number of champions, an amazing speaking ability and, believe it or not, rubber bands hanging from his face.

Albano originally hoped to make a name for himself as a boxer, but after promoter Willy Gilzenberg refused to use him due to his short stature, he turned his efforts toward professional wrestling. After being trained by the legendary Arnold Skaaland and Soldier Barry, Albano began his professional career competing in front of miniscule audiences around the New York area. He eventually worked up to more prestigious promotions in Canada and Chicago. While in the Windy City, Albano began teaming with fellow Italian Tony Altomare. Collectively known as the Sicilians, Albano & Altomare attracted great controversy due to their mafia innuendos.

A MANAGERIAL MOVE

In 1967, The Sicilians jumped to WWE where they immediately claimed the United States Tag Team Championship from Spiros Arion & Arnold Skaaland. Despite his success in the tag ranks, it was clear that Albano's wrestling skills were not going to carry him much further. So rather than settle for a career of mediocrity, Albano made the decision to jump into the managerial ranks. The move proved to be a wise one, as Albano spent the next quarter-century cementing his legacy as one of the greatest wrestling managers ever.

Albano's first client was the powerhouse Crusher Verdu. Like Albano, Verdu never seemed destined for greatness, but with Albano leading the way, he eventually earned an opportunity at Bruno Sammartino's WWE Championship. Unfortunately, Verdu failed in his attempts to unseat Sammartino, but glory was right around the corner for Albano.

In January 1971, Albano's protégé Ivan Koloff ended one of history's greatest title reigns when he defeated Sammartino for the WWE Championship. The win ended Sammartino's nearly eight-year run at the top and catapulted Albano straight to the top of the managerial ranks.

THE GOLDEN TOUCH

In the years that followed, Albano also lead many of WWE's most hated Superstars to the Intercontinental Championship. Pat Patterson, Don Muraco, and Greg Valentine all employed the services of Albano en route to claiming the Intercontinental title.

Despite all his success guiding Superstars to singles titles, Albano's greatest managerial accomplishments are from his time spent in the tag team ranks. Over the course of his career, Albano lead an amazing 17 teams to tag team titles, more than any other man in sports-entertainment history. His list of championship duos includes such legendary teams as the Valiant Brothers, the Blackjacks, the Wild Samoans, and the British Bulldogs.

Albano also helped launch the "Rock 'n' Wrestling Connection" that took America by storm in the mid-1980s. His famed friendship with rocker Cyndi Lauper landed him in the *Girls Just Want to Have Fun* music video. In turn, Lauper appeared on several WWE televised events, including the first-ever *WrestleMania*. The on-air chemistry between Albano and Lauper made national news and eventually helped propel WWE into the mainstream.

Following the success of the "Rock 'n' Wrestling Connection," Albano found himself in high demand in Hollywood. His acting credits include several episodes of *Miami Vice*, as well as a prominent role in the major motion picture *Body Slam*. Albano's most memorable role, however, was that of Nintendo legend Mario in *The Super Mario Bros. Super Show*.

Albano took his rightful place alongside wrestling's greatest when he was inducted into the WWE Hall of Fame in 1996. The honor was the ultimate sign of respect for an amazing entertainer who was often imitated, but never duplicated.

LOU THESZ

HT 6'2" **WT** 225 lbs. **FROM** St. Louis, Missouri **SIGNATURE MOVE** Lou Thesz Press

Lou Thesz debuted in St. Louis at age 16. Trained by Ray Steele and Greek Olympian George Tragos, Thesz later studied under Ad Santel to learn painful submission locks. In December 1937 he became the youngest World Heavyweight Champion in history at 21 years of age. Thesz also had historic encounters with "Nature Boy" Buddy Rogers in early 1963, which influenced the formation of the World Wide Wrestling Federation.

Thesz continued to compete throughout the 1970s all over the world as a featured competitor and special guest referee. During the 1980s he made appearances for World Wrestling Entertainment, most notably in November 1987 when he emerged the victor in a Legends Battle Royal.

Remarkably, Thesz wrestled his last match on December 26, 1990 in Japan against former student, Masahiro Chono for New Japan Pro Wrestling. He was 74 years old and became the only man to wrestle in seven different decades. Thesz was honored at *Badd Blood* along with other NWA Legends from the St. Louis area like Sam Muchnick, the Funks, Gene Kiniski, Jack Brisco, and Harley Race.

Sadly on April 28, 2002 one of professional wrestling's founding fathers passed away at 86.

Louie Spicolli

HT 5'11" **WT** 258 lbs. **FROM** Los Angeles, California **SIGNATURE MOVE** Spicolli Driver

After he developed a steady following in Mexico and independent promotions throughout the United States, Louie Spicolli made his WWE debut in 1988 and continued to appear intermittently in WWE through the mid 1990s.

In 1996 he debuted in Extreme Championship Wrestling and butted heads with the Innovator of Violence and ECW Original, Tommy Dreamer. After leaving ECW in 1997 he appeared in World Championship Wrestling and was an associate of the New World Order. Spicolli will always be fondly remembered as a gifted Superstar who gave his all whenever in the ring.

Louis Cerdan

HT 5'10" **WT** 240 lbs.

FROM Montreal, Quebec, Canada

SIGNATURE MOVE Figure-Four Leglock

TITLE HISTORY World Tag Team Champion

This French-Canadian began his WWE career in 1966 and was a close friend to then-World Champion Bruno Sammartino. For three years, Cerdan showed his fire in the ring, but in 1969 Cerdan left WWE and returned to Canada. In 1974, Cerdan made a glorious return to WWE, teaming with close friend Tony Parisi. In September 1975, the duo defeated the Blackjacks to become World Tag Team Champions. They defended the belts for six months until they crossed paths with the Executioners in May 1976. Cerdan soon left World Wrestling Entertainment and returned to the rings of the Great White North, where he retired after a stellar 25-year career.

Ludvig Borga

| HT | 6'3" | WT | 275 lbs. | FROM | Helsinki, Finland | SIGNATURE MOVE | Human Torture Rack |

This Finish powerhouse burst on the scene into World Wrestling Entertainment in 1993. The monster Borga squashed his opponents and showed little respect for the WWE rulebook. Fans quickly came to despise this individual and his spread of anti-American sentiment which resulted in him butting heads with "All-American" Lex Luger.

Borga often withstood the attacks made by many opponents. After picking up a win at *SummerSlam* against Marty Jannetty, he ended the two year undefeated streak of Tatanka, pinning him with one finger.

In early 1994 Borga left World Wrestling Entertainment to travel to Japan. He embarked on a successful professional boxing career, fighting both in the United States and Europe. In recent years he has entered the political arena in his homeland on Finland.

Luke Graham

| HT | 6'1" | WT | 219 lbs. | FROM | Charlotte, North Carolina |

| TITLE HISTORY | World Tag Team Champion, International Tag Team Champion, United States Tag Team Champion |

"Crazy" Luke Graham comes from a long line of Grahams who thrived inside the ring. His brothers are Dr. Jerry Graham and WWE Hall of Famers "Superstar "Billy Graham and Eddie Graham. Following them into the business were five of their sons, bringing the multi-generational clan to a total of nine.

Graham began teaming with his brother, Jerry, in Canada in 1963. It was during this time that fans began to recognize him as slightly deranged. Despite his efforts to convince them otherwise, Graham was constantly being called "crazy" by the fans. Infuriated by the chants, the bleached-blond Superstar would oftentimes hold his hands over his ears to drown out the sound, but that only made the crowds chant louder. Graham's greatest singles success came in 1965 when he won the prestigious WWA Heavyweight Championship from Pedro Morales. The victory proved to be a shining point in Graham's career, but paled in comparison to the groundbreaking win he would earn six years later in WWE.

In June 1971, with Tarzan Tyler as his partner, Graham turned back The Sheik & Dick the Bruiser to become one-half of WWE's first-ever World Tag Team Champions. The historic duo held the gold proudly for six months, paving the way for all the great teams that followed, including the Road Warriors, Hart Foundation, and Hardy Boys.

Luke Graham & Tarzan Tyler

| COMBINED WEIGHT | 560 lbs. | TITLE HISTORY | World Tag Team Champions, International Tag Team Champions |

All the great teams that have proudly worn the World Tag Team Championship over the past four decades have one trailblazing tandem to thank for building the titles's strong foundation. On a historic evening in June 1971, Luke Graham & Tarzan Tyler defeated The Sheik & Dick the Bruiser to become the first-ever World Tag Team Champions. Since that time, the game's best have vied to reach the same elite level, from Demolition to the Hardys.

In the six months that followed, Graham & Tyler fended off various combinations of WWE's best. Pedro Morales, Dominic DeNucci, and Chief Jay Strongbow all wanted the new titles wrapped around their waists, but it was Karl Gotch & Rene Goulet who finally unseated the champs in December 1971. In addition to the World Tag Team Championship, Graham & Tyler also held the now-defunct International Tag Team Championship in late 1971. They went their separate ways shortly after losing their titles, but will forever be remembered as the first in a long line of historic teams to be called champions.

LUMBERJACK MATCH

For decades the Lumberjack Match has been a way to keep competitors inside the ring. The match itself is traditional from a rules point of view and can be won by pinfall or submission. The ring is surrounded by other Superstars whose job is to keep the action in the ring. Once a participant is thrown out of the ring, it is the job of the "lumberjacks" around the ring to return that Superstar to the ring.

Audiences have also been treated to Lumberjill Matches which have the same set-up but include female instead of male participants. To fit the theme of the match, the Lumberjacks (or jills) sometimes come to the ring in traditional lumberjack attire. Regardless of the participants, or how they're dressed, this match is sure to take the fans on an entertaining ride.

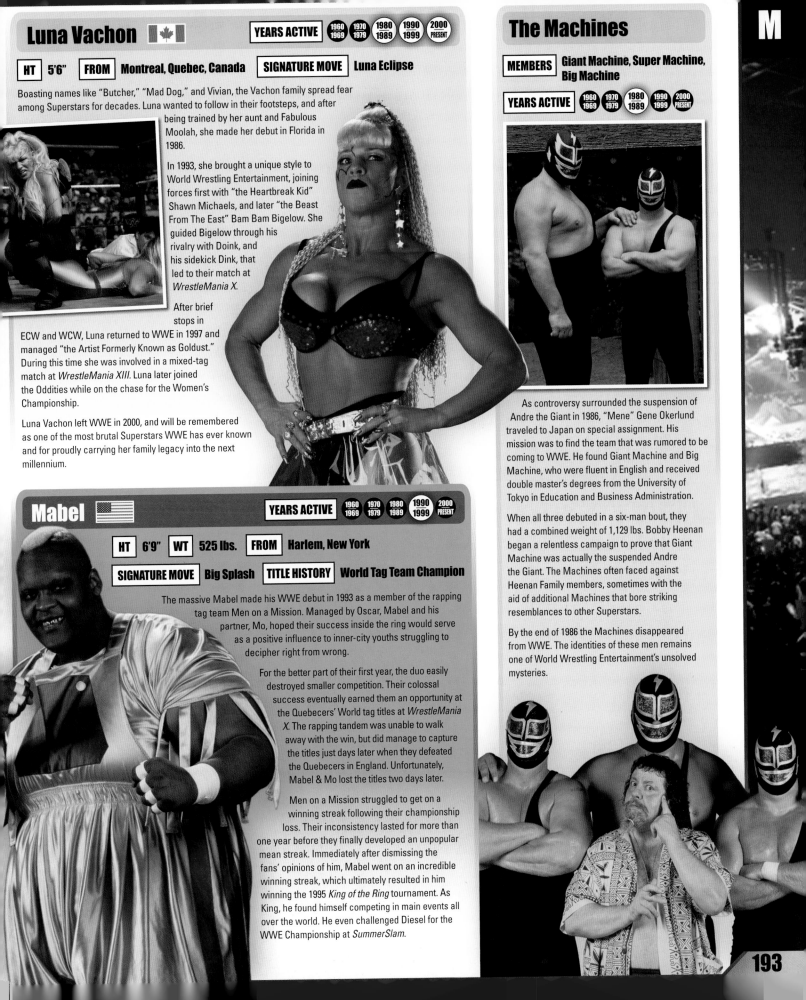

Luna Vachon 🇨🇦

YEARS ACTIVE 1960-1969 1970-1979 1980-1989 1990-1999 2000-PRESENT

HT 5'6" **FROM** Montreal, Quebec, Canada **SIGNATURE MOVE** Luna Eclipse

Boasting names like "Butcher," "Mad Dog," and Vivian, the Vachon family spread fear among Superstars for decades. Luna wanted to follow in their footsteps, and after being trained by her aunt and Fabulous Moolah, she made her debut in Florida in 1986.

In 1993, she brought a unique style to World Wrestling Entertainment, joining forces first with "the Heartbreak Kid" Shawn Michaels, and later "the Beast From The East" Bam Bam Bigelow. She guided Bigelow through his rivalry with Doink, and his sidekick Dink, that led to their match at *WrestleMania X.*

After brief stops in ECW and WCW, Luna returned to WWE in 1997 and managed "the Artist Formerly Known as Goldust." During this time she was involved in a mixed-tag match at *WrestleMania XIII.* Luna later joined the Oddities while on the chase for the Women's Championship.

Luna Vachon left WWE in 2000, and will be remembered as one of the most brutal Superstars WWE has ever known and for proudly carrying her family legacy into the next millennium.

Mabel 🇺🇸

YEARS ACTIVE 1960-1969 1970-1979 1980-1989 1990-1999 2000-PRESENT

HT 6'9" **WT** 525 lbs. **FROM** Harlem, New York

SIGNATURE MOVE Big Splash **TITLE HISTORY** World Tag Team Champion

The massive Mabel made his WWE debut in 1993 as a member of the rapping tag team Men on a Mission. Managed by Oscar, Mabel and his partner, Mo, hoped their success inside the ring would serve as a positive influence to inner-city youths struggling to decipher right from wrong.

For the better part of their first year, the duo easily destroyed smaller competition. Their colossal success eventually earned them an opportunity at the Quebecers' World tag titles at *WrestleMania X.* The rapping tandem was unable to walk away with the win, but did manage to capture the titles just days later when they defeated the Quebecers in England. Unfortunately, Mabel & Mo lost the titles two days later.

Men on a Mission struggled to get on a winning streak following their championship loss. Their inconsistency lasted for more than one year before they finally developed an unpopular mean streak. Immediately after dismissing the fans' opinions of him, Mabel went on an incredible winning streak, which ultimately resulted in him winning the 1995 *King of the Ring* tournament. As King, he found himself competing in main events all over the world. He even challenged Diesel for the WWE Championship at *SummerSlam.*

The Machines

MEMBERS Giant Machine, Super Machine, Big Machine

YEARS ACTIVE 1960-1969 1970-1979 1980-1989 1990-1999 2000-PRESENT

As controversy surrounded the suspension of Andre the Giant in 1986, "Mene" Gene Okerlund traveled to Japan on special assignment. His mission was to find the team that was rumored to be coming to WWE. He found Giant Machine and Big Machine, who were fluent in English and received double master's degrees from the University of Tokyo in Education and Business Administration.

When all three debuted in a six-man bout, they had a combined weight of 1,129 lbs. Bobby Heenan began a relentless campaign to prove that Giant Machine was actually the suspended Andre the Giant. The Machines often faced against Heenan Family members, sometimes with the aid of additional Machines that bore striking resemblances to other Superstars.

By the end of 1986 the Machines disappeared from WWE. The identities of these men remains one of World Wrestling Entertainment's unsolved mysteries.

Mad Dog Vachon 🇨🇦

| HT | 5'7" | WT | 230 lbs. | FROM | Montreal, Quebec, Canada |

| SIGNATURE MOVE | Piledriver |

| YEARS ACTIVE | 1960 1969 | 1970 1979 | 1980 1989 | 1990 1999 | 2000 PRESENT |

At only 5'7", Mad Dog Vachon was oftentimes at a disadvantage well before the opening bell ever rang. What he lacked in size, though, he made up for in determination. The savage sparkplug was known for going at his opposition with ruthless aggression. On the rare occasion he found himself on the wrong end of a beating, he'd usually resort to biting, which made Vachon one of the most hated villains of his time.

The unofficial leader of the Vachon wrestling family, the rabid Mad Dog found his greatest success competing in the AWA. Shortly after his 1986 retirement from the ring, Vachon became the victim of a horrible hit-and-run accident. He survived the tragedy, but lost his leg in the incident. Nearly one decade after the accident, WWE honored Vachon at an *In Your House* pay-per-view. During the show, Diesel actually tore Vachon's prosthetic leg from his body to use as a weapon against Shawn Michaels. The act remains one of the most infamous moments in WWE history.

Mad Maxine

| HT | 6'4" | YEARS ACTIVE | 1960 1969 | 1970 1979 | 1980 1989 | 1990 1999 | 2000 PRESENT |

Although she only competed in a handful of WWE matches, Mad Maxine will forever be remembered as one of the most frightening females to ever lace up a pair of boots. Standing at an astonishing 6-foot-4 (six-foot-seven if you include her bright green Mohawk) and sporting demonic eye makeup, Maxine instilled instant fear into her competition.

Brought into WWE by Fabulous Moolah, Maxine's sole responsibility was to strip Wendi Richter of the Women's Championship. Before the highly anticipated encounter could ever take place, however, Maxine mysteriously left WWE.

MAE YOUNG 🇺🇸

| YEARS ACTIVE | 1960 1969 | 1970 1979 | 1980 1989 | 1990 1999 | 2000 PRESENT |

| FROM | Sand Springs, Oklahoma |

Mae Young has been an influential force in sports-entertainment for seventy years. Yes, you read that right. Seventy years. A former member of her high school's boys' wrestling team, Young made her professional debut in 1939. Although she was only fifteen years old at the time, Young proved herself as a tough-as-nails competitor. In the decades that followed, Young's efforts helped pave the way for future female Superstars such as Fabulous Moolah and Judy Grable. Her success eventually lead her to becoming the first United States Women's Champion.

In addition to achieving great in-ring success, Young is known as one of the most influential trainers of both male and female Superstars. Her most noted pupil was perhaps the greatest women's wrestler of all time, Fabulous Moolah. She also helped mold the early career of Ric Drasin, the former lead guitarist of The Hollywood Vines.

Today's WWE fans best recognize Young as the fearless senior citizen who always seems to attract controversy. Her most exposing moment occurred at the 2000 *Royal Rumble* when she flashed a packed Madison Square Garden crowd.

Despite her advanced age, Young isn't afraid to mix it up in the ring. Unfortunately, however, her attempts at physicality usually land her in enormous amounts of trouble. It's not uncommon to see Young flattened by both men and women less than half her age. She was even sent off the stage and through a wooden table at the hands of Bubba Ray Dudley.

In 2008, Young's contributions to women's wrestling were recognized when she was inducted into the WWE Hall of Fame, alongside other great females Fabulous Moolah and Sherri Martel.

Magnificent Maurice

Long before "Adorable" Adrian Adonis and Lenny Lane pranced around wrestling rings in an effete fashion, Magnificent Maurice flashed a flamboyant charisma second to none. Maurice oftentimes utilized outrageous antics to get inside his opponents' heads. From there, it was easy for him to take advantage of his mystified foes, en route to victory.

Managed by the equally charismatic Grand Wizard, Maurice took part in many memorable rivalries over the years, including contests against such legends as Bobo Brazil, Pedro Morales, and Bruno Sammartino. Tragically, Magnificent Maurice's life was cut short when he was killed in an airplane crash in January 1974.

THE MAIN EVENT

After the entertainment world saw the incredible success generated by the WWE events *The Brawl To End It All* and *The War To Settle The Score* on MTV, television executives were eager to work with World Wrestling Entertainment. As the revolution known as sports-entertainment began to assault pop culture, NBC and WWE announced that professional wrestling was returning to network television for the first time in decades.

The inaugural episode of *Saturday Night's Main Event* aired on May 11, 1985 from The Nassau Coliseum in Uniondale, NY. That evening fans saw a lineup that included George "the Animal" Steele, Iron Sheik, Nikolai Volkoff, Junkyard Dog, Fabulous Moolah, "Cowboy" Bob Orton, and Hulk Hogan. A new ratings record was set on the March 14, 1987 show that saw Hulk Hogan and Andre the Giant engaged in hostile contact for the first time in a 20-man over-the-top-rope Battle Royal right before their monumental clash at *WrestleMania III*.

The success of the show was so great that in 1988 NBC began to air prime time broadcasts on Friday nights called, *The Main Event*. That first event saw Andre The Giant end the championship reign of Hulk Hogan in a rematch from *WrestleMania III*. WWE changed networks in 1991 and FOX aired both *Saturday Night's Main Event* and *The Main Event* specials in 1992 before it left the airwaves after a historic eight-year run.

REBORN IN 2006

In March 2006, WWE and *Saturday Night's Main Event* made its amazing return to network television. Audiences saw a Street Fight with Shane McMahon and Shawn Michaels, plus the battle of *WrestleMania* main eventers as John Cena & Triple H teamed against Kurt Angle, Rey Mysterio & Randy Orton.

One of the most memorable moments of Main Event's *first run in the 1980s was Hulk Hogan losing the WWE Championship, then discovering that the referee who counted him out was paid off by "Million Dollar Man" Ted DiBiase.*

In addition to the more traditional contests shown on the March 2006 show, fans were treated a beer drinking contest between Stone Cold Steve Austin and JBL.

No matter which day the show airs, *The Main Event* is sure to thrill like no other program on network television. This is a show near and dear to people's hearts, as those who grew up with it now tune in to the action sitting next to their own children.

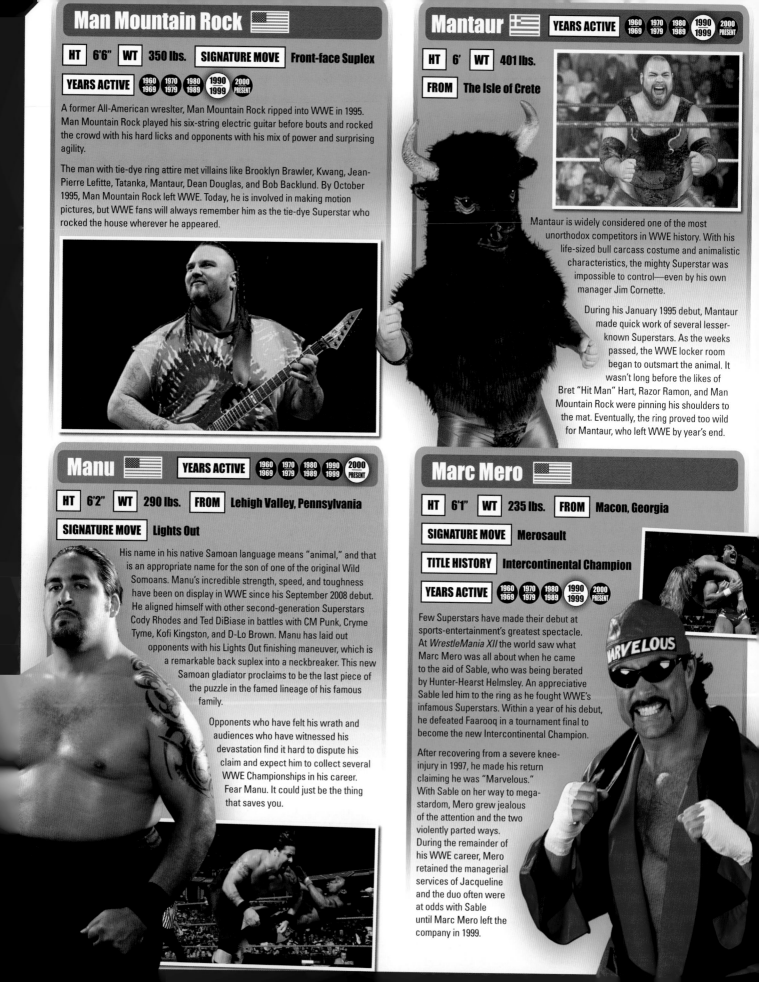

Man Mountain Rock 🇺🇸

| HT | 6'6" | WT | 350 lbs. | SIGNATURE MOVE | Front-face Suplex |

YEARS ACTIVE 1960-1969 1970-1979 1980-1989 **1990-1999** 2000-PRESENT

A former All-American wreslter, Man Mountain Rock ripped into WWE in 1995. Man Mountain Rock played his six-string electric guitar before bouts and rocked the crowd with his hard licks and opponents with his mix of power and surprising agility.

The man with tie-dye ring attire met villains like Brooklyn Brawler, Kwang, Jean-Pierre Lefitte, Tatanka, Mantaur, Dean Douglas, and Bob Backlund. By October 1995, Man Mountain Rock left WWE. Today, he is involved in making motion pictures, but WWE fans will always remember him as the tie-dye Superstar who rocked the house wherever he appeared.

Mantaur 🇬🇷 YEARS ACTIVE 1960-1969 1970-1979 1980-1989 **1990-1999** 2000-PRESENT

| HT | 6' | WT | 401 lbs. |

| FROM | The Isle of Crete |

Mantaur is widely considered one of the most unorthodox competitors in WWE history. With his life-sized bull carcass costume and animalistic characteristics, the mighty Superstar was impossible to control—even by his own manager Jim Cornette.

During his January 1995 debut, Mantaur made quick work of several lesser-known Superstars. As the weeks passed, the WWE locker room began to outsmart the animal. It wasn't long before the likes of Bret "Hit Man" Hart, Razor Ramon, and Man Mountain Rock were pinning his shoulders to the mat. Eventually, the ring proved too wild for Mantaur, who left WWE by year's end.

Manu 🇺🇸 YEARS ACTIVE 1960-1969 1970-1979 1980-1989 1990-1999 **2000-PRESENT**

| HT | 6'2" | WT | 290 lbs. | FROM | Lehigh Valley, Pennsylvania |

SIGNATURE MOVE Lights Out

His name in his native Samoan language means "animal," and that is an appropriate name for the son of one of the original Wild Somoans. Manu's incredible strength, speed, and toughness have been on display in WWE since his September 2008 debut. He aligned himself with other second-generation Superstars Cody Rhodes and Ted DiBiase in battles with CM Punk, Cryme Tyme, Kofi Kingston, and D-Lo Brown. Manu has laid out opponents with his Lights Out finishing maneuver, which is a remarkable back suplex into a neckbreaker. This new Samoan gladiator proclaims to be the last piece of the puzzle in the famed lineage of his famous family.

Opponents who have felt his wrath and audiences who have witnessed his devastation find it hard to dispute his claim and expect him to collect several WWE Championships in his career. Fear Manu. It could just be the thing that saves you.

Marc Mero 🇺🇸

| HT | 6'1" | WT | 235 lbs. | FROM | Macon, Georgia |

SIGNATURE MOVE Merosault

TITLE HISTORY Intercontinental Champion

YEARS ACTIVE 1960-1969 1970-1979 1980-1989 **1990-1999** 2000-PRESENT

Few Superstars have made their debut at sports-entertainment's greatest spectacle. At *WrestleMania XII* the world saw what Marc Mero was all about when he came to the aid of Sable, who was being berated by Hunter-Hearst Helmsley. An appreciative Sable led him to the ring as he fought WWE's infamous Superstars. Within a year of his debut, he defeated Faarooq in a tournament final to become the new Intercontinental Champion.

After recovering from a severe knee-injury in 1997, he made his return claiming he was "Marvelous." With Sable on her way to mega-stardom, Mero grew jealous of the attention and the two violently parted ways. During the remainder of his WWE career, Mero retained the managerial services of Jacqueline and the duo often were at odds with Sable until Marc Mero left the company in 1999.

Marcus Cor Von

| HT | 6'1" | WT | 265 lbs. |

FROM Detroit, Michigan

SIGNATURE MOVE Pounce

YEARS ACTIVE

1960 1969 | 1970 1979 | 1980 1989 | 1990 1999 | 2000 PRESENT

Marcus Cor Von made his WWE debut in January 2007 on ECW. According to Mr. McMahon, the presence of Superstars like Cor Von exemplified the future of the ECW brand. Shortly after his debut, "the Alpha Male" joined forces with fellow upstarts Elijah Burke, Matt Striker, and Kevin Thorn. Collectively known as the New Breed, the young stable of Superstars took exception to the veteran presence of Rob Van Dam, Tommy Dreamer, Sandman, and Sabu, also known as the ECW Originals.

At *WrestleMania 23*, Cor Von and his fellow New Breeders came up short against the Originals in an Eight Man Tag Team Match. Following the loss, Cor Von spent the majority of the next few months looking to avenge the *WrestleMania* defeat. Unfortunately, he failed to appear on ECW television after June and left WWE a few months later.

MARIA

FROM Chicago, Illinois | **YEARS ACTIVE** 1960 1969 | 1970 1979 | 1980 1989 | 1990 1999 | 2000 PRESENT

World Wrestling Entertainment audiences were first wowed by this beauty when she participated in the 2004 *Raw* Diva Search. She soon began hosting the popular "WWE Kiss Cam" segments and became a backstage correspondent during *Monday Night Raw*. In 2005, she proved she wasn't just another pretty face when she won her first official match by defeating Christy Hemme in a Lingerie Pillow Fight on *Raw*.

Maria continued to step between the ropes, facing competition such as Melina, Victoria, and Torrie Wilson. She even ended the undefeated streak of Beth Phoenix.

Maria's hobbies away from the ring include kickboxing, sewing, dancing, designing her own clothes and working on cars. She has her own column in *WWE Magazine* in which she lends her automotive expertise to readers. Maria has also appeared in many magazines that feature the most beautiful women in the world. In addition to being seen by WWE audiences each week, Maria has appeared on television shows *Family Feud*, *Project Runway*, and *Sunset Tan*.

Maria's star in the WWE gets brighter with each passing day, especially after joining the roster on *SmackDown* in 2008. Maria's dream is simple—to one day become the WWE Divas Champion.

Mark Henry

| HT | 6'1" | WT | 392 lbs. |

FROM Silsbee, Texas

SIGNATURE MOVE
World's Strongest Slam

TITLE HISTORY
ECW Champion,
European Champion

YEARS ACTIVE

1960 1969 | 1970 1979 | 1980 1989 | 1990 1999 | 2000 PRESENT

With more than a decade of WWE experience to his credit, Mark Henry has seen his share of professional ups and downs. After a high-profile weightlifting career in which he participated in the 1992 and 1996 Summer Games, he entered WWE in 1996 to much fanfare. However, an unfortunate barrage of injuries sidelined him for the majority of his early years.

Henry failed to let his physical misfortunes permanently derail him. In 2006, long after nearly every sports-entertainment insider had written him off, Henry returned to the ring more determined than ever. He spent the next year competing in high-profile matches against WWE's top names, including Batista and Rey Mysterio. He even challenged the legendary Undertaker to a Casket Match at *WrestleMania 22*.

In 2008, Henry's career continued its meteoric rise when he was drafted to ECW in June. Just days after making the move, he defeated Kane and Big Show at *Night of Champions* to capture the ECW Championship. The win proved to be the biggest of his career. Shortly after the victory, Henry aligned himself with Tony Atlas. With the historic powerhouse in his corner, Henry appears more unstoppable than ever.

Mark Jindrak

HT 6'7" **WT** 305 lbs. **FROM** Atlanta, Georgia **SIGNATURE MOVE** Mark of Excellence

Trained in WCW's Power Plant by Paul Orndorff, Mark Jindrak began his career in WCW as part of the Natural Born Thrillers. When the company was purchased by WWE in March 2001, he was soon seen on WWE programming as a member of the Alliance.

After the Alliance dissolved, Jindrak returned to WWE in late 2002 in matches against Raven and Justin Credible. During 2004, he teamed with Garrison Cade and saw action against La Resistance, Evolution, and the Dudley Boys. In March 2004, he debuted on *SmackDown* and became so impressed with himself he referred to himself as "the Reflection of Perfection." With Teddy Long in his corner, Jindrak fought Billy Gunn, Rey Mysterio, Hardcore Holly, Funaki, Charlie Haas, and Rob Van Dam. Shortly after these bouts, he aligned himself with Kurt Angle and Luther Reigns before being drafted to *Raw* in June 2005. That July, Jindrak left WWE, but still appears on cards in Japan and Mexico.

Mark Young

With solid bloodlines, and well schooled in the grappling arts, Mark Young debuted in WWE in 1986. Over the next four years, he took on the most dangerous rule-breakers sports-entertainment has ever seen. Young was a capable competitor who could mix it up between the ropes with any opponent.

His foes included Jimmy Jack Funk, Barry O, Dino Bravo, Boris Zhukov, Earthquake, and Mr. Perfect. He teamed with a number of Superstars against teams like the Islanders, Demolition, the Fabulous Rougeau Brothers, the Brain Busters, Rhythm & Blues and the Orient Express.

By September 1990, Young left WWE and toured Asia. In the early 1990s, Young retired from the ring but will be remembered as a man who took on anybody at any time.

Marty Jannetty

HT 5'11" **WT** 234 lbs. **FROM** Columbus, Georgia **SIGNATURE MOVE** Rocker Dropper

Marty Jannetty made his in-ring debut in 1984 and soon met another future star, Shawn

TITLE HISTORY Intercontinental Champion, World Tag Team Champion

Michaels. The two formed a popular duo known as the Midnight Rockers and exploded onto the tag team scene in the AWA. In June 1988, the Rockers skyrocketed to instant fame in WWE. With incredible speed, agility, quickness, and continuity, Jannetty and Michaels were considered by many as uncrowned World Tag Team Champions. Inseparable for years, Jannetty and Michaels began to drift apart. Audiences witnessed a violent split on a January 1992 episode of *The Barber Shop* when Michaels put Jannetty through the Shop's glass window.

Once Jannetty returned, the former friends traded Intercontinental Championship reigns. In January 1994 Jannetty teamed with 1-2-3 Kid to capture the World Tag Team Championship. Marty continued to appear in WWE throughout 1996 before leaving the company. In 2005, Janetty returned to team with Michaels again for a single match against La Resistance. Since then Jannetty has appeared in WWE on several occasions, most notably the 15th Anniversary episode of *Raw*.

Maryse

HT 5'8" **FROM** Montreal, Quebec, Canada

SIGNATURE MOVE French Kiss

TITLE HISTORY Divas Champion

This French-Canadian Diva was first noticed when she won the 2003 Miss Hawaiian Tropic Canada competition. A finalist in the 2006 *Raw Diva Search*, Maryse gave WWE audiences a sample of her seductive methods in May 2008 when she stole Deuce and Domino away from their manager, Cherry. The French Kiss is her devastating versions of the DDT, a move she has used to great effect in matches against the likes of Kelly Kelly, Michelle McCool, Maria, and Brie Bella.

Mascarita Sagrada

FROM Mexico

SIGNATURE MOVE Missile Dropkick

YEARS ACTIVE 1960-1969 | 1970-1979 | 1980-1989 | 1990-1999 | 2000-PRESENT

A legend in Mexico, this masked Lucha Libre star was known in Mexico and WCW before his debut in WWE on the first episode of *Shotgun Saturday Night* in 1997. The daredevil went undefeated in his first tour of duty with World Wrestling Entertainment.

In 2005, he returned to WWE as part of the newly-launched Juniors Division. Sagrada picked up where he left off and dominated his opponents. Though he left WWE in March 2006, he is one of few Superstars to go undefeated during his tenure with the company.

Matt Borne

HT 6' **WT** 241 lbs.

FROM Portland, Oregon

YEARS ACTIVE 1960-1969 | 1970-1979 | 1980-1989 | 1990-1999 | 2000-PRESENT

Second-generation Superstar Matt Borne grew up watching his father, "Tough" Tony Borne, dominate the Pacific Northwest tag team scene during the 1960s. In the early 1980s, Matt followed in his dad's footsteps, capturing the territory's tag titles on four separate occasions.

In 1985, just a few years into his career, Borne competed in the biggest match of his career when he fought Ricky Steamboat at Madison Square Garden at the first-ever *WrestleMania*. Borne failed to pick up a victory against the legendary Steamboat, but will be forever linked to the historic start of sports-entertainment's crown jewel.

Masked Superstar

YEARS ACTIVE 1960-1969 | 1970-1979 | **1980-1989** | 1990-1999 | 2000-PRESENT

HT 6'3" **WT** 291 lbs. **FROM** New York, New York

SIGNATURE MOVE Swinging neckbreaker

The Masked Superstar was as mean as he was mysterious. Hiding behind a star-covered mask, the oversized Superstar broke every rule in the book to earn several high-profile encounters during his brief WWE stay.

The man behind the mask received his first opportunity at WWE immortality in 1983 when he challenged Bob Backlund for the WWE Championship at Madison Square Garden. On that night, the Masked Superstar accomplished what few were able to do when he defeated Backlund via countout. Unfortunately, WWE titles cannot change hands on a countout.

Still searching for that elusive title, the Masked Superstar earned another opportunity at the WWE title when he challenged newly crowned titleholder Hulk Hogan in early 1984. Again, he was unable to walk away with the title, as he was disqualified for using a foreign object.

While championship glory escaped the Masked Superstar during his WWE career, he did gain great success throughout the years. Among his many accolades, the Masked Superstar was a four-time Georgia Championship Wrestling Heavyweight Champion.

Matt Hardy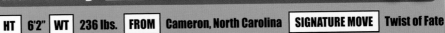

YEARS ACTIVE 1960-1969 | 1970-1979 | 1980-1989 | **1990-1999** | **2000-PRESENT**

HT 6'2" **WT** 236 lbs. **FROM** Cameron, North Carolina **SIGNATURE MOVE** Twist of Fate

TITLE HISTORY ECW Champion, World Tag Team Champion, United States Champion, European Champion, Cruiserweight Champion, Hardcore Champion

You can knock him down, kick him in the face and even steal his girl, but you will never be able to kill him. Because as Matt Hardy always says, "I will not die."

Matt Hardy has been overcoming adversity ever since he first stepped foot in a WWE ring in the mid-1990s. At the time of his debut, he was seen as nothing more than a scrawny kid who WWE's top Superstars could prove their worth against. Refusing to be held down, however, Matt, alongside his brother, Jeff, soon proved himself as a legitimate force in the tag team ranks. In fact, many of today's wrestling insiders credit the Hardy Boys for revolutionizing the art of tag team competition.

During his climb to the top, Hardy fell madly in love with WWE Diva, Lita. The two shared a long relationship until it was revealed that the fiery redhead was cheating on him with his friend, Edge. To make matters worse, Hardy was released from his WWE contract shortly thereafter. With the release, many assumed the final chapter of his career had been written. Hardy, on the other hand, saw things a bit differently.

Proving you can't keep him down, Hardy actually showed up on WWE television to attack Edge. The popularity of the rebellious act forced WWE to resign Matt. Over the next several years, the resilient Hardy achieved great success, capturing the United States Championship and his first World singles title—the ECW Championship.

Maven 🇺🇸

YEARS ACTIVE 1960–1969 | 1970–1979 | 1980–1989 | 1990–1999 | **2000 PRESENT**

HT 6'2" **WT** 220 lbs. **FROM** Chantilly, Virginia

SIGNATURE MOVE Halo DDT **TITLE HISTORY** Hardcore Champion

Originally a schoolteacher, Maven received the opportunity of a lifetime when he was chosen to participate in the WWE reality program, *Tough Enough*. After being crowned the first-ever male champion in the show's history, he was awarded a contract and immediately began his professional career. Unfortunately for the newcomer, his lack of experience cost him, as he lost several of his early matches against more seasoned competitors such as Tazz and Chris Jericho.

Despite coming up short in his early days, Maven persevered. By 2002, the former schoolteacher was beaming with confidence. He used his newfound self-assurance to eliminate the legendary Undertaker from the 2002 *Royal Rumble*. A few weeks later, he defeated the "Deadman" for the Hardcore Championship.

In November 2004, Maven parlayed an impressive *Survivor Series* appearance into a World Heavyweight Championship opportunity against Triple H. Unfortunately, Maven was unsuccessful in his bid to uncrown "The Game." Shortly after the loss, fans turned against Maven when he attacked the endearing Eugene. The former *Tough Enough* champion left WWE later that year.

Matt Striker 🇺🇸

HT 5'10" **WT** 224 lbs.

FROM Bayside, New York

YEARS ACTIVE 1960–1969 | 1970–1979 | 1980–1989 | 1990–1999 | **2000 PRESENT**

As Matt Striker molded young minds as a member of the New York City school system, he also fostered his love of sports-entertainment. To prepare himself for a life in the ring, he studied with Johnny Rodz at Gleason's Gym underneath the Brooklyn Bridge.

Matt continued to teach as his sports-entertainment career started to build, until he participated in the Angle Invitational on *Raw* the same night after calling in sick from his teaching job. When he was forced to resign, it sparked a national media frenzy. Though he may have received detention from school, the controversy launched his WWE career. In 2007, he joined ECW's New Breed in their mission to rid sports-entertainment of the ECW Originals. Striker created his own "Striker Match" which prohibits eye-gouging, hair pulling, top rope maneuvers, and the use of obscene language. In addition to his talk show segment, *Matt Striker's Classroom,* he also served as a manager for Big Daddy V before being drafted to *Raw* in 2008. Striker is currently an announcer for ECW.

Max Moon

YEARS ACTIVE 1960–1969 | 1970–1979 | 1980–1989 | **1990–1999** | 2000 PRESENT

HT 5'10" **WT** 240 lbs. **FROM** Outer Space

SIGNATURE MOVE Spinning Flying Body Press

World Wrestling Entertainment was invaded by a space traveler wearing a blue-armored suit in 1992. Max Moon defeated Superstars like the Brooklyn Brawler, Terry Taylor, Skinner, and Repo Man while enjoying a good measure of success. He continued to impress crowds wherever he appeared and became a contender to the Intercontinental Championship, held at that time by "the Heartbreak Kid" Shawn Michaels.

After a strong showing during a 1993 WWE European Tour, this cyborg from another galaxy vanished and has not been seen in World Wrestling Entertainment since.

Mean Street Posse 🇺🇸

YEARS ACTIVE	1960 1969	1970 1979	1980 1989	1990 1999	2000 PRESENT

MEMBERS Pete Gas, Rodney, Joey Abs **TITLE HISTORY** Hardcore Champion

Hailing from the "mean streets" of ritzy Greenwich, Connecticut, Pete Gas, Rodney, and Joey Abs may very well be the only three people in the history of the world to claim they are tough while wearing argyle sweater vests.

Prior to stepping foot in a WWE ring, the Mean Street Posse told tall tales of ruling the affluent streets of their hometown. Unfortunately for the Posse, childhood friends of Shane McMahon, their supposed toughness did not equate to success in WWE. Despite their inability to back up their boasts, all three Mean Street Posse members managed to permanently etch their names into the WWE record books when they briefly held—and quickly lost—the Hardcore Championship at *WrestleMania 2000*.

The Mean Street Posse faded from the WWE scene in 2001, but rest assured that patrons of Papyrus stationary store on Greenwich Avenue are shaking in their loafers at the thought of Pete Gas, Rodney & Joey Abs taking back the neighborhood.

Meat 🇺🇸

YEARS ACTIVE	1960 1969	1970 1979	1980 1989	1990 1999	2000 PRESENT

HT 6'4" **WT** 250 lbs. **SIGNATURE MOVE** Meat Grinder

Meat appeared as the submissive boy-toy to Terri and Jacqueline of Pretty Mean Sisters in 1999. A natural in the ring with an incredible physique, the man known as Meat displayed his abilities against Test, the Blue Meanie, Ken Shamrock, The Road Dogg, Val Venis, Kurt Angle, Billy Gunn, and The Godfather.

Pleasing Terri and Jacqueline took both a physical and mental toll on him. After ending his association with both Divas, Meat began using his real name, Shawn Stasiak. He left World Wrestling Entertainment by the end of 1999. He debuted in World Championship Wrestling shortly afterward, and returned to WWE in 2001 as part of the Alliance.

Mega Maniacs 🇺🇸

MEMBERS Hulk Hogan, Brutus Beefcake

COMBINED WEIGHT 573 lbs.

YEARS ACTIVE	1960 1969	1970 1979	1980 1989	1990 1999	2000 PRESENT

In the ultimate example of life imitating art, Zeus, Hulk Hogan's rival in the film *No Holds Barred*, followed the Hulkster from Hollywood to WWE. With former WWE Champion Randy "Macho Man" Savage by his side, it appeared as though nothing could stop Zeus from ending Hogan's illustrious career. Luckily for the Hulkster, longtime friend Brutus "the Barber" Beefcake stepped up to even the sides.

Collectively known as the Mega Maniacs, Hogan & Beefcake proved their dominance when they defeated Zeus & Savage at *SummerSlam 1989*. However, the devious duo simply would not go away. The two teams finally decided to settle the score in December 1989. In a unique pay-per-view event that also saw the airing of the *No Holds Barred* movie, the Mega Maniacs once again toppled Zeus & Savage, this time in a steel cage.

Several years later, the Mega Maniacs reunited to challenge Money, Inc. for the World Tag Team Championship at *WrestleMania IX*. They were unable to claim the titles after being disqualified for using Beefcake's titanium mask as a weapon.

THE MEGA POWERS

YEARS ACTIVE 1960-1969 1970-1979 **1980-1989** 1990-1999 2000-PRESENT

| **MEMBERS** Randy Savage, Hulk Hogan | **COMBINED WEIGHT** 548 lbs. | **TITLE HISTORY** WWE Championship |

The two biggest Superstars in WWE during the late 1980s were undoubtedly Randy "Macho Man" Savage and Hulk Hogan. Former rivals, Savage and Hogan patched up their differences when Miss Elizabeth persuaded "The Hulkster" to save "Macho Man" from a beating at the hands of Honky Tonk Man and the Hart Foundation. After Hogan cleared the ring of Savage's foes, the former adversaries shook hands, signifying the start of a powerful new friendship.

The new relationship helped Savage greatly, as he used help from Hogan to defeat Ted DiBiase to claim the WWE Championship at *WrestleMania IV*. Seeking retribution, DiBiase and Andre the Giant later double-teamed "Macho Man," which prompted the new WWE Champion to challenge his two attackers to a tag team match at *SummerSlam 1988*. Savage later revealed his partner to be his friend Hogan.

In a match billed as "The Mega Powers vs. The Mega Bucks," Savage & Hogan defeated DiBiase & Andre after Elizabeth removed her skirt to distract the opposition. Just when it appeared things couldn't be going any better for the Mega Powers, Savage began to develop an intense feeling of jealously over Elizabeth's friendship with Hogan. As a result, a paranoid "Macho Man" began to slowly pull back from his friendship with Hogan. Their relationship finally dissolved in early 1986 when Savage brutally attacked Hogan in the locker room following their match against the Twin Towers on *The Main Event*.

The unwarranted attack set the stage for the historic Savage vs. Hogan WWE Championship Match at *WrestleMania V*. Billed as "The Mega Powers Explode," the encounter was the culmination of a rollercoaster friendship that lasted more than one year. In the end, it was Hogan dropping his signature leg drop across the throat of Savage to claim his second WWE Championship.

Melina

YEARS ACTIVE 1960-1969 1970-1979 1980-1989 1990-1999 **2000-PRESENT**

| **HT** 5'4" | **FROM** Los Angeles, California |

The contact list on her cell phone is filled with Hollywood's top names and she only associates with WWE's elite Superstars. Wherever she goes, the paparazzi are sure to follow.

SIGNATURE MOVE California Dream

TITLE HISTORY Women's Champion

A former fashion model, Melina first made a name for herself in April 2005 when she helped guide Johnny Nitro & Joey Mercury to the WWE Tag Team Championship. During their reign on top, MNM (Melina, Nitro, Mercury) annoyed fans with their constant namedropping.

Melina's managerial credits also include leading Nitro to the Intercontinental Championship. Despite her impressive efforts outside the ring, it's the Diva's moves in between the ropes that people are buzzing about. In early 2007, Melina dedicated herself to becoming a force in the Women's Division. Within weeks, she accomplished her goal when she defeated Mickie James for the Women's Championship. Her successful reign was highlighted by a *WrestleMania 23* victory over Ashley in a Lumberjill Match. During her time in WWE, Melina has proven herself as one of the most arrogant Divas of all time, but who can blame her? She truly does have it all.

Men On A Mission

| **MEMBERS** Mo, Oscar, Mabel | **COMBINED WEIGHT** 770 lbs. |

TITLE HISTORY World Tag Team Champions

YEARS ACTIVE 1960-1969 1970-1979 1980-1989 **1990-1999** 2000-PRESENT

Managed by Oscar, Men On A Mission were a mammoth team that presented many match-up challenges for their opposition. At 300 lbs, Mo was larger than most opponents, but was nearly 200 lbs lighter than his partner, Mabel. Both Superstars were light on their feet and performed double-team moves that wowed audiences. They perfected their style and in March, 1994 defeated the Quebecers for the World Tag Team Championship.

Mabel won the 1995 *King of the Ring*. With Mabel's crown, Mo became Sir Mo and was in Mabel's corner for a match against Diesel for the WWE Heavyweight Championship. Both men took their mission elsewhere as they left WWE in 1996.

Men On A Mission were one of the more popular attractions of the WWE during the mid 1990s. They rocked the ring and their foes with an imposing physical presence that has rarely been seen in the ring.

The Mexicools 🇲🇽

YEARS ACTIVE 1960-1969 1970-1979 1980-1989 1990-1999 2000-PRESENT

MEMBERS Juventud Guerrera, Psichosis, Super Crazy

In 2005, these three crossed the border on their tricked-out John Deere tractors and rolled right into *SmackDown*. Their inspirational leader, Juventud, declared they were the true Mexican luchadores and superior Mexicools. The angry trio constantly interfered in matches on *SmackDown* and faced other factions such as the bWo and the Full Blooded Italians.

Along the way Juventud won the Cruiserweight Championship and gave the group instant credibility among WWE Superstars. In addition, Psichosis and Super Crazy were contenders for the WWE Tag Team Championship. Guerrera lost his Cruiserweight crown and eventually left WWE in January 2006. Psichosis and Super Crazy continued to team but soon disbanded when Psichosis left WWE later in the year.

Michael Bollea 🇺🇸

YEARS ACTIVE 1960-1969 1970-1979 1980-1989 1990-1999 2000-PRESENT

HT 6'4" **WT** 255 lbs. **FROM** Tampa, Florida **SIGNATURE MOVE** Full Nelson Slam

Powerful, agile, and tough as nails, Michael Bollea was a promising up-and-comer during the early 1990s. A brief run in Japan caught the attention of WWE, who were impressed with Bollea's intimidating, rugged demeanor. It didn't matter who he faced in the ring, he views all opponents the same, as the enemy. By 1998 he changed locations and appeared in WCW. In his time there, he was a part of Raven's Flock and the nWo. He remained with WCW until 2000 when he returned to the independent scene.

Michael Cole 🇺🇸

For more than a decade, Michael Cole has been seated ringside for many of WWE's most historic encounters. Starting his sports-entertainment career in 1997, Cole's earliest assignments saw him hosting such programs as *Livewire* and *Shotgun Saturday Night*. After cutting his teeth on these now-defunct shows, he landed the role of *SmackDown*'s lead announcer in 1999. Over the following nine years, Cole sat beside numerous color commentators, but eventually proved himself as the true voice of the popular brand.

In June 2008, Cole was surprisingly drafted to WWE's flagship program, *Monday Night Raw*. Within weeks of his debut, he found himself right in the thick of things. Not only did the monstrous Kane viciously attack him, but the new *Raw* announcer also teamed up with broadcast partner and WWE Hall of Famer Jerry Lawler to challenge for the World Tag Team Championship.

Prior to entering WWE, Cole's journalism career placed him in the middle of defining moments in the United States's history. While working for CBS Radio, he was on hand for the entire 51-day standoff at the Branch Davidian compound in Waco, Texas. He also covered the tragic Oklahoma City bombing in 1995, as well as three presidential elections.

Michelle McCool 🇺🇸

YEARS ACTIVE 1960-1969 1970-1979 1980-1989 1990-1999 2000-PRESENT

HT 5'10" **FROM** Palatka, Florida **TITLE HISTORY** Divas Champion

Lifelong WWE fan Michelle McCool took her first step toward realizing her dreams when she entered the 2004 Diva Search. Although she didn't win the competition, the blonde's beauty and athleticism caught the attention of WWE officials, who offered her a contract.

The former schoolteacher spent the majority of her early WWE days on the sidelines as a fitness trainer and manager, but it was clear that Michelle's exceptional athleticism would one day lead her to greatness as a competitor. In 2008, she fulfilled those expectations when she defeated Natalya at *The Great American Bash* to become the first-ever Divas Champion.

MICK FOLEY

HT	6'2"	WT	287 lbs	FROM	Long Island, New York	SIGNATURE MOVES	Mandible Claw, Double Arm D...

YEARS ACTIVE	1960 1969	1970 1979	1980 1989	1990 1999	2000 PRESENT	TITLE HISTORY	WWE Champion, World Tag Team Champion, Hardcore Champion

The story of Mick Foley is one of true genius coupled with complete insanity. He used flashes of schizophrenia to introduce the world to three entirely different personas: Mankind, Dude Love, and Cactus Jack. Collectively, the Three Faces of Foley told the story of a man who was put on this earth to become a hardcore legend.

Foley's passion for wrestling developed at a young age and grew to an obsession after he hitchhiked to a Madison Square Garden card in 1983. From the third row, Foley watched as Jimmy "Superfly" Snuka flew from the top of a fifteen-foot steel cage onto Don Muraco. "It was a defining moment in my life," wrote Foley in his 1999 autobiography, *Have a Nice Day!* "It was the day I knew without a doubt what I wanted to do with my life."

After making the inspired decision to pursue a career in professional wrestling, Foley turned to former World Tag Team Champion Dominic DeNucci for training. While learning the game from the former WWE Superstar, Foley earned spare cash competing for independent wrestling promotions, along with a few rare appearances on WWE cards in 1986, as Jack Foley.

THE BIRTH OF A HARDCORE LEGEND

Foley spent the next several years bouncing around from promotion to promotion, including the now-defunct Universal Wrestling Federation and World Class Championship Wrestling. During this time, he began to develop a cult following, largely due to his complete disregard for his own wellbeing. The more chances Foley took with his body, the more fans cheered him. It wasn't long before his hardcore style caught the attention of World Championship Wrestling officials.

As Cactus Jack, Foley made his WCW debut in late 1991 and was instantly catapulted into high-profile rivalries with Sting, Ron Simmons, and most notably Big Van Vader. The two Superstars competed in some of WCW's most brutal and bloody battles. Their March 17, 1994 encounter was so vicious that, after getting his head tangled between the ring ropes, Foley's ear tore off his head as he struggled to escape.

After leaving WCW, Foley split much of his time between Extreme Championship Wrestling and Japan. His brutal ECW encounters against Sandman and Terry Funk are the stuff of legend, while his Japan exploits bordered on illegal.

Bang bang! During his infamous Japanese days, it was not uncommon to see Foley victimized by such weapons as shards of glass, baseball bats, thumbtacks, barbed wire, and even C-4 explosives.

MANKIND COMES TO WWE

Foley made his move to WWE in early 1996, but rather than competing as the hardcore Cactus Jack, he debuted under the name of Mankind. As Mankind, Foley appeared even more deranged. He was often seen sitting in dark boiler rooms, talking to his pet rat George about the internal pain he was suffering.

Using his dreaded Mandible Claw, Mankind made short work of his early competition. The victories put him in perfect position to move up the WWE ladder. To prove his worth, Mankind soon targeted one of WWE's most successful Superstars, Undertaker. The two men spent a year competing in such revolutionary encounters as the Boiler Room Brawl and Buried Alive Match.

By mid-1997, Mankind was a bona fide main eventer. His in-ring conquests carried him to WWE Championship opportunities against Shawn Michaels, Sycho Sid, and Undertaker. He even fought to the finals of the 1997 *King of the Ring* tournament. Despite all his successes, he couldn't garner the admiration of the WWE fans. That all changed when Jim Ross began a series of probing interviews with the deranged Mankind.

THE THIRD FACE OF FOLEY

Ross' questioning revealed that a young Foley produced home videos of himself as a character called Dude Love, Foley's fun-loving alter-ego. Fans became instantly enthralled by the hippy persona, and were pleasantly shocked when he made his in-ring debut as Stone Cold Steve Austin's tag team partner in July 1997. The tie-dye-clad Dude Love & Stone Cold went on to defeat Owen Hart & British Bulldog for the World Tag Team Championship, Foley's first WWE title.

For the next several months, Foley kept his opponents on their toes, as they were never quite sure which persona they were going to face, Mankind or Dude Love. Foley took the confusion a step further in September 1997 when a vignette aired featuring Mankind and Dude Love actually talking to each other about who should face Triple H that night. In the end, they decided neither persona should face "The Game." Instead, they chose Foley's third face, Cactus Jack, to do the honors. The match marked the WWE debut of Foley's popular hardcore character.

In January 1998, Foley made history by competing in the *Royal Rumble* as all three personas. At *WrestleMania XIV*, Foley, as Cactus Jack, teamed with longtime friend Terry Funk, who competed as Chainsaw Charlie, to wrest the World Tag Team Championship belts from the New Age Outlaws in a Dumpster Match.

HELL IN A CELL

Foley's popularity reached iconic status in June 1998 when, as Mankind, he faced Undertaker in a Hell in a Cell Match. In one of the most shocking moments in sports-entertainment history, Mankind was tossed off the top of the demonic structure down to the arena floor. The blood-curdling sight caused announcer Jim Ross to scream the now-famous words, "Good God Almighty! They've killed him! With God as my witness, he is broken in half!" As if the sixteen-foot fall wasn't enough, Mankind was later thrown through the top of the cell, all the way down to the ring. A steel chair followed his descent, hitting him in the face upon impact.

In typical Foley fashion, the hardcore Superstar continued to evolve his in-ring personalities. In late 1998, Mankind went through significant changes and became a sensation with the fans, especially after debuting his sock puppet, Mr. Socko. Unfortunately for Mankind, he was as gullible as he was goofy. After accepting the newly-created Hardcore Championship as a gift from Mr. McMahon in November 1998, Mankind looked up to the WWE Chairman as a father figure. The diabolical Mr. McMahon took full advantage of this, luring the naïve Mankind close to him, then screwing him over in the finals of the WWE Championship tournament at *Survivor Series.*

WWE CHAMPION

Within weeks of his heartbreaking loss at *Survivor Series*, he gained the ultimate revenge when he upended The Rock to capture the WWE Championship on January 4, 1999. The victory saw "Mrs. Foley's baby boy" realize a boyhood dream that many assumed impossible to accomplish. The Mankind-Rock rivalry resulted in a series of brutal and bloody matches. Perhaps their most unsightly encounter occurred at the *Royal Rumble* where The Rock smashed Mankind's skull with seemingly countless steel chair shots. The force of The Rock's swings eventually rendered Mankind unconscious. Mankind reclaimed the title one week later during halftime of Super Bowl XXXIII.

Despite being nearly comatose at the hands of The Rock, Mankind found it within himself to forgive his foe and form a popular tag team known as The Rock & Sock Connection. The duo defeated Undertaker & Big Show for the World Tag Team Championship in August 1999, the first of three reigns for the combination. Mankind later presented his partner with a "This is Your Life" walk down memory lane, one of the most memorable and popular segments in *Monday Night Raw* history.

Foley captured his third and final WWE Championship when he defeated Triple H and Stone Cold Steve Austin at *SummerSlam 1999*. His reign lasted only twenty-four hours, but his rivalry with Triple H was merely beginning. The two battled for the WWE Championship in the main event of the 2000 *Royal Rumble*, and Foley put his career on the line for a final title opportunity at *No Way Out*. He lost in a brutal Hell in a Cell encounter with "The Game", but was granted a spot in the main event of *WrestleMania 2000*. The contest, which was the culmination of a fifteen-year dream for Foley, saw the hardcore Superstar compete in a Fatal Four Way Elimination Match against Triple H, The Rock, and Big Show.

With his in-ring days behind him, Foley has built a budding writing career. He is recognized for his best-selling autobiographical efforts *Have a Nice Day!, Foley is Good,* and *The Hardcore Diaries,* but has also penned many children's books, as well as adult fiction. Foley has also assumed several roles on WWE television, most notably that of commissioner, referee, and announcer. He has even made a few rare returns to the ring, including a brutal Hardcore Match against Edge at *WrestleMania 22*.

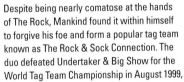

Mickie James 🇺🇸

HT	5'4"	SIGNATURE MOVE	Mick Kick

FROM	Richmond, Virginia

TITLE HISTORY	Women's Champion

YEARS ACTIVE	1960 1969	1970 1979	1980 1989	1990 1999	2000 PRESENT

The bubbly Mickie James combines the amazing athleticism found in all WWE Divas with an unmatched magnetic personality that makes her impossible not to like.

Mickie first introduced herself to WWE audiences in October 2005 when she ran to the ring to save her idol, Trish Stratus, from a vicious attack at the hands of Victoria. Over the next several months, the two Divas enjoyed a close friendship, but when Trish started to feel smothered by Mickie's admiration, the alliance turned sour and the girls engaged in a bitter rivalry. Their battles reached a peak at *WrestleMania 22* when Mickie defeated Trish for her first of many Women's Championship reigns.

The following year, with Trish no longer a member of the WWE roster, Melina emerged as Mickie's chief nemesis. The two Divas spent the first four months of 2007 battling over the Women's Championship, a title they traded three times during this period. Unfortunately, one of Mickie's championship victories over Melina lasted mere minutes, making her the owner of WWE's shortest Women's Title reign.

Despite the short reign, Mickie is widely recognized as one of the premier Divas on the WWE roster. Behind the impact of her devastating Mick Kick, there's no telling how many Women's Championships that Mickie James will end up with by the time she's done.

Mideon 🇺🇸

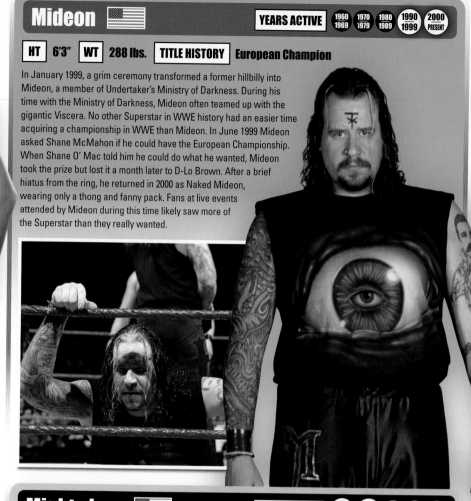

		YEARS ACTIVE	1960 1969	1970 1979	1980 1989	1990 1999	2000 PRESENT

HT	6'3"	WT	288 lbs.	TITLE HISTORY	European Champion

In January 1999, a grim ceremony transformed a former hillbilly into Mideon, a member of Undertaker's Ministry of Darkness. During his time with the Ministry of Darkness, Mideon often teamed up with the gigantic Viscera. No other Superstar in WWE history had an easier time acquiring a championship in WWE than Mideon. In June 1999 Mideon asked Shane McMahon if he could have the European Championship. When Shane O' Mac told him he could do what he wanted, Mideon took the prize but lost it a month later to D-Lo Brown. After a brief hiatus from the ring, he returned in 2000 as Naked Mideon, wearing only a thong and fanny pack. Fans at live events attended by Mideon during this time likely saw more of the Superstar than they really wanted.

Mighty Igor 🇺🇸

	YEARS ACTIVE	1960 1969	1970 1979	1980 1989	1990 1999	2000 PRESENT

FROM	Dearborn, Michigan	SIGNATURE MOVE	Bearhug

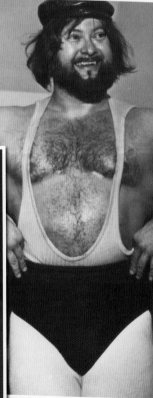

Prior to entering the world of sports-entertainment, Mighty Igor gained fame as an accomplished body builder. His immense size made him a force in the ring. However, it was his pre-match antics that oftentimes gave him the psychological advantage well before ever locking horns, as Mighty Igor was known to show off by having cinder blocks broken over his head with a sledgehammer.

Appropriately referred to as the "World's Strongest Wrestler," Mighty Igor's greatest accomplishment came when he overpowered the great Mad Dog Vachon for the AWA Championship. He only held the title for one week before losing it to Vachon, but he will forever be remembered alongside such great former AWA Champions as Verne Gagne, Nick Bockwinkel and Jerry Lawler.

Utilizing a bearhug finisher that sucked the life from his foes, Mighty Igor crossed paths with many of the industry's finest over the course of his 30-year career. Some of his most notable rivalries include The Sheik, The Masked Superstar, and Jos LeDuc.

Miguel Perez

HT 6'1" **WT** 238 lbs. **FROM** Puerto Rico **SIGNATURE MOVE** Sunset Flip

During the late 1950s, Miguel Perez shot to stardom as one-half of one of the most successful tag teams in sports-entertainment history. Along with Antonino "Argentia" Rocca, the two Superstars were main event attractions throughout the eastern seaboard for Vincent J. McMahon's Capitol Sports. Rocca and Perez were heroes everywhere as fans admired their heart, desire, and fire in the ring.

Perez stayed with McMahon when Capitol Sports became the World Wide Wrestling Federation and battled "Nature Boy" Buddy Rogers for the Heavyweight Championship. In 1968 Perez left the company and appeared in Puerto Rico where he reunited with Rocca for a time before retiring from action in 1979. For decades Miguel Perez was considered the greatest Superstar to emerge from Puerto Rico.

Mike Adamle

After career as a player in the NFL, Mike Adamle enjoyed a thirty year run in sports broadcasting, both as a studio host and sideline reporter. In 1989, he became the host of the ground-breaking "American Gladiators" program and remained with them until 1996. He was also part of the XFL broadcast team and covered the 2000 and 2004 Summer Olympic Games.

In 2008, Adamle felt it was time for a change. He kicked off his new career in sports-entertainment at the *Royal Rumble*, then went on to conduct interviews on *Raw*. That April he debuted on ECW before he eventually walked off the set with broadcast partner Tazz. Fans began to jeer the sight of Adamle, but they had no idea what was in store.

That July saw one of the most shocking events in *Raw* history when Shane McMahon promoted Mike Adamle to General Manager. During his tenure, broadcasts of WWE's flagship program were dubbed "Adamle Originals." Neither WWE fans nor its Superstars had any idea of what to expect each week. Though he resigned his post in November 2008, General Manager Adamle brought a fresh perspective to WWE during this time.

Mike Awesome

HT 6'6" **WT** 292 lbs.

FROM Tampa, Florida

SIGNATURE MOVE Awesome Bomb

TITLE HISTORY Hardcore Champion

YEARS ACTIVE

Mike Awesome had the strength to powerbomb virtually any opponent and the agility to clear the top rope while nailing opponents with a plancha. A dominant champion in ECW and Japan, Awesome sparked controversy in the beginning of the new millennium when he jumped to WCW while still reigning as ECW Champion. This resulted in Awesome, under contract with WCW, meeting Tazz, under contract with WWE, for the ECW Title at an ECW live event.

Awesome remained with WCW until the company was purchased by WWE in March 2001. In June, Awesome made his WWE debut and defeated Rhyno for the Hardcore Championship, making him the first WCW wrestler to win a championship in WWE.

After time in independent promotions and Japan, Awesome returned to WWE in 2005 at *ECW One Night Stand*. The roof of The Hammerstein Ballroom almost blew off as Awesome warred with old nemesis Masato Tanaka. Tragically, in February 2007 Mike Awesome passed away. This dynamic competitor will always be regarded as one of the most agile big men the world has ever seen.

Mike McGuirk 🇺🇸

Years before Lilian Garcia's voice became a staple on *Monday Night Raw*, the lovely Mike McGuirk introduced capacity crowds to such WWE Superstars as Hulk Hogan, Jake "the Snake" Roberts and "Hacksaw" Jim Duggan.

As a female ring announcer in the late 1980s, McGuirk oftentimes had a difficult time fitting into the male-dominated industry. On more than one occasion, the blonde voice of WWE became the target of Bobby "the Brain" Heenan's verbal barbs, but it was Harvey Wippleman and Big Bully Busick who frightened McGuirk the most. On an episode of *Wrestling Challenge*, Wippleman and The Bully verbally harassed McGuirk to the point of tears. Luckily, Sid Justice ran to the ring to fend off the frightened female's offenders.

In addition to her ring announcing duties, McGuirk also worked as a commentator on WWE's *All-American Wrestling* television program.

Mike Knox 🇺🇸

HT	6'6"	WT	293 lbs.

FROM	Phoenix, Arizona

SIGNATURE MOVE	Spinning Reverse STO

YEARS ACTIVE	1960 1969	1970 1979	1980 1989	1990 1999	2000 PRESENT

Proving you only get one chance to make a good first impression, Mike Knox's extreme unpopularity can be traced back to his initial appearance, which saw him prevent then-girlfriend Kelly Kelly from disrobing for the ECW fans. From that moment on, Knox has had a tough time gaining fan support, but that hasn't seemed to bother the near 300-pound monster, as he appears to be more focused on inflicting pain than making friends.

Just months into his career, the vicious Knox joined forces with Rated-RKO to battle Team DX at *Survivor Series 2006*. The momentum of the high-profile encounter catapulted the bushy-bearded Superstar to several victories over some of ECW's longtime favorites, including Tommy Dreamer, Stevie Richards, and Balls Mahoney.

Mil Mascaras 🇲🇽

YEARS ACTIVE	1960 1969	1970 1979	1980 1989	1990 1999	2000 PRESENT

HT	5'11"	WT	245 lbs.	FROM	Mexico City, Mexico	SIGNATURE MOVE	Plancha

Mil Mascaras is arguably the most admired masked wrestler of all time. Despite his immense popularity, however, he is difficult to identify upon appearance alone, as Mascaras rarely wears the same mask twice. Once the bell rings, however, "The Man of 1,000 Masks" has a style that is unmistakable.

Shortly after debuting in the mid-1960s, Mascaras began utilizing a high-flying style not normally associated with men of his size. His expansive repertoire of planchas and flying bodyblocks made him an instant success in Mexico. After becoming a national sensation in his homeland, Mascaras took his game international, most notably Japan and the United States, where he continued to excel.

Mascaras' reputation preceded him on his way to WWE. As a result, he was instantly propelled into main event status upon debuting. In addition to a memorable rivalry with Ernie Ladd, Mascaras challenged "Superstar" Billy Graham for the WWE Championship in 1977.

Mascaras' final in-ring WWE appearance came at the 1997 *Royal Rumble*. The masked man's unfamiliarity with the rules of the Rumble ultimately cost him, as he eliminated himself after leaping off the top rope to the outside.

"MILLION DOLLAR MAN" TED DIBIASE

HT 6'1"	**WT** 260 lbs.	**FROM** Palm Beach, Florida	**SIGNATURE MOVE** Million Dollar Dream

TITLE HISTORY World Tag Team Champion, North American Heavyweight Champion   **YEARS ACTIVE**

Ted DiBiase used his never-ending bankroll to acquire the world's most lavish possessions. He had mansions, fur coats, servants, limousines, and private jets. He even used his funds to nearly purchase the WWE Championship. In short, his spending was the stuff of legend, the legend of the "Million Dollar Man."

The obnoxiously rich Superstar first made a name for himself in 1987 when he made his now-famous claim that everybody had a price. Proving his point, DiBiase often gave fans large sums of money to perform demeaning tasks such as barking like a dog and kissing his feet.

In one of the most infamous moments in WWE history, DiBiase funded a complex ploy designed to put the WWE Championship around his waist. Prior to Andre the Giant's WWE Championship Match against Hulk Hogan in February 1988 at *The Main Event*, the "Million Dollar Man" paid Andre to hand over the championship if he won. To better Andre's chances of beating Hogan, DiBiase abducted the match's referee and replaced him with a man he paid to have plastic surgery to look like the referee. The substitute referee made several questionable calls, including the decisive pin itself, which resulted in Andre winning the WWE Championship. After the match, Andre handed the title over to DiBiase as planned. The devious scheme worked perfectly, with the exception of one thing: President Jack Tunney refused to recognize the title change.

After his failed attempts at claiming the WWE Championship, DiBiase used his impressive bank account to create his own title. In 1989, he debuted the Million Dollar Championship, a multi-million dollar prize covered in diamonds. DiBiase wore the title proudly, despite the fact that WWE refused to recognize it as an official championship.

Lost in all the talk of money is the fact that DiBiase was also an accomplished competitor. Alongside Irwin R. Schyster, DiBiase claimed three World Tag Team Championships. Toward the end of his career, DiBiase used his finances become a powerful manager. His legendary reputation as a free spender helped him lure many of the game's top names, including Sycho Sid and Steve Austin.

MILLION DOLLAR CHAMPIONSHIP

Perhaps the most controversial Championship in the history of sports-entertainment, the Million Dollar Championship was conceived by "Million Dollar Man" Ted DiBiase when he could neither buy the World Heavyweight Championship nor defeat then-champion, Hulk Hogan. This championship was never officially acknowledged by the WWE.

1989

MAR 04 Binghamton, NY

"Million Dollar Man" Ted DiBiase crowns himself Champion during an episode of *The Brother Love Show*.

1991

AUG 26 New York, NY

Vigril defeats "Million Dollar Man" Ted DiBiase.

NOV 24 Utica, NY

"Million Dollar Man" Ted DiBiase defeats Virgil via Pinfall.

From February 7, 1992 until January 8, 1996 The Million Dollar Championship was dormant.

1996

JAN 08 Newark, DE

"Million Dollar Man" Ted DiBiase awards the Million Dollar Championship to his protégé, The Ringmaster...

MAY 28 North Charleston, SC

The Ringmaster loses a Caribbean Strap Match to Savio Vega. As a result, "Million Dollar Man" Ted DiBiase had to leave World Wrestling Entertainment. The Million Dollar Championship has not been seen since.

Million Dollar Corporation

MEMBERS Nikolai Volkoff, Irwin R. Schyster, King Kong Bundy, Bam Bam Bigelow, Tatanka, 1-2-3 Kid, Sycho Sid, Xanta Klaus

YEARS ACTIVE

When "Million Dollar Man" Ted DiBiase became a manager in 1994 he was determined to acquire Superstars like he acquired assets in the business world. His first recruits were former tag team partner I.R.S. and Nikolai Volkoff. When DiBiase wanted a Superstar he more often than not persuaded them to join by interfering in their matches on their behalf and luring them with large sums of money.

If a recruited Superstar did not join the Million Dollar Corporation, they were considered an enemy of the Million Dollar Corporation. The group disbanded in 1994 after "The Ringmaster" Steve Austin lost to Savio Vega, thus eliminating the "Million Dollar Man" from World Wrestling Entertainment.

Ministry of Darkness

MEMBERS Undertaker, Faarooq, Bradshaw, Mideon, Viscera, Paul Bearer, Edge, Christian, David Heath (known in WWE as Gangrel)

TITLE HISTORY WWE Championship

YEARS ACTIVE

After more than two years apart, Undertaker and Paul Bearer reconciled in early 1999 to form the most sinister faction in WWE history. Known as The Ministry of Darkness, the group threatened to unleash a never-before-seen plague on WWE. With Faarooq & Bradshaw already in tow, Undertaker performed a series of sadistic rituals to initiate the remaining members of the group, which consisted of Mideon, Viscera, and the Brood. As a collective unit, the Ministry claimed to take orders from a "higher power," who ordered them to mentally and emotionally cripple Mr. McMahon.

The Ministry knew no boundaries when it came to their war against McMahon. They even took their devious assault to the WWE owner's private estate, where they left a burning Undertaker symbol in the yard. However, their most offensive attack came when the "Deadman" abducted McMahon's daughter. With Stephanie in custody, Undertaker threatened to join her in unholy matrimony if McMahon failed to hand over control of WWE. Luckily, Stone Cold Steve Austin saved Stephanie from the darkness.

In April 1999, the Ministry became even more powerful when they joined forces with the Corporation. The merger certainly proved to be a shock to fans, but the biggest surprise was yet to come. In June, The Ministry finally revealed the identity of the "higher power." The world watched in complete disbelief as Mr. McMahon exposed himself as the mastermind behind the entire ploy.

Miss Kitty

HT 5'3" **FROM** Memphis, Tennessee

SIGNATURE MOVE Stinkface

TITLE HISTORY Women's Champion

YEARS ACTIVE

This sweet femme debuted in August 1999 on an episode of *Monday Night Raw* as an assistant to Debra, manager of Jeff Jarrett. Audiences then saw her become the sidekick to Chyna. Before the end of the year, she stripped Ivory out of her gown and became Women's Champion in a Swimming Pool Evening Gown Match at *Armageddon 1999*. After her win, she spread the word that she would know be known as "the Kat."

Despite losing the title shortly after winning it, she appeared at *WrestleMania 2000* and at a Thong Stink Face Match at *SummerSlam*. In early 2001, she took exception to the group known as Right to Censor, and created the Right to Nudity group to oppose it. Unfortunately, after her team lost a match at *No Way Out*, the Kat was forced to join the Right to Censor. After a single appearance with Right to Censor, Kat parted ways the WWE.

Missing Link

HT 6'2" **WT** 250 lbs. **FROM** Parts Unknown

SIGNATURE MOVE Diving Headbutt

YEARS ACTIVE

One of the original oddities of sports-entertainment, the Missing Link first appeared in WWE in May 1985. He baffled audiences and Superstars with his confusing brand of violence that usually involved using his own body. Missing Link's incredible power and speed was attributed to his hunting and consumption of wild animals. Missing Link's outward appearance was so shocking it even caught the eye of *Sports Illustrated*.

Managed by Bobby Heenan and later Jimmy Hart, Missing Link was almost impossible to control. He often bashed his own head with chairs to regain his composure and grabbed the back of his hair for added force when executing one of his trademark headbutts. He only knew how to do one thing: attack anyone who stood in front of him. By the end of the year, Missing Link left WWE and traveled to World Class Championship Wrestling and Universal Wrestling Federation. He vanished after 1987 and remained in retirement until 2004 when he remerged on the independent scene. In 2006 his autobiography, *Bang Your Head: The Real Story of the Missing Link* was released. Sadly in 2007 the Missing Link passed away after a long battle with cancer.

MISSY'S MANOR

Missy Hyatt briefly appeared in WWE during the late 1980s, hosting *Missy's Manor*. Unfortunately for Hyatt, the show failed to reach the popularity of its predecessor, *Piper's Pit*. She did, however, score an interview with Bobby "the Brain" Heenan just days before his charge, Andre the Giant, went into battle against Hulk Hogan at *WrestleMania III*. Missy also grilled Randy Savage after his Intercontinental Championship loss to Ricky Steamboat. She mysteriously left WWE shortly after that interview.

Mitsu Arakawa

| HT | 5'10" | WT | 240 lbs. | FROM | Japan |

SIGNATURE MOVE Iron Claw

TITLE HISTORY International Tag Team Champion

YEARS ACTIVE 1960-1969 1970-1979 1980-1989 1990-1999 2000-PRESENT

Mitsu Arakawa wasn't very well-liked by his fellow Superstars. Whether it was a result of his consistent, illegal use of salt as a weapon or his dreaded Iron Claw, his colleagues practically refused to get in the ring with him. The fans weren't too fond of him either. In fact, many consider Arakawa to be one of the most hated villains of the 1960s.

In an attempt to avoid squaring off against him, many Superstars actually aligned themselves with Arakawa instead. Over the course of his career, he became known as one of the most sought after tag team partners in the business. His pairings resulted in ten tag team championship reigns over fifteen years. He even teamed with Professor Tanaka to capture the WWE International Tag Team Championship in June 1969. They held the titles for six months before losing to Bruno Sammartino & Battman.

The Miz

| HT | 6'1" | WT | 231 lbs. | FROM | Cleveland, Ohio |

SIGNATURE MOVE The Mizard of Oz

TITLE HISTORY WWE Tag Team Champion, World Tag Team Champion

YEARS ACTIVE 1960-1969 1970-1979 1980-1989 1990-1999 2000-PRESENT

Even before making his official WWE debut in 2006, The Miz was no stranger to television audiences. He appeared on *The Real World* and some of its spin-offs, and was a competitor in the fourth season of WWE's *Tough Enough*. While he didn't win the competition, he made enough of an impression that it wasn't long before he appeared in WWE rings in various roles, including hosting the 2006 Diva Search.

The Miz really began to shine after his move to *ECW on Sci-Fi* in 2007. The self-proclaimed chick magnet gained (and subsequently lost) the managerial services of Extreme Exposé, then faced CM Punk for the ECW championship at *Cyber Sunday*. While he came up short against CM Punk, it wasn't long before The Miz captured his first championship in WWE, after teaming with John Morrison to defeat Matt Hardy and MVP. Since that time, this co-host of *The Dirt Sheet* has enjoyed life at the top of the WWE tag team ranks.

MNM

YEARS ACTIVE 1960-1969 1970-1979 1980-1989 1990-1999 2000-PRESENT

MEMBERS Joey Mercury, Johnny Nitro, Melina

TITLE HISTORY WWE Tag Team Champions

Unlike many young newcomers, the bright lights of WWE failed to intimidate the self-proclaimed A-List celebrities MNM. With paparazzi commonplace in their everyday lives, Joey Mercury, Johnny Nitro & Melina were accustomed to the media frenzy associated with WWE. As a result, they made an instant impact upon their debut. In fact, Mercury & Nitro captured the WWE Tag Team Championship in their first match in April 2005.

Over the next year, the duo claimed the tag titles a total of three times, proving themselves as one of *SmackDown*'s greatest teams. Unfortunately, things went sour for the red-carpet trio in May 2005 when Melina & Nitro viciously attacked Mercury following a loss. Shortly after their assault, Nitro & Melina left *SmackDown* for *Raw*. As a member of the *Raw* roster, Nitro achieved great solo success, including two reigns as Intercontinental Champion.

In true Hollywood fashion, MNM premiered their thrilling sequel in November 2006 when they reunited to challenge the Hardys. Unfortunately, Mercury & Nitro were unable to duplicate the greatness of their first blockbuster. They went their separate ways soon after.

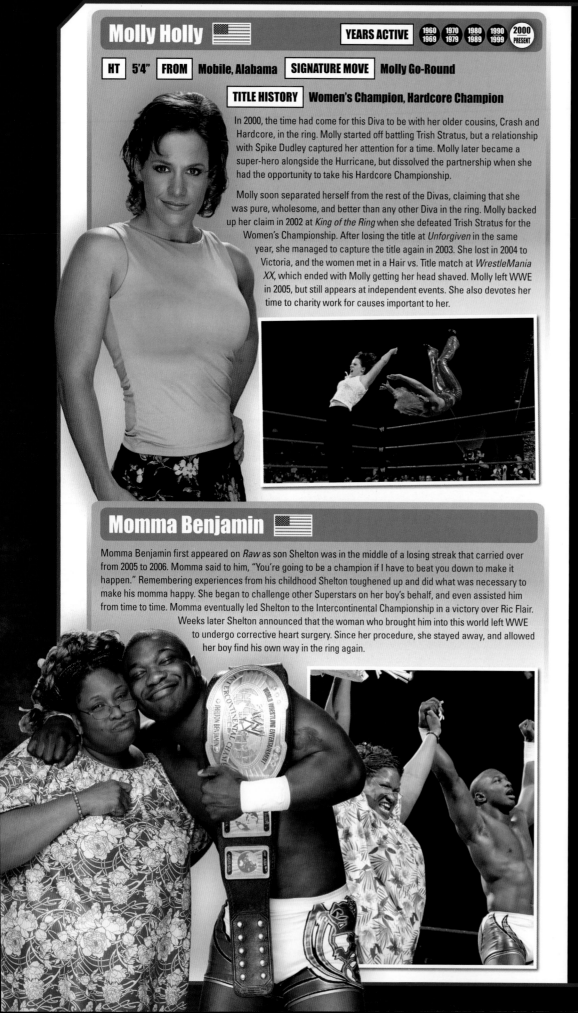

Molly Holly 🇺🇸

YEARS ACTIVE | 1960-1969 | 1970-1979 | 1980-1989 | 1990-1999 | **2000 PRESENT**

HT 5'4" **FROM** Mobile, Alabama **SIGNATURE MOVE** Molly Go-Round

TITLE HISTORY Women's Champion, Hardcore Champion

In 2000, the time had come for this Diva to be with her older cousins, Crash and Hardcore, in the ring. Molly started off battling Trish Stratus, but a relationship with Spike Dudley captured her attention for a time. Molly later became a super-hero alongside the Hurricane, but dissolved the partnership when she had the opportunity to take his Hardcore Championship.

Molly soon separated herself from the rest of the Divas, claiming that she was pure, wholesome, and better than any other Diva in the ring. Molly backed up her claim in 2002 at *King of the Ring* when she defeated Trish Stratus for the Women's Championship. After losing the title at *Unforgiven* in the same year, she managed to capture the title again in 2003. She lost in 2004 to Victoria, and the women met in a Hair vs. Title match at *WrestleMania XX*, which ended with Molly getting her head shaved. Molly left WWE in 2005, but still appears at independent events. She also devotes her time to charity work for causes important to her.

Momma Benjamin 🇺🇸

Momma Benjamin first appeared on *Raw* as son Shelton was in the middle of a losing streak that carried over from 2005 to 2006. Momma said to him, "You're going to be a champion if I have to beat you down to make it happen." Remembering experiences from his childhood Shelton toughened up and did what was necessary to make his momma happy. She began to challenge other Superstars on her boy's behalf, and even assisted him from time to time. Momma eventually led Shelton to the Intercontinental Championship in a victory over Ric Flair. Weeks later Shelton announced that the woman who brought him into this world left WWE to undergo corrective heart surgery. Since her procedure, she stayed away, and allowed her boy find his own way in the ring again.

MONEY IN THE BANK LADDER MATCH

Since its inception at *WrestleMania 21*, this innovative contest has changed the face of WWE and the fortunes of Superstars. In an otherwise standard Ladder Match, a briefcase is suspended over the ring. It contains a contract for a World Championship Match of the winner's choice anytime between that night and the following year's *WrestleMania*.

The Money In The Bank Ladder Match is a unique way for Superstars to climb the ladder of success. However, the Superstars who compete in this type of match are never again the same, physically or mentally. The matches have included anywhere from six to eight participants spanning all WWE brands. Past Money In The Bank winners include Edge, Rob Van Dam, Mr. Kennedy, and CM Punk.

Money, Inc.

MEMBERS Ted DiBiase, Irwin R. Schyster

COMBINED WEIGHT 508 lbs.

TITLE HISTORY

World Tag Team Championship

YEARS ACTIVE 1960-1969 1970-1979 1980-1989 **1990-1999** 2000-PRESENT

Among the many derogatory things you could say about Ted DiBiase is that he is arrogant, demeaning, and obnoxious. One thing you can't call him is a cheat. Otherwise, why would he choose to keep company with noted tax accountant Irwin R. Schyster?

DiBiase & Schyster first began competing as a unit in February 1992. With Jimmy "Mouth of the South" Hart as their manager, the money-hungry duo known as Money, Inc. gained instant success, capturing the World Tag Team Championship from the Legion of Doom shortly after their formation. The win ruffled the feathers of another team managed by Hart, the Natural Disasters, who believed their manager should have placed them into the championship match instead. The contention set off a fiery rivalry between the two teams.

After five months of successfully fending off Earthquake & Typhoon, Money, Inc. finally fell to the mammoth tag team in July 1992. The loss failed to set DiBiase & Schyster back, however, as they quickly reclaimed the titles a few months later. The victory gave them their second of three World Tag Team Championship reigns.

Following DiBiase's retirement in 1993, the affluent duo remained close business partners. When the "Million-Dollar Man" set out to manage his own stable of Superstars, he pinpointed I.R.S. as one of his crown jewels.

The Mongolian Stomper

HT 6'1" **WT** 260 lbs. **FROM** Mongolia **YEARS ACTIVE** **1960-1969** **1970-1979** 1980-1989 1990-1999 2000-PRESENT

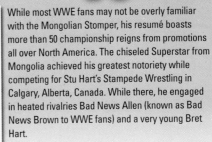

While most WWE fans may not be overly familiar with the Mongolian Stomper, his resumé boasts more than 50 championship reigns from promotions all over North America. The chiseled Superstar from Mongolia achieved his greatest notoriety while competing for Stu Hart's Stampede Wrestling in Calgary, Alberta, Canada. While there, he engaged in heated rivalries Bad News Allen (known as Bad News Brown to WWE fans) and a very young Bret Hart.

Between reigns atop Stampede Wrestling, the Mongolian Stomper achieved great success in the United States. On several occasions during the 1960s and 1970s, he nearly defeated Lou Thesz, Gene Kiniski and Harley Race for the NWA Championship.

The Mongols

YEARS ACTIVE 1960-1969 **1970-1979** 1980-1989 1990-1999 2000-PRESENT

MEMBERS Bepo, Geto **COMBINED WEIGHT** 578 lbs.

TITLE HISTORY International Tag Team Champions

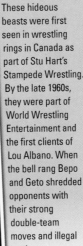

These hideous beasts were first seen in wrestling rings in Canada as part of Stu Hart's Stampede Wrestling. By the late 1960s, they were part of World Wrestling Entertainment and the first clients of Lou Albano. When the bell rang Bepo and Geto shredded opponents with their strong double-team moves and illegal tactics.

In June 1970 the pair captured the International Tag Team Championship during their Madison Square Garden debut. With the precursor to the World Tag Team Championship around their waist, the Mongols left WWE in 1971 and took the belts with them. WWE held a tournament that saw "Crazy" Luke Graham & Tarzan Tyler win on November 12, 1971. Graham & Tyler beat the Mongols at a later date, ending any question of who were the real tag team champions. After the defeat the Mongols parted ways.

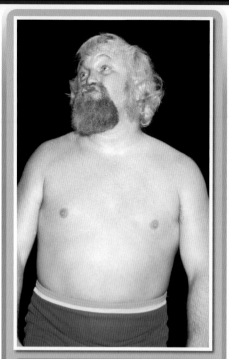

Moondog Mayne 🇺🇸

| **HT** | 6' | **WT** | 275 lbs. |

FROM Crabtree, Oregon

SIGNATURE MOVE The Bone Smash

YEARS ACTIVE 1960 1969 • 1970 1979 • 1980 1989 • 1990 1999 • 2000 PRESENT

Mayne was a crazed competitor who was unpredictable both in and out of the ring. Moondog was known for howling and chomping on pieces of broken glass during his interviews. His unorthodox means of dissecting opponents included biting them, raking their eyes, and he even took beverages from those sitting in the audience and dumped them in the face of his opponent.

Moondog debuted in WWE in 1972 and quickly set to eradicate the company's top Superstars. Mayne's "blood-eat-blood" mentality also led to many victories in Battle Royals before leaving the company in late 1973. He took his brawling ways to the west coast of the United States and became a threat everywhere he appeared. Trgically in August 1978, Moondog Mayne was killed in an automobile accident.

The Moondogs

YEARS ACTIVE 1960 1969 • 1970 1979 • 1980 1989 • 1990 1999 • 2000 PRESENT

MEMBERS Rex, Spot, King **FROM** Parts Unknown

TITLE HISTORY World Tag Team Champions

Although unorthodox in appearance, the Moondogs were one of the most skilled tag teams of the early 1980s. Managed by Capt. Lou Albano, the barrel-chested combination was known for its shaggy hair, ripped jeans and habit of gnawing on large animal bones.

Rex & King proved their bark was as big as their bite when they defeated Tony Garea & Rick Martel for the World Tag Team Championship in March 1981. A few months into their reign, however, King established himself as the runt of the litter when he ran away from WWE completely. Rex filled the vacancy with another Moondog, Spot, and the duo went on to successfully defend the tag titles for two more months.

After losing the World Tag Team Championship back to Garea & Martel in July 1981, Rex & Spot struggled to regain their momentum. The wild duo eventually moved on to moderately successful singles careers.

Mountie 🇨🇦

YEARS ACTIVE 1960 1969 • 1970 1979 • 1980 1989 • 1990 1999 • 2000 PRESENT

| **HT** | 6'1" | **WT** | 257 lbs. | **FROM** | Montreal, Quebec, Canada |

SIGNATURE MOVE Carotid Control Technique

TITLE HISTORY Intercontinental Champion

A former member of the Royal Canadian Mounted Police, this Superstar debuted in WWE in 1991. Despite claims that the world was his jurisdiction and that he upheld international law and order, the Mountie often broke the rules to earn his victories. To add insult to injry, he often handcuffed fallen opponents to the ring ropes and tasered them with his shock stick.

The Big Bossman took exception to his methods and the two former law enforcers battled for months, culminating in a Jailhouse Match at *SummerSlam 1991* with the stipulation that the loser would spend the night in a New York City jail. The Mountie lost the match and was taken away by New York's Finest.

In January 1992, the Mountie caught Bret Hart on an off night and captured the Intercontinental Championship, but held the title for only two days. By the end of 1992, the Mountie was gone from WWE, but fans will always remember him and his vow always to get his man!

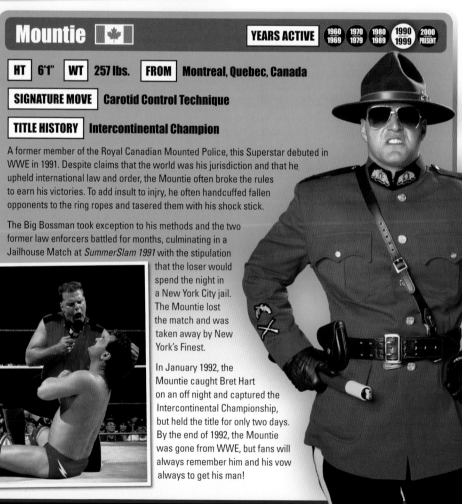

MR. FUJI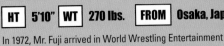

| HT | 5'10" | WT | 270 lbs. | FROM | Osaka, Japan |

SIGNATURE MOVE Bonzai Drop

TITLE HISTORY World Tag Team Champion

In 1972, Mr. Fuji arrived in World Wrestling Entertainment managed by the Grand Wizard. He quickly became known for hiding bags of ceremonial Japanese salt on his person and throwing it into the eyes of opponents. He allied himself with the dreaded Prof. Toru Tanaka, and on June 27, 1972, they began their first of three World Tag Team Championship reigns. After losing the titles for the second time, Fuji & Tanaka left WWE and stormed into the NWA, where they won numerous regional tag team championships.

In 1977, they returned with "Classy" Freddie Blassie as their new manager. Although their final championship reign ended on March 14, 1978, they remained one of wrestling's most feared teams until they separated in 1979. Fuji reappeared in WWE in 1981 with a new partner, Mr. Saito. Managed by Capt. Lou Albano, they enjoyed two reigns as World Tag Team Champions. Either alone or with a partner, Mr. Fuji was regarded as one of the world's most dangerous men and one who could not be trusted under any circumstances.

In 1985, Fuji started to dress in a black tuxedo and black top hat, carried a cane and embarked on his managerial career. Fuji also ventured into acting and received critical acclaim for his work on *Tuesday Night Titans* in the landmark skits *Fuji General* and *Fuji Vice*. At *WrestleMania IV*, he led Demolition to the World tag team titles for his first championship as a manager.

After managing multiple teams to great success, Fuji introduced the intimidating Yokozuna to WWE in 1992, then led him straight to the top of sports-entertainment. At *WrestleMania IX*, Yokozuna, with Mr. Fuji in his corner, defeated Bret Hart for the WWE Championship. Despite losing the title in a challenge to Hulk Hogan moments later, Yokozuna regained the prize at the *King of the Ring*. The devious one left WWE in 1995, but reappeared for the last time at *WrestleMania XII* with Yokozuna.

On the eve of *WrestleMania 23*, Mr. Fuji joined the WWE Hall of Fame. Mr. Fuji is one of the rare legendary figures of WWE that had as much success out of the ring as he did in it.

Mr. Fuji & Mr. Saito

| COMBINED WEIGHT | 500 lbs. |

TITLE HISTORY World Tag Team Champions

YEARS ACTIVE

By the time the 1980s rolled around, the devious Mr. Fuji had nearly two decades of in-ring experience to his credit, including two very successful stints with WWE. He could have very easily walked away from everything; instead, he chose to return to WWE in 1981 to further his already legendary legacy.

Around the same time, Mr. Saito had signed with WWE, following a near 15-year run competing for NWA territories. Like Fuji, Saito could have retired at this point as one of the greatest Japanese Superstars to ever lace up a pair of boots. Instead, he went to WWE, formed a team with Mr. Fuji and became a dominant force in the tag ranks.

Managed by Capt. Lou Albano, Fuji & Saito found success almost immediately. In October 1981, the rule-breaking combination defeated Tony Garea & Rick Martel for the World Tag Team Championship. The win gave Fuji his fourth reign with the title and Saito his first. Minus a few weeks in the summer of 1982, the Japanese tandem held the titles all the way through the following October.

Saito left WWE shortly after losing the titles, leaving his partner to fend for himself. Fuji competed briefly as a singles Superstar before embarking on one of the greatest managerial careers of all time.

Mr. Fuji & Prof. Toru Tanaka

| COMBINED WEIGHT | 545 lbs. |

TITLE HISTORY World Tag Team Champions

YEARS ACTIVE

When these two Superstars from Japan joined forces in 1972, they were already well known for their cruelty in the ring. Add the Grand Wizard as their manger and you have one of the most destructive trios in WWE history. They added to their repetoire of underhanded tactics in every match as they spent considerable time devising new ways to cheat without being discovered. In June 1972 they won their first WWE World Tag Team crown when they defeated Chief Jay Strongbow & Sonny King.

After time away from WWE they returned in 1977 with "Classy" Freddie Blassie in charge. In September, they wheedled their way to another championship reign on when they took the titles from Tony Garea & Larry Zbyzko. When Tanaka & Fuji lost the belts almost six months later, they left WWE. Winning several tag team championships among the regional territories of the National Wrestling Alliance, the two Japanese rogues parted ways by the end of 1979. Fuji continued his success both as a Superstar in the ring, and as a manager in the 1980s. Tanaka made the transition from sports-entertainment to Hollywood and appeared in dozens of films and television shows until he passed away in 2000.

The tandem of Tanaka & Fuji will always be considered one of the most ruthless and successful pairings in sports-entertainment history. Their synthesis of martial-arts, teamwork, and dirty tricks changed tag team wrestling forever.

Mr. Hughes

| **HT** 6'6" | **WT** 330 lbs. | **FROM** Kansas City, Missouri |

The scowl on his face said it all; Mr. Hughes was one mean dude. He certainly proved this during his three brief stints with WWE. Decked in dress pants,

SIGNATURE MOVE Powerslam

YEARS ACTIVE 1960 1969 | 1970 1979 | 1980 1989 | 1990 1999 | 2000 PRESENT

a button-down shirt and suspenders, Mr. Hughes made his WWE debut alongside manager Harvey Wippleman in 1993. After making an immediate impact by stealing Undertaker's signature urn, the colossal Hughes spent the next several weeks tearing through many lesser-known Superstars. Surprisingly, Mr. Hughes made a quick exit from WWE in the summer of 1993.

Four years after mysteriously leaving WWE, Mr. Hughes made his return as the bodyguard to Hunter Hearst-Helmsley, but he once again disappeared just as quickly as he arrived. In 1999, a more svelte looking Hughes reemerged as Chris Jericho's bodyguard. The no-nonsense Superstar instantly earned his money, helping Y2J defeat rival Ken Shamrock in a First Blood Match in September. In typical Hughes fashion, however, the big man once again disappeared from WWE approximately one month later.

Mr. Kennedy

| **HT** 6'2" | **WT** 235 lbs. | **TITLE HISTORY** United States Champion |

| **FROM** Green Bay, Wisconsin | **SIGNATURE MOVE** Mic Check |

YEARS ACTIVE 1960 1969 | 1970 1979 | 1980 1989 | 1990 1999 | 2000 PRESENT

After serving in the United States military, Mr. Kennedy hit the independent wrestling scene and chased his dream. Since this Superstar entered the ranks of WWE in 2005, he has truly marched to the beat of his own drum. Never before in the history of sports-entertainment has a Superstar made his own ring introductions quite like this man. Always loquacious on the microphone, Mr. Kennedy is the self-professed "future of WWE." Unfortunately for his opponents he can back up everything that comes from his mouth. He has tangled with the likes of Undertaker, Rey Mysterio, Batista, and Shawn Michaels. His first taste of WWE gold came on September 1, 2006 when he won the United States Championship in a Triple Threat Match against Finlay and Bobby Lashley.

Kennedy kept rolling and became "Mr. Money In the Bank" at *WrestleMania 23*. In 2008 he was drafted to *Raw* where he plans to continue his verbal and physical assault of Superstars.

MR. PERFECT

YEARS ACTIVE 1960 1969 | 1970 1979 | 1980 1989 | 1990 1999 | 2000 PRESENT

HALL OF FAME 2007

| **HT** 6'3" | **WT** 257 lbs. | **FROM** Robbinsdale, Minnesota | **SIGNATURE MOVE** Perfectplex |

TITLE HISTORY Intercontinental Champion

Athletically, there wasn't anything Curt Hennig couldn't do. He could hit a home run, sink a forty-foot putt, and even catch his own Hail Mary football pass. Basically, he was perfect in every way. He was Mr. Perfect.

Following a successful stint in the American Wrestling Association (AWA), Curt Hennig, the son of wrestler Larry "the Axe" Hennig, first started making a name for himself as WWE's Mr. Perfect in 1988. His first year with the company was highlighted by convincing victories over Superstars such as Red Rooster and Koko B. Ware.

By April 1990, Mr. Perfect's superior technical wrestling ability earned him a spot in a tournament designed to crown a new Intercontinental Champion. In the finals, the master of the Perfectplex turned back Tito Santana to capture his first of two Intercontinental titles. While others have held the championship longer, many consider Mr. Perfect to be the greatest Intercontinental Champion of all time.

Injuries unfortunately sidelined Mr. Perfect through much of his prime, but he didn't let that stop him from gaining a prominent role within WWE. In addition to working as color commentator for many WWE television programs, he also served as Ric Flair's advisor during his initial stint with the company.

Hennig dropped his Mr. Perfect persona in 1997 to embark on a three-year run with World Championship Wrestling (WCW). While there, he became a member of two of the most influential factions of all time, the Four Horsemen and the New World Order. Perfection returned to WWE in 2002 when Hennig competed in the *Royal Rumble*. Looking like the Mr. Perfect of old, he impressed many as one of the final four participants in the match.

Curt Hennig passed away on February 10, 2003. Four years later, he took his rightful place alongside sports-entertainment's greats when he was posthumously inducted into the WWE Hall of Fame, a perfect honor for an absolutely perfect competitor.

Mr. Saito

HT 5'11" **WT** 265 lbs.

FROM Tokyo, Japan

SIGNATURE MOVE Saito Suplex

TITLE HISTORY

World Tag Team Champion

YEARS ACTIVE

A former Japanese Olympian, Mr. Saito was admired within amateur wrestling circles for his superior technical skills. When it came to his professional career, he refused to rest solely on his previous laurels. Instead, Saito developed a punishing high-impact offense, coupled with a complete disregard for the rules, which helped round out his impressive repertoire.

Mr. Saito's impressive list of NWA championship partners includes Ivan Koloff, Mr. Sato, and Gene Kiniski. However, it wasn't until 1981 that he reached the pinnacle of tag team wrestling. Moving to WWE and teaming with Mr. Fuji, Saito captured the World Tag Team Championship from Tony Garea & Rick Martel. Sans a few weeks in the summer of 1982, the devious tandem held the titles for more than one year. Following his stay in WWE, Saito took his talents to Japan, where he proved himself as a force in both the tag team and singles ranks.

Mr. T

HT 5'10" **WT** 236 lbs.

FROM Chicago, Illinois

YEARS ACTIVE

Mr. T's sports-entertainment career only consisted of a handful of appearances, but don't let the number of times he stepped in the ring fool you. The former *A-Team* star always found himself in the middle of some of the biggest moments in WWE history.

In 1985, Mr. T teamed with friend Hulk Hogan to help usher in *WrestleMania*. The popularity of their main event victory over "Rowdy" Roddy Piper & "Mr. Wonderful" Paul Orndorff helped propel WWE to an international sensation.

The following year, Mr. T used the fame he gained as Clubber Lang in *Rocky III* to secure a boxing match against Piper at *WrestleMania 2*. Mr. T's boxing prowess proved superior, as he defeated "Hot Rod" via disqualification.

Nearly a decade later, Mr. T returned to the ring to serve as the special guest referee in the WCW Championship Match between Hogan and Ric Flair. In the end, Mr. T raised the Hulkster's hand in victory. As a result of the pre-match stipulations, the legendary Flair was forced into early—and temporary—retirement.

Mr. Wrestling II

HT 5'11" **WT** 236 lbs.

FROM Atlanta, Georgia

SIGNATURE MOVE

Running High Knee

YEARS ACTIVE

Mr. Wrestling II was one of the most popular Superstars of the southern territories during the 1970s and early 1980s. Spending the majority of his time in Georgia and Florida, the mysterious masked Superstar solidified himself as a force in both the singles and tag team ranks.

As a solo competitor, Mr. Wrestling II used his signature running high knee to claim an astonishing ten NWA Georgia Heavyweight Championships. He also won the NWA Florida Heavyweight Championship twice. A World Championship reign escaped Mr. Wrestling II during his illustrious career, but he did manage to battle NWA Champion Jack Brisco to several breathtaking draws during the 1970s.

Mr. Wrestling II was no stranger to tag team gold either. Among many of the partners the masked man captured tag titles with were Mr. Wrestling I, Tony Atlas, and "Cowboy" Bob Orton. Mr. Wrestling II's impressive career began to wind down toward the mid-1980s. In 1993, he was honored with induction into the short-lived WCW Hall of Fame.

Muhammad Hassan

HT 6'2" **WT** 245 lbs.

FROM Detroit, Michigan

SIGNATURE MOVE

Camel Clutch

YEARS ACTIVE

In 2004, this man with Middle Eastern ancestry entered WWE alongside his spokesperson, Daivari. He often interrupted the interview segments of others and verbally accosted Jim Ross and Jerry Lawler over their characterizations of him.

Hassan was last seen at the 2005 *Great American Bash* and was powerbombed through the stage by Undertaker. Muhammad Hassan will go down in WWE history books as one of the most controversial figures to appear in the company.

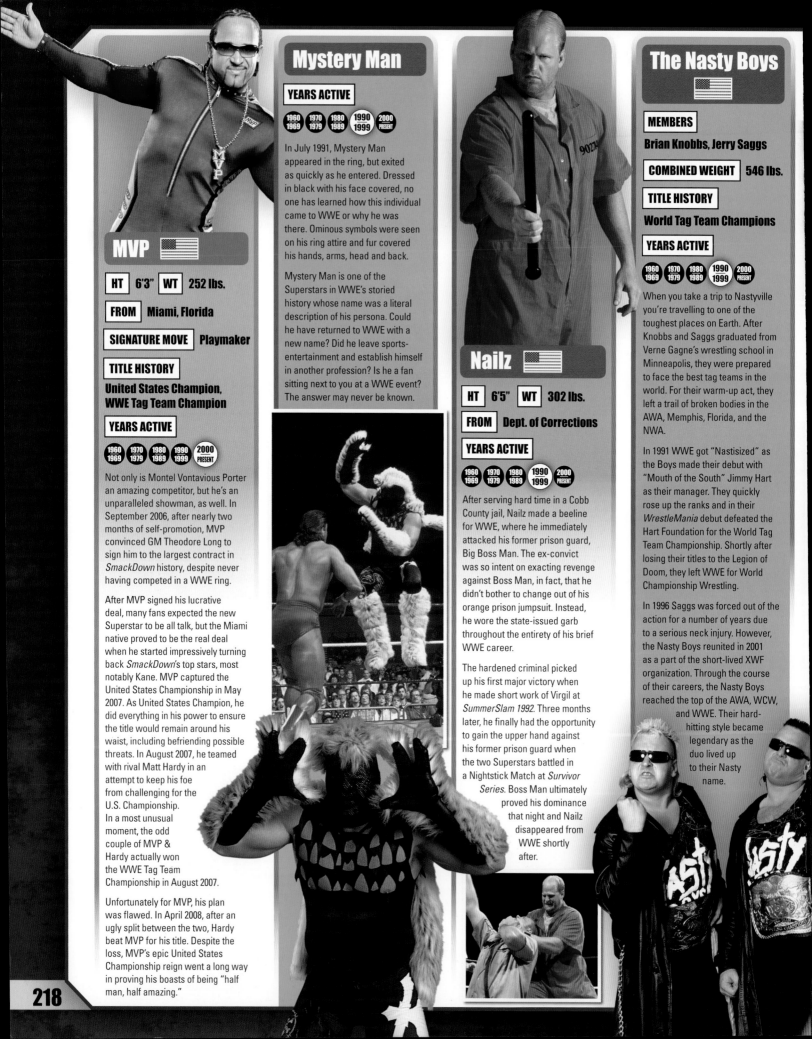

MVP 🇺🇸

| HT | 6'3" | WT | 252 lbs. |

| FROM | Miami, Florida |

| SIGNATURE MOVE | Playmaker |

TITLE HISTORY

United States Champion, WWE Tag Team Champion

YEARS ACTIVE

1960-1969 · 1970-1979 · 1980-1989 · 1990-1999 · **2000-PRESENT**

Not only is Montel Vontavious Porter an amazing competitor, but he's an unparalleled showman, as well. In September 2006, after nearly two months of self-promotion, MVP convinced GM Theodore Long to sign him to the largest contract in *SmackDown* history, despite never having competed in a WWE ring.

After MVP signed his lucrative deal, many fans expected the new Superstar to be all talk, but the Miami native proved to be the real deal when he started impressively turning back *SmackDown*'s top stars, most notably Kane. MVP captured the United States Championship in May 2007. As United States Champion, he did everything in his power to ensure the title would remain around his waist, including befriending possible threats. In August 2007, he teamed with rival Matt Hardy in an attempt to keep his foe from challenging for the U.S. Championship. In a most unusual moment, the odd couple of MVP & Hardy actually won the WWE Tag Team Championship in August 2007.

Unfortunately for MVP, his plan was flawed. In April 2008, after an ugly split between the two, Hardy beat MVP for his title. Despite the loss, MVP's epic United States Championship reign went a long way in proving his boasts of being "half man, half amazing."

Mystery Man

YEARS ACTIVE

1960-1969 · 1970-1979 · 1980-1989 · **1990-1999** · 2000-PRESENT

In July 1991, Mystery Man appeared in the ring, but exited as quickly as he entered. Dressed in black with his face covered, no one has learned how this individual came to WWE or why he was there. Ominous symbols were seen on his ring attire and fur covered his hands, arms, head and back.

Mystery Man is one of the Superstars in WWE's storied history whose name was a literal description of his persona. Could he have returned to WWE with a new name? Did he leave sports-entertainment and establish himself in another profession? Is he a fan sitting next to you at a WWE event? The answer may never be known.

Nailz 🇺🇸

| HT | 6'5" | WT | 302 lbs. |

| FROM | Dept. of Corrections |

YEARS ACTIVE

1960-1969 · 1970-1979 · 1980-1989 · **1990-1999** · 2000-PRESENT

After serving hard time in a Cobb County jail, Nailz made a beeline for WWE, where he immediately attacked his former prison guard, Big Boss Man. The ex-convict was so intent on exacting revenge against Boss Man, in fact, that he didn't bother to change out of his orange prison jumpsuit. Instead, he wore the state-issued garb throughout the entirety of his brief WWE career.

The hardened criminal picked up his first major victory when he made short work of Virgil at *SummerSlam 1992*. Three months later, he finally had the opportunity to gain the upper hand against his former prison guard when the two Superstars battled in a Nightstick Match at *Survivor Series*. Boss Man ultimately proved his dominance that night and Nailz disappeared from WWE shortly after.

The Nasty Boys 🇺🇸

MEMBERS

Brian Knobbs, Jerry Saggs

| COMBINED WEIGHT | 546 lbs. |

TITLE HISTORY

World Tag Team Champions

YEARS ACTIVE

1960-1969 · 1970-1979 · 1980-1989 · **1990-1999** · 2000-PRESENT

When you take a trip to Nastyville you're travelling to one of the toughest places on Earth. After Knobbs and Saggs graduated from Verne Gagne's wrestling school in Minneapolis, they were prepared to face the best tag teams in the world. For their warm-up act, they left a trail of broken bodies in the AWA, Memphis, Florida, and the NWA.

In 1991 WWE got "Nastisized" as the Boys made their debut with "Mouth of the South" Jimmy Hart as their manager. They quickly rose up the ranks and in their *WrestleMania* debut defeated the Hart Foundation for the World Tag Team Championship. Shortly after losing their titles to the Legion of Doom, they left WWE for World Championship Wrestling.

In 1996 Saggs was forced out of the action for a number of years due to a serious neck injury. However, the Nasty Boys reunited in 2001 as a part of the short-lived XWF organization. Through the course of their careers, the Nasty Boys reached the top of the AWA, WCW, and WWE. Their hard-hitting style became legendary as the duo lived up to their Nasty name.

Natalya Neidhart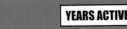

HT 5'6" **FROM** Calgary, Alberta, Canada **SIGNATURE MOVE** Sharpshooter

She is a descendant of sports-entertainment royalty, as well as a defender and graduate of the famous Hart Dungeon. Natalya is the daughter of Jim "the Anvil" Neidhart and in addition to the training from her famous family members, she is also well versed in amateur wrestling and mixed martial arts.

Natalya announced her presence in memorable fashion on the April 4, 2008 edition of *SmackDown*. She came from the crowd and aided Victoria at the expense of Michelle McCool and Cherry. Since then she and the Black Widow have been best friends as Natalya demonstrates her submission skills against her opponents. She has also made it clear that while she respects her family's incredible accomplishments, she is the future and it's all about her. Natalya offers a few words of warning to all other Divas who consider trying to make a name for themselves at her expense, "You mess with the best you go down with the rest! Yeah baby!"

Nation of Domination

MEMBERS Faarooq, The Rock, Kama, The Godfather, D-Lo Brown, Owen Hart, Crush, Savio Vega, Ahmed Johnson, Mark Henry, Clarence Mason, J.C. Ice, Wolfie D

Lead by Faarooq, the Nation of Domination was a militant group assembled to fight for the rights of black Superstars. Claiming to be held back due to the color of their skin, the controversial faction set out to gain equality "by any means necessary."

The earliest version of group contained Crush, Savio Vega, D-Lo Brown, PG-13, and Clarence Mason. When they failed to help Faarooq defeat Undertaker for the WWE Championship, the leader fired all of them, with the exception of D-Lo Brown. The new-look Nation was filled with Superstars that shared Faarooq's twisted visions: Kama, The Rock, and Mark Henry.

The Nation claimed its first piece of gold in December 1997 when The Rock was awarded the Intercontinental Championship after Stone Cold Steve Austin refused to defend the title. As the faction's only titleholder, the cocky Rock slowly began to extract leadership responsibilities from Faarooq, before finally kicking him out of the Nation altogether in early 1998.

Under The Rock's leadership, the Nation developed a more hip quality. No longer mad at the world, various members were allowed to show their true personalities. By the end of 1998, the Godfather left the Nation to pursue his budding pimping career. Shortly after that, The Rock's ego grew to epic proportions, forcing Brown and Henry to attack their leader, thus ending the Nation's existence.

Natural Disasters

MEMBERS Earthquake, Typhoon **COMBINED WEIGHT** 846 lbs.

TITLE HISTORY World Tag Team Championship

At a time when most WWE tag teams topped out at 500 pounds, Earthquake & Typhoon joined forces to create a near half-ton of total destruction. Appropriately named the Natural Disasters, the colossal duo stormed through their competition with the greatest of ease.

Prior to the Natural Disasters' formation, Typhoon spent many years competing as the hugely popular Tugboat. In 1991, he revealed a darker side when he turned on his friends, the Bushwhackers, to align himself with the hated Earthquake. Together, the Natural Disasters left such destruction in their wake that a wrecking ball would cringe.

In January 1992, Earthquake & Typhoon scored a major countout victory over the World Tag Team Champions, the Legion of Doom. By all accounts, the win should have put the Natural Disasters in line for another opportunity at the titles, but their manager Jimmy Hart put Money, Inc. in the ring with the champs instead. The move infuriated the oversized tag team, who immediately fired "The Mouth of the South." The bold move made Earthquake & Typhoon instant fan favorites and also propelled them into a heated rivalry with the new champs, DiBiase & Schyster.

The Natural Disasters gained a level of revenge when they defeated Money, Inc. for the titles in July 1992. Unfortunately, they only held the championship for three months before losing them back to DiBiase & Schyster in October.

NEW AGE OUTLAWS

MEMBERS "Road Dogg" Jesse James, "Bad Ass" Billy Gunn

COMBINED WEIGHT 548 lbs.

TITLE HISTORY World Tag Team Champions

YEARS ACTIVE

"Oh...you didn't know?"

This famous introduction brought capacity crowds around the world to their feet. In a case of good enemies, better friends, the two former enemies became a team in 1997. When Billy laid out his then-manager, the Honky Tonk Man, with a guitar, the spirit of the New Age Outlaws was born and tag team competition was about to change forever.

The New Age Outlaws became known for their abilities and antics both in and out of the ring. They quickly took aim at the top and stole the spiked shoulder pads of The Legion of Doom to get a shot at the World Tag Team Championship. Their strategy worked when they defeated Animal & Hawk for the titles.

The Outlaws then showed their mean streak when they locked Cactus Jack and Terry Funk in a dumpster and pushed the dumpster off the *Raw* stage. Their handiwork began to catch the interest of Shawn Michaels and Hunter Hearst-Helmsley as they were set to defend their titles at *WrestleMania XIV*. Though they lost to Cactus Jack & Chainsaw Charlie, they regained the titles the next night in a steel cage with a little help from their new friends.

This collaboration marked the second incarnation of D-Generation X and the Outlaws helped build the group's legacy. Though differences caused them to split in 1999, "Road Dogg" and Billy reformed to show they were still the best against the Rock 'N' Sock Connection, Edge & Christian, the Hollys, and the Dudley Boys. James & Gunn rode with DX for the final time in 2000 when they faced the Radicalz in eight-man action on *Monday Night Raw*.

Soon after, "Road Dogg" and Billy Gunn went their separate ways. Though they saw success apart, it paled in comparison to when they wreaked havoc together. The New Age Outlaws were a major attraction during WWE's Attitude Era. They changed the face of tag team competition.

The New Blackjacks

MEMBERS Blackjack Windham, Blackjack Bradshaw

COMBINED WEIGHT 565 lbs.

YEARS ACTIVE

The tag team division in World Wrestling Entertainment was given a loud wake-up call in 1998. With classic rough-house tactics matched with innovative power moves the cowboys in black became serious contenders for the World Tag Team Championship from the get-go.

The New Blackjacks had showdowns with the Godwinns, Faarooq & Kama, and the New Age Outlaws. This iteration of the classic duo did not last long. Blackjack Windham turned on Bradshaw before the end of 1998 to join Jim Cornette's collection of NWA stars.

Even though the team lasted a short period of time, Windham & Bradshaw brought traditional Texas brutality back to the ring. Their stint as the New Blackjacks paid homage to the originals and celebrated the team's legacy in sports-entertainment.

New Dream Team

MEMBERS Greg Valentine, Dino Bravo

COMBINED WEIGHT 491 lbs.

YEARS ACTIVE

Contrary to popular belief, new doesn't always mean improved. Following a *WrestleMania III* argument between original Dream Team members Brutus Beefcake and Greg Valentine, Beefcake was unceremoniously ousted from the unit and replaced with Dino Bravo. The new union, however, failed to reach the same level of success as the original duo, who once ruled WWE as World Tag Team Champions.

Managed by "Luscious" Johnny Valiant, the New Dream Team saw its greatest success early on. After several impressive showings against the Islanders, Valentine & Bravo were granted an opportunity for the Hart Foundation's World Tag Team titles. The new combination failed to capture the championship, however, and quickly slipped into obscurity. Shortly after the loss, Valentine & Bravo agreed to go their separate ways.

The New Foundation

MEMBERS

Owen Hart, Jim "The Anvil" Neidhart

COMBINED WEIGHT 508 lbs.

YEARS ACTIVE 1960-1969 1970-1979 1980-1989 1990-1999 2000-PRESENT

Jim Neidhart was left at a career crossroads after his tag team partner, Bret Hart, left the Hart Foundation to pursue singles success. Rather than attempting to find similar solo greatness, Neidhart looked to Bret's younger brother, Owen Hart, to fill the void left by the "Hit Man." Together, Owen & the Anvil adopted the name the New Foundation.

Owen's collective body of work proves that he was one of the industry's greatest tag team competitors. His impressive resumé boasts World Tag Team Championship reigns with partners Yokozuna, British Bulldog and Jeff Jarrett. On the flip side, Neidhart will forever be remembered as one-half of one of the greatest tag teams ever assembled. Together, however, the New Foundation failed to get out of the starting block.

Luckily for both Superstars, their amazing success at other points in their respective careers far overshadows the New Foundation's checkerboard ring gear and unimpressive record. Years after the New Foundation crumbled, Neidhart stood by Owen's side as the young Hart claimed the 1994 *King of the Ring.*

New Midnight Express

YEARS ACTIVE 1960-1969 1970-1979 1980-1989 1990-1999 2000-PRESENT

MEMBERS Bob Holly, Bart Gunn   **COMBINED WEIGHT** 493 lbs.

During the 1980s, manager James E. Cornette led the Midnight Express, a constantly evolving tag team consisting of such Superstars as "Beautiful" Bobby Eaton, "Sweet" Stan Lane, and "Loverboy" Dennis Condrey to tag team greatness in the NWA. A decade later, Cornette recreated the egotistical team in WWE. This time, though, he replaced its aging members with the considerably younger Bob Holly and Bart Gunn.

Known as The New Midnight Express, Holly & Gunn adopted nicknames fitting of the 1980s squad. Holly became "Bodacious" Bob, while Gunn went by "Bombastic" Bart. The name changes, however, did little in the way of creating success. The duo failed to make any real waves in WWE. Their highest-profile encounter came at *WrestleMania XV*, where they competed in the Tag Team Battle Royal, which was ultimately won by LOD 2000. By the end of 1998, less than one year into their existence, the New Midnight Express went their separate ways.

New Rockers

YEARS ACTIVE 1960-1969 1970-1979 1980-1989 1990-1999 2000-PRESENT

MEMBERS Marty Jannetty, Leif Cassidy

COMBINED WEIGHT 468 lbs.

The familiar rock n' roll theme that echoed in arenas all over the world during the late 1980s and early 1990s played again in 1996. World Wrestling Entertainment saw the thrilling tag team duo of original Rocker Marty Jannetty and newcomer Leif Cassidy take on all of the WWE's top duo's including the Godwinns, the Bodydonnas, the Smoking Gunns, and the Bushwhackers. Marty and Leif stayed true to the Rocker tradition of excellent continuity and double-team moves, and a finishing move that is still regarded as one of the most dangerous in WWE history. Despite only a brief time together, the New Rockers added another element to the legacy of the famed tandem and proved that they were in charge whenever they stepped in the ring.

IN THE MOVIES

For a period of time in the 1970s and early 1980s, narrow-minded producers only turned to professional wrestlers when they were casting a movie about the sport or needed a bulging brute to play the role of a bodyguard. Over time, thanks in large part to the on-screen efforts of Hulk Hogan, Jesse "The Body" Ventura, and "Rowdy" Roddy Piper, Hollywood executives began to recognize these Superstars as legitimate talents in the entertainment industry. Today, larger-than-life personalities such as John Cena, Stone Cold Steve Austin, and Kane continually prove their acting prowess, while remaining in high demand for various roles, including action, comedy, and drama.

WWE STUDIOS

In 2002, WWE expanded its business focus when it opened WWE Films. In July 2008, the division was renamed WWE Studios but its focus remained the same: producing filmed entertainment that features the Superstars on the WWE roster. Its first forays were co-production on many of The Rock's early movies, but starting in 2006, WWE Studios has produced a string of successful movies (*See No Evil, the Marine, The Condemned*) with at least four more planned in the near future, including *12 Rounds* starring John Cena.

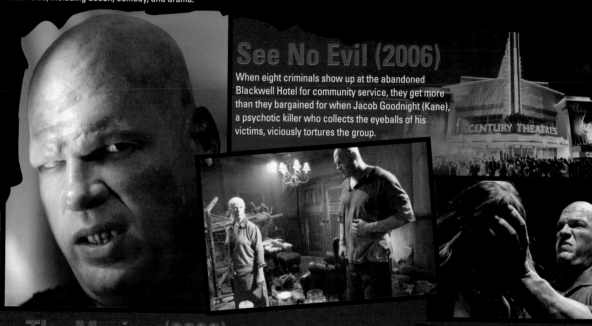

See No Evil (2006)

When eight criminals show up at the abandoned Blackwell Hotel for community service, they get more than they bargained for when Jacob Goodnight (Kane), a psychotic killer who collects the eyeballs of his victims, viciously tortures the group.

The Marine (2006)

After being unwillingly discharged from Iraq, Marine John Triton (John Cena) returns home to his beautiful wife Kate (Kelly Carlson). Shortly after their reunion, however, Kelly is kidnapped by a group of ruthless jewel thieves and Triton must do everything in his power to get her back.

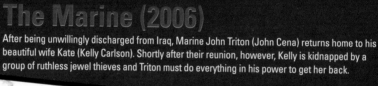

The Condemned (2007)

A wealthy television producer purchases Jack Conrad (Steve Austin) and nine other criminals to fight to the death on a deserted island. The last man standing will be granted his freedom.

WRESTLING MOVIES

Some of the more memorable movies about the industry include *The Wrestler* (1974), *Paradise Alley* (1978), the cult classic *My Breakfast with Blassie* (1983), *Body Slam* (1986), *Bad Guys* (1986), *No Holds Barred* (1989), and *Ready to Rumble* (2000). *The Wrestler* and *No Holds Barred* are notable among the group because the stars in the movies were Verne Gagne and Hulk Hogan, respectively. All the movies had cameo appearances by well-known Superstars, but most roles taken by veterans of the ring are in movies from other genres.

Superstars on the Silver Screen

Andre the Giant

Would *The Princess Bride* (1987) have been the same without Andre playing the role of gentle giant, Fezzik? While by far his most memorable role, Andre also appeared in *The Wrestling Queen* (1975), *Micki + Maude* (1984), and *Trading Mom* (1994).

Hulk Hogan

Who will ever forget Thunderlips from *Rocky III* (1982)? Outside other minor roles in many movies, Hulk Hogan can claim the starring roles in *No Holds Barred* (1989), *Suburban Commando* (1991), *Mr. Nanny* (1993), and *Santa with Muscles* (1996).

Jesse Ventura

Before he was governor of Minnesota, Jesse Ventura had roles in the movies *Predator* and *The Running Man* (1987), *No Holds Barred* (1989), and *Demoltion Man* (1993). He's made brief appearances in nearly a dozen other movies.

The Rock

After an appearance in *The Mummy Returns* (2001) led to him playing the title role in *The Scorpion King* (2002), The Rock became a Hollywood sensation. His other credits include *The Rundown* (2003), *Walking Tall* and *Be Cool* (2004), and *Doom* (2005). More recent movies have also tapped into his past as a star on the football field, such as *Gridiron Gang* (2006), and *The Game Plan* (2007).

Roddy Piper

Perhaps no Superstar has had as many movie roles as "Rowdy" Roddy Piper. *They Live* (1988) is his most memorable role, but the Rowdy one has appeared in over two dozen movies beyond his role as Nada.

Other Memorable Performances

Superstar	Movie, role
George Steele	Ed Wood (1994), Tor Johnson
Jerry Lawler	Man on the Moon (1999), Himself
Capt. Lou Albano	Wise Guys (1986), Frank Acavano
King Kong Bundy	Moving (1988), Gorgo
The Great Khali	Get Smart (2008), Dalip
Goldberg	The Longest Yard (2005), Battle
Kevin Nash	The Punisher (2004), The Russian
Stacy Keibler	Bubble Boy (2001), Working Girl
Terry Funk	Over the Top (1987), Ruker
Terry Funk	Road House (1989), Morgan
Gene Okerlund	Repossessed (1990), Himself
Dusty Rhodes	Paradise Park (1991), Deputy Johnny Morton
Big John Studd	The Marrying Man (1991), Dante
Big Show	The Waterboy (1998), Captain Insano
Rob Van Dam	Black Mask 2 (2002), The Claw
Bam Bam Bigelow	Major Payne (1995), Huge Biker
Shane McMahon	Rollerball (2002), American Media Mogul
Paul Heyman	Rollerball (2002), English Announcer
Sable	Corky Romano (2001), Female Bouncer

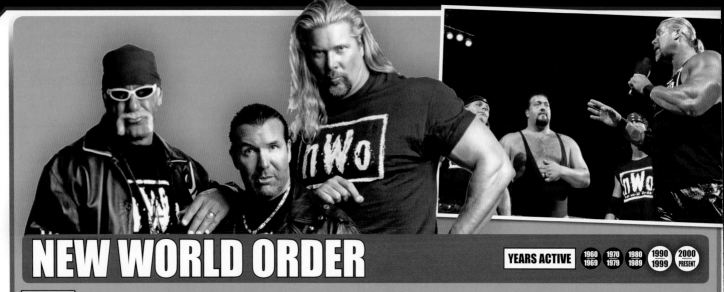

NEW WORLD ORDER

YEARS ACTIVE 1960–1969 | 1970–1979 | 1980–1989 | **1990–1999** | **2000–PRESENT**

MEMBERS Hollywood Hogan, Kevin Nash, Scott Hall, Big Show, X-Pac, Shawn Michaels, Booker T

There are a few things you can say about Mr. McMahon with complete certainty. He's a sports-entertainment icon. He's a brilliant businessman. He possesses superior physical strength. He's also made emotional decisions that lead others to question his sanity. The Chairman's questionable decision-making reached epic proportions in 2002 when rival Ric Flair assumed a leadership role within WWE. With the "Nature Boy" calling the shots, McMahon slipped into an uncontrollable depression, which caused him to diagnose WWE with, as he termed it, terminal cancer.

Unable to sit back and watch somebody else kill his creation, McMahon took matters into his own hands. With tears flowing from his eyes, a maniacal McMahon announced he was going to inject WWE with a lethal dose of poison, thus destroying the promotion before anybody else could. That lethal dose of poison? The New World Order (nWo).

In years prior to WWE's injection, the nWo ravaged WCW to the brink of destruction. Sporting more than twenty members, the rebellious faction turned a once profitable organization into a land of lawlessness. McMahon hoped the original members—Hollywood Hogan, Kevin Nash and Scott Hall—would do the same for WWE.

When the nWo arrived, they immediately targeted WWE's biggest names, Stone Cold Steve Austin and The Rock. In typical nWo fashion, they spray painted their initials onto Stone Cold's back, then used a gigantic tractor trailer to crush an ambulance carrying The Rock. The stunts set the stage for two huge *WrestleMania X8* matches. The nWo saw *WrestleMania* as their opportunity to chop down WWE's two most popular stars. By night's end, however, Stone Cold had defeated Hall, and The Rock beat Hogan. Realizing things weren't going as planned, Hall and Nash attacked Hogan, marking the end of his nWo involvement.

By all accounts, the nWo's *WrestleMania* efforts were seen as a colossal failure. In the months that followed, Hall & Nash attempted to recreate their WCW magic by recruiting ex-nWo members Big Show and X-Pac, as well as Booker T and Shawn Michaels, but their attempts proved futile and the faction soon disbanded.

Nicole Bass 🇺🇸

HT 6'2" **FROM** New York, New York

YEARS ACTIVE 1960–1969 | 1970–1979 | 1980–1989 | **1990–1999** | 2000–PRESENT

During her short WWE career, Nicole Bass proved to be a legitimate force in the Women's division. The massive Diva made her debut in March 1999, helping Sable defend the Women's Championship against Tori at *WrestleMania XV*. From there, she went on to manhandle nearly every female on the WWE roster, including Ivory, Debra and Jacqueline. Before she could string together any major victories, Bass abruptly disappeared from the WWE scene.

Nidia 🇵🇷

YEARS ACTIVE 1960–1969 | 1970–1979 | 1980–1989 | 1990–1999 | **2000–PRESENT**

HT 5'6" **FROM** Mayaguez, Puerto Rico

SIGNATURE MOVE DDT

A co-winner of the first season of *Tough Enough*, this former Diva debuted on *SmackDown* in 2002 and was revealed as the person sending letters to the Hurricane. Nidia began as a valet to her boyfriend, Jamie Noble, and demonstrated that behind every great man is an even better woman.

In time she also proved that her win on *Tough Enough* was no fluke in bouts against Torrie Wilson, Gail Kim, Dawn Marie, and Jazz. Considered a top contender for the Women's Championship, Nidia upped the ante when she showed her sexy side in the video release *Divas: Desert Heat*. In the spring of 2004 Nidia became a member of *Raw* but by November she left the company and retired from sports-entertainment shortly thereafter.

HT 6'4" **WT** 313 lbs. **FROM** The Soviet Union **SIGNATURE MOVE** The Russian Backbreaker **TITLE HISTORY** World Tag Team Champion

During his days behind the Iron Curtain, Nikolai Volkoff was a world-class amateur wrestler and bodybuilder. While attending a 1968 weightlifting competition in Vienna, Austria, Nikolai risked his life and said goodbye to everything he knew when he defected from the Soviet Union. He traveled to Calgary, Alberta, Canada and was trained for a life in the ring by legend Stu Hart. In 1970, Volkoff came to America with $50.00 in his pocket and one suit.

By 1974, Volkoff was a huge draw. A match against Bruno Sammartino broke the live gate attendance record at Madison Square Garden. During the mid 1970s, the hated Volkoff was involved in a near riot as he was discovered along with Killer Kowalski and Big John Studd to be part of the tag team championship tandem of the Executioners. After the deceptive trio was stripped of the titles, Volkoff split time between WWE, Japan and the regional territories of the NWA.

Volkoff brought the hammer and sickle of the Soviet Union with him wherever he went and demanded everyone stand as he sang the Russian National Anthem before each match.

In 1984, Nikolai returned to WWE as the first protégé of "Classy" Freddie Blassie. Blassie paired Volkoff with another anti-American rule-breaker, the Iron Sheik. As the duo spread panic throughout the United States, they became top contenders for the World Tag Team Championship. During the first championship match of the first *WrestleMania*, they defeated the U.S. Express and left New York City as champions. Their success continued to grow and on May 10, 1985 they appeared on the very first episode of *Saturday Night's Main Event*.

Following the loss of the title belts in June 1985, Nikolai focused on a return to singles action. On the October 3, 1985 episode of *Saturday Night's Main Event,* two Cold War Superpowers clashed when Nikolai challenged Hulk Hogan to a Flag Match for the WWE Championship. Volkoff then sparked a rivalry against former United States Armed Forces member Corporal Kirschner in a series of Flag Matches. After the retirement of Blassie, the managerial contractual rights for Volkoff and Iron Sheik were sold to WWE newcomer, Slick. After the "Doctor of Style" led them to a reunion at *WrestleMania III* against the Killer Bees, Nikolai and his Iranian ally soon parted ways.

Volkoff then aligned himself with another Russian monster, Boris Zhukov. With Slick in their corner, the two referred to themselves as the Bolsheviks. They were top tag title contenders and appeared at the first two *Survivor Series* events. The Russians had a violent split at *WrestleMania VI* after a humiliating 19-second loss to the Hart Foundation. As the former comrades battled, WWE fans witnessed the birth of a patriot.

During an episode of *The Brother Love Show*, newfound-friend "Hacksaw" Jim Duggan adopted Nikolai as a brother and they formed a team with the stars and stripes of the USA as their inspiration. Nikolai was then awarded a Medal of Honor from the National Boy Scouts for his contribution to world peace. Their winning ways continued as they toppled The Orient Express at *SummerSlam 1990*. Nikolai became a member of Duggan's victorious Alliance team at that November's *Survivor Series*. The two then took aim at Sgt. Slaughter when he turned his back on his country and became an Iraqi sympathizer during The Gulf War. Shortly afterward, Volkoff entered semi-retirement.

In 1995, Nikolai returned to WWE and broke the hearts of fans when he joined Ted DiBiase's Million Dollar Corporation as a low-level henchman for the greedy faction. Volkoff also appeared at *WrestleMania X-Seven*'s Gimmick Battle Royal and since then has appeared sporadically on WWE programming. In 2005, Nikolai's remarkable five-decade career was celebrated when he was inducted into the WWE Hall of Fame alongside several of his contemporaries, including former partner, the Iron Sheik.

Nikolai's combination of raw power and stunning agility were ahead of its time. He enraged fans all over the world and was a serious threat to the WWE Championship reigns of men like Bruno Sammartino, Bob Backlund, and Hulk Hogan.

Nikolai Volkoff undoubtedly contributed to the bright future of WWE and will be heralded as one of the greatest villains of all time. Now, please rise for the singing of the Russian National Anthem…

NO DISQUALIFICATION MATCH

One of the most popular and classic matches, in this contest, anything goes. Participants cannot be disqualified as a result of outside interference or illegal tactics. Superstars could throw the kitchen sink at each other without fear of repercussions. In most cases the only guideline to this type of bout is that the match must be decided by pinfall or submission in the ring.

October 17, 1999
Cleveland, OH - Gund Arena

Main Event: WWE Champion Triple H vs. Stone Cold Steve Austin, Anything Goes Match

October 22, 2000
Albany, NY - Pepsi Arena

Main Event: WWE Champion The Rock vs. Kurt Angle

October 21, 2001
St. Louis, MO - Savvis Center

Main Event: WWE Champion Stone Cold Steve Austin vs. Kurt Angle vs. Rob Van Dam, Triple Threat Match

October 20, 2002
Little Rock, AR - Alltel Arena

Main Event: WWE Champion Brock Lesnar vs. Undertaker, Hell in a Cell Match

October 19, 2003
Baltimore, MD - 1st Mariner Arena

Main Event: WWE Champion Brock

October 3, 2004
East Rutherford, NJ - Continental Airlines Arena

Main Event: WWE Champion JBL vs. Undertaker, Last Ride Match

October 9, 2005
Houston, TX - Toyota Center

Main Event: World Heavyweight Champion Batista vs. Eddie Guerrero

October 8, 2006
Raleigh, NC - RBC Center

Main Event: World Heavyweight Champion King Booker vs. Bobby Lashley vs. Finlay vs. Batista, Fatal Four Way Match

October 7, 2007
Rosemont, IL - Allstate Arena

Main Event: WWE Champion Triple H vs. Randy Orton, Last Man Standing Match

October 5, 2008
Portland, OR - Rose Gardens

Main Event: World Champion Chris Jericho vs. Shawn Michaels, Ladder Match

February 15, 1998
Houston, TX - Compaq Center

Main Event: Stone Cold Steve Austin, Cactus Jack, Chainsaw Charlie & Owen Hart vs. Triple H, Billy Gunn, Road Dogg & Savio Vega

February 27, 2000
Hartford, CT - Hartford Civic Center

Main Event: WWE Champion Triple H vs. Cactus Jack, Hell in a Cell Match

February 25, 2001
Las Vegas, NV - Thomas & Mack Center

Main Event: WWE Champion Kurt Angle vs. The Rock

February 17, 2002
Milwaukee, WI - Bradley Center

Main Event: WWE Champion Chris Jericho vs. Stone Cold Steve Austin

February 23, 2003
Montreal, Quebec, Canada - Bell Centre

Main Event: The Rock vs. Hulk Hogan

February 15, 2004
San Francisco, CA - Cow Palace

Main Event: WWE Champion Brock Lesnar vs. Eddie Guerrero

February 20, 2005
Pittsburgh, PA - Mellon Arena

Main Event: WWE Champion JBL vs. Big Show, Barbed Wire Steel Cage Match

February 19, 2006
Baltimore, MD - 1st Mariner Arena

Main Event: World Heavyweight Champion Kurt Angle vs. Undertaker

February 18, 2007
Los Angeles, CA - STAPLES Center

Main Event: WWE Champion John Cena & Shawn Michaels vs. World Heavyweight Champion Batista & Undertaker

February 17, 2008
Las Vegas, NV - Thomas & Mack Center

Main Event: Triple H vs. Jeff Hardy vs. Shawn Michaels vs. JBL vs. Chris Jericho vs. Umaga, Elimination Chamber Match

NORTH AMERICAN CHAMPIONSHIP

Despite being short-lived, the North American Heavyweight Championship is viewed by many historians as an important prize. In March 1979, after weeks of deliberation, the World Wrestling Federation Championship committee awarded Ted DiBiase the North American Heavyweight Championship.

Pat Patterson defeated Ted Dibiase on June 19, 1979. On September 1, 1979, Pat Patterson participated in a tournament held in Rio de Janiero, Brazil. His victory at the tournament unified the North American and South American Heavyweight Championships into the Intercontinental Championship. In November, 1979, Japanese wrestling star Seiji Sakaguchi resurrected the championship in Japan and defended the title until it was officially retired in April of 1981.

Nunzio

YEARS ACTIVE	1960 1969	1970 1979	1980 1989	**1990 1999**	2000 PRESENT

| **HT** | 5'7" | **WT** | 170 lbs. | **FROM** | Rockland County, New York | **SIGNATURE MOVE** | The Sicilian Slice |

TITLE HISTORY Cruiserweight Champion

To sports-entertainment fans of the extreme, this former Superstar looks familiar because in the mid-1990s he was a member of the Full Blooded Italians in the original ECW. Though the cultural make-up of the faction changed over time, he remained a constant and was a two-time ECW World Tag Team Champion with partners Tracy Smothers and Tony Mamaluke.

The fierce Nunzio debuted on *SmackDown* in 2002 and established himself as one of the most dangerous cruiserweights around. After a brief reformation of the FBI, he continued to challenge for the cruiserweight title. Nunzio had a reunion with the original FBI at 2005's *ECW One Night Stand*. On August 6, 2005 he defeated Paul London for the Cruiserweight Championship. In 2006, Nunzio went to the new Extreme Championship Wrestling. Over time, attempts to pump new life into the FBI met little success and in August 2008 Nunzio left World Wrestling Entertainment.

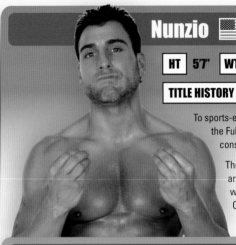

The Oddities

YEARS ACTIVE	1960 1969	1970 1979	1980 1989	**1990 1999**	2000 PRESENT

MEMBERS Giant Silva, Kurrgan, Golga, Insane Clown Posse, George "The Animal" Steele, Luna, Sable

All too often, today's judgmental society shuns individuals who may be deemed a little different. In 1998, however, a band of misfits made huge efforts towards reversing the norm when Golga, Kurrgan, and Giant Silva rallied together to form The Oddities.

Each member of The Oddities suffered from their own social shortcomings: The intellectually unstable Golga was forced to wear a mask to hide his deformed face, Kurrgan scared young children with his tree-like height and poor fashion sense, and Giant Silva, who was even taller than Kurrgan, was plain inaudible when he spoke. Despite these perceived handicaps, The Oddities proved that it was acceptable to cheer for a bunch of self-proclaimed sideshow freaks.

While fun-loving outside the ring, The Oddities were all business once the bell rang. Their most high-profile victory came at *SummerSlam 1998* when they overmatched the smaller Kaientai faction. After the match, the oddballs celebrated with their equally bizarre friends, Luna and the Insane Clown Posse, as well as a packed Madison Square Garden crowd.

In late 1998, Golga, Kurrgan, and Giant Silva were joined by the original oddity, George "The Animal" Steele. With the Hall of Famer by their side, The Oddities enjoyed their greatest success. Despite their newfound popularity, the curious combination disappeared from WWE soon after.

One Man Gang

YEARS ACTIVE	1960 1969	**1970 1979**	1980 1989	1990 1999	2000 PRESENT

| **HT** | 6'9" | **WT** | 450 lbs. | **FROM** | Halsted Street, Chicago, Illinois | **SIGNATURE MOVE** | 747 Splash |

In 1987, the "Dr. of Style" Slick brought one of the largest monsters to enter World Wrestling Entertainment. His destructive work was already known throughout the country, but the One Man Gang could not resist the opportunity for his dirty work to receive global exposure. The master of the 747 Splash was on a mission, and that mission was to destroy Hulkamania and all of those who supported it.

As One Man Gang pulled out all the stops in his matches, he began to show subtle signs of changes in behavior. In 1988 "Mean" Gene Okerlund went on special assignment to find out what was going down. Slick orchestrated a startling transformation and brought the spirit of Africa to WWE. As the lyrics of *Jive Soul Bro* pumped through his boom-box the man once known as One Man Gang was reborn and became Akeem, "the African Dream." He may have sported a new name, but his dedication to dismembering opponents never waivered.

He soon formed one of the largest teams in the history of sports-entertainment when he joined Big Boss Man to form the Twin Towers. These giants became obsessed with ending the careers of The Mega-Powers. Their attempts proved futile, and by the end of 1990, Akeem left WWE.

For the rest of the decade, One Man Gang made appearances in WCW, ECW, and in Japan. His last WWE appearance was in 2001 at the Gimmick Battle Royal during *WrestleMania X-7*. Whether he appeared as One Man Gang, or his soul brother #1 alter-ego Akeem, he was always an intimidating force in the ring.

June 12, 2005

New York, NY - Hammerstein Ballroom

Main Event: The Dudley Boyz vs. Tommy Dreamer & Sandman

June 11, 2006

New York, NY - Hammerstein Ballroom

Main Event: WWE Champion John Cena vs. Rob Van Dam

June 3, 2007

Jacksonville, FL - Veterans Memorial Arena

Main Event: WWE Champion John Cena vs. The Great Khali, Falls Count Anywhere Match

June 1, 2008

San Diego, CA - San Diego Sports Arena

Main Event: Edge vs. Undertaker, Vacant World Heavyweight Championship TLC Match

The original *One Night Stand* was a tribute to the original ECW but has since taken on a life of its own as a yearly WWE event.

Orient Express

YEARS ACTIVE 1960-1969 | 1970-1979 | 1980-1989 | **1990-1999** | 2000-PRESENT

MEMBERS Sato, Tanaka, Kato

In 1990, Mr. Fuji hand-picked the most deadly assassins from his homeland to spread terror amongst the world's greatest tag teams. Sato & Tanaka mixed under-handed tactics with martial-arts expertise to gain victories. The duo met the Rockers at *WrestleMania VI* and stole a count-out victory with assistance from their ceremonial salt. The Orient Express also took on Demolition, Hacksaw Jim Duggan & Nikolai Volkoff, the Hart Foundation, and the Legion of Doom. At *Survivor Series* they were hired by Sgt. Slaughter for his team of "Mercenaries."

Shortly after Sato returned to Japan, a third member was brought to the United States, Kato. This masked man brought power and speed to complement Tanaka's skills. By early 1992 the Orient Express returned to Japan. That was a day that WWE fans and Superstars rejoiced as they were finally safe from Fuji-orchestrated attacks at the hands of his ruthless tandem.

Orlando Jordan

YEARS ACTIVE 1960-1969 | 1970-1979 | 1980-1989 | 1990-1999 | **2000-PRESENT**

HT 6'4" **WT** 257 lbs. **FROM** Miami, Florida **SIGNATURE MOVE** Black Out

TITLE HISTORY United States Champion

For a brief period of time, Orlando Jordan was one of the most powerful Superstars on *SmackDown*. After aligning himself with JBL in August 2004, the Miami native quickly began to reap the benefits of making company with the WWE Champion. Serving as JBL's Chief of Staff, he found himself thrust into many high-profile matches.

In March 2005, Jordan picked up the biggest win of his career when he toppled John Cena on *SmackDown* to capture the coveted United States Championship. He went on to successfully defend the gold against *SmackDown*'s greatest competitors for more than five months.

Shortly after Jordan's United States Championship reign came to an end, so did his alliance with JBL. With the self-proclaimed "Wrestling God" no longer watching his back, Jordan struggled to find his way. By mid-2006, Jordan was gone from WWE entirely.

Outback Jack

YEARS ACTIVE 1960-1969 | 1970-1979 | **1980-1989** | 1990-1999 | 2000-PRESENT

HT 6'5" **WT** 300 lbs. **FROM** Humpty Doo, Australia **SIGNATURE MOVE** The Boomerang

In 1987 WWE welcomed a bushman from Australia's Northern Territory. Thanks to the survival skills learned after years with the Aborigines, Outback feared nothing—not even a saltwater croc! To prepare fans for his arrival video segments showed Jack in the Australian outback, training for his much anticipated debut.

When it came time to step through the ropes Outback Jack did not disappoint. The Boomerang, a modified version of the dangerous Enzui Lariat, put all Superstars on notice. Australia's favorite son battled against the likes of Barry Horowitz, "Iron" Mike Sharpe, Jim Neidhart, "Million Dollar Man" Ted DiBiase, and Ravishing Rick Rude.

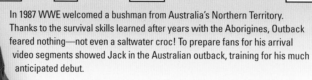

"Outlaw" Ron Bass

| HT | 6'4" | WT | 289 lbs. |

FROM Houston, Texas

SIGNATURE MOVE

Kneeling Facebuster

YEARS ACTIVE

During the 1970s Bass debuted in the National Wrestling Alliance and became quickly known as one of the toughest men around. In the 1980s he formed a successful team with fellow future WWE Superstar, Black Bart. In early 1987 Bass brought his Texan violence to WWE and threatened to end Hulkamania. Bass took on the likes of "Leapin'" Lanny Poffo, Corporal Kirschner, SD "Special Delivery" Jones, Koko B. Ware, Outback Jack, and Blackjack Mulligan.

The "Outlaw" thrived on dishing out pain and often lifted beaten opponents during the referees count to further the onslaught. His cold-blooded tenure in WWE is most remembered by his barbarous attack on Brutus "the Barber" Beefcake. Bass jumped Brutus from behind and choked him before he raked the spur from his boot across Beefcake's forehead. The attack and resulting injury left Beefcake out of action for weeks, and cost him a shot at the Intercontinental Championship at *SummerSlam 1988*. By April 1989 Bass left WWE, then retired from the ring in 1991.

OWEN HART

| HT | 5'10" | WT | 227 lbs. | **FROM** | Calgary, Alberta, Canada |

SIGNATURE MOVE Sharpshooter

TITLE HISTORY World Tag Team Champion, Intercontinental Champion, European Champion

YEARS ACTIVE

Growing up in the famed Hart wrestling family, Owen Hart could have relied on the clan's storied reputation to open doors for him. Rather than ride his family's name to the top, he paved his own path to greatness by developing one of the most technically sound offensive arsenals of all time.

Owen's career skyrocketed in 1994 after turning on his brother, Bret. The move proved unpopular with fans, but ultimately served as a launching pad for the younger Hart to finally break free from his sibling's overwhelming shadow. Owen finally accomplished his goal when he defeated Bret in their classic *WrestleMania X* showdown.

THE BLUE BLAZER

In August 1988, the Blue Blazer lit up rings with a never-before-seen blend of aerial assaults, speed, and expert grappling techniques. The masked superhero moved as if he was from another galaxy and immediately brought fans to their feet before each match as he landed in the ring via a top rope Moonsault.

At the second *Survivor Series* he was part of the winning team captained by the Ultimate Warrior. At *Wrestlemania V,* Blue Blazer had a match with Mr. Perfect that kept fans on the edge of their seats. He vanished from the WWE in 1989, but returned in the 1990s to remind fans to train, say their prayers, and drink their milk.

Following his victory over Bret, Owen began to compile an impressive list of accolades, starting with the *King of the Ring* crown in June 1994, capturing the European Championship, and two reigns as Intercontinental Champion.

Despite drawing the wrath of fans for his in-ring trickery, Owen developed a respectable reputation among his fellow Superstars. In fact, his impeccable approach to performing made him a popular tag team partner among his peers.

A tragic accident claimed the life of Owen Hart on May 23, 1999. The loss of such a great man has left a void that can never be filled. The memory of Owen's technical brilliance inside the ring and his kind, jovial nature out of it will endure in the hearts and minds of WWE fans everywhere.

Owen Hart & Yokozuna

| **COMBINED WEIGHT** | 827 lbs. |

TITLE HISTORY

World Tag Team Champions

YEARS ACTIVE

Owen Hart announced Yokozuna as his mystery partner just moments before challenging the Smokin' Gunns for the World Tag Team Championship at *WrestleMania XI*. Though they had no experience working together as a team, Hart & Yokozuna used their size advantage to unseat the longtime partners. Over the next five months, Hart and Yokozuna turned back all challengers.

When Owen Hart was supposedly unable to compete at *In Your House III*, Davey Boy Smith stepped in as Yokozuna's partner against WWE Champion Diesel & Intercontinental Champion Shawn Michaels. Towards the latter stages of the match, Hart interjected himself into the match. Diesel pinned Hart and the referee awarded the World Tag Team Championship to the challengers. The next night Clarence Mason claimed the titles could not change hands because Hart was not a legal participant in the match. Mason's eloquence persuaded the WWE to return the titles to Hart & Yokozuna. However, the emotional rollercoaster of the past twenty-four hours took its toll on the team, as they lost the titles to the Smokin' Gunns approximately one hour later. Following the loss, Yokozuna focused his attention on a singles career, while Hart formed a successful team with Davey Boy Smith.

Pampero Firpo

| HT | 5'9" | WT | 225 lbs. | FROM | Buenos Aires, Argentina | SIGNATURE MOVE | El Garfio |

Pampero Firpo was one of the original horrors of sports-entertainment. The mighty madman from the pampas of Argentina first appeared on the scene in the early 1950s. As if he was summoned from the Stone Age, Firpo's body was covered in his natural fur, while a bushy beard and wild hair obscured his head.

In 1960 he appeared in Capitol Wrestling Company and became known as a loathsome figure who was more concerned with hurting an opponent than winning a match. The wild bull vanished from the Northeast territory and traveled throughout the National Wrestling Alliance. The peculiar Pampero re-appeared in WWE in 1972 and once again took aim at fan-favorites. Firpo often screamed during his matches and became the first figure to coin the phrase "Ohh yeah!" during his fits of rage in and out of the ring. He departed again for the NWA where his wild wrath continued to earn him regional championships. His last match of public record was in October 1986 for Carlos Colon's WWC promotion in Puerto Rico. There was never any love lost between this deranged individual and other Superstars. Today words like "extreme" and "hardcore" would be used to describe Firpo's ring style and behavior.

Papa Shango

| HT | 6'6" | WT | 330 lbs. | FROM | Parts Unknown | SIGNATURE MOVE | Shoulder Breaker |

A master of voodoo, Papa Shango first began casting his mysterious spells in 1992. With a menacing skull painted over his entire face and a terrifying threat of black magic, the bizarre Superstar quickly became one of the most feared men on the WWE roster.

Though Papa Shango's time in WWE only lasted a little more than a year, he will forever be remembered for the reign of terror he unleashed on many of the promotion's biggest names, including Ultimate Warrior. Showing no fear of the former WWE Champion, Shango unleashed several supernatural spells that forced Ultimate Warrior to mysteriously double over in pain and excrete an ominous black liquid from his skull.

Unfortunately for Papa Shango, his dark voodoo rarely translated into wins. Despite standing 6' 6" and possessing a devastating shoulder breaker, Shango struggled against WWE's top-tier talent. Tito Santana, Bob Backlund, and Bret "Hit Man" Hart all picked up victories over Shango during his short tenure. In April 1993, Papa Shango strangely disappeared from the WWE scene. While nobody is certain of his whereabouts, it's safe to say the entire locker room was happy to see him go.

Pat Patterson

| HT | 6'1" | WT | 237 lbs. | FROM | Montreal, Quebec, Canada |

| TITLE HISTORY | Intercontinental Champion, Hardcore Champion, North American Champion |

After an accomplished 20 years spent competing in Montreal, San Francisco, and the Minneapolis-based AWA, Pat Patterson made his WWE debut in 1979. What followed was one of the most remarkable Hall of Fame careers of all time.

Shortly after entering WWE, Patterson made history when he won a September 1979 tournament to become the first-ever Intercontinental Champion. He held the title proudly for seven months before losing to Ken Patera in New York City. Many credit Patterson's tireless efforts in the ring for adding legitimacy to the title during its infancy.

After solidifying the Intercontinental Championship's strong foundation, Patterson engaged in one of WWE's most brutal rivalries. For much of 1981, Patterson and Sgt. Slaughter bled buckets during a vicious series of Boot Camp Matches. Their bloody rivalry culminated in the famed Madison Square Garden when Patterson defeated Slaughter in an Alley Fight that is considered one of the most brutal matches in WWE history. After hanging up his boots in 1984, Patterson continued to be a prominent WWE force working as an announcer and official. As a respected decision-maker, Patterson is credited with creating the Royal Rumble match.

The Patriot

| HT | 6'5" | WT | 275 lbs. | FROM | Columbia, South Carolina | SIGNATURE MOVE | Patriot Missile |

This man who carried the stars and stripes began his career in the early 1990s. While he made a name for himself within regional circles and even won the 1991 "Most Inspirational Wrestler of The Year Award" from *Pro Wrestling Illustrated*, he wanted to take his message of freedom to the masses.

The Patriot made his WWE debut in July, 1997 and defended the honor of America in every match. He rose through the ranks quickly and won a 20-man over-the-top-rope battle royal. The highlight of his WWE career was when he pinned Bret "Hit Man" Hart on the July 28th episode of *Monday Night Raw*. Unfortunately later that year he suffered a severe back injury that forced him to retire from the ring. Though his time in the spotlight was brief, the Patriot fought for all that was good about the American way. The fans of WWE will never forget his spirit and how he inspired everyone to be the best American they can be.

PAUL BEARER

In the words of WWE Chairman Vince McMahon, "Paul Bearer is the most unique manager in the history of the business." That's exactly what fans discovered as this creepy individual made his way to World Wrestling Entertainment in 1991. Taking over the managerial duties of Undertaker from Brother Love, this licensed mortician was the keeper of the urn from which the "Deadman" drew a mysterious power. Bearer was also often the first one seen coming through the curtain as the frightening chords of Undertaker's music haunted venues around the world.

Bearer and Undertaker embarked on a campaign of destruction, targetting WWE Superstars. The duo often reached mainstream media as seen during appearances on the *Live With Regis & Kathy Lee* television program. Paul also utilized WWE programming for his own cryptic predictions on the talk segment, *The Funeral Parlor*. The famous funeral director was also a key contributor and architect for WWE's scariest type of encounter, the Casket Match. Over the years, Bearer had periods away from the "Deadman" and managed those who opposed him such as Mankind, the Executioner, and Vader, and introduced the world to Undertaker's brother, Kane.

After an extended sabbatical from WWE, Bearer made his historic return to accompany Undertaker at *WrestleMania XX* as he fought Kane. Months later at *The Great American Bash*, Bearer was victimized by Paul Heyman. As the fate of the legendary urn rested in Heyman's hands and Undertaker faced the Dudley Boys, Bearer was encased in glass with cement up to his chest. After Undertaker's victory, he was left no choice but to pull the lever and cover his longtime manager in cement. The keeper of the urn has not been seen on WWE programming ever since.

Paul Bearer was in the death business, and business was often good. Bearer always reminded audiences to have faith in his Undertaker, and that he would always be with us whether he is seen or not. Perhaps the same can be said for the prognosticator of doom himself? Believe it, if you dare.

Paul Burchill

HT	6'4"	WT	247 lbs.	FROM	Chelsea, England

SIGNATURE MOVE	Reverse Swinging Neckbreaker

YEARS ACTIVE	1960-1969	1970-1979	1980-1989	1990-1999	2000 PRESENT

This Superstar was introduced to World Wrestling Entertainment by mentor William Regal on *SmackDown*. Regal trained this British bruiser in the grappling arts and various methods of submission wrestling to be prepared for the numerous fighting styles he would encounter in WWE.

Burchill's fury in matches against the likes of Super Crazy, Mr. Kennedy, Jeff Hardy, and Kofi Kingston lead to his moniker "the Ripper." After recovering from injuries, Burchill debuted on *Raw* in February 2008 alongside his sister, the beautiful and sadistic Katie Lea. Burchill. Burchill is poised to inflict excruciating pain on foes for years to come and become a top player in the world of sports-entertainment.

Paul Ellering

Despite only being in WWE for a brief period of time, Paul Ellering will forever be remembered by sports-entertainment fans around the world as the loud-mouthed manager of arguably the greatest tag team of all time, Legion of Doom.

Ellering introduced himself to WWE fans in 1992 when he reunited with Hawk & Animal following a brief separation. Unfortunately, the reunion didn't go quite as planned. Ellering failed to gain fans after showing up at ringside with a ventriloquist dummy named Rocco. He left WWE shortly after his debut.

Six years later, Ellering's popularity sank even more when he returned to WWE to manage LOD's chief rivals, the Disciples of Apocalypse. Ellering successfully led his new duo to victory over LOD at *Fully Loaded* in July 1998. A few months later, however, Hawk & Animal teamed with Droz to get their revenge when they defeated Ellering & DOA at *Judgment Day*.

Unfortunately, Ellering's time in WWE failed to mirror the amazing success he achieved as LOD's longtime friend and manager. While he never gained greatness inside WWE rings, the annals of sports-entertainment will forever recognize Ellering as one of the game's brightest minds.

Paul Heyman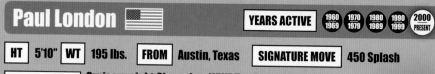

Perhaps no personality in the history of the ring was more anti-establishment than Paul Heyman. Whether it was as Paul E. Dangerously, the manager, or as a general manager or even a promoter, the rebellious New Yorker's counterculture approach to the industry made him one of the most controversial figures of all time.

After breaking into the business as a photographer, Heyman's big break came in the mid-1980s when he landed a managerial job. His first high-profile clients were Tommy Rich and Austin Idol. Over the course of his managerial career, the diabolical Heyman went on to represent many of the game's greatest names, including a young Steve Austin.

Heyman's career took a fateful turn in 1993 when he took his managerial game to Eastern Championship Wrestling. Within months of his arrival, Heyman became one of the most powerful personalities backstage, and the promotion was renamed Extreme Championship Wrestling. By the end of 1996, he had secured full control of the promotion from then-owner Tod Gordon. Under Heyman, ECW mixed hardcore action and fast-paced technical grappling with popular music to North American fans.

Despite its popularity, financial woes ultimately claimed ECW in 2001. Following its closing, Heyman emerged in WWE, where he served as an announcer, manager, and even General Manager of *SmackDown*. After the success of *ECW One Night Stand* pay-per-views in 2005 and 2006, Mr. McMahon had no choice but to reinvent the brand with Heyman back at the controls. The "Messiah of ECW" spent the next several months rebuilding his creation.

Paul London

HT	5'10"	**WT**	195 lbs.	**FROM**	Austin, Texas	**SIGNATURE MOVE**	450 Splash

YEARS ACTIVE 1960-1969 | 1970-1979 | 1980-1989 | 1990-1999 | 2000-PRESENT

TITLE HISTORY Cruiserweight Champion, WWE Tag Team Champion, World Tag Team Champion

This eccentric high-flyer is as innovative in the ring as it gets. Audiences have been captivated by this Superstar since his October 2003 debut. London is known for innovative moves like the "Dropsault" (a Moonsault and a Drop-Kick), "Mushroom Stomp" (he leaps from the middle rope over a charging opponent, then presses his feet off their back, pushing them into the corner and then lands on his feet), and the 450 Splash.

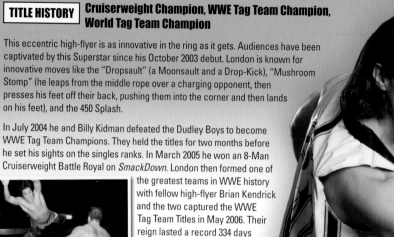

In July 2004 he and Billy Kidman defeated the Dudley Boys to become WWE Tag Team Champions. They held the titles for two months before he set his sights on the singles ranks. In March 2005 he won an 8-Man Cruiserweight Battle Royal on *SmackDown*. London then formed one of the greatest teams in WWE history with fellow high-flyer Brian Kendrick and the two captured the WWE Tag Team Titles in May 2006. Their reign lasted a record 334 days as champions. London's partner eventually turned his back on him, and he was drafted #1 to *Raw* in the 2007 Supplemental Draft.

Paul London & Brian Kendrick

COMBINED WEIGHT	380 lbs.	**YEARS ACTIVE**	1960-1969 · 1970-1979 · 1980-1989 · 1990-1999 · 2000-PRESENT

TITLE HISTORY World Tag Team Champions, WWE Tag Team Champions

To look down upon Paul London & Brian Kendrick for their relative lack of size would be to underestimate one of WWE's most athletic tandems. Sure, they never had the muscles of a Batista or the height of a Kane, but what they lacked in size, they more than made up for in cat-like quickness and an amazing aerial assault.

London & Kendrick briefly worked together in 2003, but it wasn't until they reunited in 2005 that the high-flying tandem began to realize their true potential. Sporting theatrical masks to the ring, the eccentric duo made short work of such *SmackDown* tag teams as Gymini and William Regal & Paul Burchill. Despite their impressive record, London & Kendrick weren't afforded an opportunity at true glory until the following year.

Starting in February 2006, London & Kendrick tore off five straight non-title victories over WWE Tag Team Champions MNM. Finally, at *Judgment Day 2006*, they upended the champs when it counted, giving London his second reign with the tile and Kendrick his first. They went on to hold the gold for nearly one year, longer than any other *SmackDown* team in history.

London & Kendrick were drafted from *SmackDown* to *Raw* in June 2007. The new address failed to slow the quick combination, who picked up where they left off when they captured the World Tag Team Championship while on tour in South Africa.

PAUL ORNDORFF

| HT | 6' | WT | 252 lbs. | FROM | Brandon, Florida | SIGNATURE MOVE | Piledriver |

YEARS ACTIVE 1960-1969 · 1970-1979 · 1980-1989 · 1990-1999 · 2000-PRESENT

"Mr. Wonderful" was an amazing athlete even before he trained for a career in sports-entertainment. A student of Hiro Matsuda, Orndorff applied what he learned in the NWA and was quickly noticed for his intensity, skill, and devastating piledriver.

Orndorff made his WWE debut in 1984. He associated with the likes of "Dr. D" David Schultz, "Rowdy" Roddy Piper, and "Cowboy" Bob Orton. Orndorff was selected to participate in the main event of the original *WrestleMania* against Hulk Hogan & Mr.T. His team lost the match after an Orton miscue. In the months following, Piper and Orton deserted him in the ring. He formed a bond with the Hulkster but eventually double-crossed the WWE Champion and ignited one of the most physical rivalries wrestling has ever seen. Their encounter in front of 76,000 fans at Toronto's CNE Stadium left no clear winner, so they met inside a 15-foot high Steel Cage in January, 1987 on *Saturday Night's Main Event*.

Orndorff took a hiatus from the ring, then returned with Sir Oliver Humperdink guiding his career. One of the first things he did was reconcile with Hogan and was a member of his team at the first-ever *Survivor Series*.

In 1990 he appeared in World Championship Wrestling, but a serious neck injury forced Orndorff to retire in 1996. He then became the lead trainer for WCW's Power Plant before retiring in 2000. The night before *WrestleMania 21,* the three decade career of "Mr. Wonderful" was honored as he was inducted into the WWE Hall of Fame.

Paul Roma

YEARS ACTIVE 1960-1969 · 1970-1979 · 1980-1989 · 1990-1999 · 2000-PRESENT

| HT | 5'11" | WT | 235 lbs. | FROM | Kensington, New York |

| SIGNATURE MOVE | Flying Cross Body |

This Superstar was first seen by WWE audiences in 1984, and his impressive physique and good looks quickly brought him a great deal of attention. He also became known for throwing one of the greatest dropkicks in all of sports-entertainment. In 1987 Roma became one-half of an exciting duo known as the Young Stallions. Roma and partner Jim Powers were top contenders for the World Tag Team Championship and, along with the Killer Bees, were the sole survivors at the inaugural *Survivor Series*.

The team disbanded in 1990 when Roma changed his ways and formed Power & Glory with Hercules, but that team disbanded in late 1991. Roma shocked the wrestling world in 1993 when he debuted in WCW as the fourth member of the legendary stable, the Four Horsemen. He left WCW in 1995 and after a brief return to WWE in 1997, Roma retired from the ring to pursue other interests. Today he trains ring hopefuls at his wrestling school in Connecticut.

PEDRO MORALES

YEARS ACTIVE 1960/1969 1970/1979 1980/1989 1990/1999 2000/PRESENT

| **HT** | 5'11" | **WT** | 240 lbs | **FROM** | Culebra, Puerto Rico |

TITLE HISTORY WWE Champion, World Tag Team Champion, Intercontinental Champion

While rarely mentioned in the same breath as Bruno Sammartino, Hulk Hogan, or Triple H, Pedro Morales' accomplishments are the equal of any Superstar to ever lace a pair of boots. Over the course of his nearly thirty years in the ring, the Puerto Rican legend captured the WWE, World Tag Team, and Intercontinental Championships, making him the first-ever Triple Crown Champion.

Morales made his professional debut in 1959. Still only a teenager, he spent much of his time competing on smaller cards around the New York area. It wasn't until 1963 that he made his Madison Square Garden debut, teaming with his boyhood hero Miguel Perez. As he slowly started to make a name for himself, it wasn't long before promotions nationwide were looking to add him to their rosters.

Morales eventually settled in Los Angeles and in 1971, he jumped to WWE making his debut on the same card that saw Sammartino's nearly eight-year WWE Championship reign come to an end. A mere three weeks later, Morales defeated Ivan Koloff to claim the WWE Championship, an honor he held for nearly three years. Only Sammartino, Hogan, and Bob Backlund held the championship longer.

With the title in his grasp, Morales became a hero to the large number of Puerto Rican fans living in the Northeast. In August 1980, he gave his passionate fan base even more reason to celebrate when he teamed with Bob Backlund to capture the World Tag Team Championship. Later that year, he completed the trifecta when he won his first of two Intercontinental Championships. The win made Morales the first-ever Triple Crown Champion, paving the way for future champions such as Bret Hart, Shawn Michaels, and Edge.

In 1995, Morales was honored as one of WWE's all-time elite when he was inducted into the WWE Hall of Fame by fellow Puerto Rican Superstar Savio Vega.

Perry Saturn

YEARS ACTIVE 1960/1969 1970/1979 1980/1989 1990/1999 2000/PRESENT

| **HT** | 5'10" | **WT** | 241 lbs. | **FROM** | Boston, Massachusettes |

SIGNATURE MOVE Death Valley Driver **TITLE HISTORY** European Champion, Hardcore Champion

Perry Saturn's elevator didn't go to the top floor. Whether he realized it or not, that's exactly why WWE fans loved him. It didn't matter if he was declaring his love for a mop or uttering the term "you're welcome" for no apparent reason, audiences couldn't wait to see what he would do next. When Saturn arrived in WWE alongside the Radicalz, it was easy for him to hide his less-than-impressive intellect behind his partners' superior wit. Shortly after the faction disbanded, the true Saturn was exposed. Despite his simple mind, the muscular Boston native was a legitimate powerhouse inside the ring. His extreme approach to competition, which he cultivated in ECW, lead him to two Hardcore Championship victories. He also defeated former Radicalz teammate Eddie Guerrero for the European Championship in July 2000. While Saturn's powerful Death Valley Driver certainly carried him to great heights in the ring, it was his love affair with a cleaning tool that fans will forever remember. In the summer of 2000, the tattooed Superstar dumped his beautiful girlfriend Terri in favor of, believe it or not, a mop. The relationship took a destructive turn when an upset Terri abducted the mop and threw it into a wood chipper. The broken-hearted Saturn was never able to rebound from the loss and left WWE the following year.

Pete Sanchez

YEARS ACTIVE

| **HT** | 6' | **WT** | 279 lbs. | **FROM** | San Juan, Puerto Rico | **SIGNATURE MOVE** | Cannonball |

A popular figure from the early days of World Wrestling Entertainment, Pete Sanchez was known throughout the northeast as a fiery competitor who excelled in both singles and tag team competition. Through the 1960s and 1970s Sanchez took on the likes of Crusher Verdu, the Mongols, Pampero Firpo, Stan Stasiak, Gorilla Monsoon, Blackjack Mulligan, and "Superstar" Billy Graham. He even locked-up with Ric Flair in the "Nature Boy's" WWE and Madison Square Garden debut in 1976.

Pete Sanchez continued to appear on WWE events until 1992 and remained one of the most respected journeymen to compete in the ring. Along with his opponents, Sanchez helped build the foundation to what today is the greatest sports-entertainment company in the world. With a career that spanned nearly three decades, Pete Sanchez's longevity in World Wrestling Entertainment is an accomplishment matched by few Superstars.

Peter Maivia

| HT | 5'9" | WT | 275 lbs. |

FROM The Isle of Samoa

SIGNATURE MOVE Samoan Stump Puller

YEARS ACTIVE

Sports-entertainment has had several influential families that have produced great competitors. Perhaps none is greater than the dynasty of "High Chief" Peter Maivia whose wrestling family includes his blood brothers in the Anoa'i family, his son-in-law Rocky Johnson, and his grandson, The Rock.

In early 1960, Peter moved to New Zealand to train under Steve Rickard. Maivia's charisma, toughness, power, and surprising speed led him to many championships throughout the South Pacific. Maivia also made time for Hollywood as he appeared in the 1967 James Bond film, *You Only Live Twice*. He arrived on the American mainland in 1970. He held different versions of the NWA World Tag Team Titles with Chief Billy White Wolf, Ray Stevens, and Pat Patterson.

After a brief stop in Texas, Maivia debuted in the WWE in 1977. Fans were drawn to his ring presence and the ancient Samoan tribal tattoos that covered most of his body. Maivia was a genuine Samoan High Chief and fought for the pride of his people every time he entered the ring. In 1978 Maivia broke the hearts of people everywhere when he turned on friends Chief Jay Strongbow and Bob Backlund. Managed by "Classy" Freddie Blassie, Maivia became one of the most despised men in all of sports-entertainment.

Sadly, Maivia was diagnosed with cancer in 1981, and tragically passed away in June 1982 at the age of 45. Peter Maivia created a legacy that inspired an entire culture and brought sports-entertainment some of its most storied warriors. What he began continues to live on today in the mind, body, and spirit of both his people and his fans around the world.

Pez Whatley

| HT | 5'10" | WT | 245 lbs. |

FROM Chattanooga, Tennessee

SIGNATURE MOVE The Flying Headbutt

YEARS ACTIVE 1960-1969 1970-1979 1980-1989 **1990-1999** 2000-PRESENT

This Superstar and "Pistol" was the first-ever African American amateur wrestler at the University of Tennessee at Chattanooga. Whatley made his WWE debut in 1990 and brought the fight to Superstars like "Ravishing" Rick Rude, "Million Dollar Man" Ted DiBiase, Tito Santana, "Rowdy" Roddy Piper, and Mr. Perfect. Pez left WWE in March of 1991 and returned to the ring in Japan and Amercian independents before landing in WCW. He retired from active competition in 1995 and became a trainer at WCW's Power Plant.

Sadly, in January 2005 Pez passed away following complications from a heart attack. Pez Whatley will be regarded as one of the toughest and most entertaining individuals in all of sports-entertainment history.

Phantasio

| HT | 6'3" | WT | 235 lbs. |

YEARS ACTIVE 1960-1969 1970-1979 1980-1989 **1990-1999** 2000-PRESENT

A master illusionist, Phantasio made his WWE debut on *Wrestling Challenge* in July 1995. Following a few awe-inspiring magic tricks, the WWE newcomer made short work of his opposition. After the match, the magic continued when Phantasio mysteriously removed the referee's striped underwear, despite the fact that the official was still wearing his pants.

With a 1-0 professional record to his credit, Phantasio strangely disappeared from WWE, never to be seen again. Legend claims he was the victim of a magic trick gone bad.

PIPER'S PIT

In a daring 1984 experiment, WWE executives gave noted loudmouth "Rowdy" Roddy Piper a microphone and the platform to say whatever was in his mind. The move resulted in the creation of *Piper's Pit*, the most historic interview segment in sports-entertainment history.

Despite "Hot Rod's" unfavorable approval rating, *Piper's Pit* proved to be extremely popular with fans, as they recognized the segment as the home of WWE's wackiest moments. Early in the segment's existence, Piper lured Jimmy "Superfly" Snuka to the *Pit* where he proceeded to savagely beat him with a coconut. The shocking act proved to be the first of many controversial scenes on *Piper's Pit*.

In the years that followed, many other fan favorites became victimized on the set of *Piper's Pit*. In the weeks leading up to Piper's boxing match with Mr. T at *WrestleMania 2*, Hot Rod and his bodyguard "Cowboy" Bob Orton abducted the actor's midget wrestler friend Haiti Kid. They then dragged him to the *Piper's Pit* set where they forcefully shaved his head to resemble Mr. T's unique look.

The most-noted moment in *Piper's Pit* history also helped set the stage for arguably WWE's greatest match. In early 1987, whispers of an alliance between Andre the Giant and Bobby Heenan began to circulate. The alleged union would assuredly mark the end of Andre's well-publicized friendship with Hulk Hogan. Unable to accept the rumors, Hulk Hogan appeared on *Piper's Pit* in an attempt to learn the truth. Hogan realized his worst fears when Andre confirmed his alliance with Heenan, then tore Hogan's *Hulkamania* T-shirt and crucifix from his body. The following month, the Hulkster gained a measure of revenge when he toppled Andre at *WrestleMania III*.

Piper's Pit was shelved following "Hot Rod's" first retirement from sports-entertainment in 1987. Since that time, the *Pit's* set has only been dusted off for use on WWE's biggest events, including *WrestleMania V* (with guest Morton Downey, Jr.) and *WrestleMania 21* (with guest Stone Cold Steve Austin).

Pitbulls

MEMBERS	Kid Kash, Jamie Noble	COMBINED WEIGHT	402 lbs.

YEARS ACTIVE 1960-1969 • 1970-1979 • 1980-1989 • 1990-1999 • **2000 PRESENT**

In June 2006 two former Cruiserweight Champions joined forces to ambush the tag team division on *SmackDown*. Wearing dog collars, barking, biting opponents, and attacking anything that moved in the ring, these Pitbulls were vicious and out for blood. In addition to an aggressive style, Kash and Noble displayed great speed and teamwork while showing no regard for the rules of the ring.

They battled the Mexicools and then-WWE Tag Team Champions Brian Kendrick & Paul London, and in a brief period of time became top title contenders. The Pitbulls went their own way that September when Kid Kash left World Wrestling Entertainment. While some fans are disappointed that the team never realized their full potential, tag teams throughout World Wrestling Entertainment are happy they no longer have to worry about the bite of the Pitbulls.

PJ Walker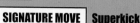

HT	6'	WT	229 lbs.	FROM	New York City

SIGNATURE MOVE	Superkick

YEARS ACTIVE 1960-1969 • 1970-1979 • 1980-1989 • **1990-1999** • 2000-PRESENT

Identified as a top prospect in the early 1990s, PJ Walker was seen on *Monday Night Raw*, and *Wrestling Challenge*. Walker was an accomplished grappler with speed, grit, and superior ring technique thanks to his training in Stu Hart's Dungeon.

As fans chanted his name, PJ took on anyone who had an open contract including Diesel, Yokozuna, Jeff Jarrett, Bam Bam Bigelow, and Undertaker. The highlight of his WWE tenure was when he beat Irwin R. Schyster on *Raw*. Walker left World Wrestling Entertainment in early 1994 to pursue other professional endeavors.

PMS

Fresh off unsuccessful romances with Marc Mero and Goldust, respectively, Jacqueline and Terri joined forces in November 1998 to exact revenge on WWE's male Superstars. Calling themselves Pretty Mean Sisters, or PMS, they used their sensuality as a weapon, using their curves, sex appeal, and questionable tactics to get what they wanted from male Superstars.

MEMBERS Terri, Jacqueline, Ryan Shamrock

Val Venis, the duo's first victim, was told he had impregnated Terri. The shocking news caused the former adult film star to run for the hills. However, PMS was not done milking the pregnancy for all it was worth. Shortly after Terri announced she was with child, D-Lo Brown accidentally knocked the mother-to-be off the ring apron, causing her to miscarry (it was later revealed that she was never pregnant in the first place). As payback, PMS forced Brown to be their servant.

The following year, Ryan Shamrock joined the sexually-charged faction. Together, the threesome adopted Meat as their sex slave. They worked the young Superstar so hard that he was too exhausted when it came time to compete, which might explain his lackluster won-loss record.

Power & Glory

MEMBERS Hercules, Paul Roma   **COMBINED WEIGHT** 519 lbs.

The "Dr. Of Style" Slick brought a new era to tag team wrestling in July 1990 when the mighty Hercules (who represented power) and Paul Roma (glory) looked for guidance as these two rule-breakers told off fans and former friends and lived by the motto, nice guys finish last.

Hercules & Roma were devastating together in the ring as they battled for supremacy and the World Tag Team Championship. They clashed with the likes of the Rockers, the Hart Foundation, and the Legion of Doom. Power & Glory often teamed in six-man action with another Slick client, the Warlord. After disappointing losses and mounting frustration, the pair split in 1991.

Powers of Pain

MEMBERS Warlord, Barbarian   **COMBINED WEIGHT** 618 lbs.

The story of the Powers of Pain is puzzling, at best. They had the look. They had the size. They even had the speed. With all these physical gifts, it is surprising that the sum of all their advantages didn't equate to championships.

Warlord & Barbarian joined WWE in 1988, following a especially successful year competing in NWA's Mid-Atlantic territory. Managed by the Baron (Baron von Raschke), the Powers of Pain quickly became favorites with the fans, who were enamored by the team's immense size and colorful face paint. The team's popularity propelled them into a lengthy rivalry with the World Tag Team Champions, Demolition.

Following several unsuccessful attempts to wrest the gold away from Ax & Smash, the Powers of Pain lured Mr. Fuji to their side. Bringing the devious manager into their camp proved unpopular with the fans, but Warlord & Barbarian saw it as an opportunity to capture the elusive World Tag Team Championship. Unfortunately, however, not even the great Mr. Fuji could lead the Powers of Pain to the titles. In 1990, after failing to achieving any success with Warlord & Barbarian, Fuji sold them separately to Slick and Bobby Heenan respectively. The sale marked the end of the Powers of Pain.

Primo

HT 5'10" **WT** 218 lbs. **FROM** San Juan, Puerto Rico   **TITLE HISTORY** WWE Tag Team Champion

Primo has some huge shoes to fill. Not only is he the younger brother of decorated Superstar Carlito, but he's also the son of Puerto Rican wrestling legend Carlos Colon. Despite all the demands that go along with being a member of the Colon wrestling family, Primo appears unfazed by the pressure.

It didn't take long for Primo to prove his worth in WWE. Only one month after making his successful debut against Charlie Haas in August 2008, the agile Puerto Rican Superstar teamed with his brother to capture the WWE Tag Team Championship from Zack Ryder & Curt Hawkins. Few Superstars have made a more immediate impact than Primo, and with many more years of active competition ahead of him, there's no telling the heights he may reach.

Prof. Toru Tanaka

HT 5'11" **WT** 280 lbs. **FROM** Hiroshima, Japan

TITLE HISTORY World Tag Team Champion, International Tag Team Champion

Famed manager Wild Red Berry lured Japanese powerhouse Prof. Toru Tanaka to the United States in the late 1960s. Tanaka was immediately looked upon as one of the most hated Superstars of his time, but the barrel-chested Superstar from the Land of the Rising Sun reveled in his role as the evil foreigner. In fact, he oftentimes intentionally incited fans by using ceremonial Japanese salts as a weapon.

Tanaka achieved most of his notoriety competing in the tag team ranks. With Mr. Fuji as his partner, Tanaka became a three-time World Tag Team Champion. The duo's first and lengthiest reign came after defeating Chief Jay Strongbow & Sonny King in June 1972. They went on to hold the titles for nearly one year.

As a singles competitor, Tanaka earned opportunities against WWE Champions Bruno Sammartino, Pedro Morales, and Bob Backlund. After retiring from the ring in the early 1980s, the Superstar parlayed his natural charisma into a successful movie career. *Pee-wee's Big Adventure, The Running Man,* and *The Last Action Hero* are just a few of the box-office hits in which Tanaka appeared.

"The Pug" Alex Porteau

HT 5'10" **WT** 226 lbs.

FROM New Orleans, Louisiana

SIGNATURE MOVE The Pugbomb

YEARS ACTIVE 1960 1969 1970 1979 1980 1989 1990 1999 2000 PRESENT

From The Big Easy, Alex Porteau started his career in the late 1980s in Fritz Von Erich's World Class Championship Wrestling. After a short tenure in World Championship Wrestling he spent the early 1990s in the GWF and Carlos Colon's World Wrestling Council. Porteau's power and technical skills earned him the opportunity to grapple with the best sports-entertainment had to offer.

In 1996 "the Pug" debuted in World Wrestling Entertainment and was a quick hit with fans everywhere. Alex battled all comers including Goldust, Mankind, Farooq, Justin Bradshaw, the Sultan, Aldo Montoya, and Vader. He was a top contender for the Intercontinental Championship until he left WWE in early 1997. Since, then he has appeared on wrestling cards in United States, Puerto Rico, and Japan.

PUNJABI PRISON MATCH

With two gigantic bamboo cages engulfing its combatants, the Punjabi Prison Match is widely considered one of the most barbaric creations ever conceived for the ring.

To win the match, a Superstar must escape both structures before his opponent. The first cage stands 16-feet tall and is equipped with doors on all four sides. Each door can only be opened once for a period of 60 seconds. If nobody makes it through the passageway in the allotted time, the door is padlocked for the remainder of the match.

The second cage is a towering 20-feet tall. Unlike the first, it does not have any doors, making the only way of escape a rush over the top, which is completely covered with razor-sharp spikes.

The first-ever Punjabi Prison Match featured Undertaker outlasting the mighty Big Show at *The Great American Bash* in 2006. The following year, Batista toppled the supposed master of the Punjabi Prison, the Great Khali, to retain his World Heavyweight Championship at *No Mercy*.

The Quebecers

MEMBERS Jacques, Pierre **COMBINED WEIGHT** 479 lbs.

TITLE HISTORY World Tag Team Champions

YEARS ACTIVE 1960 1969 1970 1979 1980 1989 1990 1999 2000 PRESENT

Managed by the obnoxious Johnny Polo, the Quebecers entered the WWE ranks in 1993. They quickly became title contenders known for their rule-breaking ways, their manager interfering in matches, and their abilities in the ring.

On an episode of *Monday Night Raw* they challenged the Steiner Brothers for the World Tag Team Championship under Province of Quebec Rules, which meant that the titles could change hands even on a disqualification. That minor change resulted in a victory when Scott Steiner lost his cool and nailed Johnny Polo with a hockey stick.

They held the titles until January 1994, and would hold them two more times before splitting in 1994 after a disappointing loss to the Headshrinkers. In the following two year span, both men left the WWE. They returned in 1998 where they competed in the Tag Team Battle Royal at *WrestleMania XIV*.

"Quickdraw" Rick McGraw

HT 5'7" **WT** 235 lbs. **FROM** Charlotte, North Carolina

After a career as a stand-out talent in the Florida and Mid-South territories during the mid-1970s, Rick McGraw debuted in World Wrestling Entertainment in May 1980. His explosive style and power made him an instant hit with the fans. Weeks later he debuted at Madison Square Garden and that energy carried him to the August Showdown At Shea where he locked-up with Greg Gagne.

McGraw often teamed with Steve Travis and with Andre the Giant on two occassions, against the Moondogs and the Wild Samoans. On his own, "Quickdraw" faced the likes of Ken Patera, Bulldog Brower, Tor Kamata, Killer Kahn, Johnny Rodz, Baron Mikel Scicluna, and Harley Race.

Tragically as McGraw's star was on the rise he passed away in November 1985. To wrestling fans, Rick McGraw will always be the energetic "Quickdraw" who brought fans to their feet and never backed down from a challenge.

Rad Radford

HT 5'11" **WT** 264 lbs. **FROM** Seattle, Washington **SIGNATURE MOVE** Northern Lights Suplex

In 1995, Rad Radford left his home in Seattle to become a WWE Superstar. As a fan of grunge bands, the flannel-clad Superstar certainly marched to the beat of his own drum. Inside the ring, he was just as sound as the most accomplished Superstar on the roster.

Armed with a devastating Northern Lights Suplex finisher, Radford picked up many wins early in his WWE stay. However, he wanted to be known for more than just victories—he also desired an amazing physique. That's when he turned to Skip & Sunny of the Bodydonnas. The fitness gurus agreed to take Radford on as a Bodydonna-in-training, but eventually fired the rotund Superstar after he failed to make any progress. Radford left WWE soon after.

The Radicalz

MEMBERS Chris Benoit, Eddie Guerrero, Dean Malenko, Perry Saturn

It's the story of one of the most-noted talent jumps in history, as Eddie Guerrero, Chris Benoit, Dean Malenko, and Perry Saturn moved en masse from WCW to WWE. Collectively known as the Radicalz, Benoit, Guerrero, Malenko, and Saturn became greatly displeased with WCW's lackluster direction in 2000. Despite Benoit being recognized as WCW Champion, the group opted to leave WCW in favor of WWE. The quartet's earliest appearances saw them sitting in the front row at WWE events, but it wasn't long before they jumped the barrier between the ring and fans to embark on their own dreams of superstardom.

Individually, each member of the Radicalz enjoyed championship-filled careers. Together, however, their success was fleeting, as the group broke apart within months of their formation. Over the next few years, the Radicalz would go on to reunite on rare occasions, including *Survivor Series 2000* where they turned back the team of Road Dogg, Billy Gunn, K-Kwik & Chyna.

Randy Orton

HT 6'4" **WT** 245 lbs. **FROM** St. Louis, Missouri **SIGNATURE MOVE** RKO

TITLE HISTORY WWE Champion, World Heavyweight Champion, Intercontinental Champion, World Tag Team Champion

As a third-generation Superstar, Randy didn't grow up in an ordinary wrestling family, he grew up an Orton. His earliest years included time with some of the greatest performers sports-entertainment has ever seen; his grandfather, "The Big O" Bob Orton, Sr., his father, "Cowboy" Bob Orton and his uncle, Barry O.

Randy made his WWE debut in 2002 on *SmackDown*, and his natural talent and charisma were recognized by Triple H and Ric Flair, who extended an invitation to the young star to join Evolution. As a part of Evolution, Orton enjoyed one of the longest Intercontinental Championship reigns in recent history. Orton also became known as "The Legend Killer" and he put the WWE on notice that no Hall of Famer, Legend, or Superstar was safe.

Every time Orton steps into the ring, he makes history. He became the youngest World Heavyweight Champion of all-time in 2004 at *SummerSlam*. The victory ushered in the "Age of Orton" in the world of sports-entertainment. In 2006, he teamed with Edge, forming Rated-RKO, and the duo captured the World Tag Team Championships. For this Triple-Crown winner domination is inevitable, victory is ensured, legacies will be advanced and glory will be obtained. It's his destiny and it's only just begun.

RANDY "MACHO MAN" SAVAGE

"OH YEAH!"

HT 6'2"	**WT** 237 lbs.	**FROM** Sarasota, Florida	

SIGNATURE MOVE Flying Elbow Drop

TITLE HISTORY Intercontinental Champion, WWE Champion

YEARS ACTIVE 1960–1969 1970–1979 1980–1989 1990–1999 2000 PRESENT

This unmistakable second-generation competitor began his full-time sports-entertainment career in 1979 after years as a Major League Baseball catching prospect.

Randy "Macho Man" Savage debuted in World Wrestling Entertainment in 1985 with "Classy" Freddie Blassie, Bobby "the Brain" Heenan, "Mouth of the South" Jimmy Hart, and Mr. Fuji vying to be his manager. He shocked the world when he signed with the unknown Miss Elizabeth. Savage came to the ring to the song *Pomp and Circumstance*, dressed in extravagant sequined robes, headbands, and wrap-around sunglasses. The "Macho Man" served notice to all that he was an elite talent when as he reached the finals of the company's first pay-per-view event, *The Wrestling Classic*.

On February 8, 1986, he used a foreign object to defeat Tito Santana for the Intercontinental Championship. The "Macho Man" did everything imaginable to keep his championship, even if it meant putting Miss Elizabeth in front of him. Savage's next opponent was more interested in his gorgeous manager than defeating him in the ring. George "the Animal" Steele entered into a string of violent matches that resulted in Savage leaving *WrestleMania 2* victorious.

In November 1986, "Macho Madness" took a dangerous turn when he crushed the larynx of Ricky Steamboat with the timekeeper's bell and put him out of commission for months. Upon Steamboat return, a championship rematch was signed for *WrestleMania III*. Despite the fact that Savage lost, this contest is regarded as one of the greatest matches in sports-entertainment history.

Months after this epic battle, Savage was the victim of an attack by the Honky Tonk Man and the Hart Foundation. When this included an assault on Miss Elizabeth, one of the most thrilling moments in WWE history followed as "Macho Madness" and Hulkamania joined forces. As Randy mowed through the WWE Championship tournament at *WrestleMania IV*, the Hulkster came to ringside for the tournament final to watch Savage's back. With a capacity crowd on its feet, "Macho Man" dropped his famous elbow on "Million-Dollar Man" Ted DiBiase and became the WWE Champion.

Sadly, miscommunication and misunderstandings led to Savage attacking Hulk Hogan in the locker room after their match against the Twin Towers on *The Main Event*. This resulted in the Mega Powers exploding at *WrestleMania V*. In one of the more hotly anticipated matches in *WrestleMania* history, Hogan defeated Savage for the title.

MACHO ROYALTY

Savage began the new decade with a new valet, Sensational Sherri. The two became royalty when he beat "King" Duggan and became the "Macho King." After a series of matches against Dusty Rhodes, Savage turned his attention to Ultimate Warrior. The two met in a Retirement Match at *WrestleMania VII*, which Savage lost. Sherri attacked her fallen client, but was chased off by a returning Miss Elizabeth. The two reunited in a wash of emotion and a "Match Made in Heaven" was set for *SummerSlam 1991*. A heartfelt ceremony turned frightful when Jake Roberts presented them a wrapped gift that contained a deadly king cobra which bit Savage. After being reinstated by Jack Tunney, Savage defeated Roberts on *Saturday Night's Main Event*.

Savage was once again tested as Ric Flair made scandalous remarks about a one-time relationship with Miss Elizabeth. At *WrestleMania VIII*, "Macho Man" not only cleared the name of his wife, but defeated Flair to become WWE Champion for the second time. Randy then made the move to the broadcast booth for WWE programs, including the first episode of *Monday Night Raw* and *WrestleMania IX*. At *WrestleMania X*, he defeated former pupil Crush in a "Falls Count Anywhere" Match.

In 1995, he traveled to World Championship Wrestling where he became a four-time WCW Champion before leaving the company in 1999. Randy later invaded the mainstream when he made his Hollywood debut as "Bonesaw McGraw" in the 2002 blockbuster *Spiderman*. In 2003, he released his rap album *Be a Man*.

Randy "Macho Man" Savage is revered as one of the greatest figures in all of sports-entertainment and a true legend in the ring. Savage combined unparalleled charisma, determination, and skill to dominate opponents. In the process, he paved the way for the next generation of Superstars. Dig It!

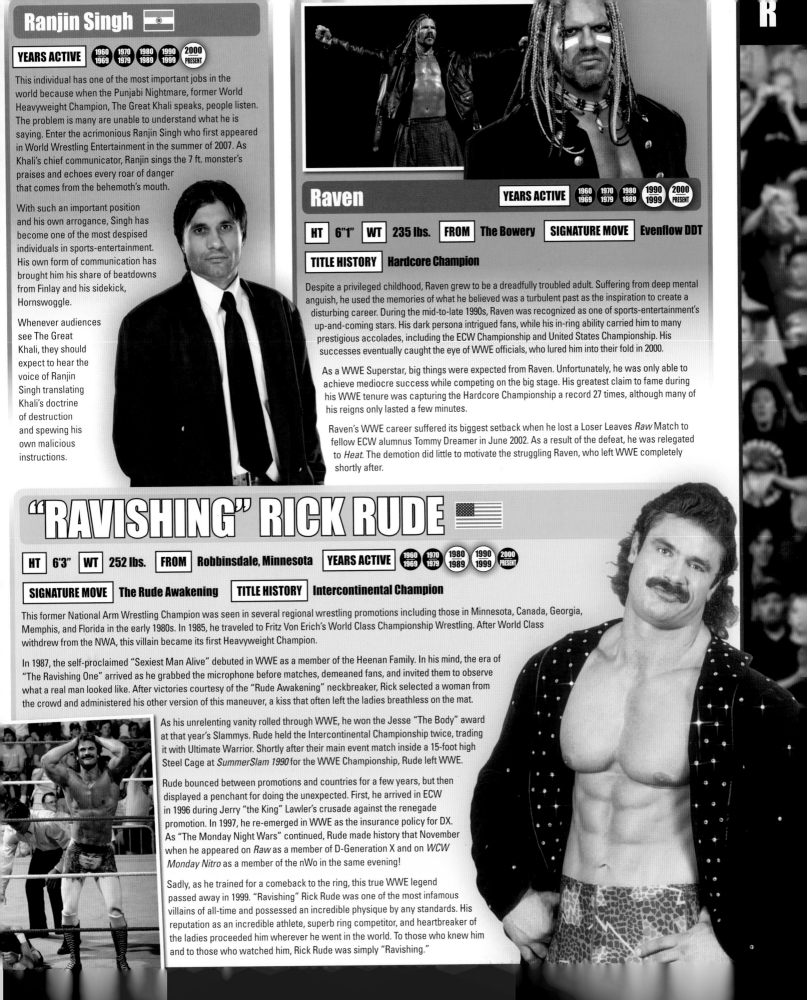

Ranjin Singh 🇮🇳

YEARS ACTIVE (1960 1969) (1970 1979) (1980 1989) (1990 1999) (**2000 PRESENT**)

This individual has one of the most important jobs in the world because when the Punjabi Nightmare, former World Heavyweight Champion, The Great Khali speaks, people listen. The problem is many are unable to understand what he is saying. Enter the acrimonious Ranjin Singh who first appeared in World Wrestling Entertainment in the summer of 2007. As Khali's chief communicator, Ranjin sings the 7 ft. monster's praises and echoes every roar of danger that comes from the behemoth's mouth.

With such an important position and his own arrogance, Singh has become one of the most despised individuals in sports-entertainment. His own form of communication has brought him his share of beatdowns from Finlay and his sidekick, Hornswoggle.

Whenever audiences see The Great Khali, they should expect to hear the voice of Ranjin Singh translating Khali's doctrine of destruction and spewing his own malicious instructions.

Raven

YEARS ACTIVE (1960 1969) (1970 1979) (1980 1989) (**1990 1999**) (2000 PRESENT)

HT 6"1" **WT** 235 lbs. **FROM** The Bowery **SIGNATURE MOVE** Evenflow DDT

TITLE HISTORY Hardcore Champion

Despite a privileged childhood, Raven grew to be a dreadfully troubled adult. Suffering from deep mental anguish, he used the memories of what he believed was a turbulent past as the inspiration to create a disturbing career. During the mid-to-late 1990s, Raven was recognized as one of sports-entertainment's up-and-coming stars. His dark persona intrigued fans, while his in-ring ability carried him to many prestigious accolades, including the ECW Championship and United States Championship. His successes eventually caught the eye of WWE officials, who lured him into their fold in 2000.

As a WWE Superstar, big things were expected from Raven. Unfortunately, he was only able to achieve mediocre success while competing on the big stage. His greatest claim to fame during his WWE tenure was capturing the Hardcore Championship a record 27 times, although many of his reigns only lasted a few minutes.

Raven's WWE career suffered its biggest setback when he lost a Loser Leaves *Raw* Match to fellow ECW alumnus Tommy Dreamer in June 2002. As a result of the defeat, he was relegated to *Heat*. The demotion did little to motivate the struggling Raven, who left WWE completely shortly after.

"RAVISHING" RICK RUDE 🇺🇸

HT 6'3" **WT** 252 lbs. **FROM** Robbinsdale, Minnesota **YEARS ACTIVE** (1960 1969) (**1970 1979**) (**1980 1989**) (1990 1999) (2000 PRESENT)

SIGNATURE MOVE The Rude Awakening **TITLE HISTORY** Intercontinental Champion

This former National Arm Wrestling Champion was seen in several regional wrestling promotions including those in Minnesota, Canada, Georgia, Memphis, and Florida in the early 1980s. In 1985, he traveled to Fritz Von Erich's World Class Championship Wrestling. After World Class withdrew from the NWA, this villain became its first Heavyweight Champion.

In 1987, the self-proclaimed "Sexiest Man Alive" debuted in WWE as a member of the Heenan Family. In his mind, the era of "The Ravishing One" arrived as he grabbed the microphone before matches, demeaned fans, and invited them to observe what a real man looked like. After victories courtesy of the "Rude Awakening" neckbreaker, Rick selected a woman from the crowd and administered his other version of this maneuver, a kiss that often left the ladies breathless on the mat.

As his unrelenting vanity rolled through WWE, he won the Jesse "The Body" award at that year's Slammys. Rude held the Intercontinental Championship twice, trading it with Ultimate Warrior. Shortly after their main event match inside a 15-foot high Steel Cage at *SummerSlam 1990* for the WWE Championship, Rude left WWE.

Rude bounced between promotions and countries for a few years, but then displayed a penchant for doing the unexpected. First, he arrived in ECW in 1996 during Jerry "the King" Lawler's crusade against the renegade promotion. In 1997, he re-emerged in WWE as the insurance policy for DX. As "The Monday Night Wars" continued, Rude made history that November when he appeared on *Raw* as a member of D-Generation X and on *WCW Monday Nitro* as a member of the nWo in the same evening!

Sadly, as he trained for a comeback to the ring, this true WWE legend passed away in 1999. "Ravishing" Rick Rude was one of the most infamous villains of all-time and possessed an incredible physique by any standards. His reputation as an incredible athlete, superb ring competitor, and heartbreaker of the ladies proceeded him wherever he went in the world. To those who knew him and to those who watched him, Rick Rude was simply "Ravishing."

RAW

On January 11, 1993, World Wrestling Entertainment and New York City made sports-entertainment history. As a raucous crowd filled The Manhattan Center, a new program debuted that was so innovative and filled with such excitement it could be called only one thing: *Raw*. For one hour, the three-man broadcast team of Vince McMahon, Randy "Macho Man" Savage, and Rob Bartlett brought the action to viewers everywhere.

Its first episode saw Superstars including Yokozuna, Koko B. Ware, the Steiner Brothers, then-Intercontinental Champion Shawn Michaels, and Undertaker. The show's audience grew and Monday nights had a new name as *Raw* became WWE's flagship program. After its first year, *Raw* was such a hit that fans demanded the show tour the United States. World Wrestling Entertainment obliged and hit the road, selling out arenas coast-to-coast every week. Whether it was the "Loser Leaves WWE" match with "Nature Boy" Ric Flair and Mr. Perfect, an unknown "Kid" who defeated Razor Ramon and added 1-2-3 to his name, or Leslie Nielsen scanning the globe for the real Undertaker, *Raw* quickly became known as a vehicle where anything could happen. Its tagline of "Uncut, Uncensored and Uncooked" paved the way for the Superstars who emerged on sports-entertainment's most thrilling stage.

As sports-entertainment evolved, WWE led the way, and *Monday Night Raw* was at the forefront. As the mid-1990s got *Raw,* its success on Monday nights reached new plateaus, and all-new Superstars, legends and phenomenons were created. The thrill of the program extended to the world of interactive software when in 1994 the first *Monday Night Raw* video game was released. With each passing week, WWE added more drama, excitement, and comedy, as was seen in January 1995 when William Shatner showed off his self-defense techniques against Jerry Lawler on an episode of *The King's Court*.

THE MONDAY NIGHT WAR BEGINS

Witnessing WWE's success, media mogul Ted Turner decided to go head-to-head with Vince McMahon and air *WCW Monday Nitro* in the same timeslot, on his own network. The Superstars knew the WWE brand had to continue to push the envelope. Historic happenings continued in February 1997 when *Raw* went to two hours as fans' thirst for excitement could not be satisfied with a single hour. Shortly thereafter, the WWE Championship changed hands for the first time on the program when Sycho Sid defeated Bret "Hit Man" Hart. The next week, the action got extreme as the original ECW Invasion saw The Manhattan Center raided by Paul Heyman, The Eliminators, Tazz, Tommy Dreamer, Sabu, The Dudley Boys, and the bWo. On March 3, 1997, World Wrestling Entertainment displayed its global reach as it introduced its first new prize since the Intercontinental Championship in 1979

when partners The British Bulldog and Owen Hart vied for the European Heavyweight Championship in Berlin, Germany.

Later that month, it became apparent the wrestling landscape had changed. With a seemingly endless budget and an abundance of underhanded tactics, World Championship Wrestling (WCW) was winning the ratings war. As World Wrestling Entertainment fought for its life, drastic times called for drastic measures. Superstars like Stone Cold Steve Austin, The Rock, Mankind, Undertaker, and D-Generation X kicked off the Attitude Era, took *Monday Night Raw* to its apex, and broke down the barriers of sports-entertainment.

September 27 was another day for WWE history books when *Monday Night Raw* emanated for the first time from Madison Square Garden in New York City. That event proved fateful when Stone Cold Steve Austin stunned Vince McMahon and fired the opening salvo in the Austin vs. McMahon conflict. The *Raw* year ended in controversy as Vince McMahon gave an exclusive interview depicting the events that led up to what has been dubbed "The Montreal Incident" and legendary hero Bret "Hit Man" Hart's exit from the company. Last but not least, Jim Ross and Jerry Lawler began a near ten-year consecutive run as the voices of the famed program.

THE ATTITUDE ERA

As *Monday Night Raw* celebrated its fifth anniversary, the battle with WCW continued. At one point WCW enjoyed eighty-four straight weeks as the top-rated sports-entertainment program. However, many within WWE felt that *Raw's* foundation was constructed to eventually unseat *Nitro* and regain its top spot in the cable television ratings. As *Raw* continued to be unpredictable and exciting each week, fans knew that once you entered the Warzone, it was on! Stone Cold Steve Austin kicked off 1998 by interrupting Vince McMahon's important announcement and came face-to-face with former heavyweight boxing champion "Iron" Mike Tyson. All hell broke loose after Austin used his unique form of sign language to communicate with the self-proclaimed "Baddest Man on the Planet." In the aftermath, all that could be heard was a vexed Vince McMahon yelling, "You ruined it damnit!" In the wake of Shawn Michaels loss at *WrestleMania XIV*, D-Generation X proclaimed a new beginning, as its new leader, Triple H, introduced his right-hand man, X-Pac. On April 13 WWE won the pivotal first battle in the ratings war since 1996 as audiences geared up for the first-ever match between the Chairman and the "Texas Rattlesnake." As the bell was ready to ring, Dude Love brought the festivities to a screeching halt thanks to his passive-aggressive tendencies and Mandible Claw.

In the following weeks, DX continued to retool and showed they ruled sports-entertainment when they crossed the Chesapeake Bay into Norfolk, VA, and invaded *WCW Monday Nitro*. The five bandits stayed on the move and added to their heated rivalry with The Nation of Domination when they mocked the entire group. In September, WWE saw the debut of Zamboni 3:16 when the world's toughest S.O.B. barreled through the gates of Detroit's Joe Louis Arena to get at his hated nemesis. Once there, Austin dove from the Zamboni, over the top rope, onto Mr. McMahon, and furthered their hate-hate relationship. Even being restrained and handcuffed by police didn't stop the former WWE Champion as he continued to lunge at the WWE Chairman.

While recovering in the hospital, Mr. McMahon's agony had only just begun when he was greeted by Mankind, who introduced the world to Mr. Socko before Stone Cold Steve Austin administered his form of alternative medicine. When it seemed that the Austin-McMahon rivalry reached its violent zenith, something else would occur to lift their mutual distain for one another. Whether the "Rattlesnake" filled a $60,000 Corvette from Mr. McMahon's prized collection with cement, or left the Chairman in urine-soaked slacks, laid-out in the center of the ring courtesy of BANG 3:16, the levels of ferocity were constantly on the rise.

The year 1999 proved to be huge for the company, as the May 10 episode of *Raw* was seen by over 8 million viewers, making it the highest-rated episode in the distinguished history of the program. As the McMahon family suffered at the eerie hands of Undertaker and the mysterious Higher Power, Vince proved that he would sacrifice anything to get the "Rattlesnake," even his own daughter. As millennium myths grew, WWE was greeted by their own countdown to the 21st Century, when Y2J interrupted the Rock and announced that *"Raw Is Jericho!"* Another record was set in September, when The Rock 'N' Sock Connection's *"Rock: This Is Your Life"* became the highest-rated segment in *Monday Night Raw* history. The Rock told everyone from his sixth grade home economics teacher to his high school sweetheart to know their role and shut their mouths.

THE MONDAY NIGHT WAR CONCLUDES

Monday Night Raw experienced dramatic growth as it approached the turn of the century. By the year 2000, World Wrestling Entertainment had reigned supreme in the Monday Night Wars. On March 26, 2001, a never-imagined event took place when Mr. McMahon informed television audiences around the globe of his purchase of World Championship Wrestling (WCW), and that the fate of the company rested in his hands. The czar of sports-entertainment added that *Monday Night Raw* and *WCW Monday Nitro* would be simulcast. However, his son Shane shocked everyone when his music hit and he was not in Cleveland, OH, at *Raw* but in Panama City, FL, on *Nitro* and announced the contract to purchases WCW did indeed have the name McMahon on it, but it read his name, not his father's. Fans soon found out that WWE was in for another war, this time one that was caused by an invasion.

In 2002, WWE Superstars and fans braced themselves for the triumphant return of Triple H at Madison Square Garden. After eight months of grueling physical rehabilitation to repair a torn quadricep, the "Cerebral Assassin" made his entry into the *Royal Rumble* official. The next month saw a meeting of past and present when Hollywood Hogan and The Rock stood eye-to-eye in the middle of the ring and set their historic *"Icon vs. Icon"* Match for *WrestleMania X-8*. In March, WWE underwent a brand division in which *Raw* and *SmackDown* became their own entities under the World Wrestling Entertainment banner. Operating within its own rules and bylaws, *Raw* instituted the position of General Manager to make the important decisions and guide the famous brand. General Managers have included WWE Hall of Famer "Nature Boy" Ric Flair, Stone Cold Steve Austin & Mick Foley in cooperative efforts, Mr. McMahon, an interim Jonathan Coachman, William Regal, and Mike Adamle. That July, unlikely worlds united as Mr. McMahon announced the new *Raw* General Manager was Eric Bischoff. A hush formed over the crowd as the one-time bitter competitors embraced. The former President of WCW listed his personal examples of ruthless aggression and guaranteed to put the "E" in WWE.

After the killing fields of the Monday Night Wars were cleared, *Monday Night Raw* continued to make its mark on sports-entertainment. On October 23, 2006, *Raw* aired its 700th episode, making it the longest running weekly entertainment show without a hiatus in the history of American broadcast television. On December 10, 2007, the show-of-shows celebrated its 15th Anniversary with a three-hour spectacular that saw the return of Stone Cold Steve Austin, Mankind, Hulk Hogan, Rob Van Dam, Sunny, The Godfather, "Million-Dollar Man" Ted DiBiase, Trish Stratus, and Howard Finkel.

Today, *Monday Night Raw* features over fifty Superstars on its roster and averages nearly five million viewers every week. The show is broadcast in one hundred thirty different countries and translated into nineteen different languages. Over the past sixteen years, *Raw* has made you laugh, cry, and jump to your feet as the greatest entertainers in the world ply their trade. This program has single-handedly changed sports-entertainment and broadcast television forever. No reruns, no off-season, no second takes or do-overs, this is World Wrestling Entertainment, and on Monday nights it *Raw*.

RAY "THE CRIPPLER" STEVENS

| HT | 5'8" | WT | 235 lbs. | FROM | San Francisco, California |

| SIGNATURE MOVE | Bombs Away Knee-Drop |

YEARS ACTIVE

The man who first became known as "the Blonde Bomber" began his career in 1950. Stevens' early dastardly acts made him one of the most loathed men in the business. However, by the mid 1960s he teamed with Pat Patterson to form one of the most revered tag teams in history, the Blonde Bombers.

In the 1970s Stevens spent most of his time in the AWA and NWA before heading to World Wrestling Entertainment in 1980. Ray had the distinction of having co-managers in Lou Albano and "Classy" Freddie Blassie. He showed how he got his nickname when he viciously attacked Jimmy "Superfly" Snuka and administered two piledrivers to him on the concrete floor after Snuka was declared a free man on *Roger's Corner*. Stevens soon returned to the AWA as a competitor and broadcaster until he retired in 1992. On April 5, 1995 Stevens' impact was recognized when the mayors of San Francisco and Oakland jointly declared it "Ray Stevens Day."

In May 1996, one of sports-entertainment's true pioneers passed away at his California home. Ray Stevens, a master at his craft and consummate performer, left a lasting impression within the world of sports-entertainment.

RAZOR RAMON

YEARS ACTIVE

| HT | 6'7" | WT | 287 lbs. | FROM | Miami, Florida | SIGNATURE MOVE | Razor's Edge |

| TITLE HISTORY | Intercontinental Champion |

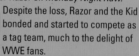

During his introductory interviews in 1992, Razor Ramon proclaimed that he was the only real man in the WWE and that if you wanted to be like Razor, you had to do like Razor and take whatever you want. Known as "the Bad Guy," Ramon was both hated for his attitude and respected for his abilities in the ring.

Despite his impressive win-loss record, Razor Ramon may be best remembered for being the victim of one of the greatest upsets in WWE history. The unknown Kid (who later became known as X-Pac) scored an improbable victory over Razor on *Monday Night Raw*. Despite the loss, Razor and the Kid bonded and started to compete as a tag team, much to the delight of WWE fans.

Over the rest of Razor Ramon's WWE tenure, he held the Intercontinental Championship multiple times and often faced off against Shawn Michaels. At *WrestleMania X* "the Bad Guy" defeated "the Heartbreak Kid" in a legendary Ladder Match regarded by many as one of the greatest sports-entertainment moments in history.

In 1996 Razor Ramon left WWE and signed with WCW. He appeared under his real name, Scott Hall, alongside Kevin Nash and Hulk Hogan. The trio formed the nWo and changed the face of sports-entertainment forever. After his time in WCW, Hall made stops in ECW and in Japan, then briefly reformed the nWo in WWE in 2002. Whether the tooth-pick is being flicked from Razor Ramon or Scott Hall, people know they just got hit with a little bit of his oozing machismo.

Rene Dupree

YEARS ACTIVE 1960-1969 | 1970-1979 | 1980-1989 | 1990-1999 | **2000 PRESENT**

HT 6'3" **WT** 260 lbs. **FROM** Paris, France **SIGNATURE MOVE** Dupree Bomb

TITLE HISTORY World Tag Team Champion, WWE Tag Team Champion

Nobody loved Rene Dupree more than, well, Rene Dupree. The cocky Superstar believed he was greatest Superstar to ever grace a WWE ring. Unfortunately for his detractors, Dupree's early ring efforts certainly backed his boasts. In June 2003, a little more than a month after his in-ring debut, Dupree and his partner, Sylvain Grenier, defeated Kane & Rob Van Dam to capture the World Tag Team Championship. The victory proved historic, as it put Dupree in the record books as the youngest tag champ in WWE history (at 19 years old). Collectively known as La Resistance, Dupree & Grenier dominated the *Raw* tag team division until he was drafted to *SmackDown* in March 2004.

As a member of *SmackDown*, Dupree continued his tag team excellence; this time with partner Kenzo Suzuki. The new duo defeated Billy Kidman & Paul London for the WWE Tag Team Championship in September 2004. They held the titles for three months before losing to Rey Mysterio & RVD. Following the loss, Dupree struggled to get back on track. He bounced around from *SmackDown* to *Raw* to *ECW* before finally being released from WWE in July 2007.

Red Bastien

HT 6' **WT** 190 lbs.

FROM Bottineau, North Dakota

YEARS ACTIVE 1960-1969 | 1970-1979 | 1980-1989 | 1990-1999 | 2000 PRESENT

At just 16, Red Bastien developed a love for fighting while wrestling and boxing in carnivals. Before he could turn his passion into a career, Bastien was drafted into the Navy. He spent his time in the military beefing up for what he hoped would be a profitable professional career. By the time his commitment to the Navy was finished, he had added 30 pounds to his frame, which was greatly needed considering he was considerably smaller than most pros.

As a professional, Bastien was dedicated to constantly improving his craft. Over time, he eventually became recognized as one of the game's toughest men. He then combined his rugged persona with lightning-fast speed, which he acquired while training with noted Mexican speed merchant Manuel Barintez.

Bastien's career took him all over the world, but it was in the United States that he gained his greatest fame, especially in the tag team ranks. Teaming with his brother Lou, he enjoyed five tag team title reigns. In later years, he went on to form championship combinations with several other Superstars, including Hercules Cortez, who he won the AWA Tag Team Championship with in May 1971.

Rene Goulet

YEARS ACTIVE 1960-1969 | **1970-1979** | **1980-1989** | 1990-1999 | 2000 PRESENT

HT 6' **WT** 236 lbs. **FROM** Nice, France

SIGNATURE MOVE Claw

TITLE HISTORY World Tag Team Champion

By the time WWE's mainstream boom of the 1980s came along, Rene Goulet's glory days were behind him. The self-proclaimed No. 1 Frenchman spent much of the Hulkamania era falling to up-and-coming fan favorites such as "Leaping" Lanny Poffo and Hillbilly Jim, but longtime WWE fans actually remember Goulet as a serious threat to all titleholders during the 1970s.

Goulet formed a formidable tandem with fellow foreigner Karl Gotch of Germany in 1971. Together, they defeated Luke Graham & Tarzan Tyler to become the second-ever World Tag Team Champions in December 1971. Fans and insiders alike predicted a lengthy reign for Goulet & Gotch. Surprisingly, however, they were unseated by Baron Mikel Scicluna & King Curtis only two months later.

After the loss, Goulet left WWE to tour the globe. He competed in Japan, Australia, and Germany before returning to WWE in the early 1980s. Unfortunately by this time, the aged "Master of the Claw" rarely had the opportunity to apply his feared finisher.

REPO MAN

HT 6'2" **WT** 290 lbs.

SIGNATURE MOVE The Crowbar

YEARS ACTIVE 1960-1969 | 1970-1979 | 1980-1989 | 1990-1999 | 2000 PRESENT

In 1991, this Superstar was introduced to WWE audiences in vignettes that showed him repossessing cars from garages and parking lots. His services were retained by "Million Dollar Man" Ted DiBiase to acquire the Million Dollar Championship from DiBiase's former bodyguard, Virgil.

The man with his black mask and bull rope terrorized fans and Superstars like Big Bossman, British Bulldog, "Hacksaw" Jim Duggan, Tito Santana, Jimmy "Superfly" Snuka, Sgt. Slaughter, and "Rowdy" Roddy Piper until he left World Wrestling Entertainment in Spring 1993.

In recent years Repo Man has resurfaced in WWE most notably at *WrestleMania X-7* in the Gimmick Battle Royal and in December 2007 for the *Raw 15th Anniversary* special. The imprint this individual left on WWE is as permanent as the tire tracks on his ring attire. The Repo Man will always be right around the corner. It's just a matter of if you see him or not.

REY MYSTERIO

HT 5'6" **WT** 175 lbs. **FROM** San Diego, California

SIGNATURE MOVE 619, West Coast Pop **YEARS ACTIVE** 1960-1969 | 1970-1979 | 1980-1989 | 1990-1999 | 2000 PRESENT

TITLE HISTORY World Heavyweight Champion, Cruiserweight Champion, WWE Tag Team Champion

Many fans of sports-entertainment first saw this phantasmic Lucha Libre star during his 1995 stay in ECW. He began to receive national acclaim the next year when he joined WCW and became its Cruiserweight Champion. Rey was at the forefront of the Cruiserweight revolution and appeared on WCW programming until the final episode of *Monday Nitro*.

After a short stint in Mexico, Rey prepared for his debut on sports-entertainment's global stage. In 2002 Mysterio flew into WWE and landed on *SmackDown* where he immediately battled Kurt Angle and soon after became WWE Tag Team Champions with Edge. After *WrestleMania XX* he reclaimed the Tag Team Championship, first with Rob Van Dam, then Eddie Guerrero. At *WrestleMania 21*, Rey and Eddie had the first-ever match between tag champion partners.

After the tragic loss of his close friend Eddie Guerrero, Rey focused on winning a World title in Eddie's honor. At *WrestleMania 22* Rey's dream became reality after he defeated Kurt Angle and Randy Orton in a Triple Threat Match, showing that he could beat anybody at any time.

For more than 15 years Rey Mysterio has made the impossible, possible. Today he is one of the WWE's premier Superstars and has no intention of slowing down anytime soon. Rey holds it down for the 619, for his friends and family and for the underdog in everyone.

Rhyno

HT	5'10"	**WT**	275 lbs.

FROM Detroit, Michigan

SIGNATURE MOVE Gore

TITLE HISTORY Hardcore Champion, United States Champion

YEARS ACTIVE (1960 1969) (1970 1979) (1980 1989) (1990 1999) **(2000 PRESENT)**

Billed as half man and half beast, Rhyno entered WWE in 2001 with the distinction of being the original ECW's final champion. His reputation preceding him, fans demanded he live up to his lofty hardcore reputation. Refusing to disappoint WWE's rabid fans, Rhyno immediately proved he was extreme when he defeated the mighty Kane for the Hardcore Championship on *SmackDown*. He went on to win the title two more times during his WWE tenure, once from Chris Jericho and once from Test.

In July 2001, Rhyno reverted back to his ECW roots when he joined forces with Stephanie and Shane McMahon's Alliance of ECW and WCW Superstars. As a member of The Alliance, Rhyno became Stephanie's pet, largely because he refused to allow Y2J to verbally berate her. The rivalry led to a *SummerSlam* showdown between the two Superstars. Despite coming out on the losing end, the match is widely regarded as a highlight of Rhyno's WWE career. Undeterred by the loss, the "Man-Beast" defeated Tajiri the following month for the United States Championship (which was still considered part of WCW at the time).

Proving he will always be tied to the original ECW, Rhyno's final WWE appearance took place at *One Night Stand* in 2005. He battled Sabu in a thrilling throwback to his hardcore days.

RHYTHM & BLUES

MEMBERS	Honky Tonk Man, Greg Valentine	**COMBINED WEIGHT**	514 lbs.

YEARS ACTIVE (1960 1969) (1970 1979) **(1980 1989)** **(1990 1999)** (2000 PRESENT)

Former Intercontinental Champions Honky Tonk Man & Greg Valentine joined forces in 1989 to help manager Jimmy Hart in his battle against the Hart Foundation. Though not officially recognized as Rhythm & Blues yet, the duo battled Bret Hart & Jim Neidhart at *WrestleMania V*. The Hart Foundation walked away victorious that night, but it didn't deter Honky Tonk Man & Valentine from continuing to make music together.

A few months after the loss, Valentine began his transformation from a no-nonsense professional to Elvis look-alike. He dyed his hair jet black, donned oversized sunglasses, and began carrying around a classic guitar. With the makeover complete, Valentine officially joined forces with Honky Tonk Man; Rhythm & Blues was born.

The tone-deaf duo appeared to care more about their fledgling music careers than they did about competing in the ring. As a result, Rhythm & Blues failed to score any major hits in the tag ranks. They did, however, manage to debut their single "Hunka, Hunka, Honky Love" at *WrestleMania VI*. Unfortunately for Honky Tonk Man & Valentine, the Bushwhackers crashed the performance, and destroyed their guitars.

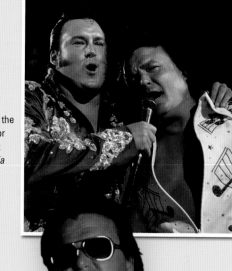

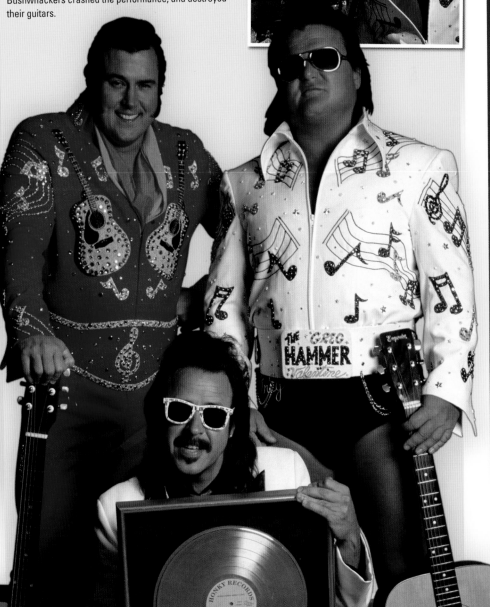

RIC FLAIR

| HT | 6'1" | WT | 243 lbs. | FROM | Charlotte, North Carolina | SIGNATURE MOVE | Figure-Four Leglock |

YEARS ACTIVE 1960-1969 1970-1979 1980-1989 1990-1999 2000 PRESENT

TITLE HISTORY WWE Champion, Intercontinental Champion, World Tag Team Champion

Over the course of his thirty-five years inside the ring, Ric Flair orchestrated arguably the greatest career in the history of sports-entertainment. With an unprecedented sixteen World Championships to his credit, the man known as the "Nature Boy" truly epitomizes what it means to be a champion between the ropes. Flair also lived like a champion outside the ring, earning an unparalleled reputation as a "... kiss-stealing, wheeling, dealing, jet-flying, limousine-riding son-of-a-gun."

As a youngster growing up in Minneapolis, Flair became so unruly that his parents were forced to send him to boarding school. While there, Flair interacted with some of the area's most affluent kids, which he claims helped contribute to the lavish lifestyle he later embraced. After boarding school, while bouncing around from job to job, he had the opportunity to meet his friend's father, Verne Gagne, who was also the promoter of the American Wrestling Association (AWA). With no promises of a future career, Gagne agreed to let Flair take part in his wrestling camp.

In late 1972, Flair enrolled in Gagne's ten-week wrestling school, but quit after only one day when the cardiovascular exercises proved to be too much. Luckily, Flair later reconsidered his decision and returned to the camp, which also produced such greats as The Iron Sheik, Greg Gagne, and Ken Patera.

After completing his training, Flair earned an opportunity to compete in Gagne's AWA. In his first-ever match, he battled George "Scrap Iron" Gadaski to a ten-minute draw at the Minneapolis Auditorium. The inexperienced Flair managed to form relationships that would eventually benefit him greatly, especially the close friendship he developed with the great Wahoo McDaniel.

When McDaniel moved south to compete in the Mid-Atlantic territory, he recommended his new promoters take a close look at his young friend. In April 1974, Flair was on his way to North Carolina, a state that would eventually adopt the moniker "Flair Country" as a tribute to the man who cemented his amazing legacy in the Tar Heel State.

While competing for Mid-Atlantic, Flair finally started to make a name for himself. He defeated Paul Jones for the Television Championship in February 1975. With a title belt around his waist, Flair's future couldn't look brighter. However, tragedy struck one Sunday afternoon when the plane Flair was traveling on tragically crashed to the ground. The accident claimed the life of the pilot, and seriously injured wrestlers Johnny Valentine and Bob Bruggers, as well as announcer David Crockett. Flair broke his back in three places, causing doctors to claim he may never walk again, let alone wrestle. Unable to accept a life without wrestling, Flair persevered and was back in the ring six months and ten days later.

> ## "WHETHER YOU LIKE IT OR YOU DON'T LIKE IT, LEARN TO LOVE IT, BECAUSE IT'S THE BEST THING GOING TODAY."

THE NATURE BOY

Flair adopted a new style upon returning to the ring. Following the advice of George Scott, he patterned his persona after the legendary Buddy Rogers. He even adopted Rogers' nickname, "Nature Boy." As the "Nature Boy," Flair demonstrated an unquenchable thirst for the best the world had to offer.

Life was also good for Flair inside the ring. After capturing numerous titles, including the prestigious United States Championship, Flair reached the sports-entertainment pinnacle when he defeated Dusty Rhodes for the National Wrestling Alliance (NWA) Championship on September 17, 1981. The victory put Flair on the map as one of the time's most accomplished competitors. However, after touring the globe and competing against such legends as Harley Race, Kerry Von Erich, and Ricky Steamboat every single night, Flair proved himself as one of the greatest Superstars in the world.

THE FOUR HORSEMEN

In 1986, Flair made a decision that would forever alter the face of sports-entertainment, when he aligned himself with Tully Blanchard, Arn Anderson, Ole Anderson, and J.J. Dillon. Collectively known as The Four Horsemen, the well-dressed faction of bullies controlled the gold in the Mid-Atlantic territory. Blanchard held the United States Championship, the Andersons controlled the NWA Tag Team Championship, while Flair maintained a stranglehold on the NWA Championship. The unstoppable unit plowed through their competition, laying the groundwork for future great factions, such as the New World Order and D-Generation X.

By decade's end, Flair had become a multiple-time NWA Champion. If had decided to retire then, he would have walked away as one of the finest to ever step foot in a ring. However, there was plenty more for the "Nature Boy" to accomplish. Surprisingly, however, he was forced to find a new place of employment for the next chapter of his legendary story.

THE "REAL WORLD HEAVYWEIGHT CHAMPION"

After Ted Turner purchased Jim Crockett Promotions and renamed it World Championship Wrestling, the billionaire made a series of questionable decisions that rubbed his competitors the wrong way, including hiring Jim Herd to run the wrestling operation. Unable to accept Herd's decisions and perceived disrespect of the industry, Flair left WCW. The wrestling world was sent into a frenzy when Bobby Heenan announced to the world on *Wrestling Challenge* that a great champion was on his way to WWE and then displayed the WCW Championship belt, shocking millions of viewers. Flair soon debuted on WWE television with the WCW Championship belt in tow, claiming to be the "real World Champion." Flair displayed the title proudly, while fans and Superstars alike observed in utter disbelief.

For years, fans and experts wondered how a match between Flair and Hulk Hogan, the two greatest competitors of their era, would play out. Fans would savor pondering a question that looked like it would never be answered. With Flair in WWE, however, such fantasy became reality.

A mere three months after making his WWE debut, Flair put any doubt surrounding his championship claims to rest when he captured the WWE Championship by winning the 1992 *Royal Rumble*. Flair's victory put him in elite company, as he joined another "Nature Boy," Buddy Rogers, as the only men to capture both the NWA and WWE Championships. Flair enjoyed a second WWE Championship reign before finally falling to former confidant Mr. Perfect in a Loser Leaves WWE Match in January 1993.

"The Dirtiest Player in the Game" gets an assist from Mr. Perfect.

BACK IN WORLD CHAMPIONSHIP WRESTLING

Following the loss, Flair returned to WCW and picked up right where he left off. He defeated Vader at *Starrcade 1993* to reclaim the WCW Championship, which was followed by an impressive win over Sting months later. Hulk Hogan and Flair renewed their epic rivalry at the 1994 *Bash at the Beach*. Though the result was not in Flair's favor, the star-studded encounter, which featured Shaquille O'Neal in Hogan's corner, will forever be remembered as one of sports-entertainment's most historic matches.

Despite going on to reclaim his WCW Championship and eventually reunite the Four Horsemen, internal politics caused Flair to become disenchanted with WCW. He spent the final years of the promotion's existence extremely unhappy. By the time WCW closed its doors, Flair's heart had already left the great sport he spent decades loving.

NEW LIFE IN WWE

When WWE purchased WCW, Flair's passion for competition quickly resurfaced. Now over 50 years old, the "Nature Boy" miraculously located the fountain of youth and sipped from it for the following seven years.

Perhaps Flair's greatest accomplishment during his second WWE run was his union with Triple H, Batista, and Randy Orton. Collectively known as Evolution, the faction was built using ideologies borrowed from The Four Horsemen. During their successful time together, the well-dressed stable controlled WWE's championship scene. Years later, both Batista and Orton credited Flair's guidance with helping them achieve World Championship status.

Flair's unprecedented in-ring career came to an end on March 30, 2008. One day after being the first active Superstar ever inducted into the WWE Hall of Fame, Shawn Michaels defeated the "Nature Boy" at *WrestleMania XXIV*. The historic match officially signified the end of an era that can never be duplicated.

Hogan and Flair battled in sold-out arenas across the country, and while they thrilled fans, a clear winner was never determined

RICK MARTEL

HT 6' **WT** 230 lbs. **FROM** Montreal, Quebec, Canada

TITLE HISTORY World Tag Team Champion **YEARS ACTIVE**

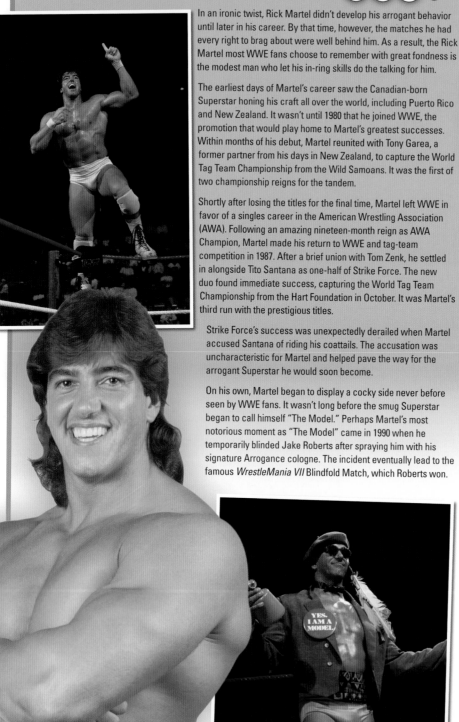

In an ironic twist, Rick Martel didn't develop his arrogant behavior until later in his career. By that time, however, the matches he had every right to brag about were well behind him. As a result, the Rick Martel most WWE fans choose to remember with great fondness is the modest man who let his in-ring skills do the talking for him.

The earliest days of Martel's career saw the Canadian-born Superstar honing his craft all over the world, including Puerto Rico and New Zealand. It wasn't until 1980 that he joined WWE, the promotion that would play home to Martel's greatest successes. Within months of his debut, Martel reunited with Tony Garea, a former partner from his days in New Zealand, to capture the World Tag Team Championship from the Wild Samoans. It was the first of two championship reigns for the tandem.

Shortly after losing the titles for the final time, Martel left WWE in favor of a singles career in the American Wrestling Association (AWA). Following an amazing nineteen-month reign as AWA Champion, Martel made his return to WWE and tag-team competition in 1987. After a brief union with Tom Zenk, he settled in alongside Tito Santana as one-half of Strike Force. The new duo found immediate success, capturing the World Tag Team Championship from the Hart Foundation in October. It was Martel's third run with the prestigious titles.

Strike Force's success was unexpectedly derailed when Martel accused Santana of riding his coattails. The accusation was uncharacteristic for Martel and helped pave the way for the arrogant Superstar he would soon become.

On his own, Martel began to display a cocky side never before seen by WWE fans. It wasn't long before the smug Superstar began to call himself "The Model." Perhaps Martel's most notorious moment as "The Model" came in 1990 when he temporarily blinded Jake Roberts after spraying him with his signature Arrogance cologne. The incident eventually lead to the famous *WrestleMania VII* Blindfold Match, which Roberts won.

Ricky Ortiz

HT 6'3" **WT** 246 lbs.

FROM Paradise Valley, Arizona

SIGNATURE MOVE The Big O

YEARS ACTIVE

As a child growing up in Paradise Valley, the imagination of Atlas Ortiz was consumed with another man from the Arizona desert, "Superstar" Billy Graham. A stand-out four sport athlete, Ortiz closely followed World Wrestling Entertainment and dreamed of being part of the WWE.

When ECW General Manager Theodore Long launched his "New Superstar Initiative" the powerful, charismatic Ortiz debuted in the Land of Extreme in July 2008. His nickname "Ricky" soon stuck and the large muscled, big-haired Superstar showed he was on his way to big things in the ring. After an impressive debut victory over Armondo Estrada, Ortiz also faced the likes of Carlito, Gavin Spears, and Chavo Guerrero. With the fans strongly behind him anytime he laces up the boots, this blue-chipper's career is built on discipline, self-reliance, courage, and an unmatched energy.

RICKY "THE DRAGON" STEAMBOAT

R

| HT | 5'10" | WT | 235 lbs. | FROM | Honolulu, Hawaii | TITLE HISTORY | Intercontinental Champion | YEARS ACTIVE | 1960 1969 | 1970 1979 | 1980 1989 | 1990 1999 | 2000 PRESENT |

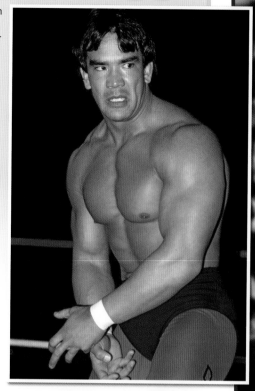

Ricky Steamboat had a unique career that saw him spend his prime bouncing around from promotion to promotion. Despite never staying in one place for very long, "the Dragon" became immensely popular, thanks in large part to his involvement in what many consider the greatest match in sports-entertainment history, and firmly established himself among the all-time greats.

After successful stints in the AWA and NWA, Steamboat arrived in WWE in 1985. Within months of his debut, "the Dragon" earned a spot on the inaugural *WrestleMania* card, defeating Matt Borne with a flying crossbody. Following *WrestleMania*, Steamboat successfully proved his worth against Jake Roberts and fellow Hawaiian Don Muraco.

WWE's championship committee finally took note of Steamboat's success and afforded him an opportunity at Randy Savage's Intercontinental Championship in late 1986. Unfortunately for Steamboat, the match ended when "Macho Man" savagely crushed the challenger's larynx with the ring bell from the top rope. The heinous act not only kept Steamboat from competing for months, but also threatened his chances of ever speaking again.

Luckily Steamboat was able to make a full recovery. With revenge occupying his every thought, Steamboat challenged Savage for the Intercontinental Championship at *WrestleMania III*. In the end, it was Steamboat gaining the ultimate measure of retribution, defeating "Macho Man" for the title in a match many believe to be the greatest of all time.

The following year, Steamboat returned to the NWA, where he battled Ric Flair in arguably the greatest series of matches ever witnessed, and enjoyed a three-month reign as NWA Champion. Steamboat briefly rejoined WWE in 1991. While he failed to recreate the same in-ring success as his initial WWE run, "the Dragon" did manage to amaze crowds with his fire-breathing pre-match rituals. Steamboat's in-ring days came to an end in 1994. Following his retirement, he settled into a backstage producer role with WWE. In his new position, Steamboat disseminates his years of superior wrestling knowledge to the Superstars of today.

Right to Censor

| MEMBERS | Steven Richards, Val Venis, The Goodfather, Bull Buchanon, Ivory |

| YEARS ACTIVE | 1960 1969 | 1970 1979 | 1980 1989 | 1990 1999 | 2000 PRESENT |

In the summer of 2000 World Wrestling Entertainment was raided by a self-righteous collection of transformed Superstars that had more conviction for convenience than all politicians put together. Spear-headed by Steven Richards, this faction brainwashed those who at one time loved the pageantry and glitz of sports-entertainment into believing life was about a tireless campaign to cover-up Divas and remove weapons from the ringside area during matches.

Despite their unpopular acts they did achieve success in the ring as Ivory became Women's Champion in November 2000. Days later Bull Buchanan & the Goodfather became World Tag Team Champions. However, everyone started to tire of their pontification and WWE had enough of Right To Censor. Each member lost their match at *Wrestlemania X-7* and soon after a Last Ride from Undertaker on their leader, they disappeared from WWE television.

Though fans may be reluctant to admit it, Right To Censor sent the following message to the self-proclaimed moralists of society: perhaps before proclaiming how everyone else should live, they should take a long look at themselves.

| **Rikishi** | | YEARS ACTIVE | 1960 1969 | 1970 1979 | 1980 1989 | 1990 1999 | 2000 PRESENT |

| HT | 6'1" | WT | 423 lbs. | FROM | Samoa |

| SIGNATURE MOVE | Stinkface |

| TITLE HISTORY | World Tag Team Champion, WWE Tag Team Champion, Intercontinental Champion |

The fans' love affair with Rikishi was similar to a ride on a wild rollercoaster. One minute, his fun-loving persona carried them to great heights; the next, his reprehensible actions brought them crashing down, only to be thrust back up again when he had a change of heart.

Despite wearing a revealing thong to the ring, the massive Rikishi immediately won over fans upon his debut in 1999. Alongside Too Cool, the Samoan Superstar oftentimes broke out into a contagious dance that always got audiences moving their feet. His popularity eventually lead to an Intercontinental Championship reign in June 2000.

Rikishi's approval rating took a huge hit in late 2000 when it was revealed that he ran over Stone Cold Steve Austin with a car. While the vicious attack certainly put the big man in bad standing with the fans, it also helped catapult him to main event status. Over the next few months, Rikishi found himself across the ring from many of WWE's all-time greats, including The Rock, Undertaker, and Stone Cold Steve Austin.

Toward the end of 2001, Rikishi began to slowly regain the fans' trust. Then, in December, he completely won them over when he performed one of the most disgusting acts ever seen on television. With the hated Mr. McMahon sitting battered in the corner of the ring, Rikishi delivered a gag-inducing Stinkface to the WWE Chairman.

"Road Dogg" Jesse James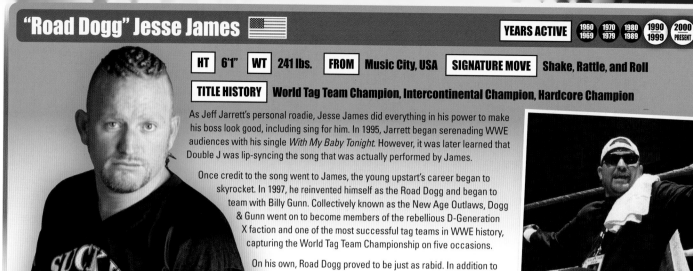

HT 6'1" **WT** 241 lbs. **FROM** Music City, USA **SIGNATURE MOVE** Shake, Rattle, and Roll

TITLE HISTORY World Tag Team Champion, Intercontinental Champion, Hardcore Champion

As Jeff Jarrett's personal roadie, Jesse James did everything in his power to make his boss look good, including sing for him. In 1995, Jarrett began serenading WWE audiences with his single *With My Baby Tonight*. However, it was later learned that Double J was lip-syncing the song that was actually performed by James.

Once credit to the song went to James, the young upstart's career began to skyrocket. In 1997, he reinvented himself as the Road Dogg and began to team with Billy Gunn. Collectively known as the New Age Outlaws, Dogg & Gunn went on to become members of the rebellious D-Generation X faction and one of the most successful tag teams in WWE history, capturing the World Tag Team Championship on five occasions.

On his own, Road Dogg proved to be just as rabid. In addition to being the third in a long line of Superstars to hold the Hardcore Championship, he also topped Val Venis in March 1999 to become Intercontinental Champion.

Roadkill

HT 6' **WT** 323 lbs.

FROM Lancaster, Pennsylvania

Roadkill can count his number of WWE televised appearances on one hand. Outside of a few losing efforts on *Velocity* and the reborn ECW in 2006, the "Angry Amish Warrior" doesn't have much WWE experience. However, he can certainly look back at his efforts in the original ECW with great fondness.

While competing in the original ECW, Roadkill formed an unlikely, yet successful tandem, with Danny Doring. In December 2000, Roadkill & Doring bested Tony Mamaluke & Little Guido for the ECW Tag Team Championship. The duo remained champions until the promotion closed its doors in the spring of 2001.

Rob Conway

HT 6'2" **WT** 230 lbs. **FROM** Atlantic City, New Jersey **SIGNATURE MOVE** Neckbreaker **TITLE HISTORY** World Tag Team Champion

After brief appearances with the WWE, Conway made his presence felt in August 2003 when he disguised himself as a US serviceman and attacked the Dudley Boys to reveal himself as the third member of La Resistance. Conway turned on his native USA and was introduced as being from the Province of Quebec. He formed a dangerous tag team with Sylvain Grenier and won the World Tag Team Championship on three separate occasions. The two rule-breakers parted ways in 2005 when they couldn't keep their egos in check. Conway returned to singles competition and later became part of the anti-ECW crusade. He started to refer to himself as "Con Man," but his fast talk got him in hot water during the WWE Homecoming. After interrupting a Legends Ceremony, Conway felt the effects of the Von Erich Claw followed by a "Superfly" Splash.

Conway spent much of 2006 on the end of a horrid losing streak. In January 2007, he proclaimed he would quit if he didn't defeat Jeff Hardy. After a disappointing twelve second loss, WWE Chairman Mr. McMahon appeared and fired Conway on the spot.

ROB VAN DAM

| HT | 6' | WT | 235 lbs. | FROM | Battle Creek, Michigan |

SIGNATURE MOVE Five-Star Frog Splash **YEARS ACTIVE** 1960-1969 1970-1979 1980-1989 **1990-1999** **2000-PRESENT**

TITLE HISTORY WWE Champion, ECW Champion, World Tag Team Champion, WWE Tag Team Champion, Intercontinental Champion, European Champion, Hardcore Champion

Considered by many to be sports-entertainment's ultimate risk taker, Rob Van Dam utilized a lethal combination of acrobatic offense and martial arts to mold a WWE career that was truly one of a kind. A standout in ECW, "Mr. Monday Night" made his highly-anticipated WWE debut in 2001. Although a member of The Alliance at the time, he managed to gain the admiration of the fans through his awe-inspiring aerial assault, which was highlighted by electrifying moves such as the Van Terminator, Rolling Thunder, and Five-Star Frog Splash. It wasn't long before Van Dam's innovative offense was driving him to championship opportunities.

RVD won his first major piece of WWE hardware at *WrestleMania X8* when he beat William Regal for the Intercontinental Championship. Subsequent victories saw him claim nearly every other singles championship in WWE, including the now-defunct European and Hardcore championships. He also proved to be a force in the tag team ranks, winning titles with partners Kane, Booker T, and Rey Mysterio.

In 2006, RVD's career finally reached the pinnacle so many predicted when he won the thrilling Money in the Bank Ladder Match at *WrestleMania 22*. As "Mr. Money in the Bank," RVD was afforded the opportunity to challenge for a World Championship at the time and location of his choosing. He chose wisely.

In front of a large ECW fan base at *One Night Stand*, RVD challenged the normally popular John Cena for the WWE Championship. The ECW faithful nearly booed Cena out of the arena, but not before RVD could defeat him for the WWE Championship first. A few days later, Paul Heyman also awarded the rechristened ECW Championship to RVD, making him the first Superstar to hold both titles simultaneously.

RVD quietly left WWE in the summer of 2007. While he no longer entertains WWE audiences, many fans look back at his time on *Raw, SmackDown,* and especially in ECW with great fondness. In fact, some might say he was the "Whole Dam Show."

Rob Van Dam & Kane

| COMBINED WEIGHT | 560 lbs. |

TITLE HISTORY World Tag Team Champions

YEARS ACTIVE 1960-1969 1970-1979 1980-1989 1990-1999 **2000-PRESENT**

These two Superstars from opposite sides of the sports-entertainment spectrum came together in 2003. At the end of March, RVD and "the Big Red Monster" became World Tag Team Champions when they beat the Dudley Boyz and Lance Storm & Chief Morley in a Three-Team Elimination Match. As champions they seemed unbeatable with amazing attacks from the air courtesy of Van Dam, and brutal power moves from Kane. They fended off the challenge of La Resistance until a loss to the French-Canadians at *Bad Blood*. The loss created some hard feelings between RVD and Kane and, as is the case all too often, the lingering bad feelings spilled into the ring, and at one point Kane considered setting his former partner on fire! After a No Holds Barred match at *SummerSlam*, and a Steel Cage Match, they went their separate ways for good.

THE ROCK

| HT | 6'5" | WT | 275 lbs. | FROM | Miami, Florida |

SIGNATURE MOVE The People's Elbow

YEARS ACTIVE 1960–1969 1970–1979 1980–1989 **1990–1999 2000–PRESENT**

TITLE HISTORY WWE Champion, Intercontinental Champion, World Tag Team Champion

Dwayne Johnson grew up in a family of wrestling royalty. His father, future WWE Hall of Famer Rocky Johnson, was one of the most popular Superstars in the industry. His maternal grandfather, future WWE Hall of Famer High Chief Peter Maivia, was the patriarch of the famous Maivia family, one of professional wrestling's toughest competitors who also appeared in the 1967 James Bond classic, *You Only Live Twice*.

Because he idolized his father, grandfather and WWE Hall of Famers Andre The Giant, Hulk Hogan, Jimmy "Superfly" Snuka, and "Nature Boy" Ric Flair, it was only natural Dwayne thought about a life in both sports and entertainment. After a childhood of mischief, Dwayne was an All-American on the gridiron at Freedom High School in Bethlehem, PA. The young Johnson went on to the University of Miami and in 1991 was part of the Hurricanes NCAA Championship team. After a brief career in the Canadian Football League, Johnson entered the industry in which his family played such a significant role for so many decades.

" *KNOW YOUR ROLE AND SHUT YOUR MOUTH!* "

Trained by his father, along with Pat Patterson, Dwayne exceeded all expectations and soon cut his teeth in the United States Wrestling Association. While there, he learned his craft and stared across the ring at Jerry Lawler.

A ROCKY START

At the 1996 *Survivor Series,* a capacity Madison Square Garden crowd witnessed this first third-generation Superstar make his way to the ring. As a tribute to his grandfather and father, he chose the name Rocky Maivia. As the next Maivia emerged the sole survivor, this Superstar was set to take the sports-entertainment world by storm. Within three months of his debut, Rocky captured the Intercontinental Championship when he defeated Hunter Hearst-Helmsley on a special episode of *Thursday Raw.*

As the tone of sports-entertainment changed, the fans' cheers suddenly turned to jeers as they chanted "Rocky Sucks" and "Die Rocky Die." Shortening his name to "The Rock" and referring to himself in the third person, he became one of the most detested figures in all of WWE and a member of The Nation of Domination. The anger from the fans fueled his fire to succeed, and his undiluted arrogance enraged crowds everywhere. The Rock dubbed himself "The People's Champion" and made it clear he would reach the top of World Wrestling Entertainment by any means necessary. The Rock soon physically removed Faarooq as Nation leader and became the self-appointed ruler of The Nation, citing the term leader was beneath him. In the summer of 1998, The Nation began a fierce rivalry against D-Generation X to decide which was the dominant faction in WWE. The two leaders met in the King of the Ring tournament. After The Rock pinned rival Triple H, both crews threw fists of fury as pure bedlam flooded the ring.

The Rock's career gained momentum and he left The Nation to construct his own path to glory. He invited all Superstars to "Go One-on-One with The Great One," and in the process became the object of Mr. McMahon's intense scrutiny. "The People's Champion" went into the *Survivor Series'* 16-man tournament for the WWE Championship a heavy favorite. In the tournament finals against Mankind, the 26-year-old showed the perseverance and poise of a seasoned veteran. After he locked-in the Sharpshooter, the bell unexpectedly rang and their collusion became known. The McMahons courted The Rock and made "The People's Champion," "The Corporate Champion." A confused Mankind got his final explanation courtesy of a blindside beating by the newly crowned champion. This event led to a string of classic clashes between the two, and though Mankind temporarily regained the championship, the sight of a jubilant Mankind brought out an even more barbarous "Brahma Bull." Their most sadistic bout was the Last Man Standing Match at the *St. Valentine's Day Massacre.*

As millions (and millions) of The Rock's fans continued to smell what he was cookin', his opponents headed down Jabroni Drive, hung a left on Know Your Role Boulevard, and were checked directly into the Smackdown Hotel.

When neither man answered the ten-count, the match was ruled a draw and they met the next night on *Raw* in a Ladder Match, won by The Rock. Afterward, "The Most Electrifying Man in Sports-Entertainment" put his problems with Mankind behind him and focused on a new enemy.

At *WrestleMania XV,* the "Great One" took on the anti-establishment Stone Cold Steve Austin for the WWE Championship. The carnage in Philadelphia, proved to be the beginning of one of the greatest rivalries in WWE history. Despite a loss to the "Texas Rattlesnake," The Rock truly became "The People's Champion" when he left The Corporation and went his own way. As the mystique of The Rock grew, audiences continued to marvel at his undeniable charisma and wildly entertaining interview segments. As he entered the summer of 1999, he resumed war with a familiar foe, Triple H. When former enemy Mankind was looking for a friend, he treated The Rock to a parade of his past on an episode of "Rock: This is Your Life." In the process, the two joined forces as The Rock N' Sock Connection and surprised everyone with their continuity and resolve when they defeated Undertaker & Big Show for the World Tag Team Championship.

THE GREAT ONE AT #1

After he won the 2000 *Royal Rumble,* The Rock's popularity rose to new heights each week on WWE programming. He wrote his autobiography, *The Rock Says,* which reached No. 1 on the prestigious New York Times Bestseller List. He hosted *Saturday Night Live,* gave a special address at the Republican National Convention, and appeared in hip-hop legend Wyclef Jean's famous video, "It Doesn't Matter". By 2001, The Rock was considered an absolute multimedia superstar as he appeared in the feature film, *The Mummy Returns* and later starred in its highly successful prequel, *The Scorpion King,* which was commemorated with a wax statue of "The Great One" at Madame Tussaud's famous gallery in New York City.

The Rock challenging someone to go one-on-one with the Great One.

Of course, The Rock didn't sever his ties with WWE during this time. The Rock secured the fate of World Wrestling Entertainment at the 2001 *Survivor Series* as he captained Team WWE and destroyed The Alliance. This defense of his first love became indisputable in February 2002, when WWE was injected with the lethal poison of the nWo. The path taken by Hogan, Hall, and Nash left The Rock no choice but to do what was needed for the company's survival. At *Wrestlemania X-8,* he defeated Hollywood Hulk Hogan in their epic fantasy turned reality Icon vs. Icon Match. In 2003, The Rock's Hollywood stock continued to rise, but he may have saved his greatest act for *WrestleMania XIX,* when he defeated his long-time nemesis Stone Cold Steve Austin.

The Rock returned to Hollywood for *The Rundown* with Christopher Walken, but returned to WWE in 2004 to reform the Rock N' Sock Connection, and battle Evolution at *WrestleMania XX.* The Rock's international following grew and he continued to electrify movie screens as the main draw in multiple Hollywood blockbusters.

After three years away from WWE, The Rock appeared on *Monday Night Raw* in a taped segment in which he gave his prediction to the Battle of The Billionaires Match at *WrestleMania 23.* In 2008, he returned to World Wrestling Entertainment and inducted his father, Rocky Johnson, and late grandfather High Chief Peter Maivia into the WWE Hall of Fame.

THE ROCK 'N' SOCK CONNECTION

MEMBERS	The Rock, Mankind	**COMBINED WEIGHT**	562 lbs.

| **TITLE HISTORY** | World Tag Team Champions | **YEARS ACTIVE** | 1960-1969 | 1970-1979 | 1980-1989 | **1990-1999** | 2000-PRESENT |

Know your role, and have a nice day.

What do you get when you take a third-generation Superstar and combine him with a Hardcore Legend? You get the Rock 'N' Sock Connection. These two gifted performers and former adversaries were brought together by chance in August 1999 after Undertaker and Big Show attacked The Rock. As their success grew, the unlikely pair became closer, Mankind wanted to surprise his new friend that September. On what would be a ratings record-setting segment on *Monday Night Raw,* Mankind treated The Rock to a special *"This is Your Life."*

While The Rock grew tired of the team and accused Mankind of stealing his catchphrases and signature moves, there was always something about the odd couple that brought a smile to his face. Even after Mankind wrongfully accused "The Great One" of throwing his New York Times best-seller, *Have A Nice Day,* in the trash and letting him defend the World Tag Team Championship on his own, they were always able to get back on the same page. The popular tandem reunited from time-to-time as called for up until Mick Foley's retirement from the ring in 2000. When all hope was lost for Foley, who was outnumbered in his fight against Evolution, the three-time World Tag Team Champions reformed on sports-entertainment's most famed stage for the last time at *WrestleMania XX.* The packed Madison Square Garden crowd saw the Rock 'N' Sock Connection battle "Nature Boy" Ric Flair, Batista & Randy Orton in a Handicap Match.

This duo ignited World Wrestling Entertainment and continuously showed that no matter the odds, the Rock 'N' Sock Connection could come together at any given time and take care of business. To this day, audiences fondly recall their thrilling matches and entertaining interviews.

Rockabilly

HT	6'4"	**WT**	268 lbs.

| **YEARS ACTIVE** | 1960-1969 | 1970-1979 | 1980-1989 | **1990-1999** | 2000-PRESENT |

Following three World Tag Team Championship reigns with his brother Bart, Billy Gunn tried his hand at singles competition in 1997. His initial attempt at solo glory was one he'd likely rather forget. Managed by Honky Tonk Man, Gunn adopted the identity of a 1950s rocker known as Rockabilly. It was during this period of his career that Gunn first came in contact with Jesse James. While the two were in the midst of a brief rivalry, they decided they were better off ending their war peacefully and forming a tag team. Their union resulted in the end of Rockabilly and the formation of the New Age Outlaws.

THE ROCKERS

| MEMBERS | Shawn Michaels, Marty Jannetty | COMBINED WEIGHT | 455 lbs. |

YEARS ACTIVE

The Rockers are seen by many as the greatest tag team never to win titles in WWE. While this is an astonishing fact, it's even harder to grasp the idea that Shawn Michaels & Marty Jannetty almost never had an opportunity to prove themselves in WWE.

After opening eyes while competing as the Midnight Rockers in the AWA, Michaels & Jannetty made the move to WWE in 1987. The good-looking tandem had dreams of dominating the stacked tag division. WWE, however, didn't share the same dream and fired the youngsters after only two weeks.

With their tails between their legs, Michaels & Jannetty left, not knowing if they would get another opportunity at greatness. The high-flying duo continued to work on their game for the better part of a year before WWE officials agreed to give them another look. By the summer of 1988, Michaels & Jannetty re-debuted as the Rockers, and the rest is sports-entertainment history.

The Rockers achieved early success, turning back such highly celebrated duos as the Brain Busters and the Rougeau Brothers. By 1990, their incredible teamwork earned them the reputation of tag team specialists. However, despite all their wins, they were never given a serious opportunity to claim the World Tag Team Championship.

In October 1990, the Rockers were finally granted a high-profile championship shot against the Hart Foundation at *Saturday Night's Main Event*. The match proved to be one of the most controversial tag team encounters of all time, as the Rockers actually left the arena that night with the titles. The championship switch, however, was later stricken from the record after the match was ruled unsafe, due to a ring rope breaking during the bout.

That was the closest the Rockers ever came to claiming the World Tag Team Championship. By 1992, Michaels believed he had outgrown his role in the Rockers. To prove his point, he kicked his longtime partner through the window of *The Barber Shop*, thus signifying the end of the popular tag team. In recent years, the duo has reunited on occasion, giving fans a glimpse at what made the Rockers such a groundbreaking and memorable tandem.

Rockin' Robin

| HT | 5'7" |

| FROM | Charlotte, North Carolina |

| SIGNATURE MOVE | Bulldog |

| TITLE HISTORY | Women's Champion |

YEARS ACTIVE

Rockin' Robin made her WWE debut on one of the biggest stages possible when she joined the Fabulous Moolah's stable to turn back Sensational Sherri and her team of Divas at the 1987 *Survivor Series*.

The athletic brunette spent the next several months utilizing her devastating bulldog finisher to open the eyes of WWE officials. After racking up an impressive win-loss record, Robin finally earned an opportunity at the Women's Championship. Capitalizing on her big break, she upended Sherri for the championship in France in October 1988.

Proving her championship victory was no fluke, Robin handily defeated challenger Judy Martin at the 1989 *Royal Rumble*. A few months later, she established herself as a multi-talented Diva when she opened *WrestleMania V* with a stirring rendition of "America the Beautiful."

Robin remained Women's Champion until she left WWE in 1990. As a result of her departure, WWE deemed the title inactive. It was later reintroduced in December 1993.

ROCKY JOHNSON 🇨🇦

HT 6'2"	**WT** 243 lbs.	**FROM** Toronto, Ontario, Canada

SIGNATURE MOVE The Dropkick **TITLE HISTORY** World Tag Team Champion

YEARS ACTIVE 1960-1969 1970-1979 1980-1989 1990-1999 2000-PRESENT

This soulman started out as a boxer and decided to enter professional wrestling during the mid-1960s. After success in both the singles and tag team ranks throughout the National Wrestling Alliance and overseas, Rocky Johnson made his World Wrestling Entertainment debut in 1983. From his first match, audiences knew he was a special performer and sports-entertainment's first "Rock" was one of the most popular members of the WWE roster. Fans admired his style that combined speed, acrobatics, power, and mat wrestling. Rocky was also admired by the daughter of High Chief Peter Maivia, one of his tag team partners. They two were married, and had a son in 1972.

Johnson matched up against the likes of "Superstar" Billy Graham, the Wild Samoans, Mr. Fuji, the Magnificent Muraco, Baron Mikel Scicluna, George "The Animal" Steele, and Big John Studd. On November 15, 1983, he and "Mr. USA" Tony Atlas made history in Allentown, Pennsylvania when they defeated the Wild Samoans to become the first-ever World Tag Team Champions of African descent. They proudly defended the titles for five months and became one of the most popular duos in the annals of WWE.

After leaving the WWE in 1985, Rocky Johnson, along with Pat Patterson, trained his son for a career in sports-entertainment. During his son's debut as Rocky Maivia, things got heated and Mr. Johnson was not afraid to get into the mix and help his son fend off foes.

The night before *Wrestlemania XXIV,* the career that was fueled by courage and desire was immortalized when Rocky Johnson was inducted into the WWE Hall of Fame by his son, now known as The Rock.

ROGERS' CORNER

"Nature Boy" Buddy Rogers was one of the greatest performers sports-entertainment will ever know. For decades he was the only man to hold both NWA and WWE Championships. Rogers returned to WWE in 1982 and soon after he saved protégé Jimmy "Superfly" Snuka from Capt. Lou Albano, he debuted his talk show segment *Rogers' Corner*.

Rogers' Corner was where Superstars discussed their careers, and shared their opinions and future intentions with the great "Nature Boy." Whenever things got contentious, Rogers was quick to let guests know that he had no problem straightening things out, his way.

Ron "Faarooq" Simmons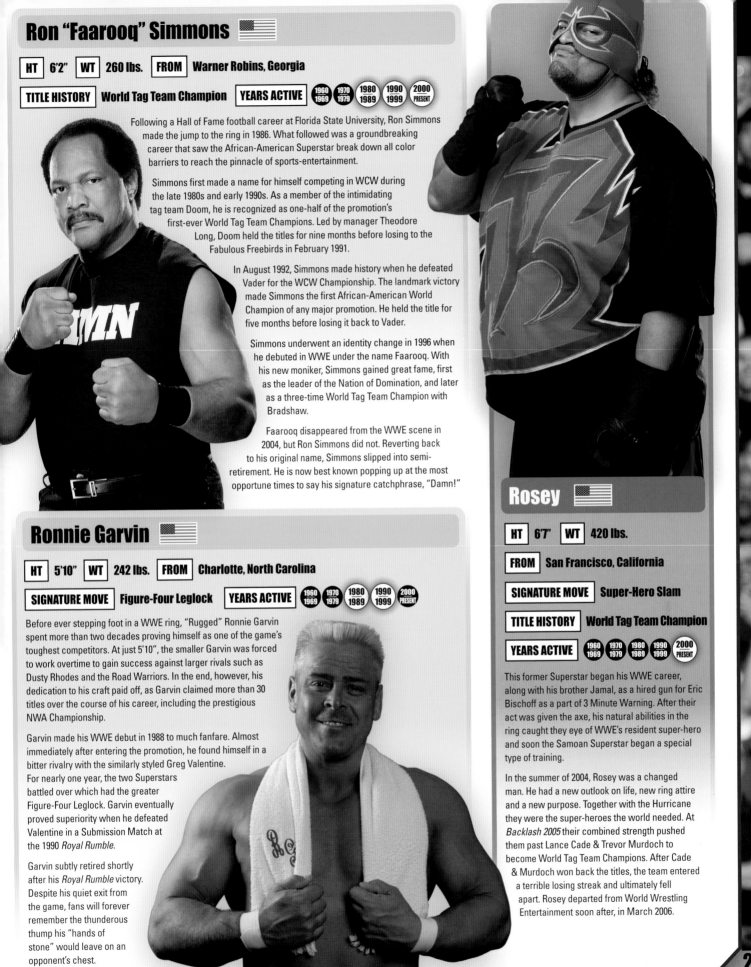

HT	6'2"	WT	260 lbs.	FROM	Warner Robins, Georgia

TITLE HISTORY	World Tag Team Champion	YEARS ACTIVE	1960 1969	1970 1979	1980 1989	1990 1999	2000 PRESENT

Following a Hall of Fame football career at Florida State University, Ron Simmons made the jump to the ring in 1986. What followed was a groundbreaking career that saw the African-American Superstar break down all color barriers to reach the pinnacle of sports-entertainment.

Simmons first made a name for himself competing in WCW during the late 1980s and early 1990s. As a member of the intimidating tag team Doom, he is recognized as one-half of the promotion's first-ever World Tag Team Champions. Led by manager Theodore Long, Doom held the titles for nine months before losing to the Fabulous Freebirds in February 1991.

In August 1992, Simmons made history when he defeated Vader for the WCW Championship. The landmark victory made Simmons the first African-American World Champion of any major promotion. He held the title for five months before losing it back to Vader.

Simmons underwent an identity change in 1996 when he debuted in WWE under the name Faarooq. With his new moniker, Simmons gained great fame, first as the leader of the Nation of Domination, and later as a three-time World Tag Team Champion with Bradshaw.

Faarooq disappeared from the WWE scene in 2004, but Ron Simmons did not. Reverting back to his original name, Simmons slipped into semi-retirement. He is now best known popping up at the most opportune times to say his signature catchphrase, "Damn!"

Ronnie Garvin

HT	5'10"	WT	242 lbs.	FROM	Charlotte, North Carolina

SIGNATURE MOVE	Figure-Four Leglock	YEARS ACTIVE	1960 1969	1970 1979	1980 1989	1990 1999	2000 PRESENT

Before ever stepping foot in a WWE ring, "Rugged" Ronnie Garvin spent more than two decades proving himself as one of the game's toughest competitors. At just 5'10", the smaller Garvin was forced to work overtime to gain success against larger rivals such as Dusty Rhodes and the Road Warriors. In the end, however, his dedication to his craft paid off, as Garvin claimed more than 30 titles over the course of his career, including the prestigious NWA Championship.

Garvin made his WWE debut in 1988 to much fanfare. Almost immediately after entering the promotion, he found himself in a bitter rivalry with the similarly styled Greg Valentine. For nearly one year, the two Superstars battled over which had the greater Figure-Four Leglock. Garvin eventually proved superiority when he defeated Valentine in a Submission Match at the 1990 *Royal Rumble*.

Garvin subtly retired shortly after his *Royal Rumble* victory. Despite his quiet exit from the game, fans will forever remember the thunderous thump his "hands of stone" would leave on an opponent's chest.

Rosey

HT	6'7"	WT	420 lbs.

FROM	San Francisco, California

SIGNATURE MOVE	Super-Hero Slam

TITLE HISTORY	World Tag Team Champion

YEARS ACTIVE	1960 1969	1970 1979	1980 1989	1990 1999	2000 PRESENT

This former Superstar began his WWE career, along with his brother Jamal, as a hired gun for Eric Bischoff as a part of 3 Minute Warning. After their act was given the axe, his natural abilities in the ring caught they eye of WWE's resident super-hero and soon the Samoan Superstar began a special type of training.

In the summer of 2004, Rosey was a changed man. He had a new outlook on life, new ring attire and a new purpose. Together with the Hurricane they were the super-heroes the world needed. At *Backlash 2005* their combined strength pushed them past Lance Cade & Trevor Murdoch to become World Tag Team Champions. After Cade & Murdoch won back the titles, the team entered a terrible losing streak and ultimately fell apart. Rosey departed from World Wrestling Entertainment soon after, in March 2006.

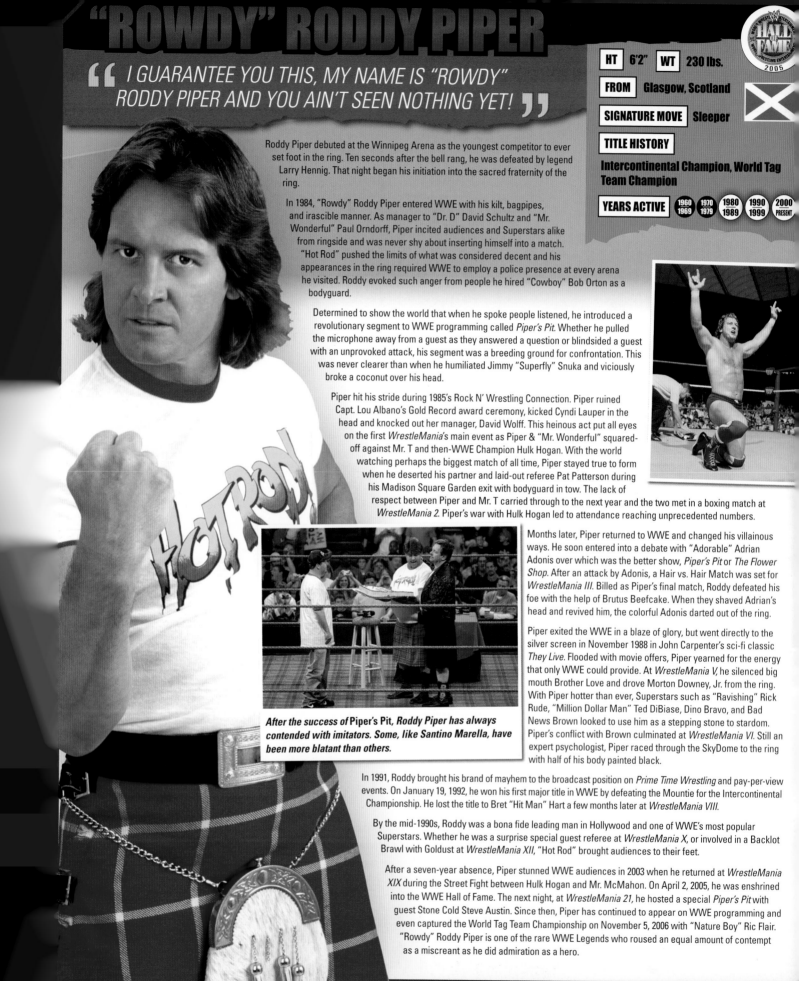

"ROWDY" RODDY PIPER

> " I GUARANTEE YOU THIS, MY NAME IS "ROWDY" RODDY PIPER AND YOU AIN'T SEEN NOTHING YET! "

HT	6'2"	WT	230 lbs.

FROM Glasgow, Scotland

SIGNATURE MOVE Sleeper

TITLE HISTORY
Intercontinental Champion, World Tag Team Champion

YEARS ACTIVE | 1960 1969 | 1970 1979 | 1980 1989 | 1990 1999 | 2000 PRESENT |

Roddy Piper debuted at the Winnipeg Arena as the youngest competitor to ever set foot in the ring. Ten seconds after the bell rang, he was defeated by legend Larry Hennig. That night began his initiation into the sacred fraternity of the ring.

In 1984, "Rowdy" Roddy Piper entered WWE with his kilt, bagpipes, and irascible manner. As manager to "Dr. D" David Schultz and "Mr. Wonderful" Paul Orndorff, Piper incited audiences and Superstars alike from ringside and was never shy about inserting himself into a match. "Hot Rod" pushed the limits of what was considered decent and his appearances in the ring required WWE to employ a police presence at every arena he visited. Roddy evoked such anger from people he hired "Cowboy" Bob Orton as a bodyguard.

Determined to show the world that when he spoke people listened, he introduced a revolutionary segment to WWE programming called *Piper's Pit*. Whether he pulled the microphone away from a guest as they answered a question or blindsided a guest with an unprovoked attack, his segment was a breeding ground for confrontation. This was never clearer than when he humiliated Jimmy "Superfly" Snuka and viciously broke a coconut over his head.

Piper hit his stride during 1985's Rock N' Wrestling Connection. Piper ruined Capt. Lou Albano's Gold Record award ceremony, kicked Cyndi Lauper in the head and knocked out her manager, David Wolff. This heinous act put all eyes on the first *WrestleMania*'s main event as Piper & "Mr. Wonderful" squared-off against Mr. T and then-WWE Champion Hulk Hogan. With the world watching perhaps the biggest match of all time, Piper stayed true to form when he deserted his partner and laid-out referee Pat Patterson during his Madison Square Garden exit with bodyguard in tow. The lack of respect between Piper and Mr. T carried through to the next year and the two met in a boxing match at *WrestleMania 2*. Piper's war with Hulk Hogan led to attendance reaching unprecedented numbers.

Months later, Piper returned to WWE and changed his villainous ways. He soon entered into a debate with "Adorable" Adrian Adonis over which was the better show, *Piper's Pit* or *The Flower Shop*. After an attack by Adonis, a Hair vs. Hair Match was set for *WrestleMania III*. Billed as Piper's final match, Roddy defeated his foe with the help of Brutus Beefcake. When they shaved Adrian's head and revived him, the colorful Adonis darted out of the ring.

Piper exited the WWE in a blaze of glory, but went directly to the silver screen in November 1988 in John Carpenter's sci-fi classic *They Live*. Flooded with movie offers, Piper yearned for the energy that only WWE could provide. At *WrestleMania V*, he silenced big mouth Brother Love and drove Morton Downey, Jr. from the ring. With Piper hotter than ever, Superstars such as "Ravishing" Rick Rude, "Million Dollar Man" Ted DiBiase, Dino Bravo, and Bad News Brown looked to use him as a stepping stone to stardom. Piper's conflict with Brown culminated at *WrestleMania VI*. Still an expert psychologist, Piper raced through the SkyDome to the ring with half of his body painted black.

After the success of Piper's Pit, Roddy Piper has always contended with imitators. Some, like Santino Marella, have been more blatant than others.

In 1991, Roddy brought his brand of mayhem to the broadcast position on *Prime Time Wrestling* and pay-per-view events. On January 19, 1992, he won his first major title in WWE by defeating the Mountie for the Intercontinental Championship. He lost the title to Bret "Hit Man" Hart a few months later at *WrestleMania VIII*.

By the mid-1990s, Roddy was a bona fide leading man in Hollywood and one of WWE's most popular Superstars. Whether he was a surprise special guest referee at *WrestleMania X*, or involved in a Backlot Brawl with Goldust at *WrestleMania XII*, "Hot Rod" brought audiences to their feet.

After a seven-year absence, Piper stunned WWE audiences in 2003 when he returned at *WrestleMania XIX* during the Street Fight between Hulk Hogan and Mr. McMahon. On April 2, 2005, he was enshrined into the WWE Hall of Fame. The next night, at *WrestleMania 21*, he hosted a special *Piper's Pit* with guest Stone Cold Steve Austin. Since then, Piper has continued to appear on WWE programming and even captured the World Tag Team Championship on November 5, 2006 with "Nature Boy" Ric Flair. "Rowdy" Roddy Piper is one of the rare WWE Legends who roused an equal amount of contempt as a miscreant as he did admiration as a hero.

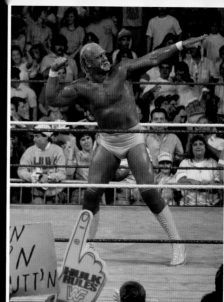

Every year since 1988, one Superstar has earned a shot at the World Heavyweight or WWE Championship at *WrestleMania* after being the last man in the ring after the match for which the event is named: the *Royal Rumble*. The list of past winners reads like a "Who's Who" of sports-entertainment, including Hulk Hogan, Bret Hart, Ric Flair, Shawn Michaels, Stone Cold Steve Austin, and even Mr. McMahon himself.

January 24, 1988
Hamilton, Ontario, Canada - Copps Coliseum

Royal Rumble Winner:
"Hacksaw" Jim Duggan

January 15, 1989
Houston, TX - The Summit

Royal Rumble Winner:
Big John Studd

January 21, 1990
Orlando, FL - Orlando Arena

Royal Rumble Winner:
Hulk Hogan

January 19, 1991
Miami, FL - Miami Arena

Royal Rumble Winner:
Hulk Hogan

January 19, 1992
Albany, NY - Knickerbocker Arena

Royal Rumble Winner:
Ric Flair

January 24, 1993
Sacramento, CA - ARCO Arena

Royal Rumble Winner:
Yokozuna

January 22, 1994
Providence, RI - Providence Civic Center

Royal Rumble Winner:
Bret "Hit Man" Hart and Lex Luger

January 22, 1995
Tampa, FL - USF Sun Dome

Royal Rumble Winner:
Shawn Michaels

January 21, 1996
Fresno, CA - Selland Arena

Royal Rumble Winner:
Shawn Michaels

January 19, 1997
San Antonio, TX - Alamodome

Royal Rumble Winner:
Stone Cold Steve Austin

January 18, 1998
San Jose, CA - San Jose Arena

Royal Rumble Winner:
Stone Cold Steve Austin

January 24, 1999
Anaheim, CA - Arrowhead Pond

Royal Rumble Winner:
Mr. McMahon

January 23, 2000
Anaheim, CA - Arrowhead Pond

Royal Rumble Winner:
The Rock

January 21, 2001
New Orleans, LA - New Orleans Arena

Royal Rumble Winner:
Stone Cold Steve Austin

January 20, 2002
Atlanta, GA - Philips Arena

Royal Rumble Winner:
Triple H

January 19, 2003
Boston, MA - Fleet Center

Royal Rumble Winner:
Brock Lesnar

January 24, 2004
Philadelphia, PA - Wachovia Center

Royal Rumble Winner:
Chris Benoit

January 30, 2005
Fresno, CA - Save Mart Arena

Royal Rumble Winner:
Batista

January 29, 2006
Miami, FL - American Airlines Arena

Royal Rumble Winner:
Rey Mysterio

January 28, 2007
San Antonio, TX - AT&T Center

Royal Rumble Winner:
Undertaker

January 27, 2008
New York, NY - Madison Square Garden

Royal Rumble Winner:
John Cena

R-Truth

HT 6'2" **WT** 228 lbs. **FROM** Charlotte, North Carolina **TITLE HISTORY** Hardcore Champion

Growing up in the rough streets of North Carolina, R-Truth chose a life of crime as a way to make a name for himself. His imprudence ultimately landed him behind bars. Now a free man, R-Truth has recognized the wrongs of his past and considers himself a stronger man after paying his debt to society.

R-Truth first appeared in WWE in 1999 as K-Kwik alongside Road Dogg. Today, the reformed Superstar exudes an optimism that spreads throughout arenas all over the world. With his infectious smile and charismatic rapping, R-Truth has become an instant fan favorite. His unparalleled agility and athleticism inside the ring has made him a legitimate threat to *SmackDown's* titleholders.

Ryan Braddock

YEARS ACTIVE 1960 1969 1970 1979 1980 1989 1990 1999 **2000 PRESENT**

HT 6'4" **WT** 262 lbs. **FROM** Chicago, Illinois **SIGNATURE MOVE** Lariat

Rough, tough, and ready for anything that comes his way, this young Superstar showed in his WWE debut against Big Show that he's afraid of nothing. With an aggressive fighting style for a new era of competitor, Ryan Braddock has seen action against *SmackDown* Superstars of various shapes and sizes including Festus, Ricky Ortiz, and Super Crazy.

As this tough guy from the South Side of Chicago smashes competition on his way up the championship ranks, watch out for Ryan Braddock, it might just save your career!

Ryan Shamrock

YEARS ACTIVE 1960 1969 1970 1979 1980 1989 **1990 1999** 2000 PRESENT

HT 5'6" **FROM** Sacramento, California

With her quiet demeanor and innocent smile, Ryan Shamrock certainly played the part of a proper young woman. In reality, Ken Shamrock's little sister was anything but pure. Just weeks after making her first WWE appearance, Ryan was co-starring in Val Venis' latest flick, *Sister Act*. Proving her act of indiscretion was not a momentary lapse of judgment, the leggy blonde later intentionally left the blinds to her SkyDome hotel room open so that *Raw* fans could witness the couple in their most intimate moments. In typical fashion, Val Venis eventually kicked young Ryan to the curb. Refusing to be a victim, the jilted Diva later joined forces with Terri and Jacqueline in the male-bashing faction Pretty Mean Sisters. As a member of PMS, Ryan used her sexuality to get whatever she wanted from the male Superstars.

Saba Simba

YEARS ACTIVE 1960 1969 1970 1979 1980 1989 **1990 1999** 2000 PRESENT

HT 6'2" **WT** 250 lbs. **FROM** Africa

In the early 1990s, a mountain of a man emerged on the WWE scene under the moniker of Saba Simba. Clad in a giant feather headdress and leopard print tights, Saba Simba was billed as an African tribal warrior. He struggled to pick up wins and was quickly gone from WWE, but not before he was able to compete in the 1991 *Royal Rumble*.

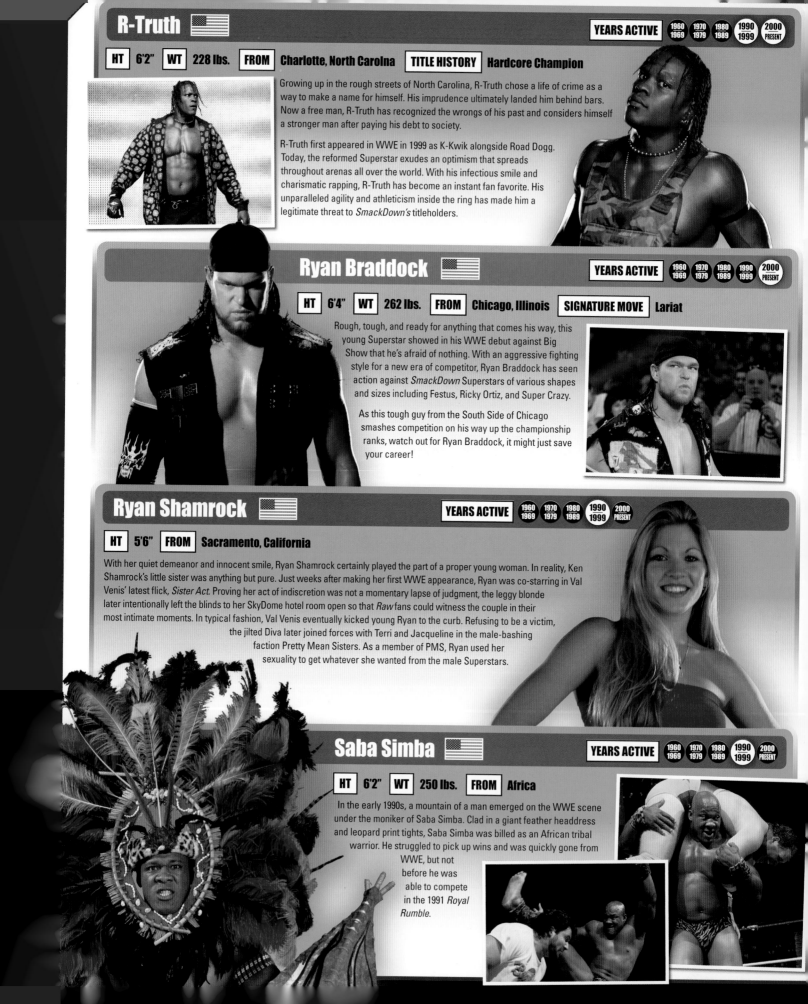

SABLE

HT 5'6" **FROM** Jacksonville, Florida **SIGNATURE MOVE** Sable Bomb

TITLE HISTORY Women's Champion

Although women competed for decades in WWE rings before her, Sable is considered by many as a pioneer. Behind her amazing athleticism and spine-jarring Sable Bomb, the blonde bombshell became the sixteenth Women's Champion in WWE history. Despite her impressive in-ring accolades, however, Sable will be long remembered for being the first of many beautiful Divas to bare it all in *Playboy*.

Sable's earliest WWE days were spent by the side of Hunter Hearst-Helmsley, but when he began to mistreat the fair-haired Diva, her husband, Marc Mero, ran to her aid. For the better part of the next two years, the loving couple shared a strong bond both on and off the air.

By 1998, the spotlight began to shine brightest on Sable, leaving Mero's star to fade. Jealous of his wife's popularity, Mero tried everything in his power to dim her bright career and hide her voluptuous curves. His attempts eventually backfired when Sable escaped from his grasp, delivering a Sable Bomb in the process.

Sable then went on to achieve never-before-seen success. Her first step toward greatness was capturing the Women's Championship from Mero's new lady, Jacqueline. In the months that followed, the new champ rode her popularity all the way to Hollywood, landing guest roles on a few television programs.

Sable's inevitable break into mainstream came when she landed the cover of *Playboy* in April 1999. The overwhelming success of her spread led to two more covers, but more importantly, helped pave the way for future Divas. Sable made a shocking return to WWE in 2003, when she was featured in another *Playboy* spread—this time with Torrie.

Sabu

HT 6' **WT** 235 lbs. **FROM** Bombay, Michigan

SIGNATURE MOVE Arabian Facebuster

Trained by his Hall of Fame uncle, The Sheik, Sabu knew no fear inside the ring. Possessing a complete disregard for his own wellbeing, the maniacal Superstar gained a cult-like following while competing in ECW in the mid-to-late 1990s.

Over the course of his lengthy ECW career, Sabu captured every piece of hardware the promotion offered, including three reigns with the prestigious ECW Championship. Despite his golden resumé, Sabu is best remembered for the abundance of injuries he suffered. Sliced open by barbed wire and shards of broken tables, his scarred body proudly displays permanent memories of his vicious battles.

Sabu competed at *ECW One Night Stand* in 2006. Battling Rey Mysterio for the World Heavyweight Championship, he used his extreme style of competition to take Mysterio to the limit. In the end, the match was declared a no-contest after both men crashed through a table, rendering them unable to compete.

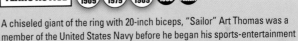

Following the success of his *One Night Stand* appearance, Sabu entered WWE's revived version of ECW. He used the brand's premiere episode to reintroduce himself as one of ECW's supreme Superstars, winning an Extreme Battle Royal to earn the right to challenge John Cena for the WWE Championship at *Vengeance*. He ultimately lost to Cena, but successfully reminded fans that he was the "Suicidal, Homicidal, Genocidal, Death-Defying Maniac."

"Sailor" Art Thomas

HT 6'6" **WT** 265 lbs. **FROM** Fitchburg, Wisconsin

SIGNATURE MOVE Bearhug

A chiseled giant of the ring with 20-inch biceps, "Sailor" Art Thomas was a member of the United States Navy before he began his sports-entertainment career in 1943. During the 1950s Thomas became one of the most beloved performers in the world and one of the first Superstars of African descent.

In the early 1960s Thomas contended for the NWA Heavyweight Championship held at the time by "Nature Boy" Boddy Rogers. In 1963 Thomas made his WWE debut dazzling the fans in the northeast with his physique, power, and quickness. For the next seven years "Sailor" appeared for WWE in singles competition and formed thrilling tandems with Bruno Sammartino and Bobo Brazil.

He continued his sports-entertainment career until his retirement early in the 1980s. Sadly, this cultural icon and legend of the ring passed away in 2003. "Sailor" Art Thomas was a hero to all and touched fans throughout the world over the course of his career.

Salvatore Bellamo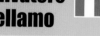

HT 6'2" **WT** 290 lbs.

FROM Italy

SIGNATURE MOVE
Running Splash

YEARS ACTIVE

Known as the "Wildman", Italian Superstar Salvatore Bellomo gained moderate WWE success upon his arrival in the early 1980s. During this time, his greatest claim to fame was filling in for his injured friend Junkyard Dog on an in-ring edition of *Piper's Pit.* As a guest of "Rowdy" Roddy Piper, Bellomo was the target of severe verbal barbs from both Piper and "Mr. Wonderful" Paul Orndorff. Finally, after the verbal attack turned physical, the injured JYD dragged himself to the ring to fend off Bellomo's adversaries.

After his WWE days came to a close, Bellomo brought his signature running splash finisher to ECW. As a member of the Philadelphia-based promotion, the "Wildman" became a brief member of the Full Blooded Italians stable. With his in-ring days behind him, Bellomo now works in Belgium as a trainer to Superstars of tomorrow.

Salvatore Sincere

HT 6'3" **WT** 262 lbs.

FROM
Philadelphia, Pennsylvania

SIGNATURE MOVE
Sincerely Yours

YEARS ACTIVE

Arrogant, charismatic, and with a bodybuilder's physique, Salvatore Sincere entered WWE in 1996. Sincere battled Superstars such as Barry Horowitz, Savio Vega, Rocky Maivia, Jake Roberts, Shawn Michaels, and Undertaker. While battilng over the services of Sable, Marc Mero revealed Salvatore's real name was Tom Brandi, which lead to Salvatore often using that name while competing until he left WWE in April 1998.

Whichever name was announced to audiences, whether a villain or fan favorite, this rugged soldier brought the same grit and fight to the ring. Today, he still appears at independent events all over the United States.

Sam Houston

HT 6'1" **WT** 227 lbs.

FROM Waco, Texas

YEARS ACTIVE

Sam Houston liked to dance just as much as he liked to wrestle. Upon his debut in 1987, he caught the attention of fans with his pre-match dance steps. Once the bell rang, he was all business.

Houston's WWE career was highlighted by decisive victories in rivalries with Barry Horowitz and Danny Davis. Unfortunately, he had trouble keeping up with WWE's more skilled competitors. Houston did, however, compete in the first-ever *Royal Rumble* Match in 1988. He was also a member of Ultimate Warrior's *Survivor Series* team later that year.

Samu

HT 6'4" **WT** 260 lbs.

FROM Isle of Samoa

SIGNATURE MOVE
Flying Head-butt

TITLE HISTORY
World Tag Team Champion

YEARS ACTIVE

This young monster appeared in Canada, Puerto Rico, and in the United States, managed by the ever-agitating Paul E. Dangerously. In 1992, Samu and his cousin Fatu entered WWE under the name the Headshrinkers. Managed by Afa and later co-managed by Lou Albano. They won the World Tag Team Championship in April 1994, but lost them in August. Soon after their title, Samu left the company. In 1996 he appeared in Extreme Championship Wrestling and remains active on the independent scene.

Samula

| **HT** 6'4" | **WT** 260 lbs. | **FROM** Isle of Samoa | **TITLE HISTORY** World Tag Team Champion |

Samula comes from a long line of successful Samoan Superstars. As a member of the famed Anoa'i family, which also includes Afa, Sika, Peter Maivia, and The Rock, Samula was born into wrestling greatness.

At the young age of 20, Samula was thrust into the WWE spotlight. With his Uncle Sika sidelined by injury, Samula became the third member of the legendary Wild Samoans tag team. While Sika rehabbed his injury, Samula teamed with his father, Afa, to help defend the World Tag Team Championship. Samula also gained some success as a singles Superstar before finally leaving WWE in 1985.

The Sandman

| **HT** 6'4" | **WT** 240 lbs. | **FROM** Philadelphia, Pennsylvania |

SIGNATURE MOVE The White Russian Legsweep

This Singapore Cane swingin', cigarette smokin', beer-chuggin' maniac was one of the primary reasons the "E" stood for Extreme in ECW. In his six years with ECW he was a five-time ECW Champion and Tag Team Champion. The Sandman was also seen by WWE audiences during ECW's first invasion of WWE in 1996. In 1999 Sandman left the world of barbed-wire and blood and went to WCW but returned home by the end of the year. After ECW's closure in 2001 he toured the globe.

When the hardcore revolution arose from the ashes in 2005, culminating at *ECW One Night Stand*, the Sandman made a dramatic entrance highlighted by the entire arena singing along with his entrance music, Sandman flattening an empty can against his head, and Joey Styles noting, "He's already busted open, and the match hasn't begun yet!" After appearing at *One Night Stand* in 2006, he became a key figure in WWE's re-launch of ECW. As a part of the ECW Originals, he stood victorious in the ring at *WrestleMania 23* after defeating the New Breed. That June, he became the first ECW Original to be drafted away from the brand to *Raw*, where he appeared until he left WWE in September 2007.

Santino Marella

| **HT** 5'10" | **WT** 227 lbs. | **FROM** Calabria, Italy |

SIGNATURE MOVE Neckbreaker

TITLE HISTORY Intercontinental Championship

Proving that miracles can happen, Santino Marella turned a front row seat into a golden opportunity when he answered Mr. McMahon's challenge for any WWE fan to step into the ring with Intercontinental Champion Umaga. With a little help from Bobby Lashley, Marella defeated Umaga for the title in one of the most improbable moments in WWE history.

With sold-out arenas chanting his name, the young Italian somehow managed to turn back the most skilled veterans. Suddenly, Marella's magical momentum began to disappear, and with each mounting loss, an ugly side of Marella began to emerge. Despite his new annoyingly insecure attitude, Marella managed to strike the fancy of Maria. The two quickly engaged in an intense affair that ultimately proved to be too much for Marella to handle. Their relationship reached its climax when the beautiful Maria was chosen to pose nude for *Playboy* magazine. Marella did everything in his power to sabotage Maria's moment; but in the end, it was their love affair that fizzled, as the Raw Diva had no choice but to walk away for good. Marella has since sought comfort in the arms of Beth Phoenix, who carried him to the Intercontinental Championship at *SummerSlam* in 2008.

Sapphire

In 1989, longtime fan Sapphire bought a ticket to a WWE live event that changed her life forever. While sitting ringside, the superfan was spotted by Dusty Rhodes. Admiring her enthusiasm, the "American Dream" pulled her from her seat and took her on as his valet.

As Rhodes' second, Sapphire escorted her man to the ring and sat ringside while he climbed the WWE ladder. As a sign of loyalty to Rhodes, she even wore matching yellow polka dots. As time went on, Sapphire's involvement increased. It wasn't long before the one-time fan soon became an in-ring competitor. At *WrestleMania VI*, Sapphire teamed with Rhodes to defeat Randy Savage & Sensational Sherri in WWE's first-ever Mixed Tag Team Match.

In the summer of 1990, Sapphire began to receive extravagant gifts from an unknown source. Week after week, she was seen with new diamond rings, bracelets and necklaces. She claimed she had no idea where the gifts were coming from. At *SummerSlam 1990*, Sapphire proved that everybody has a price for the "Million-Dollar Man" when she turned her back on Rhodes to join forces with Ted DiBiase.

Savio Vega

YEARS ACTIVE: 1960-1969, 1970-1979, 1980-1989, **1990-1999**, 2000-PRESENT

HT 5'11" **WT** 260 lbs. **FROM** South Bronx, New York **SIGNATURE MOVE** Spinning Heel Kick

Savio Vega made a big splash in his debut at May 1995's *In Your House*. After saving Razor Ramon from a brutal beating at the hands of Jeff Jarrett and the Roadie, the two became tag team partners. After Razor Ramon left WWE, Vega continued to make an impression within the singles ranks against the likes of Hunter Hearst-Helmsley and Steve Austin, then known as the Ringmaster.

In 1997 he briefly joined the Nation of Domination, but after he was forcibly expelled, Vega created a group of his own, Los Baricuas. Vega also competed in 1998's *Brawl For All* Tournament before leaving World Wrestling Entertainment later in the year. He returned to his homeland of Puerto Rico where he has been a huge star since his early days in sports-entertainment.

Scott Casey

YEARS ACTIVE: 1960-1969, 1970-1979, **1980-1989**, 1990-1999, 2000-PRESENT

HT 6' **WT** 230 lbs. **FROM** Amarillo, Texas **SIGNATURE MOVE** Bulldog

Trained by the legendary Dory Funk, Sr., Scott Casey showcased his talents in various promotions worldwide over the course of his 30 years in the ring. The rugged Texan's days of constantly bouncing around finally settled, however, when he signed a WWE contract in 1987.

Casey's greatest WWE highlight saw him team with "Hacksaw" Jim Duggan, Jake Roberts, Tito Santana, & Ken Patera at the 1988 *Survivor Series*. After a brutal 30-minute battle, Casey's team succumbed to the mighty combination of Andre the Giant, "Ravishing" Rick Rude, Mr. Perfect, Dino Bravo & Harley Race. Casey failed to achieve much success after *Survivor Series*, but will forever have the memory of competing alongside many future Hall of Famers on one of the biggest stages around. After retiring from WWE in 1990, Casey began working as a trainer to future Superstars. He is credited for helping shape the career of a young Booker T.

Scott Putski

YEARS ACTIVE: 1960-1969, 1970-1979, 1980-1989, **1990-1999**, 2000-PRESENT

HT 5'9" **WT** 275 lbs. **FROM** Austin, Texas **SIGNATURE MOVE** Polish Hammer

Scott Putski grew up in the sports-entertainment world of his father "Polish Power" Ivan Putski. In the early 1990s, Scott began his professional career and even toured Japan. In 1997, Scott Putski debuted in WWE on *Monday Night Raw* and had fans on their feet once his name was announced. His rivalry against Brian Christopher escalated to a father and son affair. On an episode of *Raw*, father and son teams of Scott Putski & "Polish Power" Ivan Putski clashed against Christopher & Jerry Lawler. Scott soon left WWE and appeared in WCW in 1998 before returning to the North American independent scene.

Scott Steiner

YEARS ACTIVE: 1960-1969, 1970-1979, 1980-1989, **1990-1999**, 2000-PRESENT

HT 6'1" **WT** 265 lbs. **FROM** Detroit, Michigan **SIGNATURE MOVE** Steiner Recliner

TITLE HISTORY World Tag Team Champion

Scott Steiner was an All-American in freestyle wrestling at the University of Michigan. He was trained for a career in the pro ranks by The Sheik. After working for local promotions in 1986, he joined his older brother Rick in Jim Crockett Promotions.

From 1992 to 1994 they appeared in World Wrestling Entertainment and became World Tag Team Champions as well as wrestled on the debut episode of *Monday Night Raw* in 1993. After a short stay in ECW the brothers returned to WCW in 1996. Soon they reclaimed the WCW Tag Team Titles, but Scott turned on his brother and joined the nWo as the genetic freak, "Big Poppa Pump."

Steiner shined on his own and won virtually every WCW Championship before it shut down in March of 2001. Steiner rejoined WWE at the 2002 *Survivor Series*. The General Managers of *SmackDown* and *Raw* vied for him, with Eric Bischoff eventually signing him to *Raw*. Steiner became a top challenger for the World Heavyweight Championship held by Triple H. Though trumping "The Game" in pose-downs and arm-wrestling contests, Steiner was unable to get the title away from him. In 2004 Steiner and WWE mutually parted ways. He remains active, and occasionally reunites with his brother. No matter where he goes, he always gives a shout-out to all his freaks. In the words of the man with the largest arms in the world, "Holla if ya hear me!"

Scotty 2 Hotty

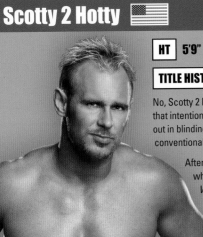

HT 5'9" **WT** 209 lbs. **FROM** Westbrook, Maine **SIGNATURE MOVE** The Worm

TITLE HISTORY World Tag Team Champion, WWE Tag Team Champion, Light Heavyweight Champion

No, Scotty 2 Hotty didn't stick his finger in a light socket. He actually styled his hair like that intentionally. No, he never got dressed in the dark. He purposely decked himself out in blinding neon attire. While the common man may choose to do things a bit more conventionally, Scotty's colorful personality was the driving force behind his success.

After several non-descript years competing in WWE, Scotty's fortunes changed when he was randomly paired with Grandmaster Sexay to compete in *WrestleMania XIV*'s Tag Team Battle Royal. The new pairing liked each other so much they couldn't stop showing their admiration for each other. Eventually, they molded themselves into Too Cool, an over-the-top hip-hop tandem severely short on hip.

Despite their inability to act even remotely cool, Too Cool emerged as fan favorites. With close friend Rikishi by their side, the threesome regularly broke into dance routines that always brought the fans to their feet. The team's popularity reached even greater heights when they defeated Edge & Christian for the World Tag Team Championship in May 2000. Several years later, Scotty would team with Rikishi to claim *SmackDown*'s WWE Tag Team Championship.

On his own, Scotty was equally impressive. Using his popular Worm signature move, he successfully turned back noted rivals Billy Gunn, Crash Holly, and D-Lo Brown. He even defeated Dean Malenko for the Light Heavyweight Championship in April 2000.

Scotty Goldman

HT 6'1" **WT** 242 lbs. **FROM** Deerfield, Illinois

Week after week, Scotty Goldman continues to fall to gigantic Superstars such as the Great Khali and Vladimir Kozlov. Despite the beatings he continually receives, Goldman always accepts his fate with a smile. In fact, in his relatively short period of time in WWE, the happy-go-lucky Superstar has made a name for himself as a bit of a joker. If you don't believe it, just look at his tights. With words like "boom" and "pow" stitched onto them, they look more like the pages of a comic book than ring gear.

SD "Special Delivery" Jones

HT 6'1" **WT** 265 lbs. **FROM** Antigua in the West Indies **SIGNATURE MOVE** Jumping Headbutt

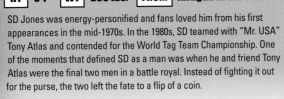

SD Jones was energy-personified and fans loved him from his first appearances in the mid-1970s. In the 1980s, SD teamed with "Mr. USA" Tony Atlas and contended for the World Tag Team Championship. One of the moments that defined SD as a man was when he and friend Tony Atlas were the final two men in a battle royal. Instead of fighting it out for the purse, the two left the fate to a flip of a coin.

SD was always popular with the fans, as shown in LJN's 1986 toyline. He was in such demand, that his figure had two variants: one with a red shirt and one with a yellow shirt! SD remained with WWE until his retirement in 1988. He brought smiles to fans faces once again in 2006 when he inducted friend and former partner Tony Atlas into the WWE Hall of Fame.

MERCHANDISE & MEMORABILIA

Whether its clothing emblazoned with their favorite superstar's logo, trading cards, home videos, or action figures cast in the likenesses of the industry's greatest attractions, fans have always found a way to feel closer to their heroes of the ring. While far from a comprehensive list, the following pages provide a brief look at some of the items created by the WWE for its fans.

Bring the Action Into Your Home

As great of an experience as live events are, you weren't able to watch your favorite matches over and over until the advent of the home video player and Coliseum Home Video. Today, the video tape has given way to DVDs and WWE On Demand but the excitement remains the same.

From the first Coliseum Video release to today, WWE collections have always been top-sellers.

Printed Materials

The printed programs from its first events were the earliest form of memorabilia from the WWE, but they're not the only printed items available. Since 1984, the WWE has produced a monthly or bi-monthly magazine, and also creates special editions of the magazine throughout the year. Other printed WWE merchandise include collector's cards, posters, and official WWE Lunch Boxes, carried by WWE fans wherever they go.

WWE Toys

In 1984 World Wrestling Entertainment and LJN launched the first line of action figures. Fans around the world couldn't wait to get their hands on the first edition which included Hillbilly Jim, Hulk Hogan, Andre the Giant, Jimmy "Superfly" Snuka, Big John Studd, Junkyard Dog, the Iron Sheik, Nikolai Volkoff, and "Rowdy" Roddy Piper. Each Superstar came with a mini-poster, bio card, and accessories true to their larger than life personas like Cowboy Bob Orton's hat, Terry Funk's branding iron, and pets like Damian and Frankie. With the WWE ring also available fans could slam, zing and fling their favorite Superstars from pillar to post.

Since the initial toys were released, WWE has continued to build its presence in the toy aisle with additional figures and even entirely new toylines. Working with multiple companies over the past two decades has led to the creation of toys for fans of all ages.

Tonka produced the "Wrestling Buddies." These could be used as pillows or as practice partners as fans cuddled up or locked up with Hulk Hogan, Ultimate Warrior, Jake Roberts, "Million Dollar Man" Ted DiBiase, and Big Boss Man among others.

Wearing Your Favorite Superstar

While shirts are the most popular item, they're not the only option for fans who want to show support for their favorite Superstars. Pajamas, hats, headbands, and even armbands have been made available to WWE fans.

While not technically clothing, WWE fans have been able to purchase replica WWE Championship belts since the 1980s. The original belts not only paid homage to the greats of the ring with the name and tenure of each previous champion, but they also featured the face of the championship belt in either its gold form, or the picture of then-Heavyweight Champion, Hulk Hogan.

SGT. SLAUGHTER

" AT-TEN-HUT "

To the millions of fans that watched him compete over his thirty-year career, Sgt. Slaughter remains a champion and pop-culture icon. After serving in the Marine Corps, Sgt. Slaughter worked as a roofer in Minnesota. During this time, a chance meeting with American Wrestling Association (AWA) promoter Verne Gagne changed his life. Impressed by his size and strength, Gagne convinced the roofer to take up wrestling.

Upon his debut in 1974, Sgt. Slaughter fell back on his time serving in the Marine Corps. He wore military fatigues, a whistle, and sunglasses. In 1980, Vincent J. McMahon called Sgt. Slaughter to offer him a spot with WWE. Slaughter jumped at the opportunity and went on to have one of the most spectacular debuts in wrestling history. Prior to making his entrance in the arena, Slaughter asked McMahon to play the Marine Corps Hymn over the loudspeakers. The song garnered a huge reaction from the fans in attendance and marked the first use of entrance music in wrestling history.

BIG NAME COMPETITION

Impressed by Sarge's ability to draw huge reactions from fans, McMahon watched the newcomer rocket straight to the top of the card. It wasn't long before he challenged Bob Backlund for the WWE Championship. Slaughter was even given the distinction of competing against Bruno Sammartino in the legend's final Madison Square Garden match.

Under the guidance of famed manager the Grand Wizard, Slaughter engaged in a brutal and bloody rivalry with Pat Patterson. In truly revolutionary fashion, the two Superstars battled for bragging rights in an infamous Alley Fight at Madison Square Garden that did not feature a referee. The match came to a stunning conclusion when the Grand Wizard, fearing the worst for his battered protégé, threw in the towel.

In early 1984, WWE fans began to recognize Slaughter as a hero when he stood up to the Iron Sheik and his manager "Ayatollah" Freddie Blassie. The Sarge's patriotic change of heart marked the end of an epic love-hate relationship between Slaughter and the fans. It also sparked the beginning of an amazing rivalry with the Iron Sheik that sold out arenas across the country.

A REAL AMERICAN HERO?

Shortly after his rivalry with the Iron Sheik, Slaughter left WWE. The decision to return to Minnesota caused Slaughter to miss out on the nationwide phenomenon WWE became in the mid-1980s. Ironically, the Sarge gained national exposure of his own when he became the spokesperson for the G.I. Joe line of toys. The new role saw the Sarge become a household name while being featured in cartoons, comic books, and as multiple action figures.

Slaughter made his return to WWE in 1990. When news of his comeback began to circulate, fans couldn't wait to once again cheer their hero. Unfortunately, Slaughter gave them no reason to celebrate, as he denounced his country to become an Iraqi sympathizer. The move shocked WWE fans, who needed a hero during the tumultuous times of the Persian Gulf War.

Matters became worse for the American fans when Slaughter defeated Ultimate Warrior for the coveted WWE Championship at the *Royal Rumble* in 1991. The victory resulted in Slaughter becoming even more hated than he was during his early days in sports-entertainment. It wasn't long before his family was receiving death threats.

Luckily, American hero Hulk Hogan saved the day when he defeated Slaughter for the WWE Championship at *WrestleMania VII*. Following the loss, Slaughter begged for his country back. The fans ultimately forgave the Marine Corps drill sergeant, who was given the opportunity to finish his competitive career with the support of his fans.

After retirement, Slaughter assumed several prominent roles within WWE, including Commissioner and road producer. In 2004, he was recognized with induction into the WWE Hall of Fame, a fitting honor for a man who was both a wrestling great and real American hero.

HT	6'6"	WT	305 lbs.

FROM Paris Island, South Carolina

SIGNATURE MOVE Cobra Clutch

TITLE HISTORY WWE Champion

YEARS ACTIVE 1960-1969 1970-1979 1980-1989 1990-1999 2000-PRESENT

The Shadow

YEARS ACTIVE 1960-1969 1970-1979 1980-1989 1990-1999 2000-PRESENT

As Vincent J. McMahon and "Toots" Mondt transformed Capitol Sports into World Wrestling Entertainment, a kinetic energy spread through the entire wrestling world. As grapplers from all over vied for employment, one surfaced with an unknown origin with an unknown identity and an unknown past. All he went by was the Shadow.

This stealth-like individual was a hazard to opposing Superstars like Miguel Perez, Bruno Sammartino, Pedro Morales, Bobo Brazil, and Gorilla Monsoon. During this time Shadow also joined forces with other dangerous figures like Dr. Jerry Graham and Hans Mortier. By the end of 1963 the Shadow disappeared into thin air. It has been over 45 years since the silhouette of this man was seen in a wrestling ring. Or has it appeared again and no one knew it?

The Shadow's influence lingered after his last appearance as nearly two decades later a tag team emerged from nowhere and called themselves the Shadows. The duo took on the likes of the Young Stallions and the Fabulous Rougeau Brothers during their brief time in WWE.

Shadow Douglas

YEARS ACTIVE 1960-1969 1970-1979 1980-1989 1990-1999 2000-PRESENT

HT	6'1"	WT	241 lbs.	FROM	Pittsburgh, Pennsylvania

SIGNATURE MOVE Belly-to-Belly Suplex

Trained by Dominic DeNucci, Douglas first made a name for himself in the Universal Wrestling Federation. Shane Douglas was a fan favorite who was highly regarded for his exciting, high-flying style and tough as nails, never say die attitude.

In the spring of 1990 Shane Douglas debuted in WWE and impressed fans in bouts against Buddy Rose, Brooklyn Brawler, Haku, Dino Bravo, Barbarian, Undertaker, and Greg Valentine. While he contended for the Intercontinental Championship, his resiliency was best shown during the 1991 *Royal Rumble,* when he lasted almost 30 minutes before being eliminated. By August 1991, Shane left the company but stayed busy in the ring in other promotions.

In 1994, after winning a Three Way Dance against Terry Funk and Sabu, Shane Douglas threw down his newly won NWA Championship and was immediately named champion of the upstart ECW promotion, which began the movement that made the group a grassroots phenomenon.

SHANE MCMAHON

Most individuals would collapse under the pressure of being the son of a famous father. This dynamic figure thrives on it. Shane McMahon dreamed of one day following in the extraordinary path walked by his father, grandfather, and great grandfather in the amazing world of sports-entertainment. It was commonplace in the McMahon household for Shane to share a meal or conversation with the pioneers and legends of the business. His childhood experiences were unique as he carried the bags of Superstars from the locker room and appeared in WWE merchandise catalogues. As an adolescent, Shane spent school vacations and summers stocking the company warehouse, and was a member of the ring crew as well as a referee and an announcer.

After he graduated from Boston University in 1993, Shane furthered his experience into the various levels of World Wrestling Entertainment business. The fourth generation McMahon needed to work harder than everyone else and studied the intricacies of television production, sales, marketing, and international business development. In 1998 he was a driving force in the company's new exploration into the world of digital media and led the team that launched WWE.com, which today exceeds 14.5 million monthly unique visitors worldwide.

This time in Shane's career brought about interesting circumstances. While he was building an impressive resumé amongst the top professionals in the industry, he also began to entertain audiences in the ring as well as became a creative contributor. As the rivalry between his father and Stone Cold Steve Austin defined the Attitude Era, Shane was often involved in defending the McMahon name and adopted the alias, Shane-O-Mac. While he later became a critical member of the Corporation, he made history on the February 15, 1999 episode of *Monday Night Raw* when he became the first McMahon to capture a WWE championship by covering X-Pac for the European title. Shane battled with X-Pac for the European prize and though he held the European Championship for almost two months, he retired it on an episode of *Sunday Night Heat*. While he continued to appear in the corners of his associates and as a special guest referee, Shane mixed it up in the ring with the likes of Triple H, Mankind, Ken Shamrock, and Test. The master of the Greenwich Street Fight ended 1999 by winning the prestigious Rookie of the Year Award from *Pro Wrestling Illustrated*.

WCW UNDER NEW OWNERSHIP

In 2001 Shane rocked the foundation of sports-entertainment when he announced that he purchased the shares of rival World Championship Wrestling (WCW). The brash McMahon rode that momentum into the granddaddy of them all and beat his father at *WrestleMania X-7* in a Street Fight. Shortly after Shane led the invasion of WWE and came extremely close to ruling the world of sports-entertainment.

In 2003 he returned to the public eye in the wake of his

Shannon Moore 🇺🇸

HT 5'9" **WT** 207 lbs. **FROM** Whispering Pines, North Carolina

SIGNATURE MOVE The Halo

Originally introduced to wrestling by childhood friends the Hardy Boys, this former Superstar appeared in their North Carolina-based OMEGA promotion. Moore debuted in WWE in 2002 and soon became a devout follower of Matt Hardy's way of life known as "Mattitude." As a follower (called an "MF'er") Moore appeared at ringside for Hardy's matches. Moore found a subordinate of his own, who was known as a "Moore-On."

After Hardy and Shannon parted ways he took on a variety of opponents and participated in the Cruiserweight Open at *WrestleMania XX*. In 2005 he tapped into the punk in him and rocked-out in several locations with his mohawk haircut, elaborate body art and piercings. The self-labeled "Prince of Punk" spread his messages of non-conformity to WWE fans. After spending much of 2005 making appearances on the independant circuit, Moore returned to WWE in 2006 as part of ECW before moving to *SmackDown*. Leaving the "Prince of Punk" in his past, he remained a consistent contender for the Cruiserweight Championship.

HT 6'2" **WT** 236 lbs.

FROM Greenwich, Connecticut

SIGNATURE MOVE Coast-To-Coast

TITLE HISTORY

European Champion, Hardcore Champion

father's match with Hulk Hogan at *WrestleMania XIX*. That July he began his tenure as Executive Vice President of WWE Global Media, overseeing international TV distribution, live event bookings, digital media, consumer products, and publishing. Shane once again performed multiple tasks as he wiped the mat with Eric Bischoff at *SummerSlam*, and danced with Chris Jericho. In recent years Shane has remained a force behind the scenes and in front of the cameras.

Shane avenged Kane's senseless attack on his mother, Linda, in a Last Man Standing Match at Unforgiven and in the first-ever Ambulance Match at Survivor Series.

Just as his father brought WWE from a regional operation to a national enterprise recognized around the world, Shane is expanding WWE's global business and continues to contribute to its North American success. While honoring the legacies of those before him, Shane remains dedicated to blazing his own trail into the annals of sports-entertainment. Today, he is a main ingredient to the success of World Wrestling Entertainment. However, don't think he's gone totally corporate. If the situation calls for it, you'll see him on *Monday Night Raw* or a pay-per-view leaping from a venues highest available point down on a beaten opponent just to prove his point. This business leader does it all, and he's just getting started!

Sharmell 🇺🇸

Formerly a member of WCW's Nitro Girls dance team, Sharmell waited four years after WCW closed its doors before making her WWE debut in 2005. Once she got there, she quickly made up for lost time, stopping at nothing to ensure a victory for her man, Booker T.

While she certainly wasn't known for her in-ring prowess, Sharmell did manage to land a match on the biggest card of 2006. At *WrestleMania 22*, she teamed with Booker to battle Boogeyman in a Handicap Match. The loving couple not only walked away with the loss that night, but Sharmell also left the event with a lingering taste of worms in her mouth.

Sharmell failed to let the *WrestleMania 22* defeat derail her man. The following month, she lead him to victory in the *King of the Ring* tournament, which was immediately followed by a World Heavyweight Championship victory over Rey Mysterio at *The Great American Bash*.

SHAWN MICHAELS

" *THE HEARTBREAK KID* "

HT	6'1"	WT	225 lbs.

FROM San Antonio, Texas

SIGNATURE MOVE Sweet Chin Music

TITLE HISTORY WWE Champion, World Heavyweight Champion, World Tag Team Champion, Intercontinental Champion, European Champion

YEARS ACTIVE (1960 1969) (1970 1979) (1980 1989) (1990 1999) (2000 PRESENT)

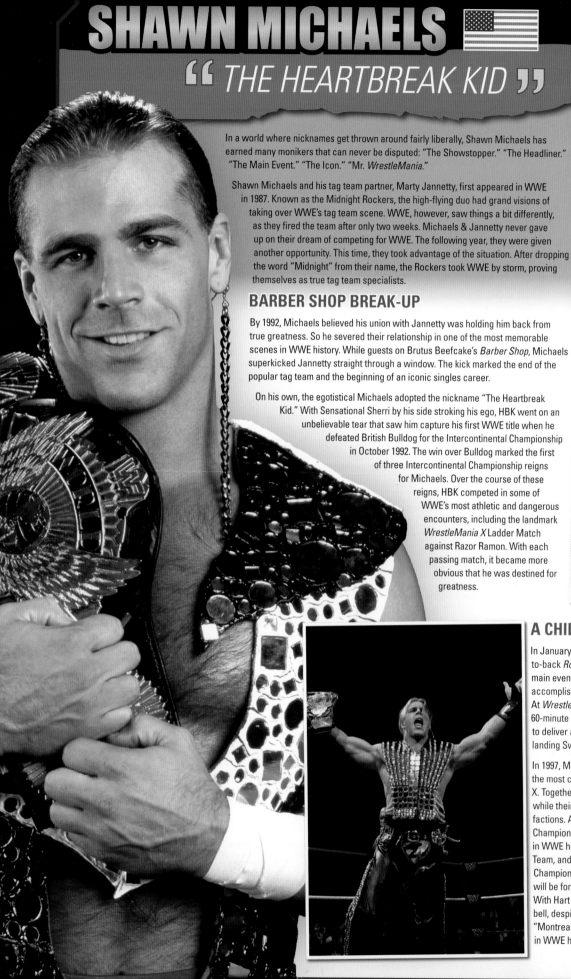

In a world where nicknames get thrown around fairly liberally, Shawn Michaels has earned many monikers that can never be disputed: "The Showstopper." "The Headliner." "The Main Event." "The Icon." "Mr. *WrestleMania*."

Shawn Michaels and his tag team partner, Marty Jannetty, first appeared in WWE in 1987. Known as the Midnight Rockers, the high-flying duo had grand visions of taking over WWE's tag team scene. WWE, however, saw things a bit differently, as they fired the team after only two weeks. Michaels & Jannetty never gave up on their dream of competing for WWE. The following year, they were given another opportunity. This time, they took advantage of the situation. After dropping the word "Midnight" from their name, the Rockers took WWE by storm, proving themselves as true tag team specialists.

BARBER SHOP BREAK-UP

By 1992, Michaels believed his union with Jannetty was holding him back from true greatness. So he severed their relationship in one of the most memorable scenes in WWE history. While guests on Brutus Beefcake's *Barber Shop*, Michaels superkicked Jannetty straight through a window. The kick marked the end of the popular tag team and the beginning of an iconic singles career.

On his own, the egotistical Michaels adopted the nickname "The Heartbreak Kid." With Sensational Sherri by his side stroking his ego, HBK went on an unbelievable tear that saw him capture his first WWE title when he defeated British Bulldog for the Intercontinental Championship in October 1992. The win over Bulldog marked the first of three Intercontinental Championship reigns for Michaels. Over the course of these reigns, HBK competed in some of WWE's most athletic and dangerous encounters, including the landmark *WrestleMania X* Ladder Match against Razor Ramon. With each passing match, it became more obvious that he was destined for greatness.

A CHILDHOOD DREAM REALIZED

In January 1996, he last eliminated Diesel to become a back-to-back *Royal Rumble* winner. The victory put HBK back in the main event of *WrestleMania* and gave him the opportunity to accomplish his boyhood dream of becoming WWE Champion. At *WrestleMania XII*, he faced Bret "Hit Man" Hart in a grueling 60-minute Iron Man Match that required sudden-death overtime to deliver a conclusive winner. Michaels scored the win after landing Sweet Chin Music and became WWE Champion.

In 1997, Michaels teamed with longtime friend Triple H to form the most controversial faction in WWE history, D-Generation X. Together, HBK and Triple H spat in the face of authority while their unparalleled popularity set the bar for all future factions. As a member of DX, HBK captured the European Championship, making him the first-ever Grand Slam Champion in WWE history (he held the WWE, Intercontinental, World Tag Team, and European titles during his career), but it was a WWE Championship victory over Bret Hart at *Survivor Series 1997* that will be forever remembered for its controversial conclusion. With Hart caught in a Sharpshooter, the referee called for the bell, despite the fact that the "Hit Man" never submitted. The "Montreal Incident" remains arguably the most infamous event in WWE history.

RETIREMENT? NO, REJUVENATION!

Back injuries forced Michaels into early retirement in 1998. During this time, he became a very spiritual person, which helped him overcome his personal demons. He also used this time to rest his battered back. By 2002, a reinvigorated HBK got the itch to compete again.

When he returned, Michaels found himself embedded in a bloody rivalry against former friend Triple H. Amazingly, he showed no sign of ring rust, defeating "The Game" at *SummerSlam 2002*. A few months later, Michaels last eliminated Triple H in an unforgiving Elimination Chamber Match that saw HBK claim the World Heavyweight Championship.

Over the next several years, the renewed Michaels worked effortlessly to recreate the magic of his earlier years. In typical HBK fashion, he found himself in the spotlight of WWE's biggest matches, including his match at *WrestleMania XXIV* where he sent Ric Flair into retirement. There's no telling when Shawn Michaels will finally decide to stop tuning up the band, but when he does, he will undoubtedly gain entry into the prestigious WWE Hall of Fame.

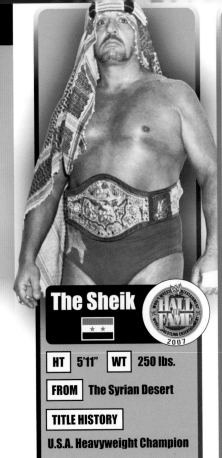

The Sheik

HALL OF FAME 2007

| HT | 5'11" | WT | 250 lbs. |

FROM The Syrian Desert

TITLE HISTORY

U.S.A. Heavyweight Champion

YEARS ACTIVE

A true pioneer of hardcore wrestling, the Sheik left a legacy that fans are reminded of every time a Superstar breaks a table or swings a flaming baseball bat. Considered by many as the father of extreme, many believe there never would have been an ECW without his vicious vision.

Using anything he could get his hands on as a weapon, the Sheik made a name for himself competing in Detroit, Toronto, and Japan. While wrestling in the Midwest, he began a bitter rivalry with Bobo Brazil, which lasted more than thirty years. Over the course of their bloody rivalry, the Sheik captured the now-defunct United States Heavyweight Championship twice, once in 1969 and once in 1977.

Amazingly, the Sheik managed to wrestle into the 1990s, despite already celebrating his seventieth birthday. The twilight of his hardcore career saw him compete in many classic ECW encounters against Kevin Sullivan and Tazz, who would later go on to become a heated rival of Sabu, The Sheik's nephew. In 2007, The Sheik's innovative approach to hardcore competition was recognized with induction into the WWE Hall of Fame.

SHELTON BENJAMIN

| HT | 6'2" | WT | 248 lbs. | FROM | Orangeburg, South Carolina |

SIGNATURE MOVE T-bone Suplex

TITLE HISTORY Intercontinental Champion, United States Champion, WWE Tag Team Champion

YEARS ACTIVE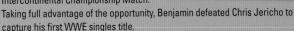

Shelton Benjamin claims to be sports-entertainment's "Gold Standard." By looking at his in-ring exploits and championship resumé, it's hard to argue against that claim. After refusing to fall into the dangerous drug scene of Orangeburg, SC, Benjamin attended the University of Minnesota, where he became a national amateur wrestling powerhouse. Following graduation, he parlayed his college success into a WWE contract, thus fulfilling a lifelong dream of becoming a Superstar.

Alongside partner Charlie Haas, Benjamin debuted in December 2002 as a part of the powerful Team Angle faction. In less than two months, Benjamin & Haas proved their dominance, defeating Los Guerreros for the WWE Tag Team Championship. Dubbing themselves as "The World's Greatest Tag Team," they would go on to capture the titles one more time before the WWE Draft sent Benjamin to *Raw*, which forced the athletic tandem to split.

With a shocking victory over Triple H in his debut match, Benjamin's *Raw* career had an electric start. The victory put the newcomer on the map as one of the brand's top singles stars. It also opened the eyes of many WWE fans, who voted Benjamin into *Taboo Tuesday*'s Intercontinental Championship Match. Taking full advantage of the opportunity, Benjamin defeated Chris Jericho to capture his first WWE singles title.

In November 2007, following an impressive *Raw* career, Benjamin jumped to ECW. Benjamin used his time in ECW to cement his status as one of history's most athletic competitors. His breathtaking efforts in the *WrestleMania XXIV* Money in the Bank Ladder Match will live on highlight reels for generations to come.

Just when it seemed Benjamin was hitting his ECW stride, the 2008 WWE Draft once again sent the Superstar packing. In typical Shelton Benjamin fashion, however, he refused to be deterred by the move. Within one month of his debut, Benjamin defeated Matt Hardy to claim the United States Championship.

Over the years, Benjamin has developed a swagger, but who can blame him? With his unparalleled athleticism and penchant for making a powerful first impression, the successful Superstar has every right to call himself the "Gold Standard."

SHERRI MARTEL

HT 5'7" **FROM** New Orleans, Louisiana

SIGNATURE MOVE Sleeper **TITLE HISTORY** Women's Champion

YEARS ACTIVE

World Wrestling Entertainment turned "Sensational" when Sherri debuted on July 24, 1987 and pinned her mentor, the Fabulous Moolah, for the WWE Women's Championship. As champion, Sherri successfully defended her crown for over 15 months against challengers such as Velvet McIntyre, Angie Minelli, Desiree Peterson, and Debbie Combs. Sherri also continued to battle Moolah and the two captained opposing teams at the first *Survivor Series*. She was finally dethroned in October 1988 in Paris, France by Rockin' Robin.

Sherri transitioned to managing some of WWE's most infamous rule-breakers in the early 1990s. Her first client was Randy "Macho Man" Savage. When he pinned "King Hacksaw" Jim Duggan, Savage became a King and Sherri, his Queen. In 1991 "Million-Dollar Man" Ted DiBiase enlisted her expert services and later a new bad boy signed her, "The Heartbreak Kid" Shawn Michaels. In 1993, Sherri left WWE.

Later in the year and into 1994, she toured the independent circuit. That spring, she signed a contract with WCW and became "Sensuous" Sherri at the side of "Nature Boy" Ric Flair in his war against Sting and Hulk Hogan. Later she became "Sister" Sherri and guided Harlem Heat to an amazing seven World Tag Team Championship reigns before leaving the company in the summer of 1997.

In 2005, she returned to WWE on *SmackDown* during the Shawn Michaels/Kurt Angle conflict. On April 1, 2006, the 30-year career of the girl whose dream began with a ring of a bell in a barn was celebrated as she was inducted into the WWE Hall of Fame by DiBiase.

Sadly, Sherri passed away in June 2007 while visiting her mother in Alabama. This pioneer was as tough as nails, but those around her remember her for her big heart. Sensational Sherri is the only woman to ever hold both AWA and WWE Women's titles and was a legitimate force both in and out of the ring. She was the forerunner to the WWE Divas of today and her legacy lives on through them. DiBiase described her—and all who knew her remember her—as "truly priceless."

Shohei "Giant" Baba

HT 6'10" **WT** 310 lbs.

FROM Sanjo, Nigata, Japan

SIGNATURE MOVE Running Yakuza Kick

YEARS ACTIVE

When a shoulder injury ended his baseball career, Giant Baba looked to make a name for himself in the ring. In 1959 he trained alongside Antonio Inoki with the founding father of *puroresu*, Rikidozan. Both future legends debuted in September, 1959 and dominated the Japanese scene for the next thirty years. He debuted in WWE in 1964, challenging Bruno Sammartino for the Heavyweight Championship.

Over the next decade, Baba competed against the biggest names in sports-entertainment all over the world. In December 1974, Baba defeated Jack Brisco to become the first-ever Japanese NWA Heavyweight Champion. Baba made history in 1975 when he faced Bruno Sammartino in a "Champion vs. Champion" bout marking the first time the WWE Championship was defended in Japan.

In January 1990 Vince McMahon appeared at an All-Japan event at Korauken Hall and announced a Wrestling Summit at Tokyo's Egg Dome featuring WWE, and the biggest names in Japan. Baba was instrumental in co-promoting shows with WWE in Japan and teamed with Andre the Giant to defeat Demolition.

On January 31, 1999 this legend passed away days after his 61st birthday. Shohei "Giant" Baba was one of sports-entertainment's leading ambassadors and brightest stars who was honored by all those who knew him in Japan and around the world.

SHOWDOWN AT SHEA

Showdown At Shea was a series of three supercards held at Shea Stadium. Each event had at least two title matches, while the undercard was filled with the biggest names in wrestling.

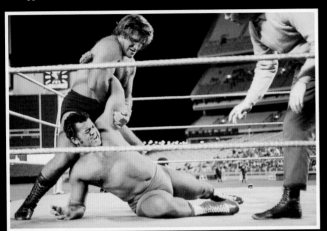

September 30, 1972

Main Event: WWE Champion Pedro Morales and Bruno Sammartino battled to a draw (curfew)

June 25, 1976

Main Event: Andre the Giant defeated Chuck Wepner via countout in a Wrestler vs. Boxer Match

Antonio Inoki fought Muhammad Ali to a draw in a Wrestler vs. Boxer Match

August 9, 1980

Main Event: Bruno Sammartino defeated Larry Zbyszko in a Steel Cage Match

Sid Justice

YEARS ACTIVE 1960–1969 1970–1979 1980–1989 **1990–1999** 2000–PRESENT

HT 6'8" **WT** 320 lbs. **FROM** West Memphis, Arkansas

SIGNATURE MOVE Powerbomb **TITLE HISTORY** World Heavyweight Champion

An early master of the chokeslam and powerbomb, this monster first appeared in WCW as Sid Vicious. Shortly after his 1991 debut in WWE as Sid Justice, he was announced as the special guest referee for the main event match at *SummerSlam 1991*. While he appeared to be on the side of Hulk Hogan, fans caught a glimpse of his true nature at the 1992 *Royal Rumble* when he eliminated Hogan in hopes of capturing the WWE Championship. They met at *Wrestlemania VIII* as part of the double main event. After the encounter, Sid abruptly left WWE and soon returned to World Championship Wrestling.

In 1995, he resurfaced in WWE as Sycho Sid, the new bodyguard for Shawn Michaels. After a mishap cost his boss the WWE Championship, Sid attacked Michaels the next night on *Raw* when he was told his services were no longer needed. After his tenure with the Million Dollar Corporation, Sid was not seen in WWE until June 1996. He patched things up with HBK and teamed with him and Ahmed Johnson against Camp Cornette. Sid captured the WWE Championship on two different occassions, but his second reign ended at the hands of Undertaker at *WrestleMania XIII*. Sid departed WWE in 1996, then appeared in ECW in 1998 before going to World Championship Wrestling, where he held different championships. Although a horrific injury halted his career for a few years, he has been a fixture on the independent scene since 2004.

Simon Dean

YEARS ACTIVE 1960–1969 1970–1979 1980–1989 1990–1999 **2000–PRESENT**

HT 5'10" **WT** 210 lbs. **FROM** Clearwater, Florida **SIGNATURE MOVE** Simonizer

Fitness guru Simon Dean first began shilling his Simon System to WWE viewers in late 2004. Decked out in bright colors, the annoying salesman claimed his "patented" system could transform any couch potato into a lean, mean, fighting machine.

Despite purchasing valuable advertising time on WWE television, Dean's infomercials failed to turn the Simon System into a profitable product. As sales for the system sank, so did Dean's career. It wasn't long before the unsuccessful salesman began losing to nearly every Superstar he faced, including Gunnar Scott, Tatanka, and the dress-wearing Vito.

Realizing his in-ring career wasn't taking off like he hoped, Dean turned to managing in 2006. Unfortunately, however, his protégés, the Gymini, were just as unsuccessful in the ring as he was. Dean finally walked away from the ring completely later that year.

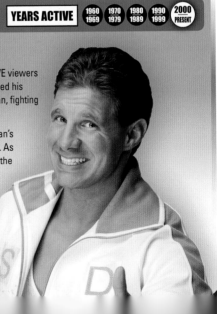

Sir Oliver Humperdink

YEARS ACTIVE 1960-1969 1970-1979 **1980-1989** 1990-1999 2000-PRESENT

With his long red beard, bright flowing hair, and outrageously colored suits, Sir Oliver Humperdink became one of the game's most easily recognized managers. While his WWE timeline only spanned one year, Humperdink's flamboyant persona left a lasting impression that will be remembered for generations.

His biggest win as a manager came when he was awarded the services of Bam Bam Bigelow in 1987. Bigelow was easily the largest Superstar in Humperdink's stable, which also housed Hall of Famer "Mr. Wonderful" Paul Orndorff. In November 1987, Humperdink led his duo into action in the first-ever *Survivor Series* pay-per-view main event. Bigelow & Orndorff teamed with WWE Champion Hulk Hogan, Don Muraco & Ken Patera to take on Andre the Giant, Rick Rude, Butch Reed, One Man Gang & King Kong Bundy. Andre last eliminated Bigelow to pick up the victory for his squad. By 1988, Humperdink had left WWE in favor of a managerial career in the NWA. While there, he guided the careers of the Fabulous Freebirds, among others.

SIX-MAN TAG MATCH

This contest features two teams of three Superstars where, unless specified, standard tag team rules apply. Victory is achieved by pinfall, submission, count-out, or disqualification.

These bouts can also feature Texas Tornado rules where all six participants are in the ring at once or Elimination rules, where defeated Superstars must leave the ring area and the match continues until one team does not have any members remaining.

Skinner 🇺🇸

YEARS ACTIVE 1960-1969 1970-1979 1980-1989 **1990-1999** 2000-PRESENT

HT 6' **WT** 215 lbs. **FROM** The Everglades **SIGNATURE MOVE** Gatorbreaker

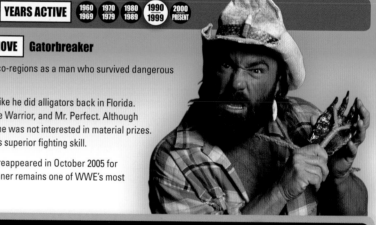

Skinner emerged from the sawgrass prairies of one of the world's most diverse eco-regions as a man who survived dangerous encounters with the dangerous predators that inhabit the Everglades.

Skinner entered WWE in 1991 and he immediately set to taking down Superstars like he did alligators back in Florida. Audiences witnessed Skinner brawl with Undertaker, Tatanka, Crush, Sid, Ultimate Warrior, and Mr. Perfect. Although Skinner was a contender for both the Intercontinental and WWE Championships he was not interested in material prizes. His trophy was taking something from a fallen opponent and keeping it to show his superior fighting skill.

In 1993 Skinner returned to the Everglades and his familiar wild surroundings. He reappeared in October 2005 for *WWE Raw Homecoming* and then again in 2007 for the *Raw 15th Anniversary*. Skinner remains one of WWE's most unusual Superstars nearly two decades after his debut.

Skull Murphy 🇨🇦

YEARS ACTIVE **1960-1969** 1970-1979 1980-1989 1990-1999 2000-PRESENT

HT 6'1" **WT** 265 lbs. **FROM** Hamilton, Ontario, Canada **SIGNATURE MOVE** Heart Punch

TITLE HISTORY United States Tag Team Champion

Long before Stone Cold Steve Austin made the bald head a widely recognized fashion of the ring, John Joseph Murphy proudly sported the hairless cranium. The Canadian Superstar, however, didn't have much of a choice, as a childhood disease left him permanently hairless. Murphy chose to embrace the unique trait, though; he even adopted the moniker "Skull."

As Skull Murphy, the bald Superstar became one of the ring's most hated personalities during the 1950s and 1960s. Utilizing a devastating heart punch, Murphy was able to claim many NWA singles titles, but it was in the tag team ranks that he gained his greatest notoriety.

As a 14-time tag team titlist, Murphy was accustomed to wearing gold around his waist. His biggest victory came in May 1963 when he teamed with Brute Bernard to defeat Buddy Austin & Great Scott for the United States Tag Team Championship. They held the titles for six months before being unseated by WWE Hall of Famers Killer Kowalski & Gorilla Monsoon.

| HT | 3'7" | WT | 86 lbs. | FROM | Montreal, Quebec, Canada |

SIGNATURE MOVE Hanging Vertical Suplex

Always in impeccable physical condition, Sky Low Low was revered as "the Little Atlas of the Wrestling World." His performances became legendary; he fought in front of Queen Elizabeth of the United Kingdom and King Farouk of Egypt. Sky Low Low amazed fans by standing on top of his head without using his hands for balance.

Sky Low Low's mixture of strength, speed, and devilish tactics brought him great success in the ring. He was the first-ever NWA Midget World Champion, capturing the title in 1949. He made his WWE debut in 1963, where he battled the likes of Little Beaver, Farmer Pete, Tiny Tim, Pancho Lopez, Jamaica Kid, Irish Jackie and Cowboy Bradley.

His career continued for decades, reaching the Hulkamania era. He even appeared in the classic Mixed-Tag Match at *WrestleMania III*. Sadly in November 1998 this sports-entertainment pioneer passed away. Sky Low Low was a special type of performer with an endless imagination that always brought audiences to their feet.

THE SLAMMY AWARDS

Much like the television industry does with the popular Emmy Awards, WWE rewards excellence in sports-entertainment with their semi-annual Slammy Awards. The prestigious awards ceremony, which was created by the Academy of Wrestling Arts & Science, can be traced all the way back to 1986. The inaugural ceremony focused largely on the musical efforts on *The Wrestling Album*. The night's big winner was Junkyard Dog, who walked away with the award for Best Single Performer.

The following year, the Slammys altered its categories to include the mat, as well as music. In the end, few remembered the winners and losers. Instead, the 1987 Slammy Awards are mainly remembered for Mr. McMahon's now-embarrassing rendition of "Stand Back." McMahon's musical act almost single-handedly sent the Slammys into a nine-year hiatus. When it finally returned in 1996, however, some of WWE's all-time greatest names walked away with golden statuettes, including Shawn Michaels, Bret Hart, and Freddie Blassie, who was honored with the Lifetime Achievement Award.

In 1997, Arnold Skaaland followed Blassie's lead when he too was given the Lifetime Achievement Award. Other 1997 winners include Rocky Maivia for Best Sensation and Sable for Best Dressed and Miss Slammy. Following the 1997 ceremony, The Slammy Awards took another hiatus, but the prestigious honor returned in 2008. For the first time ever, the new millennium version of the Slammys included fan voting on WWE.com.

Slick 🇺🇸

While his academic record may dispute it, Slick arrived in WWE in 1986 claiming to be a doctor—a "Doctor of Style," that is. The impeccably dressed manager introduced himself to WWE audiences when he dipped into his "pockets of green" to purchase half interest in the legendary "Classy" Freddie Blassie's stable of Superstars. The innovative merger gave the newcomer instant credibility, as he was thrust into the spotlight alongside such greats as the Iron Sheik and Nikolai Volkoff. He eventually added Butch Reed to his list of clients before finally assuming full ownership of Blassie's crop. Within months, the "Doctor of Style" assembled one of the most dominant forces in WWE.

Always looking to make a buck, Slick became a popular recording artist in 1987. With his hit single, *Jive Soul Bro*, Slick attempted to convince everybody that he was an honest man. His claims fell on deaf ears among the fans of WWE.

In the early 1990s, Slick took an unexpected leave of absence from WWE. When he returned, the normally fast-talking manager was barely recognizable. Instead of his traditional claims of greatness, the manager presented a more reserved personality. Renamed Reverend Slick, he preached the importance of good over evil.

SMACK DOWN

For nearly a decade, *SmackDown* has been known as the larger-than-life two-hour weekly extravaganza where classic rivalries are conceived and Superstars are created. Regardless of changes on its roster, Superstars know that when they step through the blue ropes, they're entering the ring to perform on one of WWE's brightest stages.

This program debuted in 1999 as a one-time special and was such a hit that it became a weekly program that added two more hours of incredible WWE action. Its first episode featured Superstars the Blue Blazer, Big Show, Mankind, the New Age Outlaws, Triple H, The Rock, Stone Cold Steve Austin, and Undertaker.

In early 2002, World Wrestling Entertainment underwent a brand division and *SmackDown* became its own brand with exclusive Superstars, championships, management, announcers, and pay-per-view events. While initially the Undisputed WWE Champion and Women's Champion were to defend their titles on both shows, then-champion Brock Lesnar defied the decree and made his title exclusive to *SmackDown*. *Raw* created its own title, the World Heavyweight Championship, and the Women's Championship became exclusive to the Monday night program. As a result of the Brand Division, WWE implemented an annual Draft Lottery, where members of their respective rosters could be exchanged. The hit program has had strong leaders such as Stephanie McMahon, Paul Heyman, Kurt Angle, Theodore Long, and Vickie Guerrero.

On April 20, 2007 *SmackDown* celebrated its 400th episode. That October, history was made once again when it was announced that *SmackDown* and *ECW* began a talent exchange and Superstars would appear on both brands. 2008 held many major developments for the program. In January, *SmackDown* began to be broadcast in high-definition. In June, Triple H and Jim Ross moved to the brand via the Draft Lottery. In July, the new Divas Championship was won by Michelle McCool. In August, Tazz joined J.R. at the broadcast booth.

The title for SmackDown was inspired by one of The Rock's popular catchphrases; the "Brahma Bull" often referred to SmackDown as "The Rock's show."

Smasher Sloan 🇺🇸

YEARS ACTIVE (1960 1969) (1970 1979) (1980 1989) (1990 1999) (2000 PRESENT)

WT 275 lbs. **FROM** Butte, Montana **TITLE HISTORY** United States Tag Team Champion

Son of wrestler Whitey Whitler, Smasher Sloan made his professional debut in 1965. Shortly after becoming a pro, the second-generation Superstar teamed with Baron Mikel Scicluna to defeat Johnny Valentine & Antonio Pugliese in controversial fashion to claim the United States Tag Team Championship. They held the titles for two months before losing the gold back to Pugliese and his new tag team partner, Spiros Arion.

After losing the titles, Sloan left WWE to compete in various other North American promotions. When he was unable to recreate the success he found in WWE, he began to compete under a mask using several different monikers, including The Beast. Sloan made a brief and unsuccessful return to WWE in 1972. Competing mainly as a singles Superstar, he failed to become a legitimate force in the promotion. Sloan retired from wrestling shortly after.

The Smokin' Gunns 🇺🇸

YEARS ACTIVE (1960 1969) (1970 1979) (1980 1989) (1990 1999) (2000 PRESENT)

MEMBERS Billy, Bart **COMBINED WEIGHT** 534 lbs. **TITLE HISTORY** World Tag Team Champions

These cowboys arrived in WWE in 1993 and were an instant sensation. At that year's *King of the Ring* they joined the Steiner Brothers to defeat the Headshrinkers and Money Inc. The Smokin' Gunns climbed the tag team championship ladder while fans everywhere cheered their appearances. At the 1994 *Survivor Series* they joined Lex Luger's "Guts & Glory" team to battle Ted DiBiase's Million Dollar Corporation.

In January 1995 Billy and Bart defeated Bob "Spark Plug" Holly & 1-2-3 Kid to become World Tag Team Champions. Although they lost the belts at *WrestleMania XI*, they regained the titles in September. Unfortunately, Billy suffered a serious neck injury and they were forced to forfeit the belts.

After Billy recovered, the Gunns refocused their efforts. With an assist from Sunny, the duo won their third World Tag Team Championship from the Godwinns at *In Your House 8: Beware of Dog*. Sunny joined the brothers, adding her considerable experience as a manager to the team. Unfortunately, her presence became a mixed blessing, as she was the cause of infighting between the brothers. They split in October 1996 when Billy walked out on Bart.

THE SNAKE PIT

In September 1986 audiences were treated to the twisted prophecies of a man who walked in eternal darkness. Jake "the Snake" Roberts invited all to come into his Pit. As his snake Damien slithered amongst friends, Roberts' guests included all of WWE's top Superstars and some who even challenged "the Snake" while in the Pit's unruly confines.

Roberts always professed that the DDT is like life, cruel but fair. Many times he showed audiences around the globe we were living in his world. By July 1987 "the Snake" decided to solely focus on dominating WWE rings. Fans and Superstars alike will forever heed the words of Roberts spoken from his Pit pulpit, "We're not born from the original sins, but we may well be the original sinners. Enter the Snake Pit if you dare..."

Snitsky 🇺🇸

YEARS ACTIVE (1960 1969) (1970 1979) (1980 1989) (1990 1999) (2000 PRESENT)

HT 6'8" **WT** 307 lbs. **FROM** Nesquehoning, Pennsylvania **SIGNATURE MOVE** Pump Handle Slam

While this deranged monster might not be runway model material, he is perfect for the WWE. Well, he's perfect for himself, but is the exact opposite for the audiences he terrifies and Superstars he massacres! Since 2004, Snitsky has inflicted pain on the Superstars of World Wrestling Entertainment. Snitsky has displayed his sadistic tendencies against the likes of John Cena, Kane, and Big Show. In 2007, he moved to ECW and during his time there he faced CM Punk, Balls Mahoney, Matt Striker, and even took Hardcore Holly out of action after breaking his arm. He wants to be challenged. He needs to test his skills to ensure he can inflict pain on as many different types of people as time will permit. After all, it's what gives him ultimate pleasure.

Sonny Boy Hayes

YEARS ACTIVE 1960–1969 1970–1979 1980–1989 1990–1999 2000–PRESENT

| **HT** | 4'6" | **WT** | 76 lbs. |

Sonny Boy Hayes brought experience, toughness and heart to WWE's midget wrestling ranks in 1967. His matches against the likes of Little Beaver, Sky Low Low, Little Boy Blue, Little Tokyo, Lord Littlebrook, Little John, Tiger Jackson, and Butch Cassidy were filled with non-stop action.

While mainly known as a singles competitor, Hayes teamed with Superstars like Cowboy Bradley, Haiti Kid, Farmer Jerome, Tahiti Kid, and Poncho Boy. At one time he was a co-holder of the briefly sanctioned NWA Midget World Tag Team Championship with partner Little Louie, which was defended occasionally on WWE cards.

Sonny King

YEARS ACTIVE 1960–1969 **1970–1979** 1980–1989 1990–1999 2000–PRESENT

TITLE HISTORY World Tag Team Champion

Sonny King arrived in WWE in 1971 and showed from the start that he was ready for anything. During the early portion of 1972 he teamed up with Chief Jay Strongbow. In May, 1972 the duo won the World Tag Team Championships at Madison Square Garden. King and Strongbow defended the belts for one month until they were defeated by Prof. Toru Tanaka and Mr. Fuji. By spring 1973 King left the company but remained a force throughout the territories of the National Wrestling Alliance. In the early 1980s he became a manager and shared his methods of success with up-and-coming competitors. WWE fans will always remember him as a great singles contender and part of one of the most popular teams of the 1970s.

Spike Dudley

YEARS ACTIVE 1960–1969 1970–1979 1980–1989 **1990–1999** **2000–PRESENT**

| **HT** | 5'8" | **WT** | 150 lbs. | **FROM** | New York City | **SIGNATURE MOVE** | Dudley Dog |

TITLE HISTORY World Tag Team Champion, Cruiserweight Champion, European Champion, Hardcore Champion

As the runt of the Dudley litter, Spike Dudley entered WWE with awfully low expectations, but over the course of his career, the half-brother of Bubba Ray and D-Von Dudley proved that size doesn't matter. Spike made an immediate impact when he helped his brothers defeat Edge & Christian for the World Tag Team Championship in March 2001. Unfortunately, the brotherly love didn't last long, as he eventually turned his back on his brothers and the ECW-WCW Alliance to stay by the side of his girlfriend Molly Holly and WWE. His decision to follow his heart resulted in a bitter Dudley family feud. Teaming with Tazz, Spike eventually gained the ultimate retribution over his bullying brothers when he pinned Bubba Ray to gain his brothers' cherished World Tag Team Championship. In addition to his success in the tag team division, Spike also achieved notoriety as a singles competitor. Not only did he capture both the European and Hardcore Championships, but he also defeated Rey Mysterio for the Cruiserweight Championship in July 2004.

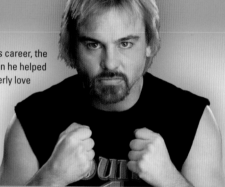

Spirit Squad

YEARS ACTIVE 1960–1969 1970–1979 1980–1989 1990–1999 **2000–PRESENT**

MEMBERS Kenny, Johnny, Nicky, Mikey, Mitch

TITLE HISTORY World Tag Team Championship

In a locker room overflowing with testosterone, Spirit Squad knew they would have difficulty fitting in. So rather than making futile attempts at changing people's opinions of them, the male cheerleaders chose to focus on the one thing they could control: their actions in the ring.

The quintet of Superstars first began annoying fans with their uncoordinated routines in January 2006. Lacking self-awareness, the group believed their horrible chants were brilliant. Spirit Squad's talents in the ring, however, were amazing. Within months of their debut, the high-flyers defeated Kane & Big Show for the World Tag Team Championship.

Despite their comical exterior, Spirit Squad possessed a vicious mean streak. In May 2006, all five members of the crew nearly crippled Shawn Michaels when they targeted his knee with a steel chair. Luckily for HBK, Triple H saved him from certain doom. The rescue served as a launching pad for a D-Generation X revival, and landed the cheerleaders in a bitter rivalry with the reunited faction.

In late 2006, Spirit Squad hit an uncharacteristic losing streak. Cryme Tyme, Eugene, Sgt. Slaughter and a whole host of others lined up to topple the annoying faction. Finally, at *Cyber Sunday*, Ric Flair & "Rowdy" Roddy Piper defeated the group to capture the World Tag Team Championship. Shortly after the loss, longtime rivals DX packed Spirit Squad into a shipping crate and sent them off to OVW in Louisville.

Spiros Arion

YEARS ACTIVE 1960-1969 | 1970-1979 | 1980-1989 | 1990-1999 | 2000-PRESENT

HT 6'5" **WT** 260 lbs. **FROM** Athens, Greece **SIGNATURE MOVE** Atomic Drop

TITLE HISTORY United States Tag Team Champion

The man known throughout the world as "the Iron Greek" appeared in WWE rings in 1966. Spiros Arion's fiery Mediterranean nature made him one of the most popular Superstars in the northeast. In December, 1966 he won his first championship in WWE when he and Antonio Pugliese won the United States Tag Team Championship. In 1967 Arion's close friendship with Bruno Sammartino led to another United States Tag Team reign. Over the next few years Arion traveled the globe, then returned to WWE in 1974. Sadly, Spiros turned on his mentor and fell under the sinister influence of "Classy" Freddie Blassie. Filled with hate, Spiros became a treacherous and crafty villain aligned with slime such as the Wolfman, Bobby Duncum, and Waldo Von Erich.

The Spoiler

YEARS ACTIVE 1960-1969 | 1970-1979 | 1980-1989 | 1990-1999 | 2000-PRESENT

HT 6'4" **WT** 293 lbs. **FROM** Parts Unknown **SIGNATURE MOVE** Iron Claw

Don Jardine made his in-ring debut at the young age of 15. He spent more than ten years competing under his given name, as well such aliases as The Butcher and Sonny Cooper. Then in 1967, famed promoter Fritz Von Erich gave him the name "The Spoiler." From there, Jardine went on to become one of the most well-known masked Superstars of all time.

The Spoiler was a double threat in the ring. At 6'4" and nearly 300 pounds, he possessed immense strength, but he was also very athletic for a man of his size. In fact, The Spoiler perfected the top-rope walk decades before Undertaker made it popular in WWE rings. As a member of WWE, The Spoiler used his feared Iron Claw to eventually earn an opportunity at Pedro Morales' WWE Championship. He was unable to unseat the champ, but the match will forever hold historical significance, as the Spoiler was forced to compete without his trademark mask due to Madison Square Garden regulations.

STACY KEIBLER

YEARS ACTIVE 1960-1969 | 1970-1979 | 1980-1989 | 1990-1999 | 2000-PRESENT

HT 5'11" **FROM** Baltimore, Maryland

At more than 41 inches in length, Stacy Keibler's legs seem to go on forever. Just like her entrance theme suggests, she certainly knows how to use them. A former Baltimore Ravens cheerleader, Stacy broke into sports-entertainment by winning a WCW contest designed to find a new Nitro Girl. Within months of her debut, it was clear that the leggy Diva was destined to become much more than a member of an ensemble dance team. She soon broke free from the Nitro Girls to become the valet, Miss Hancock.

Following WWE's acquisition of WCW, Stacy remained loyal to her roots and joined The Alliance. While the faction of WCW and ECW Superstars was universally despised, WWE fans found it hard to boo the beautiful newcomer, especially after seeing her during the *Invasion* pay-per-view.

Stacy's early managerial efforts saw her guide the careers of Bubba Ray and D-Von Dudley. Known as the "Duchess of Dudleyville," she often distracted her team's opposition. The sexy ploy carried the Dudleys to numerous victories, but when it resulted in a loss for Bubba Ray & D-Von, the team drove the Diva through a table, signifying the end of their relationship.

Stacy's managerial career also landed her by the side of Scott Steiner and Test, but it was her in-ring action that truly excited audiences. In March 2004, she competed in the biggest match of her career when she participated in *WrestleMania XX*'s Playboy Evening Gown Match. Despite never having graced the pages of *Playboy* (she's rumored to have declined numerous invitations), Stacy's participation made it one of the event's most memorable matches.

The popularity Stacy gained while competing in WWE rings eventually led her to a career in Hollywood. Her most well-known role saw the Diva dance all the way to the final episode of ABC's hit series *Dancing with the Stars*. She also landed recurring roles on *George Lopez* and *What About Brian*.

The Stalker

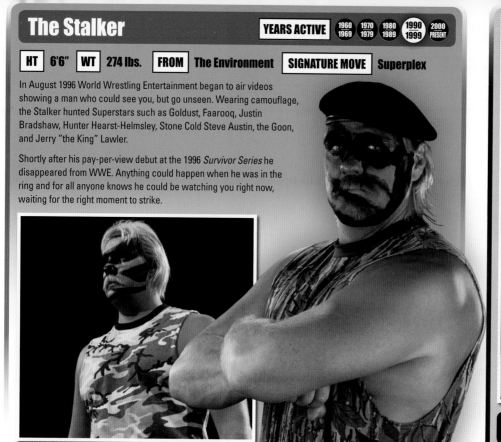

| HT | 6'6" | WT | 274 lbs. | FROM | The Environment | SIGNATURE MOVE | Superplex |

YEARS ACTIVE 1960-1969 | 1970-1979 | 1980-1989 | **1990-1999** | 2000-PRESENT

In August 1996 World Wrestling Entertainment began to air videos showing a man who could see you, but go unseen. Wearing camouflage, the Stalker hunted Superstars such as Goldust, Faarooq, Justin Bradshaw, Hunter Hearst-Helmsley, Stone Cold Steve Austin, the Goon, and Jerry "the King" Lawler.

Shortly after his pay-per-view debut at the 1996 *Survivor Series* he disappeared from WWE. Anything could happen when he was in the ring and for all anyone knows he could be watching you right now, waiting for the right moment to strike.

Stan Hansen

| HT | 6'4" | WT | 321 lbs. | FROM | Borger, Texas | SIGNATURE MOVE | The Lariat |

YEARS ACTIVE 1960-1969 | **1970-1979** | **1980-1989** | **1990-1999** | 2000-PRESENT

Stan Hansen began wrestling in the early 1970s in Amarillo. In 1976 the double-tough roughneck arrived in WWE, courtesy "Classy" Freddie Blassie, who was trying to eliminate Bruno Sammartino. On April 26th in the main event at Madison Square Garden he broke Sammartino's neck when he connected with his Lariat clothesline. After this brutal attack, Hansen gained a reputation as a vicious bounty hunter. Though they settled their score at the Showdown At Shea, more despicable attacks took place against the likes of Ivan Putski and Gorila Monsoon.

Hansen returned to WWE in 1981 and hunted the WWE and Intercontinental Titles, calling out respective champions Bob Backlund and Pedro Morales. He left WWE in 1982 and spent time in Georgia, the AWA, and Japan. In April 1990 Hansen fought Hulk Hogan in the main event of the Wrestling Summit. He briefly appeared in WCW and even stopped in ECW in 1993. His final match was in 2000 against Genichiro Tenryu. Stan Hansen was a rare individual whose home territory was the world. The bad man from Borger left a legacy that may never be duplicated.

Stan Stasiak

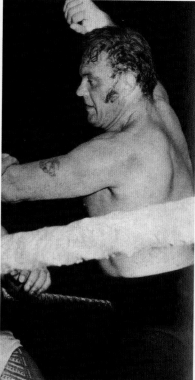

| HT | 6'4" | WT | 270 lbs. |

| FROM | Buzzard Creek, Oregon |

| SIGNATURE MOVE | Heart Punch |

| TITLE HISTORY | WWE Champion |

YEARS ACTIVE 1960-1969 | 1970-1979 | 1980-1989 | 1990-1999 | 2000-PRESENT

Stan Stasiak's name will never be mentioned alongside the greats that held the WWE Championship, but his nine-day stint with the prestigious title is recognized as one of the promotion's most significant reigns, as it served as an historic bridge between Pedro Morales' and Bruno Sammartino's lengthy runs with the title.

Stasiak made his professional debut in Quebec, Canada, in 1958. Known for his long sideburns and rugged offensive approach, he quickly earned the moniker "the Crusher." Over the next several years, he bounced back and forth between territories in Canada and the United States' Pacific Northwest. During this time, Stasiak became known for his paralyzing heart punch, but it wasn't until he took his game to the Northeast that he truly became immortal.

In December 1973, Stan "the Man" forever cemented his name in sports-entertainment lore when he defeated Pedro Morales for the WWE Championship in Philadelphia. The victory made him the fifth champion in WWE history; and while his reign only lasted a little more than a week, he spent the rest of his life being recognized as one of the few Superstars lucky enough to have reached the sport's zenith.

STEEL CAGE MATCH

This match type has been a part of World Wrestling Entertainment from its early days. For decades it has been the most brutal match in sports-entertainment and the ultimate form of confrontation. Whether in a singles or tag team setting, the object is simple: to declare a winner once and for all. The cold, hard steel can be used as a weapon and as a barrier designed to keep the combatants inside its steel confines, as well as block any possible outside interference. A competitor earns the victory by either walking out of the cage door or climbing over the top of the cage.

Arguably the greatest Steel Cage Match ever was Jimmy "Superfly" Snuka's match against the Magnificent Muraco to settle their score in October 1983 at Madison Square Garden. This match was a bloodbath from the early going and saw the most incredible feat take place after the contest. Bleeding profusely, "Superfly" climbed to the top of the cage and leaped down onto a bloodied and bashed Muraco on the canvas.

Over the years their have been numerous historic battles involving legends, giants, and icons. Though they all have their own unique story, one thing remains true for each bloody battle: combatants know when they sign a contract for a Steel Cage match there is nowhere to run and nowhere to hide. Whether championships are on the line or vendettas need to be settled, anyone who enters the 15-foot-high steel cage is in store for a battle that will leave its mark on the participants.

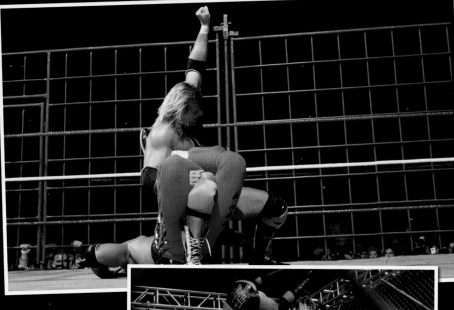

Steel Cage Matches pit opponents with grudges against one another, and no encounters are more brutal than when it's a a rivalry born of a broken heart or when family members face each other, such as the Hart brothers battling for respect.

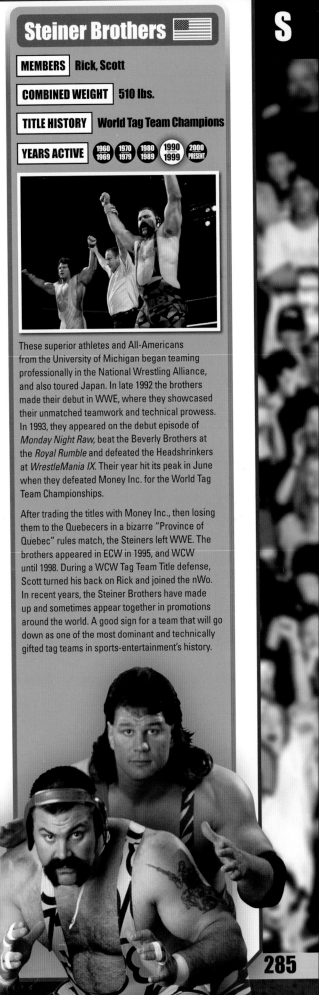

Steiner Brothers 🇺🇸

MEMBERS	Rick, Scott
COMBINED WEIGHT	510 lbs.
TITLE HISTORY	World Tag Team Champions
YEARS ACTIVE	1960–1969 1970–1979 1980–1989 **1990–1999** 2000–PRESENT

These superior athletes and All-Americans from the University of Michigan began teaming professionally in the National Wrestling Alliance, and also toured Japan. In late 1992 the brothers made their debut in WWE, where they showcased their unmatched teamwork and technical prowess. In 1993, they appeared on the debut episode of *Monday Night Raw,* beat the Beverly Brothers at the *Royal Rumble* and defeated the Headshrinkers at *WrestleMania IX.* Their year hit its peak in June when they defeated Money Inc. for the World Tag Team Championships.

After trading the titles with Money Inc., then losing them to the Quebecers in a bizarre "Province of Quebec" rules match, the Steiners left WWE. The brothers appeared in ECW in 1995, and WCW until 1998. During a WCW Tag Team Title defense, Scott turned his back on Rick and joined the nWo. In recent years, the Steiner Brothers have made up and sometimes appear together in promotions around the world. A good sign for a team that will go down as one of the most dominant and technically gifted tag teams in sports-entertainment's history.

STEPHANIE MCMAHON

FROM Greenwich, Connecticut

TITLE HISTORY
Women's Champion

YEARS ACTIVE 1960-1969 1970-1979 1980-1989 1990-1999 2000-PRESENT

Proving the apple doesn't fall far from the tree, Stephanie McMahon has transformed herself into one of the most powerful personalities in sports-entertainment. With an intoxicating combination of beauty and brains, she demands nothing short of excellence. If she doesn't get it from others, Stephanie isn't afraid to step in the ring and beat it out of somebody, much like her father, WWE Chairman Vince McMahon.

Stephanie was introduced to WWE in early 1999 when the sadistic Undertaker abducted her as a means to get to her father. With the innocent Stephanie firmly in his possession, the "Deadman" arranged for a ceremony that would forever lock the two in unholy matrimony. Luckily for Stephanie, an unlikely hero made the save when noted McMahon nemesis Stone Cold Steve Austin ran to the ring and attacked Undertaker.

LOVE LIFE PUT TO THE TEST

Following the horrifying Undertaker incident, Stephanie found love in the form of a WWE Superstar, Test. The relationship helped put a smile back on her face, but also managed to infuriate her protective older brother, Shane. Looking out for what he believed were his sister's best interests, Shane attempted to put an end to the fiery love affair when he battled Test in a Love Her or Leave Her Match at *SummerSlam 1999*. In the end, Test won the match and the right to continue his romance with Stephanie.

The strong bond between Stephanie and Test eventually lead to an engagement. The young lovers planned to wed in November 1999, but just before they could exchange vows, one Superstar made a very revealing objection. Armed with video evidence, Triple H exposed the shocking truth that Stephanie was already a married woman.

In an attempt to salvage his daughter's good name, an irate Mr. McMahon battled Triple H at *Armageddon* in December 1999. Unfortunately for the WWE Chairman, however, "The Game" wasn't his only opponent that night, as his daughter shocked the sports-entertainment world when she helped Triple H defeat her father. After the match, Stephanie jumped into the arms of her husband, proving the two had been in cahoots all along.

MCMAHON-HELMSLEY ERA

Together, Stephanie and Triple H went on to become one of the most power-hungry couples ever. The husband-and-wife team began a ruthless dictatorship that controlled all of WWE. Abusing their power as much as possible, they were both conveniently placed in situations that would benefit them most. As a result, it wasn't long before Triple H had regained the WWE Championship, and Stephanie claimed the Women's Championship.

In July 2001, Stephanie elevated the rivalry with her father to new heights. After already breaking his heart in 1999, Stephanie revealed herself as the new owner of ECW, which she merged with her brother's WCW to form The Alliance. Stephanie and Shane's goal was simple: Put their father and WWE out of business forever.

The Alliance began as a very serious threat to Mr. McMahon's empire, as many of his major Superstars jumped ship to Stephanie's camp, including Stone Cold and William Regal. In the end, however, The Alliance was forced to disband when they were defeated by Team WWE at *Survivor Series 2001*.

With the loss, Stephanie was finally forced out of sports-entertainment, or so it seemed. In January 2002, she used a faux pregnancy to weasel her way back into WWE, alongside her husband, Triple H. Her plan eventually backfired, however, when "The Game" learned of the hoax. Following the emotional rollercoaster, an enraged Triple H demanded a divorce from his conniving wife.

BACK IN POWER

In July 2002, Stephanie returned to prominence when she took over the reigns of *SmackDown*. As the brand's General Manager, she acquired some of sports-entertainment's biggest names, including Hulk Hogan, Brock Lesnar, and Undertaker. She is also credited with creating the WWE Tag Team Championship and resurrecting the prestigious United States Championship.

Stephanie's time in office came to a painful end when she lost an "I Quit" Match to her father at *No Mercy 2003*. While she refused to submit to her father, the match ultimately ended when Stephanie's mother, Linda, couldn't bear to watch the brutality any longer. As a result, she threw in the towel, signifying the end of Stephanie's time on *SmackDown*. Following the loss, Stephanie limited her public appearances in favor of assuming several executive roles behind the scenes. On occasion, however, she reappears when the situation calls for a strong leader.

Steve Blackman

YEARS ACTIVE 1960-1969 1970-1979 1980-1989 1990-1999 2000-PRESENT

HT 6'2" **WT** 245 lbs. **FROM** Annville, Pennsylvania

TITLE HISTORY Hardcore Champion

When Steve Blackman walked to the ring with his eskrima and kendo sticks in hand, everybody knew danger lurked ahead, but it was Blackman's bare hands and mastery of martial arts more than anything else that earned him the nickname "the Lethal Weapon."

Blackman's no-nonsense approach to competition made him a natural fit for WWE's hardcore division, as there were few Superstars that could match his intensity and training with martial arts weaponry. One thing Blackman couldn't combat, however, was being out-manned. In August 2000, "the Lethal Weapon" lost his Hardcore Championship to Shane McMahon when the WWE heir enlisted the help of several other Superstars to help his cause. Later that month at *SummerSlam*, Blackman regained the title after knocking McMahon off the top of the TitanTron onto the arena floor approximately fifty feet below. Blackman then jumped off the structure onto McMahon's limp body for the win. The image of "the Lethal Weapon" flying through the air remains one of Blackman's greatest career highlights.

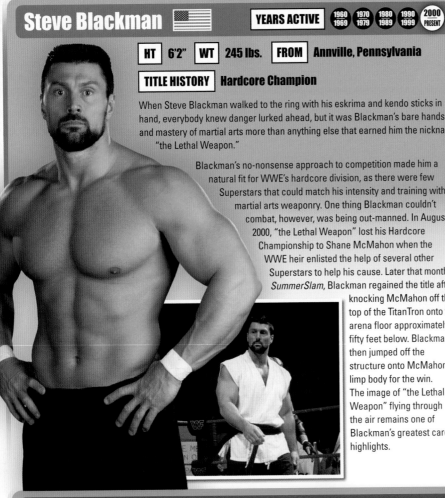

Steve "Dr. Death" Williams

HT 6'1" **WT** 285 lbs. **FROM** Norman, Oklahoma

SIGNATURE MOVE Oklahoma Stampede **YEARS ACTIVE** 1960-1969 1970-1979 1980-1989 1990-1999 2000-PRESENT

Steve Williams was an All-American in amateur wrestling and football at the University of Oklahoma. After training by "Cowboy" Bill Watts, "Dr. Death" became famous all over North America and Japan, winning titles at virtually every stop he made.

In 1998 Williams arrived in sports-entertainment's most competitive landscape, World Wrestling Entertainment. He was an early favorite to win the Brawl For All Tournament, but he suffered a severe hamstring tear. He returned in 1999 alongside Jim Ross, but soon left for WCW and Japan. In 2003, Williams made surprise appearances for WWE and after a heroic fight against throat cancer in 2004, came back to WWE rings through 2006.

2007 was a huge year for Williams. He was inducted into the George Tragos/Lou Thesz Professional Wrestling Hall of Fame and penned his inspirational autobiography titled *"How Dr. Death Became Dr. Life."*

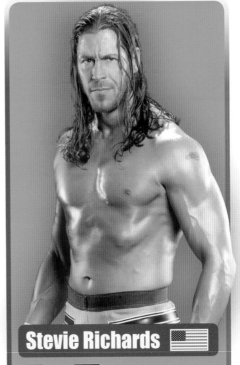

Stevie Richards

HT 6'2" **WT** 230 lbs.

FROM Philadelphia, Pennsylvania

SIGNATURE MOVE Stevie Kick

TITLE HISTORY Hardcore Champion

YEARS ACTIVE 1960-1969 1970-1979 1980-1989 1990-1999 2000-PRESENT

Often referred to as a clueless putz, Stevie Richards must've done something right, as many experts give him partial credit for the early success of ECW. In fact, Richards owns the distinction of competing in ECW's first-ever match, battling Jimmy Jannetty to a 20-minute draw in 1992.

Following an eventful ECW career, which saw him claim two tag team championship reigns, Richards briefly competed in WCW before ultimately landing in WWE. He spent his earliest WWE days mocking fellow Superstars, similar to his popular bWo persona from ECW. After poking fun at the likes of Dude Love, Richards made a shocking transformation. He traded in his cutoff jean shorts for more formal attire and became leader of Right To Censor. As the head of RTC, Steven Richards protested against WWE's risqué content.

Luckily for Richards fans, the movement lasted less than a year. After the faction broke up, Richards returned to the extreme style of competition that initially gained him great fame. In April 2002, he defeated fellow ECW alumnus Tommy Dreamer for the Hardcore Championship. It was his first of 21 reigns with the title. Only Crash Holly and Raven boast more reigns than Richards.

After the retirement of the Hardcore Championship, Richards became a regular on *Heat*. While WWE's highest-profile encounters rarely occurred there, Richards took full advantage of his opportunity; he even proclaimed himself *Heat*'s General Manger, though he was never officially appointed the role.

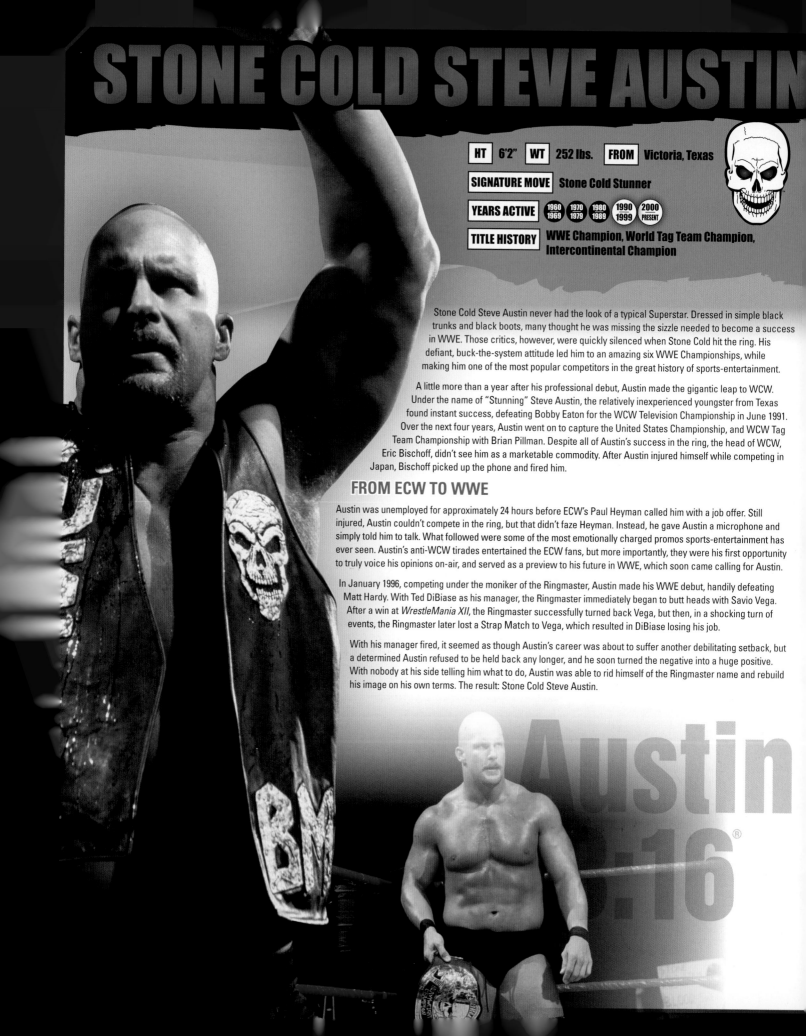

STONE COLD STEVE AUSTIN

HT	6'2"	WT	252 lbs.	FROM	Victoria, Texas

SIGNATURE MOVE Stone Cold Stunner

YEARS ACTIVE 1960–1969 1970–1979 1980–1989 1990–1999 2000–PRESENT

TITLE HISTORY WWE Champion, World Tag Team Champion, Intercontinental Champion

Stone Cold Steve Austin never had the look of a typical Superstar. Dressed in simple black trunks and black boots, many thought he was missing the sizzle needed to become a success in WWE. Those critics, however, were quickly silenced when Stone Cold hit the ring. His defiant, buck-the-system attitude led him to an amazing six WWE Championships, while making him one of the most popular competitors in the great history of sports-entertainment.

A little more than a year after his professional debut, Austin made the gigantic leap to WCW. Under the name of "Stunning" Steve Austin, the relatively inexperienced youngster from Texas found instant success, defeating Bobby Eaton for the WCW Television Championship in June 1991. Over the next four years, Austin went on to capture the United States Championship, and WCW Tag Team Championship with Brian Pillman. Despite all of Austin's success in the ring, the head of WCW, Eric Bischoff, didn't see him as a marketable commodity. After Austin injured himself while competing in Japan, Bischoff picked up the phone and fired him.

FROM ECW TO WWE

Austin was unemployed for approximately 24 hours before ECW's Paul Heyman called him with a job offer. Still injured, Austin couldn't compete in the ring, but that didn't faze Heyman. Instead, he gave Austin a microphone and simply told him to talk. What followed were some of the most emotionally charged promos sports-entertainment has ever seen. Austin's anti-WCW tirades entertained the ECW fans, but more importantly, they were his first opportunity to truly voice his opinions on-air, and served as a preview to his future in WWE, which soon came calling for Austin.

In January 1996, competing under the moniker of the Ringmaster, Austin made his WWE debut, handily defeating Matt Hardy. With Ted DiBiase as his manager, the Ringmaster immediately began to butt heads with Savio Vega. After a win at *WrestleMania XII*, the Ringmaster successfully turned back Vega, but then, in a shocking turn of events, the Ringmaster later lost a Strap Match to Vega, which resulted in DiBiase losing his job.

With his manager fired, it seemed as though Austin's career was about to suffer another debilitating setback, but a determined Austin refused to be held back any longer, and he soon turned the negative into a huge positive. With nobody at his side telling him what to do, Austin was able to rid himself of the Ringmaster name and rebuild his image on his own terms. The result: Stone Cold Steve Austin.

" ...AND THAT'S THE BOTTOM LINE, 'CAUSE STONE COLD SAID SO! "

PAY PER VIEW VICTORIES

It didn't take long for Stone Cold to prove he was the "toughest S.O.B." in all of WWE. Just one month after remaking his image, Austin defeated Jake Roberts to become the 1996 WWE King of the Ring. After the match, Austin made a victory speech that would forever change the face of sports-entertainment.

Austin's post-match rant was an instant rage. Within days, Austin 3:16 T-shirts were everywhere. Stone Cold fans soon started dressing like their hero, making it impossible to walk through the mall without seeing a bald-headed, goatee-wearing fan in jeans and a black T-shirt. Not since Hulkamania had WWE been taken over by such a phenomenon.

"You sit there and you thump your bible, you say your prayers, and it didn't get you anywhere. Talk about your Psalms, talk about John 3:16; Austin 3:16 says I just whipped your ass."

As a result of his *King of the Ring* victory, Stone Cold was afforded opportunities that were denied him while in WCW, which lead to friction between him and Bret "Hit Man" Hart. After last eliminating Hart to win the 1997 *Royal Rumble*, Stone Cold squared off against his rival in a Submission Match at *WrestleMania 13*. While the result did not go in his favor, the sight of Stone Cold profusely bleeding to the point of losing consciousness proved to be one of the most memorable images in WWE history.

Several other members of the famed Hart family muscled their way into the historic rivalry, including Bret's brother Owen. While competing against the younger Hart at *SummerSlam 1997*, Stone Cold suffered a career-threatening injury when a piledriver delivered by Owen broke his neck. Miraculously, Austin was able to recover just enough to roll Owen up for the win and the Intercontinental Championship. Unfortunately for Stone Cold, the severity of his injury forced him to relinquish the title. Upon returning to the ring later that year, however, Stone Cold gained retribution by defeating Owen to become a two-time Intercontinental Champion.

At the *D-Generation X* pay-per-view in December 1997, Stone Cold defeated The Rock to retain his title. By all accounts, the victory should have silenced The Rock's quest to become Intercontinental Champion. The next night on *Raw*, however, Mr. McMahon demanded Stone Cold defend his title against the same man he defeated twenty-four hours earlier. When a defiant Austin refused to give in to McMahon's demands, the Chairman of WWE stripped Stone Cold of the Intercontinental Championship. A fired-up Austin responded by knocking Mr. McMahon out of the ring, officially igniting one of the greatest rivalries in the history of sports-entertainment—Stone Cold vs. Mr. McMahon.

THE ATTITUDE ERA PERSONIFIED

After winning the 1998 Royal Rumble, Stone Cold challenged Shawn Michaels for the WWE Championship in the main event of *WrestleMania XIV*. With Mike Tyson serving as the match's special enforcer, Austin floored HBK with his signature Stone Cold Stunner. Three seconds later, Stone Cold was celebrating his first of six WWE Championship reigns in front of a capacity crowd in Boston's FleetCenter.

The victory infuriated Mr. McMahon, who now had a beer-drinking, middle-finger gesturing Superstar representing his company as its champion. Unable to stand by and allow Stone Cold to act in such a rebellious fashion, McMahon demanded that the new titleholder act more like a "corporate champion". The authority-defying Austin had other plans, however. In typical Stone Cold fashion, he delivered a Stunner to his boss and continued to drink beers while flipping the middle finger.

Stone Cold and Mr. McMahon continued their heated rivalry for the better part of the next three years. However, in April 2001, Austin did the unthinkable. While competing against The Rock at *WrestleMania X-Seven*, Stone Cold actually aligned himself with the man he tried to destroy for so many years. With assistance from Mr. McMahon, Austin defeated The Rock for the WWE Championship that fateful night. After the match, the former rivals actually shook hands and shared a beer.

Stone Cold's shocking allegiance to Mr. McMahon left his dedicated followers scratching their heads while attempting to digest their hero's heinous actions. Just when it appeared as though things couldn't get any worse, Stone Cold dropped another bomb three months later when he turned his back on the entire WWE locker room to join the WCW/ECW Alliance.

Stone Cold's defection from WWE ultimately proved to be an unsuccessful venture. After the Alliance was forced to disband, he found himself right back on the WWE roster. The fans were happy to see him back, but unsure about whether they could trust him again. Stone Cold quickly put all their misgivings to rest the best way he knew how: attacking Mr. McMahon.

POST-WRESTLING CAREER

Chronic neck injuries began to take their toll on Stone Cold Steve Austin in 2002. After taking off the second half of the year, he returned to WWE in 2003 to battle The Rock at *WrestleMania XIX*. Despite a valiant effort, Austin came up short in what was ultimately his final official WWE match.

Stone Cold's in-ring career may be behind him, but he still manages to steal the spotlight every time he steps foot inside a WWE arena. While serving as guest referee for the Goldberg vs. Brock Lesnar *WrestleMania XX* match, Austin received one of the loudest ovations of the night after delivering the Stunner to both Goldberg and Lesnar. The following year at *WrestleMania 21*, Carlito and "Rowdy" Roddy Piper suffered the same fate. At *WrestleMania 23*, Stone Cold even Stunned billionaire Donald Trump.

Since hanging up his boots, much of Stone Cold's time is dedicated to his budding movie career. The final script to his Hollywood story has yet to be completed, but if he's half as successful in theaters as he was in the ring, he will undoubtedly become a box-office hit.

STRAP MATCH

To win a Strap Match, a Superstar must touch all four corners of the ring uninterrupted and in succession. The only catch is that he must accomplish this feat while attached to his opponent by a long leather strap.

Over the years, many other devices have been used to connect the battling Superstars, including bullropes and chains. Regardless of the material, the rules remain the same and the device is always used as a weapon. The most historic match of this variety took place at *The Great American Bash 2004* when JBL and Eddie Guerrero were united by a thick Texas bullrope. Both Superstars used the device to choke their opponent. In the end, it was a bloody JBL touching all four corners first to claim the coveted WWE Championship from Guerrero.

Variations of the rules sometimes allow for pinfalls or submissions to end the contest. In one of the match's earliest displays, "Rowdy" Roddy Piper defeated Greg Valentine in a Dog Collar Match at *Starrcade 1983*. The match was so severe that both men suffered partial hearing loss. More recent matches have witnessed Savio Vega beat Steve Austin in 1996, Triple H defeat The Rock in 1999, and Randy Orton top Dusty Rhodes in 2007.

STREET FIGHT

This type of match has no rules, so anything goes. A Street Fight isn't limited to the ring; the action could spill out on the floor, into the crowd, behind the arena, or wherever it sweeps the participants. In recent years Street Fights have become more popular as the conflicts in World Wrestling Entertainment become more heated, so when it comes time to settle a grudge, Superstars don't want to be limited by what they can do to inflict pain on their opponents.

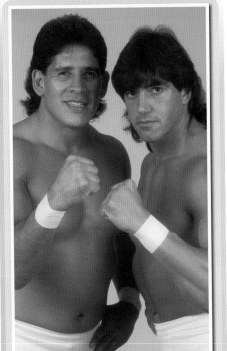

Strike Force

MEMBERS	Tito Santana, Rick Martel

COMBINED WEIGHT	460 lbs.

TITLE HISTORY	World Tag Team Championship

Prior to joining forces, both Tito Santana and Rick Martel enjoyed successful singles careers, which is why it was no surprise to see them achieve greatness as a unit. They first began teaming together in 1987 after Santana ran to the ring to save Martel from a double-team attack at the hands of the Islanders. From that point on, they became known as Strike Force, a good looking tandem whose sound technical skills carried them all the way to the top of the tag team division.

After defeating the Hart Foundation for the World Tag Team Championship in October 1987, Strike Force looked near unstoppable. Many predicted a lengthy reign for the duo, but after only five months with the gold, the impact of Mr. Fuji's cane caused Santana & Martel to lose their titles to Demolition at *WrestleMania IV*. The loss proved to be a major setback for the popular tag team, as they struggled to regain their momentum.

After a brief hiatus, Strike Force reunited to battle the Brain Busters at *WrestleMania V*. In a shocking turn of events, Martel turned on his partner during the match, marking the official end of Strike Force. Over the next several years, the two Superstars engaged in an emotional rivalry that never saw a clear-cut winner.

The Strongbows

MEMBERS	Chief Jay, Jules

TITLE HISTORY	World Tag Team Champions

In 1982 Chief Jay Strongbow tapped his brother Jules for help to face WWE's rule-breakers and bring audiences to their feet. Their high-flying moves, ground-attacks, and double-team actions paved the road of their success. In June 1982 they defeated Mr. Fuji & Mr. Saito for the World Tag Team Championship. Over the next few months they traded title reigns with the hired Japanese guns. Their final title reign ended in March 1983 when they lost to the Wild Samoans. Shortly after the loss the Chief retired from the ring and Jules left WWE and spent the rest of his career competing on the Independent scene.

The Strongbows are warmly remembered as two of the most honorable heroes in WWE history and an exciting duo. When great brother tag team combinations are mentioned, Chief Jay and Jules Strongbow undoubtedly make the list!

The Sultan

HT	6'3"	WT	295 lbs.	FROM	The Middle East	SIGNATURE MOVE	Camel Clutch

When this masked Superstar was first seen in 1997 some experts speculated that his face was deformed. After his impressive debut win against Jake Roberts, the focus was off of his mask and turned to his dangerous array of maneuvers in the ring. Mentored by the Iron Sheik and Mr. Bob Backlund, Sultan was well versed in submission wrestling, mat techniques, and rule-breaking.

Although he met foes like Phineas Godwinn, Yokozuna, Goldust, Undertaker, and Bret Hart, Sultan's greatest battle was with Rocky Maivia over the Intercontinental Championship. The two Superstars settled their score at *WrestleMania 13*. By early 1998 Sultan returned to the home of the one-time Persian Empire and has not been on World Wrestling Entertainment programming since.

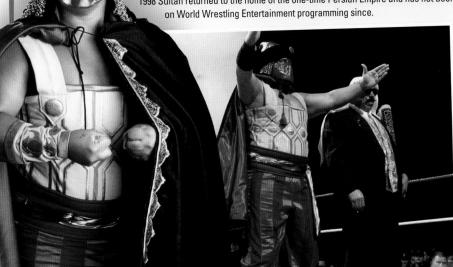

WWE SummerSlam

August 29, 1988
New York, NY - Madison Square Garden

Main Event: Mega Powers (Hulk Hogan & Randy "Macho Man" Savage (with Miss Elizabeth)) vs. Mega Bucks ("Million Dollar Man" Ted DiBiase & Andre The Giant (with Virgil & Bobby Heenan))

August 28, 1989
East Rutherford, NJ - The Meadowlands Arena

Main Event: Hulk Hogan & Brutus "The Barber" Beefcake (with Miss Elizabeth) vs. Randy "Macho Man" Savage & Zeus (with Sensational Sherri)

August 27, 1990
Philadelphia, PA - The Spectrum

Main Event: WWE Champion Ultimate Warrior vs. "Ravishing" Rick Rude in a Steel Cage Match

August 26, 1991
New York, NY - Madison Square Garden

Main Event: Hulk Hogan & Ultimate Warrior vs. Sgt. Slaughter, Colonel Mustafa, & Gen. Adnan in the Match Made In Hell (Handicap Tag Team Match with Sid Justice as special guest referee)

August 29, 1992
London, England - Wembley Stadium

Main Event: British Bulldog vs. Intercontinental Champion Bret "Hit Man" Hart

August 30, 1993
Auburn Hills, MI - The Palace At Auburn Hills

Main Event: Lex Luger vs. WWE Champion Yokozuna (with Mr. Fuji & Jim Cornette) via count out

August 29, 1994
Chicago, IL - The United Center

Main Event: Undertaker (with Paul Bearer) vs. "Undertaker" (with "Million Dollar Man" Ted DiBiase)

August 27, 1995
Pittsburgh, CA - Pittsburgh Civic Arena

Main Event: WWE Champion Diesel vs. King Mabel (with Sir Mo)

August 18, 1996
Cleveland, OH - Gund Arena

Main Event: WWE Champion Shawn Michaels (with Jose Lothario) vs. Vader (with Jim Cornette)

August 3, 1997
East Rutherford, NJ - Continental Airlines Arena

Main Event: Bret "Hit Man" Hart vs. WWE Champion Undertaker with Shawn Michaels as special guest referee

August 30, 1998
New York, NY - Madison Square Garden

Main Event: WWE Champion Stone Cold Steve Austin defeated Undertaker

August 22, 1999
Minneapolis, MN - Target Center

Main Event: Mankind vs. Triple H (with Chyna) vs. WWE Champion Stone Cold Steve Austin in a Triple Threat Match with Jesse "The Body" Ventura as special guest referee

August 27, 2000
Raleigh, NC - Raleigh Entertainment and Sports Arena

Main Event: WWE Champion The Rock vs. Kurt Angle vs. Triple H in a Triple Threat Match

August 29, 2001
San Jose, CA - Compaq Center

WCW Main Event: The Rock vs. WCW Champion Booker T (with Shane McMahon)

WWE Main Event: Kurt Angle vs. WWE Champion Stone Cold Steve Austin

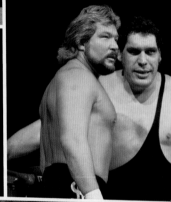

August 25, 2002
Uniondale, NY - Nassau Coliseum

Main Event: Brock Lesnar (with Paul Heyman) vs. WWE Champion The Rock

August 24, 2003
Phoenix, AZ - America West Arena

SmackDown Main Event: WWE Champion Kurt Angle vs. Brock Lesnar

Raw Main Event: World Heavyweight Champion Triple H (with Ric Flair) vs. Kevin Nash vs. Goldberg vs. Chris Jericho vs. Randy Orton vs. Shawn Michaels in an Elimination Chamber Match

August 15, 2004
Toronto, ON - Air Canada Centre

SmackDown Main Event: WWE Champion JBL (with Orlando Jordan) vs. Undertaker via disqualification

Raw Main Event: Randy Orton vs. World Heavyweight Champion Chris Benoit

August 21, 2005
Washington DC - MCI Center

Main Event: Hulk Hogan vs. Shawn Michaels

August 20, 2006
Boston, MA - TD Banknorth Garden

Main Event: WWE Champion Edge (with Lita) vs. John Cena

August 26, 2007
East Rutherford, NJ - Continental Airlines Arena

Main Event: WWE Champion John Cena vs. Randy Orton

August 17, 2008
Indianapolis, IN - Conseco Fieldhouse

Main Event: Undertaker vs. Edge in a Hell in a Cell Match

SUNNY

A life-long fan, Sunny did everything she could to learn the art of managing within the world of sports-entertainment. One day she got a call that made all of her dreams come true. This ground-breaker began her sports-entertainment career in Smokey Mountain Wrestling in the early 1990s.

In the summer of 1995, Sunny debuted as the manager of fellow Bodydonna, Skip. This fabulous female shined brighter than any before her as audiences were captivated by her striking beauty, charisma, and confidently energetic persona. As her career expanded Sunny was a broadcast correspondent, a ring announcer, color commentator, and ambassador during her time with WWE. There was nothing Sunny couldn't do and she was more than happy to remind people of that whenever she had the opportunity. In 1996 Sunny brought Faarooq to WWE, was the most downloaded woman on America Online, and won two Slammy Awards.

After guiding Skip and his brother Zip to the tag team titles at *WrestleMania XII*, Sunny left the team behind after they lost to the Godwinns a few months later. Sunny's stay with the Godwinns came to a sudden halt when she helped the Smokin' Gunns win the match and claim the World Tag Team Championship. However, she caused problems between the brothers which ultimately led to losing the belts to Owen Hart & Yokozuna.

In 1998, she rejuvenated the Legion of Doom and re-christened them L.O.D. 2000 as they won the Tag Team Battle Royal at *WrestleMania XIV*. She left WWE later in 1998, but resurfaced in ECW and WCW over the next few years before taking a break from sports-entertainment in 2001.

During the *Raw 15th Anniversary* the original Diva returned to WWE for the first time in almost a decade, with her theme song *I Know You Want Me* sent shivers down the spines of the male fans around the world. She will always fondly be recognized as one of the first Divas in World Wrestling Entertainment history, and many feel the best.

Super Crazy

HT	5'8"	WT	200 lbs.

FROM Tulancingo, Hidalgo, Mexico

SIGNATURE MOVE Moonsault

He's super. He's crazy. He's Super Crazy.

The appropriately named Super Crazy was inked to a WWE contract after executing a moonsault off the second balcony of New York's Hammerstein Ballroom at *ECW One Night Stand*. Alongside Juventud and Psicosis, Super Crazy made his WWE debut as a member of the Mexicools faction. Despite being rule breakers in the ring, the Mexicools high-flying style made them instant fan favorites.

In late 2006, Super Crazy left *SmackDown* in favor of a singles career on *Raw*. The extreme luchador made an instant impact, defeating Chris Masters several times within his first month on the roster. After a year of amazing *Raw* audiences in singles matches, Super Crazy returned to tag action, teaming with the legendary "Hacksaw" Jim Duggan in late 2007.

The next year, Super Crazy was shipped from *Raw* to ECW in the 2008 Supplemental Draft. The move sent him back to the rings of "The Land of the Extreme," where he first made a name for himself 10 years earlier.

"SUPERSTAR" BILLY GRAHAM

> *I AM THE REFLECTION OF PERFECTION. I AM THE SENSATION OF THE NATION. THE NUMBER-ONE CREATION.*

HT 6'4"	**WT** 275 lbs.
FROM	Paradise Valley, Arizona
SIGNATURE MOVE	Bearhug
TITLE HISTORY	WWE Champion
YEARS ACTIVE	1960–1969 · 1970–1979 · 1980–1989 · 1990–1999 · 2000 PRESENT

As a high-school track and field star, "Superstar" Billy Graham held national records for discus and shot-put events and was groomed for the 1964 Olympic Games. After he won the Teenage Mr. America contest, Graham landed in Santa Monica in 1968 and trained at the original Gold's Gym with future movie star and Governor of California, Arnold Schwarzenegger. After attempts at pro football left him uninspired, Graham traveled to Calgary, Alberta, Canada, and trained with the legendary Stu Hart. In 1975 "Superstar" Billy Graham debuted in World Wrestling Entertainment determined to take Earth on a magnificent vision quest. Wearing a psychedelic kaleidoscope of tie-dye outfits, feathered boas, sunglasses, and a sun-kissed tan, Graham was the finest physical specimen the world had ever seen.

Brought to the ring by the Grand Wizard, Graham hunted then-champion Bruno Sammartino for wrestling's richest honor. On April 30, 1977, Graham met Sammartino for the WWE Championship in Baltimore, Maryland, where both men fought beyond the brink of exhaustion. As Sammartino barraged Graham in the corner, the challenger moved with the cunning of a viper. Graham swept Sammartino's feet out from under him, pinned his shoulders to the mat and put his feet on the top rope for added (and illegal) leverage to win the WWE Championship. The landscape changed as "Superstar" held its most prestigious trophy and transcended pop culture.

Six months later, Graham had a series of title matches against Dusty Rhodes that sold out Madison Square Garden and electrified the wrestling world. On February 20, 1978, Graham's feet once again changed history as he lost the WWE Championship to Bob Backlund despite Graham's foot being on the bottom rope as the referee counted three. Devastated in defeat, Billy took a sabbatical from competition and returned to Arizona. During this fall from grace, he became detached from reality and spiraled into the dangerous world of drug abuse.

In 1982, Graham returned to WWE as a martial arts expert with a new look, complete with shaved head, black mustache and black karate pants. Once again managed by the Grand Wizard, Graham chased Backlund in unsuccessful attempts to regain the WWE Championship. A dejected Graham left WWE again and briefly appeared in the NWA. While there, he brought back the popular technicolor appearance and poetic flow with a new two-toned goatee. In 1987, "Superstar" made his triumphant WWE return to swarms of adoring fans.

Unfortunately, years of competition had taken its toll and Graham was in dire need of hip replacement surgery. He returned to the ring for a short time before his litany of injuries forced him to leave the ring permanently. With the desire to inspire, Graham managed Don Muraco and was his inspiration for a newfound attitude. Graham also used his gift of gab in the broadcast booth and provided commentary for *SummerSlam 1988*. Sadly, Graham's body continued to break down and he was no longer physically able to perform for the company in any capacity. Graham was forced to leave the profession he so dearly loved at age 45. While on the outside looking in, WWE experienced extraordinary success. "Superstar" once again battled depression, bitterness, and drug addition. The once admired sports-entertainment visionary was trapped underneath a mountainous valley of regret and anger.

Soon, Graham was facing another obstacle as he was in dire need of a liver replacement. Things looked so grim he considered planning his own funeral in 2002, but luckily, a suitable donor was found. As he enjoyed a new lease on life, Graham was invigorated like never before and started his crusade for organ donor awareness. After being estranged from WWE for 14 years, Graham had a joyous reunion with Vince McMahon backstage at *SummerSlam 2003*. In March 2004, Graham finally found his rightful place in history alongside the immortals of sports-entertainment when he was inducted into the WWE Hall of Fame. To the delight of his fans, he continues to appear on WWE programming and in January 2006, he penned his autobiography titled, *Tangled Ropes*.

There was never a finer physical specimen or as masterful a communicator than "Superstar" Billy Graham. He was the ultimate entertainer and an original like no other who defeated all contenders and pretenders. Graham's unparalleled influence and success touched generations as seen with Hulk Hogan and Jesse "The Body" Ventura. The only question that remains is how great could he have been if he blessed us with his presence 20 years later?

"Superstar" Billy Graham possessed a physique chiseled from granite and a cornucopia of catchphrases that were so innovative, people wrote down his words to study and recite them as if they were their own.

SURVIVOR SERIES

November 16, 2003

Dallas, TX - American Airlines Center

Main Event: World Heavyweight Champion Goldberg vs. Triple H (with Ric Flair)

November 14, 2004

Cleveland, OH - Gund Arena

SmackDown Main Event:
Eddie Guerrero, Rob Van Dam, Big Show & John Cena vs. Kurt Angle, Mark Jindrak, Luther Reigns & Carlito

Survivors:
Eddie Guerrero, Big Show, and John Cena

Raw Main Event: Randy Orton, Chris Benoit, Chris Jericho & Maven vs. Triple H (with Ric Flair), Batista, Edge & Snitsky

Survivor: Randy Orton

November 27, 2005

Detroit, MI - Joe Louis Arena

Main Event: Team SmackDown (Batista, Rey Mysterio, JBL, Bobby Lashley & Randy Orton) vs. Team Raw (Shawn Michaels, Kane, Big Show, Carlito & Chris Masters) in a Classic Survivor Series Match

Survivor: Randy Orton

November 26, 2006

Philadelphia, PA - Wachovia Center

Main Event: Batista vs. World Heavyweight Champion King Booker (with Queen Sharmell)

November 18, 2007

Miami, FL - American Airlines Arena

Main Event: World Heavyweight Champion Batista vs. Undertaker, in a Hell In A Cell Match

November 23, 2008

Boston, MA - TD Banknorth Garden

Main Event: John Cena vs. World Heavyweight Champion Chris Jericho

November 26, 1987

Richfield, OH - Richfield Coliseum

Main Event: Andre the Giant, One Man Gang, King Kong Bundy, "The Natural" Butch Reed & "Ravishing" Rick Rude vs. Hulk Hogan, Paul Orndorff, Don Muraco, Ken Patera & Bam Bam Bigelow

Sole Survivor: Andre the Giant

November 24, 1988

Richfield, OH - Richfield Coliseum

Main Event: Hulk Hogan, "Macho Man" Randy Savage, Hercules, Koko B. Ware & Hillbilly Jim vs. "Million Dollar Man" Ted DiBiase, Akeem, Big Bossman, Haku & Red Rooster

Survivors: Hulk Hogan and "Macho Man" Randy Savage

November 23, 1989

Rosemont, IL - The Rosemont Horizon

Main Event: The Ultimate Warriors (Ultimate Warrior, Jim Neidhart, & the Rockers) vs. the Heenan Family (Andre the Giant, Bobby Heenan, Haku, & Arn Anderson)

Sole Survivor: Ultimate Warrior

November 22, 1990

Hartford, CT - Hartford Civic Center

Main Event: Hulk Hogan, Ultimate Warrior & Tito Santana vs. "The Model" Rick Martel, Power & Glory, the Warlord & "Million Dollar Man" Ted DiBiase, in a Survivors Match

Survivors:
Ultimate Warrior and Hulk Hogan

November 27, 1991

Detroit, MI - Joe Louis Arena

Main Event: Undertaker (with Paul Bearer) vs. WWE Champion Hulk Hogan

November 25, 1992

Richmond, OH - Richfield Coliseum

Main Event: WWE Heavyweight Champion Bret "Hit Man" Hart vs. Shawn Michaels

November 24, 1993

Boston, MA - Boston Garden

Main Event: The All Americans (Lex Luger, the Steiner Brothers & Undertaker) vs. The Foreign Fanatics (Quebecer Jacques, Yokozuna, Ludvig Borga & Crush)

Sole Survivor: Lex Luger

November 23, 1994

San Antonio, TX - Freeman Coliseum

Main Event: Undertaker (with Paul Bearer) vs. Yokozuna (with Mr. Fuji & Jim Cornette) in a Casket Match

November 19, 1995

Landover, MD - U.S. Air Arena

Main Event: Bret "Hit Man" Hart vs. WWE Champion Diesel in a No Disqualification Match

November 17, 1996

New York, NY - Madison Square Garden

Main Event: Sid vs. WWE Champion Shawn Michaels (with Jose Lothario)

November 9, 1997

Montreal, Quebec Canada - Molson Centre

Main Event: Shawn Michaels vs. WWE Champion Bret Hart

After Shawn Michaels applied this Sharpshooter to Bret Hart, sports-entertainment was never the same again.

November 15, 1998

St. Louis, MO - Kiel Center

Main Event: The Rock vs. Mankind in the WWE Championship Tournament Finals

November 14, 1999

Detroit, MI - Joe Louis Arena

Main Event: Big Show vs. The Rock vs. Triple H, Triple Threat Match for the WWE Championship

November 19, 2000

Tampa, FL - Ice Palace

Main Event: Stone Cold Steve Austin vs. Triple H, No Disqualification Match

November 18, 2001

Greensboro, NC - Greensboro Coliseum

Main Event: WWE (The Rock, Chris Jericho, Big Show, Kane & Undertaker) vs. The Alliance (Stone Cold Steve Austin, Kurt Angle, Shane McMahon, Booker T & Rob Van Dam), in an Elimination Match

Sole Survivor: The Rock

November 17, 2002

New York, NY - Madison Square Garden

SmackDown Main Event: Big Show defeated WWE Champion Brock Lesnar

Raw Main Event: Shawn Michaels vs. World Heavyweight Champion Triple H vs. Booker T vs. Rob Van Dam vs. Chris Jericho vs. Kane, in an Elimination Chamber Match for the World Heavyweight Championship

Swede Hanson

HT 6'5" **WT** 307 lbs. **FROM** Slaughter Creek, North Carolina **SIGNATURE MOVE** Bearhug

A former Golden Gloves competitor, this giant was trained by the legendary George Tragos and debuted in Vincent J. McMahon's Capitol Wrestling in the late 1950s, often facing off against Bruno Sammartino. In the early 1960s, Swede ventured to Jim Crockett Promotions where he was part of one of the most famous tandems in professional wrestling history with Rip Hawk. In 1979 the man known as "Big Swede" returned to World Wrestling Entertainment, managed by Freddy Blassie. He reignited his battle with Bruno Sammartino and warred with Ivan Putski, Chief Jay Strongbow, Gorilla Monsoon, Andre the Giant, Tito Santana, and Pedro Morales, but his main objective was to end the Heavyweight Championship reign of Bob Backlund. Swede remained with WWE until 1985. He retired from the ring one year later.

Swede Hanson passed away in 2002. His career was legendary and spanned four decades. Tough guys may come and go as time continues on but no one will ever forget the "Big Swede."

Sweet Daddy Siki

HT 5'10" **WT** 245 lbs. **FROM** Montgomery, Texas

Sweet Daddy Siki was born in Texas, but cemented his legacy while competing north of the border in Canada. After several non-descript years of competing in New Mexico, Los Angeles, and Japan, Siki moved to Toronto where he became one of the country's most admired Superstars of the 1960s and 1970s.

While competing for Calgary's Stampede Wrestling, Siki defeated Dave Ruhl to capture the organization's North American Heavyweight Championship in September 1970. He held the title for six months before being toppled by the great Abdullah the Butcher. During the twilight of his career, Siki began to train future competitors out of Sully's Gym in Toronto. During this time, he helped shape the career of a very young Edge. The "Rated-R Superstar" later went on to achieve amazing success as both a WWE Champion and World Heavyweight Champion.

SWS/WWE SUPERCARDS

In 1990 and 1991, WWE teamed up with Super World of Sports, a Japanese promotion, to hold a series of events that often saw WWE competitors facing an opponent from Japan.

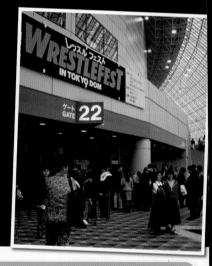

WRESTLING SUMMIT
April 13, 1990
Tokyo Dome, Tokyo, Japan

Main Event: Shohei "Giant" Baba & Andre the Giant vs. Demolition in a Non-Title Special Tag Team Challenge Match

WRESTLEFEST
March 30, 1991
Tokyo Dome, Tokyo, Japan

Main Event: The Legion of Doom vs. Hulk Hogan & Genichiro Tenryu in a Special Tag Team Challenge Match

SUPERWRESTLE
December 12, 1991
Tokyo Dome, Tokyo, Japan

Main Event: Hulk Hogan vs. Genichiro Tenryu in a Special Challenge Match

Sylvan Grenier

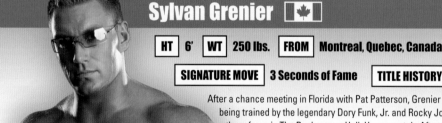

HT 6' **WT** 250 lbs. **FROM** Montreal, Quebec, Canada

SIGNATURE MOVE 3 Seconds of Fame **TITLE HISTORY** World Tag Team Champion

After a chance meeting in Florida with Pat Patterson, Grenier changed from a supermodel to a sports-entertainer. After being trained by the legendary Dory Funk, Jr. and Rocky Johnson, Grenier made his WWE debut at *No Way Out 2003* as the referee in The Rock versus Hulk Hogan match. After an appearance at *WrestleMania XIX* as the referee for Mr. McMahon, the self-proclaimed prized treasure of North America soon formed the French elitist group known as La Resistance with Renee Dupree. In June, he and Dupree defeated Rob Van Dam & Kane to capture the World Tag Team Championship.

Towards the end of the year Sylvan suffered a severe neck injury, but he returned to WWE in March 2004 and rejoined La Resistance. In August 2005 Grenier became a member of *SmackDown* and the Ambassador to Quebec. He briefly changed his name to Sylvan and took aim at people's lack of fashion sense. In February 2007 Grenier briefly reunited with Dupree in ECW before he ultimately parted ways with WWE that August.

TAG TEAM MATCH

The first match to evolve from the standard one on one competition, a tag team match is when a minimum of two individuals square off against an opposing team of the same number of participants. The teams are often Superstars who are connected by a common cause or shared antagonists. Regardless of the circumstances, tag team matches are always exciting and usually a breeding ground for mayhem and chaos.

Throughout time tag team matches have seen virtually countless additions, stipulations and modifications. Virtually any type of match can be successfully applied to a tag team setting.

ELIMINATION

When a Superstar is pinned, disqualified, counted out, or submits, that Superstar is eliminated from further participation in the match. The contest continues until all members of one team are eliminated.

FOUR CORNERS

Four teams compete with one member of two of the participating teams starting. Anyone could be tagged in by anyone else at anytime and be subject to count out or disqualification if they refuse to accept the tag. When a wrestler is pinned that team is eliminated. The last team is the winner.

HANDICAP

When one team has an advantage, typically an additional team member.

INTERGENDER

When a team has both men and women and either can face-off against the other.

MIXED

A team that features both men and women where the two competitors in the ring must be of the same gender.

TEXAS TORNADO

All participants fight in the ring at the same time. Though it involves teams, there are no tags necessary.

Sylvester Terkay

HT	6'6"	**WT**	320 lbs.

FROM Big Bear, California

YEARS ACTIVE

1960-1969 | 1970-1979 | 1980-1989 | 1990-1999 | **2000 PRESENT**

An accomplished mixed martial artist, Sylvester Terkay made the jump to sports-entertainment in July 2006. With corner man Elijah Burke backing him, the Superstar dubbed "the Man Bear" made quick work of his fellow *SmackDown* Superstars, including Matt Hardy and Tatanka.

In November 2006, Terkay left *SmackDown* in favor of the competition found on ECW. The move proved to be a mistake, as his initial ECW match also marked his first-ever loss. Outside of a victory at *December to Dismember*, "the Man Bear" struggled to make waves as a member of the ECW roster.

Tajiri

HT	5'9"	**WT**	205 lbs.

FROM Japan

SIGNATURE MOVE Tarantula

TITLE HISTORY

World Tag Team Champion, WWE Tag Team Champion, Cruiserweight Champion, Light Heavyweight Champion

YEARS ACTIVE

1960-1969 | 1970-1979 | 1980-1989 | **1990-1999** | **2000 PRESENT**

After nearly a decade of professional experience in Japan and Mexico, Tajiri graced American rings in 1998. As a member of ECW, he reminded fans of the Great Muta with flying somersaults and roundhouse kicks. When financial woes closed ECW's doors in 2001, Tajiri followed many of his colleagues to WWE. Initially, he served as the sidekick to WWE Commissioner William Regal. Tajiri exhibited a tremendous sense of humor, but there was nothing funny about his in-ring skills.

If the ref wasn't looking, "the Japanese Buzzsaw" was never above spitting a blinding green mist into the eyes of his competition. His combination of talent and a little rule breaking propelled Tajiri to numerous singles titles, including four combined runs with the now-defunct Cruiserweight and Light Heavyweight Championships.

Over the course of his five-year stay with WWE, Tajiri was also considered a top tag team talent. In May 2003, he teamed with Eddie Guerrero to claim the WWE Tag Team Championship from Shelton Benjamin & Charlie Haas. A few years later, alongside longtime associate William Regal, he bested La Resistance for the World Tag Team Titles in his home country of Japan.

Taka Michinoku 🇯🇵

HT 5'8" **WT** 201 lbs. **FROM** Iwate, Japan

SIGNATURE MOVE Michinoku Driver

TITLE HISTORY Light Heavyweight Champion

Trained by the legendary Great Sasuke, Taka Michinoku first arrived in the United States courtesty the bWo and ECW. A master of high-flying assaults, martial-arts, lucha libre, and grappling, he collected his share of admirers.

At *In Your House: Calgary Stampede* Taka made his debut in a thrilling contest against his mentor. In December, 1997 Michinoku defeated Brian Christopher to become the first WWE Light Heavyweight Champion in the finals of a tournament. Taka set a new championship standard as he defended the prize for more than 10 months before losing it to Christian.

Around this time he turned on partner Val Venis and joined the ranks of Kaientai, most often working with Funaki. Taka continued to appear in WWE into 2002 before returning to Japan where he remains one of the country's most popular Superstars. Taka Michinoku will be remembered by WWE audiences as one who took the Light Heavyweight Championship to new heights and brought a special brand of evil to the ring, indeed!

Tank Morgan

Fans who witnessed the beatings delivered by Tank Morgan may forever hold the images of his battered opponents in their minds. The opponents who took the beatings likely relive them in their worst nightmares. A detested villain, Morgan barreled into WWE in October 1966. He used power, agility, and cunning to further his ambitions to destroy his competition. His brutal, but effective methods made him a top challenger for the Heavyweight Championship held by Bruno Sammartino. The two Superstars brawled throughout the northeast and pushed one another to the limit of their physical endurance.

Though Tank never held the championship, he continued to ruin the lives of WWE heroes on his own as well as with associates of the treacherous sort, such as Luke Graham, Bull Ortega, Smasher Sloan, Gorilla Monsoon, and Baron Mikel Scicluna. Morgan left WWE in 1967 and toured the National Wrestling Alliance, developing a soft-spot in his black heart for its Hawaiian territory.

Tarzan Tyler 🇺🇸

HT 6'3" **WT** 270 lbs. **FROM** Miami Beach, Florida

TITLE HISTORY World Tag Team Champion, International Tag Team Champion

After nearly one decade of competing in Canadian wrestling rings, Tarzan Tyler took his game to the United States during the 1960s. Clad in multi-colored trunks and sporting bleached blonde hair, Tyler would incite the crowds by breaking nearly every rule in the book. For years, fans suspected he illegally loaded his boots, making them nearly lethal weapons. Referees, however, were unable to confirm the allegations.

As a singles star, Tyler engaged in many world championship rivalries. In the early 1960s, he challenged American Wrestling Association Champion Verne Gagne for the title on numerous occasions. Later, Tyler tried to wrest the National Wrestling Alliance Title from champions Lou Thesz and Dory Funk Jr. Tyler's greatest claim to fame came as a tag competitor. Teaming with Crazy Luke Graham, he turned back Dick the Bruiser & The Sheik in June 1971 to become WWE's first-ever World Tag Team Champions.

Tatanka 🇺🇸

This Native American warrior was a renowned body builder before he entered the ring. After winning several bodybuilding competitions along the east coast of the United States, he trained at Larry Sharpe's Monster Factory.

HT 6'2" **WT** 285 lbs. **FROM** Pembroke, North Carolina

SIGNATURE MOVE The Indian Death Drop

After appearing in regional promotions, Tatanka came to WWE in 1992. Pushed by his Lumbee tribe war cry, his opponents knew that when he went on his war dance, it marked the beginning of the end for them. He enjoyed a lengthy undefeated streak where he didn't suffer a loss until September 1993 after Ludvig Borga used a steel chair on Tatanka's back when the referee was distracted.

Tatanka earned so much respect that Chief Jay Strongbow became his mentor and presented him with a Lumbee tribe chief headdress. Unfortunately, something in Tatanka snapped at *SummerSlam 1994* when he turned on Lex Luger and joined the Million Dollar Corporation. In 1995 Tatanka left WWE to take care of his family, but he made a surprise return at the 1996 *Royal Rumble*. Afterwards, Tatanka departed WWE again, and spent the next ten years on the independent scene. He made an amazing return to *Raw* in 2005 and for the next two years reminded audiences of the warrior he always was.

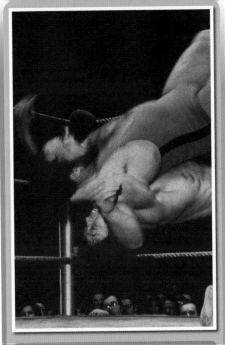

Tatsumi Fujinami

HT	6'	**WT**	238 lbs.

FROM Oita, Japan

SIGNATURE MOVE Dragon Sleeper

TITLE HISTORY Junior Heavyweight Champion, International Heavyweight Champion, International Tag Team Champion

YEARS ACTIVE 1960 1969 1970 1979 1980 1989 1990 1999 2000 PRESENT

Tatsumi Fujinami's career started in 1971. His intensity and superior technical abilities quickly earned him the nickname "the Dragon." He developed revolutionary moves including the Dragon Sleeper, Dragon Suplex, and Dragon Backbreaker. In the late 1970s Fujinami arrived in North America competing in Mexico and Jim Crockett Promotions before his WWE debut in 1976. He defeated Jose Estrada in his debut to become WWE Light Heavyweight Champion.

Fujinami's fame brought him to the 1980 Showdown At Shea where he defeated Lucha Libre legend Chavo Guerrero. In August, 1982 Fujinami defeated Gino Brito to capture the prized International Heavyweight Championship with its lineage dating back to Antonino "Argentina" Rocca. Fujinami made headlines in the United States when he opposed "Nature Boy" Ric Flair for a historic "Champion v. Champion" match at the first-ever WCW SuperBrawl in 1991.

Fujinami continues to be active in Japan, and has even started his own promotion. Tatsumi Fujinami is one of the greatest legends to ever do battle in professional wrestling on any continent and his influence goes beyond time periods and cultures.

Tazz

HT	5'9"	**WT**	240 lbs.

FROM Red Hook section of Brooklyn

TITLE HISTORY World Tag Team Champion, Hardcore Champion

YEARS ACTIVE 1960 1969 1970 1979 1980 1989 1990 1999 2000 PRESENT

Tazz was widely regarded as one of the most dangerous competitors of his time. Though undersized by most standards, his offensive attack was pure dynamite. Known as "the Human Suplex Machine," Tazz's rise to the top started in 1993 when he joined ECW. Over the next six years, he defined himself as a true ECW icon, winning every piece of hardware the promotion offered. He even proudly carried his own FTW Championship, a title he created in 1998. He was known to challenge opponents to "...win if you can; survive if I let you."

Tazz made his WWE debut in 1999, beating the undefeated Kurt Angle. The win started Tazz's WWE career on the right foot, but little did anybody realize the extreme Superstar still had some ECW fight left in him. A few months after his WWE debut, Tazz returned to ECW and defeated Mike Awesome for the ECW Championship. The victory was truly historic, considering Tazz, under contract with WWE at the time, defeated Mike Awesome, a Superstar employed by WCW.

Towards the end of his in-ring career, Tazz began serving as a part-time commentator on *Sunday Night Heat*. His tell-it-like-it-is approach to announcing made him popular with the fans and it wasn't long before he was the permanent color commentator on *SmackDown*.

Proving he could do just about anything, Tazz added trainer to his impressive list of accomplishments. In 2001, he joined the cast of *Tough Enough* to train aspiring Superstars. His list of pupils includes Christopher Nowinski and fellow announcer Josh Mathews.

Ted Arcidi

HT	5'11"	**WT**	285 lbs.

FROM Boston, Massachusetts

YEARS ACTIVE 1960 1969 1970 1979 1980 1989 1990 1999 2000 PRESENT

The sports-entertainment world has seen many Superstars falsely claim to be the world's strongest man. In 1985, Ted Arcidi proved his bold assertion when he became the first human being to ever bench press more than seven-hundred pounds. The awesome Arcidi put up 705 pounds, breaking the world record once held by Bruno Sammartino.

The record-breaking feat caught the eyes of WWE officials, who quickly signed Arcidi to a contract. Within moments of the ink drying, the solid block of a man took to the ring. Arcidi quickly engaged in rivalries with fellow toughmen Hercules and Big John Studd.

Arcidi's impressive strength earned him a spot in the famed WWE/NFL Battle Royal at *WrestleMania 2*. While he didn't win the competition, he did impress those watching, as it took the combination of Hillbilly Jim, B. Brian Blair, and Danny Spivey to eliminate him.

VIDEO GAMES

As WWE's brand of sports entertainment took the globe on a never-ending roller coaster ride, another industry began to assault pop-culture as well. The video game business which began in the 1970's as basic computer games and then coin-operated arcade machines started an in-home craze during the early 1980s. While many believe the professional wrestling games that were released in the early 1980s for both arcade and home play were inspired by WWE, they were not officially licensed by World Wrestling Entertainment.

That all changed in 1987 when the first officially licensed WWE video game was released for the Commodore 64 Computer Games System titled, *Micro League Wrestling*. A turn-based strategic simulation, *Micro League* was one of the first video games to feature real, digitized video. The game also allowed you to defend the Heavyweight Championship of Hulk Hogan or try to dethrone him. In addition to authentic WWE Superstar moves, Vince McMahon and Jesse Ventura provided ringside commentary and interviews. The series became so popular it spawned a follow-up in the form of 1989's *Micro League: WWE Superstars 2* as well as later titles on the Commodore such as *WWE WrestleMania* and *WWE European Rampage*.

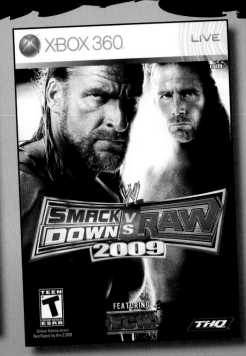

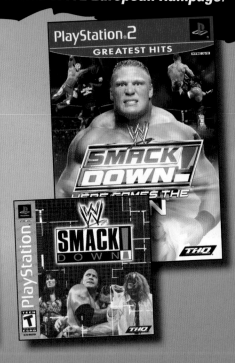

GAMES FOR THE HOME CONSOLES

After millions of letters and fan-driven campaigns, the power and excitement of WWE was finally brought to home video gaming consoles for the first time in 1988. Published by Acclaim Entertainment, *WWE WrestleMania* was released on the Nintendo Entertainment System. The game featured six of the biggest names in sports entertainment from the era including Randy "Macho Man" Savage, "Million Dollar Man" Ted DiBiase, Bam Bam Bigelow, Honky Tonk Man, Andre the Giant, and Hulk Hogan. Each Superstar had their own attacks and trademark finishing maneuvers as well as character icons that gave added health when picked up by the player. The game revolved around a tournament to win the WWE Heavyweight Championship and also sported a 6-player, turn-based tournament so gamers could test one another's skills.

The demand for WWE licensed software continued to grow and arcade gamers saw a revolutionary product explode onto the scene in 1989. Developed by Technos, the coin-op was an instant classic and, as the follow-up to Nintendo's *WrestleMania*, made its way to systems in 1990's *WWE WrestleMania Challenge*. It offered a career mode and Survivor Series mode. Technos returned to the ring with 1991's *WrestleFest* and once again arcades were packed.

After successful releases like *WWE Superstars* went portable on handheld systems, WWE gaming reached a new level of power on the 16-bit Sega Genesis and Super Nintendo Entertainment Systems with offerings from 1992–1995 like *Super WrestleMania, Royal Rumble, Monday Night Raw,* and *WrestleMania: The Arcade Game*. During this exciting time fans faithful to the original Nintendo saw its last release in 1993's, *King of the Ring. Monday Night Raw* made its way to additional systems like Sega's Game Gear and 32X platforms, and *WrestleMania* followed suit on those systems and received an additional boost in graphics and processing power on the Sega Saturn, PC, Sony PlayStation and at the arcade. *In Your House: There Goes The Neighborhood* released in 1996 had similar success, but no one knew what was in the works.

In June 1998, professional wrestling video gaming changed forever as *WWE Warzone* appeared for the Sony PlayStation, Nintendo 64, and Game Boy systems. With a robust Career Mode, Superstar entrances and running commentary gamers were hooked. For all its innovation, *Warzone* is credited for unleashing the first-ever Create-A-Wrestler mode where gamers created their own character and brought them to the top of sports-entertainment. This form of customization has become the most popular feature for games in the genre. After *Attitude* was released for the PlayStation, Nintendo 64, Game Boy, and Sega DreamCast in 1999, it was time for another software publisher to take the most powerful sports and entertainment property into the next millennium and meet the rising product and technological demands of the fans.

THQ TAKES OVER

THQ Inc., through its joint venture with JAKKS Pacific, Inc., made a splash with their first WWE licensed effort for the Nintendo 64 and Game Boy Color with *WrestleMania 2000* in November 1999. One of the first products with a lenticular package back cover, gamers could choose from over 50 Superstars, a variety of match types and Create-A-Wrestler. These features made the title a best-seller and set a tone for the type of products members of the WWE fan nation could expect. The start of the year 2000 did not disappoint as *Royal Rumble* hit the DreamCast and the very first *SmackDown* made its way to the Sony PlayStation as a critical and commercial success. The new era of WWE had arrived with an incredible grappling system, new match types, backstage areas, Superstar facial expressions, dynamic television presentation and a remarkably deep Career Mode. Audiences realized the level of detail they were living in when, for the first-time ever, The Rock's right elbow pad was thrown off his arm while performing The People's Elbow. By the end of the year, fans were able to layout jabronis in the heavily anticipated *SmackDown 2: Know Your Role* for the Sony PlayStation with Create-A-Stable and the first-ever Create-A-Taunt plus Table, Ladders & Chairs Match. Fans were then treated to the final WWE product for the Nintendo 64, aptly named *No Mercy*. With over 65 Superstars, un-lockable Hall of Famers, various match types and one of the deepest Career and Create-A-Wrestler modes in the history of wrestling games, *No Mercy* is considered by genre purists, experts, aficionados, and button mashers as the greatest pure playing wrestling game of all-time.

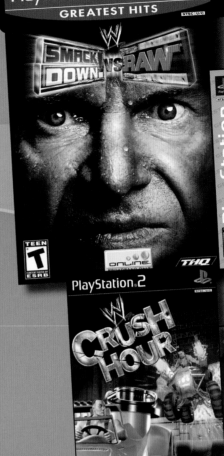

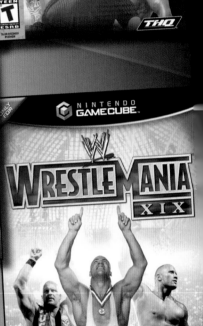

SMACKDOWN VS RAW

While *SmackDown* established its dominance in the genre on the Sony PlayStation 2 with releases *Just Bring It* and *Shut Your Mouth*. WWE hit the Xbox with one of the most anticipated titles on the platform in 2002's *Raw*. Anticipation on new gaming systems became a specialty as that same year *Wrestlemania X-8* debuted on Nintendo's GameCube. The next year saw major releases like *SmackDown: Here Comes The Pain*, *WrestleMania XIX*, *Raw 2* and a game that put Superstars behind the wheel of their favorite combat vehicles in *Crush Hour*. These titles helped solidify WWE's reputation as one of the most powerful brands in any gaming genre on any system.

Unlike many other entertainment entities, World Wrestling Entertainment is ever-changing. To maintain its ultra high standards of quality, the products must reflect what goes on in that ever-changing world. In 2004, the brand extension hit interactive platforms when *SmackDown v. Raw* hit the PlayStation 2 while *Day of Reckoning* entered the GameCube ranks and *WrestleMania 21* launched on the Xbox. After *SmackDown v. Raw 2006* and *Day of Reckoning 2* in 2005, *SmackDown v. Raw* became the sole controller of WWE gaming. In 2007, video gamers got all they could handle as *SmackDown v. Raw* made history as it appeared on all platforms: Sony PlayStation 2, Sony PlayStation 3, Sony PlayStation Portable, Nintendo Wii, Nintendo DS, Mobile, and Xbox 360.

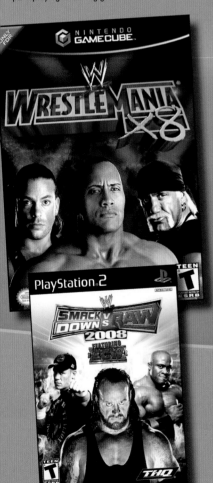

The WWE video game releases continue to push the technological limits of the hardware platforms on which they appear. Most recently, Superstars came to life in *SmackDown v. Raw 2009* while fans new and old alike await the video game arrival of *Legends of WrestleMania*. With each release the bar for sports entertainment gaming is set to all-new standards as the interactive drama and excitement of World Wrestling Entertainment is lived out in the hands of gamers. Today, no interactive software platform is considered complete without a World Wrestling Entertainment title in its library.

As the world of video gaming continues to evolve, so does the world of sports-entertainment. The two industries that have complemented one another so well for almost a quarter century continue to strive for innovation while crossing cultural and geographic boundaries every step of the way.

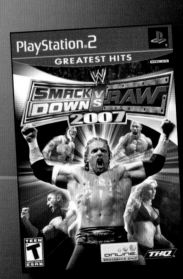

Ted DiBiase

| HT | 6'3" | WT | 235 lbs. |

FROM Palm Springs, Florida

SIGNATURE MOVE

Cobra Clutch Legsweep

TITLE HISTORY

World Tag Team Champion

YEARS ACTIVE

 1960 1969 1970 1979 1980 1989 1990 1999 **2000 PRESENT**

While growing up, Ted DiBiase watched his father, the "Million Dollar Man," prove that everyone has a price. He started to dream of taking the DiBiase name into the next millennium. After graduating college in 2005, Ted began training under Harley Race.

By 2007 Ted was generating a buzz in the WWE developmental system . In May 2008, the third generation Superstar made his debut on *Raw* and guaranteed he would become a champion in his first match. At *Night of Champions*, he delivered when Cody Rhodes turned on his partner Hardcore Holly and joined DiBiase to capture the World Tag Team Championship. In addition to Rhodes, DiBiase has aligned himself with other men of distinguished sports-entertainment lineages including Manu and Randy Orton. Whether part of a rare collection of Superstars or on his own, Ted DiBiase is poised to leave his own footprints in WWE. Of course, those imprints will be priceless.

Tekno Team 2000

| **MEMBERS** | Travis, Troy | **COMBINED WEIGHT** | 480 lbs. |

YEARS ACTIVE  1960 1969 1970 1979 1980 1989 **1990 1999** 2000 PRESENT

Following successful collegiate football careers with the University of Louisville, Travis and Troy reunited in 1995 to compete in WWE's heated tag team division. Dressed in shiny silver jackets and ultramodern elbow and knee pads, the agile duo claimed to be the team of the future. Unfortunately for them, their record said otherwise.

After picking up easy victories over combinations such as Brooklyn Brawler & Barry Horowitz, Travis & Troy found defeating the Smokin' Gunns and other top-notch tandems quite difficult. In 1996, the futuristic tag team disappeared from WWE completely.

TEN MAN TAG MATCH

This chaotic contest includes five Superstars on two teams where, unless otherwise stipulated, normal tag team match rules apply. A team can realize victory by pinfall, submission, count out or disqualification. Ten Man Tag matches can also have caveats including elimination rules where once a participant loses the fall he or she must return to the locker room area and the match continues until one team does not have any members remaining. The contest can also feature Texas Tornado rules where all ten Superstars are in the ring at the same time.

Terri Runnels

| HT | 5' |

FROM Gainesville, Florida

YEARS ACTIVE

 1960 1969 1970 1979 1980 1989 **1990 1999** **2000 PRESENT**

Movie buff Goldust introduced the world to his leading lady at the 1996 *Royal Rumble*. Calling herself Marlena, she sat in her director's chair and watched her masterpiece unfold, as Goldust beat Razor Ramon for the Intercontinental Championship. In the months that followed, the bizarre duo pushed the limits of acceptable social behavior, including public displays of affection and posing almost completely nude for *Raw Magazine*. Unfortunately for Marlena, what she assumed to be a storybook romance revealed itself as horror in November 1997. While a stipulation forced Marlena to be by the side of Brian Pillman for thirty days, Goldust was out making magic with the exotic Luna. The affair crushed Marlena's spirit, but gave Terri Runnels new life.

With "Marlena" a distant memory, Terri joined forces with Jacqueline and Ryan Shamrock to form Pretty Mean Sisters. Together, PMS used their sexuality to prey on WWE's male Superstars. Despite her petite frame, Terri held her own in the ring, highlighted by her victory at *WrestleMania 2000* when she defeated the Kat in one-on-one action. During her time with WWE, Terri, also known as the Horny Little She-Devil, worked as a backstage interviewer and manager.

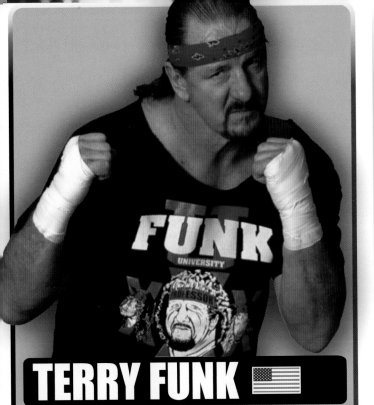

TERRY FUNK

| HT | 6'1" | WT | 247 lbs. |

| FROM | The Double Cross Ranch, Amarillo, Texas |

| TITLE HISTORY | World Tag Team Champion |

| YEARS ACTIVE | 1960 1969 | 1970 1979 | 1980 1989 | 1990 1999 | 2000 PRESENT |

A man sees the world through a different set of eyes when growing up on the Double-Cross Ranch. Raised in a wrestling family, Terry Funk wanted to follow the career path of his famous father Dory Funk Sr. and brother, Dory Funk Jr. In 1965, Terry was regarded as one of the brightest stars in the National Wrestling Alliance. He combined rough housing, mat skills, and a mean streak a mile wide to become a legend in North America and Japan. In 1985 Terry came to WWE with his brothers, Dory and Hoss. In the late 1980s, he returned to the NWA for a classic "I Quit" Match with "Nature Boy" Ric Flair.

As the 1990s began, Funk became the backbone of the upstart ECW promotion, leading the revolution in sports-entertainment. In 1998, Funk joined his friend Mick Foley in WWE, and captured the World Tag Team Championships under their demented alter-egos, Chainsaw Charlie and Cactus Jack.

As the years went on this legend of the squared circle just got tougher and crazier. After penning his autobiography, *Terry Funk: More Than Just Hardcore* in 2005, he returned to WWE for *One Night Stand* in 2006 to join Tommy Dreamer & Beulah against Mick Foley, Edge & Lita.

Some Superstars graduated from the School of Hard Knocks; Terry Funk, the icon who's meaner than a Texas rattlesnake, tougher than shoe leather, and more dangerous than a hallow-eyed scorpion, built that institution brick-by-brick with his bare hands.

Terry Gibbs

| HT | 6' | WT | 240 lbs. | FROM | Tampa, Florida |

| SIGNATURE MOVE | Inverted Atomic Drop |

| YEARS ACTIVE | 1960 1969 | 1970 1979 | 1980 1989 | 1990 1999 | 2000 PRESENT |

This tough customer was known in regions within the National Wrestling Alliance and Puerto Rico's World Wrestling Council before his WWE debut in November 1984. Over the next four years Terry Gibbs was seen against the premier Superstars on programs like *Championship Wrestling, All-Star Wrestling,* and *Prime-Time Wrestling.*

Gibbs took on individuals like Mr. Wrestling II, Hillbilly Jim, SD Jones, Barry Windham, Ultimate Warrior, and Hulk Hogan. By the late 1980s Gibbs left WWE and returned to the Independent scene. Terry Gibbs was one of the fixtures of WWE programming during the early days of Hulkamania and will be remembered as a rule-breaker who would do anything to win a match.

Terry Taylor

| HT | 6'1" | WT | 225 lbs. | FROM | Vero Beach, Florida |

| SIGNATURE MOVE | Scorpion Death Lock |

| YEARS ACTIVE | 1960 1969 | 1970 1979 | 1980 1989 | 1990 1999 | 2000 PRESENT |

This Superstar began his career in the late 1970s and made his WWE debut in October 1980, defeating Jose Estrada. Over the next eight years he expanded and honed his abilities in various territories in North America before returning to World Wrestling Entertainment in 1988. In his first match back, he attacked partner Sam Houston after a loss to Los Conquistadors.

Soon Taylor became a member of the Heenan Family and was greeted by jeers from fans at every turn. In 1989 he appeared as "the Red Rooster" but quickly grew tired of Bobby Heenan's verbal abuse. After facing the Brooklyn Brawler in a series of matches, he left WWE in June 1990. Taylor spent the next few years in WCW, and held various titles during his time there.

In 1992 he returned to WWE as "Terrific" Terry Taylor and used a new move to put away opponents, the Gutwrench Sit-out Powerbomb. Taylor also became a broadcaster for WWE television before he left the company again in 1993. After his departure from WWE, Taylor shifted his focus from in-ring work to calling the action and interviewing Superstars. In 1998, he returned to WWE to conduct backstage interviews but departed for WCW when he was given the opportunity to host *WCW Saturday Night.*

During competitive prime, Terry Taylor was a versatile performer with a great deal of technical wrestling ability and the gift of gab when given the microphone.

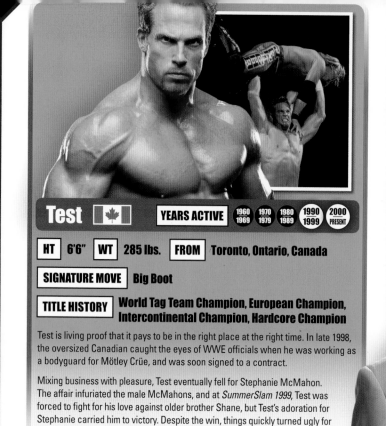

Test 🍁 YEARS ACTIVE (1960-1969) (1970-1979) (1980-1989) **1990-1999** **2000 PRESENT**

HT 6'6"	**WT** 285 lbs.	**FROM**	Toronto, Ontario, Canada

SIGNATURE MOVE Big Boot

TITLE HISTORY World Tag Team Champion, European Champion, Intercontinental Champion, Hardcore Champion

Test is living proof that it pays to be in the right place at the right time. In late 1998, the oversized Canadian caught the eyes of WWE officials when he was working as a bodyguard for Mötley Crüe, and was soon signed to a contract.

Mixing business with pleasure, Test eventually fell for Stephanie McMahon. The affair infuriated the male McMahons, and at *SummerSlam 1999*, Test was forced to fight for his love against older brother Shane, but Test's adoration for Stephanie carried him to victory. Despite the win, things quickly turned ugly for the young lovers when Stephanie concocted a devious plan to leave Test and marry Triple H.

Refusing to be derailed by a broken heart, Test persevered. Over the next several years, he engaged in many high-profile encounters. His most notable match took place at *Survivor Series 2001* where he unsuccessfully defended his Intercontinental Championship against Edge's U.S. Title in a Unification Match. Test's WWE career also saw him capture the European and Hardcore Championships, as well as the World Tag Team Titles with Booker T.

Theodore Long

YEARS ACTIVE (1960-1969) (1970-1979) (1980-1989) **1990-1999** **2000 PRESENT**

Mr. Long cut his teeth in the professional wrestling business working his way up from a starting position with the ring crew to become a referee in the National Wrestling Alliance. He went from ring official to manager and managed many of the organizations top stars to prominent roles within the company.

After a hiatus from the business, he appeared on WWE programming in 1999 as Teddy Long, the referee. Long continued to call the action straight down the middle until he took on the role of conspirator. He quickly collected a group of Superstars known as "Thuggin' & Buggin' Enterprises suggesting "Don't be drinkin' that hatorade."

In 2004 Long moved up the corporate ladder, and made history when he became the first African-American General Manager of *SmackDown*. The man brought a host of ideas with him to give the fans what they wanted. Two of his most successful acts were implementing the "New Talent Initiative" and bringing back the *King of the Ring* Tournament.

As the tensions between *Raw* and *SmackDown* arose, Long represented his brand at *Survivor Series 2005* where he won the "Battle of the GM's" against Eric Bischoff. Long continued to shake things up on Friday Nights and keep Superstars in check. In June 2008 he changed work nights but not titles when he was announced as the new General Manager of ECW. Now can you dig that or what, playa? Holla holla holla!

THIS TUESDAY IN TEXAS

LOCATION Freeman Coliseum, San Antonio, TX **DATE** December 3, 1991

Following Undertaker's controversial WWE Championship victory over Hulk Hogan at *Survivor Series 1991*, WWE President Jack Tunney called for an immediate rematch. Unable to wait for January's *Royal Rumble*, he created the impromptu *This Tuesday in Texas* event, which was held on December 3, 1991.

Ironically, the Undertaker-Hogan rematch proved to be just as controversial as their *Survivor Series* encounter. The match fell apart when Tunney, who was seated ringside to ensure justice, was inadvertently knocked out. With Tunney unconscious, action quickly got out of hand, highlighted by Hogan temporarily blinding Undertaker with the ashes from the "Deadman's" signature urn. In the end, it was Hogan picking up the win, but Tunney later declared the WWE Championship vacant due to the madness that arose during the match. The following month, Ric Flair outlasted 29 other Superstars to win the *Royal Rumble* and the vacant WWE Championship.

This Tuesday in Texas also featured the emotional return of Randy "Macho Man" Savage. Following his *WrestleMania VII* loss to Ultimate Warrior, Savage had been forced into an early retirement. However, when Jake "the Snake" Roberts pushed his venomous cobra on the "Macho Man," Tunney had no choice but to reinstate Savage for a *This Tuesday in Texas* encounter. In the record books, Savage earned the pinfall victory, but Roberts walked away with the psychological win. After the match, "the Snake" delivered three DDTs to his opponent. He then forced Elizabeth to beg for her man's safety before grabbing her by the hair and slapping her across the face.

In other *This Tuesday in Texas* action, Intercontinental Champion Bret Hart successfully defended his title against the undefeated Skinner, Ted DiBiase teamed with Repo Man to defeat Virgil & Tito Santana, and Davey Boy Smith beat The Warlord via pinfall.

Following the event, WWE did not hold another Tuesday night pay-per-view until the interactive *Taboo Tuesday* in 2004.

Tiffany

HT 5'6" **FROM** New Orleans, Louisiana

This beautiful Diva debuted in World Wrestling Entertainment in 2008 as the Executive Assistant to ECW General Manager Theodore Long. Since she's come on board her acumen for business, marketing, and maintaining strong relationships have made her a valued employee to Mr. Long.

Tiffany is a young executive determined to use her many skills and make an impact wherever she decides to go within WWE. She is capable of making tough decisions quickly for the betterment of audiences and Superstars. Her professional demeanor and razor sharp wit is a tremendous aid for Theodore Long as he revolutionizes ECW.

Tiger Chung Lee

HT 6'4" **WT** 289 lbs. **FROM** Korea

A master of martial arts, Tiger Chung Lee made a name for himself early on in his career while competing in Japan. While there, he and tag team partner Kintaro Ohki traded the All Japan International Tag Team Championship twice with Giant Baba & Jumbo Tsuruta.

After losing the titles for the final time in May 1978, Tiger Chung Lee made his way to the United States where he briefly wrestled for the National Wrestling Alliance before finally landing in WWE.

Affectionately referred to as "the Chunger" by WWE Hall of Famer Gorilla Monsoon, Tiger Chung Lee proved his toughness almost immediately when he broke solid bricks on live television using only his bare hands. Unfortunately, his toughness failed to translate into victories, as Tiger Chung Lee oftentimes walked away from his WWE matches with the loser's share of the purse.

Tiger Jeet Singh

HT 6'3" **WT** 265 lbs. **FROM** Punjab, India **SIGNATURE MOVE** Tiger Claw

Tiger Jeet Singh was a famous bodybuilder in his native India before he emigrated to Canada in 1965. Over the next few years, he became one of the most feared men of the ring. His match in 1967 at the Maple Leaf Gardens against Bruno Sammartino was such a huge draw that thousands of fans were turned away after the arena reached its capacity.

For the next three decades, Tiger Jeet Singh continued to maul opponents all over the world. His popularity was greatest in Japan, where he fought in the IWA "King of the Death Match" tournament with fellow Superstars Terry Funk, Cactus Jack, and Terry "Bam Bam" Gordy.

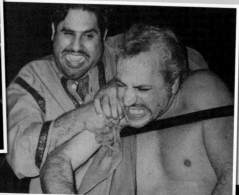

Singh appeared in the crowd at *SummerSlam 1997* alongside his son, Tiger Ali Singh. Tiger Jeet managed his son into the Attitude Era before returning to terrorize foes overseas. Today, he remains one of the greatest figures in all of Japan and an influence to all rule-breakers who step into the ring.

Tiger Mask

YEARS ACTIVE **1960 1969** **1970 1979** **1980 1989** **1990 1999** **2000 PRESENT**

| HT | 5'8" | WT | 198 lbs. | FROM | Japan | SIGNATURE MOVE | Tiger Suplex | TITLE HISTORY | Junior Heavyweight Champion |

Originally a Japanese comic book superhero, Tiger Mask came to life in 1981 when he debuted in New Japan Pro Wrestling. With superior mat skills and high-flying aerial assaults, the furry masked Superstar was a legitimate double threat in the ring. Tiger Mask's legendary rivalries with fellow technicians Bret Hart and Chris Adams made news all over the world, but it was his battles with Dynamite Kid that resonated most. In January 1982, he defeated Dynamite Kid in Japan to capture the WWE Junior Heavyweight Championship. Over the next several years, the two Superstars engaged in a global battle for junior heavyweight supremacy. In all, Tiger Mask held the title three times during the course of their epic rivalry.

Tiger Mask simply wowed American audiences during his rare United States appearances. Never before had they seen such innovative high-flying offense. Some even say his unique approach helped motivate many of the today's Superstars, including Rey Mysterio.

By the mid-1980s, Tiger Mask lost his passion to compete. Still relatively young at the time, he walked away from the sport at the height of his popularity. Over the next several years, many Japanese Superstars donned the furry mask, claiming to be Tiger Mask. However, true sports-entertainment historians only recognize the original as the true Tiger Mask.

TITO SANTANA

YEARS ACTIVE **1960 1969** **1970 1979** **1980 1989** **1990 1999** **2000 PRESENT**

HALL OF FAME 2004

| HT | 6'2" | WT | 234 lbs. | FROM | Tocula, Mexico | SIGNATURE MOVE | Flying Forearm |

| TITLE HISTORY | Intercontinental Champion; World Tag Team Champion |

A two-time Intercontinental and World Tag Team Champion, Tito Santana pieced together an impressive career that spanned decades. Along the way, he displayed class and a sound technical ability that made him one of the game's elite.

While Santana is most recognized for the success he experienced during the 1980s, his first taste of WWE superstardom actually came in the late 1970s. During a brief stay with the promotion, he teamed with Ivan Putski to claim the World Tag Team Championship from the Valiant Brothers. Santana & Putski held the titles for close to six months before losing to the Samoans. Following the loss, Santana took an extended leave from WWE.

In 1983, Santana returned to WWE and immediately found himself back in the title hunt. This time, he had eyes for Don Muraco's Intercontinental Championship. After a few unsuccessful tries, Santana was finally able to end Muraco's lengthy reign in February 1984. The win gave Santana his first of two Intercontinental Championships.

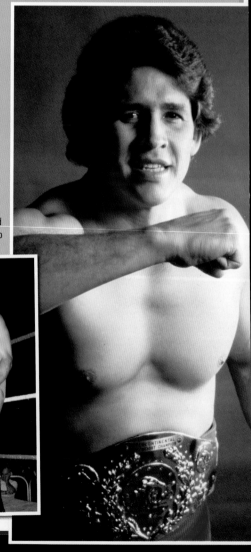

Between runs with the Intercontinental Championship, Santana made history when he defeated the Executioner in the first-ever *WrestleMania* match. He went on to earn a spot on the first nine *WrestleMania* cards (although his *WrestleMania IX* match was untelevised). Only Hulk Hogan can make the same claim.

Santana returned to his tag team roots in 1987, teaming with fellow fan favorite Rick Martel. Known as Strike Force, the duo defeated the Hart Foundation for the World Tag Team Championship in October. The popular tag team operated as a successful unit until April 1989 when Martel turned on Santana at *WrestleMania V*.

Following Strike Force's untimely demise, Santana adopted a bullfighting persona. Aptly named El Matador, Santana enjoyed a bit of a resurgence to his maturing career. El Matador's highest-profile encounter came at *WrestleMania VIII* when he fell to an up-and-coming Shawn Michaels.

In 2004, Santana assumed his rightful place alongside sports-entertainment's greatest when he was inducted into the WWE Hall of Fame.

TL Hopper

| HT | 5'10" | WT | 235 lbs. | YEARS ACTIVE | 1960-1969 | 1970-1979 | 1980-1989 | **1990-1999** | 2000-PRESENT |

This plumber-turned-performer first appeared in World Wreslting Entertainment in 1996. His appearances in the ring were heralded by the sound of a flushing toilet, and he never strayed far from Betsy, his beloved plunger. During his tenure with WWE, he battled the likes of the Stalker, Aldo Montoya, the Bushwhackers, Marc Mero, and the Godwinns. He was also involved in a match where he teamed up with Billy Gunn to face Bart Gunn & Freddie Joe Floyd after the Smoking Gunns' tumultuous split. After less than a year competing in WWE, TL Hopper left the the company to return to his former profession.

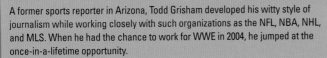

TLC (TABLES, LADDERS & CHAIRS) MATCH

Since 2000, the Tables, Ladders and Chairs Match has provided some of the most exciting and death-defying moments in sports-entertainment. In this type of match, tables, ladders, and chairs are all legal. The object of the match is to ascend to the top of the ladder and capture the item that hangs from the ceiling before your opponent can do the same.

These matches have become incredibly popular, mostly due to the teams who inspired the first TLC match, the Hardy Boys, Edge & Christian, and the Dudley Boys.

Todd Grisham

A former sports reporter in Arizona, Todd Grisham developed his witty style of journalism while working closely with such organizations as the NFL, NBA, NHL, and MLS. When he had the chance to work for WWE in 2004, he jumped at the once-in-a-lifetime opportunity.

As a member of WWE's esteemed announce team, Grisham has done it all. He's best known for his hard-hitting line of questioning as *Raw*'s backstage interviewer, but has also served as *Heat*'s play-by-play man and host of WWE.com's now-defunct webcast *Byte This!* Most recently, Grisham has been named the lead announcer for ECW.

Tom Magee

| HT | 6'5" | WT | 275 lbs. | FROM | Winnipeg, Manitoba, Canada |

| YEARS ACTIVE | 1960-1969 | 1970-1979 | **1980-1989** | **1990-1999** | 2000-PRESENT |

Holding a black belt in karate, and world titles in competitive bodybuilding, Tom Magee trained for the ring with the incomparable Stu Hart. After appearing in Japan, Magee took his impressive physique and charisma to WWE.

Magee debuted in World Wrestling Entertainment in 1986 and jumped right into the mix taking on Jimmy Jack Funk, Terry Gibbs, Tiger Chung Lee, Ron Bass, Barry O, Iron Mike Sharpe, and Bret "Hit Man" Hart. Magee left WWE in 1990 and pursued a career as an actor. Today, he lends his training expertise to bodybuilding hopefuls.

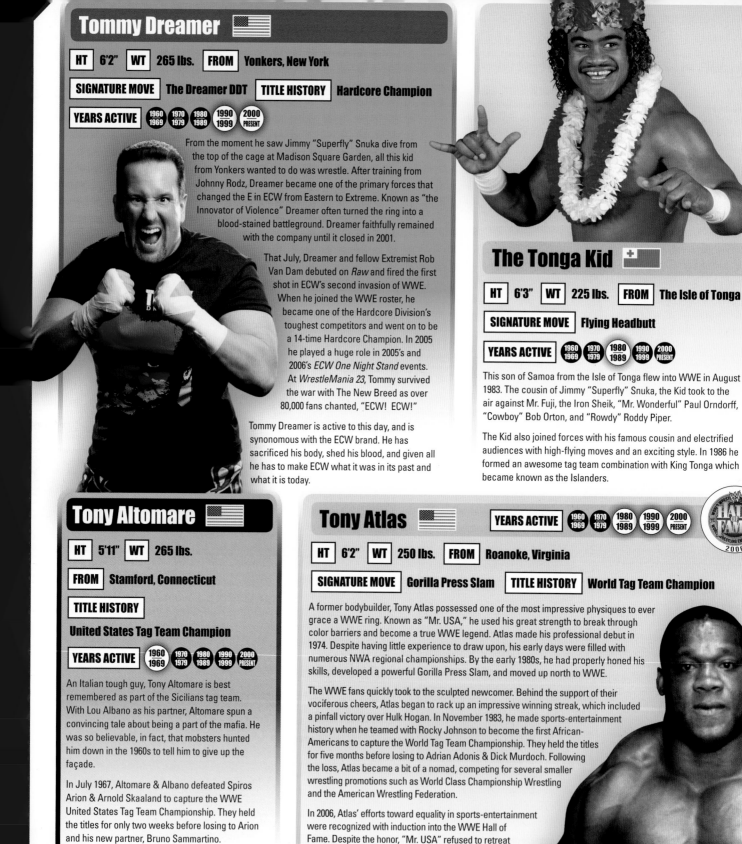

Tommy Dreamer 🇺🇸

| **HT** | 6'2" | **WT** | 265 lbs. | **FROM** | Yonkers, New York |

| **SIGNATURE MOVE** | The Dreamer DDT | **TITLE HISTORY** | Hardcore Champion |

YEARS ACTIVE 1960/1969 · 1970/1979 · 1980/1989 · **1990/1999** · **2000/PRESENT**

From the moment he saw Jimmy "Superfly" Snuka dive from the top of the cage at Madison Square Garden, all this kid from Yonkers wanted to do was wrestle. After training from Johnny Rodz, Dreamer became one of the primary forces that changed the E in ECW from Eastern to Extreme. Known as "the Innovator of Violence" Dreamer often turned the ring into a blood-stained battleground. Dreamer faithfully remained with the company until it closed in 2001.

That July, Dreamer and fellow Extremist Rob Van Dam debuted on *Raw* and fired the first shot in ECW's second invasion of WWE. When he joined the WWE roster, he became one of the Hardcore Division's toughest competitors and went on to be a 14-time Hardcore Champion. In 2005 he played a huge role in 2005's and 2006's *ECW One Night Stand* events. At *WrestleMania 23*, Tommy survived the war with The New Breed as over 80,000 fans chanted, "ECW! ECW!"

Tommy Dreamer is active to this day, and is synonomous with the ECW brand. He has sacrificed his body, shed his blood, and given all he has to make ECW what it was in its past and what it is today.

The Tonga Kid 🇹🇴

| **HT** | 6'3" | **WT** | 225 lbs. | **FROM** | The Isle of Tonga |

| **SIGNATURE MOVE** | Flying Headbutt |

YEARS ACTIVE 1960/1969 · 1970/1979 · **1980/1989** · 1990/1999 · **2000/PRESENT**

This son of Samoa from the Isle of Tonga flew into WWE in August 1983. The cousin of Jimmy "Superfly" Snuka, the Kid took to the air against Mr. Fuji, the Iron Sheik, "Mr. Wonderful" Paul Orndorff, "Cowboy" Bob Orton, and "Rowdy" Roddy Piper.

The Kid also joined forces with his famous cousin and electrified audiences with high-flying moves and an exciting style. In 1986 he formed an awesome tag team combination with King Tonga which became known as the Islanders.

Tony Altomare 🇺🇸

| **HT** | 5'11" | **WT** | 265 lbs. |

| **FROM** | Stamford, Connecticut |

TITLE HISTORY

United States Tag Team Champion

YEARS ACTIVE **1960/1969** · 1970/1979 · 1980/1989 · 1990/1999 · 2000/PRESENT

An Italian tough guy, Tony Altomare is best remembered as part of the Sicilians tag team. With Lou Albano as his partner, Altomare spun a convincing tale about being a part of the mafia. He was so believable, in fact, that mobsters hunted him down in the 1960s to tell him to give up the façade.

In July 1967, Altomare & Albano defeated Spiros Arion & Arnold Skaaland to capture the WWE United States Tag Team Championship. They held the titles for only two weeks before losing to Arion and his new partner, Bruno Sammartino.

Shortly after the loss, Albano hung up his boots and began managing. This left Altomare to fend for himself. On his own, the Italian Superstar's star began to fade. As the losses began to pile up, he started to investigate other ways to earn a living. He briefly served as a referee and a trainer. One of his most noted pupils was Steve Blackman.

Tony Atlas 🇺🇸

YEARS ACTIVE **1960/1969** · **1970/1979** · **1980/1989** · **1990/1999** · **2000/PRESENT**

WWE HALL OF FAME 2006

| **HT** | 6'2" | **WT** | 250 lbs. | **FROM** | Roanoke, Virginia |

| **SIGNATURE MOVE** | Gorilla Press Slam | **TITLE HISTORY** | World Tag Team Champion |

A former bodybuilder, Tony Atlas possessed one of the most impressive physiques to ever grace a WWE ring. Known as "Mr. USA," he used his great strength to break through color barriers and become a true WWE legend. Atlas made his professional debut in 1974. Despite having little experience to draw upon, his early days were filled with numerous NWA regional championships. By the early 1980s, he had properly honed his skills, developed a powerful Gorilla Press Slam, and moved up north to WWE.

The WWE fans quickly took to the sculpted newcomer. Behind the support of their vociferous cheers, Atlas began to rack up an impressive winning streak, which included a pinfall victory over Hulk Hogan. In November 1983, he made sports-entertainment history when he teamed with Rocky Johnson to become the first African-Americans to capture the World Tag Team Championship. They held the titles for five months before losing to Adrian Adonis & Dick Murdoch. Following the loss, Atlas became a bit of a nomad, competing for several smaller wrestling promotions such as World Class Championship Wrestling and the American Wrestling Federation.

In 2006, Atlas' efforts toward equality in sports-entertainment were recognized with induction into the WWE Hall of Fame. Despite the honor, "Mr. USA" refused to retreat into retirement. Instead, he continued to compete on independent wrestling cards and eventually worked his way back to WWE. In 2008, he revealed himself as the manager of ECW Champion Mark Henry. For the first time in his WWE career, he found himself on the wrong side of the fans' admiration. However, the lack of cheers hasn't stopped Atlas from guiding Henry toward the same level of greatness "Mr. USA" achieved during his heyday.

Tony Garea

| HT | 6'2" | WT | 246 lbs. |

FROM Auckland, New Zealand

SIGNATURE MOVE

The Octopus Hold

TITLE HISTORY

World Tag Team Champion

YEARS ACTIVE

This sensational athlete debuted in World Wrestling Entertainment in 1972. His accomplishments within the ranks of tag team wrestling set him apart from every other Superstar before or since. Over the next eight years Garea enlisted other great men like Dean Ho, Larry Zbyszko, and Rick Martel to capture tag team gold against the likes of the Valiant Brothers, the Yukon Lumberjacks, the Wild Samoans, and the Moondogs.

Garea continued his in-ring career until his retirement from the ring in 1986. During this time he also dabbled in announcing as a commentator alongside Vince McMahon on episodes of *Championship Wrestling*. Garea then made the transition to WWE's front office and was often seen breaking apart violent brawls on WWE programming. Today he is still a valued WWE employee who is often out scouting for the next WWE Superstar.

In his career, Garea was a five-time World Tag Team Champion, and his success with partner Rick Martel was celebrated in June 2007 at *Vengeance: Night of Champions*. Tony Garea will go down in WWE history as a legend of tag team wrestling and one of its most decorated competitors. His abilities and heart made him a favorite among fans, and a difficult individual for opposing Superstars to beat.

Tony Chimel

Today, Tony Chimel is best recognized as the ring announcer for ECW, but his sports-entertainment career started long before the extreme brand even came into existence. Back in the early 1980s, Chimel parlayed his friendship with Gorilla Monsoon's son into a job setting up wrestling rings. In 1999, he permanently moved in front of the cameras when he defeated legendary ring announcer Howard Finkel for the right to introduce *SmackDown*'s Superstars. Chimel spent the next eight years on *SmackDown* before taking his game to ECW in September 2007.

Tony Garea & Rick Martel

COMBINED WEIGHT 471 lbs.

TITLE HISTORY

World Tag Team Champions

YEARS ACTIVE

During the 1970s, Tony Garea was one of WWE's most-noted tag team competitors. A champion alongside Haystacks Calhoun, Larry Zbyzsko, and Dean Ho, the perception was that he could carry any Superstar to the promised land. Despite this recognition, none of Garea's teams were considered sports-entertainment's most popular. That all changed when he joined forces with Rick Martel, a Superstar he first teamed with while competing in New Zealand years earlier.

Garea & Martel gained instant admiration from the fans from the first time they appeared together in WWE in 1980. Amazingly, they also won the World Tag Team Championship almost as quickly, defeating the Wild Samoans in November 1980. The win gave Garea his fourth title reign and Martel his first. They remained champions for the next four months before being dethroned by the savage Moondogs.

Following the championship loss, Garea & Martel maintained their popularity while dedicating themselves to regaining the gold. A short four months later, they reclaimed the titles from the Moondogs. Shortly after their second reign with the World Tag Team Championship came to an end, Martel left WWE to compete in Montreal. Garea went on to team with other Superstars, such as Eddie Gilbert, and Lanny Poffo, but he was unable to recreate the magic he had with Martel.

Tony Mamaluke

| HT | 5'10" | WT | 150 lbs. |

FROM Bensonhurst, Brooklyn

SIGNATURE MOVE

Sicilian Stretch

YEARS ACTIVE

After a brief stint in WCW, Tony Mamaluke made his mark in ECW as part of the Full Blooded Italians. He became ECW World Tag Team Champions with Little Guido and remained a star until ECW closed its doors in March 2001.

Tony spent the next few years appearing at independent events throughout the United States. In 2005 he appeared with the FBI at *ECW One Night Stand*. When WWE relaunched ECW, Mamaluke was a part of it. After *One Night Stand 2006* he was seen on *ECW On Sci-Fi* fighting the likes of Sabu, Test, and Mike Knox. In January 2007 Mamaluke and World Wrestling Entertainment severed ties and he returned to the independent circuit where he can be seen competing today.

Tony Parisi

YEARS ACTIVE 1960–1969, 1970–1979, 1980–1989, 1990–1999

HT 5'11" **WT** 241 lbs. **FROM** Cosenza, Italy

TITLE HISTORY World Tag Team Champion, United States Tag Team Champion, International Heavyweight Champion

Early in his WWE career, Tony Parisi, then known as Antonio Pugliese, was billed as the cousin of the legendary Bruno Sammartino. The family ties helped lend legitimacy to the newcomer's career and within weeks of his 1966 debut, the proud Italian was co-holder of the now-defunct United States Tag Team Championship with Johnny Valentine.

In mid-1967, Parisi left WWE to compete in various territories throughout the United States and Australia. When he finally returned several years later, he periodically teamed with Sammartino before forming a championship combination with Louis Cerdan. The new pairing defeated the Blackjacks for the World Tag Team Championship in November 1975. They held the titles for six months before being upended by the Executioners. Parisi's lone WWE singles title came in 1982 when he was awarded the short-lived International Heavyweight Championship. After losing the gold in August, the Italian Superstar moved to Canada where he spent the twilight of his in-ring career.

Too Cool

YEARS ACTIVE 1960–1969, 1970–1979, 1980–1989, 1990–1999, 2000–PRESENT

MEMBERS Scotty 2 Hotty, "Grandmaster Sexay" Brian Christopher, Rikishi

TITLE HISTORY World Tag Team Champions

In the late 1990s Scotty 2 Hotty and Grandmaster Sexay were a pair of hip-hoppers who stood out from the pack who called themselves Too Hot. In 2000, after taking on the name Too Cool, they were joined by Rikishi and became a three-man squad that was a huge hit with fans who cheered as much for the trio's wins as they did their post-match celebratory dance.

In May, 2000 Too Cool showed they were too good when they defeated Edge & Christian to became World Tag Team Champions. Though Rikishi eventually left to follow a darker path, Scotty and Grandmaster continued to thrill until 2001 when Brian Christopher and WWE parted ways. Rikishi and Scotty reunited in 2004, but it did not recapture the magic of their first stint together.

Tor Kamata

YEARS ACTIVE 1960–1969, 1970–1979, 1980–1989, 1990–1999, 2000–PRESENT

HT 6'3" **WT** 350 lbs. **FROM** The South Pacific Islands **SIGNATURE MOVE** Big Splash

Tor Kamata toured the globe many times over during the course of his thirty-year career, but it was his time spent in Canada's Stampede Wrestling that fans will remember most. While competing for Stampede Wrestling, the hated Tor Kamata, who often used salt as a weapon to blind his foes, captured the prestigious North American Heavyweight Championship on three separate occasions. He also teamed with Sugi Siti to win the promotion's International Tag Team Championship in February 1972.

Later that year, Kamata competed in one of sports-entertainment's first Ladder Matches. With Cowboy Dan Kroffat as his opponent, Kamata did everything in his power to claw his way up the ladder towards the bag of money. In the end, it was Kroffat who walked away the winner. In the late 1970s, Kamata joined WWE under the tutelage of Freddie Blassie. His brief WWE career was highlighted by several memorable matches with an up-and-coming Bob Backlund.

Tori

YEARS ACTIVE 1960–1969, 1970–1979, 1980–1989, 1990–1999, 2000–PRESENT

HT 5'9" **FROM** Portland, Oregon **SIGNATURE MOVE** Tori-Plex

This former Diva morphed from a bodybuilder into a wrestling machine and burst into the spotlight in 1998. Tori faced the likes of Luna, Jacqueline, and Sable and also showed her skills in Mixed Tag matches with partners Val Venis and Al Snow before going after Ivory's Women's Championship.

In late 1999 Tori became romantically involved with "the Big Red Monster" Kane but eventually left him for high-flying bad boy, X-Pac. Her ring savvy later served her well as she became a trainer on the first season of *Tough Enough*. By 2001 Tori left World Wrestling Entertainment. Today she is a yoga guru and makes the occasional appearance on the independent wrestling scene.

TORRIE WILSON

FROM Boise, Idaho **YEARS ACTIVE** 1960-1969 1970-1979 1980-1989 1990-1999 2000-PRESENT

This WWE Diva grew up a competitive athlete and dancer. She was passionate about nutrition and fitness and in 1998 won the prestigious Miss Galaxy competition. Torrie began her career in sports-entertainment with WCW in 1999 and was a manager through late 2000. Torrie joined the WCW invasion of WWE in June of 2001, and first appeared on *SmackDown* in a segment with WWE Chairman Vince McMahon. Her in-ring debut was in a Bra and Panties Match, teaming with Stacy Kiebler against Lita and Trish Stratus at *Invasion*.

Despite being a part of the enemy, this breathtaking blonde became an instant sensation with audiences all over the globe. She returned to managing when she aligned herself with "Japanese Buzzsaw" Tajiri. From there she moved on to more Diva-centric pursuits like ruling Lingerie, Bra and Panties, and Paddle On A Pole Matches.

In May of 2003 Torrie adorned the cover of Playboy and set a new standard of beauty for the magazine. As the issue achieved incredible success, she returned to the cover for a second time in March 2004. On this occasion however she brought a partner in crime with her, the intoxicating Sable.

Torrie's fame continued to skyrocket during 2005 when she joined *Raw* and participated in Mixed Tag, Evening Gown, Kimono, Santa's Little Helper, and Lumberjill Matches. In June 2006, she defeated Candice Michelle in the first-ever Wet & Wild Match where the winner graced the cover of WWE's Summer Special Magazine. Torrie followed that pictorial in September by appearing on the cover of FHM Magazine. Wilson went from cover girl to calendar girl in FHM's 2007 Calendar. She was also listed in its *Sexiest Women In The World* issue. Torrie entered the fashion world when she unveiled her own clothing line called "Officially Jaded."

To the dismay of her fans worldwide, Torrie and WWE parted ways in May 2008. Torrie Wilson will forever be remembered for her charisma, athleticism, and dedication to sports-entertainment.

Want to know what it's like to try to become a WWE Superstar? Do you think you have what it takes to be a part of the greatest sports-entertainment company in the history of human civilization? In June 2001 fans of sports-entertainment had the opportunity to enter a competition-based television program. Over 4,000 audition tapes were sent into World Wrestling Entertainment and from that enormous pool, 230 individuals were invited to WWE New York. Out of that number, 13 were selected to compete in the inaugural season that saw an expert training staff led by Al Snow and included Tori, Jacqueline, and Tazz. During the show's tenure it produced several memorable moments and future Superstars.

The pioneering program's final season took place in 2004 in cooperation with *SmackDown*. In addition to the prize of a WWE contract, the winner also received $1,000,000. The standard that Tough Enough set is seen today with every prospective trainee that embarks on a career in the squared circle.

During its four seasons *Tough Enough* gave the world a small glimpse of the grueling physical and mental toll sports entertainment takes and what you need to even have a chance of making it to the big time.

WINNERS

Season 1: Maven Huffman & Nidia Guenard

Season 2: Linda Miles & Jackie Gayda

Season 3: John Hennigan & Matt Cappotelli

Season 4: Daniel Pruder

Trinity

 **YEARS ACTIVE** 1960-1969 1970-1979 1980-1989 1990-1999 2000-PRESENT

FROM Boise, Idaho

You didn't have to look hard to see that Trinity was a dangerous Diva. With peaking biceps and yellow police tape strapped across her sculpted chest, it was practically written all over her. The stuntwoman-turned-Diva made her debut in June 2006 as the manager of ECW's Full Blooded Italians. Before she could make her mark, an unfortunate knee injury sidelined her for close to three months. When Trinity finally returned, her chances to assert herself in the ring were limited.

TRIPLE H

| HT | 6'4" | WT | 260 lbs. | FROM | Greenwich, Connecticut | SIGNATURE MOVE | Pedigree |

YEARS ACTIVE 1960-1969 | 1970-1979 | 1980-1989 | 1990-1999 | 2000-PRESENT

TITLE HISTORY WWE Champion, World Heavyweight Champion, World Tag Team Champion, Intercontinental Champion, European Champion

Triple H has captured every major championship, headlined multiple *WrestleMania* events, won the *Royal Rumble*, become King of the Ring and even spearheaded two of WWE's most influential factions. However, these achievements didn't happen by chance. They are the result of an unparalleled commitment to excellence that propelled Triple H past controversy and career-threatening injuries to become one of the greatest of all time.

Triple H was a lanky 135 pounds at the age of 14 when he received a gym membership that would change his life forever. Over the next several years, Triple H committed himself to becoming bigger and stronger. His dedication eventually lead to numerous bodybuilding crowns, including the prestigious Mr. Teen New Hampshire.

Looking for advice on breaking into wrestling, Triple H turned to former Superstar Ted Arcidi. The two men developed a friendship while working out together at the same gym in New Hampshire. Arcidi pointed Triple H in the direction of Killer Kowalski, who agreed to train him.

After one year of working with Kowalski, Triple H competed on an independent wrestling card that happened to have a legend quietly sitting in the stands. As a favor to Big John Studd, Pat Patterson went to the event to scout out one of Studd's protégés. While he was there, however, Patterson couldn't help but be amazed by the skill of Triple H.

WWE COMES CALLING

Triple H was thrilled by Patterson's compliments, but knew he still had some seasoning to do. However, it didn't take long for word of his outstanding matches, which included a stint in WCW, to reach Vince McMahon, who signed the young star.

Outside the ring, Helmsley began to form close bonds with several of his fellow Superstars, most notably Shawn Michaels, Kevin Nash (known then as Diesel) and Scott Hall (known then as Razor Ramon), the group became known as "The Kliq." On their final night together in Madison Square Garden (Hall and Nash were on their way to join WCW), all four members of "The Kliq" shared a heartfelt embrace in the center of the ring. The controversial stunt infuriated Mr. McMahon. As a result, McMahon punished Helmsley, relegating him to near-meaningless matches.

Lesser Superstars would never have rebounded from McMahon's wrath, but Helmsley refused to stay down, using his in-ring talent to force his way back to the top. Five months after the MSG incident, he earned an Intercontinental Championship opportunity against Marc Mero. Capitalizing on this rare opportunity to prove his worth, Helmsley defeated Mero for the first of many singles titles in WWE.

For weeks, WWE television aired vignettes featuring Triple H as Hunter Hearst-Helmsley, an American blue blood from Greenwich, Connecticut.

By 1997, the successful Helmsley became the target of many Superstars. To combat their attacks, he employed the services of a muscle-bound bodyguard. *Her* name was Chyna. With his new enforcer watching his back, Helmsley continued to post impressive wins, including a victory over Mankind to win the prestigious *King of the Ring* tournament.

FORMING D-GENERATION X

As 1997 continued to roll on, Helmsley began to shed his American blue blood persona and WWE fans were shocked at what they saw. The one-time snob from Greenwich, Connecticut, had transformed into one of the most rebellious and controversial Superstars in recent history. By the end of September, the new Triple H brought his backstage friendship with Shawn Michaels in front of the television cameras. Together, they pushed the envelope and formed one of the most notorious factions of all time: D-Generation X.

Controversy followed DX, who were not afraid to spit in the face of authority. The constant sophomoric jabs at then Commissioner Sgt. Slaughter was one of the main reasons the authority figure demanded to be ringside for Triple H's *WrestleMania XIV* battle against Owen Hart. *WrestleMania XIV* also marked the temporary end of Michaels' career, which logically should have meant the demise of DX. However, rather than letting HBK's inability to compete demolish a good thing, Triple H simply retooled the controversial faction the following night on *Raw*. Added to the new-and-improved DX were Billy Gunn, Road Dogg, and longtime friend X-Pac. Triple H lead the new DX into action for one year before finally turning his back on them at *WrestleMania XV*.

" *I AM THE GAME, AND I AM THAT DAMN GOOD!* "

"The Game" made his highly-anticipated return at Madison Square Garden in January 2002. The WWE crowd in attendance welcomed him back with a sustained standing ovation. Three weeks later, Triple H put an exclamation point on his return when he won the *Royal Rumble*. He followed that up by defeating Chris Jericho at *WrestleMania X8* to reclaim the WWE Championship.

Later that year, Shawn Michaels made a surprising return to WWE. With HBK back in the picture, everybody, including Michaels, assumed a DX reunion was in the works. "The Game," however, saw things a bit differently. The former friends met in a series of memorable battles, including a bloody Three Stages of Hell Match at *Armageddon* that saw Triple H defeat HBK to reclaim the World Heavyweight Championship.

THE GAME A.K.A. THE CEREBRAL ASSASSIN

Less than five months after turning his back on DX, Triple H reached the summit of the sports-entertainment world when he defeated Mankind for the WWE Championship. By the end of the year, the cerebral Triple H managed to advance his career and personal life in one fell swoop when he married Mr. McMahon's daughter, Stephanie. The announcement of their union sickened the WWE Chairman, especially after learning "The Game" apparently drugged his little girl to get her to go through with the ceremony.

Mr. McMahon had one opportunity to make everything right for his daughter when he battled Triple H at *Armageddon*. Just when it appeared as though the Chairman was going to clear his daughter's good name, however, Stephanie shocked the world by attacking her own father and running into the arms her new husband. What followed was the infamous McMahon-Helmsley Era, one of the most blatant abuses of power in sports-entertainment history. With Stephanie at his side, Triple H was able to piece together an impressive string of victories, including a *WrestleMania 2000* win over Big Show, The Rock, and Mick Foley in a Four Corners Match.

Proving anything can happen in WWE, Triple H teamed with the unlikeliest of Superstars when he joined forces with longtime rival Stone Cold Steve Austin in 2001. Collectively known as "The Two-Man Power Trip," Triple H and Stone Cold controlled the championship scene at the time, as Triple H once again wore the Intercontinental title, while Austin was WWE Champion. They added even more titles to their resumes when they defeated Kane & Undertaker for the World Tag Team Championship in April 2001.

THE END OF "THE GAME"?

The golden duo seemed almost unstoppable, until Triple H suffered a career-threatening injury when his left quadriceps tore completely off the bone during a tag team match. The severity of the injury caused noted orthopedic surgeon Dr. James Andrews to predict the end of "The Game's" career. Triple H refused believe Andrews' prognosis and began an exhausting eight months of rehabilitation.

THE EVOLUTION OF SPORTS-ENTERTAINMENT

Triple H accomplished a lifelong dream when he joined forces with childhood hero, Ric Flair, to form Evolution in early 2003. With Batista and Randy Orton, the well-dressed stable had the feel of a present-day Four Horsemen. At *Armageddon 2003*, they proved their greatness when all four members walked away with a title. Triple H defeated Goldberg and Kane for the World Heavyweight Championship, Orton beat Rob Van Dam to claim the Intercontinental Championship, and Flair & Batista toppled the Dudley Boys for the World Tag Team Championship.

The following year, the original D-Generation X (Triple H and Shawn Michaels) made their triumphant WWE return. In typical DX fashion, the duo targeted authority, most notably Mr. McMahon. The controversial faction's most-noted moment saw them shove the Chairman's face into the bare behind of Big Show at *Unforgiven*.

Unfortunately, Triple H suffered another debilitating setback when he tore his right quadriceps in January 2007. With nothing left to prove, Triple H could have easily walked away from sports-entertainment following the injury. Instead, he duplicated the dedication he showed in 2001 and returned to the ring after eight grueling months of rehabilitation. Upon his return, he faced King Booker in a battle of ring royalty. In the end, Triple H turned back Booker, proving he was the true "King of Kings".

By 2005, individual interests derailed Evolution's success, causing an ugly breakup of the faction. Triple H spent much of the year battling his former allies, including an unsuccessful World Heavyweight Championship defense against Batista at WrestleMania 21.

TRISH STRATUS

FROM Toronto, Ontario, Canada **SIGNATURE MOVE** Stratusfaction **TITLE HISTORY** Women's Champion, Hardcore Champion

Her beauty was astonishing; combined with her strength and natural athleticism, Trish Stratus redified WWE Diva for a new generation. She began her career as a top fitness model, appearing in many magazines. She grew up as a fan of sports-entertainment, and after college, she attended Ron Hutchison's wrestling school to pursue a dream.

She made her debut on *Sunday Night Heat* in March of 2000. She became the manager of Test & Albert, and Val Venis. After she parted with her stable of Superstars, she became involved with WWE Chairman Vince McMahon in an affair that did not sit well with other members of his family, particularly his daughter. The tension between mistress and daughter reached a boiling point at 2001's *No Way Out*. When Stephanie emerged victorious, Vince turned on Trish the next night on *Raw*. Trish had her revenge at *WrestleMania X-7* when she wheeled Linda McMahon to ringside for the Father vs. Son Streetfight between Shane and Vince, costing Vince the match.

Trish began to focus on competition within the women's division. At the 2001 *Survivor Series* she won her first (of seven) Women's Championships in the Six-Pack Challenge. After she lost three months later to Jazz at *No Way Out*, she managed to briefly hold the Hardcore Championship. Over the next few years Trish evolved as a performer and her dedication and hard work were recognized by fans when she was voted WWE.com *Babe of the Year* from 2002-2004. She was voted Diva of the Decade at *Raw's 10th Anniversary* in 2003.

In October 2005 Trish met her biggest fan in Mickie James. As James' friendship turned to infatuation, she turned on Trish and defeated her for the Women's Championship at *WrestleMania 22*. In August of 2006 Trish signed a contract to face Lita for the Women's Championship at *Unforgiven* after confirming that it would be her final match. With Toronto's Air Canada Centre chanting her name, Trish forced Lita to submit to the finishing move made famous by Bret "Hit Man" Hart, the Sharpshooter. An emotional Trish bid her devoted fans farewell and her storied WWE career came to a close.

During her time in WWE, Trish Stratus redefined "Diva" and took the women's division to all-new levels. Her formula for success was simple: 33% Beauty + 34% Brains + 33% Brawn = 100% Stratusfaction guaranteed.

The Truth Commission

MEMBERS The Jackyl, Kurrgan the Interrogator, Recon, Sniper, Tank, The Commandant

Introduced to WWE audiences by the Commandant in 1997, Recon, Sniper, Tank & Kurrgan displayed a style of South African guerilla warfare that struck fear into the WWE locker room. Shortly after their debut, however, the frightening faction went through a bit of restructuring when the Jackyl assumed leadership responsibilities from the Commandant, and Tank was relieved of his duties. The new-look Truth Commission proved to be equally as dangerous as the original.

At a towering seven-foot tall, Kurrgan proved to be the monster solo Superstar of the group, while Recon & Sniper competed mainly as a tag team. The entire Commission managed to make a rare appearance as an entire unit at the 1997 *Survivor Series* when they defeated the Disciples of Apocalypse.

Despite their success at *Survivor Series*, the Truth Commission struggled in the early parts of 1998. Unhappy with his team's performance, the Jackyl frequently ordered the monstrous Kurrgan to attack Recon & Sniper. The infighting eventually proved to be too much, as the faction slowly crumbled.

TUESDAY NIGHT TITANS

One of the major contributors to WWE forging into the uncharted waters of sports-entertainment in 1984 was a program that brought a breath of fresh air into a classic television format. With host Vince McMahon and faithful sidekick Lord Alfred Hayes, *Tuesday Night Titans* brought audiences the lives of their most beloved and despised WWE Superstars both in and out of the ring.

In front of a live studio audience, McMahon and Hayes took fans on a wild ride that included Superstar interviews, action in the ring and countless golden moments including the Hart Foundation on "The Mating Game," the wedding of Paul "Butcher" Vachon, Kamala eating a live chicken, and Mr. Fuji and the Magnificent Muraco starring in "Fuji Vice" and "Fuji General." Other memorable episodes saw "This is Your Life" with Nikolai Volkoff, "Baffle The Brain" with Bobby Heenan, and "Rowdy" Roddy Piper become the ultimate Scrooge as Roddy Ebenezer Piper.

Considered by many as classic television, *Tuesday Night Titans* showed that anything can and often would happen in World Wrestling Entertainment. Over time one word has consistently been used to describe this show of shows: EXPLOSIVE!

Tugboat

YEARS ACTIVE	1960 1969	1970 1979	1980 1989	**1990 1999**	2000 PRESENT

HT 6'3" **WT** 384 lbs. **SIGNATURE MOVE** Big Splash

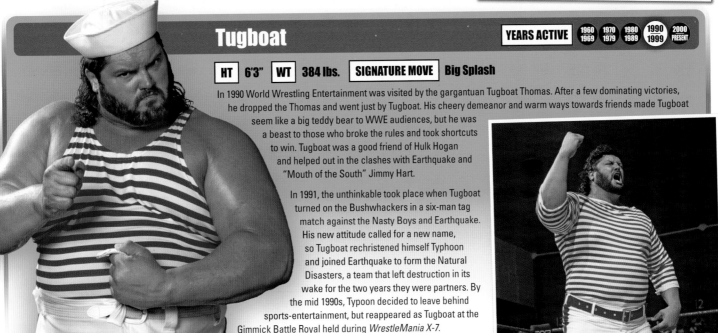

In 1990 World Wrestling Entertainment was visited by the gargantuan Tugboat Thomas. After a few dominating victories, he dropped the Thomas and went just by Tugboat. His cheery demeanor and warm ways towards friends made Tugboat seem like a big teddy bear to WWE audiences, but he was a beast to those who broke the rules and took shortcuts to win. Tugboat was a good friend of Hulk Hogan and helped out in the clashes with Earthquake and "Mouth of the South" Jimmy Hart.

In 1991, the unthinkable took place when Tugboat turned on the Bushwhackers in a six-man tag match against the Nasty Boys and Earthquake. His new attitude called for a new name, so Tugboat rechristened himself Typhoon and joined Earthquake to form the Natural Disasters, a team that left destruction in its wake for the two years they were partners. By the mid 1990s, Typoon decided to leave behind sports-entertainment, but reappeared as Tugboat at the Gimmick Battle Royal held during *WrestleMania X-7*.

TUXEDO MATCH

Despite sharing its rules with the popular Evening Gown Match, the Tuxedo Match is one of the least liked encounters in all of sports-entertainment. Like the Evening Gown encounter, the Tuxedo Match is won by the first competitor to successfully strip his opponent's formalwear. Rather than revealing a curvaceous WWE Diva, the Superstar left standing in the ring is usually a male announcer or manager.

One of WWE's first high-profile Tuxedo Matches pitted ring announcer Howard Finkel against manager Harvey Wippleman at *Raw*'s second anniversary. With the Bushwhackers in his corner, The Fink successfully disrobed Wippleman to win the contest. Following the victory, Finkel was widely recognized as the King of the Tuxedo Match.

Despite his lofty reputation, the Fink was unable to strip Lilian Garcia in the first-ever Tuxedo vs. Evening Gown Match in 2002. As a result of the loss, Finkel was forced to relinquish his *Raw* ring announcing duties to Lilian.

The Twin Towers

| YEARS ACTIVE | 1960 1969 | 1970 1979 | **1980 1989** | 1990 1999 | 2000 PRESENT |

MEMBERS Akeem, Big Boss Man **COMBINED WEIGHT** 800 lbs.

In 1988, Slick brought together his two largest Superstars to form one colossal team he called the Twin Towers. Over the next year, the mighty Akeem & Big Boss Man used their overwhelming size to manhandle WWE's smaller competition.

Alone, Akeem and Boss Man weren't going to win any popularity contests. Together, they were even more hated, especially after they handcuffed Hulk Hogan to a ring post at *Survivor Series 1988* and proceeded to beat him. Following the savage attack, the Twin Towers engaged in a high-profile rivalry with the Hulkster and his newfound friend, Randy Savage.

Unfortunately for Akeem & Boss Man, the popular pairing of Hogan & Savage proved superior when they defeated the oversized team on *The Main Event* in February 1989. While discouraging, the loss failed to set back the Twin Towers. They rebounded nicely with a major victory over the Rockers on the year's biggest stage, *WrestleMania V*.

As 1989 came to a close, Boss Man became unhappy with Slick's handling of the team. Akeem, on the other hand, didn't share the same feelings. Their disagreement eventually lead to a complete breakup when Boss Man attacked his partner. Following their inevitable dissolution, Boss Man defeated Akeem at *WrestleMania VI*. The victory won over the fans, as Boss Man went on to enjoy an amazing WWE career. Akeem never recovered from the loss and was gone from WWE shortly after.

TWO-OUT-OF-THREE FALLS MATCH

For decades a Two-out-of-Three Falls Match has been considered a true test of endurance. The winner is the first Superstar who records two falls. Traditionally falls are awarded like that of a traditional match: pinfall, submission, count out, or disqualification.

It is important to note that championship matches that are in this form usually follow standard championship match rules in that the title does not change hands if one of the victor's falls were determined by count out or disqualification. These matches are customarily held one after the other with a brief break between falls. However, it has been seen where the contests are held over the course of multiple events.

Tyson Tomko

| YEARS ACTIVE | 1960 1969 | 1970 1979 | 1980 1989 | 1990 1999 | **2000 PRESENT** |

HT 6'6" **WT** 275 lbs. **FROM** Jacksonville, Florida

SIGNATURE MOVE Big Boot

If there was a problem, Tyson Tomko could solve it. Introduced to WWE fans in April 2004, the behemoth known as the "Problem Solver" was brought in by Christian with the purpose of protecting "Captain Charisma" and his beautiful girlfriend, Trish Stratus, against Chris Jericho. A man of few words, Tomko used his unique appearance to intimidate fellow Superstars. In addition to sporting a bald skull and pointy goatee, his entire upper body was covered in tattoos. Coupled with his immense size, Tomko truly was an unmistakable figure.

In January 2005, Tomko teamed with Christian to challenge William Regal & Eugene for the World Tag Team Championship. A reign atop the tag scene was not to be, however, as Eugene rolled up Tomko to retain the titles. It was the closest the tattooed Superstar came to claiming a WWE championship.

After Christian was drafted to *SmackDown* in June 2005, Tomko went on to gain moderate success on *Raw*. Using his big boot to knock opponents unconscious, he racked up an impressive string of victories. Tomko eventually went on to form a tag team with Snitsky before leaving WWE in the spring of 2006.

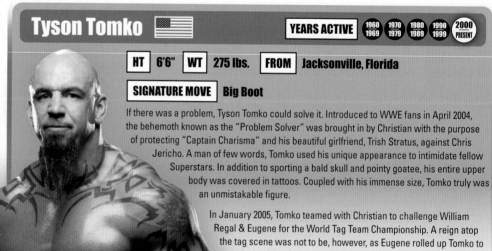

ULTIMATE WARRIOR

HT 6'2" **WT** 280 lbs. **FROM** Parts Unknown **TITLE HISTORY** WWE Champion, Intercontinental Champion

With unmatched energy, Ultimate Warrior exploded on the WWE scene in 1987. In record time, the face-painted Superstar became a household name and sports-entertainment icon. Ultimate Warrior had a natural charisma that was undeniable. His high-energy entrances and chiseled frame made him an instant hit with fans, while his high threshold for pain and unparalleled power struck instant fear into opponents. Within months of his debut, he had turned back many of WWE's top names on his way to becoming one of the company's top draws.

At *SummerSlam 1988*, Ultimate Warrior ended Honky Tonk Man's record 15-month Intercontinental Championship reign when he toppled the titleholder in a mere 30 seconds. The dominant victory proved that nobody was safe from the Ultimate Warrior's intensity. With the Intercontinental Championship around his waist, the Ultimate Warrior became one of WWE's most marketable Superstars. It wasn't long before arenas were filled with Ultimate Warrior T-shirts; fans even began to paint their faces like their eccentric hero.

Ultimate Warrior's superhuman strength carried him to a nearly eight-month Intercontinental Championship reign. It eventually took outside interference from Bobby Heenan for "Ravishing" Rick Rude to wrest the title from Ultimate Warrior at *WrestleMania V*. He later reclaimed the gold from Rude at *SummerSlam 1989*.

Ultimate Warrior's second stint with the Intercontinental Championship proved to be even more popular with the fans, setting the stage for an inevitable showdown with WWE Champion Hulk Hogan. WWE's two most popular Superstars finally met at *WrestleMania VI* in an historic encounter dubbed The Ultimate Challenge. With both titles on the line, Ultimate Warrior defeated Hogan in front of more than 67,000 screaming fans in Toronto's SkyDome. The victory was capped off by an amazing fireworks display, a precursor to the pyrotechnics seen on a weekly basis on today's WWE television.

Following the *WrestleMania* win, Ultimate Warrior spent the next nine months proudly defending the WWE Championship. His whirlwind reign was eventually silenced when Sgt. Slaughter, with some help from Randy Savage, defeated him at the 1991 *Royal Rumble*. Rather than set his sights on reclaiming the prize, Ultimate Warrior focused his attention on gaining revenge from Savage. He finally accomplished the ultimate retribution when he defeated Savage in a Retirement Match at *WrestleMania VII*.

Umaga

HT 6'4" **WT** 350 lbs. **FROM** The Isle of Samoa **SIGNATURE MOVE** Samoan Spike

TITLE HISTORY Intercontinental Champion

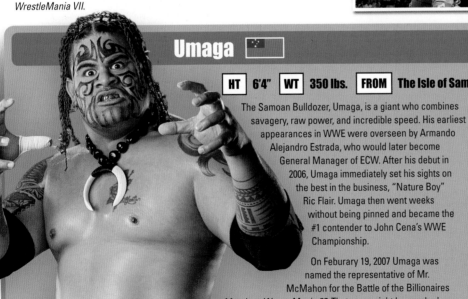

The Samoan Bulldozer, Umaga, is a giant who combines savagery, raw power, and incredible speed. His earliest appearances in WWE were overseen by Armando Alejandro Estrada, who would later become General Manager of ECW. After his debut in 2006, Umaga immediately set his sights on the best in the business, "Nature Boy" Ric Flair. Umaga then went weeks without being pinned and became the #1 contender to John Cena's WWE Championship.

On Feburary 19, 2007 Umaga was named the representative of Mr. McMahon for the Battle of the Billionaires Match at *WresteMania 23*. That same night he crushed Jeff Hardy to become the Intercontinental Champion. At *Backlash*, Umaga teamed with Mr. McMahon again. When the duo defeated the team of Bobby Lashley and Shane McMahon, the WWE Chairman became the new ECW Champion. No one is quite sure what drives Umaga to act as he does. Quite often, his opponents are too dazed from their encounters with him to give it much thought.

The Un-Americans 🇨🇦 🇬🇧

MEMBERS Lance Storm, Christian, Test, William Regal

TITLE HISTORY World Tag Team Champions

Led by Lance Storm, this collection of resident malcontents formed in June 2002 on *SmackDown*. Claiming that Canadians have been discriminated against in World Wrestling Entertainment since the company's early days, this group spewed anti-American rhetoric wherever they traveled. Their antics were hammered home in the ring as they failingly attempted on several occasions to burn the American flag. The Un-Americans' plans were thwarted by the likes of Booker T., Goldust, Bradshaw, Kane, Rey Mysterio, Rikishi, Edge, Undertaker, and Hulk Hogan.

The group did see success as Christian & Lance Storm captured the World Tag Team Championship on July 21, 2002 from Edge & Hollywood Hogan. They held the title for two months and the group experienced added power from WWE gold. However, when they lost the titles two months later the team eventually crumbled.

Uncle Elmer

HT 6'10" **WT** 430 lbs. **FROM** Mississippi **SIGNATURE MOVE** Big Splash

Uncle Elmer was a simple man. The only things he needed to be happy were a good meal and the affection of his family. He loved those around him so much, in fact, that he would unleash his mass on any Superstar that threatened to mess with them. Introduced to WWE audiences in 1985, Uncle Elmer proudly stood by the side of his nephew, Hillbilly Jim,

and later Cousin Luke and Cousin Junior. As far as technical wrestling skills were concerned, the big man didn't necessarily have any. Furthermore, he was as slow as a turtle, but he did possess a more than 400-pound frame that struck fear into his competition. His size was such a factor, in fact, that he once beat an opponent in just six seconds after dropping all his weight on him.

In a world where weddings rarely go as planned, Uncle Elmer actually pulled it off when he married his longtime girlfriend Joyce on *Saturday Night's Main Event* in October 1985. The nuptials feature some major star power, as Elmer's wedding party consisted of both Hulk Hogan and Andre the Giant.

The following year, the newlywed competed in the biggest match of his career when he lost to Adrian Adonis at *WrestleMania 2*. Shortly afterwards, he retreated back to his bride and farm in Mississippi.

Uncle Zebakiah

This managerial ruffian first appeared in World Wrestling Entertainment in 1995 as the manager of Jacob & Eli Blu. Zebakiah was an ultimate strategist who preached the importance of rule-breaking and permanently hurting opponents. He also had no issue with interfering on behalf of his team as they became top contenders for the World Tag Team Championship.

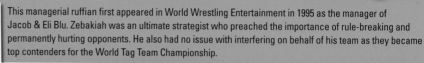

When the Blu Brothers left the company in 1996, Zebakiah brought in one of the hardest-hitting Superstars to ever enter the ring, Justin "Hawk" Bradshaw. As Zebakiah led Bradshaw to the ring with whip and bull-rope they were branding opponents as the Texan became a top contender for both the Intercontinental and Heavyweight Championships. In late 1996 Uncle Zebakiah returned to the mountains and has not been seen in World Wrestling Entertainment since.

Undertaker (see page 314)

UNFORGIVEN

April 26, 1998

Greensboro, North Carolina - Greensboro Coliseum

Main Event: Dude Love vs. WWE Champion Stone Cold Steve Austin

September 26, 1999

Charlotte, North Carolina - Charlotte Coliseum

Main Event: Triple H vs. The Rock vs. Mankind vs. Big Show vs. British Bulldog vs. Kane in a Six Pack Challenge Match for the vacant WWE Championship

September 24, 2000

Philadelphia, Pennsylvania - First Union Center

Main Event: The Rock (Champion) vs. Chris Benoit vs. Undertaker vs. Kane in a Fatal Four Way for the WWE Championship

September 23, 2001

Pittsburgh, Pennsylvania - Mellon Arena

Main Event: Kurt Angle vs. WWE Champion Stone Cold Steve Austin

September 22, 2002

Los Angeles, California - Staples Center

Main Event: WWE Champion Brock Lesnar vs. Undertaker

September 21, 2003

Hershey, Pennsylvania - Giant Centre

Main Event: Goldberg vs. World Heavyweight Champion Triple H

September 12, 2004

Portland, Oregon - Rose Garden

Main Event: Triple H vs. World Heavyweight Champion Randy Orton

September 18, 2005

Oklahoma City, Oklahoma - Ford Center

Main Event: Kurt Angle vs. WWE Champion John Cena by Disqualification

September 17, 2006

Toronto, Ontario, Canada - Air Canada Centre

Main Event: John Cena vs. WWE Champion Edge in a Tables, Ladders & Chairs Match

September 16, 2007

Memphis, Tennessee - FedEx Forum

Main Event: Undertaker vs. Mark Henry

September 7, 2008

Cleveland, Ohio - Quicken Loans Arena

Main Event: Championship Scramble Matches for the ECW, WWE, and World Heavyweight Championships

---

The Union

YEARS ACTIVE 1960-1969 1970-1979 1980-1989 **1990-1999** 2000-PRESENT

MEMBERS Mankind, Big Show, Ken Shamrock, Test

People all over the world hate their bosses. They huddle in corners of the office and whisper about how unfairly they're treated or how little they're compensated. Rarely do these employees have the courage to voice their feelings aloud to their superiors. When four Superstars felt this way, however, they refused to sit back silently. Instead, they formed a union and waged war on their boss.

In May 1999, former Corporation members Mankind, Big Show, Ken Shamrock, and Test banded together to form the "Union of People You Oughta Respect, Son". According to Mankind, the initials of The Union spelled out U.P.Y.O.U.R.S., a blatant sign of disrespect for their former boss, Shane McMahon. Upon their debut, the 2x4-carrying Superstars immediately engaged in a rivalry with Shane's Corporate Ministry.

The Union was able to gain some of the respect they were looking for when they defeated Corporate Ministry members Big Boss Man, Viscera, Faarooq & Bradshaw at the *Over The Edge* pay-per-view. The stable silently disbanded shortly after the win.

UNDERTAKER

HT	6'10½"	WT	295 lbs	FROM	Death Valley	SIGNATURE MOVE	Tombstone Piledriver

YEARS ACTIVE	1960 1969	1970 1979	1980 1989	1990 1999	2000 PRESENT	TITLE HISTORY	WWE Champion, World Heavyweight Champion, World Tag Team Champion, Hardcore Champion

From darkness, he emerged to build a dynasty second to none. He is the "Deadman." He is the "Phenom." He is the "Lord of Darkness." He is Undertaker. The mysterious Superstar from Death Valley was unveiled to WWE audiences at the 1990 *Survivor Series*. Alongside manager Brother Love, Undertaker made an immediate impact, eliminating Koko B. Ware from competition within two minutes of his career getting underway. Over the next two decades, the "Deadman's" domination in the ring lead to multiple World Championships, as well as an unblemished *WrestleMania* record.

DEADMAN WALKING

The first chapter in Undertaker's remarkable *WrestleMania* epic was penned in Los Angeles in 1991. Under the tutelage of new manager Paul Bearer, the "Phenom" used the Tombstone Piledriver to destroy Jimmy "Superfly" Snuka. The victory marked the first of a record number of *WrestleMania* wins, and also catapulted the "Deadman" straight to main-event status.

Undertaker spent the next several months using caskets and his mysteriously powerful urn to exploit his opponents' fear of their own mortality. He tore through every Superstar put in his path and in November 1991, at *Survivor Series*, he challenged Hulk Hogan for the WWE Championship. In the end, even the Hulkster's immortality was no match for the "Deadman," as Undertaker defeated Hogan for his first reign as WWE Champion.

Ric Flair's interference in Undertaker's WWE Championship victory ultimately caused President Jack Tunney to order a rematch at *This Tuesday in Texas*. Hogan wound up walking away from the event with the WWE Championship, but the controversial conclusion to the match caused Tunney to later vacate the title.

Following his WWE Championship reign, Undertaker faced a series of colossal competitors looking to rid WWE of the "Deadman." The four-hundred pound Kamala nearly accomplished the task during WWE's first-ever Coffin Match at the 1992 *Survivor Series*. Undertaker was able to avoid Kamala's offensive onslaught en route to picking up the ground-breaking win. The following year, the "Phenom" toppled the near eight-foot Giant Gonzalez at *WrestleMania IX*.

TWO UNDERTAKERS!

Many believed Undertaker had finally met his match when he squared off against WWE Champion Yokozuna at the 1994 *Royal Rumble*. The encounter saw Undertaker victimized by not only the mighty Yokozuna, but a posse of oversized Superstars, including Bam Bam Bigelow and Diesel. Many assumed the defeat, which saw Undertaker stuffed into a ringside casket, meant the demise of the "Deadman." However, as Yokozuna's gang pushed the casket up the aisle, an eerie smoke began to fill the arena, followed by the familiar gong of Undertaker's entrance theme. The "Deadman" then appeared on the TitanTron to proclaim, "I will not rest in peace."

Despite his promise of a return to dominance, Undertaker was nowhere to be seen for the first half of 1994. By summer, however, Ted DiBiase claimed to have found the "Phenom." DiBiase's declaration shocked Paul Bearer, who claimed to have found him too. The two men agreed to have their Undertakers square off against each other at *SummerSlam 1994*. In the end, Bearer's Undertaker proved to be the real "Phenom," defeating DiBiase's fake after hitting him with three Tombstones.

Undertaker's 1994 disappearance caused

him to miss *WrestleMania X*, but his dark dominance returned the following year when he defeated the massive King Kong Bundy in Hartford, Connecticut. The victory improved the "Phenom's" impressive WrestleMania record to a perfect 4-0. The following year, he handily defeated Diesel.

Following his defeat of Diesel, Undertaker became the target of WWE newcomer Mankind. The two Superstars spent the next year competing in one of the most innovative rivalries in sports-entertainment history. Their intense rivalry sparked the advent of two revolutionary match types, the Boiler Room Brawl and Buried Alive Match. It also marked the shocking end to one of the closest alliances of all time when Paul Bearer clobbered Undertaker with his urn at *SummerSlam 1996*.

Despite losing his manager to Mankind, Undertaker continued to post an impressive record, which earned him a WWE Championship opportunity against Sycho Sid at *WrestleMania 13*. Following a skull-crushing Tombstone, the "Phenom" covered Sid to reclaim the title he lost more than five years earlier. The victory catapulted Undertaker back to the top of the sports-entertainment scene. He spent the next five months successfully defending the title against the likes of Stone Cold Steve Austin and Vader.

FAMILY TIES

An errant steel chair shot at the hands of special referee Shawn Michaels allowed Bret "Hit Man" Hart to dethrone Undertaker at *SummerSlam 1997*. Yearning for revenge, the "Deadman" shifted his focus from the WWE Championship scene to destroying HBK. After a series of inconclusive contests, the two Superstars agreed to settle the score in the first-ever Hell in a Cell Match at *Badd Blood*. Once locked inside the satanic structure, Undertaker released all his frustrations on Michaels, but just when it appeared as though victory was certain, Undertaker came face to face with a familiar figure from the past that cost him the match. That figure was Kane.

In the months leading up to Kane's shocking debut, Paul Bearer, in an attempt to blackmail Undertaker, threatened to uncover a disturbing secret from the "Deadman's" past. When Undertaker refused to give in to the demands, Bearer finally revealed that the "Phenom" set fire to his family's funeral parlor twenty years earlier, killing his mother and father. In the years that followed the blaze, Undertaker assumed his younger brother also perished in the fire. At *Badd Blood*, Undertaker's assumption proved to be dead wrong, as his disfigured sibling appeared from out of nowhere to brutally attack him.

In the months following the shocking revelation, Undertaker refused to step in the ring with his flesh and blood. However, after Kane attempted to send him to a fiery grave at the 1998 *Royal Rumble*, Undertaker had no choice but to respond with force. The two brothers finally squared off at *WrestleMania XIV*. Undertaker won the emotional battle, but the war between the two was just heating up. Undertaker and Kane went on to engage in some of the most bitter battles ever seen, including several Inferno Matches that forced the "Big Red Monster" to relive his charring childhood.

By 1999, Undertaker adopted an even darker, more demonic demeanor. He also made the unpopular decision to reconcile with Paul Bearer to form the Ministry of Darkness, which included Mideon, Viscera, the Acolytes, and the Brood. Claiming to serve a "higher power", Undertaker unleashed a never-before-seen assault on the entire WWE. Nobody was safe from the "Deadman's" wicked wrath, not even Stephanie McMahon, who was abducted by Undertaker in April 1999. Luckily for Stephanie, Stone Cold Steve Austin rescued her from further assault. The heroics, however, landed Stone Cold in a WWE Championship defense against Undertaker the following month. The "Phenom" defeated Stone Cold for the WWE Championship, his third reign with the prestigious championship.

A FRESH START

Leaving his "Deadman" persona in the dust, he reemerged at *Judgment Day* riding a motorcycle. Recognized as the "American Bad Ass," the new Undertaker was equally imposing. Following an impressive victory over Triple H at *WrestleMania X-Seven*, Undertaker formed an alliance with brother and longtime rival Kane. Known as the Brothers of Destruction, the duo spent the next several months dominating the tag team scene, capturing the World and WCW Tag Team Championships a total of three times.

After being forced out of action for eight months, a very different Undertaker returned to the ring in May 2000.

More than a decade after defeating Hulk Hogan for his first WWE Championship, Undertaker challenged the Hulkster for the same prize at *Judgment Day 2002*. Much like that fateful night back in November 1991, he used a steel chair to claim the title from Hogan. Undertaker held the gold for more than two months before The Rock beat him and Kurt Angle in a Triple Threat Match to win the title.

The fiery family hostility between Undertaker and Kane reignited in late 2003. This time, however, Kane appeared to walk away the victor when he helped Mr. McMahon bury his brother alive at *Survivor Series*. As mounds of dirt covered Undertaker's seemingly lifeless body, many assumed they had finally seen the end of Undertaker.

THE DEADMAN RETURNS

Proving you can't kill what's already dead, Undertaker made his triumphant return to WWE at *WrestleMania XX*. He defeated Kane to improve his WrestleMania record to an astonishing 12-0. The "Phenom's" iconic status made him the perfect target for the brash youngster Randy Orton. The third-generation Superstar saw Undertaker's spotless *WrestleMania* record as an opportunity to permanently etch his name into the WWE history books. Unfortunately for the self-appointed "Legend Killer", he became unlucky victim number thirteen.

By 2007, there were two glaring holes on the Undertaker's impressive resumé: He had never won a *Royal Rumble* or captured the World Heavyweight Championship. In January 2007, he filled in one hole when he last eliminated Shawn Michaels to win the *Royal Rumble* Match. Winning that match allowed him to meet Batista at *WrestleMania 23* for the World Heavyweight Championship, which he won after a Tombstone Piledriver. Undertaker duplicated his efforts the following year when he toppled Edge at *WrestleMania XXIV* to become a two-time World Heavyweight Champion.

UNITED STATES CHAMPIONSHIP

Today's fans recognize the United States Championship as the title defended in WWE arenas by the likes of Matt Hardy, Montel Vontavious Porter, and Mr. Kennedy. However, what many might not realize is that the U.S. Championship actually had its start in the NWA in 1975.

Harley Race, Terry Funk, Magnum T. A. and a host of other legendary names drove the highways of the southern United States in the 1970s and 80s, defending the title in small arenas in Florida, North Carolina and Virginia. When the U.S. Championship became exclusive to World Championship Wrestling in 1991, the gold began to be defended nationwide on a more regular basis. Sting, Rick Rude, and Dustin Rhodes began to introduce the title to fans west of the Mississippi River and north of the Mason-Dixon Line.

WWE fans first became familiar with the U.S. Championship when WWE purchased WCW in 2001. Unfortunately, fans had less than one year to truly appreciate the title, as it was unified with the Intercontinental Championship when Edge defeated Test in November 2001.

For nearly two years, the U.S. Championship sat dormant, but in July 2003, Stephanie McMahon breathed life back into the historic championship. Eddie Guerrero defeated Chris Benoit in the finals of a tournament to crown a new titleholder to the revived championship. Since that time, the title has found its way around the waists of such names as Booker T, Big Show, and John Cena.

1975

JAN 01 Tallahassee, FL
Harley Race defeats Johnny Weaver
Harley Race beat Johnny Weaver in the finals of a tournament to crown a new United States Champion.

JULY 03 Greensboro, NC
Johnny Valentine defeats Harley Race

Injuries forced Johnny Valentine to vacate the United States Championship in October 1975.

NOV 09 Greensboro, NC
Terry Funk defeats Paul Jones
Terry Funk beat Paul Jones in the finals of a tournament to crown a new United States Champion.

1978

JAN 01 Greensboro, NC
Blackjack Mulligan defeats Ricky Steamboat

MAR 19 Greensboro, NC
Mr. Wrestling defeats Blackjack Mulligan

APR 09 Greensboro, NC
Ric Flair defeats Mr. Wrestling

DEC 18 Toronto, Ontario
Ricky Steamboat defeats Ric Flair

1979

APR 01 Greensboro, NC
Ric Flair defeats Ricky Steamboat

1982

MAY 21 Richmond, VA
Wahoo McDaniel defeats St. Slaughter

JUNE 07 Greensville, SC
Sgt. Slaughter is awarded United States Championship

After an injury forced Wahoo McDaniel to vacate the United States Championship, Sgt. Slaughter was declared the new champion.

AUG 22 Charlotte, NC
Wahoo McDaniel defeats Sgt. Slaughter

NOV 4 Norfolk, VA
Greg Valentine defeats Wahoo McDaniel

OCT 07 Charlotte, NC
Wahoo McDaniel defeats Manny Fernandez
Wahoo McDaniel beat Manny Fernandez in the finals of a tournament to crown a new United States Champion.

1985

MAR 23 Charlotte, NC
Magnum T.A. defeats Wahoo McDaniel

JULY 21 Charlotte, NC
Tully Blanchard defeats Magnum T.A.

NOV 28 Greensboro, NC
Magnum T.A. defeats Tully Blanchard

Magnum T.A. was stripped of the United States Championship in May 1985 after attacking NWA President Bob Geigel.

1989

FEB 20 Chicago, IL
Lex Luger defeats Barry Windham

MAR 07 Nashville, TN
Michael Hayes defeats Lex Luger

MAR 22 Bluefield, WV
Lex Luger defeats Michael Hayes

1990

OCT 27 Chicago, IL
Stan Hansen defeats Lex Luger

DEC 16 St. Louis, MO
Lex Luger defeats Stan Hansen

1994

AUG 24 Cedar Rapids, IA
Ricky Steamboat defeats Steve Austin

Injury forced Ricky Steamboat to vacate the United States Championship.

SEPT 18 Roanoke, VA
Steve Austin is awarded the United States Championship

SEPT 18 Roanoke, VA
Jim Duggan defeats Steve Austin

DEC 27 Nashville, TN
Vader defeats Jim Duggan

Vader was stripped of the United States Championship by WCW Commissioner Nick Bockwinkel in April 1995.

1997

MAR 16 Charleston, SC
Dean Malenko defeats Eddie Guerrero

JUNE 09 Boston, MA
Jeff Jarrett defeats Dean Malenko

AUG 21 Nashville, TN
Steve McMichael defeats Jeff Jarrett

SEPT 15 Charlotte, NC
Curt Hennig defeats Steve McMichael

DEC 28 Washington, DC
Diamond Dallas Page defeats Curt Hennig

1999

FEB 08 Buffalo, NY
Roddy Piper defeats Bret Hart

FEB 21 Oakland, CA
Scott Hall defeats Roddy Piper

WCW President Ric Flair stripped Scott Hall of the United States Championship on March 18.

APR 11 Tacoma, WA
Scott Steiner defeats Booker T
Scott Steiner beat Booker T in the finals of a tournament to crown a new United States Champion.

WCW President Ric Flair stripped Scott Steiner of the United States Championship on July 5.

JULY 05 Atlanta, GA

DEC 20 Baltimore, MD
Jeff Jarrett defeats Chris Benoit

Injury forced Jeff Jarrett to vacate the United States Championship on January 16.

2000

JAN 17 Columbus, OH
Jeff Jarrett is awarded the United States Championship

One night after being stripped of the United States Championship, Jeff Jarrett was given the title back by WCW Commissioner Kevin Nash. Jarrett was stripped of the title again on April 10, when WCW heads Vince Russo and Eric Bischoff vacated all titles.

APR 16 Chicago, IL
Scott Steiner defeats Sting

continued on next page

After using a banned maneuver on Mike Awesome, Steiner was stripped of the title by WCW Commissioner Ernest Miller on July 9.

JULY **18** — Auburn Hills, MI
Lance Storm defeats Mike Awesome
Lance Storm beat Mike Awesome in the finals of a tournament to crown a new United States Champion.

SEPT **22** — Amarillo, TX
Terry Funk defeats Lance Storm

SEPT **23** — Lubbock, TX
Lance Storm defeats Terry Funk

OCT **29** — Las Vegas, NV
Gen. Rection defeats Jim Duggan
Gen. Rection pinned Jim Duggan to win the United States Championship in a Handicap Match. Duggan's partner in the match was then-champion Lance Storm.

NOV **13** — London, England
Lance Storm defeats Gen. Rection

NOV **26** — Milwaukee, WI
Gen. Rection defeats Lance Storm

After stripping Scott Steiner of the United States Championship, WCW President Ric Flair gave the title to his son, David.

AUG **09** — Boise, ID
Chris Benoit defeats David Flair

SEPT **12** — Winston-Salem, NC
Sid Vicious defeats Chris Benoit

OCT **24** — Las Vegas, NV
Goldberg defeats Sid Vicious

OCT **25** — Phoenix, AZ
Bret Hart defeats Goldberg

NOV **08** — Indianapolis, IN
Scott Hall defeats Bret Hart
Scott Hall beat Bret Hart for the United States Championship in a Ladder Match that also included Goldberg and Sid Vicious.

Injury forced Scott Hall to vacate the United States Championship on December 19.

DEC **19** — Washington, DC
Chris Benoit is awarded the United States Championship

1998

APR **19** — Denver, CO
Raven defeats Diamond Dallas Page

APR **20** — Colorado Springs, CO
Goldberg defeats Raven

Goldberg vacated the United States Championship on July 6, 1998 after winning the WCW Championship.

JULY **20** — Salt Lake City, UT
Bret Hart defeats Diamond Dallas Page

AUG **10** — Rapid City, SD
Lex Luger defeats Bret Hart

AUG **13** — Fargo, ND
Bret Hart defeated Lex Luger

OCT **26** — Phoenix, AZ
Diamond Dallas Page defeats Bret Hart

NOV **30** — Chattanooga, TN
Diamond Dallas Page defeats Bret Hart

Bret Hart defeats Diamond Dallas Page

1995

JUNE **18** — Dayton, OH
Sting defeats Meng
Sting beat Meng in the finals of a tournament to crown a new United States Champion.

NOV **13** — Tokyo, Japan
Kensuke Sasaki defeats Sting

DEC **27** — Nashville, TN
One Man Gang defeats Kensuke Sasaki

1996

JAN **29** — Canton, OH
Konnan defeats One Man Gang

JULY **07** — Daytona Beach, FL
Ric Flair defeats Konnan

Injury forced Ric Flair to vacate the United States Championship in September 1996.

DEC **29** — Nashville, TN
Eddie Guerrero defeats Diamond Dallas Page
Eddie Guerrero beat Diamond Dallas Page in the finals of a tournament to crown a new United States Champion.

Lex Luger vacated the United States Championship on July 14, 1991 after winning the WCW Championship.

1991

AUG **25** — Atlanta, GA
Sting defeats Steve Austin
Sting beat Steve Austin in the finals of a tournament to crown a new United States Champion.

NOV **19** — Savannah, GA
Rick Rude defeats Sting

Injury forced Rick Rude to vacate the United States Championship in December 1992.

1993

JAN **11** — Atlanta, GA
Dustin Rhodes defeats Ricky Steamboat

Rhodes was forced to vacate the title in May 1993 after a title defense against Rick Rude ended in a double pinfall.

AUG **30** — Atlanta, GA
Dustin Rhodes defeats Rick Rude

DEC **27** — Charlotte, NC
Steve Austin defeats Dustin Rhodes

1986

AUG **17** — Charlotte, NC
Nikita Koloff defeats Magnum T.A.
Nikita Koloff beat Magnum T.A. in the finals of a tournament to crown a new United States Champion.

1987

JULY **11** — Greensboro, NC
Lex Luger defeats Nikita Koloff

NOV **26** — Chicago, IL
Dusty Rhodes defeats Lex Luger

Dusty Rhodes was stripped of the United States Championship in April 1987 after attacking Jim Crockett.

1988

MAY **13** — Houston, TX
Barry Windham defeats Nikita Koloff
Barry Windham beat Nikita Koloff in the finals of a tournament to crown a new United States Champion.

1983

APR **01** — Greensboro, NC
Ric Flair defeats Ricky Steamboat

APR **16** — Greensboro, NC
Roddy Piper defeats Greg Valentine

APR **30** — Greensboro, NC
Greg Valentine defeats Roddy Piper

DEC **14** — Shelby, NC
Dick Slater defeats Greg Valentine

1984

APR **21** — Greensboro, NC
Ricky Steamboat defeats Dick Slater

JUNE **24** — Greensboro, NC
Wahoo McDaniel defeats Ricky Steamboat

Wahoo McDaniel was forced to vacate the United States Championship after Tully Blanchard interfered in McDaniel's match.

After winning the NWA World Tag Team Championship in August 1979, Ric Flair was forced to vacate the United States Championship.

1980

SEPT **01** — Charlotte, NC
Jimmy Snuka defeats Ricky Steamboat
Jimmy Snuka beat Ricky Steamboat in the finals of a tournament to crown a new United States Champion.

1981

JAN **27** — Raleigh, NC
Roddy Piper defeats Ric Flair

AUG **08** — Greensboro, NC
Ric Flair defeats Roddy Piper

OCT **04** — Charlotte, NC
Wahoo McDaniel defeats Roddy Piper

Injury forced Wahoo McDaniel to vacate the United States Championship in September 1981.

Sgt. Slaughter defeats Ricky Steamboat
Sgt. Slaughter beat Ricky Steamboat in the finals of a tournament to crown a new United States Champion.

NOV **27** — Greensboro, NC
Paul Jones defeats Terry Funk

1976

MAR **13** — Greensboro, NC
Blackjack Mulligan defeats Paul Jones

OCT **16** — Greensboro, NC
Paul Jones defeats Blackjack Mulligan

DEC **15** — Greensboro, NC
Blackjack Mulligan defeats Paul Jones

1977

JULY **07** — Norfolk, VA
Bobo Brazil defeats Blackjack Mulligan

JULY **29** — Norfolk, VA
Ric Flair defeats Bobo Brazil

OCT **23** — Greensboro, NC
Ricky Steamboat defeats Ric Flair

U

2001

JAN 14 — Indianapolis, IN

Shane Douglas defeats Gen. Rection

FEB 05 — Tupelo, MS

Rick Steiner defeats Shane Douglas

MAR 18 — Jacksonville, FL

Booker T defeats Rick Steiner

JULY 26 — Pittsburgh, PA

Chris Kanyon is awarded the United States Championship

Chris Kanyon was given the United States Championship by then-champion Booker T.

SEPT 10 — San Antonio, TX

Tajiri defeats Chris Kanyon

SEPT 23 — Pittsburgh, PA

Rhyno defeats Tajiri

OCT 22 — Kansas City, MO

Kurt Angle defeats Rhyno

NOV 12 — Boston, MA

Edge defeats Kurt Angle

Edge beat Test to unify the United States and Intercontinental Championships on November 18. The title was declared inactive until Stephanie McMahon revived it in July 2003.

2003

JULY 27 — Denver, CO

Eddie Guerrero defeats Chris Benoit

Eddie Guerrero beat Chris Benoit in the finals of a tournament to crown a new United States Champion.

OCT 19 — Baltimore, MD

Big Show defeats Eddie Guerrero

2004

MAR 14 — New York, NY

John Cena defeats Big Show

After attacking SmackDown General Manager Kurt Angle, John Cena was stripped of the United States Championship on July 8.

JULY 29 — Cincinnati, OH

Booker T defeats Rob Van Dam

Booker T last eliminated Rob Van Dam to win the United States Championship in an 8-man Elimination Match that also included Billy Gunn, Rene Dupree, Kenzo Suzuki, John Cena, Charlie Haas, and Luther Reigns.

OCT 03 — East Rutherford, NJ

John Cena defeats Booker T

OCT 07 — Boston, MA

Carlito defeats John Cena

NOV 18 — Dayton, OH

John Cena defeats Carlito

2005

MAR 03 — Albany, NY

Orlando Jordan defeats John Cena

AUG 21 — Washington, DC

Chris Benoit defeats Orlando Jordan

OCT 21 — Reno, NV

Booker T defeats Chris Benoit

Booker T was forced to vacate the United States Championship after a title defense against Chris Benoit ended with a double pinfall.

2006

JAN 13 — Philadelphia, PA

Booker T defeats Chris Benoit

Substituting for Booker T, Randy Orton beat Chris Benoit. As a result, Booker T was named new United States Champion.

FEB 19 — Baltimore, MD

Chris Benoit defeats Booker T

APR 02 — Chicago, IL

JBL defeats Chris Benoit

MAY 26 — Bakersfield, CA

Bobby Lashley defeats JBL

JULY 14 — Minneapolis, MN

Finlay defeats Bobby Lashley

SEPT 01 — Reading, PA

Mr. Kennedy defeats Bobby Lashley

Mr. Kennedy pinned Bobby Lashley to win the United States Championship in a Triple Threat Match that also included then-champion Finlay.

OCT 13 — Jacksonville, FL

Chris Benoit defeats Mr. Kennedy

2007

MAY 20 — St. Louis, MO

Montel Vontavious Porter defeats Chris Benoit

2008

APR 27 — Baltimore, MD

Matt Hardy defeats Montel Vontavious Porter

JULY 20 — Uniondale, NY

Shelton Benjamin defeats Matt Hardy

The U.S. Express

YEARS ACTIVE — 1960–1969 · 1970–1979 · **1980–1989** · 1990–1999 · 2000–PRESENT

| MEMBERS | Barry Windham, Mike Rotundo | COMBINED WEIGHT | 505 lbs. | TITLE HISTORY | World Tag Team Championship |

Blessed with boy-next-door good looks, Barry Windham & Mike Rotundo teamed up in 1984 and quickly became America's sweethearts. Collectively referred to as the U.S. Express, they became known for fending off WWE's most devious Superstars.

A mere three months after making their WWE debut, the U.S. Express defeated Adrian Adonis & Dick Murdoch to win the World Tag Team Championship. Following the win, the patriotic pairing began to use Rick Derringer's single *Real American* as their theme song. Hulk Hogan would later adopt the song as his own, using it for the majority of his career.

Behind some outside interference from "Classy" Freddie Blassie, the U.S. Express lost their titles to The Iron Sheik & Nikolai Volkoff at the inaugural *WrestleMania*. Unable to stand by and allow the rule-breaking Iranian and Russian parade around the United States with the gold, Windham & Rotunda focused on exacting revenge. They finally accomplished their goal in June 1985 when they regained the titles from their rivals.

Later that year, Windham left WWE to return to the Florida territories. The U.S. Express would reunite more than twenty years later, though, when they signed on to battle Sheik & Volkoff in a *WrestleMania* rematch. Unfortunately, the match never got underway, as Jillian interrupted to sing *Born in the U.S.A.*

VADER

HT	6'5"	WT	450 lbs.	FROM	The Rocky Mountains

SIGNATURE MOVE Vader Splash, Vader Bomb

YEARS ACTIVE 1960-1969 · 1970-1979 · 1980-1989 · **1990-1999** · 2000 PRESENT

Before ever stepping foot in a WWE ring, the man they call Vader earned a worldwide reputation as a bona fide tough man. At well over four hundred pounds, he possessed the power of a super heavyweight, while also owning the unbelievable ability to fly through the air like a cruiserweight.

The three-time WCW Champion made his WWE debut at the 1996 *Royal Rumble*. Despite being eliminated by Shawn Michaels, Vader made a remarkable showing, eliminating an impressive list of Superstars. Following his debut, the mastodon assaulted both Superstars and WWE officials. He even attacked WWE President Gorilla Monsoon, which earned him a brief suspension.

Upon returning to the ring, Vader's path of destruction left many of WWE's biggest names laying in his wake, including Yokozuna, Razor Ramon, and Sycho Sid. His impressive victories over WWE's elite eventually earned him a WWE Championship match against Shawn Michaels at *SummerSlam*. Vader defeated the champ at the event, but the victory came by countout, which meant the title could not change hands. Realizing his client would not be awarded the title, Jim Cornette demanded the match be restarted. Vader won again, this time by disqualification. As expected, Cornette cried for another restart, which he received. However, this time HBK defeated Vader via pinfall to mark the official end to the wild encounter.

The following year, Vader traded in Cornette for Paul Bearer. The move proved to be a wise one, as his new manager helped him gain a huge victory over the legendary Undertaker at the 1997 *Royal Rumble*. Bearer also paired Vader with Mankind in an attempt to claim a tag team championship. The duo nearly dethroned Owen Hart & Davey Boy Smith at *WrestleMania 13*, but fell just short after the match was declared a double countout. Following losses to Edge and Bradshaw in late 1998, Vader disappeared from the WWE scene completely.

Val Venis

HT	6'4"	WT	245 lbs.

FROM Las Vegas, Nevada

SIGNATURE MOVE Money Shot

TITLE HISTORY
Intercontinental Champion, European Champion, World Tag Team Champion

YEARS ACTIVE 1960-1969 · 1970-1979 · 1980-1989 · **1990-1999** · **2000 PRESENT**

"Hello Ladies!"

Val Venis made his debut with a towel around his waist and gyrations before his matches that left female fans in a hypnotic trance. The Big Valbowski often made waves in WWE by seducing the wives and sisters of other Superstars and managers. His actions resulted in battles against Kaientai, Goldust, and Ken Shamrock.

At *St. Valentine's Day Massacre* Venis, with an assist from Billy Gunn, defeated Ken Shamrock for the Intercontinental Title. Val Venis claimed his other singles title at *Armageddon 1999*. He defeated British Bulldog and D-Lo Brown in a Triple Threat Match to win the European Championship.

In 2000, Venis became the antithesis of his former self when he joined the Right To Censor. After the group fell apart and he took some time away from WWE, Val returned as the Chief of Staff to *Raw* GM Eric Bischoff. Not wanting the association with Bischoff to tarnish the name he cultivated earlier in his career, he operated under the name Chief Morley.

Working as an authority figure ultimately left Val unsatisfied, so he returned to his true calling, making the ladies swoon while showing off his impressive in-ring repertoire.

The Valiant Brothers

MEMBERS Jimmy Valiant, Johnny Valiant, Jerry Valiant

COMBINED WEIGHT 490 lbs.

TITLE HISTORY
World Tag Team Championship

YEARS ACTIVE 1960-1969 · **1970-1979** · 1980-1989 · 1990-1999 · 2000 PRESENT

"Handsome" Jimmy & "Luscious" Johnny Valiant were two of the most charismatic characters of the 1970s. With their bleached blond hair and outrageous ring attire, they had a magnetic personality that made them tough not to like, even though you weren't supposed to.

Jimmy's career kicked off in 1964. Johnny followed the lead, making his debut in 1967. Initially singles stars, the brothers turned to tag team competition at the turn of the decade. They gained some level of success early, capturing a title while competing in Indianapolis.

The flamboyant duo made their WWE debut in early 1974. Within days of their arrival, they defeated Dean Ho & Tony Garea for the World Tag Team Championship. They would go on to hold the titles for more than one year, longer than any other tandem at that time. Demolition's reign of the late 1980s is the only one to top Jimmy & Johnny in length.

After a brief hiatus, the Valiants returned to WWE in 1978. This time, however, Jimmy stepped aside and brother "Gentleman" Jerry stepped in. With Jimmy serving as manager, Johnny & Jerry defeated Larry Zbyzsko & Tony Garea for the World Tag Team Championship in March 1979.

Jimmy & Johnny Valiant took their rightful place alongside the all-time best when they were inducted into the WWE Hall of Fame in 1996.

V

VENGEANCE

December 9, 2001

San Diego, CA - San Diego Sports Arena

Main Event: Chris Jericho vs. Stone Cold Steve Austin in a World Heavyweight Championship Unification Match

July 21, 2002

Detroit, MI - Joe Louis Arena

Main Event: The Rock vs. WWE Champion Undertaker vs. Kurt Angle in a Triple Threat Match

July 27, 2003

Denver, CO - Pepsi Arena

Main Event: Kurt Angle vs. Big Show vs. WWE Champion Brock Lesnar in a Triple Threat, No Disqualification Match

July 11, 2004

Hartford, CT - Hartford Civic Center

Main Event: World Heavyweight Champion Chris Benoit vs. Triple H

June 26, 2005

Las Vegas, NV - Thomas & Mack Center

Main Event: World Heavyweight Champion Batista vs. Triple H in Hell in a Cell Match

June 25, 2006

Charlotte, NC - Charlotte Bobcats Area

Main Event: D-Generation X vs. the Spirit Squad in a 5-On-2 Handicap, Non-Title Match

VENGEANCE: NIGHT OF CHAMPIONS

June 24, 2007

Houston, TX - Toyota Center

Main Event: WWE Champion John Cena vs. Booker T vs. Mick Foley vs. Randy Orton vs. Bobby Lashley in a WWE Championship Challenge

NIGHT OF CHAMPIONS

June 29, 2008

Dallas, TX - American Airlines Center

Main Event: WWE Champion Triple H vs. John Cena

| HT | 5'11" | WT | 215 lbs. | FROM | Robbinsdale, Minnesota | SIGNATURE MOVE | Gagne Sleeper Hold |

Verne Gagne was one of the top amateur athletes in the United States during the 1940s. At the University of Minnesota he was a four-time Big Ten Conference Champion and a two-time NCAA National Champion, and held a spot on the 1948 Olympic team. After a short tenure with the Green Bay Packers, Gagne entered sports-entertainment in 1950. His first major championship was the NWA World Junior Heavyweight Championship.

During the 1960s, while still active in the ring, Verne became a promoter and eventual owner of the AWA, leading it to new heights. From 1972 to 1979 Verne made special appearances for World Wrestling Entertainment in Madison Square Garden and battled Eddie Graham, Mr. Fuji, the Valiant Brothers, and Nikolai Volkoff. In 1981, Verne retired from the ring but did lace-up the boots on occasion if foes overstepped their bounds. Throughout his career, Verne honed many budding Superstars' in-ring talents and the list of individuals he taught reads like a veritable Who's Who of sports-entertainment.

In 1991 the AWA closed its doors after an astonishing 31 years of operation. Verne has enjoyed life away from the ring but was called back under the bright lights in April 2006 when he was enshrined amongst the immortals in the WWE Hall of Fame.

Verne Gagne dedicated his life to the advancement of sports-entertainment. Over his four decades in the business, he showed that he was a dynamic performer in the ring, and an inventive business mind behind the scenes.

Vickie Guerrero

As the widow of WWE Hall of Famer Eddie Guerrero, Vickie Guerrero was a beloved figure when she entered WWE. It wasn't long, however, before she revealed a darker side. Fans everywhere were shocked when Vickie turned into a power-hungry witch who would stop at nothing to get what she wants.

Vickie became a regular on WWE television during the emotional rivalry between Rey Mysterio and Chavo Guerrero in 2006. Appearing as a neutral party, she pleaded with them to call a truce. However, she later aligned with her nephew to defeat Mysterio.

In May 2007, Vickie was awarded the position of *SmackDown*'s Assistant General Manager. She eventually gained full control when her boss, Theodore Long, suffered a heart attack. As a protégé of the popular Long, Vickie slowly began to regain the fans' trust again. Vickie, however, then revealed a torrid tryst with Edge. The cunning GM proceeded to abuse her power to ensure the "Rated-R Superstar" would become World Heavyweight Champion.

With championship gold strapped around her lover's waist, Vickie began to build a powerful faction around her, starting with Edge look-alikes Curt Hawkins and Zack Ryder. She later added Chavo and Bam Neely. Collectively known as La Familia, the faction quickly snatched up additional championships, as Chavo claimed the ECW Championship and Hawkins & Ryder won the WWE Tag Team titles.

Victor Rivera

YEARS ACTIVE 1960 1969 | 1970 1979 | 1980 1989 | 1990 1999 | 2000 PRESENT

| HT | 6'2" | WT | 240 lbs. | FROM | Puerto Rico | SIGNATURE MOVE | Cannonball |

| TITLE HISTORY | International Tag Team Champion, World Tag Team Champion |

Victor Rivera's career began in the late 1960s, but he rose to prominence in December 1969 when he was awarded Bruno Sammartino's half of the International Tag Team Championship with partner the Battman. Rivera also traveled the National Wrestling Alliance in the early 1970s, mainly in the Los Angeles Territory. In March 1975 Victor worked with Dominic DeNucci to defeat the Valiant Brothers for the World Tag Team Championship. Rivera split time for the rest of the decade in the NWA and WWE and made his last WWE appearance in 1989. Victor Rivera will be remembered forever by fans as a beloved champion who fought on the side of good for three decades.

Victoria 🇺🇸

HT 5'8"

FROM San Bernardino, California

SIGNATURE MOVE

Widow's Peak

TITLE HISTORY

Women's Champion

YEARS ACTIVE

 1960 1969 1970 1979 1980 1989 1990 1999 **2000 PRESENT**

In 2002, WWE was introduced to Victoria, who quickly proved she was a different type of Diva. She gained notoriety when she nailed Trish Stratus in the back with a steel chair. That November, she beat Trish for the Women's Championship and held the prize for almost five months, often with the help of Steven Richards.

Almost a year after winning her first championship this dangerous black widow kept spun her web of pain in the first-ever Women's Steel Cage Match where she defeated Lita. Victoria's winning ways continued for many months, including a second title run that started in February 2004. That March, Victoria faced Molly Holly in a Hair vs. Title match at WrestleMania XX.

In June of 2007 Victoria found herself on *SmackDown* where she continues to strive for the WWE Divas Championship and aims to crush any Diva foolish enough to stand in her way.

VINCENT J. MCMAHON

The global phenomenon known today as WWE would not exist had it not been for Vincent J. McMahon. The father of current WWE Chairman Vincent K. McMahon, the elder McMahon used his keen business acumen and unparalleled passion for wrestling to lay the groundwork for what would become the most successful sports-entertainment company in the history of the world.

The son of Rose and Jess McMahon, Vincent J. was born on July 6, 1915 in Harlem. He spent much of his childhood roaming the backstage hallways of Madison Square Garden while his father Jess, an accomplished boxing promoter, booked the famed arena with some of the era's biggest names, including Jack Johnson, Jack Delaney, and Paul Berlenbach.

In the early 1930s, Vince's father took an uncharacteristic step back from the boxing world to focus his attention on promoting wrestling events. Little did anybody know at the time that Jess's decision would greatly impact generations of McMahons to follow, as well as millions of wrestling fans.

Vince had his first taste of working in the business in 1935 when he began promoting fights out of Hempstead, Long Island. Unfortunately for the up-and-coming promoter, his career was put on hold before it ever took off when he was shipped to North Carolina to serve in the Coast Guard. While there, he met and married a young girl named Vicki. While the marriage didn't last long, they did have two sons together, Vincent and Rod.

Following his divorce, Vince was eager to get back into the wrestling business in a major way. However, successful promoter Toots Mondt controlled the New York territory, so Vince was forced to take his ambition elsewhere. He eventually settled on Washington, D.C.

CAPITOL WRESTLING CORPORATION

Upon arrival, Vince purchased a small dilapidated venue he later called Capitol Arena; and on January 7, 1953, he put on the first-ever Capitol Wrestling Corporation event. Like most startups, Capitol Wrestling experienced its share of growing pains, but the company took its first real step towards greatness when Vince decided to embrace television, a new technology at the time.

On January 5, 1956, Capitol Wrestling produced its first-ever television program. The show was an instant hit. Within six months, Capitol Wrestling was in high demand as far north as the prestigious New York market, which was controlled by Mondt at the time. Some of the regular weekly viewers of Capitol Wrestling included General Douglas MacArthur and former First Lady Bess Truman.

Proving that timing is everything, Vince miraculously was able to promote Capitol Wrestling shows at Madison Square Garden while Mondt had his promoter's license temporarily suspended. Vince's wrestling product was an instant hit with Northeast fans, which infuriated Mondt and many other of the area's promoters. While those promoters were busy pouting, Vince used his television product to take over the territory.

FORGING AN ALLIANCE

By 1960, Vince was the sole survivor of the promoters' battle for the Northeast. Vince welcomed former adversary Mondt into Capitol Wrestling as a partner. In what would eventually prove to be one of the most important talent signings in sports-entertainment history, Capitol Wrestling assumed the booking rights to Buddy Rogers in 1960. One year later, Rogers captured the National Wrestling Alliance (NWA) Championship. The victory provided an amazing opportunity for Vince to use Rogers' drawing power to sell out Madison Square Garden time after time. Realizing he had a hot commodity on his hands, Vince also only allowed Rogers to defend his title outside of the Northeast on very rare occasions. This didn't sit well with the other NWA promoters, who eventually demanded Rogers cease his reign. The promoters got their wish when Lou Thesz defeated Rogers for the title in Toronto on January 24, 1963.

WORLD WIDE WRESTLING FEDERATION

Vince refused to recognize the title change, claiming a championship could not change hands during a one-fall match (championship matches were traditionally two-out-of-three falls at this time). To further show his dissatisfaction, Vince made the perilous decision to withdraw Capitol Wrestling from the NWA and start his own independent wrestling promotion. Shortly thereafter, the World Wide Wrestling Federation was born, and Buddy Rogers was its first champion.

After buying out Mondt in 1969, Vince proved his generosity by splitting his former partner's shares and offering them to longtime confidants Gorilla Monsoon, Arnold Skaaland, and Phil Zacko. Together, they brought professional wrestling into the 1970s and ushered in such legendary names as Andre the Giant, Pedro Morales, and "Superstar" Billy Graham.

After nearly 50 years in the business, Vince decided it was time to retire in 1982. The successful promoter planned on passing on the company to Monsoon, but his ambitious son Vincent K. had other plans. Just prior to Monsoon assuming leadership, the young McMahon convinced his father and his partners to sell the entire company to him.

Over the next several years, Vince watched his son incorporate the same formula for success he used when taking over the Northeast decades prior. The only difference was that Vincent K. wasn't interested in simply ruling a single territory. Instead, the determined entrepreneur intended on taking over the entire nation, and eventually the globe.

The young McMahon's plans to put other wrestling promotions out of business originally didn't sit well with his father, who grew up in a business that only knew separate territories. Furthermore, the elder McMahon had friends in many of the other territories his son planned on taking over. As a result, the father-son duo butted heads over the company's future on several occasions. In the end, after seeing his son gain amazing success in a short period of time, Vince came around and offered his support to Vincent K.

On January 23, 1984, Vince walked the halls of his home away from home, Madison Square Garden, for the final time. In the main event of the evening, a young newcomer called Hulk Hogan defeated the Iron Sheik for the WWE Championship. A proud Vince watched as The Hulkster's victory instantly ushered in his son's new vision of sports-entertainment.

On May 27, 1984, Vincent J. McMahon passed away after a battle with pancreatic cancer. He was 68.

In the months following Vince's death, Vincent K. took his company to heights never imagined before, thanks in large part to the unbelievable success of the first-ever *WrestleMania* at Madison Square Garden. Like his father before him, Vincent K. also embraced technological advances when he made his product available on pay-per-view. These early moves help build the foundation for today's sports-entertainment empire known as WWE, but none of it would have been possible had it not been for the foresight and groundwork put in place by the father of WWE, Vincent J. McMahon.

VINCENT K. MCMAHON

| HT | 6'2" | WT | 248 lbs. | FROM | Greenwich, Connecticut | SIGNATURE MOVE | Power Walk |

YEARS ACTIVE 1960/1969 1970/1979 1980/1989 1990/1999 2000/PRESENT

TITLE HISTORY WWE Champion, ECW Champion

Vince McMahon did not meet his biological father until the age of 12, an event that would forever change the direction of his life. From that day, he became enamored with professional wrestling. However, the elder McMahon wanted his son to become either a physician or attorney and sent a protesting Vince to military school. As Vince grew up, major career influences continued to be the wrestling kind. He even patterned himself after the extravagant Superstar, Dr. Jerry Graham and at one point bleached his hair blond to duplicate the looks of the good doctor. After graduating from college, he married the love of his life and entrepreneurial muse Linda Marie Edwards. Vince's unwavering ambition propelled him to do everything he could to get into the business he prized above all else. His father did everything he could to keep him out. After a few years as a reluctant traveling salesman, Vince's dream finally came true.

In 1971, Vince McMahon had one chance to prove himself in the arena he longed to enter. Failure would put him out of the business forever; success meant a ticket to the main event. Thankfully, his effort in Bangor, Maine was a huge success, and Vince became the third generation McMahon promoter. As he learned the ropes of the business, another opportunity came his way in 1972. Right before a show was to go on the air, then-announcer Ray Morgan tried to hold up the McMahons for more money. The elder McMahon promptly showed Ray the way out. As the door closed for Mr. Morgan, it opened for the young Vince McMahon, and he became the new voice of WWE. As hundreds of thousands of fans watched every week on television, few people knew the major role Vince was playing behind the scenes. For the remainder of the 1970s he was a driving force behind the company's success, responsible for an almost quadruple increase in its television syndication. Vince's innovative implementation of his father's business formula prepared him to turn the corner, and catapult the company into the era of sports-entertainment.

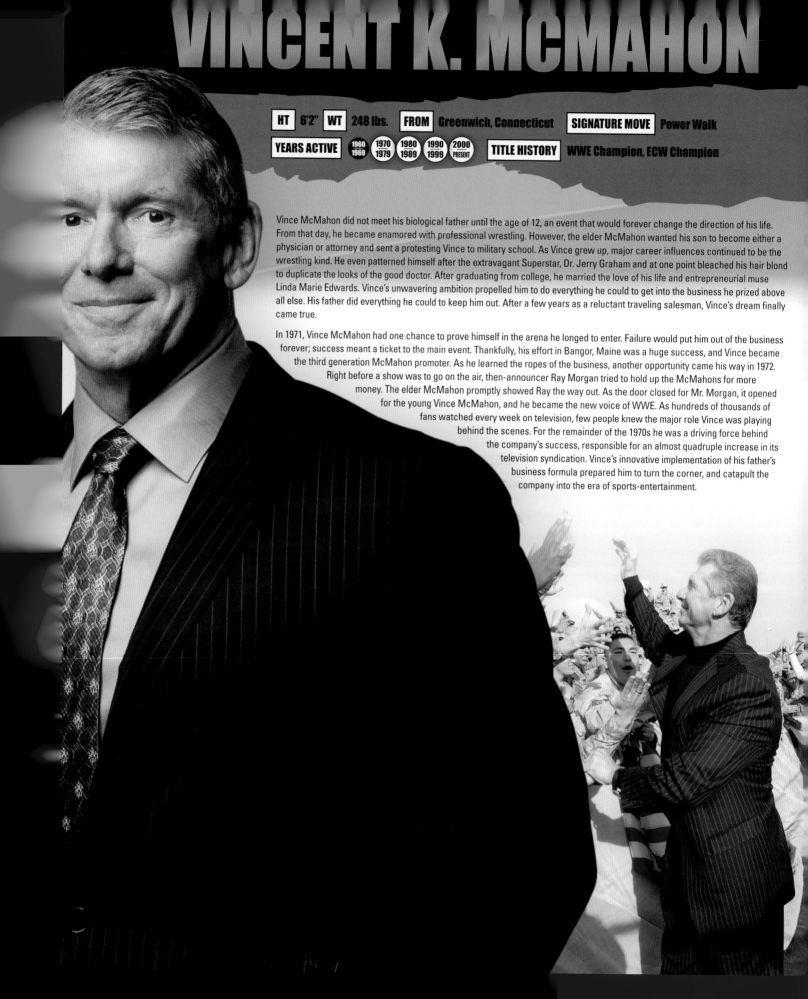

TITAN SPORTS AND HULKAMANIA

In 1980, the entrepreneurial McMahon edged toward the pinnacle as he incorporated Titan Sports. In 1982, he and his wife, Linda, acquired Capital Wrestling Company shares, taking control of World Wrestling Entertainment, and ultimately changing the model of the professional wrestling business. Vince adopted the formula his father created for dominance in the Northeast section of the United States and began implementing key initiatives to expand the company's reach. As he took the first steps toward expansion, Vince approached many of the members of the old wrestling territory fiefdoms and offered them buy-outs. Set in their ways and resting on past laurels, they laughed him out of their offices. They didn't see that the days of great moments in the ring being confined to a specific geographic area were quickly coming to an end. In a classic example of "He who laughs last, laughs loudest," Vince flexed his entrepreneurial muscle and assembled a world-class roster of Superstars. His vision of global expansion was complete when he orchestrated the return of the 6'7", 303 lbs. Hulk Hogan. Audiences were captivated by Hogan, and with McMahon as the brains, and Hulk Hogan providing the brawn, the two made an unstoppable team. As every ring of the bell brought an amazing match, World Wrestling Entertainment steamrolled through the United States, breaking down the imaginary walls that had protected the territory system against legitimate competition for decades.

In 1985, with Hulkamania running wild, and wrestling experiencing its second "Golden Age," the driven McMahon rolled the dice and bet it all on a one-time experiment called *WrestleMania*. This star-studded event garnered global attention as it featured Muhammad Ali, Liberace, The Rockettes, Billy Martin, and Mr. T. The happening became an annual phenomenon, and today *WrestleMania* is considered the greatest sports-entertainment spectacle on Earth. After the success of *WrestleMania*, McMahon brought WWE to network television with a bi-monthly replacement for *Saturday Night Live* called *Saturday Night's Main Event*. A company that was once a successful regional entity was now a global entertainment powerhouse. WWE exploded with television programs, pay-per-view events, a monthly magazine, home video, action figures, official Superstar merchandise, and interactive video game software. The era of sports-entertainment had arrived and tens of millions of fans around the globe were watching World Wrestling Entertainment with an indescribable fervor.

In 1987 he achieved the unthinkable and packed 93,173 fans into the Pontiac Silverdome to see Hulk Hogan battle Andre the Giant for the WWE Championship in the main event of *WrestleMania III*. As Hogan took his step towards immortality, WWE solidified its position as the premiere sports-entertainment company in the world.

SPORTS-ENTERTAINMENT, LIVE ON TV!

As McMahon and his Superstars marched into the 1990s setting records for live crowd attendance, pay-per-view buy rate revenue, cable television ratings, and licensed merchandise sales, McMahon once again changed the face of broadcast television. In January 1993, he launched *Monday Night Raw*. In 1995, media magnate Ted Turner chose to go head-to-head with Vince McMahon and broadcast his competing *WCW Monday Nitro* during the same time-slot on his own network, which lead to the Monday Night Wars.

After a number of duplicitous gambits and billions of dollars, World Championship Wrestling (WCW) became a formidable opponent, and took the lead in the sports-entertainment television ratings. Now Vince was fighting for his company and his livelihood. He reinvented and reconfigured his entrepreneurial game plan, adding a new persona to the mix. Once again, he would literally and figuratively change the face of sports-entertainment.

At the 1997 *Survivor Series*, in the wake of "The Montreal Incident," Vince wiped Bret "Hit Man" Hart's spit off his face and in that one fell swoop, Vince McMahon, the broadcaster, morphed into "Mr. McMahon," and an infamous, wicked character was born. Since Vince always believed adaptation is the key to survival, the Attitude Era bombarded television sets everywhere and a rivalry between "Mr. McMahon" and Stone Cold Steve Austin propelled WWE to fantastical heights. Now Vince McMahon was recognized for his maniacal acts in the ring, as well as for his dramatic business accomplishments outside it. In 1999, World Wrestling Entertainment made history when it became a publicly traded company. Now that its fans could truly be part of the company's success, WWE proved that it ruled Wall Street and the world.

A NEW MILLENIUM

In March 2001, the WWE emerged as the victor of the Monday Night Wars after the McMahon family acquired WCW. In November 2001, riding the wave of success from earlier in the year, Vince created a club that required a specific act to join. Unlike other groups characterized by prestige and distinction, the Vince McMahon Kiss My Ass Club was designed for individuals to kiss the Chairman's bare posterior or suffer the threat of suspension or termination.

Vince started the year 2003 on a crusade to kill the cultural ideology he helped create—the red and yellow of Hulkamania. This led to a Street Fight at *WrestleMania XIX* between the Chairman and future WWE Hall of Famer. This flight of fisticuffs was 20 years in the making and as the bell rang, the line between entertainment and reality was obliterated. As two decades of history blended into one historic moment the two men annihilated each other and donned the proverbial crimson mask. This battle showed once again that "Mr. McMahon" will do anything to entertain the fans. On September 18, the entrepreneurial pioneer in promoting, television, marketing, and business took his rightful place —next to his father— among the greatest figures of the world's most famous arena. Inducted in by his children Shane and Stephanie, Vince McMahon became a member of the Madison Square Garden Hall of Fame. In March 2008 Vince joined entertainment immortals when he received a star on the Hollywood Walk of Fame.

Despite all the accolades for his mastery behind-the-scenes and in front of the camera, there is another side of the WWE Chairman which humbles his most vocal opponents: his boundless philanthropy and patriotism. Vince McMahon works with the Special Olympics; he launched a non-partisan campaign to help Americans register to vote; he travels to the Middle East each year with Superstars to host the *Tribute To The Troops* program; and along with his wife, Linda, he is on the Honorary National Board of The Make-A-Wish Foundation. For the WWE Chairman, it's not just about giving back. It's about leading by example.

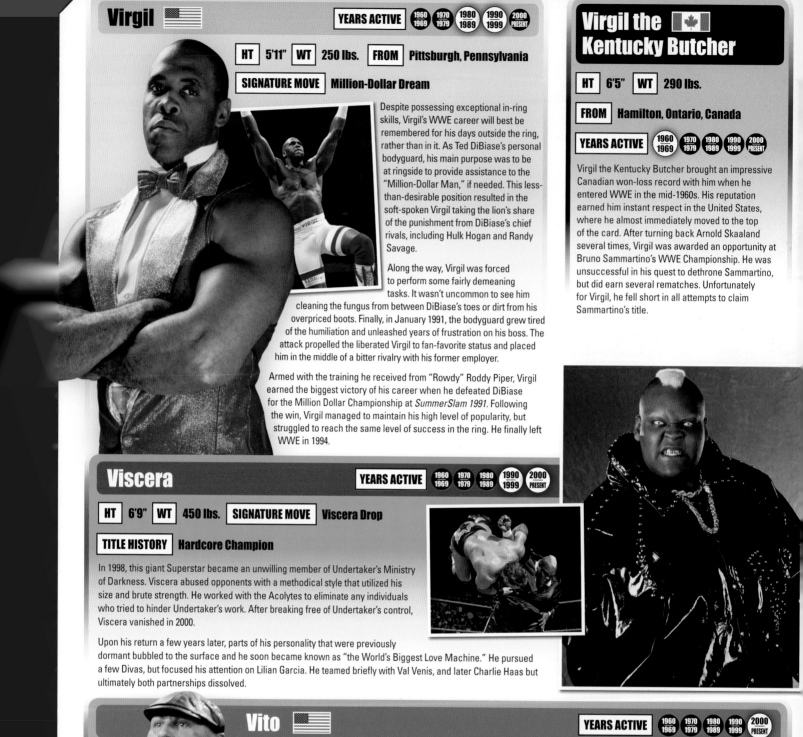

Virgil 🇺🇸

| **YEARS ACTIVE** | 1960 1969 | 1970 1979 | **1980 1989** | **1990 1999** | 2000 PRESENT |

| **HT** 5'11" | **WT** 250 lbs. | **FROM** Pittsburgh, Pennsylvania |

SIGNATURE MOVE Million-Dollar Dream

Despite possessing exceptional in-ring skills, Virgil's WWE career will best be remembered for his days outside the ring, rather than in it. As Ted DiBiase's personal bodyguard, his main purpose was to be at ringside to provide assistance to the "Million-Dollar Man," if needed. This less-than-desirable position resulted in the soft-spoken Virgil taking the lion's share of the punishment from DiBiase's chief rivals, including Hulk Hogan and Randy Savage.

Along the way, Virgil was forced to perform some fairly demeaning tasks. It wasn't uncommon to see him cleaning the fungus from between DiBiase's toes or dirt from his overpriced boots. Finally, in January 1991, the bodyguard grew tired of the humiliation and unleashed years of frustration on his boss. The attack propelled the liberated Virgil to fan-favorite status and placed him in the middle of a bitter rivalry with his former employer.

Armed with the training he received from "Rowdy" Roddy Piper, Virgil earned the biggest victory of his career when he defeated DiBiase for the Million Dollar Championship at *SummerSlam 1991*. Following the win, Virgil managed to maintain his high level of popularity, but struggled to reach the same level of success in the ring. He finally left WWE in 1994.

Virgil the Kentucky Butcher 🇨🇦

| **HT** 6'5" | **WT** 290 lbs. |

| **FROM** Hamilton, Ontario, Canada |

| **YEARS ACTIVE** | **1960 1969** | 1970 1979 | 1980 1989 | 1990 1999 | 2000 PRESENT |

Virgil the Kentucky Butcher brought an impressive Canadian won-loss record with him when he entered WWE in the mid-1960s. His reputation earned him instant respect in the United States, where he almost immediately moved to the top of the card. After turning back Arnold Skaaland several times, Virgil was awarded an opportunity at Bruno Sammartino's WWE Championship. He was unsuccessful in his quest to dethrone Sammartino, but did earn several rematches. Unfortunately for Virgil, he fell short in all attempts to claim Sammartino's title.

Viscera

| **YEARS ACTIVE** | 1960 1969 | 1970 1979 | 1980 1989 | **1990 1999** | 2000 PRESENT |

| **HT** 6'9" | **WT** 450 lbs. | **SIGNATURE MOVE** Viscera Drop |

TITLE HISTORY Hardcore Champion

In 1998, this giant Superstar became an unwilling member of Undertaker's Ministry of Darkness. Viscera abused opponents with a methodical style that utilized his size and brute strength. He worked with the Acolytes to eliminate any individuals who tried to hinder Undertaker's work. After breaking free of Undertaker's control, Viscera vanished in 2000.

Upon his return a few years later, parts of his personality that were previously dormant bubbled to the surface and he soon became known as "the World's Biggest Love Machine." He pursued a few Divas, but focused his attention on Lilian Garcia. He teamed briefly with Val Venis, and later Charlie Haas but ultimately both partnerships dissolved.

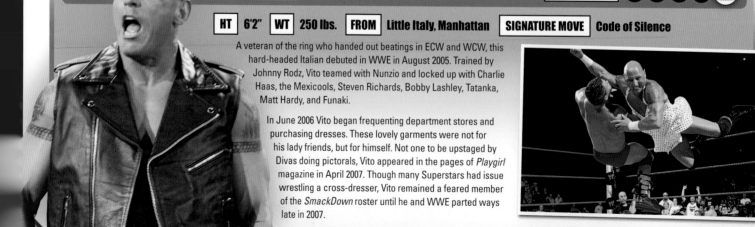

Vito 🇺🇸

| **YEARS ACTIVE** | 1960 1969 | 1970 1979 | 1980 1989 | 1990 1999 | **2000 PRESENT** |

| **HT** 6'2" | **WT** 250 lbs. | **FROM** Little Italy, Manhattan | **SIGNATURE MOVE** Code of Silence |

A veteran of the ring who handed out beatings in ECW and WCW, this hard-headed Italian debuted in WWE in August 2005. Trained by Johnny Rodz, Vito teamed with Nunzio and locked up with Charlie Haas, the Mexicools, Steven Richards, Bobby Lashley, Tatanka, Matt Hardy, and Funaki.

In June 2006 Vito began frequenting department stores and purchasing dresses. These lovely garments were not for his lady friends, but for himself. Not one to be upstaged by Divas doing pictorals, Vito appeared in the pages of *Playgirl* magazine in April 2007. Though many Superstars had issue wrestling a cross-dresser, Vito remained a feared member of the *SmackDown* roster until he and WWE parted ways late in 2007.

Vivian Vachon

HT 5'7" **FROM** Montreal, Quebec, Canada

Wrestling flowed through Vivian Vachon's veins. As the sister of legendary Superstars Mad Dog and Butcher Vachon, competing in the ring was her main focus from a young age. Still a teenager, Vivian made her professional debut in the late 1960s. A few years later, she gained her greatest accolade when she captured the AWA Women's Championship in November 1971.

Many consider Vivian to be one of the supreme female competitors of the 1970s, despite the fact that she retired midway through the decade. Vachon made a brief return to the ring in 1986 when she toured Japan with brother Mad Dog. Adding acting to her resume, Vivian also starred in the 1975 motion picture *Wrestling Queen*.

Vladamir Kozlov

HT 6'8" **WT** 302 lbs. **FROM** Moscow, Russia **SIGNATURE MOVE** Battering Ram Head Butt

Judo, sambo, and kickboxing are just a few of the fighting styles Vladimir Kozlov perfected prior to his April 2008 debut. After spending the first few months of his WWE career decimating *SmackDown* Superstars Festus, Jamie Noble, and Jimmy Wang Yang, among others, Kozlov began demanding better competition. Armed with his patented battering ram head butt, the mighty Russian started targeting WWE's top stars, including Triple H and Jeff Hardy.

With a have-no-fear attitude and multiple offensive weapons, there's no telling how many bodies Kozlov will lay waste to on his way to the top of the WWE roster.

Wahoo McDaniel

HT 6'2" **WT** 265 lbs. **FROM** Midland, Texas **SIGNATURE MOVE** Tomahawk Chop

A former football player, most notably with the New York Jets and Miami Dolphins, Wahoo McDaniel first began his in-ring career in the 1960s during the off-season. It wasn't until his time on the gridiron ended that the proud Native American began to cement his legacy as one of the toughest men to grace the ring.

Trained by the legendary Dory Funk, Sr., McDaniel rarely competed in WWE. Choosing to leave the Northeast territory to fellow Native American Chief Jay Strongbow, McDaniel instead spent the majority of his career in the Mid-Atlantic region. Armed with a devastating chop, a move perfected by various Indian Superstars, he battled many of the region's top names, including Ric Flair, Johnny Valentine, and Dory Funk, Jr.

In August 1981, McDaniel defeated Roddy Piper for the United States Championship. Unfortunately, an injury at the hands of Abdullah the Butcher forced McDaniel to vacate the championship shortly after his victory. Over the next three years, however, he went on to capture the title four more times.

Waldo Von Erich

HT 6' **WT** 260 lbs. **FROM** Germany

SIGNATURE MOVE Blitzkrieg

TITLE HISTORY

United States Tag Team Champion

YEARS ACTIVE

When this merciless remnant of the Third Reich entered WWE in 1963 audiences throughout the northeastern United States were horrified. The brother of Fritz Von Erich, Waldo operated in the ring with a controlled fury that ended careers of countless heroes. People watched in fear as Von Erich threatened favorite son Bruno Sammartino in sold-out arenas from Maine to Washington DC.

In 1965 Waldo teamed with Gene Kiniski and defeated Dr. Jerry & "Crazy" Luke Graham to capture the WWE United States Tag Team Championship. Even after he lost the title, Von Erich continued his assault and recruited "Classy" Freddie Blassie as his manager in battles against Chief Jay Strongbow and Andre the Giant. Waldo Von Erich retired from the ring in 1979, but will be remembered as a dangerous threats to any champion in any era.

The Warlord

HT 6'5" **WT** 323 lbs.

FROM Parts Unknown

SIGNATURE MOVE Full Nelson

YEARS ACTIVE

Few teams in WWE history could match strength with colossal duo of Warlord & Barbarian. Collectively known as the Powers of Pain, the muscular tandem amazed audiences with their incredible athleticism and frightening face paint.

After tangling with legendary tag teams the Hart Foundation and Demolition, including a failed attempt at unseating Ax & Smash for the World Tag Team Championship at *WrestleMania V*, the Powers of Pain went their separate ways. With manager Slick guiding him, Warlord's singles career looked bright early on. He even defeated former Intercontinental Champion Tito Santana at *SummerSlam 1990*. Unfortunately, that's where the success stopped.

Over the next several years, Warlord found himself on the wrong end of rivalries with "Texas Tornado" Kerry Von Erich and fellow strongman British Bulldog. Despite coming up short, however, Warlord did push Bulldog to the limit during their encounter at *WrestleMania VII*.

Waylon Mercy

HT 6'7" **WT** 290 lbs.

SIGNATURE MOVE Sleeperhold

YEARS ACTIVE

A man of few words but a variety of violent actions, Waylon Mercy came to WWE in 1995. He claimed to be a peaceful person and friend to all mankind. During his slow walk to the ring he shook hands with fans, ring announcers, referees, and opponents alike with an eerily calm demeanor. His interviews sent chills down people's spines as he stated, "Lives are gonna be in Waylon Mercy's hands."

When the bell rang Waylon became a man possessed and attacked opponents in a fit of rage. By October of that year Waylon was forced to leave the ring after feeling the bone-crushing effects from Diesel's Jacknife Powerbomb. Waylon Mercy was not a man to be trusted, associated with, or challenged. He could snap at the slightest move or word and make people pay dearly for such offenses.

WENDI RICHTER

| **HT** | 5'8" | **FROM** | Dallas, Texas | **SIGNATURE MOVE** | Swinging Arm Wrench |

TITLE HISTORY Women's Champion

YEARS ACTIVE 1960-1969 | 1970-1979 | **1980-1989** | 1990-1999 | 2000 PRESENT

Well Dunn

| **MEMBERS** | Timothy Well, Steve Dunn |

| **COMBINED WEIGHT** | 470 lbs. |

YEARS ACTIVE 1960-1969 | 1970-1979 | 1980-1989 | **1990-1999** | 2000 PRESENT

A well known team in the southeastern United States, Timothy Well & Steven Dunn debuted in the big time in the summer of 1993. Determined to show their talents where the world could see them, Well Dunn combined excellent tag team wrestling with relentless rule-breaking tactics.

The duo attacked the likes of the Smoking Gunns, Men On A Mission, the Bushwhackers, 1-2-3 Kid & Bob "Spark Plugg" Holly, the Headshrinkers, and the Allied Powers. Despite being contenders for WWE tag team titles, they were never able to win the prizes and left World Wrestling Entertainment in the spring of 1995.

Wendi Richter came to World Wrestling Entertainment in 1984 and was an exciting addition to the WWE roster with an impressive combination of size, agility, and power. She took audiences on a thrilling ride as she soon joined forces with Cyndi Lauper to form a groundbreaking alliance called "the Rock N' Wrestling Connection." Wendi Richter became a pop-culture phenomenon during WWE's growth into a global brand of sports-entertainment.

On July 23, 1984 Wendi ended the almost 30 year championship reign of her former mentor, Fabulous Moolah, at *The Brawl To End It All*. Despite losing to Leilani Kai, Wendi Richter remained the main attraction in the women's division. Their rematch, won by Richter, took place at the first *WrestleMania*.

Wendi lost the title in controversial fashion to the Spider, who was revealed to be Fabulous Moolah. The loss devastated her, and it proved to be Wendi Richter's last match in World Wrestling Entertainment.

Wild Red Berry

YEARS ACTIVE 1960-1969 | **1970-1979** | 1980-1989 | 1990-1999 | 2000 PRESENT

| **FROM** | Pittsburg, Kansas |

Boxer-turned-wrestler Red Berry had a reputation for being a bit outrageous. In fact, it was his unorthodox style that eventually lead to his nickname. After spending three days in a tree outside Memorial Hall in Kansas, the local newspaper dubbed Berry a "wild man." The description was perfect, and Wild Red Berry was born.

Standing only five-foot-eight, Berry had to find creative ways to win his matches, which is why he oftentimes turned to rule breaking. His defiant in-ring actions made him one of the most hated Superstars of the 1930s, 1940s, and 1950s. Berry didn't care, as his disregard for authority eventually lead to him more than fifteen championship reigns over the course of his lengthy career.

Berry continued his deviant behavior long after his in-ring career came to a close. As manager to such top stars as Gorilla Monsoon, the Fabulous Kangaroos, and Bull Ramos, Berry was not above using his signature cane as a weapon.

THE WILD SAMOANS

YEARS ACTIVE 1960–1969 · 1970–1979 · 1980–1989 · 1990–1999 · 2000 PRESENT

MEMBERS Afa, Sika · **COMBINED WEIGHT** 645 lbs. · **TITLE HISTORY** World Tag Team Champions

In the early 1970s, Afa started training with his uncle, High Chief Peter Maivia, and Rocky Johnson. Afa took what he learned and trained his brother, Sika. From there the two began a 30 year reign of terror that may never be duplicated. They tore through Stu Hart's Stampede Wrestling as well as the territories of the NWA.

In the fall of 1979, the Samoans were brought to World Wrestling Entertainment by Capt. Lou Albano. Afa & Sika ripped apart opponents and were so dominant that even as individuals they were both contenders for the WWE Championship. On April 12, 1980, they defeated "Polish Power" Ivan Putski & Tito Santana for their first World Tag Team Championship. They held the titles for five months until at the 1980 mega-event Showdown at Shea, the dream team of WWE Champion Bob Backlund & Pedro Morales beat them in a Best 2-out-of-3 Falls contest. The duo had to vacate the titles because of a rule at the time that didn't allow Backlund to hold two championships simultaneously. A tournament was arranged to crown new champs, and the Samoans defeated Tony Garea & Rene Goulet to regain the World Tag Team titles. After a loss to Garea & Rick Martel, they soon departed from WWE.

For the next two years, they dominated the Mid-South and Mid-Atlantic Wrestling scenes. However, after a call from Albano, the Wild Samoans were back in WWE frightening audiences, speaking in ancient Samoan tongues, and consuming raw fish. Their third and final title reign came at the expense of Jay & Jules Strongbow in March 1983. By 1984, they left the company.

Sika briefly returned as a singles competitor in 1992. Afa returned to manage the Headshrinkers and with Capt. Lou, and co-managed them to the World Tag Team Championship. Shortly after he left WWE, Afa opened The Wild Samoan Training Center, and today it is regarded as one of the best wrestling schools in the world.

WrestleMania 23 saw the Wild Samoans take their rightful place among the immortals of sports-entertainment when they were inducted into the WWE Hall of Fame.

William Regal

YEARS ACTIVE 1960–1969 · 1970–1979 · 1980–1989 · 1990–1999 · 2000 PRESENT

HT 6'2" · **WT** 240 lbs. · **FROM** Blackpool, England · **SIGNATURE MOVE** Regal Stretch

TITLE HISTORY World Tag Team Champion, Intercontinental Champion, European Champion, Hardcore Champion

A former King of the Ring, William Regal looks down upon the WWE roster as a group of filthy peasants. Rather than carry himself as a true monarch, the smug Superstar has proven to be nothing but a royal pain.

Luckily for Regal, he backs up his arrogant behavior with superior in-ring skills, which he developed as a teenager while competing in carnivals across the United Kingdom. By the time he reached WWE in mid-1998, he had already established himself as a legitimate technical threat in his home country of England, as well as WCW. If for some reason his natural ability failed to carry him to victory, the sly Brit was never above dipping into his tights to grab his deadly set of brass knuckles.

Over the course of his career, Regal has assumed numerous leadership responsibilities, including WWE Commissioner and *Raw* General Manager. However, it's his championship resume that's most impressive. In addition to runs with the now-defunct European and Hardcore Championships, he defeated Edge to capture the prestigious Intercontinental Championship at *Royal Rumble 2002*. He is also a noted tag team competitor, winning titles with partners Lance Storm, Eugene and Tajiri.

Willie Gilzenberg

In the early 1960s Vince McMahon, Sr. and his partners were looking to break Capitol Wrestling free from the National Wrestling Alliance. One of the key figures in this transformation was an individual who had a reputation as a sharp businessman and a pioneering promoter. When McMahon needed a savvy administrator to handle dealing with promoters, venue executives, the public and his vast array of Superstars, Willie Gilzenberg was the man for the job.

Willie was a successful promoter based out of Newark, New Jersey. As McMahon's first President, Gilzenberg influenced the careers of some of the most pivotal figures in sports-entertainment such as Antonino "Argentina" Rocca, "Nature Boy" Buddy Rogers, Bruno Sammartino, and Swede Hanson.

Sadly on November 15, 1978 this innovator of great attractions passed away. Willie Gilzenberg set the standard for the on-air positions of authority seen for decades on WWE programming.

The Wizard

| 1960 1969 | 1970 1979 | **1980 1989** | 1990 1999 | 2000 PRESENT |

His brutally scarred forehead served as a reminder of the bloody battles he competed in during his days as an active competitor; but while the cavernous ditches in The Wizard's skull were certainly disturbing, it was his relationships with the wild Kamala and Sika that freaked out fans the most.

For a brief period of time during the mid-1980s, the four-hundred-pound manager not only served as Kamala and Sika's representation, but more importantly their voices. While the untamed Superstars shouted unintelligible noises, The Wizard stood by their side to translate their offensive words.

Unlike the *Grand* Wizard (the Hall of Fame manager with whom he is oftentimes confused), The Wizard failed to bring his protégés to great success. After a brief stint by the sides of Kamala and Sika, he disappeared from the WWE scene.

The Wolfman

HT 6'2"   **WT** 260 lbs.

FROM The Wilds of Canada

SIGNATURE MOVE Hanging Neckbreaker

YEARS ACTIVE | 1960 1969 | **1970 1979** | 1980 1989 | 1990 1999 | 2000 PRESENT |

Ushered to the ring on a chain by Lou Albano, this Superstar debuted in 1970, and appeared to be half man and half beast. According to his manager, he was raised amongst the wolves of the Great White North. Once he was released from his chain the Wolfman's behavior could not be predicted and his animalistic tendencies were only controllable by Albano.

After many of his victories, television stations throughout the northeast demanded that WWE place a large X on the screen due to Wolfman's proclivity for chewing on fallen opponents and ring ropes. These disturbing acts along with lunging at referees frightened all who witnessed them and stayed in the backs of the minds of his opponents. By the late 1970s Wolfman fled WWE and returned to the Canadian wilderness. It has been over 30 years since he has been seen by humans and his location remains unknown.

WOMEN'S CHAMPIONSHIP

For more than a half of a century, the Women's Championship has been recognized as sports-entertainment's top prize for female competition. It was originally introduced to fans in September 1956, when Fabulous Moolah defeated Judy Grable to be crowned the first-ever Women's Champion. Moolah went on to maintain a firm grasp of the title for the next 27 years before finally being upended by Wendi Richter in 1984.

Despite suffering through two three-year periods of inactivity (1990-93, 1995-98), the Women's Championship is as strong as ever, thanks in large part the level of athleticism brought to the ring by recent titleholders Trish Stratus, Victoria, and Mickie James.

Women's World Tag Team Championship

The Women's World Tag Team Championship provided some of the greatest bouts in tag team wrestling history. World Wrestling Federation rings all over the world saw these femme fatales clash to capture tag team gold.

1983
- **MAY 01** — Calgary, Alberta, Canada — Velvet McIntyre & Princess Victoria are recognized as Champions

1985 — In early 1985 Princess Victoria gives her half of the championship to Desiree Peterson.
- **AUG 15** — Cairo, Egypt — The Glamour Girls defeat Velvet McIntyre & Desiree Peterson.

1988
- **JAN 24** — Hamilton, Ontario, Canada — The Jumping Bomb Angels defeat The Glamour Girls in a Best 2-out-of-3 Falls Match.
- **JUNE 08** — Omiya, Japan — The Glamour Girls defeat The Jumping Bomb Angels.
- **JAN 24** — Hamilton, Ontario, Canada — The Jumping Bomb Angels defeat The Glamour Girls in a Best 2-out-of-3 Falls Match.

In mid-1989 the Women's Tag Team Championship was retired.

WORLD HEAVYWEIGHT CHAMPIONSHIP

For close to four decades, WWE recognized only one World Champion. However, when then-WWE Champion Brock Lesnar chose to become exclusive to *SmackDown* in 2002, *Raw* was left without a top Superstar. General Manager Eric Bischoff quickly rectified the situation by dusting off the old WCW Championship and bringing it to *Raw*. He awarded the gold to Triple H, making him the first-ever World Heavyweight Champion in WWE history.

The World Heavyweight Championship remained *Raw*'s top prize until June 2005 when then-champ Batista was drafted to *SmackDown*. The change in scenery had no ill-effect on the title's prestige, as many of *SmackDown*'s top names went on to capture to gold, including Undertaker, Kurt Angle, and Edge.

2002
- **SEPT 02** — Milwaukee, WI — Triple H is awarded the World Heavyweight Championship by *Raw* General Manager Eric Bischoff
- **AUG 15** — Toronto, Ontario — Randy Orton defeats Chris Benoit
- **SEPT 12** — Portland, OR — Triple H defeats Randy Orton
- **JULY 23** — Indianapolis, IN — King Booker defeats Rey Mysterio
- **NOV 26** — Philadelphia, PA — Batista defeats King Booker

2008
- **MAR 30** — Orlando, FL — Undertaker defeats Edge
- *SmackDown* General Manager Vickie Guerrero strips Undertaker of the World Heavyweight Championship in May.

WOMEN'S CHAMPIONSHIP TIMELINE

1956
- **SEPT 18** — Baltimore, MD — Fabulous Moolah defeats Judy Grable — *Fabulous Moolah beat Judy Grable in the finals of a tournament to crown a new Women's Champion.*

1984
- **JULY 23** — New York, NY — Wendi Richter defeats Fabulous Moolah

1985
- **FEB 18** — New York, NY — Lelani Kai defeats Wendi Richter
- **MAR 31** — New York, NY — Wendi Richter defeats Lelani Kai
- **NOV 25** — New York, NY — Fabulous Moolah defeats Wendi Richter

1994
- **NOV 27** — Tokyo, Japan — Bull Nakano defeats Alundra Blayze — *Alundra Blayze beat Heidi Lee Morgan in the finals of a tournament to crown a new Women's Champion.*

1995
- **APR 03** — Poughkeepsie, NY — Alundra Blayze defeats Bull Nakano
- **AUG 27** — Pittsburgh, PA — Bertha Faye defeats Alundra Blayze
- **OCT 23** — Brandon, Manitoba — Alundra Blayze defeats Bertha Faye
- *The Women's Championship was deemed inactive in December 1995 after Alundra Blayze left WWE.*

1998
- **SEPT 21** — Sacramento, CA — Jacqueline defeats Sable

2003
- **MAR 30** — Seattle, WA — Trish Stratus defeats Victoria — *Trish Stratus pinned Victoria to become Women's Champion in a Triple Threat Match that also included Jazz.*
- **FEB 03** — Detroit, MI — Jacqueline defeats Hervina
- **MAR 30** — San Antonio, TX — Stephanie McMahon defeats Jacqueline
- **AUG 21** — Lafayette, LA — Lita defeats Stephanie McMahon
- **NOV 02** — Rochester, NY — Ivory defeats Lita — *Ivory pinned Lita to become Women's Champion in a Fatal Four Way Match that also included Trish Stratus and Jacqueline.*

2001
- **APR 01** — Houston, TX — Chyna defeats Ivory
- *Chyna was stripped of the Women's Championship upon leaving WWE in November 2001.*

- **APR 27** — Worcester, MA
- **JUNE 30** — Buffalo, NY — Jazz defeats Trish Stratus
- **JULY 28** — Colorado Springs, CO — Molly Holly defeats Gail Kim
- Gail Kim wins the Women's Championship — *Gail Kim last eliminated Victoria to become Women's Champion in a 7-Diva Battle Royal that also included Molly Holly, Trish Stratus, Ivory, Jacqueline and then-champion Jazz.*

- **SEPT 17** — Toronto, Ontario — Trish Stratus defeats Lita — *Trish Stratus retired after the match, vacating the Women's Championship.*
- **NOV 05** — Cincinnati, OH — Lita defeats Mickie James — *Lita beat Mickie James in the finals of a tournament to crown a new Women's Champion.*
- **NOV 26** — Philadelphia, PA — Mickie James defeats Lita

2007
- **FEB 19** — Bakersfield, CA — Melina defeats Mickie James
- **APR 24** — Paris, France — Mickie James defeats Melina — *Mickie James beat Melina to become Women's Champion in a Triple Threat Match that also included Victoria.*
- **APR 24** — Paris, France — Melina defeats Mickie James

World Heavyweight Championship

2007
- **JUNE 01** — San Diego, CA — Edge defeats Undertaker
- **JUNE 30** — Oklahoma City, OK — CM Punk defeats Edge
- **SEP 07** — Cleveland, OH — Chris Jericho becomes World Heavyweight Champion. *Chris Jericho pinned Kane in a Championship Scramble Match that also included Batista, JBL, and Rey Mysterio.*
- **OCT 26** — Phoenix, AZ — Batista defeats Chris Jericho
- **NOV 03** — Tampa, FL — Chris Jericho defeats Batista
- **NOV 23** — Boston, MA — John Cena defeats Chris Jericho

2007
- **APR 01** — Detroit, MI — Undertaker defeats Batista
- **MAY 08** — Pittsburgh, PA — Edge defeats Undertaker
- **JULY 17** — Laredo, TX — The Great Khali wins World Heavyweight Championship. *The Great Khali last eliminated Kane and Batista in a Battle Royal to crown the new World Heavyweight Champion.*
- **SEPT 16** — Memphis, TN — Batista defeats the Great Khali. *Batista pinned The Great Khali to win the World Heavyweight Championship in a Triple Threat Match that also included Rey Mysterio.*
- **DEC 16** — Pittsburgh, PA — Edge defeats Batista. *Edge pinned Batista to win the World Heavyweight Championship in a Triple Threat Match that also included Undertaker.*

> Raw General Manager Eric Bischoff declares the World Heavyweight Championship vacant in December 2004 after a controversial ending to a title defense.

2005
- **JAN 09** — Puerto Rico — Triple H defeats Randy Orton. *Triple H pinned Randy Orton in an Elimination Chamber Match that also included Edge, Chris Benoit, Chris Jericho, and Batista.*
- **APR 03** — Los Angeles, CA — Batista defeats Triple H

2006
- **JAN 01** — Philadelphia, PA — Kurt Angle wins World Heavyweight Championship. *Kurt Angle last eliminated Mark Henry in a Battle Royal to crown the new World Heavyweight Champion.*
- **APR 02** — Chicago, IL — Rey Mysterio defeats Randy Orton. *Rey Mysterio pinned Randy Orton to win the World Heavyweight Championship in a Triple Threat Match that also included Kurt Angle.*

2003
- **NOV 11** — New York, NY — Shawn Michaels defeats Triple H. *Shawn Michaels last eliminated Triple H in an Elimination Chamber Match that also included Chris Jericho, Kane, Booker T, and Rob Van Dam.*
- **DEC 15** — Fort Lauderdale FL — Triple H defeats Shawn Michaels

2004
- **SEPT 21** — Hershey, PA — Goldberg defeats Triple H
- **DEC 14** — Orlando, FL — Triple H defeats Goldberg. *Triple H pinned Goldberg in a Triple Threat Match that also included Kane.*

2004
- **MAR 14** — New York, NY — Chris Benoit defeats Triple H. *Chris Benoit forced Triple H to tap out to win the World Heavyweight Championship in a Triple Threat Match that also included Shawn Michaels.*

Women's Championship

2008
- **JUNE 24** — Houston, TX — Candice defeats Melina
- **OCT 07** — Chicago, IL — Beth Phoenix defeats Candice

2008
- **APR 14** — London, England — Mickie James defeats Beth Phoenix
- **AUG 18** — Indianapolis, IN — Beth Phoenix becomes Women's Champion. *In an intergender Winner Takes All Match, Santino Marella & Beth Phoenix defeated Kofi Kingston & Mickie James.*

2004
- **FEB 23** — Omaha, NE — Victoria defeats Lita. *Victoria last eliminated Lita to become Women's Champion in a Fatal Four Way Elimination Match that also included Jazz, Jacqueline, Molly Holly.*
- **JUNE 13** — Columbus, OH — Trish Stratus defeats Lita. *Trish Stratus pinned Lita to become Women's Champion in a Fatal Four Way Match that also included Gail Kim and then-champion Victoria.*
- **DEC 06** — Charlotte, NC — Lita defeats Trish Stratus

2005
- **JAN 09** — Puerto Rico — Trish Stratus defeats Lita

2006
- **APR 02** — Chicago, IL — Mickie James defeats Trish Stratus
- **AUG 14** — Charlottesville, VA — Lita defeats Mickie James

2002
- **NOV 18** — Greensboro, NC — Trish Stratus defeats Ivory. *Trish Stratus pinned Ivory to become Women's Champion in a Six-Pack Challenge Match that also included Jazz, Jacqueline, Molly Holly, and Lita.*
- **FEB 04** — Las Vegas, NV — Jazz defeats Trish Stratus
- **MAY 13** — Toronto, Ontario — Trish Stratus defeats Jazz. *Trish Stratus pinned Jazz to become Women's Champion in a Tag Team Match where Bubba Ray Dudley teamed with Stratus and Steven Richards teamed with Jazz.*
- **JUNE 23** — Los Angeles, CA — Molly Holly defeats Trish Stratus
- **SEPT 22** — Columbus, OH — Trish Stratus defeats Molly Holly
- **NOV 17** — New York, NY — Victoria defeats Trish Stratus

1999
- **NOV 15** — St. Louis, MO — Sable defeats Jacqueline
- **MAY 10** — Orlando, FL — Debra defeats Sable
- **JUNE 14** — Worcester, MA — Ivory defeats Debra
- **OCT 17** — Cleveland, OH — Fabulous Moolah defeats Ivory
- **OCT 25** — Providence, RI — Ivory defeats Fabulous Moolah
- **DEC 12** — Sunrise, FL — The Kat defeats Ivory. *The Kat won the Women's Championship by besting Jacqueline, B.B., and Ivory in an Evening Gown in a Pool Match.*

2000
- **JAN 31** — Pittsburgh, PA — Hervina defeats The Kat

1986
- **JULY 03** — Brisbane, Australia — Velvet McIntyre defeats Fabulous Moolah
- **JULY 09** — Sydney, Australia — Fabulous Moolah defeats Velvet McIntyre

1987
- **JULY 24** — Houston, TX — Sherri Martel defeats Fabulous Moolah

1988
- **OCT 07** — Paris, France — Rockin' Robin defeats Sherri Martel

> Rockin' Robin held the Women's Championship until 1990 when the title was deemed inactive.

1993
- **DEC 13** — Poughkeepsie, NY — Alundra Blayze defeats Heidi Lee Morgan

World Martial Arts Heavyweight Championship

The Martial Arts Heavyweight Championship was awarded to Japanese *puroresu* legend Antonio Inoki by Vincent J. McMahon. The belt was defended all over the world until 1985, when it solely appeared in Japan. This championship was for skilled competitors with specialties in a variety of fighting disciplines.

The championship would be retired by Antonio Inoki during the middle of his second title reign. However, in 1990 a new championship was created by New Japan Pro Wrestling called The Greatest 18 Championship. This title was represented with the same Martial Arts Heavyweight Championship belt that was given to Inoki in 1978 by Vince McMahon, Sr.

1978

DEC 18 — New York, NY

Antonio Inoki makes his debut with the championship and successfully defends the title against Texas Red at Madison Square Garden.

MAY 25 — Osaka, Japan

Antonio Inoki defeats Shota Chochoshvili

1989

APR 24 — Tokyo, Japan

Shota Chochoshvili defeats Antonio Inoki

WORLD TAG TEAM CHAMPIONSHIP

With more than three decades of legends linked to its lineage, the World Tag Team Championship is recognized as the most historic prize in all of tag team wrestling. In its first decade of existence, Hall of Famers like the Blackjacks and the Valiants wore the championship proudly before passing the torch to the flashier teams of the 1980s.

Demolition and the Hart Foundation dominated the tag team scene in the 1980s, forging many unforgettable rivalries with the British Bulldogs, Strike Force, and the Brain Busters. The memorable matches between these teams began to catch the attention of many young, aspiring superstars. As a result, striving to become a tag-team specialist, which was once looked upon as a secondary achievement by some, quickly became en vogue.

Before long, the fans growing up in awe of the great tag teams of the 1980s were Superstars themselves. Teams like the Hardy Boys and Edge & Christian were living their lifelong dreams as World Tag Team Champions, while introducing a new highflying, have-no-fear attitude to the tag team division that is so popular today.

1971

JUNE 03 — New Orleans, LA

Luke Graham & Tarzan Tyler defeat Dick the Bruiser & the Sheik

DEC 06 — New York, NY

Luke Graham & Tarzan Tyler beat Dick the Bruiser & the Sheik in the finals of a tournament to crown new World Tag Team Champions.

1972

Karl Gotch & Rene Goulet defeat Luke Graham & Tarzan Tyler

1975

MAY 13 — Philadelphia, PA

Victor Rivera & Dominic DeNucci defeat Jimmy & Johnny Valiant

Pat Barrett became Dominic DeNucci's partner when Victor Rivera left the WWE in June 1975.

AUG 26 — Philadelphia, PA

The Blackjacks defeat Dominic DeNucci & Pat Barrett

NOV 08 — Philadelphia, PA

Tony Parisi & Louis Ceran defeat the Blackjacks

1978

MAR 14 — Philadelphia, PA

Dino Bravo & Dominic DeNucci defeat Professor Tanaka & Mr. Fuji

JUNE 26 — New York, NY

The Yukon Lumberjacks defeat Dino Bravo & Dominic DeNucci

NOV 21 — Allentown, PA

Tony Garea & Larry Zbyszko defeat the Yukon Lumberjacks

1981

NOV 08 — Philadelphia, PA

Tony Garea & Rick Martel defeat the Samoans

MAR 17 — Allentown, PA

The Moondogs defeat Tony Garea & Rick Martel

JULY 21 — Allentown, PA

Tony Garea & Rick Martel defeat the Moondogs

OCT 13 — Allentown, PA

Mr. Fuji & Mr. Saito defeat Tony Garea & Rick Martel

1985

JAN 21 — Hartford, CT

Mike Rotundo & Barry Windham defeat Adrian Adonis & Dick Murdoch

MAR 31 — New York, NY

The Iron Sheik & Nikolai Volkoff defeat Mike Rotundo & Barry Windham

JUNE 17 — Poughkeepsie, NY

Mike Rotundo & Barry Windham defeat the Iron Sheik & Nikolai Volkoff

AUG 24 — Philadelphia, PA

Brutus Beefcake & Greg Valentine defeat Mike Rotundo & Barry Windham

1990

APR 01 — Toronto, Ontario

Demolition defeat Andre the Giant & Haku

AUG 27 — Philadelphia, PA

The Hart Foundation defeat Demolition

1991

MAR 24 — Los Angeles, CA

The Nasty Boys defeat the Hart Foundation

AUG 26 — New York, NY

The Legion of Doom defeat the Nasty Boys

1994

JAN 10 — Richmond, VA

Marty Jannetty & 1-2-3 Kid defeat the Quebecers

JAN 17 — New York, NY

The Quebecers defeat Marty Jannetty & 1-2-3 Kid

MAR 29 — London, England

Men on a Mission defeat the Quebecers

MAR 31 — Sheffield, England

The Quebecers defeat Men on a Mission

SEPT 07 — Louisville, KY

The Headbangers last eliminated Owen Hart & Davey Boy Smith in a Fatal Four Way Elimination Match that also included the Legion of Doom and the Godwinns.

SEPT 25 — Grand Rapids, MI

The World Tag Team Championship was returned to Owen Hart & Yokozuna after their lawyer threatened legal action if the duo was not recognized as rightful champs.

SEPT 25 — Grand Rapids, MI

The Smokin' Gunns defeat Owen Hart & Yokozuna

An injury to Billy Gunn's neck forced the Smokin' Gunns to vacate the World Tag Team Championship on February 15, 1996.

OCT 05 — St. Louis, MO

The Godwinns defeat the Headbangers

OCT 07 — Topeka, KS

The Legion of Doom defeat the Godwinns

NOV 24 — Fayetteville, NC

New Age Outlaws defeat the Legion of Doom

1998

MAR 29 — Boston, MA: Cactus Jack & Chainsaw Charlie defeat New Age Outlaws

Cactus Jack & Chainsaw Charlie were forced to vacate the World Tag Team Championship on March 30, due to a controversial ending to their title victory.

MAR 30 — Albany, NY: New Age Outlaws defeat Cactus Jack & Chainsaw Charlie in a Steel Cage Match to crown new World Tag Team Champions.

JULY 13 — East Rutherford, NJ: Kane & Mankind defeat New Age Outlaws

JULY 26 — Fresno, CA: Stone Cold Steve Austin & Undertaker defeat Kane & Mankind

AUG 10 — Omaha, NE: Kane & Mankind beat Stone Cold Steve Austin & Undertaker to win the World Tag Team Championship in a Fatal Four Way Match that also included the New Age Outlaws and the Rock & D'Lo Brown.

continued on next page

1996

MAR 31 — Anaheim, CA: The Bodydonnas defeat the Godwinns in the finals of a tournament to crown new World Tag Team Champions.

MAY 19 — New York, NY: The Godwinns defeat the Bodydonnas

MAY 26 — Florence, SC: The Smokin' Guns defeat The Godwinns

SEPT 22 — Philadelphia, PA: Owen Hart & Davey Boy Smith defeat The Smokin' Guns

1997

MAY 25 — Evansville, IN: Stone Cold Steve Austin & Shawn Michaels defeat Owen Hart & Davey Boy Smith

An injury to Shawn Michaels forced Stone Cold Steve Austin & HBK to vacate the World Tag Team Championship in July 1997.

JULY 14 — San Antonio, TX: Stone Cold Steve Austin & Dude Love defeat Owen Hart & Davey Boy Smith

APR 26 — Burlington, VT: The Headshrinkers defeat the Quebecers

AUG 28 — Indianapolis, IN: Diesel & Shawn Michaels defeat the Headshrinkers

Diesel & Shawn Michaels were forced to vacate the World Tag Team Championship on November 23, 1994, after they were unable to co-exist as a team.

1995

JAN 22 — Tampa, FL: Bob Holly & 1-2-3 Kid defeat Bam Bam Bigelow & Tatanka in the finals of a tournament to crown new World Tag Team Champions.

JAN 23 — Palmetto, FL: The Smokin' Guns defeat Bob Holly & 1-2-3 Kid

APR 02 — Hartford, CT: Owen Hart & Yokozuna defeat the Smokin' Guns

SEPT 24 — Saginaw, MI: Diesel & Shawn Michaels defeat Owen Hart & Yokozuna

1992

FEB 07 — Denver, CO: Money, Inc. defeat the Legion of Doom

JULY 20 — Worcester, MA: Natural Disasters defeat Money, Inc.

OCT 13 — Regina, Saskatchewan: Money, Inc. defeats Natural Disasters

1993

JUN 14 — Columbus, OH: The Steiners defeat Money, Inc.

JUNE 16 — Rockford, IL: Money, Inc. defeat the Steiners

JUNE 19 — St. Louis, MO: The Steiners defeat Money, Inc.

SEPT 13 — New York, NY: The Quebecers defeat the Steiners

1986

APR 07 — Rosemont, IL: The British Bulldogs defeat Brutus Beefcake & Greg Valentine

1987

JAN 26 — Tampa, FL: The Hart Foundation defeat the British Bulldogs

OCT 27 — Syracuse, NY: Strike Force defeat the Hart Foundation

1988

MAR 27 — Atlantic City, NJ: Demolition defeat Strike Force

1989

JULY 18 — Worcester, MA: Brain Busters defeat Demolition

OCT 02 — Wheeling, WV: Demolition defeat Brain Busters

DEC 13 — Huntsville, AL: Andre the Giant & Haku defeat Demolition

1982

JUNE 28 — New York, NY: Jules & Chief Jay Strongbow defeat Mr. Fuji & Mr. Saito

JULY 13 — Allentown, PA: Mr. Fuji & Mr. Saito defeat Jules & Chief Jay Strongbow

OCT 26 — Allentown, PA: Jules & Chief Jay Strongbow defeat Mr. Fuji & Mr. Saito

1983

MAR 08 — Allentown, PA: The Samoans defeat Jules & Chief Jay Strongbow

NOV 15 — Allentown, PA: Tony Atlas & Rocky Johnson defeat the Samoans

1984

APR 17 — Hamburg, PA: Adrian Adonis & Dick Murdoch defeat Tony Atlas & Rocky Johnson

1979

MAR 06 — Allentown, PA: Johnny & Jerry Valiant defeat Tony Garea & Larry Zbyszko

OCT 22 — New York, NY: Ivan Putski & Tito Santana defeat Johnny & Jerry Valiant

1980

APR 12 — Philadelphia, PA: The Samoans defeat Ivan Putski & Tito Santana

AUG 09 — New York, NY: Bob Backlund & Pedro Morales defeat the Samoans

Shortly after winning the World Tag Team Championship, Bob Backlund & Perdro Morales were forced to vacate the title due to Backlund already holding the WWE Championship.

SEPT 09 — Allentown, PA: The Samoans defeat Tony Garea & Rene Goulet in the finals of a tournament to crown new World Tag Team Champions.

1976

MAY 11 — Philadelphia, PA: The Executioners defeat Tony Parisi & Louis Cerdan

The Executioners were stripped of the World Tag Team Championship in December 1976 when they illegally used a third Executioner during a match.

DEC 07 — Philadelphia, PA: Chief Jay Strongbow & Billy White Wolf win the World Tag Team Championship

Chief Jay Strongbow & Billy White Wolf won a three-team tournament to capture the World Tag Team Championship. The tournament also included The Executioners, and Nikolai Volkoff & Tor Kamata.

Injury forced Strongbow & Wolf to vacate the titles in August 1977.

1977

SEPT 27 — Philadelphia, PA: Professor Tanaka & Mr. Fuji defeat Tony Garea & Larry Zbyszko in the finals of a tournament to crown new World Tag Team Champions.

1973

FEB 01 — Philadelphia, PA: Mikel Scicluna & King Curtis defeat Karl Gotch & Rene Goulet

MAY 22 — New York, NY: Chief Jay Strongbow & Sonny King defeat Mikel Scicluna & King Curtis

JUNE 27 — Philadelphia, PA: Professor Tanaka & Mr. Fuji defeat Chief Jay Strongbow & Sonny King

MAY 30 — Hamburg, PA: Tony Garea & Haystacks Calhoun defeat Professor Tanaka & Mr. Fuji

NOV 14 — Hamburg, PA: Professor Tanaka & Mr. Fuji defeat Tony Garea & Haystacks Calhoun

1974

SEPT 11 — Philadelphia, PA: Tony Garea & Dean Ho defeat Professor Tanaka & Mr. Fuji

MAY 08 — Hamburg, PA: Jimmy & Johnny Valiant defeat Tony Garea & Dean Ho

AUG 30 — New York, NY
New Age Outlaws defeat Mankind

NOV 04 — Philadelphia, PA
Mankind & Al Snow defeat Crash & Hardcore Holly

DEC 10 — Birmingham, AL
Edge & Christian beat The Dudley Boys in a Four Corners Match that also included Road Dogg & K-Kwik and then-champions Bull Buchanan & Goodfather.

MAY 21 — San Jose, CA
Chris Benoit & Chris Jericho defeat Stone Cold Steve Austin & Triple H

MAY 19 — Nashville, TN
Rico & Rikishi defeat Billy & Chuck

MAR 24 — Sacramento, CA
Lance Storm & Chief Morley are awarded the World Tag Team Championship

OCT 19 — Milwaukee, WI
Chris Benoit & Edge defeat Sylvain Grenier & Rob Conway

SEPT 18 — Oklahoma City, OK
Lance Cade & Trevor Murdoch defeat the Hurricane & Rosey

JUNE 04
Lance Cade & Trevor Murdoch defeat Hardy Boys

DEC 14 — Tacoma, WA
Big Boss Man & Ken Shamrock defeat New Age Outlaws

NOV 08 — State College, PA
New Age Outlaws defeat Mankind & Al Snow

DEC 18 — Greenville, SC
The Rock & Undertaker defeat Edge & Christian

JUNE 21 — Orlando, FL
The Dudley Boys defeat Chris Benoit & Chris Jericho

JUNE 06 — Oklahoma City, OK
Billy & Chuck defeat Rico & Rikishi

MAR 31 — Seattle, WA
Kane & Rob Van Dam last eliminated Lance Storm & Chief Morley to win the World Tag Team Championship in an Elimination Match that also included the Dudley Boys.

NOV 01 — Peoria, IL
Sylvain Grenier & Rob Conway defeat Chris Benoit

NOV 01 — San Diego, CA
Big Show & Kane defeat Lance Cade & Trevor Murdoch

SEPT 05
Paul London & Kendrick defeat Cade & Trevor

1999

JAN 25 — Phoenix, AZ
Owen Hart & Jeff Jarrett defeat Big Boss Man & Ken Shamrock

2000

JAN 25 — Phoenix, AZ
Owen Hart & Jeff Jarrett defeat Big Boss Man & Ken Shamrock

DEC 21 — Charlotte, NC
Edge & Christian defeat The Rock & Undertaker

JULY 09 — Atlanta, GA
The APA defeat the Dudley Boys

JULY 04 — Boston, MA
Hulk Hogan & Edge defeat Billy & Chuck

JUNE 15 — Houston, TX
Sylvain Grenier & Rene Dupree defeat Kane & Rob Van Dam

NOV 15 — Indianapolis, IN
Eugene & William Regal beat Sylvain Grenier & Rob Conway to win the World Tag Team Championship in an Elimination Match that also included Rhyno & Tajiri.

2006

APR 03 — Chicago, IL
Spirit Squad defeat Big Show & Kane

SEPT 08
Lance Cade & Trevor Murdoch defeat London & Brian

MAR 30 — Uniondale, NY
Kane & X-Pac defeat Owen Hart & Jeff Jarrett

FEB 27 — Hartford, CT
The Dudley Boys defeat New Age Outlaws

2001

JAN 21 — New Orleans, LA
The Dudley Boys defeat Edge & Christian

AUG 09 — Los Angeles, CA
Kanyon & Diamond Dallas Page defeat the APA

JULY 21 — Detroit, MI
Christian & Lance Storm defeat Hulk Hogan & Edge

SEPT 21 — Hershey, PA
The Dudley Boys defeat Sylvain Grenier, Rene Dupree & Rob Conway

2005

JAN 16 — Winnipeg, Manitoba
Sylvain Grenier & Rob Conway defeat William Regal & Jonathan Coachman

NOV 05 — Cincinnati, OH
Ric Flair & Roddy Piper defeat Spirit Squad

DEC 10
Cody Rhodes & Holly defeat & Trevor Murdoch

MAY 31 — Moline, IL
The Acolytes defeat Kane & X-Pac

APR 02 — Anaheim, CA
Edge & Christian beat The Dudley Boys and The Hardy Boys in a Triple Threat Ladder Match to win the World Tag Team Championship.

MAR 05 — Washington, DC
The Hardy Boys defeat The Dudley Boys

AUG 19 — San Jose, CA
Undertaker & Kane defeat Kanyon & Diamond Dallas Page

SEPT 23 — Anaheim, CA
Kane & the Hurricane defeat Christian & Lance Storm

DEC 14 — Orlando, FL
Ric Flair & Batista defeat the Dudley Boys

> **Sylvain Grenier & Rob Conway beat William Regal & Jonathan Coachman for the World Tag Team Championship in a match where Jonathan Coachman filled in for an injured Eugene.**

NOV 13 — Manchester, England
Edge & Randy Orton defeat Ric Flair & Roddy Piper

20

JUNE 29
Ted DiBiase & Cody Rhodes defeat Hardcore Holly

JUNE 29 — Fayetteville, NC
The Hardy Boys defeat the Acolytes

MAY 29 — Vancouver, British Columbia
Too Cool defeat Edge & Christian

MAR 19 — Albany, NY
Edge & Christian defeat the Hardy Boys

SEPT 17 — Nashville, TN
The Dudley Boys defeat Undertaker & Kane

OCT 14 — Montreal, Quebec
Christian & Chris Jericho defeat Kane & the Hurricane

FEB 07 — Tokyo, Japan
Tajiri & William Regal defeat Sylvain Grenier & Rob Conway

2007

JAN 29 — Dallas, TX
John Cena & Shawn Michaels defeat Edge & Randy Orton

AUG 04
Batista & John defeat Ted DiBiase & Cody Rhodes

JULY 25 — Buffalo, NY
The Acolytes defeat the Hardy Boys

MAR 19 — Albany, NY
The Dudley Boys defeat Edge & Christian

OCT 22 — Kansas City, MO
The Rock & Chris Jericho defeat the Dudley Boys

DEC 15 — Fort Lauderdale, FL
Booker T & Goldust last eliminated Christian & Chris Jericho to win the World Tag Team Championship in a Fatal Four Way Elimination Match that also included the Dudley Boys and Lance Storm & William Regal.

Ric Flair & Batista last eliminated The Dudley Boyz to win the World Tag Team Championship in a Tag Team Turmoil Match that also included The Hurricane & Rosey, Mark Jindrak & Garrison Cade, La Resistance, Val Venis & Lance Storm and Scott Steiner & Test.

AUG 11
Ted DiBiase & Cody Rhodes defeat Batista & John

AUG 09 — Rosemont, IL
Kane & X-Pac defeat the Acolytes

NOV 01 — Cincinnati, OH
Booker T & Test defeat The Rock & Chris Jericho

OCT 27 — Tucson, AZ: CM Punk & Kofi Kingston defeat Ted DiBiase & Cody Rhodes

APR 02 — Dayton, OH: The Hardy Boys win the World Tag Team Championship

The Hardy Boys last eliminated Lance Cade & Trevor Murdoch to win the World Tag Team Championship in a 10-team Battle Royal that also included Tommy Dreamer & Sandman, Brian Kendrick & Paul London, William Regal, Chavo Guerrero & Gregory Helms, Johnny Nitro & The Miz, Viscera & Val Venis, Kevin Thorn & Marcus Cor Von and then-champions John Cena & Shawn Michaels.

MAY 01 — Manchester, NH: The Hurricane & Rosey defeat Sylvain Grenier & Rob Conway

The Hurricane & Rosey beat Sylvain Grenier & Rob Conway to win the World Tag Team Championship in a Tag Team Turmoil Match that also included The Heart Throbs, Simon Dean & Maven and then-champions Tajiri & William Regal.

2003 2004

FEB 16 — Bakersfield, CA: Booker T & Rob Van Dam defeat Ric Flair & Batista

MAR 22 — Detroit, MI: Ric Flair & Batista defeat Booker T & Rob Van Dam

APR 19 — Calgary, Alberta: Chris Benoit & Edge defeat Ric Flair & Batista

MAY 31 — Montreal, Quebec: Sylvain Grenier & Rob Conway defeat Chris Benoit & Edge

JAN 06 — Phoenix, AZ: William Regal & Lance Storm defeat Booker T & Goldust

JAN 19 — Boston, MA: The Dudley Boys defeat William Regal & Lance Storm

JAN 20 — Providence, RI: William Regal & Lance Storm defeat the Dudley Boys

An injury to William Regal forced the duo to vacate the World Tag Team Championship on March 24.

NOV 12 — Boston, MA: The Hardy Boys defeat Booker T & Test

NOV 18 — Greensboro, NC: The Dudley Boys defeat the Hardy Boys

The Dudley Boys beat the Hardy Boys in a Steel Cage Match to unify the World and WCW Tag Team Championships.

2002

JAN 07 — New York, NY: Tazz & Spike Dudley defeat the Dudley Boys

FEB 21 — Rockford, IL: Billy & Chuck defeat Tazz & Spike Dudley

APR 01 — Houston, TX: Edge & Christian beat the Dudley Boys and the Hardy Boys in a Tables, Ladders and Chairs Match to win the World Tag Team Championship.

APR 19 — Nashville, TN: Undertaker & Kane defeat Edge & Christian

APR 29 — Chicago, IL: Stone Cold Steve Austin & Triple H defeat Undertaker & Kane

JUNE 25 — Boston, MA: Edge & Christian last eliminated Too Cool to win the World Tag Team Championship in Four Corners Elimination Match that also included the Hardy Boys and Test & Albert.

SEPT 24 — Philadelphia, PA: The Hardy Boys defeat Edge & Christian

OCT 22 — Albany, NY: Edge & Christian defeat the Hardy Boys

OCT 23 — Hartford, CT: The Hardy Boys defeat Edge & Christian

NOV 06 — Houston, TX: Bull Buchanan & Godfather defeat the Hardy Boys

AUG 22 — Minneapolis, MN: Undertaker & Big Show defeat Kane & X-Pac

AUG 30 — Boston, MA: Mankind & The Rock defeat Undertaker & Big Show

SEPT 09 — Albany, NY: Undertaker & Big Show defeat Mankind & The Rock

SEPT 20 — Houston, TX: Mankind & The Rock defeat Undertaker & Big Show

SEPT 23 — Dallas, TX: New Age Outlaws defeat Mankind & The Rock

OCT 14 — Birmingham, AL: Mankind & The Rock defeat New Age Outlaws

OCT 18 — Columbus, OH: Crash & Hardcore Holly defeat Mankind & The Rock

World Wide Wrestling Federation United States Heavyweight Championship

The World Wide Wrestling Federation United States Heavyweight Championship was the company's first iteration of a United States title and was passionately battled for during its existence. From 1963 to 1977, this championship was held by names such as WWE Hall of Famers Bobo Brazil, The Sheik, and Pedro Morales.

1963

Bobo Brazil is recognized as the first United States Heavyweight Champion.

JUNE — Philadelphia, PA

Johnny Barend defeats Bobo Brazil

1969

JAN — Salisbury, MD

The Sheik defeats Bobo Brazil

JULY — Philadelphia, PA

Bobo Brazil defeats Johnny Barend

1971

JAN — Los Angeles, CA

Pedro Morales defeats Fred Blassie in the Tournament Finals

FEB

Bobo Brazil defeats The Shiek in a Texas Death Match

On February 8, 1971, Pedro Morales forfeits the title when he becomes the World Wide Wrestling Federation Heavyweight Champion.

FEB 15

Bobo Brazil is recognized as champion for the fourth time and would go on to hold the championship until it was removed from the World Wide Wrestling Federation.

World Wide Wrestling Federation United States Tag Team Championship History

This tag team championship traces its lineage back to the Northeast territory of the National Wrestling Alliance. In 1963, the championship became a part of the World Wide Wrestling Federation and held by teams including WWE Hall of Famers Killer Kowalski & Gorilla Monsoon, Dr. Jerry & Luke Graham, The Sicilians, and Bruno Sammartino & Spiros Arion before being retired in 1967.

1963

MAR 07 — Washington D.C.

Buddy Austin & the Great Scott defeat "Nature Boy" Buddy Rogers & Johnny Barend in a Best 2-out-of-3 Falls Match.

Austin replaced Sanchez after Sanchez injured himself while losing the 1st fall.

MAY 16 — Washington D.C.

Skull Murphy & Brute Bernard defeat Buddy Austin & the Great Scott

NOV 14 — Washington D.C.

Killer Kowalski & Gorilla Monsoon defeat Skull Murphy & Brute Bernard

DEC 28 — Teaneck, N.J.

Chris & John Tolos defeat Killer Kowalski & Gorilla Monsoon.

1964

FEB 16 — New Haven, CT

Don McClarity & Vittorio Apollo defeat Chris & John Tolos

JUNE 06 — Washington D.C.

Dr. Jerry & Luke Graham defeat Don McClarity & Vittorio Apollo

1965

FEB 04 — Washington D.C.

Gene Kiniski & Waldo Von Erich defeat Dr. Jerry & Luke Graham

APR 06 — Washington D.C.

Gorilla Monsoon & Cowboy Bill Watts defeat Gene Kiniski & Waldo Von Erich

AUG 07 — Washington D.C.

Dr. Bill Miller & Dan Miller defeat Gorilla Monsoon & Cowboy Bill Watts

1966

FEB 21 — New York, NY

Antonio Pugliese & Johnny Valentine defeat Dr. Bill Miller & Dan Miller

SEPT 22 — Washington D.C.

Dr. Bill Miller & Dan Miller defeat Antonio Pugliese & Johnny Valentine.

DEC 08 — Washington D.C.

Spiros Arion & Antonio Pugliese defeat Dr. Bill Miller & Dan Miller

In July 1967, Antonio Pugliese abruptly leaves the United States. Sprios Arion chooses Arnold Skaaland as his new tag team partner to defend the championship.

1967

JULY 10 — Atlantic City, N.J.

The Sicilians defeat Chuck Richards (substitute for Spiros Arion) and Arnold Skaaland

JULY 24 — Atlantic City, N.J.

Bruno Sammartino & Spiros Arion defeat The Sicilians

In late 1967, Bruno Sammartino vacates his half of the championship to concentrate on his World Heavyweight Champion title defenses. The United States Tag Team Championship would remain vacant and eventually vanish from the World Wide Wrestling Federation.

The World's Greatest Tag Team

 **YEARS ACTIVE**

MEMBERS Shelton Benjamin, Charlie Haas

COMBINED WEIGHT 497 lbs.

TITLE HISTORY WWE Tag Team Champions

The exchanging of gifts continued for Kurt Angle on the day after Christmas 2002. It was on this day that Paul Heyman presented the former gold medalist with the athletic tandem of Shelton Benjamin & Charlie Haas, collectively known as Team Angle. Their main responsibility was to help Angle retain his WWE Championship at all costs. The duo, however, was able to capture titles of their own when they defeated Los Guerreros for the WWE Tag Team Championship in February 2003.

After losing the titles back to Eddie Guerrero and his new partner, Tajiri, in May 2003, Team Angle found themselves in an uncharacteristic slump. As a result, Angle fired them as his associates. On their own, Benjamin & Haas dubbed themselves the World's Greatest Tag Team and quickly duplicated their earlier success when they regained the WWE Tag Team Championship from Guerrero & Tajiri. The duo was forced to go their separate ways when Benjamin was sent to *Raw* via the WWE Draft in March 2004. They briefly reformed a few years later on *Raw*.

WWF WrestleMania

World Wrestling Entertainment approached a pivotal time in its existence. To make the crucial turn to sports-entertainment complete, Vince McMahon rolled the dice. If he was to succeed in turning his WWE into an international entity, the initial *WrestleMania* needed to be a hit. This was a closed-circuit spectacle that saw the greatest Superstars in sports-entertainment meet in the legendary Madison Square Garden.In addition, celebrities such as Billy Martin, Liberace, the Rockettes, and Muhammad Ali contributed in turning the wrestling event into a spectacle.

Nearly twenty-five years later, it's safe to say the gamble paid off and the world of sports-entertainment has never been the same.

Madison Square Garden; New York, NY

MAR 31 **1985**

Tito Santana defeated the Executioner

David Sammartino (with Bruno Sammartino) vs. Brutus Beefcake (with "Luscious" Johnny Valiant) went to a no contest

Ricky "The Dragon" Steamboat defeated Matt Borne

King Kong Bundy (with Jimmy Hart) defeated SD "Special Delivery" Jones

BODYSLAM CHALLENGE

Andre the Giant defeated Big John Studd

INTERCONTINENTAL CHAMPIONSHIP MATCH

Junkyard Dog defeated Intercontinental Champion Greg "the Hammer" Valentine (with Jimmy Hart) via count-out

WORLD TAG TEAM CHAMPIONSHIP MATCH

Nikolai Volkoff & Iron Sheik (with "Classy" Freddie Blassie) defeated World Tag Team Champions US Express (with Lou Albano) to become new champions

WOMEN'S CHAMPIONSHIP MATCH

Wendi Richter (with Cyndi Lauper) defeated Women's Champion Leilani Kai (with Fabulous Moolah) to become new champion

MAIN EVENT

Hulk Hogan & Mr. T (with Jimmy "Superfly" Snuka) defeated "Rowdy" Roddy Piper & "Mr. Wonderful" Paul Orndorff (with "Cowboy" Bob Orton)

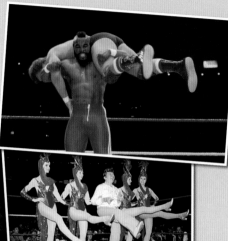

WWF WrestleMania 2

The unbelievable response to *WrestleMania* left WWE no choice but to make it an annual extravaganza. The stakes were raised as this event emanated from three locations simultaneously across the United States. After Ray Charles sang "America the Beautiful" to kick off the event, audiences saw a match decided with the sweet science, a battle royal with WWE and NFL Superstars, and the first *WrestleMania* title defense inside a 15-foot high Steel Cage!

Nassau Veteran's Memorial Coliseum; Uniondale, NY
The Rosemont Horizon; Rosemont, IL
The Sports Arena; Los Angeles, CA

APR 07 **1986**

"Mr. Wonderful" Paul Orndorff versus the Magnificent Muraco (with Mr. Fuji) went to a double count-out

INTERCONTINENTAL CHAMPIONSHIP MATCH

Intercontinental Champion Randy "Macho Man" Savage (with Elizabeth) defeated George "the Animal" Steele

Jake "The Snake" Roberts defeated George Wells

BOXING MATCH

Mr. T (with Joe Frazier and Haiti Kid) defeated "Rowdy" Roddy Piper (with "Cowboy" Bob Orton) by Disqualification

WOMEN'S CHAMPIONSHIP MATCH

The Fabulous Moolah defeated Women's Champion Velvet McIntyre to become new champion

FLAG MATCH

Corporal Kirchner defeated Nikolai Volkoff (with "Classy" Freddie Blassie)

WWE AND NFL BATTLE ROYAL

Andre the Giant was the last man standing. The other entrants were Jimbo Covert (Chicago Bears), Pedro Morales, Tony Atlas, Ted Arcidi, Harvey Martin (Dallas Cowboys), Dan Spivey, Hillbilly Jim, King Tonga, Iron Sheik, Ernie Holmes (Pittsburgh Steelers), Big John Studd, B. Brian Blair, Jumpin' Jim Brunzell, Bill Fralic (Atlanta Falcons), Bret "Hit Man" Hart, Jim "the Anvil" Neidhart, Russ Francis (San Francisco 49ers), Bruno Sammartino, and William "Refrigerator" Perry (Chicago Bears)

WORLD TAG TEAM CHAMPIONSHIP MATCH

The British Bulldogs (with Captain Lou Albano and Ozzy Osbourne) defeated World Tag Team Champions the Dream Team (with "Luscious" Johnny Valiant) to become new champions

Ricky "The Dragon" Steamboat defeated Hercules

"Adorable" Adrian Adonis (with Jimmy Hart) defeated Uncle Elmer

Terry & Hoss Funk (with Jimmy Hart) defeated Tito Santana & Junkyard Dog

STEEL CAGE MATCH FOR THE WWE CHAMPIONSHIP

WWE Champion Hulk Hogan defeated King Kong Bundy (with Bobby "The Brain" Heenan)

WRESTLEMANIA III

As WWE set a new indoor attendance record of 93,173 it proved that it was "Bigger, Better & Badder" than any other sports-entertainment company past or present. It continued its tradition of star-studded happenings as "the Queen of Soul" Aretha Franklin kicked off the historic day with her rendition of "America The Beautiful." The scores that were to be settled received global media attention, and Superstars became legends as they battled on this epic occasion.

Pontiac SliverDome; Pontiac, MI

MAR 29 **1987**

MATCH RESULTS

Can Am Connection defeated "Cowboy" Bob Orton & The Magnificent Muraco (with Mr. Fuji)

FULL NELSON CHALLENGE

Billy Jack Haynes versus Hercules (with Bobby "the Brain" Heenan) went to a double count-out

Hillbilly Jim, Little Beaver, & Haiti Kid defeated King Kong Bundy, Lord Littlebrook, & Little Tokyo by Disqualification

"LOSER MUST BOW" MATCH

"King" Harley Race (with Bobby Heenan and Fabulous Moolah) defeated Junkyard Dog

The Dream Team (with "Luscious" Johnny Valiant & Dino Bravo) defeated The Rougeau Brothers

HAIR VS. HAIR MATCH

"Rowdy" Roddy Piper defeated "Adorable" Adrian Adonis (with Jimmy Hart)

The Hart Foundation & "Dangerous" Danny Davis (with Jimmy Hart) defeated The British Bulldogs & Tito Santana

"The Natural" Butch Reed (with Slick) defeated Koko B. Ware

INTERCONTINENTAL CHAMPIONSHIP MATCH

Ricky "the Dragon" Steamboat (with George "the Animal" Steele) defeated Intercontinental Champion Randy "Macho Man" Savage (with Elizabeth) to become new champion

Honky Tonk Man (with Jimmy Hart) defeated Jake "the Snake" Roberts (with Alice Cooper)

Nikolai Volkoff & Iron Sheik (with Slick) defeated Killer Bees by Disqualification

WWE CHAMPIONSHIP MATCH

WWE Champion Hulk Hogan defeated Andre the Giant (with Bobby Heenan)

WRESTLEMANIA IV

Where there's chaos, there's opportunity. The fate of sports-entertainment's richest prize hung in the balance as the vacant WWE Championship was to be awarded at the end of a one-night tournament. The biggest names in sports-entertainment gathered for the event, but only one would emerge from Atlantic City the new undisputed Champion of the World!

Trump Plaza, Atlantic City; NJ

MAR 27 **1988**

MATCH RESULTS

BATTLE ROYAL

Bad News Brown defeated Bret "Hit Man" Hart, Jim "The Anvil" Neidhart, Jim Powers, Paul Roma, Sika, "Dangerous" Danny Davis, Sam Houston, Hillbilly Jim, B. Brian Blair, Jumpin' Jim Brunzell, Ray Rougeau, Jacques Rougeau, Junkyard Dog, Ken Patera, Ron Bass, "King" Harley Race, Nikolai Volkoff, Boris Zhukov, and George "The Animal" Steele

Ultimate Warrior defeated Hercules (with Bobby "the Brain" Heenan)

INTERCONTINENTAL CHAMPIONSHIP MATCH

Brutus "the Barber" Beefcake defeated Intercontinental Champion Honky Tonk Man (with Jimmy Hart and Peggy Sue) by Disqualification

The Islanders & Bobby Heenan defeated the British Bulldogs & Koko B. Ware (with Matilda)

WORLD TAG TEAM CHAMPIONSHIP MATCH

Demolition (with Mr. Fuji) defeated World Tag Team Champions Strike Force to become new champions

WWE CHAMPIONSHIP TOURNAMENT

Round One Matches

"Million Dollar Man" Ted DiBiase (with Virgil and Andre The Giant) defeated "Hacksaw" Jim Duggan

Don "the Rock" Muraco (with "Superstar" Billy Graham) defeated Dino Bravo (with Frenchy Martin) by Disqualification

Greg "the Hammer" Valentine (with Jimmy Hart) defeated Ricky "The Dragon" Steamboat

Randy "Macho Man" Savage (with Elizabeth) defeated "The Natural" Butch Reed (with Slick)

One Man Gang (with Slick) defeated Bam Bam Bigelow (with Sir Oliver Humperdink)

"Ravishing" Rick Rude (with Bobby Heenan) vs. Jake "The Snake" Roberts went to a draw

Round Two Matches

Hulk Hogan vs. Andre The Giant (with Bobby "The Brain" Heenan, "Million Dollar Man" Ted DiBiase and Virgil) ended in a Double Disqualification

"Million Dollar Man" Ted DiBiase (with Virgil) defeated Don "the Rock" Muraco (with "Superstar" Billy Graham)

Randy "Macho Man" Savage (with Elizabeth) defeated Greg "the Hammer" Valentine (with Jimmy Hart)

Round Three Match

Randy "Macho Man" Savage (with Elizabeth) defeated One Man Gang (with Slick) by Disqualification

WWE CHAMPIONSHIP TOURNAMENT FINAL MATCH

Randy "Macho Man" Savage (with Elizabeth & Hulk Hogan) defeated "Million Dollar Man" Ted DiBiase (with Virgil & Andre the Giant) to become new champion

MATCH RESULTS

Over 19,000 fans attended the event, and millions around the world tuned in to see WWE legends go to war. The main event featured Hulk Hogan and Randy "Macho Man" Savage, who once battled together as the Mega-Powers, face off for Savage's WWE Championship. *WrestleMania IV* and *WrestleMania V* remain the only *WrestleMania* events to date that have originated from the same venue in consecutive years.

Hercules defeated "King" Haku (with Bobby "the Brain" Heenan)

The Twin Towers (with Slick) defeated The Rockers

"Million Dollar Man" Ted DiBiase (with Virgil) versus Brutus "the Barber" Beefcake ended in a double count-out

The Bushwhackers defeated the Fabulous Rougeau Brothers (with Jimmy Hart)

Mr. Perfect defeated Blue Blazer

HANDICAP MATCH FOR THE WORLD TAG TEAM CHAMPIONSHIP

World Tag Team Champions Demolition defeated Powers of Pain & Mr. Fuji

Dino Bravo (with Frenchy Martin) defeated "Rugged" Ronnie Garvin

The Brain Busters (with Bobby Heenan) defeated Strike Force

Jake "the Snake" Roberts defeated Andre the Giant (with Bobby Heenan) by Disqualification (Big John Studd was special guest referee)

The Hart Foundation defeated Rhythm & Blues (with Jimmy Hart)

INTERCONTINENTAL CHAMPIONSHIP MATCH

"Ravishing" Rick Rude (with Bobby Heenan) defeated Intercontinental Champion Ultimate Warrior to become new champion

Bad News Brown versus "Hacksaw" Jim Duggan ended in a no contest

Red Rooster defeated Bobby Heenan (with the Brooklyn Brawler)

WWE CHAMPIONSHIP MATCH

Hulk Hogan defeated WWE Champion Randy "Macho Man" Savage with Elizabeth in a neutral corner to become new champion

Trump Plaza; Atlantic City, NJ

APR 02 **1989**

MATCH RESULTS

The first *WrestleMania* of the 1990s brought about many firsts for the world's greatest annual entertainment event. This was the first time *WrestleMania* was held outside the United States, the first time the main event saw a "Title versus Title" bout, and the first time two fan favorites clashed as 67,678 fans traveled to SkyDome and to witness "The Ultimate Challenge."

"The Model" Rick Martel defeated Koko B. Ware

WORLD TAG TEAM CHAMPIONSHIP MATCH

Demolition defeated World Tag Team Champions Colossal Connection (with Bobby "the Brain" Heenan) to become new champions

Earthquake (with Jimmy Hart) defeated Hercules

Brutus "the Barber" Beefcake defeated Mr. Perfect (with The Genius)

"Rowdy" Roddy Piper vs. Bad News Brown went to a no contest

The Hart Foundation defeated the Bolsheviks

The Barbarian (with Bobby Heenan) defeated Tito Santana

MIXED TAG TEAM MATCH

Dusty Rhodes & Saphire (with Elizabeth) defeated Randy "Macho King" Savage & Queen Sherri

The Orient Express (with Mr. Fuji) defeated The Rockers by count-out

"Hacksaw" Jim Duggan defeated Dino Bravo (with Earthquake)

MILLION DOLLAR CHAMPIONSHIP MATCH

Million Dollar Champion "Million Dollar Man" Ted DiBiase (with Virgil) defeated Jake "the Snake" Roberts by count-out

Big Boss Man defeated Akeem (with Slick)

"Ravishing" Rick Rude (with Bobby Heenan) defeated Jimmy "Superfly" Snuka

TITLE VS. TITLE MATCH

Intercontinental Champion Ultimate Warrior defeated WWE Champion Hulk Hogan to retain Intercontinental Championship and become new WWE Champion

Toronto SkyDome; Toronto, Ontario, Canada

APR 01 **1990**

WRESTLEMANIA VII

The United States of America was at war and the WWE Championship was in the hands of an enemy sympathizer. Patriots everywhere pulled for Hulk Hogan once again to be the hero and bring sports-entertainment's richest prize back home. This historic event also saw the first-ever Blindfold Match, a King's career on the line, and as "the Eighth Wonder of the World" made his final *WrestleMania* appearance, Undertaker made his debut.

Sports Arena; Los Angeles, CA

MAR 24 | **1991**

MATCH RESULTS

The Rockers defeated Haku & The Barbarian (with Bobby "the Brain" Heenan)

Texas Tornado defeated Dino Bravo

British Bulldog defeated Warlord (with Slick)

WORLD TAG TEAM CHAMPIONSHIP MATCH

The Nasty Boys (with Jimmy Hart) defeated World Tag Team Champions the Hart Foundation to become new champions

BLINDFOLD MATCH

Jake "the Snake" Roberts defeated "The Model" Rick Martel

Undertaker (with Paul Bearer) defeated Jimmy "Superfly" Snuka

RETIREMENT MATCH

Ultimate Warrior defeated Randy "Macho King" Savage (with Queen Sherri)

Genichiro Tenryu & Koji Kitao defeated Demolition

Intercontinental Championship Match

Big Boss Man defeated Intercontinental Champion Mr. Perfect (with Bobby Heenan) by Disqualification

Earthquake defeated Greg "the Hammer" Valentine

Legion of Doom defeated Power & Glory (with Slick)

Virgil (with "Rowdy" Roddy Piper) defeated "Million Dollar Man" Ted DiBiase by count-out

The Mountie (with Jimmy Hart) defeated Tito Santana

WWE CHAMPIONSHIP MATCH

Hulk Hogan defeated WWE Champion Sgt. Slaughter (with General Adnan) to become new champion

MATCH RESULTS

WRESTLEMANIA VIII

Over 62,000 crazed fans flocked to the Hoosier Dome to see the first *WrestleMania* featuring a double main-event. While the "Macho Man" fought to clear the name of the one he loved and become a two-time WWE Champion, Hulk Hogan defended WWE against the Superstar who sought to rule the world. In the end, audiences were jolted to their feet as they saw the return of Ultimate Warrior.

Hoosier Dome; Indianapolis, IN

APR 05 | **1992**

Shawn Michaels (with Sensational Sherri) defeated "El Matador" Tito Santana

Undertaker (with Paul Bearer) defeated Jake "the Snake" Roberts

INTERCONTINENTAL CHAMPIONSHIP MATCH

Bret "Hit Man" Hart defeated Intercontinental Champion "Rowdy" Roddy Piper to become new champion

"Hacksaw" Jim Duggan, Sgt. Slaughter, Virgil & Big Boss Man defeated The Mountie, Repo Man & Nasty Boys (with Jimmy Hart)

FIRST MAIN EVENT— WWE CHAMPIONSHIP MATCH

Randy "Macho Man" Savage (with Elizabeth) defeated WWE Champion "Nature Boy" Ric Flair (with Mr. Perfect) to become new champion

Tatanka defeated "The Model" Rick Martel

WORLD TAG TEAM CHAMPIONSHIP MATCH

Natural Disasters defeated World Tag Team Champions Money Inc. (with Jimmy Hart) by count-out

Owen Hart defeated Skinner

SECOND MAIN EVENT

Hulk Hogan defeated Sid Justice (with Harvey Wippleman) by Disqualification

MATCH RESULTS

The ninth annual *WrestleMania* was the first to be held outdoors and hosted the world's biggest Toga Party. "The Brain" entered Caesar's Palace on a camel, Jim Ross made his WWE debut dressed in a toga, and fans heard the voice of Finkus Maximus announce Superstars on their way to the ring. Who would leave the Greco-Roman coliseum victorious? Could the Mega-Maniacs get revenge on Money Inc? Could anyone stand up to the seemingly unstoppable Japanese force of Yokozuna?

Caesar's Palace; Las Vegas, NV

APR 04 **1993**

INTERCONTINENTAL CHAMPIONSHIP MATCH

Tatanka defeated Intercontinental Champion Shawn Michaels (with Luna Vachon) by count-out

The Steiner Brothers defeated the Headshrinkers (with Afa)

Doink defeated Crush

Razor Ramon defeated Bob Backlund

WORLD TAG TEAM CHAMPIONSHIP MATCH

World Tag Team Champions Money Inc. defeated Hulk Hogan & Brutus "the Barber" Beefcake (with Jimmy Hart) by disqualification

"The Narcissist" Lex Luger defeated Mr. Perfect

Undertaker (with Paul Bearer) defeated Giant Gonzales (with Harvey Wippleman) by disqualification

WWE CHAMPIONSHIP MATCH[1]

Yokozuna (with Mr. Fuji & Jim Cornette) defeated WWE Champion Bret "Hit Man" Hart to become new champion

[1] After the match, Hulk Hogan defeated Yokozuna to become new champion

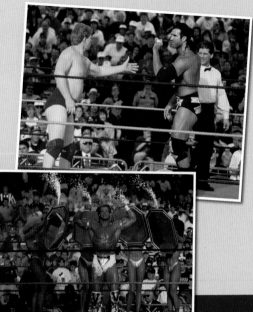

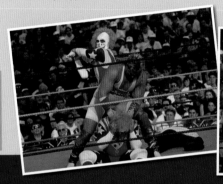

MATCH RESULTS

The event celebrating a decade of sports-entertainment dominance took place back where it all began as *WrestleMania X* returned to Madison Square Garden. This event exceeded all expectations as fans witnessed a unique mixed tag match, an all-out brawl, and the ladder match that set the standard for all future encounters of its kind.

Madison Square Garden; New York, NY

MAR 20 **1994**

Owen Hart defeated Bret "Hit Man" Hart

MIXED TAG TEAM MATCH

Bam Bam Bigelow & Luna Vachon defeated Doink & Dink

FALLS COUNT ANYWHERE MATCH

Randy "Macho Man" Savage defeated Crush (with Mr. Fuji)

WOMEN'S CHAMPIONSHIP MATCH

Women's Champion Alundra Blayze defeated Leilani Kai

WWE CHAMPIONSHIP MATCH

Yokozuna (Champion, with Mr. Fuji and Jim Cornette) defeated Lex Luger by disqualification, with special guest referee, Mr. Perfect

LADDER MATCH FOR THE INTERCONTINENTAL CHAMPIONSHIP

Intercontinental Champion Razor Ramon defeated Shawn Michaels

WORLD TAG TEAM CHAMPIONSHIP MATCH

Men on a Mission (with Oscar) defeated World Tag Team Champions the Quebecers (with Johnny Polo) by count-out

Earthquake defeated Adam Bomb (with Harvey Wippleman)

WWE CHAMPIONSHIP MATCH

Bret "Hit Man" Hart defeated WWE Champion Yokozuna (with Mr. Fuji & Jim Cornette) to become new champion

The only *WrestleMania* to be held in WWE's home state continued the tradition of an awesome array of contests and celebrities. With stars in attendance, from Pamela Anderson and Jenny McCarthy to hip-hop legends Salt-N-Peppa, millions tuned in all over the world to see the WWE Championship on the line, a Superstar quit and a type of main event that will never be duplicated.

Hartford Civic Center; Hartford, CT

APR 02 1995

MATCH RESULTS

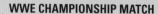

Lex Luger & British Bulldog defeated Eli & Jacob Blu (with Uncle Zebekiah)

INTERCONTINENTAL CHAMPIONSHIP MATCH

Razor Ramon (with 1-2-3 Kid) defeated Jeff Jarrett (with the Roadie) by disqualification

Undertaker (with Paul Bearer) defeated King Kong Bundy (with "Million Dollar Man" Ted DiBiase)

WORLD TAG TEAM CHAMPIONSHIP MATCH

Owen Hart & Yokozuna (with Mr. Fuji & Jim Cornette) defeated World Tag Team Champions Smoking Gunns to become new champions

I QUIT MATCH

Bret "Hit Man" Hart defeated Bob Backlund

WWE CHAMPIONSHIP MATCH

WWE Champion Diesel defeated Shawn Michaels to retain

Lawrence Taylor (with Ken Norton, Jr., Carl Banks, Rickey Jackson, Steve McMichael, Chris Spielman, & Reggie White) defeated Bam Bam Bigelow (with the Million Dollar Corporation)

Following in *WrestleMania* tradition, the bar for the world's greatest entertainment spectacle was raised as WWE legends returned, and two Superstars solidified their legendary status in a 60 Minute Iron Man Match. The capacity crowd at Arrowhead Pond also saw the *WrestleMania* debuts of Steve Austin and Triple H, a sign that an era filled with attitude was on the horizon.

Arrowhead Pond; Anaheim, CA

MAR 31 1996

MATCH RESULTS

Owen Hart, British Bulldog, & Vader (with Jim Cornette) defeated Yokozuna, Jake "the Snake" Roberts, & Ahmed Johnson

HOLLYWOOD BACKLOT BRAWL

"Rowdy" Roddy Piper defeated Goldust (with Marlena)

The Ringmaster (with "Million Dollar Man" Ted DiBiase) defeated Savio Vega

Ultimate Warrior defeated Hunter Hearst Helmsley (with Sable)

Undertaker (with Paul Bearer) defeated Diesel

IRON MAN MATCH FOR THE WWE CHAMPIONSHIP

Shawn Michaels (with Jose Lothario) defeated WWE Champion Bret "Hit Man" Hart in overtime to become new champion

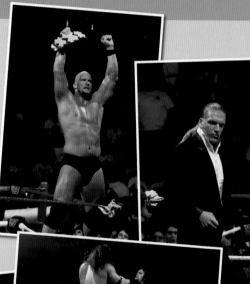

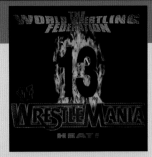

MATCH RESULTS

Eleven years after hosting a portion of *WrestleMania 2*, Chicago's Rosemont Horizon was once again the site of sports-entertainment's annual crown jewel in 1997. The 18,197 in attendance witnessed a Submission Match that

will be remembered as one of the greatest battles of all time. Trapped in the Sharpshooter, Stone Cold refused to submit to his rival, even with blood spewing from his forehead. Austin refused to give up, but the blood loss became too great for him to overcome and he passed out.

Rosemont Horizon; Chicago, IL

MAR 23 **1997**

NO. 1 CONTENDERS TAG TEAM FATAL FOUR WAY ELIMINATION MATCH

The Headbangers defeated the Godwinns (with Hillbilly Jim), the New Blackjacks, and Phil Lafon & Doug Furnas

INTERCONTINENTAL CHAMPIONSHIP MATCH

Intercontinental Champion Rocky Maivia defeated the Sultan (with Bob Backlund & Iron Sheik) to retain

Hunter Hearst-Helmsley (with Chyna) defeated Goldust (with Marlena)

WORLD TAG TEAM CHAMPIONSHIP MATCH

World Tag Team Champions Owen Hart & British Bulldog vs. Mankind & Vader went to a double countout

SUBMISSION MATCH

Bret "Hit Man" Hart defeated Stone Cold Steve Austin, with Special Guest Referee Ken Shamrock

CHICAGO STREET FIGHT

Ahmed Johnson & Legion of Doom defeated the Nation of Domination

WWE CHAMPIONSHIP MATCH

Undertaker defeated WWE Champion Sycho Sid to become WWE Champion

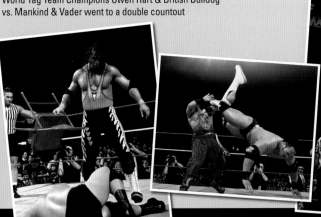

MATCH RESULTS

Tagged "DX-raided," *WrestleMania XIV* was supposed to be the site of D-Generation X's greatest triumph. With special enforcer Mike Tyson already announcing his allegiance to Shawn Michaels heading into the WWE Championship Match, it looked like an HBK win was a mere formality. With Austin's dream just three seconds away, Tyson hit the ring to make the three count and officially usher in the Austin era. Also, the 19,028 on hand saw Kane and Undertaker's first

encounter. Prior to the match, guest ring announcer Pete Rose poked fun at the Boston crowd for the Red Sox inability to win a World Series. His words not only angered the crowd, but set something off in Kane, who delivered a Tombstone to baseball's all-time hits leader.

FleetCenter; Boston, MA

MAR 29 **1998**

TAG TEAM BATTLE ROYAL

Legion of Doom (with Sunny) defeated Savio Vega & Miguel Perez, Jose Estrada & Jesus Castillo, New Midnight Express, Truth Commission, Bradshaw & Chainz, D-Lo Brown & Mark Henry, the Quebecers, Rock n' Roll Express, Faarooq & Kama, the Headbangers, Scott Taylor & Brian Christopher, the Godwinns, and D.O.A.

LIGHT HEAVYWEIGHT CHAMPIONSHIP MATCH

Light Heavyweight Champion Taka Michinoku defeated Aguila

EUROPEAN CHAMPIONSHIP MATCH

European Champion Triple H defeated Owen Hart

MIXED TAG TEAM MATCH

Marc Mero & Sable defeated The Artist Formerly Known as Goldust & Luna

INTERCONTINENTAL CHAMPIONSHIP MATCH

Intercontinental Champion The Rock (with the Nation of Domination) defeated Ken Shamrock via disqualification

DUMPSTER MATCH FOR THE WORLD TAG TEAM CHAMPIONSHIP

Cactus Jack & Terry Funk defeated World Tag Team Champions New Age Outlaws to become new champions

Undertaker defeated Kane

WWE CHAMPIONSHIP MATCH

Stone Cold Steve Austin defeated WWE Champion Shawn Michaels to become new champion

MATCH RESULTS

Despite Stone Cold Steve Austin's unparalleled popularity, Mr. McMahon failed to recognize him as a worthy representative of WWE. In September 1998, he declared the title vacant after Stone Cold Steve Austin had been simultaneously pinned by Undertaker and Kane. At *WrestleMania XV*, the 19,514 fans inside the First Union Center watched Stone Cold Steve Austin face The Rock. *WrestleMania XV* also hosted arguably the most one-sided match to ever take place in a WWE ring as Bart

Gunn, who won the Brawl For All Tournament, faced Butterbean, with boxing great Vinny Pazienza serving as referee. Elsewhere, Pete Rose sought revenge from Kane for his *WrestleMania XIV* humiliation. Things didn't go as planned, and the "Big Red Monster" planted Rose with a Tombstone for the second year in a row.

First Union Center; Philadelphia, PA

MAR 28 | **1999**

TRIPLE THREAT MATCH FOR THE HARDCORE CHAMPIONSHIP

Hardcore Holly defeated Al Snow and Hardcore Champion Billy Gunn to become new champion

WORLD TAG TEAM CHAMPIONSHIP MATCH

World Tag Team Champions Owen Hart & Jeff Jarrett (with Debra) defeated D-Lo Brown & Test (with Ivory)

BRAWL FOR ALL

Butterbean defeated Bart Gunn by knockout, with guest referee Vinny Pazienza

REFEREE MATCH

Mankind defeated Big Show via disqualification to become referee for main event

FATAL FOUR WAY MATCH FOR THE INTERCONTINENTAL CHAMPIONSHIP

Intercontinental Champion Road Dogg defeated Val Venis, Ken Shamrock and Goldust (with Blue Meanie & Ryan Shamrock)

Kane defeated Triple H via disqualification

WOMEN'S CHAMPIONSHIP MATCH

Women's Champion Sable defeated Tori

EUROPEAN CHAMPIONSHIP MATCH

European Champion Shane McMahon defeated X-Pac

HELL IN A CELL MATCH

Undertaker (with Paul Bearer) defeated Big Boss Man

WWE CHAMPIONSHIP MATCH

Stone Cold Steve Austin defeated WWE Champion The Rock to become new champion

MATCH RESULTS

With a McMahon in every corner for the main event and 19,776 fans in attendance, the WWE Championship Match at *WrestleMania 2000* certainly had the makings of a volatile situation. Accompanied by Stephanie, WWE Champion Triple H defended his title against The Rock (with Vince), Big Show (with Shane), and Mick Foley (with Linda) in a Fatal Four Way Elimination Match. However, the World Tag Team Championship Match stole the show. The champion

Dudley Boys battled Edge & Christian and the Hardy Boys in a thrilling Ladder Match. Throughout the epic encounter, tables and chairs also made their way into the fray, leading many to consider this encounter the precursor to the famed TLC Match.

Arrowhead Pond; Anaheim, CA

APR 02 | **2000**

Big Boss Man & Bull Buchanan defeated The Godfather & D-Lo Brown (with Ice-T)

HARDCORE BATTLE ROYAL

Hardcore Holly was the final winner of the Hardcore Championship Battle Royal, which also included Hardcore Champion Crash Holly, Viscera, Tazz, Kaientei, Mean Street Posse, the Headbangers, and the Acolytes

Test & Albert (with Trish Stratus) defeated Al Snow & Steve Blackman (with Chester McCheeserton)

LADDER MATCH FOR THE WORLD TAG TEAM CHAMPIONSHIP

Edge & Christian defeated the Hardy Boys and the Dudley Boys to become new champions

CATFIGHT

Terri defeated the Kat

Too Cool & Chyna defeated the Radicalz

TWO-FALL TRIPLE THREAT MATCH FOR THE INTERCONTINENTAL & EUROPEAN CHAMPIONSHIPS

Chris Benoit defeated Chris Jericho and Intercontinental Champion Kurt Angle to become new Intercontinental Champion

Chris Jericho defeated Chris Benoit and European Champion Kurt Angle to become new European Champion

Kane & Rikishi defeated Road Dogg & X-Pac

FATAL FOUR WAY ELIMINATION MATCH FOR THE WWE CHAMPIONSHIP

WWE Champion Triple H (with Stephanie McMahon) defeated The Rock (with Mr. McMahon), Mick Foley (with Linda McMahon), and Big Show (with Shane McMahon)

MATCH RESULTS

As *WrestleMania* transformed into a true global phenomenon, Mr. McMahon watched from the sidelines as the sport's greatest became legends at the extravaganza he created. In 2001, he decided it was his turn to step into the ring. In the midst of a bitter divorce from his wife Linda, Mr. McMahon began a very public love affair with Trish Stratus. Viewing the relationship as the ultimate sign of disrespect, son Shane challenged his father to a Street Fight. For the second year in a row, Edge & Christian captured the World Tag Team Championship in an epic encounter. In front of 67,925 fans, they successfully out-climbed the Hardy Boys and Dudley Boys to become unofficial Kings of the TLC Match.

Astrodome; Houston, TX

APR 01 2001

INTERCONTINENTAL CHAMPIONSHIP MATCH

Intercontinental Champion Chris Jericho defeated William Regal

Bradshaw, Faarooq & Tazz defeated Right to Censor

TRIPLE THREAT MATCH FOR THE HARDCORE CHAMPIONSHIP

Kane defeated Big Show and Hardcore Champion Raven to become new champion

EUROPEAN CHAMPIONSHIP MATCH

Eddie Guerrero defeated European Champion Test to become new champion

Kurt Angle defeated Chris Benoit

WOMEN'S CHAMPIONSHIP MATCH

Chyna defeated Women's Champion Ivory to become new champion

STREET FIGHT

Shane McMahon defeated Mr. McMahon, with special guest referee, Mick Foley

TLC MATCH FOR THE WORLD TAG TEAM CHAMPIONSHIP

Edge & Christian defeated the Hardy Boys and World Tag Team Champions the Dudley Boys to become new champions

GIMMICK BATTLE ROYAL

Iron Sheik defeated Nikolai Volkoff, Kamala, Doink, Repo Man, Brother Love, The Bushwhackers, Jim Cornette, Duke "The Dumpster" Droese, Tugboat, Sgt. Slaughter, Kim Chee, One Man Gang, Hillbilly Jim, The Goon, Michael Hayes, Gobbledly Gooker, and Earthquake

Undertaker defeated Triple H

WWE CHAMPIONSHIP MATCH

Stone Cold Steve Austin defeated WWE Champion The Rock to become new champion

MATCH RESULTS

For the second time in WWE history, *WrestleMania* went international when the eighteenth annual event took place in front of 68,237 fans inside Toronto's SkyDome. Nine years after making his last *WrestleMania* appearance, Hulk Hogan returned to the spotlight to battle The Rock. *WrestleMania X8* proved to be a tough night for the nWo. Not only did Hogan falter, but Scott Hall also came up short in his contest against Stone Cold Steve Austin. By the end of the night, the nWo was a mere shell of itself, as Hall and Kevin Nash attacked Hogan, officially marking the beginning of the end for the feared faction.

SkyDome; Toronto, Ontario, Canada

MAR 17 2002

INTERCONTINENTAL CHAMPIONSHIP MATCH

Rob Van Dam defeated Intercontinental Champion William Regal to become new champion

EUROPEAN CHAMPIONSHIP MATCH

European Champion Diamond Dallas Page defeated Christian

HARDCORE CHAMPIONSHIP

Utilizing the 24/7 rule, Spike Dudley, The Hurricane, Mighty Molly, Maven, and Christian all scored pinfalls to win the Hardcore Championship during the night

Kurt Angle defeated Kane

Undertaker defeated Ric Flair

Edge defeated Booker T

Stone Cold Steve Austin defeated Scott Hall (with Kevin Nash)

FATAL FOUR WAY ELIMINATION MATCH FOR THE WORLD TAG TEAM CHAMPIONSHIP

World Tag Team Champions Billy & Chuck defeated the Hardy Boys, the Dudley Boys, and the APA

ICON VS. ICON MATCH

The Rock defeated Hulk Hogan

TRIPLE THREAT MATCH FOR THE WOMEN'S CHAMPIONSHIP

Women's Champion Jazz defeated Trish Stratus and Lita

UNDISPUTED WWE CHAMPIONSHIP MATCH

Triple H defeated WWE Champion Chris Jericho to become new champion

In 2003, one of the greatest *WrestleMania* rivalries continued when The Rock squared off against Stone Cold Steve Austin for the third time. On the eve of the epic encounter, a combination of anxiety, nerves, and heart palpitations hospitalized the "Texas Rattlesnake." Despite waking up that morning in a hospital bed, Stone Cold battled the Rock in front of 54,097, but in the end, it was Austin falling to three Rock Bottoms.

In the months leading up to WrestleMania XIX, Hulk Hogan and Mr. McMahon engaged in a bitter rivalry over which man was most responsible for WWE's enormous success. In a battle for bragging rights, the two powerful personalities faced off in a Street Fight. WrestleMania XIX

also marked the first time that both the World Heavyweight and WWE Championships were contested in the same *WrestleMania*. While Triple H retained his title, Brock Lesnar delivered a now-infamous Shooting Star Press to top Kurt Angle for the WWE Championship.

Safeco Field; Seattle, WA

MAR 30 | **2003**

CRUISERWEIGHT CHAMPIONSHIP MATCH

Cruiserweight Champion Matt Hardy defeated Rey Mysterio

HANDICAP MATCH

Undertaker defeated A-Train & Big Show

TRIPLE THREAT MATCH FOR THE WOMEN'S CHAMPIONSHIP

Trish Stratus defeated Jazz and Women's Champion Victoria to become new champion

TRIPLE THREAT MATCH FOR THE WORLD TAG TEAM CHAMPIONSHIP

World Tag Team Champions Team Angle defeated Los Guerreros and Chris Benoit & Rhyno to retain

Shawn Michaels defeated Chris Jericho

CAT FIGHT

Stacy Keibler, Torrie Wilson and the Miller Light Cat Fight Girls battled to a no contest

WORLD HEAVYWEIGHT CHAMPIONSHIP MATCH

World Heavyweight Champion Triple H defeated Booker T

STREET FIGHT

Hulk Hogan defeated Mr. McMahon

The Rock defeated Stone Cold Steve Austin

WWE CHAMPIONSHIP MATCH

Brock Lesnar defeated WWE Champion Kurt Angle to become new champion

MATCH RESULTS

With over 20,000 fans on hand on its twentieth anniversary, *WrestleMania* returned to Madison Square Garden, the home of the inaugural *WrestleMania*. WrestleMania XX was John Cena's *WrestleMania* debut, and the site of the start of his first title reign. It was also the last time Goldberg and Brock Lesnar would compete in a WWE ring. Prior to their match, fans caught wind

that both Superstars would be leaving WWE following *WrestleMania*. To the delight of fans, the real highlight came after the bout when special referee Stone Cold Steve Austin hit both men with a Stone Cold Stunner.

Madison Square Garden; New York, NY

MAR 14 | **2004**

UNITED STATES CHAMPIONSHIP MATCH

John Cena defeated United States Champion Big Show to become new champion

FATAL FOUR WAY MATCH FOR THE WORLD TAG TEAM CHAMPIONSHIP

World Tag Team Champions Booker T & Rob Van Dam defeated the Dudley Boys, La Resistance, and Mark Jindrak & Garrison Cade to retain

HANDICAP MATCH

Batista, Randy Orton, & Ric Flair defeated The Rock & Mick Foley

PLAYBOY EVENING GOWN MATCH

Sable & Torrie Wilson defeated Stacy Keibler & Miss Jackie

CRUISERWEIGHT OPEN FOR THE CRUISERWEIGHT CHAMPIONSHIP

Ultimo Dragon defeated Shannon Moore; Jamie Noble defeated Ultimo Dragon; Jamie Noble defeated Funaki; Jamie Noble defeated Nunzio; Billy Kidman defeated Jamie Noble; Rey Mysterio defeated Billy Kidman; Rey Mysterio defeated Tajiri; Cruiserweight Champion Chavo Guerrero defeated Rey Mysterio

Goldberg defeated Brock Lesnar, with special guest referee Stone Cold Steve Austin

FATAL FOUR WAY MATCH FOR THE WWE TAG TEAM CHAMPIONSHIP

WWE Tag Team Champions Scotty 2 Hotty & Rikishi defeated APA, World's Greatest Tag Team, and the Basham Brothers

WOMEN'S CHAMPIONSHIP MATCH

Women's Champion Victoria defeated Molly Holly

WWE CHAMPIONSHIP MATCH

WWE Champion Eddie Guerrero defeated Kurt Angle

Undertaker defeated Kane

TRIPLE THREAT MATCH FOR THE WORLD HEAVYWEIGHT CHAMPIONSHIP

Chris Benoit defeated Shawn Michaels and World Heavyweight Champion Triple H to become new champion

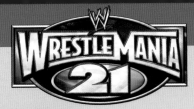

MATCH RESULTS

Rey Mysterio defeated Eddie Guerrero

MONEY IN THE BANK LADDER MATCH

Edge defeated Chris Benoit, Chris Jericho, Christian, Kane, and Shelton Benjamin

LEGEND VS. LEGEND KILLER MATCH

Undertaker defeated Randy Orton

WOMEN'S CHAMPIONSHIP MATCH

Women's Champion Trish Stratus defeated Christy Hemme

Kurt Angle defeated Shawn Michaels

SUMO MATCH

Akebono defeated Big Show

WWE CHAMPIONSHIP MATCH

John Cena defeated WWE Championship JBL to become new champion

WORLD HEAVYWEIGHT CHAMPIONSHIP MATCH

Batista defeated World Heavyweight Champion Triple H to become new champion

Emanating from Los Angeles, California, *WrestleMania 21* was aptly tagged "*WrestleMania* Goes Hollywood." Even with celebrities Sylvester Stallone, Carmen Electra, and Adam Sandler among the 20,193 in attendance, the true stars of the night were Batista and John Cena. After his 2005 *Royal Rumble* victory, Batista shocked the wrestling world when he chose to battle fellow Evolution member Triple H for the World Heavyweight Championship. John Cena claimed his first world title in WWE, allowing him to usher in the modern "spinner" championship belt that is seen today. *WrestleMania 21* also marked the beginning of the annual tradition known as the Money in the Bank Ladder Match. Big Show took part in a *WrestleMania* first when he signed on to compete in a Sumo Match against the famed Akebono.

STAPLES Center; Los Angeles, CA

APR 05 2005

MATCH RESULTS

WORLD TAG TEAM CHAMPIONSHIP MATCH

World Tag Team Champions Big Show & Kane defeated Carlito & Chris Masters to retain

MONEY IN THE BANK LADDER MATCH

Rob Van Dam defeated Ric Flair, Finlay, Shelton Benjamin, Bobby Lashley, and Matt Hardy

UNITED STATES CHAMPIONSHIP MATCH

JBL defeated United States Champion Chris Benoit to become new champion

HARDCORE MATCH

Edge (with Lita) defeated Mick Foley

HANDICAP MATCH

Boogeyman defeated Booker T & Sharmell

WOMEN'S CHAMPIONSHIP MATCH

Mickie James defeated Women's Champion Trish Stratus to become new champion

CASKET MATCH

Undertaker defeated Mark Henry

NO HOLDS BARRED MATCH

Shawn Michaels defeated Mr. McMahon

TRIPLE THREAT MATCH FOR THE WORLD HEAVYWEIGHT CHAMPIONSHIP

Rey Mysterio defeated Randy Orton and World Heavyweight Champion Kurt Angle to become new champion

PLAYBOY PILLOW FIGHT

Torrie Wilson defeated Candice Michelle

WWE CHAMPIONSHIP MATCH

WWE Champion John Cena defeated Triple H

Despite being one of the smallest Superstars on the WWE roster, Rey Mysterio took the event's "Big Time" theme literally. Competing in a World Heavyweight Championship Triple Threat Match against Kurt Angle and Randy Orton, the undersized underdog won the title. After defeating Big Show and Rob Van Dam in the *Road to WrestleMania* Tournament, momentum was clearly on Triple H's side heading into his WWE Championship Match with John Cena. Shockingly, so was half of the crowd, as the normally-popular Cena was booed by a good portion of the 17,159 fans in attendance.

Allstate Arena; Chicago, IL

APR 02 2006

MATCH RESULTS

The "Battle of the Billionaires" ruled the mainstream media heading into *WrestleMania 23*. With every major news outlet keeping a sharp eye on WWE, both Donald Trump and Mr. McMahon agreed to put their signature heads of hair on the line in front of over 80,000 fans at Detroit's Ford Field. For the second straight year, WWE Champion John Cena walked into the *WrestleMania* main event facing a divided crowd, as he took on the iconic Shawn Michaels. Elsewhere, Undertaker advanced his perfect *WrestleMania* record to 15-0 when he defeated Batista for the World Heavyweight Championship.

Ford Field; Detroit, MI

APR 01 **2007**

MONEY IN THE BANK LADDER MATCH
Mr. Kennedy defeated CM Punk, King Booker, Edge, Randy Orton, Finlay, Matt Hardy, and Jeff Hardy

The Great Khali defeated Kane

UNITED STATES CHAMPIONSHIP MATCH
United States Champion Chris Benoit defeated Montel Vontavious Porter

WORLD HEAVYWEIGHT CHAMPIONSHIP MATCH
Undertaker def World Heavyweight Champion Batista to become new champion

The ECW Originals (Tommy Dreamer, Sandman, Sabu & Rob Van Dam) defeated the New Breed (Elijah Burke, Marcus Cor Von, Matt Striker & Kevin Thorn)

BATTLE OF THE BILLIONAIRES, HAIR VS. HAIR MATCH
Bobby Lashley (representing Donald Trump) defeated Umaga (representing Mr. McMahon), with special guest referee, Stone Cold Steve Austin

LUMBERJILL MATCH FOR THE WOMEN'S CHAMPIONSHIP
Women's Champion Melina defeated Ashley

WWE CHAMPIONSHIP MATCH
WWE Champion John Cena defeated Shawn Michaels

MATCH RESULTS

Held outdoors in Orlando's famed Citrus Bowl, *WrestleMania XXIV* proved to be the "Biggest *WrestleMania* Under the Sun." Unfortunately for Ric Flair, it also marked the day the sun set on his legendary career. After a loss to Shawn Michaels, a tearful Flair thanked the fans and his family for their decades of support before riding off into the sunset. Three years after falling to Akebono in a sumo match, Big Show stepped out of his traditional wrestling arena yet again, this time to battle acclaimed boxer Floyd "Money" Mayweather.

Citrus Bowl; Orlando, FL

MAR 30 **2008**

BELFAST BRAWL
JBL defeated Finlay

MONEY IN THE BANK LADDER MATCH
CM Punk defeated Chris Jericho, Carlito, Montel Vontavious Porter, Shelton Benjamin, John Morrison, and Mr. Kennedy

BATTLE FOR BRAND SUPREMACY
Batista defeated Umaga

ECW CHAMPIONSHIP MATCH
Kane defeated ECW Champion Chavo Guerrero to become new champion

CAREER THREATENING MATCH
Shawn Michaels defeated Ric Flair

BUNNYMANIA LUMBERJILL MATCH
Melina & Beth Phoenix defeated Maria & Ashley

TRIPLE THREAT MATCH FOR THE WWE CHAMPIONSHIP
WWE Champion Randy Orton defeated Triple H and John Cena

THE BIGGEST VS. THE BEST
Floyd "Money" Mayweather defeated Big Show via knockout

WORLD HEAVYWEIGHT CHAMPIONSHIP MATCH
Undertaker defeated World Heavyweight Champion Edge to become new champion

THE WRESTLING CLASSIC

LOCATION Rosemont Horizon, Rosemont, IL   **DATE** November 7, 1985

The *Wrestling Classic*, also known as WrestleVision, was the first pay per view event WWE made available on a large scale (*WrestleMania* came first but was available in a limited number of markets). The Wrestling Classic is also the name of the tournament that took place at the event. Sixteen Superstars (Adrian Adonis, Corporal Kirschner, Dynamite Kid, Nikolai Volkoff, Randy Savage, Ivan Putski, Ricky Steamboat, Davey Boy Smith, Junkyard Dog, Iron Sheik, Moondog Spot, Terry Funk, Tito Santana, the Magnificent Muraco, Paul Orndorff, & "Cowboy" Bob Orton) began the night. Junkyard Dog emerged victorious over Randy Savage at the end of the tournament with a hard-fought count-out victory.

The only match of the night that did not involve the tournament was a WWE Championship Match between Hulk Hogan and "Rowdy" Roddy Piper, who lost after being disqualified due to the interference of "Cowboy" Bob Orton.

WWE CHAMPIONSHIP

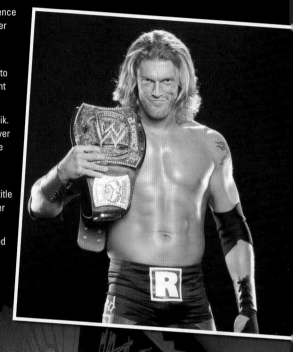

Widely recognized as the top prize in all of sports-entertainment, the WWE Championship began its historic existence on April 29, 1963, when Buddy Rogers defeated Antonino Rocca in the finals of a tournament to crown the first-ever titleholder.

Many memorable reigns followed Rogers' inaugural tour of duty with the WWE Championship, but none were as lengthy as Bruno Sammartino's first run with the title. Sammartino defeated Rogers on May 17, 1963, and went on to hold the gold until January 18, 1971, when he was finally upended by Ivan Koloff. Sammartino's reign of nearly eight years is a record many sports-entertainment insiders believe will never be broken.

The WWE Championship reached iconic levels in January 1984, when Hulk Hogan won the title from The Iron Sheik. Almost immediately after Hogan strapped the gold around his waist for the first time, Hulkamania began to take over the nation. It wasn't long before kids across the United States starting donning Hogan's signature headband, while The Hulkster found himself on countless magazine covers, including *Sports Illustrated*.

In the years that followed, such great names as Ric Flair and Bret Hart climbed the elusive WWE Championship mountain. In March 1998, the defiant Stone Cold Steve Austin captured the WWE Championship and brought the title to heights once thought unimaginable. His popularity quickly became a global phenomenon, as fans the world over tuned into *Raw* at record rates to watch the workingman's champion.

Stone Cold Steve Austin's championship days ended in September 2001, but Superstars like The Rock, Triple H, and John Cena have worked long and hard to maintain the WWE Championship's remarkable reputation.

WWE CHAMPIONSHIP TIMELINE

1963
APR 29 — Rio de Janeiro — Buddy Rogers defeated Antonino Rocca in the finals of a tournament to be crowned the first-ever WWE Champion.

MAY 17 — New York, NY — Bruno Sammartino defeats Buddy Rogers

1971
JAN 01 — New York, NY — Ivan Koloff defeats Bruno Sammartino

FEB 08 — New York, NY — Pedro Morales defeats Ivan Koloff

1973
DEC 01 — Philadelphia, PA — Stan Stasiak defeats Pedro Morales

DEC 10 — New York, NY — Bruno Sammartino defeats Stan Stasiak

WWE President Jack Tunney vacated the title after learning Ted DiBiase had paid a corrupt referee to have plastic surgery in order to look like the official referee assigned to the match.

MAR 27 — Atlantic City, NJ — Randy Savage beat Ted DiBiase in the finals of a 14-man tournament to crown a new WWE Champion.

1989
APR 02 — Atlantic City, NJ — Hulk Hogan defeats Randy Savage

1990
APR 01 — Toronto, Ontario — Ultimate Warrior defeats Hulk Hogan

1991
JAN 19 — Miami, FL — Sgt. Slaughter defeats Ultimate Warrior

1993
APR 04 — Las Vegas, NV — Yokozuna defeats Bret Hart

APR 04 — Las Vegas, NV — Hulk Hogan defeats Yokozuna

JUNE 13 — Dayton, OH — Yokozuna defeats Hulk Hogan

1994
MAR 20 — New York, NY — Bret Hart defeats Yokozuna

NOV 23 — San Antonio, TX — Bob Backlund defeats Bret Hart

NOV 26 — New York, NY — Diesel defeats Bob Backlund

1995
NOV 19 — Landover, MD — Bret Hart defeats Diesel

AUG 03 — East Rutherford, NJ — Bret Hart defeats Undertaker

NOV 09 — Montreal, Quebec — Michaels defeats Bret Hart

1998
MAR 29 — Boston, MA — Stone Cold Steve Austin defeats Shawn Michaels

JUNE 28 — Pittsburgh, PA — Kane defeats Stone Cold Steve Austin

JUNE 29 — Cleveland, OH — Stone Cold Steve Austin defeats Kane

Mr. McMahon vacates the title in September 1998 after a controversial ending to a Triple Threat Match featuring Stone Cold Steve Austin, Undertaker, and Kane.

NOV 15 — St. Louis, MO — The Rock defeats Mankind in the finals of a 14-man tournament to crown a new WWE Champion.

AUG 23 — Ames, IA — Triple H defeats Mankind

SEPT 16 — Las Vegas, NV — Mr. McMahon defeats Triple H

Mr. McMahon vacates the title on September 20.

SEPT 26 — Charlotte, NC — Triple H pins The Rock to win the WWE Championship in a Six-Pack Challenge Match that also included Mankind, British Bulldog, Big Show, and Kane.

NOV 14 — Detroit, MI — Big Show pins Triple H to win the WWE Championship in a Triple Threat Match that also included The Rock.

2000
JAN 03 — Miami, FL — Triple H defeats Big Show

APR 30 — Washington, DC — The Rock defeats Triple H

DEC 09 — San Diego, CA — Chris Jericho defeats Stone Cold Steve Austin

2002
MAR 17 — Toronto, Ontario — Triple H defeats Chris Jericho

APR 21 — Kansas City, MO — Hulk Hogan defeats Triple H

MAY 19 — Nashville, TN — Undertaker defeats Hulk Hogan

JULY 21 — Detroit, MI — The Rock pins Kurt Angle to win the WWE Championship in a Triple Threat Match that also included then-champion Undertaker.

AUG 25 — Uniondale, NY — Brock Lesnar defeats The Rock

NOV 17 — New York, NY — Big Show defeats Brock Lesnar

DEC 15 — Fort Lauderdale, FL — Kurt Angle defeats Big Show

2003
MAR 30 — Seattle, WA — Brock Lesnar defeats Kurt Angle

JULY 27 — Denver, CO — Kurt Angle pins Brock Lesnar to win the WWE Championship in a Triple Threat Match that also included Big Show.

SEPT 18 — Raleigh, NC — Brock Lesnar defeats Kurt Angle

2004
FEB 15 — San Francisco, CA — Eddie Guerrero defeats Brock Lesnar

JUNE 27 — Norfolk, VA — JBL defeats Eddie Guerrero

2005
APR 03 — Los Angeles, CA — John Cena defeats JBL

2006
JAN 08 — Albany, NY — Edge defeats John Cena

JAN 29 — Miami, FL — John Cena defeats Edge

JUNE 11 — New York, NY — Rob Van Dam defeats John Cena

JULY 03 — Philadelphia, PA — Edge pins Rob Van Dam to win the WWE Championship in a Triple Threat Match that also included John Cena.

SEPT 17 — Toronto, Ontario — John Cena defeats Edge

2007
OCT 07 — Chicago, IL — Randy Orton is awarded the WWE Championship

Mr. McMahon awarded the WWE Championship to Randy Orton after an injury at the hands of Orton forced John Cena to surrender the title.

OCT 07 — Chicago, IL — Triple H defeats Randy Orton

OCT 07 — Chicago, IL — Randy Orton defeats Triple H

2008
APR 27 — Baltimore, MD — Triple H pins Randy Orton to win the WWE Championship in a Fatal Four Way Match that also included John Cena and JBL.

HUSTLE LOYALTY RESPECT

JOHN CENA

1977

APR 30 — Baltimore, MD
Superstar Billy Graham defeats Bruno Sammartino

1978

FEB 20 — New York, NY
Bob Backlund defeats Superstar Billy Graham

1983

DEC 26 — New York, NY
The Iron Sheik defeats Bob Backlund

1984

JAN 23 — New York, NY
Hulk Hogan defeats The Iron Sheik

1988

FEB 05 — Indianapolis, IN
Andre the Giant defeats Hulk Hogan

MAR 24 — Los Angeles, CA
Hulk Hogan defeats Sgt. Slaughter

NOV 27 — Detroit, MI
Undertaker defeats Hulk Hogan

DEC 03 — San Antonio, TX
Hulk Hogan defeats Undertaker

WWE President Jack Tunney vacated the title due to controversy surrounding Hulk Hogan's victory over Undertaker.

1992

JAN 19 — Albany, NY
Ric Flair last eliminated Sid Justice to win the Royal Rumble and the WWE Championship.

APR 05 — Indianapolis, IN
Randy Savage defeats Ric Flair

SEPT 01 — Hershey, PA
Ric Flair defeats Randy Savage

OCT 12 — Saskatoon, Saskatchewan
Bret Hart defeats Ric Flair

1996

MAR 31 — Anaheim, CA
Shawn Michaels defeats Bret Hart

NOV 17 — New York, NY
Sid defeats Shawn Michaels

1997

JAN 19 — San Antonio, TX
Shawn Michaels defeats Sid

Injuries force Shawn Michaels to vacate the title shortly after his victory.

FEB 16 — Chattanooga, TN
Bret Hart last eliminates Undertaker in a Fatal Four Way Match that also included Vader and Stone Cold Steve Austin.

FEB 16 — Chattanooga, TN
Bret Hart last eliminates Undertaker in a Fatal Four Way Match that also included Vader and Stone Cold Steve Austin.

FEB 17 — Nashville, TN
Sid defeats Bret Hart

MAR 23 — Chicago, IL
Undertaker defeats Sid

1999

JAN 04 — Worcester, MA
Mankind defeats The Rock

JAN 24 — Anaheim, CA
The Rock defeats Mankind

JAN 31 — Tucson, AZ
Mankind defeats The Rock

FEB 15 — Birmingham, AL
The Rock defeats Mankind

MAR 28 — Philadelphia, PA
Stone Cold Steve Austin defeats The Rock

MAY 23 — Kansas City, MO
Undertaker defeats Stone Cold Steve Austin

JUNE 28 — Charlotte, NC
Stone Cold Steve Austin defeats Undertaker

AUG 22 — Minneapolis, MN
Mankind pins Stone Cold Steve Austin to win the WWE Championship in a Triple Threat Match that also included Triple H.

MAY 21 — Louisville, KY
Triple H defeats The Rock

JUNE 25 — Boston, MA
The Rock defeats Mr. McMahon

The Rock, Undertaker and Kane battled Triple H, Shane and Mr. McMahon in a six-man tag team match. Pre-match stipulations stated that if anybody on Triple H's team lost, he would lose his WWE Championship. The Rock pinned Mr. McMahon to win the title.

OCT 22 — Albany, NY
Kurt Angle defeats The Rock

2001

FEB 25 — Las Vegas, NV
The Rock defeats Kurt Angle

APR 01 — Houston, TX
Stone Cold Steve Austin defeats The Rock

SEPT 23 — Pittsburgh, PA
Kurt Angle defeats Stone Cold Steve Austin

OCT 08 — Indianapolis, IN
Stone Cold Steve Austin defeats Kurt Angle

WWE TAG TEAM CHAMPIONSHIP

Once it was decided by World Wrestling Entertainment brass in 2002 that the World Tag Team Championship would be exclusive to the *Raw* brand, then-*SmackDown!* General Manager Stephanie McMahon created her own version of the Tag Team Championship. She stated that the first team to wear these prestigious belts could only do so if they survived a brutal tournament. The duo that emerged victorious was Kurt Angle and Chris Benoit. Since that historic tournament several outstanding tag teams have staked claim to this prominent championship including the Dudley Boys, Los Guerreros, the World's Greatest Tag Team, and John Morrison & The Miz.

2002

OCT 20 — Little Rock, AR
Kurt Angle and Chris Benoit defeat Edge & Rey Mysterio in the tournament to crown the first-ever WWE Tag Team Champions.

NOV 07 — Manchester, NH
Edge & Rey Mysterio defeat Kurt Angle & Chris Benoit

NOV 17 — New York, NY
Los Guerreros defeat Edge & Rey Mysterio

2003

FEB 06 — Philadelphia, PA
The World's Greatest Tag Team defeat Los Guerreros

MAY 18 — Charlotte, NC
Eddie Guerrero & Taijiri defeat the World's Greatest Tag Team

JULY 03 — Rochester, NY
The World's Greatest Tag Team defeat Eddie Guerrero & Taijiri

SEPT 18 — Raleigh, NC
Los Guerreros defeat The World's Greatest Tag Team

OCT 23 — Albany, NY
The Basham Brothers defeat Los Guerreros

2004

FEB 05 — Cleveland, OH
Scotty 2 Hotty & Rikishi defeat the Basham Brothers

APR 22 — Kelowna, BC
Charlie Haas & Rico defeat Scotty 2 Hotty & Rikishi

JUNE 17 — Chicago, IL
The Dudley Boys defeat Charlie Haas & Rico

JULY 08 — Winnipeg, Manitoba
Billy Kidman & Paul London defeat the Dudley Boys

SEPT 09 — Tulsa, OK
Kenzo Suzuki & Renee Dupree defeat Billy Kidman & Paul London

DEC 09 — Greenville, SC
Rob Van Dam & Rey Mysterio defeat Kenzo Suzuki & Renee Dupree

2005

JAN 13 — Tampa, FL
The Basham Brothers defeat Rob Van Dam & Rey Mysterio

FEB 20 — Pittsburgh, PA
Rey Mysterio & Eddie Guerrero defeat The Basham Brothers

APR 21 — New York, NY
MNM defeat Rey Mysterio & Eddie Guerrero

JULY 25 — Buffalo, NY
Animal & Heidenreich defeat MNM

OCT 28 — San Francisco, CA
MNM defeat Road Warrior Animal & Heidenreich

DEC 16 — Springfield, MA
Batista & Rey Mysterio defeat MNM

DEC 30 — Uncasville, CT
MNM defeat Batista & Rey Mysterio

2006

MAY 21 — Phoenix, AZ
Brian Kendrick & Paul London defeat MNM

2007

APR 20 — Milan, Italy
Deuce & Domino defeat Brian Kendrick & Paul London

AUG 31 — Albany, NY
MVP & Matt Hardy defeat Deuce & Domino

NOV 16 — Wichita, KS
John Morrison & the Miz defeat MVP & Matt Hardy

2008

JUL 20 — Uniondale, NY
Curt Hawkins & Zach Ryder defeat John Morrison & the Miz

SEP 20 — Columbus, OH
Carlito & Primo Colon defeat Curt Hawkins & Zach Ryder

Xanta Claus

| HT | 6'2" | WT | 305 lbs. | FROM | The South Pole |

| SIGNATURE MOVE | Nutcracker Suite |

During the December 17, 1995 *In Your House* Pay-Per-View it appeared that Santa Claus was giving gifts to young fans around the ring with the help of Savio Vega. "Million Dollar Man" Ted DiBiase appeared and disparaged both Santa and his helper. Just as his verbal exchange with Vega ended, the Million Dollar Man's twisted sense of holiday gift giving presented itself. Suddenly, Santa attacked Savio Vega and viciously beat him in front of the capacity crowd.

Thanks to Jim Ross, audiences soon learned that this individual claimed to be the twin brother of Santa Claus and went by the name "Xanta Claus." He hailed from the South Pole, stole presents from good children and used underhanded maneuvers to put away opponents. While Xanta Claus had a brief tenure in the WWE history, his despicable actions during his television debut made a lasting impression.

X-Factor

| MEMBERS | X-Pac, Albert, Justin Credible | COMBINED WEIGHT | 775 lbs. |

| TITLE HISTORY | Light Heavyweight Championship, Cruiserweight Championship, Intercontinental Championship |

X-Factor may not sit atop historians' lists of greatest factions of all time, but what many fail to remember is the rapid rate in which the group snatched up championships. In all, X-Factor compiled an astonishing four championship reigns during their brief eight-month union.

The leader of the group, X-Pac, enjoyed two Light Heavyweight Championship reigns before unifying the title with the Cruiserweight Championship in July 2001. Albert attained the group's greatest success when he used his patented Baldo Bomb to defeat Kane for the Intercontinental Championship in June 2001. Finally, the faction's most extreme Superstar, Justin Credible, was a perennial contender for the Hardcore Championship, which he eventually captured eight times after X-Factor split up.

Together, X-Factor's biggest victory came when they defeated Bubba Ray, D-Von & Spike Dudley at *Backlash 2001*. The faction began to slowly crumble after Credible left X-Pac & Albert to join forces with the WCW/ECW Alliance.

YOKOZUNA 🇯🇵

| **HT** 6'4" | **WT** 600 lbs. | **FROM** The Land of the Rising Sun |

SIGNATURE MOVE Bonzai Drop **YEARS ACTIVE** 1960-1969 1970-1979 1980-1989 1990-1999 2000-PRESENT

TITLE HISTORY WWE Champion, World Tag Team Champion

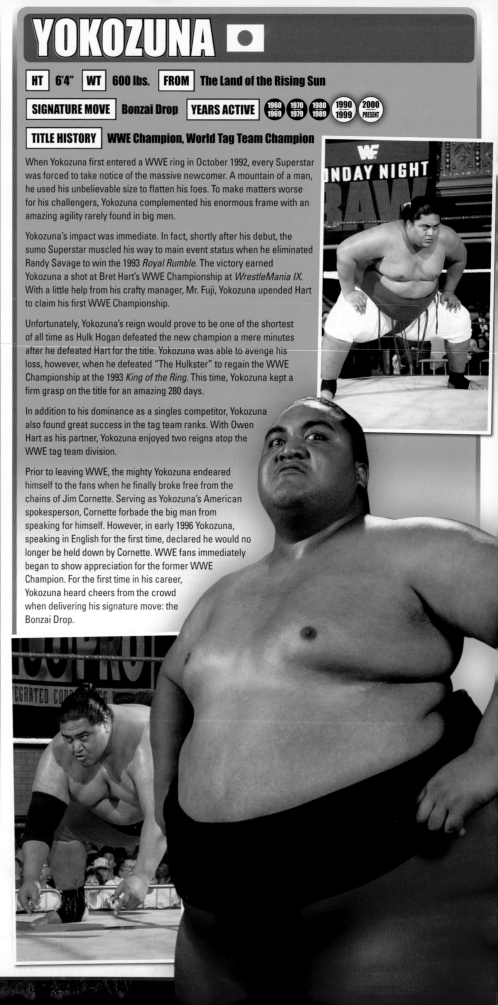

When Yokozuna first entered a WWE ring in October 1992, every Superstar was forced to take notice of the massive newcomer. A mountain of a man, he used his unbelievable size to flatten his foes. To make matters worse for his challengers, Yokozuna complemented his enormous frame with an amazing agility rarely found in big men.

Yokozuna's impact was immediate. In fact, shortly after his debut, the sumo Superstar muscled his way to main event status when he eliminated Randy Savage to win the 1993 *Royal Rumble*. The victory earned Yokozuna a shot at Bret Hart's WWE Championship at *WrestleMania IX*. With a little help from his crafty manager, Mr. Fuji, Yokozuna upended Hart to claim his first WWE Championship.

Unfortunately, Yokozuna's reign would prove to be one of the shortest of all time as Hulk Hogan defeated the new champion a mere minutes after he defeated Hart for the title. Yokozuna was able to avenge his loss, however, when he defeated "The Hulkster" to regain the WWE Championship at the 1993 *King of the Ring*. This time, Yokozuna kept a firm grasp on the title for an amazing 280 days.

In addition to his dominance as a singles competitor, Yokozuna also found great success in the tag team ranks. With Owen Hart as his partner, Yokozuna enjoyed two reigns atop the WWE tag team division.

Prior to leaving WWE, the mighty Yokozuna endeared himself to the fans when he finally broke free from the chains of Jim Cornette. Serving as Yokozuna's American spokesperson, Cornette forbade the big man from speaking for himself. However, in early 1996 Yokozuna, speaking in English for the first time, declared he would no longer be held down by Cornette. WWE fans immediately began to show appreciation for the former WWE Champion. For the first time in his career, Yokozuna heard cheers from the crowd when delivering his signature move: the Bonzai Drop.

X-Pac 🇺🇸

| **HT** 6'1" | **WT** 212 lbs. |

FROM Minneapolis, Minnesota

SIGNATURE MOVE 1-2-3 Kick

TITLE HISTORY World Tag Team Champion, European Champion, Light Heavyweight Champion, Cruiserweight Champion

YEARS ACTIVE 1960-1969 1970-1979 1980-1989 1990-1999 2000-PRESENT

Making his WWE debut in the spring of 1993 as the Kid, he made an immediate impact during an episode of *Monday Night Raw* when he beat Razor Ramon. Renamed the 1-2-3 Kid, he teamed with Marty Jannetty to win the World Tag Team Championship. Sadly, WWE's shy hero soon took a new career direction as a member of Ted DiBiase's Million Dollar Corporation.

In late 1996, the 1-2-3 Kid left WWE and stunned audiences when he appeared in the front row of an episode of *WCW Monday Nitro,* calling himself Syxx. In March 1998, his contract was suddenly terminated, but he didn't stay gone for long. During an episode of *Monday Night Raw*, Triple H introduced the latest recruit to DX, X-Pac. Though later Triple H turned on him, which caused a split within DX, X-Pac later rejoined the group. Partnering with Kane, the duo won the World Tag Team Championship. When he returned from injury, DX had dissolved and in 2001 he formed the short-lived X-Factor with Justin Credible and Albert.

He was the only Superstar to ever wear both the WCW Cruiserweight and WWE Light Heavyweight championships at once when he defeated Billy Kidman. Plagued by injuries, X-Pac was out of action and released from WWE that August. Since his recovery, he has brought his mix of martial arts and aerial maneuvers to arenas all over the world.

The Young Stallions

YEARS ACTIVE 1960-1969 · 1970-1979 · **1980-1989** · 1990-1999 · 2000-PRESENT

| MEMBERS | Paul Roma, Jim Powers | COMBINED WEIGHT | 481 lbs. |

No strangers to WWE audiences, these two former singles competitors joined forces in the late 1980s. As a cohesive unit, Roma & Powers were an exciting combination during one of the greatest eras of tag team wrestling. They battled the Hart Foundation over the rights of use to the theme song *Crank It Up,* when Jimmy Hart claimed the tune was intended for his men.

The shining moment for the Young Stallions came at the 1987 *Survivor Series* when, along with the Killer Bees, they were the sole survivors in the tag team elimination match. They also appeared in the 20-Man Over the Top Rope Battle Royal at *WrestleMania IV* before taking on top teams like the Brain Busters, the Fabulous Rougeaus, and the Twin Towers.

Unfortunately for their fans, mounting losses turned frustration into fighting and the Stallions fell apart. Paul Roma became a member of Power & Glory while Jim Powers returned to singles action.

The Yukon Lumberjacks

YEARS ACTIVE 1960-1969 · **1970-1979** · 1980-1989 · 1990-1999 · 2000-PRESENT

| MEMBERS | Eric, Pierre | COMBINED WEIGHT | 551 lbs. | TITLE HISTORY | World Tag Team Champions |

Managed by Capt. Lou Albano, the Yukon Lumberjacks spent a brief, but successful time competing in WWE. Eric & Pierre made their WWE debut in 1978. Shortly after their initial appearance, the bearded duo defeated the legendary Dominic DeNucci & Dino Bravo in New York City to capture the World Tag Team Championship. Behind Eric's devastating big boot and Pierre's Cobra Clutch, the Yukon Lumberjacks sawed through all challengers before finally losing the titles to Tony Garea & Larry Zbyszko in November 1978.

The Yukon Lumberjacks split up shortly after losing the World Tag Team Championship. Eric went on to compete for various southern United States promotions, while Pierre achieved most of his notoriety wrestling in Canada.

Zach Gowen

YEARS ACTIVE 1960-1969 · 1970-1979 · 1980-1989 · 1990-1999 · **2000-PRESENT**

| HT | 6'1" | WT | 169 lbs. | FROM | Flint, Michigan | SIGNATURE MOVE | Unisault |

When Zach Gowen was eight years old he lost his left leg to cancer. He was a WWE fan and dreamed of meeting Hulk Hogan. Through the years Zach followed sports-entertainment and became an amateur wrestler in high school. In May 2003, his life-long dream came true when he appeared on *SmackDown* and held the American Flag for Mr. America. He intervened on America's behalf when he was jumped by Roddy Piper and Sean O' Haire. Piper exposed Zach's condition when he pulled off his prosthetic limb.

Zach's spent a year in WWE fending off Big Show, Brock Lesnar, and the manipulative Mr. McMahon. In early 2004, Zach and World Wrestling Entertainment parted ways, but he was recognized for his achievements by *Pro Wrestling Illustrated* who named Zach the 2003 "Rookie of the Year" and "Most Inspirational Wrestler of the Year."

Zeus

YEARS ACTIVE 1960-1969 · 1970-1979 · **1980-1989** · 1990-1999 · 2000-PRESENT

| HT | 6'5" | WT | 300 lbs. | FROM | Parts Unknown |

During the filming of *No Holds Barred* reports spread that tensions were high on the set between Hulk Hogan and the man known as "the Human Wrecking Machine," Zeus. In the spring of 1989, Zeus appeared in WWE with Slick, and attacked Hulk Hogan before his Steel Cage Match with Big Boss Man. Zeus claimed that he was the real star of *No Holds Barred* and that he was going to destroy Hulk Hogan.

Zeus continued to stalk Hogan in arenas around the nation and joined forces with Randy Savage. They challenged the team of Hogan & Brutus Beefcake at *SummerSlam '89*. The battle didn't end there as the four men brought others into the fray at that November's *Survivor Series*. Zeus made his last appearance with World Wrestling Entertainment in December 1989 in No Holds Barred—The Match. Zeus appeared months later in Puerto Rico and later appeared briefly in WCW as Z-Gangsta. Today, the man once known as Zeus can be seen in many movies and television programs.

Z

INDEX

#

1-2-3 Kid (see X-Pac)
3-Minute Warning _____ 8
8-Ball _____ 80

A

Abs, Joey _____ 67, 156, 201
Adam Bomb _____ 8
Adamale, Mike _____ 207
Adams, Brian _____ 177
Adonis, Adrian _____ 8, 9, 87, 128
Afa _____ 336
Akeem (see One Man Gang)
Albano, Lou _____ 190
Albert _____ 10, 361
Alliance, The _____ 11
Allied Powers _____ 11
Altomare, Tony _____ 308
Anderson, Arn _____ 42, 128
Andre the Giant _____ 12, 66, 128
Angle, Kurt _____ 177
Animal _____ 183
Antonio _____ 128
APA, The _____ 15
Apollo, Argentina _____ 15
Arakawa, Mitsu _____ 211
Arcidi, Ted _____ 299
Ariel _____ 15
Arion, Spiros _____ 283
Armageddon _____ 15
Ashley _____ 18
Atlas, Tony _____ 308
Austin, Stone Cold Steve _____ 85, 288
Avatar _____ 19
Awesome, Mike _____ 207
Ax _____ 76

B

Baba, Shohei "Giant" _____ 276
Backlash _____ 19
Backlund, Bob _____ 34
Bad Blood _____ 19
Barbarian _____ 21, 128, 237
Barber Shop, The _____ 21
Basham Brothers _____ 23, 56
Basham, Danny _____ 23
Basham, Doug _____ 23
Bass, Nicole _____ 224
Bass, "Outlaw" Ron _____ 229
Bastien, Red _____ 245
Batista _____ 24, 98
Battle Kat _____ 25
Battle Royal _____ 25
Battman _____ 26
Bearer, Paul _____ 210, 231
Beast, The _____ 26
Beefcake, Brutus _____ 50, 84, 201
Bella, Brie _____ 44
Bella, Nikki _____ 44
Bellamo, Salvatore _____ 264
Benjamin, Momma _____ 212
Benjamin, Shelton _____ 275, 344
Benoit, Chris _____ 61, 239
Berry, Wild Red _____ 335
Berzerker, The _____ 27

Beverly Brothers, The _____ 27
Beverly, Beau _____ 27
Beverly, Blake _____ 27
Big Boss Man _____ 28, 67, 316
Big Daddy V _____ 28
Big Event, The _____ 29
Big Machine _____ 193
Big Man Steel _____ 30
Big Show _____ 30, 67, 224, 319
Bigelow, Bam Bam _____ 20, 210
Billy the Kid _____ 32
Bischoff, Eric _____ 93
Black Bart _____ 33
Blackjack Bradshaw _____ 220
Blackjack Lanza _____ 33
Blackjack Mulligan _____ 33
Blackjack Windham _____ 220
Blackjacks, The _____ 33
Blackman, Steve _____ 287
Blair, B. Brian _____ 172
Blanchard, Tully _____ 42, 128
Blassie, Freddie _____ 105
Blayze, Alundra _____ 11
Blu Brothers _____ 33
Blu, Eli _____ 33
Blu, Jacob _____ 33
Blue Blazer _____ 229
Blue Meanie _____ 34, 56, 156
Body Shop, The _____ 38
Bodydonna, Skip _____ 39
Bodydonna, Zip _____ 39
Bodydonnas, The _____ 39
Bollea, Michael _____ 203
Bolo Mongol _____ 39
Bolsheviks, The _____ 39
Booger, Bastian _____ 23
Boogeyman _____ 40
Booker T _____ 40, 224
Boone, Brady _____ 42
Borga, Ludvig _____ 192
Borne, Matt _____ 199
Bourne, Evan _____ 95
Bra & Panies Match _____ 41
Braddock, Ryan _____ 262
Bradshaw, Justin "Hawk" _____ 166
Brain Busters _____ 42
Brakkus _____ 42
Brandi, Tom (see Sincere, Salvatore)
Bravo, Dino _____ 80, 82, 84, 220
Brazil, Bobo _____ 38
Brisco Brothers _____ 44
Brisco, Gerald _____ 44, 67
Brisco, Jack _____ 44
British Bulldogs _____ 45
Brito, Gino _____ 112
Brody, Bruiser _____ 47
Brood, The _____ 46
Brooke _____ 46, 99
Brooklyn Brawler, The _____ 46, 128
Brother Love _____ 47
Brother Love Show, The _____ 47
Brothers of Destruction, The _____ 47
Brower, Bulldog _____ 54
Brown, Bad News _____ 19
Brown, D-Lo _____ 81, 188, 251

Brown, Luke _____ 171
Brunzell, Jim _____ 172
Brute Bernard _____ 50
Buchanon, Bull _____ 51, 251
Bundy, King Kong _____ 128, 174, 210
Bunkhouse Brawl _____ 54
Burchill, Katie Lea _____ 169
Burchill, Paul _____ 231
Buried Alive Match _____ 54
Burke, Elijah _____ 91
Bush, Barbara (B.B.) _____ 21
Bushwackers _____ 55
Busick, Big Bully _____ 28
Butch _____ 55
Butterbean _____ 55
bWo _____ 56

C

Cabinet, The _____ 56
Cactus Jack (see Foley, Mick)
Cade, Lance _____ 179
Calhoun, Haystacks _____ 127
Camp Cornette _____ 56
Canadian Heavyweight Championship _____ 56
Can-Am Connection _____ 57
Candice _____ 57
Cannon, Crybaby _____ 69
Cappetta, Gary Michael _____ 108
Carlito _____ 57
Carlito's Cabana _____ 58
Carpentier, Edouard _____ 91
Casey, Scott _____ 266
Cassidy, Lance _____ 179
Cassidy, Leif _____ 221
Castillo, Jesus _____ 189
Cena, John _____ 158
Cerdan, Louis _____ 191
Chainz _____ 80
Chaz _____ 188
Cherry _____ 59
Chief White Owl _____ 61
Chimel, Tony _____ 309
Christian _____ 46, 63, 90, 210, 318
Christopher, Brian _____ 310
Chyna _____ 64, 67, 77
Clark, Bryan _____ 177
Cleavage, Beaver _____ 26
CM Punk _____ 65
Coach, The _____ 65
Coachman, Jonathan _____ 162
Cobra, The _____ 65
Col. Mustafa _____ 66
Cole, Michael _____ 203
Colon, Carlos _____ 58
Colossal Connection, The _____ 66
Commandant, The _____ 314
Conway, Rob _____ 178, 252
Cor Von, Marcus _____ 197
Cornette, Jim _____ 56, 152
Corporal Kirschner _____ 66
Corporation, The _____ 67
Costello, Al _____ 100
Cousin Junior _____ 131
Cousin Luke _____ 131
Credible, Justin _____ 166, 361

Cruiserweight Championship _____ 70
Crush _____ 68, 76, 80, 219
Cryme Tyme _____ 69
Cutting Edge, The _____ 72
Cyber Sunday _____ 72

D

Daivari _____ 72
Davis, Danny _____ 73
Dawn Marie _____ 74
Dean Douglas _____ 75
Dean, Simon _____ 277
Debra _____ 75
December to Dismember _____ 76
DeFazio, Johnny _____ 160
Delany, Colin _____ 66
DelRay, Jimmy _____ 128
Demento, Damien _____ 72
Demolition _____ 76
DeMott, Bill _____ 31
DeNucci, Dominic _____ 82
Deuce _____ 76
D-Generation X _____ 77
DiBiase, "Million Dollar Man" Ted _____ 209, 213
DiBiase, Ted _____ 302
Dick the Bruiser _____ 79
Dick, Chad _____ 79
Dick, James _____ 79
Dicks, The _____ 79
Diesel _____ 79, 80, 176, 224
Dink the Clown _____ 80
Disciples of Apocalypse, The _____ 80
Diva's Championship _____ 81
Doink _____ 81
Domino _____ 76
Doring, Danny _____ 73
Douglas, Shane _____ 271
Dream Team, The _____ 84
Dreamer, Tommy _____ 308
Droese, Duke "the Dumpster" _____ 85
Droz _____ 84
Dude Love (see Foley, Mick)
Dudley Boys, the _____ 85
Dudley, Bubba Ray _____ 85
Dudley, D-Von _____ 85
Dudley, James _____ 148
Dudley, Spike _____ 282
Duggan, "Hacksaw" Jim _____ 120
Duncum, Bobby _____ 35
Dunn, Steve _____ 335
Dupree, Rene _____ 178, 245
Dykstra, Kenny _____ 171, 282
Dynamite Kid _____ 86

E

Earthquake _____ 87, 219
East-West Connection, The _____ 87
ECW _____ 88
ECW Championship _____ 88
Edge _____ 46, 90, 210
Eight-Man Tag Match _____ 91
El Olympico _____ 91
Elimination Chamber _____ 92
Elimination Match _____ 92
Elizabeth _____ 92

ACKNOWLEDGMENTS

Kevin Sullivan

Above all else, I would like to thank my wife Caryn for supporting me during this project. My passion to make this book a must-read for all sports-entertainment fans unfortunately left her to tackle her pregnancy practically on her own. Luckily for me, she overlooked my selfishness and supported me the entire time. Thank you, Caryn. You are the strongest and most beautiful woman I know.

I would also like to thank my parents, Lorraine and Joe, for supporting my WWE addiction while growing up. My mother bought me my first action figure, an LJN version of the Iron Sheik; and my father, who inexplicably loved the Bushwhackers, sacrificed his weekends to take me to live events, including WrestleMania V and X.

Thank you to my sister, Amy, for using her connections to get me my first job with WWE in 1998.

It's been an honor to work with Ken Schmidt, Brian Saliba, Leigh Davis, and the entire DK Publishing team. The book you are holding in your hands looks so impressive because of their endless dedication to make it the best it could possibly be.

Thank you to my WWE family. For ten years, I had the honor of being surrounded by the most creative team ever assembled. Special thanks to Mike Archer for mentoring me for all those years; Dean Miller for including me in this project; Chris Chambers for being so much more than a boss; and Michael Cole for making the twenty-hour workdays a little more enjoyable. Of course, I would be remiss if I didn't mention the talented team at WWE.com: John Cerilli, Phil Speer, Lucas Swineford, Mike McAvennie, Craig Tello, Zack Zeigler, Bryan Robinson, Ken O'Brien, Jim Monsees, Jennifer Spear and the rest of the gang (Sorry, guys. There are just too many of you to list. It's hard to believe that we all fit into that .com trailer).

Thank you to the McMahon family for taking a chance on a kid like me and giving me the tools needed to climb the corporate ladder.

Finally, thank you Brian Shields for being an amazing co-author. I'm looking forward to working with you again in the future.

WORLD WRESTLING ENTERTAINMENT, INC. CREDITS

Director, Home Entertainment & Books
Dean Miller

Photo Department
Frank Vitucci, Joshua Tottenham, Jamie Nelson, Lea Girard, Melissa Halladay

Legal
Lauren Middlen, Jim Coplit

WWE would like to thank Jennifer Good, Steve Pantaleo, Lauren Dienes-Middlen, Kevin Caldwell, Frank Vitucci, and Josh Tottenham for their tireless efforts to complete this manuscript, as well as Donna Goldsmith, Jim Coplit, Joel Satin, Kevin Hennessy, Jamie Nelson, Lear Girard, Melissa Halladay, Julie Cominsky, and Ann Vozzella for their support.

Brian Shields

As one of my favorite authors, Steve Martin once wrote, "If writing is so solitary, why are there so many people to thank?"

It's been an awesome experience to write about something I've loved since I was a child. I am profoundly grateful to have been part of this extraordinary project and to work with such gifted individuals.

I would like to thank the incredible team at WWE, especially Dean "The Dream" Miller for this amazing opportunity, along with the fantastic group at DK Publishing, my editor Ken Schmidt, Leigh Davis, Tim Fitzpatrick, and Brian Saliba. I hope this is the first of many collaborations. Rave reviews for my co-author Kevin Sullivan. I couldn't have asked for a better tag team partner for a project of this magnitude.

Profound appreciation goes to Mike Archer who has been a champion of my work for more than a decade and an incredible influence. Sincere gratitude to Christopher J. Ostuni, best friend, confidant, trusted business partner, and consigilieri. Thanks for everything, always.

I'm eternally grateful to the Breen and Eibeler families, who shepherded my first career steps. A special thank you to Tom Bass, Christina Recchio, Rich LaRocca, Dorian Rehfield, Frank Chiechi, John Ma and Evan Stein for their endless encouragement way back when. Boundless thanks to Kevin Brannan, Patrick Scanlon, Nique Fajors and Andrew Newburg for being incredible mentors and better friends.

To every Superstar past, present and future: your sacrifice, commitment and unique talent to do what most people only dream of—you were my true inspiration. There wouldn't have been a book to write without your existence. You are wondrous storytellers.

I have saved the best for last: To my mother Barbara, the most important person in my life, who taught me how to write, how to live and how to become a person. I can't thank you enough for everything you've given to your children for a better life and for always believing in me, despite giving you countless reasons not to while growing up. When I think of the strides I've made as a human being I think of the person you are and realize how far I have to go.

DK

DK would like to thank Tim Fitzpatrick, Tim Amrhein, Areva, David Bartley, Tim Cox, Christian Sumner, Brian Shotton, and JJ Fadd from D-town for their assistance on this project.

Photographs on pages 9, 10, 14, 15, 16, 17, 18, 22, 26, 31, 32, 33, 35, 39, 41, 47, 48, 49, 50, 52, 53, 54, 59, 62, 68, 69, 78, 79, 82, 84, 88, 91, 93, 98, 99, 100, 105, 109, 116, 117, 118, 121, 127, 143, 144, 150, 160, 161, 163, 164, 168, 169, 171, 173, 182, 191, 192, 206, 207, 208, 213, 214, 215, 217, 227, 230, 234, 235, 238, 244, 245, 263, 275, 276, 277, 278, 279, 281, 282, 283, 284, 294, 296, 298, 299, 305, 306, 309, 310, 325, 328, 329, 333, 334, 345, 346, 347, 348, 349, 350, 351, 352, 353, 354, 355, 356 courtesy of *Pro Wrestling Illustrated* Photographs. All other photos copyright World Wrestling Entertainment.